GENERALISED ANXIETY DISORDER IN ADULTS:

MANAGEMENT IN PRIMARY, SECONDARY AND COMMUNITY CARE

National Clinical Guideline Number 113

National Collaborating Centre for Mental Health
commissioned by the

National Institute for Health & Clinical Excellence

published by
The British Psychological Society and The Royal College of Psychiatrists

British Library Cataloguing-in-Publication Data

A catalogue record for this book is available from the British Library.

ISBN-: 978-1-904671-42-8

Printed in Great Britain by Stanley L. Hunt (Printers) Ltd.

Additional material: data CD-Rom created by Pix18 (www.pix18.co.uk)

developed by	National Collaborating Centre for Mental Health The Royal College of Psychiatrists 4th Floor, Standon House 21 Mansell Street London E1 8AA www.nccmh.org.uk
commissioned by	National Institute for Health and Clinical Excellence MidCity Place, 71 High Holborn London WC1V 6NA www.nice.org.uk
published by	The British Psychological Society St Andrews House 48 Princess Road East Leicester LE1 7DR www.bps.org.uk

and

The Royal College of Psychiatrists
17 Belgrave Square
London
SW1X 8PG
www.rcpsych.ac.uk

CONTENTS

Contents

GUIDELINE DEVELOPMENT GROUP MEMBERS

Professor John Cape (Guideline Chair)
Head of Psychological Therapies, Camden and Islington NHS Foundation Trust, London

Professor Tim Kendall (Guideline Facilitator)
Director, National Collaborating Centre for Mental Health, and Medical Director and Consultant Psychiatrist, Sheffield Health and Social Care NHS Foundation Trust

Ms Henna Bhatti
Research Assistant, National Collaborating Centre for Mental Health

Dr Marta Buszewicz
Senior Lecturer, Research Department of Primary Care and Population Health, University College London

Ms Melissa Chan
Systematic Reviewer, National Collaborating Centre for Mental Health

Professor Carolyn Chew-Graham
Professor of Primary Care, University of Manchester

Professor Philip Cowen
Professor of Psychopharmacology, University of Oxford

Ms Esther Flanagan
Project Manager, National Collaborating Centre for Mental Health (2009 to 2010)

Ms Laura Gibbon
Project Manager, National Collaborating Centre for Mental Health (2010 to 2011)

Ms Joanna Hackman
Service user member

Ms Marie Halton
Research Assistant, National Collaborating Centre for Mental Health

Ms Jill Keegan
Carer member, Islington Carers Centre

Guideline Development Group members

Ms Judy Leibowitz
Consultant Clinical Psychologist and Clinical Lead, Camden Psychological
Therapies Service, London

Professor Karina Lovell
Professor in Mental Health, University of Manchester

Dr Ifigeneia Mavranezouli
Senior Health Economist, National Collaborating Centre for Mental Health

Dr Nick Meader
Systematic Reviewer, National Collaborating Centre for Mental Health

Ms Catherine O'Neill
Service user member, Anxiety UK

Professor Paul Salkovskis
Professor of Clinical Psychology and Applied Science, University of Bath and
Clinical Director, Centre for Anxiety Disorders and Trauma, Maudsley Hospital

Professor Jan Scott
Professor of Psychological Medicine, University of Newcastle

Ms Sarah Stockton
Senior Information Scientist, National Collaborating Centre for Mental Health

Dr Clare Taylor
Editor, National Collaborating Centre for Mental Health

1   PREFACE

This guideline is a partial update of the first guideline on anxiety published in December 2004, which looked at the management of generalised anxiety disorder (GAD) and panic disorder, with or without agoraphobia (NICE, 2004a). The present guideline updates part of the original guideline on the management of GAD; panic disorder is not included.[1] Other anxiety disorders for which there are NICE guidelines are post-traumatic stress disorder (PTSD) and obsessive-compulsive disorder (OCD) (NICE, 2005a; 2005b). The guideline does not address the management of GAD in children and young people.

The scope for this guideline (see Appendix 1 for more details) also includes the partial update of NICE Technology Appraisal 97, *Computerised Cognitive Behaviour Therapy for Depression and Anxiety* (NICE, 2006). This update focuses on computerised cognitive behavioural therapy (CCBT) for panic disorder only.

The guideline recommendations have been developed by a multidisciplinary team of healthcare professionals, people who have experienced anxiety problems, a carer and guideline methodologists, after careful consideration of the best available evidence. It is intended that the guideline will be useful to clinicians and service commissioners in providing and planning high-quality care for people with GAD, while also emphasising the importance of the experience of care for them and their carers.

Although the evidence base is rapidly expanding, there are a number of major gaps, and further revisions of this guideline will incorporate new scientific evidence as it develops. The guideline makes a number of research recommendations specifically to address gaps in the evidence base. In the meantime, it is hoped that the guideline will assist clinicians, people with GAD and their carers by identifying the merits of particular treatment approaches where the evidence from research and clinical experience exists.

1.1   NATIONAL GUIDELINES

1.1.1   What are clinical practice guidelines?

Clinical practice guidelines are 'systematically developed statements that assist clinicians and patients in making decisions about appropriate treatment for specific conditions' (Mann, 1996). They are derived from the best available research evidence,

---

[1]For copyright reasons this publication contains the evidence and recommendations for GAD only; the evidence and recommendations for panic disorder were developed by the National Collaborating Centre for Primary Care in 2004 and can be found in the original NICE guideline (NICE, 2004b) and in the updated guideline on the NICE website: http://guidance.nice.org.uk/CG113/Guidance

using predetermined and systematic methods to identify and evaluate the evidence relating to the specific condition in question. Where evidence is lacking, the guidelines incorporate statements and recommendations based upon the consensus statements developed by the Guideline Development Group (GDG).

Clinical guidelines are intended to improve the process and outcomes of healthcare in a number of different ways. They can:

- provide up-to-date evidence-based recommendations for the management of conditions and disorders by healthcare professionals
- be used as the basis to set standards to assess the practice of healthcare professionals
- form the basis for education and training of healthcare professionals
- assist people with GAD and their carers in making informed decisions about their treatment and care
- improve communication between healthcare professionals, people with GAD and their carers
- help identify priority areas for further research.

1.1.2   Uses and limitations of clinical guidelines

Guidelines are not a substitute for professional knowledge and clinical judgement. They can be limited in their usefulness and applicability by a number of different factors: the availability of high-quality research evidence, the quality of the methodology used in the development of the guideline, the generalisability of research findings and the uniqueness of individuals with GAD.

Although the quality of research in this field is variable, the methodology used here reflects current international understanding on the appropriate practice for guideline development (Appraisal of Guidelines for Research and Evaluation Instrument [AGREE]; www.agreetrust.org; AGREE Collaboration, 2003), ensuring the collection and selection of the best research evidence available and the systematic generation of treatment recommendations applicable to the majority of people with GAD. However, there will always be some people and situations for which clinical guideline recommendations are not readily applicable. This guideline does not, therefore, override the individual responsibility of healthcare professionals to make appropriate decisions in the circumstances of the individual, in consultation with the person with GAD or their carer.

In addition to the clinical evidence, cost-effectiveness information, where available, is taken into account in the generation of statements and recommendations of the clinical guidelines. While national guidelines are concerned with clinical and cost effectiveness, issues of affordability and implementation costs are to be determined by the National Health Service (NHS).

In using guidelines, it is important to remember that the absence of empirical evidence for the effectiveness of a particular intervention is not the same as evidence for ineffectiveness. In addition, and of particular relevance in mental health, evidence-based treatments are often delivered within the context of an overall treatment programme including a range of activities, the purpose of which may be to help engage the person and provide an appropriate context for the delivery of specific interventions. It is important to maintain and enhance the service context in which these interventions are delivered; otherwise the specific benefits of effective interventions will be lost. Indeed, the importance of organising care in order to support and encourage a good therapeutic relationship is at times as important as the specific treatments offered.

1.1.3   Why develop national guidelines?

The National Institute for Health and Clinical Excellence (NICE) was established as a Special Health Authority for England and Wales in 1999, with a remit to provide a single source of authoritative and reliable guidance for patients, professionals and the public. NICE guidance aims to improve standards of care, diminish unacceptable variations in the provision and quality of care across the NHS, and ensure that the health service is patient centred. All guidance is developed in a transparent and collaborative manner, using the best available evidence and involving all relevant stakeholders.

NICE generates guidance in a number of different ways, three of which are relevant here. First, national guidance is produced by the Technology Appraisal Committee to give robust advice about a particular treatment, intervention, procedure or other health technology. Second, NICE commissions public health intervention guidance focused on types of activity (interventions) that help to reduce people's risk of developing a disease or condition, or help to promote or maintain a healthy lifestyle. Third, NICE commissions the production of national clinical practice guidelines focused upon the overall treatment and management of a specific condition. To enable this latter development, NICE has established four National Collaborating Centres in conjunction with a range of professional organisations involved in healthcare.

1.1.4   The National Collaborating Centre for Mental Health

This guideline has been commissioned by NICE and developed within the National Collaborating Centre for Mental Health (NCCMH). The NCCMH is a collaboration of the professional organisations involved in the field of mental health, national patient and carer organisations, and a number of academic institutions and NICE. The NCCMH is funded by NICE and is led by a partnership between the Royal College of Psychiatrists and the British Psychological Society's Centre for Outcomes Research and Effectiveness.

1.1.5   From national guidelines to local implementation

Once a national guideline has been published and disseminated, local healthcare groups will be expected to produce a plan and identify resources for implementation, along with appropriate timetables. Subsequently, a multidisciplinary group involving commissioners of healthcare, primary care and specialist mental health professionals, people with GAD and carers should undertake the translation of the implementation plan locally taking into account both the recommendations set out in this guideline and the priorities set in the National Service Framework for Mental Health (Department of Health [DH], 1999) and related documentation. The nature and pace of the local plan will reflect local healthcare needs and the nature of existing services; full implementation may take a considerable time, especially where substantial training needs are identified.

1.1.6   Auditing the implementation of guidelines

This guideline identifies key areas of clinical practice and service delivery for local and national audit. Although the generation of audit standards is an important and necessary step in the implementation of this guidance, a more broadly based implementation strategy will be developed. Nevertheless, it should be noted that the Care Quality Commission will monitor the extent to which Primary Care Trusts, trusts responsible for mental health and social care, and Health Authorities have implemented these guidelines.

1.2   THE NATIONAL GENERALISED ANXIETY DISORDER GUIDELINE

1.2.1   Who has developed this guideline?

The GDG was convened by the NCCMH and supported by funding from NICE. The GDG included service user and carer representatives, and professionals from psychiatry, clinical psychology and general practice.

Staff from the NCCMH provided leadership and support throughout the process of guideline development, undertaking systematic searches, information retrieval, appraisal and systematic review of the evidence. Members of the GDG received training in the process of guideline development from NCCMH staff, and the service user and carer representatives received training and support from the NICE Patient and Public Involvement Programme. The NICE Guidelines Technical Adviser provided advice and assistance regarding aspects of the guideline development process.

All GDG members made formal declarations of interest at the outset, which were updated at every GDG meeting (see Appendix 3). The GDG met a total of 14 times throughout the process of guideline development. It met as a whole, but key topics were led by a national expert in the relevant topic. The GDG was supported by the NCCMH technical team, with additional expert advice from special advisers where needed. The group oversaw the production and synthesis of research evidence before presentation. All statements and recommendations in this guideline have been generated and agreed by the whole GDG.

1.2.2   For whom is this guideline intended?

This guideline is relevant for adults with GAD as the primary diagnosis and covers the care provided by primary, community, secondary, tertiary and other healthcare professionals who have direct contact with, and make decisions concerning the care of, adults with GAD.

The guideline will also be relevant to the work, but will not specifically cover the practice, of those in:
- occupational health services
- social services
- forensic services
- the independent sector.

The experience of anxiety problems can affect the whole family. The guideline recognises the role of families and carers in the treatment and support of people with GAD.

1.2.3   Specific aims of this guideline

The guideline makes recommendations for the treatment and management of GAD. It aims to:
- improve access and engagement with treatment and services for people with GAD
- evaluate the role of specific psychological and psychosocial interventions in the treatment of GAD
- evaluate the role of specific pharmacological interventions in the treatment of GAD
- integrate the above to provide best-practice advice on the care of people with GAD and their family and carers
- promote the implementation of best clinical practice through the development of recommendations tailored to the requirements of the NHS in England and Wales.

1.2.4   The structure of this guideline

The guideline is divided into chapters, each covering a set of related topics. The first three chapters provide an introduction to guidelines, the topic of GAD and the methods used to update this guideline. Chapters 5 to 8 provide the evidence that underpins the recommendations about the treatment and management of GAD, with Chapter 4 providing personal accounts from people with anxiety problems and carers, giving an insight into their experience of GAD. Chapter 9 reviews the evidence for computerised cognitive behavioural therapy for panic disorder.

Each evidence chapter begins with a general introduction to the topic that sets the recommendations in context. Depending on the nature of the evidence, narrative reviews or meta-analyses were conducted, and the structure of the chapters varies accordingly. Where appropriate, details about current practice, the evidence base and any research limitations are provided. Where meta-analyses were conducted, information is given about the review protocol and studies included in the review. Clinical evidence summaries are then used to summarise the data presented. Health economic evidence is then presented (where appropriate), followed by a section (from evidence to recommendations) that draws together the clinical and health economic evidence and provides a rationale for the recommendations. On the CD-ROM, further details are provided about included/excluded studies and the evidence (see Table 1 for details).

Table 1: Appendices on CD-ROM

Review protocols	Appendix 7
Economic plan	Appendix 14
Clinical study characteristics tables	Appendix 15
Clinical evidence forest plots	Appendix 16
Methodology checklists for economic studies	Appendix 17
GRADE evidence profiles	Appendix 18

2 GENERALISED ANXIETY DISORDER

2.1 INTRODUCTION

This guideline is concerned with the treatment and management of adults with a diagnosis of GAD in primary and secondary care. GAD is one of a range of anxiety disorders including panic disorder (with and without agoraphobia), PTSD, OCD, social phobia, specific phobias (for example, of spiders) and acute stress disorder.

GAD commonly coexists with other anxiety disorders and with depressive disorders, as well as a variety of physical health disorders. 'Pure' GAD in the absence of another anxiety or depressive disorder is less typical than comorbid GAD. This guideline is relevant to both people with pure and comorbid GAD. The NICE guideline on case identification and referral for common mental health disorders will provide further guidance on identification (NICE, 2011).

2.2 THE DISORDER

2.2.1 Symptoms, presentation and patterns of illness

Anxiety is a prominent symptom of many psychiatric disorders but it is only comparatively recently that several distinct anxiety disorders have been recognised in classificatory systems. The key feature of GAD is worry and apprehension that is out of proportion to the circumstances. The worries are typically widespread, involve everyday issues and have a shifting focus of concern. The affected person finds the worries difficult to control, and this can result in decreased occupational and social functioning (Tyrer & Baldwin, 2006; Bitran *et al.*, 2009).

As well as worry that is excessive, generalised and difficult to control, people with GAD experience other psychological and somatic symptoms of anxiety. Psychological symptoms include irritability, poor concentration, increased sensitivity to noise and sleep disturbance, typically difficulty falling asleep. Somatic symptoms of GAD can manifest in many different ways. For example, an overactive autonomic nervous system can lead to sweating, dry mouth, palpitations, urinary frequency, epigastric discomfort and frequent and/or loose bowel motions, while hyperventilation may result in feelings of shortness of breath and dizziness. Increased muscle tension is a common accompaniment of persistent anxiety and may be experienced as restlessness, inability to relax, headaches and aching pains, particularly in the shoulders and back (Gelder *et al.*, 2006).

GAD is frequently comorbid with other mental disorders, which can complicate its presentation. The rates of comorbidity vary between studies with estimates of between 68 and 93% of comorbidity with another axis 1 mental health disorder (Carter *et al.*, 2001; Hunt *et al.*, 2002; ESEMeD/MHEDEA 2000 Investigators,

2004). Comorbid disorders that are particularly common include depressive disorders (specifically major depression and dysthymia), other anxiety disorders (especially panic disorder, social phobia and specific phobias) and somatoform disorders (Bitran *et al.*, 2009; Carter *et al.*, 2001; Hunt *et al.*, 2002; Grant *et al.*, 2005; Kessler *et al.*, 2005b). There is also significant comorbidity with substance misuse especially among men (Grant *et al.*, 2005; Kessler *et al.*, 2005b).

GAD also often co-occurs with physical health problems such as arthritis and gastrointestinal and respiratory disorders and may mimic the presentation of some physical conditions (for example, hyperthyroidism) (Culpepper, 2009; Roy-Byrne *et al.*, 2008; Sareen *et al.*, 2006). Due to the somatic symptoms of anxiety, which are central to GAD, and physical comorbidities, people with GAD who present in primary care may emphasise somatic problems or sleep disturbance, rather than excessive worry or psychological symptoms of anxiety (Rickels & Rynn, 2001).

2.2.2   Course and prognosis

Most clinical studies suggest that GAD is typically a chronic condition with low rates of remission over the short and medium-term. Evaluation of prognosis is complicated by the frequent comorbidity with other anxiety disorders and depression, which worsen the long-term outcome and accompanying burden of disability (Tyrer & Baldwin, 2006). In the Harvard-Brown Anxiety Research Program, which recruited participants from Boston hospitals, the mean age of onset of GAD was 21 years, although many participants had been unwell since their teens. The average duration of illness in this group was about 20 years and despite treatment the outcome over the next 3 years was relatively poor, with only one in four showing symptomatic remission from GAD (Yonkers *et al.*, 1996). The proportion of people who became free from all psychiatric symptomatology was smaller, about one in six. In people who remitted from GAD the risk of relapse over the next year was about 15%, increasing to about 30% in those who achieved only partial symptomatic remission (Yonkers *et al.*, 1996).

The participants in the above study were recruited from hospital services and may not be representative of GAD in general. In a naturalistic study in the UK, Tyrer and colleagues (2004) followed up people with anxiety and depression identified in psychiatric clinics in primary care and found that 12 years later 40% of those initially diagnosed with GAD had recovered, in the sense that they no longer met criteria for any *Diagnostic and Statistical Manual of Mental Disorders* 3rd edition (DSM-III; American Psychiatric Association [APA], 1980) psychiatric disorder. The remaining participants remained symptomatic, but GAD was still the principal diagnosis in only 3% of trial participants; in the vast majority conditions such as dysthymia, major depression and agoraphobia were now more prominent. This study confirms the chronic and fluctuating symptomatic course of GAD in clinically-identified people. It should be noted, however, that the majority of people with GAD in the community do not seek medical help for their symptoms (Wittchen & Jacobi, 2005), and the course of the illness in these circumstances is not established.

2.2.3   Disability and mortality

As is the case with major depression, GAD is associated with a substantial burden of disability, equivalent to that of other chronic conditions such as arthritis and diabetes (Wittchen, 2002). Outcome studies suggest that anxiety disorders are more chronic than other common mental disorders (Tyrer *et al.*, 2004) and there is evidence that comorbid depression and anxiety has a worse prognosis, with more associated disability and more persistent symptoms than either depression or anxiety disorders alone (Kroenke *et al.*, 2007). There is also evidence in the community that anxiety disorders are independently associated with several physical conditions, and this comorbidity is significantly associated with poor quality of life and disability (Sareen *et al.*, 2006). This morbidity comes with high associated health and social costs (Simon *et al.*, 1995).

Studies have shown that the presence of GAD is also associated with significant impairments in occupational and social functioning. For example, over 30% of people with GAD showed an annual reduction of work productivity of 10% or more compared with 8% of people with major depression. The figure for people with comorbid GAD and depression was over 45% (Wittchen *et al.*, 2000). A large part of the economic cost of anxiety disorders is attributable to the costs of non-medical psychiatric treatment. People with GAD have increased numbers of visits not only to primary care doctors but also to hospital specialists, particularly gastroenterologists (Kennedy & Schwab, 1997; Wittchen, 2002). This may be a consequence of the distressing somatic symptoms which many people with GAD experience.

GAD also carries a considerable cost in personal suffering – in the Harvard-Brown Anxiety Research Program noted above, one third of people had never married and unemployment was higher than average (Yonkers *et al.*, 1996). Suicidal ideation and suicide attempts are significantly increased in GAD compared with the general population, particularly in women, and this increase is still greater in the presence of comorbid major depression (Cougle *et al.*, 2009).

2.2.4   Incidence and prevalence

The estimated proportion of people in England with GAD was 4.4% in the most recent *Adult Psychiatric Morbidity in England* survey (McManus *et al.*, 2009), a figure that has varied little across the three survey years 1993, 1997 and 2007. This figure is at the upper end of estimates of point and annual prevalence of 2.1 to 4.4% in English speaking countries (Grant *et al.*, 2005; Hunt *et al.*, 2002; Kessler & Wang, 2008) with lower rates of 0.8 to 2.2% reported from other European countries (Lieb *et al.*, 2005; Wittchen & Jacobi 2005). Worldwide estimates of the proportion of people who are likely to experience GAD in their lifetime vary between 0.8% and 6.4% (Lieb *et al.*, 2005; Grant *et al.*, 2005; Kessler & Wang, 2008).

Prevalence rates have generally been found to be between 1.5 and 2.5 times higher in women than men. In the *Adult Psychiatric Morbidity in England* survey (McManus *et al.*, 2009), the rates were 3.4% for men and 5.3% for women. In terms of age, epidemiological studies have generally found GAD to be less common in older age groups (over 55 years) although there are some exceptions. Some studies have also found GAD to be less common in younger adults (younger than 35 years).

Evidence from the US on ethnicity and race differences in GAD rates is inconsistent, with studies finding increased (Blazer *et al.*, 1991), decreased (Grant *et al.*, 2005) and no difference (Wittchen *et al.*, 1994) in rates between white and one or more of black, Asian and Hispanic groups. Numbers of minority ethnic groups sampled in the *Adult Psychiatric Morbidity in England* survey (McManus *et al.*, 2009) were too small to draw conclusions about possible differences, although proportions of the black and South Asian groups with GAD in the sample (both male and female) were higher than the equivalent proportions for white interviewees.

Socioeconomic factors associated with GAD are lower household income (Grant *et al.*, 2005; McManus *et al.*, 2009), lack of tertiary qualifications (Hunt *et al.*, 2002) and unemployment (Hunt *et al.*, 2002). Divorce, separation and death of a partner are also associated with an increased likelihood of GAD.

2.2.5   Diagnosis

Diagnostic criteria and methods of classification of anxiety disorders have changed substantially over the years. Historically what we now consider to be GAD was subsumed under 'anxiety neurosis'. It first appeared as a separate diagnosis in 1980 with the introduction of DSM-III (APA, 1980). In DSM-III it was a residual category to be used only when an anxiety disorder could not be classified under another diagnosis. It was only with the DSM-III revision in 1987 (DSM-III-R; APA, 1987) that it became a well defined condition in its own right. DSM-III-R also changed the DSM-III minimum duration requirement from 1 month to 6 months and introduced excessive worry as a central feature. Some of the developments in DSM-III-R were later reflected in the *International Classification of Diseases – the Classification of Mental and Behavioural Disorders* 10th revision (ICD-10; World Health Organization [WHO], 1992), although without the same focus on worry. The introduction of DSM-IV in 1994 (APA, 1994) further streamlined and refined the criteria, in particular focusing less on somatic symptoms of anxiety and replacing the DSM-III-R criterion that the worry is 'unrealistic' with a criterion that the worry is 'difficult to control'.

DSM-IV and ICD-10 have overlapping but different diagnostic features for GAD. DSM-IV emphasises worry ('apprehensive expectation'), including the feature that the worry is difficult to control, while ICD-10 focuses more on somatic symptoms of anxiety, particularly autonomic reactivity and tension. DSM-IV requires two major symptoms (6 months or more of excessive anxiety and worry, occurring on more days than not, about a number of events and activities and difficulty controlling the worry) and three or more additional symptoms from a list of six. ICD-10, as operationalised in the *ICD-10 Diagnostic Criteria for Research* (ICD-10-DCR; WHO, 1993), requires 6 months or more prominent tension, worry and feelings of apprehension, and four from a list of 22 symptoms, of which at least one must be from a list of four autonomic symptoms (palpitations, sweating, trembling, dry mouth).

In line with the previous guideline on GAD (NICE, 2004a) and other NICE guidelines on anxiety disorders and depression (NICE, 2005a, b; 2009b) the GDG used DSM-IV, rather than ICD-10 to define the diagnosis of GAD, because the evidence base for treatments nearly always uses DSM-IV.

As there is now greater recognition of the need to consider 'subthreshold' depression in terms of human and economic costs and the risk of future major depression (Rowe & Rapaport, 2006), there has also been recent attention given to subthreshold GAD. Relaxing the DSM-IV requirements of duration, excessive worry and/or three associated symptoms more than doubles the estimated prevalence of GAD (Ruscio *et al.*, 2007). Cases of subthreshold GAD have similar but reduced comorbidities, with persistence, impairment and sociodemographic correlates all being significantly associated with an elevated risk of subsequent psychopathology (Kessler *et al.*, 2005a; Ruscio *et al.*, 2007). The implication is that, in clinical practice, identification of subthreshold GAD may be helpful for prevention of future disorder.

2.3   AETIOLOGY

The aetiology of GAD is multifactorial and involves psychological, social and biological factors. Interpretation of experimental data is complicated by changes in diagnostic practice and the frequent occurrence of comorbidity, particularly with major depression (Yonkers *et al.*, 1996). On the other hand, anxiety (or more precisely, fear) is readily modelled in animal experimental studies, and the brain circuitry relevant to fear has been characterised in both animals and humans (Engel *et al.*, 2009). One influential formulation ('the theory of triple vulnerability') regards GAD as arising from three distinct kinds of vulnerability: a generalised biological, a generalised psychological and a specific psychological vulnerability (Barlow, 2000; Bitran *et al.*, 2009).

Anxiety disorders run in families. For example, a family study found that the risk of GAD in first-degree relatives of people with GAD was five times that in control groups (Noyes *et al.*, 1987), although specific genes conferring vulnerability to GAD have not yet been reliably identified. Indeed the genes involved in the transmission of GAD appear to increase susceptibility to other anxiety disorders such as panic disorder and agoraphobia as well as major depression (Kendler, 1996; Hettema *et al.*, 2001; 2005). There is also genetic overlap between GAD and the temperamental trait of neuroticism, which is itself a predisposing factor for GAD (Hettema *et al.*, 2004). Overall the findings suggest that genetic factors play a significant though moderate role in the aetiology of GAD, that these factors predispose people to a range of anxiety and depressive disorders rather than GAD specifically, and that environmental factors are important in determining the nature of the emotional disorder experienced by a particular person.

Generalised anxiety disorder

Several environmental factors are known to predispose individuals to GAD. These can act remotely or as contemporaneous triggers to the disorder. For example, good parenting experiences are important in providing children with a secure base from which to explore the world, and problems in child-parent attachment have been linked to feelings of diminished personal control of potentially threatening events (Barlow, 2000). Such feelings could plausibly contribute to the risk of experiencing anxiety disorders. Studies suggest that adults with GAD report experiencing parental styles characterised by overprotection and lack of emotional warmth (Silove *et al.*, 1991). Similar findings have been reported in other anxiety disorders and depression (Parker *et al.*, 1995), which suggest that certain parenting styles may act as a psychological vulnerability factor for a range of subsequent emotional disorders. Similar comments apply to other kinds of childhood adversity such as neglect, abuse, maternal depression and family disruption, which increase the risk of experiencing GAD in adulthood as well as other anxiety and depressive disorders (Brown & Harris, 1993; Halligan *et al.*, 2007; Safren *et al.*, 2002). More recent stressful life events are also known to be involved in the onset of emotional disorders including GAD (Roemer *et al.*, 1996). A study by Kendler and colleagues (2003) showed that stressful life events characterised by loss increased the risk of both depression and GAD; however, life events characterised by 'danger' (where the full import of the event was yet to be realised) were more common in those who subsequently developed GAD.

Particular coping and cognitive styles also predispose individuals to the development of GAD, although it is not always easy to distinguish predisposition from the abnormal cognitions seen in the illness itself. As noted above, it is believed that people who lack a sense of control of events and personal effectiveness, perhaps through early life experiences, are more prone to anxiety disorders (Barlow, 2000). Such individuals may also demonstrate trait-like cognitive biases in the form of increased attention to potentially threatening stimuli, overestimation of environmental threat and enhanced memory of threatening material. This has been referred to as the 'looming cognitive style', which appears to be a general psychological vulnerability factor for a number of anxiety disorders (Reardon & Nathan, 2007). More recent cognitive formulations have focused on the process of worrying itself, which is of central importance in the diagnosis of GAD. Studies suggest that people at risk of GAD use worry as a positive coping strategy to deal with potential threats, whereby the person worries until they feel reassured that they have appraised all possible dangers and identified ways of dealing with them. However, this can lead to 'worry about worry', when individuals come to believe, for example, that worrying in this way, while necessary for them, is also uncontrollable and harmful. This 'metacognitive belief' may constitute a transitionary stage between excessive, but normal, worrying and GAD (Wells, 2005).

Studies of both animal and human subjects suggest that the amygdala plays a central role in the processing of information relevant to threat and fear (Le Doux, 2000). Activation of the amygdala can occur prior to conscious appreciation of threat but there are strong connections between the amygdala and areas of prefrontal cortex involved in the conscious experience and regulation of emotion (Le Doux, 2000; Phillips *et al.*, 2003). Another structure involved in anxiety is the hippocampus, which is important in relating fearful memories to their environmental context (Fanselow, 2000). The hippocampus forms part of a 'behavioural inhibition system', which is activated by potential threats, and has the ability in these circumstances to suspend ongoing behaviours (Gray, 1982). Brain imaging studies of individuals with high trait anxiety and people with GAD have shown exaggerated responses in both the amygdala and prefrontal cortex during presentation of emotionally threatening stimuli (Bishop *et al.*, 2004; Nitschke *et al.*, 2009). It is therefore possible that pre-existing abnormalities in this circuitry might predispose people to GAD and other anxiety disorders.

The neural circuitry involved in fear and anxiety is modulated by brain neurotransmitters and other chemical mediators including hormones (Dedovic *et al.*, 2009). A relevant hormonal system is the hypothalamo-pituitary-adrenal axis (HPA), which regulates cortisol secretion. Adversity experienced in childhood and current stresses can alter the pattern of cortisol secretion in adult life, and there is an extensive literature on the role of HPA axis dysfunction in major depression (for example, Pariante & Lightman, 2008). HPA axis activity in people with GAD has been much less studied but there is some evidence that GAD, like depression, is associated with excessive glucocorticoid secretion (Mantella *et al.*, 2008). The monoamine neurotransmitters, serotonin and noradrenaline, can alter fear processes in animals and have extensive inputs to the relevant neural circuitry, including the amygdala and the behavioural inhibition system (Bitran *et al.*, 2009; Garner *et al.*, 2009). In addition, selective serotonin reuptake inhibitors (SSRIs) are widely used in the treatment of GAD (Baldwin *et al.*, 2005). Despite this there is only modest evidence that abnormalities in serotonin and noradrenaline are involved in the pathophysiology of GAD, though more work needs to be carried out with ligand neuroimaging to resolve this issue (Garner *et al.*, 2009). In the same way, pharmacological manipulation of gamma-aminobutyric acid (GABA) neurones and their associated benzodiazepine receptors clearly have profound effects on the experience of fear and anxiety in animals and humans (Kalueff & Nutt, 2007) but again there is only modest evidence that abnormalities in GABA neurotransmission or benzodiazepine receptor function are involved in the aetiology of GAD (Garner *et al.*, 2009).

Overall there is good evidence that both genetic factors and early life difficulties can predispose people to a range of emotional disorders, including GAD. More specific risk factors for GAD, presumably occurring in combination with these more generalised vulnerabilities, include certain kinds of life events and particular individual cognitive styles involving the use of worrying as a coping strategy. The neural circuitry involved in fear and anxiety has been well delineated in brain imaging studies and abnormalities in both people with GAD and non-clinical subjects with high trait anxiety have been described in relevant brain regions. It seems likely that these neural changes are associated with abnormal cognitions, such as increased attention to threat, that are seen in people with GAD and those at risk of the disorder. There is much knowledge on how particular neuropharmacological manipulations can influence anxiety. While this information has proved helpful in developing pharmacological treatment, the role of neurotransmitters and other chemical mediators in the aetiology of GAD is currently unclear.

2.4   TREATMENT AND MANAGEMENT IN THE NHS

2.4.1   Detection, recognition and referral in primary care

Relative to its prevalence in the community, GAD is more common in primary care occurring in about 5% of attendees, and is the most common anxiety disorder seen in this setting. A recent international review of some of the larger general population surveys reported 12-month prevalence rates of 5.6 to 18.1% for anxiety disorders, of which GAD and panic disorder together accounted for over half of the prevalence figures (Baumeister & Hartner, 2007).

General practitioner (GP) rates of diagnosis and treatment of anxiety disorders are much lower than expected from the prevalence figures (Wittchen & Jacobi, 2005). Wittchen and colleagues (2002) found that recognition rates by primary care practitioners were only 34.4% for pure GAD and 43% for GAD with comorbid depression. There are likely to be a variety of reasons why GPs are poor at recognising anxiety disorders in their patients. People with GAD may have symptoms of anxiety, worry, tension, irritability or tiredness, about which they feel reluctant to complain to their GP because they do not view these symptoms as being 'medical', or the GP may identify these as symptoms of a more general malaise and not specifically consider or ask about anxiety as a possible cause (Arroll & Kendrick, 2009). In addition, many people may present with somatic symptoms associated with their anxiety, considering these to be more legitimate or more troubling. It appears that people with anxiety disorders are often frequent users of primary care resources, but if the anxiety component of their problem is not detected they may not receive the correct treatment and may undergo unnecessary and costly investigations, in particular for their physical symptoms (Hales *et al.*, 1997). Recognition is increased by factors such as older age, presentation of other psychological problems, and enhanced knowledge, skills and attitudes of practitioners in primary care (Tylee & Walters, 2007).

There is evidence that GPs may not offer effective evidence-based treatments to people with anxiety disorders as often as may be indicated, and that the treatments offered are more likely to be pharmacological, rather than psychological therapies such as cognitive behavioural therapy (CBT) (Stein *et al.*, 2004) due to limited availability of such treatments, although this may be changing with increased access to psychological therapies through the Improving Access to Psychological Therapies programme (IAPT).[2] The majority of treatments offered for anxiety disorders are likely to be based in primary care and may involve the GP and/or a low-intensity psychological therapist such as a primary care mental health worker or the practice counsellor. Self-help bibliotherapy and web-based interventions may be effective for some people with GAD, although referral to secondary care practitioners, such as a high-intensity psychological therapist, may occur for those more severely affected. Referral to secondary care psychiatric mental health services is likely to be rare and reserved for people with the most treatment-resistant symptoms and severe functional impairment.

---

[2] www.iapt.nhs.uk

In summary, there is evidence that GAD is currently significantly under-detected and under-treated in UK primary care settings. This is a potentially serious omission, given the functional impairment and chronicity that can be associated with this diagnosis, particularly when comorbid with depression or physical health problems. There needs to be an increased emphasis on encouraging people to actively present their anxiety symptoms, and for their GPs to be more attuned to this diagnosis (particularly in people known to have depression or a chronic physical health problem) and the need to provide effective evidence-based treatments as early as possible in the course of this disorder before it becomes a long-term problem.

2.4.2 Assessment and co-ordination of care

Primary care and mental health practitioners need to have skills in the identification of GAD and its differentiation from other anxiety and depressive disorders in order to assess GAD and provide appropriate treatment. Assessment involves evaluation of GAD symptoms, especially worry and somatic symptoms of anxiety, the duration of these symptoms, and the extent of the person's functional impairment and distress and their coping resources. Assessment also needs to include evaluation of the symptoms of other anxiety and depressive disorders (especially panic disorder, hypochondriasis, OCD, social phobia, major depressive disorder and dysthymic disorder) given both the overlap of symptoms (for differential diagnosis) and the comorbidity between GAD and these other disorders.

The majority of treatment takes place in primary care or is linked with primary care, usually by either being directly provided by GPs or by psychological practitioners in liaison with GPs. GPs are accordingly central to the coordination of care. Ensuring a clear collaborative treatment plan between GP and psychological practitioners is important. For a small minority of people with very severe disorders, treatment may be provided by a multi-professional team in secondary care with coordination of care through the Care Programme Approach (CPA).

2.4.3 Aims and non-specific effects of treatment and placebo

The aim of treatment for GAD is to relieve symptoms, restore function and prevent relapse. The latter goal is important because GAD manifests as a chronic, relapsing condition and recurrence of illness is common, even when short-term treatment has apparently been successful (Yonkers *et al.*, 1996). In clinical trials, the outcome of treatment is often determined on standardised rating scales and can be divided into 'response' (where the symptom score has dropped by at least 50%) and 'remission' (almost complete relief of symptoms). In the treatment of depression, remission rather than response is now seen as the preferred goal because people who are essentially asymptomatic have improved functional outcomes and less risk of relapse. It seems probable that similar considerations will apply to the treatment of GAD.

Many people with GAD have had symptoms for long periods of time. Nevertheless, in short-term studies of medication, pill placebo treatment in the context of the clinical care provided by a controlled trial is certainly beneficial for a proportion of people. For example, in a 12-week placebo-controlled trial of escitalopram and paroxetine, just over 40% of participants responded to placebo and about 30% reached remission (Baldwin *et al.*, 2006). In contrast, naturalistic follow-up studies of people with GAD in the community have found considerably lower remission rates than this, at about 15% a year (Yonkers *et al.*, 1996). This suggests that either GAD, despite its chronicity, can respond well to pill placebo and non-specific aspects of good clinical management, or that the people who participate in placebo-controlled trials are not typical of the broad range of people with GAD in the community. In addition, it is not known whether people who respond to a placebo in the short-term will maintain this level of improvement whereas there is some evidence that continuing drug treatment that proved effective in the short-term can help prevent relapse (Baldwin *et al.*, 2005).

Non-specific effects of treatment are also important in assessing the benefits of psychological therapies such as CBT and applied relaxation. Often such treatments are assessed against 'waitlist' or 'treatment as usual' control groups, which means that the non-specific effects of factors such as increased professional support and instillation of hope will augment the specific effects of a particular therapy. Thus a meta-analysis showed that while CBT was superior to waitlist control in the treatment of GAD, its superiority to supportive psychological therapy could not be clearly demonstrated (Hunot *et al.*, 2007).

Consistent with this, a substantial number of other approaches have been employed to help people with anxiety disorders, such as exercise, prayer and homeopathic and herbal remedies (Jorm *et al.*, 2004). This suggests that numerous non-medical approaches, provided they carry meaning and hope for the person concerned, can enable individuals to use their own coping and healing capacities to overcome anxiety symptoms. At present it is not possible to identify those people who will respond to non-specific, as opposed to specific, pharmacological and psychological treatments. In the treatment of depression it appears that the response to placebo lessens as the condition becomes symptomatically more severe (Khan *et al.*, 2005); this means that the specific benefits of antidepressants are greater in the most severely ill people. Whether the same is true in people with GAD is not clear.

2.4.4   Pharmacological treatments

Placebo-controlled trials indicate that a wide range of medicines with differing pharmacological properties can be effective in the treatment of GAD (Baldwin *et al.*, 2005). Traditionally, benzodiazepine drugs, such as diazepam, were employed for this purpose but it became clear that their use was commonly associated with the development of tolerance and dependence (Royal College of Psychiatrists, 2005). For this reason they are now recommended only for short-term use (2 to 4 weeks). Another drug specifically licensed for the treatment of GAD is buspirone, which acts on a particular subtype of serotonin receptor. However, like benzodiazepines, buspirone is recommended for short-term use only (British Medical Association & the Royal Pharmaceutical Society of Great Britain, 2009).

In recent years antidepressants such as SSRIs have been increasingly used to treat GAD (Baldwin *et al.*, 2005). Unlike benzodiazepines, antidepressants do not relieve anxiety from the beginning of treatment and a period of some weeks often needs to elapse before significant clinical improvement is seen. Tolerance and dependence do not seem to be a problem with antidepressant treatment, though it should be noted that, like benzodiazepines, antidepressants can cause discontinuation symptoms on abrupt withdrawal (MHRA, 2004). As well as SSRIs, serotonin noradrenaline reuptake inhibitors (SNRIs), such as venlafaxine and duloxetine, are also effective in GAD, as are the older and less selective tricyclic antidepressants (TCAs), such as imipramine. However, TCAs are not as well tolerated as newer antidepressant agents and are more dangerous in overdose (Baldwin *et al.*, 2005).

In addition to the antidepressants, other compounds also have efficacy in the treatment of GAD. These include the antihistamine hydroxyzine, and the anticonvulsant drug pregabalin, which binds to a subtype of calcium channel in the brain (Baldwin *et al.*, 2005). Both conventional antipsychotic drugs and the newer 'atypical' antipsychotic agents have also been used in the treatment in GAD, both as a sole therapy and as an 'add-on' to SSRI therapy when the latter has proved ineffective (Pies, 2009). However, the greater side-effect burden of antipsychotic drugs means that their use is currently restricted to people with refractory conditions, with prescribing guided by secondary care.

While many drug treatments have been demonstrated to be effective in GAD relative to placebo, there are very few comparative studies between active pharmacological agents. In addition there are no reliable clinical or biological predictors of treatment response in individuals. For this reason the selection of pharmacological treatment is usually made on the basis of the side-effect profile and the history of medication response in a particular individual.

2.4.5   Psychological treatments

Developments in psychological treatments for GAD have tended to parallel changes in the conceptualisation and diagnostic criteria for GAD, moving from a more general approach to more specific interventions.

Early psychological treatments for GAD tended to involve non-specific interventions such as supportive psychotherapy and relaxation training. Initial cognitive behavioural packages for the treatment of GAD (Borkovec & Costello, 1993; Barlow *et al.*, 1992) focused on the treatment of persistent anxious arousal and often included a number of interventions such as applied relaxation, imagery rehearsal (imaginal practice of coping skills in response to anxiety), stimulus control (establishing increased control over worry) and cognitive approaches based on the work of Beck and colleagues (1985).

More recent adaptations of CBT have emphasised the specific role of worry in GAD and have tried to focus treatment more on the processes thought to underlie the disorder. An example of this is CBT targeting the intolerance of uncertainty (Dugas *et al.*, 2007) or the metacognitive therapy developed by Wells (1999), which emphasises the importance of the beliefs people have about worry and attempts to modify these.

Borkovec and colleagues (2002) have augmented existing CBT protocols with interpersonal/psychodynamic strategies to address problematic relationship patterns often found in people with GAD and the implications of the avoidance theory of worry, suggesting that people with GAD worry in order to avoid experiencing negative emotions.

Other adaptations of CBT have integrated acceptance-based and mindfulness approaches into treatment for GAD, incorporating the acceptance and experience of frequently avoided emotions into treatment protocols (Orsillo *et al.*, 2003).

2.4.6   Stepped care

Stepped care (Scogin *et al.*, 2003) is a framework that is increasingly being used in the UK to specify best practice in the design of clinical pathways to care. Stepped care is designed to increase the efficiency of service provision and therefore benefit patient populations. The basic principle is that patients presenting with a common mental health disorder will 'step through' progressive levels of treatment as necessary, with the expectation that many of these patients will recover or improve while undergoing less intensive treatments. The key features of stepped care are that treatments delivered first should be the least restrictive and that the model is self-correcting. The definition of 'least restrictive' may refer to the impact on patients in terms of cost and personal inconvenience, but can also refer to the amount of specialist therapist time required (that is, treatment intensity). High-intensity treatments are reserved for patients who do not benefit from low-intensity treatments, or for those who can be accurately predicted to not benefit from such treatments. 'Self-correcting' in this context means that the decisions about treatment provision and the effects of treatment are monitored systematically, and changes are made ('stepping up') if current treatments are not achieving significant health gain. Thus, stepped care has the potential for deriving the greatest benefit from available therapeutic resources (Bower & Gilbody, 2005).

Successful implementation of a stepped-care model is crucial for effective implementation of the NICE guidelines (Lovell & Bee, 2008). There are two conceptualisations of the stepped-care model. The first is a sequential model, where all people move through the steps in a systematic way, regardless of severity, need or choice. All patients initially receive an evidence-based low-intensity treatment and only 'step up' if and when they have not benefited from the low-intensity treatments offered. The second model is a stratified or multiple-access model, which allows patients to access more intensive treatment initially, without having received less intensive interventions first (Lovell & Richards, 2000). Stratified stepped-care models have been incorporated into previous NICE guidelines, where stratification has been determined by the person's degree of functional impairment (as in the NICE guideline on OCD and body dysmorphic disorder; NICE, 2005b) or severity of the disorder (as in the NICE guidelines on depression; NICE, 2009b; 2009c).

2.4.7 The economic cost of anxiety disorders – focus on generalised anxiety disorder

Anxiety disorders place a significant burden on individuals as well as on the healthcare system. Andlin-Sobocki and colleagues (2005) estimated the cost of anxiety disorders in Europe using published epidemiological and economic data from 28 European countries. Data on healthcare resource utilisation (medication, hospitalisation and outpatient care) and productivity losses due to sick leave associated with anxiety disorders were based on a German national health survey. The estimated total cost of anxiety disorders in Europe was reported to reach €41 billion (2004 prices). The average annual additional cost per person with GAD (relative to a person without an anxiety disorder) was estimated at €1,628 in 2004; of this, 76% was associated with provision of healthcare services and the remaining 24% with productivity losses due to sick leave (Andlin-Sobocki & Wittchen, 2005). The additional per-person cost of GAD was found to be the highest among respective costs of other anxiety disorders, such as panic disorder, agoraphobia, social phobia and OCD.

Only limited data on the healthcare resource utilisation by people with anxiety disorders exist in the UK. According to the Hospital Episode Statistics, in the financial year 2007 to 2008, 8,682 admissions were reported for phobic and other anxiety disorders in England, resulting in 121,359 inpatient bed days; of these, 747 admissions and 16,733 bed days were attributed specifically to GAD (NHS, The Information Centre, 2009). According to the most recent *Adult Psychiatric Morbidity in England* survey (McManus *et al.*, 2009), only 34% of people with GAD were receiving any kind of treatment for their condition at the time of the survey. Of them, 53% were receiving medication, 21% counselling or other psychological therapy, and 26% a combination of drugs and psychological treatment. In addition, 1% of respondents with GAD reported that they had used inpatient services for their condition over the past 3 months, 8% had used outpatient services during the same period, while 25% had used community or day care services during the past year.

A number of studies have estimated the cost of anxiety disorders in the US. DuPont and colleagues (1998) estimated this cost at $46.6 billion in 1990, which accounted for 31.5% of the total cost of mental disorders in the country. The estimated cost was incurred by healthcare resource utilisation such as mental health services, medication, hospitalisation, nursing homes and outpatient visits (23.1%), productivity losses (76.1%) and, to a lesser extent, by provision of other services such as criminal justice services, incarceration, social welfare administration, as well as family care-giving (0.8%). Greenberg and colleagues (1999) provided a more up-to-date figure of the cost of anxiety disorders in the US, at $63.1 billion in 1998.

A retrospective, multivariate analysis of data derived from a large claims database in the US demonstrated that people with anxiety disorders are more likely to use outpatient mental health services compared with a control group; they are also more likely to visit medical specialists such as cardiologists and neurologists and to use hospital services, including accident and emergency services. Furthermore, compared with controls, people with anxiety disorders were found to miss more days of work or to have a short-term disability (Marciniak *et al.*, 2004). According to the same analysis, the total medical cost per person with any anxiety disorder was estimated at $6,475 in 1999 (Marciniak *et al.*, 2005). The multivariate model indicated that, controlling for demographics and other disease states, GAD was associated with an increase of $2,138 in the total medical cost per person.

An Australian study (Andrews *et al.*, 2004) estimated the total annual cost of routine treatment for GAD in Australia at AUS$112.3 million in 1997 prices, based on the results of a national survey of mental health and wellbeing, and an estimated treatment coverage of only 38%. By applying optimal treatment (as achieved by operationalising detailed clinical practice guidelines and expert reviews) and increasing treatment coverage to 70%, the total annual direct medical cost of GAD was expected to rise to AUS$205.1 million.

Anxiety disorders are associated with a wide range of comorbidities, which result in a substantial increase in total healthcare costs. Souêtre and colleagues (1994) estimated the total direct and indirect costs incurred by people with GAD, with and without comorbidities, using data on 999 people participating in a French cross-sectional study. Controlling for confounding variables, the prevalence of healthcare utilisation in terms of hospitalisation, laboratory tests and medications and the respective medical costs were found to be significantly higher in people with GAD and other comorbidities, as opposed to those with GAD without comorbidities. Moreover, comorbidities were associated with increased absenteeism from work. In particular, comorbid depression (Marciniak *et al.*, 2005; Wetherell *et al.*, 2007; Zhu *et al.*, 2009) and physical pain (Olfson & Gameroff, 2007; Zhu *et al.*, 2009) have been found to have a significant impact on treatment costs incurred by people with GAD.

Efficient use of available healthcare resources will maximise the health benefits for people with GAD and can potentially reduce costs to the healthcare system and society in the long term.

3   METHODS USED TO DEVELOP THIS GUIDELINE

3.1   OVERVIEW

The development of this guideline drew upon methods outlined by NICE (NICE, 2009a). A team of healthcare professionals, lay representatives and technical experts known as the Guideline Development Group (GDG), with support from NCCMH staff, undertook the development of a patient-centred, evidence-based guideline. There are six basic steps in the process of developing a guideline:

- Define the scope, which sets the parameters of the guideline and provides a focus and steer for the development work.
- Define review (clinical) questions considered important for practitioners and service users.
- Develop criteria for evidence searching and search for evidence.
- Design validated protocols for systematic review and apply to evidence recovered by the search.
- Synthesise and (meta-) analyse data retrieved, guided by the review questions, and produce evidence profiles and summaries.
- Answer review questions with evidence-based recommendations for clinical practice.

The clinical practice recommendations made by the GDG are therefore derived from the most up-to-date and robust evidence base for the clinical and cost effectiveness of the treatments and services used in the treatment and management of GAD. In addition, to ensure a service user and carer focus, the concerns of service users and carers have been highlighted and addressed by recommendations agreed by the whole GDG.

3.2   THE SCOPE

Guideline topics are selected by the Department of Health and the Welsh Assembly Government, which identify the main areas to be covered by the guideline in a specific remit (see NICE, 2009a). The NCCMH developed a scope for the guideline based on the remit.

The purpose of the scope is to:

- provide an overview of what the guideline will include and exclude
- identify the key aspects of care that must be included
- set the boundaries of the development work and provide a clear framework to enable work to stay within the priorities agreed by NICE, NCCMH and the remit from the Department of Health/Welsh Assembly Government
- inform the development of the review questions and search strategy

- inform professionals and the public about expected content of the guideline
- keep the guideline to a reasonable size to ensure that its development can be carried out within the allocated period.

The draft scope was subject to consultation with registered stakeholders over a 4-week period. During the consultation period, the scope was posted on the NICE website (www.nice.org.uk). Comments were invited from stakeholder organisations and the Guideline Review Panel (GRP). Further information about the GRP can also be found on the NICE website. The NCCMH and NICE reviewed the scope in light of comments received, and the revised scope (see Appendix 1) was signed off by the GRP.

3.3   THE GUIDELINE DEVELOPMENT GROUP

The GDG consisted of professionals in psychiatry, clinical psychology, nursing and general practice, academic experts in psychiatry and psychology, and service user and carer representatives from service user and carer organisations. The guideline development process was supported by staff from the NCCMH, who undertook the clinical and health economics literature searches, reviewed and presented the evidence to the GDG, managed the process, and contributed to drafting the guideline.

3.3.1   Guideline Development Group meetings

Eleven GDG meetings were held between June 2009 and September 2010. During each day-long GDG meeting, in a plenary session, review questions and clinical and economic evidence were reviewed and assessed, and recommendations formulated. At each meeting, all GDG members declared any potential conflicts of interest, and service user and carer concerns were routinely discussed as part of a standing agenda.

3.3.2   Topic groups

The GDG divided its workload along clinically relevant lines to simplify the guideline development process, and certain GDG members were asked to undertake guideline work in that area of clinical practice. As the GDG was relatively small, there were no defined topic groups for the clinical evidence on pharmacological and psychological interventions; however there was a topic group that looked at service user and carer experience through personal accounts and qualitative literature. This group managed the evidence appraisal prior to presenting it to the GDG as a whole.

3.3.3   Service users and carers

Individuals with direct experience of services gave an integral service-user focus to the GDG and the guideline. The GDG included service user and carer representatives who contributed as full GDG members to writing the review questions, helping to ensure that the evidence addressed their views and preferences, highlighting sensitive issues and terminology relevant to the guideline, and bringing service-user research to the attention of the GDG. In drafting the guideline, they contributed to writing the guideline's introduction (Chapter 2) and the review of experience of care (Chapter 4), and they identified recommendations from the service user and carer perspective.

3.3.4 National and international experts

National and international experts in the area under review were identified through the literature search and through the experience of the GDG members. These experts were contacted to recommend unpublished or soon-to-be published studies in order to ensure up-to-date evidence was included in the development of the guideline. They informed the group about completed trials at the pre-publication stage, systematic reviews in the process of being published, studies relating to the cost effectiveness of treatment and trial data if the GDG could be provided with full access to the complete trial report. Appendix 5 lists researchers who were contacted.

3.4 REVIEW QUESTIONS

Review (clinical) questions were used to guide the identification and interrogation of the evidence base relevant to the topic of the guideline. Before the first GDG meeting, draft review questions were prepared by NCCMH staff based on the scope and an overview of existing guidelines, and discussed with the guideline Chair. The draft review questions were then discussed by the GDG at the first few meetings and amended as necessary. Questions submitted by stakeholders were also discussed by the GDG and the rationale for not including questions was recorded in the minutes. The final list of review questions can be found in Appendix 6.

For questions about interventions, the PICO (patient, intervention, comparison and outcome) framework was used. This structured approach divides each question into four components: the patients (the population under study), the interventions (what is being done), the comparisons (other main treatment options) and the outcomes (the measures of how effective the interventions have been) (see Text Box 1).

In some situations, the prognosis of a particular condition is of greater importance than its general significance in relation to specific interventions. Areas where this is particularly likely to occur relate to assessment of risk, for example, in terms of behaviour modification or screening and early intervention.

To help facilitate the literature review, a note was made of the study design type that is most appropriate for answering each question. There are four main types of review question of relevance to NICE guidelines. These are listed in Text Box 2. For each type of question, the best primary study design varies, where 'best' is interpreted as 'least likely to give misleading answers to the question'. It should be noted that, in all cases, a well-conducted systematic review of the appropriate type of study is likely to yield a better answer than a single study.

Deciding on the best design type to answer a specific clinical or public health question does not mean that studies of different design types addressing the same question were discarded.

Text Box 1: Features of a well-formulated question on effectiveness intervention – the PICO guide

Patients/population	Which patients or population of patients are we interested in? How can they be best described? Are there subgroups that need to be considered?
Intervention	Which intervention, treatment or approach should be used?
Comparison	What is/are the main alternative/s to compare with the intervention?
Outcome	What is really important for the patient? Which outcomes should be considered: intermediate or short-term measures; mortality; morbidity and treatment complications; rates of relapse; late morbidity and readmission; return to work, physical and social functioning and other measures such as quality of life; general health status?

Text Box 2: Best study design to answer each type of question

Type of question	Best primary study design
Effectiveness or other impact of an intervention	Randomised controlled trial (RCT); other studies that may be considered in the absence of an RCT are the following: internally/ externally controlled before and after trial, interrupted time-series
Accuracy of information (for example, risk factor, test, prediction rule)	Comparing the information against a valid gold standard in a randomised trial or inception cohort study
Rates (of disease, patient experience, rare side effects)	Cohort, registry, cross-sectional study

3.5   SYSTEMATIC CLINICAL LITERATURE REVIEW

The aim of the clinical literature review was to systematically identify and synthesise relevant evidence from the literature in order to answer the specific review questions developed by the GDG. Thus, clinical practice recommendations are evidence-based, where possible, and, if evidence is not available, informal consensus methods are used (see Section 3.5.9) and the need for future research is specified.

3.5.1   Methodology – Scoping searches

A broad preliminary search of the literature was undertaken in April 2009 to obtain an overview of the issues likely to be covered by the scope, and to help define key areas.[3] Searches were restricted to clinical guidelines, health technology assessment reports, key systematic reviews and RCTs, and were conducted in the following databases and websites:

- *British Medical Journal* (*BMJ*) Clinical Evidence
- Canadian Medical Association (CMA) Infobase (Canadian guidelines)
- Clinical Policy and Practice Program of the New South Wales Department of Health (Australia)
- Clinical Practice Guidelines (Australian Guidelines)
- Cochrane Central Register of Controlled Trials (CENTRAL)
- Cochrane Database of Abstracts of Reviews of Effects (DARE)
- Cochrane Database of Systematic Reviews (CDSR)
- Excerpta Medica Database (EMBASE)
- Guidelines International Network (G-I-N)
- Health Evidence Bulletin Wales
- Health Management Information Consortium (HMIC)
- Health Technology Assessment (HTA)
- Medical Literature Analysis and Retrieval System Online (MEDLINE/MEDLINE In-Process)
- National Health and Medical Research Council (NHMRC)
- National Library for Health (NLH)[4]
- New Zealand Guidelines Group
- NHS Centre for Reviews and Dissemination (CRD)
- Organizing Medical Networked Information (OMNI) Medical Search
- Scottish Intercollegiate Guidelines Network (SIGN)
- Turning Research Into Practice (TRIP)
- United States Agency for Healthcare Research and Quality (AHRQ)
- Websites of NICE and the National Institute for Health Research (NIHR) HTA programme for guidelines and HTAs in development.

---

[3]A second scoping search was conducted in June 2009, as a result of changes made to the scope.
[4]Since the scoping searches were conducted the name of this database has changed to NHS Evidence Health Information Resources.

3.5.2   The review process

The previous guideline on GAD and panic disorder (NICE, 2004a) was evaluated by the review team in liaison with NICE. It was agreed that the methodology utilised by the guideline was not consistent with the current NICE guideline manual (NICE, 2009a). It was subsequently decided that the review process would consider all evidence from inception to the present date (which may include data already reviewed in the previous guideline) using methodology more consistent with the current version of the NICE guideline manual, as described below.

At this point, the review team, in conjunction with the GDG, developed an evidence map that detailed all comparisons necessary to answer the review questions. The initial approach taken to locating primary-level studies depended on the type of review question and availability of evidence.

The GDG classified each review question into one of three groups: 1) questions concerning good practice; 2) questions likely to have little or no directly relevant evidence; 3) questions likely to have a good evidence base. Questions concerning good practice were answered by the GDG using informal consensus. For questions that were unlikely to have a good evidence base, a brief descriptive review was initially undertaken, and then the GDG used informal consensus to reach a decision (see Section 3.5.9). For questions with a good evidence base, the review process depended on the type of key question, as described below.

3.5.3   Systematic literature searches

After the review questions were formulated, a systematic search strategy was developed to locate all the relevant evidence. The balance between sensitivity (the power to identify all studies on a particular topic) and specificity (the ability to exclude irrelevant studies from the results) was carefully considered, and a decision made to utilise highly sensitive strategies to identify as complete a set as possible of clinically relevant studies.

In order to ensure comprehensive coverage, search terms for GAD were kept purposely broad to help counter dissimilarities in bibliographic databases in thesaurus terms and indexing practices, and (often) imprecise reporting of study populations by authors in the titles and abstracts of records. It was observed that broader searching retrieved significantly more relevant records than would have been achieved through the use of more specific terms. A broad search for panic was similarly constructed for evidence relating to the effectiveness of CCBT.

A stepwise approach to formulising the searches was implemented at all times, and attempts were made to eradicate duplication of effort in areas of overlapping coverage. Searches were restricted to systematic reviews, meta-analyses, RCTs and qualitative research, and were conducted in the following bibliographic databases:
- Allied and Complementary Medicine Database (AMED)
- CDSR
- CENTRAL
- Cumulative Index to Nursing and Allied Health Literature (CINAHL)

- DARE
- EMBASE
- HTA database
- International Bibliography of the Social Sciences (IBSS)
- MEDLINE/MEDLINE In-Process
- Psychological Information Database (PsycINFO).

Search strategies were initially developed for MEDLINE and subsequently translated for use in other databases/search interfaces.

3.5.4   The search process for questions concerning interventions

For questions relating to interventions, the initial evidence base was formed from well-conducted RCTs that addressed at least one of the review questions. Although there are a number of difficulties with the use of RCTs in the evaluation of interventions in mental health, the RCT remains the most important method for establishing treatment efficacy (this is discussed in more detail in the appropriate clinical evidence chapters). For other review questions, searches were conducted for the appropriate study design (see above).

Where the evidence base was large, recent high-quality English-language systematic reviews were used primarily as a source of RCTs (see Appendix 10 for quality criteria used to assess systematic reviews). However, in some circumstances existing datasets were utilised. Where this was the case, data were cross-checked for accuracy before use. New RCTs meeting inclusion criteria set by the GDG were incorporated into the existing reviews and fresh analyses performed.

Reference Manager
Citations from each search were downloaded into Reference Manager (a software product for managing references and formatting bibliographies) and all duplicates removed. Records were then screened against the inclusion criteria of the reviews before being quality appraised. The unfiltered search results were saved and retained for future potential re-analysis to help keep the process both replicable and transparent.

Search filters
The search filters utilised in work for this guideline are adaptations of filters designed by the CRD, the Health Information Research Unit of McMaster University, Ontario, and the University of Alberta. Each filter comprises medical subject headings (MeSH), explosions (exp), subheadings (sh), and text words (ti,ab/tw) based on various research design features and characteristics. The qualitative research filter was developed in-house. Each filter comprises index terms relating to the study type(s) and associated text words for the methodological description of the design(s).

Date restrictions
Systematic database searches were initially conducted between April and November 2009 up to the most recent searchable date. Search updates were generated on a 6-monthly basis, with the final re-runs carried out 7 weeks before the guideline consultation.

After this point, studies were only included if they were judged by the GDG to be exceptional (for example, if the evidence was likely to change a recommendation).

Other search methods

Other search methods involved scanning the reference lists of all eligible publications (systematic reviews, stakeholder evidence and included studies) for more published reports and citations of unpublished research, sending lists of studies meeting the inclusion criteria to subject experts (identified through searches and by the GDG) and asking them to check the data for completeness, and provide information of any additional published or unpublished research for consideration (see Appendix 5). Tables of contents of key journals were checked for studies that might have been missed by the database and reference list searches, and key papers in the Science Citation Index (prospectively) were tracked over time for further useful references.

Full details of the search strategies and filters used for the systematic review of clinical evidence are provided in Appendix 8.

Sifting

After the initial search results were scanned liberally to exclude irrelevant papers, the review team used a purpose-built 'study information' database to manage both the included and the excluded studies (eligibility criteria were developed after consultation with the GDG). Double checking of all excluded studies was not done routinely, but a selection of abstracts was checked to ensure reliability of the sifting. For questions without good-quality evidence (after the initial search), a decision was made by the GDG about whether to: (i) repeat the search using subject-specific databases (for example, Education Resources Information Center [ERIC], Cambridge Scientific Abstracts [CSA] – Sociological Abstracts); (ii) conduct a new search for lower levels of evidence; or (iii) adopt a consensus process (see section 3.5.9). Future guidelines will be able to update and extend the usable evidence base starting from the evidence collected, synthesised and analysed for this guideline.

Study selection

All primary-level studies included after the first scan of citations were acquired in full and evaluated for eligibility as they were being entered into the study information database. More specific eligibility criteria were developed for each review question and are described in the relevant clinical evidence chapters. Eligible systematic reviews and primary-level studies were critically appraised for methodological quality (see Appendices 10 and 12). The eligibility of each study was confirmed by at least one member of the GDG.

For some review questions, it was necessary to prioritise the evidence with respect to the UK context (that is, external validity). To make this process explicit, the GDG took into account the following factors when assessing the evidence:
● participant factors (for example, gender, age and ethnicity)
● provider factors (for example, model fidelity, the conditions under which the intervention was performed and the availability of experienced staff to undertake the procedure)

- cultural factors (for example, differences in standard care and differences in the welfare system).

It was the responsibility of GDG members to decide which prioritisation factors were relevant to each review question in light of the UK context and then decide how they should modify their recommendations.

Unpublished evidence

The GDG used a number of criteria when deciding whether or not to accept unpublished data. First, the evidence must have been accompanied by a trial report containing sufficient detail to properly assess the quality of the data. Second, the evidence must have been submitted with the understanding that data from the study and a summary of the study's characteristics would be published in the full guideline. Therefore, the GDG did not accept evidence submitted as commercial in confidence. However, the GDG recognised that unpublished evidence submitted by investigators might later be retracted by those investigators if the inclusion of such data would jeopardise publication of their research.

3.5.5   Data extraction

Study characteristics and outcome data were extracted from all eligible studies, which met the minimum quality criteria, using a bespoke database and Review Manager (The Cochrane Collaboration, 2008) (see Appendix 15b–e).

In most circumstances, for a given outcome (continuous and dichotomous), where more than 50% of the number randomised to any group were lost to follow-up, the data were excluded from the analysis (except for the outcome 'leaving the study early', in which case, the denominator was the number randomised). Where possible, dichotomous efficacy outcomes were calculated on an intention-to-treat basis (that is, a 'once-randomised-always-analyse' basis). Where there was good evidence that those participants who ceased to engage in the study were likely to have an unfavourable outcome, early withdrawals were included in both the numerator and denominator. Adverse effects as reported by the study authors were entered into Review Manager because it was usually not possible to determine whether early withdrawals had an unfavourable outcome. Where there were limited data for a particular review, the 50% rule was not applied. In these circumstances the evidence was downgraded due to the risk of bias.

Where some of the studies failed to report standard deviations (for a continuous outcome), and where an estimate of the variance could not be computed from other reported data or obtained from the study author, the following approach was taken[5]:

- When the number of studies with missing standard deviations was less than a third and when the total number of studies was at least ten, the pooled standard deviation was imputed (calculated from all the other studies in the same meta-analysis that used the same version of the outcome measure). In this case, the appropriateness

---

[5]Based on the approach suggested by Furukawa and colleagues (2006).

of the imputation was made by comparing the standardised mean differences (SMDs) of those trials that had reported standard deviations against the hypothetical SMDs of the same trials based on the imputed standard deviations. If they converged, the meta-analytical results were considered to be reliable.

● When the conditions above could not be met, standard deviations were taken from another related systematic review (if available). In this case, the results were considered to be less reliable.

The meta-analysis of survival data, such as time to any mood episode, was based on log hazard ratios and standard errors. Since individual patient data were not available in included studies, hazard ratios and standard errors calculated from a Cox proportional hazard model were extracted. Where necessary, standard errors (SEs) were calculated from confidence intervals (CIs) or p-value according to standard formulae (see Higgins & Green, 2009). Data were summarised using the generic inverse variance method using Review Manager.

Consultation with another reviewer or members of the GDG was used to overcome difficulties with coding. Data from studies included in existing systematic reviews were extracted independently by one reviewer and cross-checked with the existing dataset. Where possible, two independent reviewers extracted data from new studies. Where double data extraction was not possible, data extracted by one reviewer were checked by the second reviewer. Disagreements were resolved with discussion. Where consensus could not be reached, a third reviewer or GDG members resolved the disagreement. Masked assessment (that is, blind to the journal from which the article comes, the authors, the institution and the magnitude of the effect) was not used since it is unclear that doing so reduces bias (Jadad *et al.*, 1996; Berlin, 2001).

3.5.6   Synthesising the evidence

Where possible, meta-analysis was used to synthesise the evidence using Review Manager. If necessary, reanalyses of the data or sub-analyses were used to answer review questions not addressed in the original studies or reviews.

Dichotomous outcomes were analysed as relative risks (RR) with the associated 95% CI (for an example, see Figure 1). A relative risk (also called a risk ratio) is the ratio of the treatment event rate to the control event rate. An RR of 1 indicates no

Figure 1: Example of a forest plot displaying dichotomous data

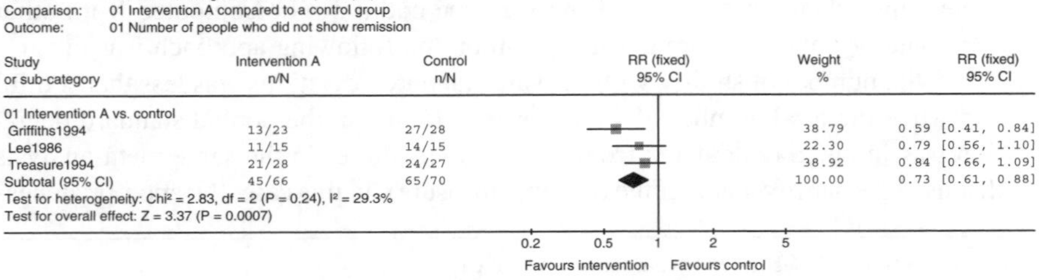

Review: NCCMH clinical guideline review (Example)
Comparison: 01 Intervention A compared to a control group
Outcome: 01 Number of people who did not show remission

Study or sub-category	Intervention A n/N	Control n/N	RR (fixed) 95% CI	Weight %	RR (fixed) 95% CI
01 Intervention A vs. control					
Griffiths1994	13/23	27/28		38.79	0.59 [0.41, 0.84]
Lee1986	11/15	14/15		22.30	0.79 [0.56, 1.10]
Treasure1994	21/28	24/27		38.92	0.84 [0.66, 1.09]
Subtotal (95% CI)	45/66	65/70		100.00	0.73 [0.61, 0.88]

Test for heterogeneity: Chi² = 2.83, df = 2 (P = 0.24), I² = 29.3%
Test for overall effect: Z = 3.37 (P = 0.0007)

    0.2   0.5   1   2   5
    Favours intervention   Favours control

Figure 2: Example of a forest plot displaying continuous data

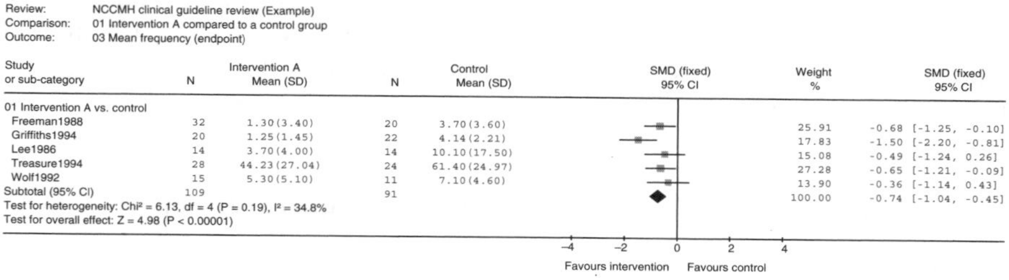

Review: NCCMH clinical guideline review (Example)
Comparison: 01 Intervention A compared to a control group
Outcome: 03 Mean frequency (endpoint)

Study or sub-category	N	Intervention A Mean (SD)	N	Control Mean (SD)	SMD (fixed) 95% CI	Weight %	SMD (fixed) 95% CI
01 Intervention A vs. control							
Freeman1988	32	1.30(3.40)	20	3.70(3.60)		25.91	-0.68 [-1.25, -0.10]
Griffiths1994	20	1.25(1.45)	22	4.14(2.21)		17.83	-1.50 [-2.20, -0.81]
Lee1986	14	3.70(4.00)	14	10.10(17.50)		15.08	-0.49 [-1.24, 0.26]
Treasure1994	28	44.23(27.04)	24	61.40(24.97)		27.28	-0.65 [-1.21, -0.09]
Wolf1992	15	5.30(5.10)	11	7.10(4.60)		13.90	-0.36 [-1.14, 0.43]
Subtotal (95% CI)	109		91			100.00	-0.74 [-1.04, -0.45]

Test for heterogeneity: Chi² = 6.13, df = 4 (P = 0.19), I² = 34.8%
Test for overall effect: Z = 4.98 (P < 0.00001)

```
        -4      -2       0       2       4
        Favours intervention   Favours control
```

difference between treatment and control. In Figure 1 the overall RR of 0.73 indicates that the event rate (that is, non-remission rate) associated with intervention A is about three quarters of that associated with the control intervention or, in other words, the relative risk reduction is 27%.

The CI shows with 95% certainty the range within which the true treatment effect should lie and can be used to determine statistical significance. If the CI does not cross the 'line of no effect', the effect is statistically significant.

Continuous outcomes were analysed using the mean difference (MD), or SMD when different measures were used in different studies to estimate the same underlying effect (for an example, see Figure 2). If reported by study authors, intention-to-treat data, using a method such as 'last observation carried forward', were preferred over data from completers.

To check for consistency of effects among studies, both the I^2 statistic and the chi-squared test of heterogeneity, as well as a visual inspection of the forest plots were used. The I^2 statistic describes the proportion of total variation in study estimates that is due to heterogeneity (Higgins & Thompson, 2002). The I^2 statistic was interpreted in the following way based on Higgins and Green (2009):

- 0 to 40%: might not be important
- 30 to 60%: may represent moderate heterogeneity
- 50 to 90%: may represent substantial heterogeneity
- 75 to 100%: considerable heterogeneity.

Two factors were used to make a judgement about importance of the observed value of I^2: (i) the magnitude and direction of effects, and (ii) the strength of evidence for heterogeneity (for example, p-value from the chi-squared test, or a confidence interval for I^2).

Publication bias
To explore the possibility that the results entered into each meta-analysis suffered from publication bias, data from included studies were entered, where there was sufficient data, into a funnel plot. Asymmetry of the plot was taken to indicate possible publication bias and investigated further.

Where necessary, an estimate of the proportion of eligible data that were missing (because some studies did not include all relevant outcomes) was calculated for each analysis.

Included/excluded studies tables, generated automatically from the study database, were used to summarise general information about each study (see Appendix 15b–e). Where meta-analysis was not appropriate and/or possible, the reported results from each primary-level study were also presented in the included studies table (and included, where appropriate, in a narrative review).

3.5.7   Presenting the data to the Guideline Development Group

Study characteristics tables and, where appropriate, forest plots generated with Review Manager were presented to the GDG in order to prepare a Grades of Recommendation Assessment, Development and Evaluation (GRADE) evidence profile table for each review and to develop recommendations.

GRADE evidence profile tables
A GRADE evidence profile was used to summarise both the quality of the evidence and the results of the evidence synthesis (see Table 2 for an example of an evidence profile). For each outcome, quality may be reduced depending on the following factors:
● **study design** (RCT, observational study, or any other evidence)
● **limitations** (based on the quality of individual studies; see Appendix 10 for the quality checklists)
● **inconsistency** (see section 3.5.6 for how consistency was measured)
● **indirectness** (that is, how closely the outcome measures, interventions and participants match those of interest)
● **imprecision** (based on the confidence interval around the effect size).
    For observational studies, the quality may be increased if there is a large effect, plausible confounding would have changed the effect, or there is evidence of a dose-response gradient (details would be provided under the 'other considerations' column). Each evidence profile also includes a summary of the findings: number of patients included in each group, an estimate of the magnitude of the effect, and the overall quality of the evidence for each outcome.
    The quality of the evidence was based on the quality assessment components (study design, limitations to study quality, consistency, directness and any other considerations) and graded using the following definitions:
● **High** = Further research is very unlikely to change our confidence in the estimate of the effect
● **Moderate** = Further research is likely to have an important impact on our confidence in the estimate of the effect and may change the estimate
● **Low** = Further research is very likely to have an important impact on our confidence in the estimate of the effect and is likely to change the estimate
● **Very low** = Any estimate of effect is very uncertain.
    For further information about the process and the rationale of producing an evidence profile table, see GRADE Working Group (2004).

Table 2: Example of GRADE evidence profile

No. of studies	Design	Limitations	Inconsistency	Indirectness	Imprecision	Other considerations	Intervention	Control	Relative (95% CI)	Absolute	Quality
Outcome 1											
6	Randomised trial	No serious limitations	No serious inconsistency	No serious indirectness	Serious[1]	None	8/191	7/150	RR 0.94 (0.39 to 2.23)	0 fewer per 100 (from 3 fewer to 6 more)	⊕⊕⊕○ MODERATE
Outcome 2											
6	Randomised trial	No serious limitations	No serious inconsistency	No serious indirectness	Serious[2]	None	55/236	63/196	RR 0.44 (0.21 to 0.94)[3]	18 fewer per 100 (from 2 fewer to 25 fewer)	⊕⊕⊕○ MODERATE
Outcome 3											
3	Randomised trial	No serious limitations	No serious inconsistency	No serious indirectness	No serious imprecision	None	83	81	–	MD –1.51 (–3.81 to 0.8)	⊕⊕⊕⊕ HIGH
Outcome 4											
3	Randomised trial	No serious limitations	No serious inconsistency	No serious indirectness	Serious[4]	None	88	93	–	SMD –0.26 (–0.56 to 0.03)	⊕⊕⊕○ MODERATE
Outcomes											
4	Randomised trial	No serious limitations	No serious inconsistency	No serious indirectness	Serious[4]	None	109	114	–	SMD –0.13 (–0.6 to 0.34)	⊕⊕⊕○ MODERATE

[1] The upper confidence limit includes an effect that, if it were real, would represent a benefit that, given the downsides, would still be worth it.
[2] The lower confidence limit crosses a threshold below which, given the downsides of the intervention, one would not recommend the intervention.
[3] Random-effects model.
[4] 95% CI crosses the minimal importance difference threshold.

3.5.8 Forest plots

Each forest plot displayed the effect size and CI for each study as well as the overall summary statistic. The graphs were organised so that the display of data in the area to the left of the 'line of no effect' indicated a 'favourable' outcome for the treatment in question (see Appendix 16).

3.5.9 Method used to answer a review question in the absence of appropriately designed, high-quality research

In the absence of appropriately designed, high-quality research, or where the GDG were of the opinion (on the basis of previous searches or their knowledge of the literature) that there were unlikely to be such evidence, an informal consensus process was adopted. This process focused on those questions that the GDG considered a priority.

Informal consensus

The starting point for the process of informal consensus was that members of the GDG identified, with help from the systematic reviewer, a narrative review that most directly addressed the review question. Where this was not possible, a brief review of the recent literature was initiated.

This existing narrative review or new review was used as a basis for beginning an iterative process to identify lower levels of evidence relevant to the review question and to lead to written statements for the guideline. The process involved a number of steps:

1. A description of what is known about the issues concerning the review question was written by one of the GDG members.
2. Evidence from the existing review or new review was then presented in narrative form to the GDG and further comments were sought about the evidence and its perceived relevance to the review question.
3. Based on the feedback from the GDG, additional information was sought and added to the information collected. This may include studies that did not directly address the review question but were thought to contain relevant data.
4. If, during the course of preparing the report, a significant body of primary-level studies (of appropriate design to answer the question) were identified, a full systematic review was done.
5. At this time, subject possibly to further reviews of the evidence, a series of statements that directly addressed the review question were developed.
6. Following this, on occasions and as deemed appropriate by the GDG, the report was then sent to appointed experts outside the GDG for peer review and comment. The information from this process was then fed back to the GDG for further discussion of the statements.

7. Recommendations were then developed and could also be sent for further external peer review.
8. After this final stage of comment, the statements and recommendations were again reviewed and agreed upon by the GDG.

3.5.10   Forming the clinical summaries and recommendations

Once the GRADE evidence profiles relating to a particular review question were completed, summary evidence tables were developed (these tables are presented in the evidence chapters). Finally, the systematic reviewer in conjunction with GDG members produced a clinical evidence summary.

After the GRADE profiles and clinical summaries were presented to the GDG, the associated recommendations were drafted. In making recommendations, the GDG took into account the trade-off between the benefits and downsides of treatment as well as other important factors, such as economic considerations, social value judgements[6], the requirements to prevent discrimination and to promote equality[7], and the GDG's awareness of practical issues (Eccles *et al.*, 1998; NICE, 2009a).

Finally, to show clearly how the GDG moved from the evidence to the recommendations, each chapter has a section called 'from evidence to recommendations'. Underpinning this section is the concept of the 'strength' of a recommendation (Schunemann *et al.*, 2003). This takes into account the quality of the evidence but is conceptually different. Some recommendations are 'strong' in that the GDG believes that the vast majority of healthcare professionals and patients would choose a particular intervention if they considered the evidence in the same way that the GDG has. This is generally the case if the benefits clearly outweigh the harms for most people and the intervention is likely to be cost effective. However, there is often a closer balance between benefits and harms, and some patients would not choose an intervention whereas others would. This may happen, for example, if some patients are particularly averse to some side effect and others are not. In these circumstances the recommendation is generally weaker, although it may be possible to make stronger recommendations about specific groups of patients. The strength of each recommendation is reflected in the wording of the recommendation, rather than by using labels or symbols.

Where the GDG identified areas in which there are uncertainties or where robust evidence was lacking, they developed research recommendations. Those that were identified as 'high-priority' were included in the NICE version of the guideline; the full set of research recommendations can be found at the end of each evidence chapter.

---

[6]See NICE's Social Value Judgements: Principles for the Development of NICE Guidance: www.nice.org.uk/aboutnice/howwework/socialvaluejudgements/socialvaluejudgements.jsp
[7]See NICE's equality scheme: www.nice.org.uk/aboutnice/howwework/NICEEqualityScheme.jsp

3.6 HEALTH ECONOMICS METHODS

The aim of health economics was to contribute to the guideline's development by providing evidence on the cost effectiveness of interventions covered in this guideline. This was achieved by:
- a systematic literature review of existing economic evidence
- decision-analytic economic modelling.

Systematic reviews of economic literature were conducted in all areas covered by the guideline. Economic modelling was undertaken in areas with likely major resource implications, where the current extent of uncertainty over cost effectiveness was significant and economic analysis was expected to reduce this uncertainty, in accordance with the NICE guidelines manual (NICE, 2009a). Prioritisation of areas for economic modelling was a joint decision between the health economist and the GDG. The rationale for prioritising review questions for economic modelling was set out in an economic plan agreed between NICE, the GDG, the health economist and the other members of the technical team; the economic plan is presented in Appendix 14. The following economic questions were selected as key issues that were addressed by economic modelling:
- cost effectiveness of low and high-intensity psychological interventions for people with GAD
- cost effectiveness of pharmacological interventions for people with GAD
- cost effectiveness of CCBT for people with panic disorder.

In addition, literature on the health-related quality of life of people with GAD and panic disorder was systematically searched to identify studies reporting appropriate health state utility scores that could be utilised in a cost-utility analysis.

The rest of this section describes the methods adopted in the systematic literature review of economic studies. Methods employed in economic modelling are described in the respective sections of the guideline.

3.6.1 Search strategy for economic evidence

Scoping searches
A broad preliminary search of the literature was undertaken in April 2009 to obtain an overview of the issues likely to be covered by the scope, and help define key areas. Searches were restricted to economic studies and health technology assessment reports, and conducted in the following databases:
- EMBASE
- HTA database
- MEDLINE/MEDLINE In-Process
- NHS Economic Evaluation Database (NHS Economic Evaluation Database [EED])

Any relevant economic evidence arising from the clinical evidence scoping searches was also made available to the health economist during the same time frame.

Systematic literature searches

After the review questions were formulated, a systematic search strategy was developed to locate all the relevant evidence. The balance between sensitivity (the power to identify all studies on a particular topic) and specificity (the ability to exclude irrelevant studies from the results) was carefully considered, and a decision made to utilise highly sensitive strategies to identify as complete a set as possible of relevant studies.

In order to ensure comprehensive coverage, search terms for GAD were kept purposely broad to help counter dissimilarities in bibliographic databases in thesaurus terms and indexing practices, and (often) imprecise reporting of study populations by authors in the titles and abstracts of records. It was observed that broader searching retrieved significantly more relevant records than would have been achieved through the use of more specific terms. A broad search for panic was similarly constructed for evidence relating to the effectiveness of CCBT.

A stepwise approach to formulising the searches was implemented at all times, and attempts made to eradicate duplication of effort in areas of overlapping coverage. Searches were restricted to economic studies and health technology assessment reports, and conducted in the following databases:

- CINAHL
- EconLit (the American Economic Association's electronic bibliography)
- EMBASE
- HTA database
- MEDLINE/MEDLINE In-Process
- NHS Economic Evaluation Database (NHS EED)
- PsycINFO.

Any relevant economic evidence arising from the clinical searches was also made available to the health economist during the same time frame.

Reference Manager

Citations from each search were downloaded into Reference Manager and duplicates removed. Records were then screened against the inclusion criteria of the reviews before being quality appraised. The unfiltered search results were saved and retained for future potential re-analysis to help keep the process both replicable and transparent.

Search filters

The search filter for health economics is an adaptation of a filter designed by CRD. The filter comprises medical subject headings (MeSH), explosions (exp), subheadings (sh), and text words (ti,ab/tw) based on various research design features and characteristics.

Date restrictions

Systematic database searches were initially conducted between April and November 2009 up to the most recent searchable date. Search updates were generated on a 6-monthly basis, with the final re-runs carried out 7 weeks before the guideline consultation. After this point, studies were only included if they were judged by the GDG to be exceptional (for example, the evidence was likely to change a recommendation).

Other search methods

Other search methods involved scanning the reference lists of all eligible publications (systematic reviews, stakeholder evidence and included studies from the economic and clinical reviews) to identify further studies for consideration.

Full details of the search strategies and filter used for the systematic review of health economic evidence are provided in Appendix 11.

3.6.2   Inclusion criteria for economic studies

The following inclusion criteria were applied to select studies identified by the economic searches for further consideration:

- Only studies from Organisation for Economic Co-operation and Development countries were included, as the aim of the review was to identify economic information transferable to the UK context.
- Selection criteria based on types of clinical conditions and patients as well as interventions assessed were identical to the clinical literature review.
- Studies were included provided that sufficient details regarding methods and results were available to enable the methodological quality of the study to be assessed, and provided that the study's data and results were extractable.
- Full economic evaluations that compared two or more relevant options and considered both costs and consequences (that is, cost–consequence analysis, cost-effectiveness analysis, cost–utility analysis or cost–benefit analysis), as well as costing analyses that compared only costs between two or more interventions, were included in the review.
- Economic studies were included if they used clinical effectiveness data from an RCT, a cohort study, or a systematic review and meta-analysis of clinical studies. Studies that had a mirror-image design were excluded from the review.
- Studies were included only if the examined interventions were clearly described. This involved the dosage and route of administration and the duration of treatment in the case of pharmacological therapies; and the types of healthcare professionals involved as well as the frequency and duration of treatment in the case of psychological interventions. Evaluations in which medications were treated as a class were excluded from further consideration.

3.6.3   Applicability and quality criteria for economic studies

All economic papers eligible for inclusion were appraised for their applicability and quality using the methodology checklist for economic evaluations recommended by the NICE guidelines manual (NICE, 2009a), which is shown in Appendix 12 of this guideline. The methodology checklist for economic evaluations was also applied to the economic models developed specifically for this guideline. All studies that fully or partially met the applicability and quality criteria described in the methodology checklist were considered during the guideline development process, along with the results of the economic modelling conducted specifically for this guideline. The completed methodology checklists for all economic evaluations considered in the guideline are provided in Appendix 17.

3.6.4   Presentation of economic evidence

The economic evidence considered in the guideline is provided in the respective evidence chapters, following presentation of the relevant clinical evidence. The references to included studies as well as the evidence tables with the characteristics and results of economic studies included in the review, are provided in Appendix 15f. Methods and results of economic modelling undertaken alongside the guideline development process are presented in the relevant evidence chapters. Characteristics and results of all economic studies considered during the guideline development process (including modelling studies conducted for this guideline) are summarised in economic evidence profiles accompanying respective GRADE clinical evidence profiles in Appendix 18.

3.6.5   Results of the systematic search of economic literature

The titles of all studies identified by the systematic search of the literature were screened for their relevance to the topic (that is, economic issues and information on health-related quality of life of people with GAD). References that were clearly not relevant were excluded first. The abstracts of all potentially relevant publications (136 references) were then assessed against the inclusion criteria for economic evaluations by the health economist. Full texts of the studies potentially meeting the inclusion criteria (including those for which eligibility was not clear from the abstract) were obtained. Studies that did not meet the inclusion criteria, were duplicates, were secondary publications of one study, or had been updated in more recent publications were subsequently excluded. Economic evaluations eligible for inclusion (that is, five studies on interventions for GAD and two studies on CCBT for panic disorder) were then appraised for their applicability and quality using the methodology checklist for economic evaluations. Of these, five economic studies fully or partially met the applicability and quality criteria set by NICE. These studies, together with the cost and cost-utility analyses conducted specifically for this guideline, were considered during the formulation of the guideline recommendations.

3.7   STAKEHOLDER CONTRIBUTIONS

Professionals, service users, and companies have contributed to and commented on the guideline at key stages in its development. Stakeholders for this guideline include:
- service user/carer stakeholders: the national service user and carer organisations that represent people with GAD

- professional stakeholders: the national organisations that represent healthcare professionals who are providing services to people with GAD
- commercial stakeholders: the companies that manufacture medicines used in the treatment of GAD
- Primary Care Trusts
- Department of Health and Welsh Assembly Government.

Stakeholders have been involved in the guideline's development at the following points:

- commenting on the initial scope of the guideline and attending a briefing meeting held by NICE
- contributing possible review questions and lists of evidence to the GDG
- commenting on the draft of the guideline.

3.8   VALIDATION OF THE GUIDELINE

Registered stakeholders had an opportunity to comment on the draft guideline, which was posted on the NICE website during the consultation period. Following the consultation, all comments from stakeholders and others were responded to, and the guideline updated as appropriate. The GRP also reviewed the guideline and checked that stakeholders' comments had been addressed.

Following the consultation period, the GDG finalised the recommendations and the NCCMH produced the final documents. These were then submitted to NICE. NICE then formally approved the guideline and issued its guidance to the NHS in England and Wales.

4 EXPERIENCE OF CARE

4.1 INTRODUCTION

This chapter provides an overview of the experience of people with GAD and other anxiety problems, and their families/carers. The first section comprises first-hand personal accounts written by people with GAD and other anxiety problems and carers; the accounts provide some experiences of having a diagnosis of GAD, accessing services, having treatment and caring for someone with an anxiety problem. It should be noted that these accounts are not representative of the experiences of people with GAD and therefore can only ever be illustrative. The second section of the chapter includes a review of the qualitative and quantitative literature, which provides a basis for the recommendations, which appear in the final section.

4.2 PERSONAL ACCOUNTS – PEOPLE WITH GENERALISED ANXIETY DISORDER

4.2.1 Introduction

The writers of the personal accounts were contacted primarily through the service user and carer representatives on the GDG and through various agencies that had access to people with GAD and other anxiety problems. The people who were approached to write the accounts were asked to consider a number of questions when composing their narratives. These included:

- When were you diagnosed with GAD and how old were you?
- How did you feel about the diagnosis? How has your diagnosis affected you in terms of stigma and within your community?
- Do you think that any life experiences led to the onset of the condition? If so, please describe if you feel able to do so.
- When did you seek help from the NHS and whom did you contact? (Please describe this first contact.) What helped or did not help you gain access to services? If you did not personally seek help, please explain how you gained access to services.
- What possible treatments were discussed with you?
- Do you have any language support needs, including needing help with reading or speaking English? If so, did this have an impact on your receiving or understanding a diagnosis of GAD or receiving treatment?
- What treatment(s) did you receive? Please describe both drug treatment and psychological therapy.
- Was the treatment(s) helpful? (Please describe what worked for you and what didn't work for you.)

- How would you describe your relationship with your practitioner(s)? (GP/community psychiatric nurse/psychiatrist, and so on.)
- Did you use any other approaches to help your GAD in addition to those provided by NHS services, for example private treatment? If so please describe what was helpful and not helpful.
- Did you attend a support group and was this helpful? Did any people close to you help and support you?
- How has the nature of the condition changed over time?
- How do you feel now?
- If your condition has improved, do you use any strategies to help you to stay well? If so, please describe these strategies.
- In what ways has GAD affected your everyday life (such as schooling, employment and making relationships) and the lives of those close to you?

Each author signed a consent form allowing their account to be reproduced in this guideline. Six personal accounts from people with GAD were received in total. The majority of individuals who provided an account experienced long-standing anxiety symptoms and often a delay in obtaining a diagnosis of GAD (which may have been compounded by co-existing mental health problems or misrecognition of their anxiety symptoms). However, once diagnosed most expressed a sense of relief. Most individuals also reported adverse impacts on many areas of their lives, particularly on relationships, self-esteem, social interaction, employment and education. Limitations placed on life choices were also commonly experienced, particularly when choosing careers and friendships. The individuals detailed a range of helpful approaches to managing their anxiety, including both NHS and non-NHS prescribed treatments (psychological and pharmacological) and personal coping strategies (exercise, managing diet, relaxation, talking to people who share common experiences and receiving non-judgmental support). Unhelpful factors included stigma and general unsupportive attitudes from healthcare professionals, family members, friends or colleagues (for example, being told to 'pull yourself together'). Individuals were dissatisfied with the lack of treatment options: antidepressants were frequently offered first, leaving people to seek psychological therapy independently and/or privately. People felt that it was important for them that the right treatment should be offered at the right time.

4.2.2   Personal account A

I was diagnosed with GAD in 2004 aged 39. My husband and I had recently moved so that my husband could take up a new job that would significantly develop his career. I had recently accepted voluntary redundancy from my job, so it was the right time for us to move. We moved into a small flat whilst we sold our house. We had no garden and only one car. I had no job and no friends in the area and as a result of the change and my newfound isolation I had a bad bout of anxiety which resulted in me seeing my new GP. My anxiety symptoms included insomnia, excessive worrying about my health (constantly checking my body for new symptoms and worrying that minor symptoms were indicative of a more serious illness), panic attacks, feeling tense and unable to relax, and being easily startled and upset. On an intellectual level I knew the feelings were not rational and that the reality was quite different, but I couldn't control the anxious response and it made me feel powerless and trapped in my anxious feelings. Fortunately for me my new GP had a special interest in anxiety and depression so he was very understanding.

Despite only receiving a diagnosis in 2004, I have been suffering from symptoms of anxiety all my life – it just wasn't recognised as such. From the age of 17 I have also suffered intermittently with panic attacks. It was a huge relief to get a proper diagnosis. Instead of being labelled unsympathetically by family and my GPs as a 'highly strung, nervous child', a 'stressed out, panicky teenager' and a 'jumpy, angst-ridden university student', I could finally say that I had 'generalised anxiety disorder' and 'panic disorder', which were medical conditions that could be treated and controlled. For many years prior to the diagnosis, the main advice I had received from my GP was to 'learn to relax more' and from my parents to 'snap out of it'. Labelling a person with a disease or condition sometimes isn't helpful for recovery, but it helped me by making my anxiety seem real and authentic, rather than a stupid flight of fancy.

In 2004 my GP offered me antidepressants, which I refused, and attendance at a NHS-run stress-management course, which I accepted. The course was useful in expanding my repertoire of coping strategies and it helped to shorten the bout of anxiety that I was experiencing. Prior to the course I used to manage my anxiety via rest, healthy eating and regular exercise. The course provided me with additional skills, such as assertiveness training, time management skills and relaxation exercises. I have since been offered antidepressants by two other GPs, but I still refuse them. In my experience, antidepressants are always the first treatment option offered by GPs. For me, they mask the symptoms and don't help me get to the root cause of the anxiety. I have never been offered counselling by any GP, but I have paid for counselling myself. When I asked several GPs about counselling they told me that there was a waiting list and I could be waiting up to 6 months to see someone. I am currently seeing a counsellor who uses CBT and I am finding it very helpful, so much so that my anxiety has been reduced to much lower levels.

Both my grandmother and my mother displayed anxiety symptoms as I was growing up. My grandmother lived with us all her life and she was a very anxious person. She took Valium for over 25 years and had bouts of deep anxiety. It is possible therefore that I learned to be anxious, but GAD could have been inherited. As well as having GAD and panic attacks, I suffer from anxiety about my health and about illness in general. This has only been a serious problem in the last 5 years or so but I think it started as a child. Both my mother and my father had serious illnesses when I was growing up and neither of them coped particularly well with them. There was always a lot of anxiety in the air at these times and I think I learned to fear illness of any kind.

Over the years my anxiety symptoms have changed. I get far fewer panic attacks now, but I still get attacks of unspecific anxiety that come out of the blue. As mentioned before, I have started to get more anxious about my health too, which has resulted in me seeing my GP more often because of concerns that mild symptoms of illness are actually symptoms of something much more sinister, like cancer. I also worry and fret about the health of my family and friends and I am terrified of them dying.

I try to eat healthily and I exercise regularly, which involves walking for 30 minutes every day and taking more vigorous exercise three times per week. When I have an attack of anxiety it can be quite crippling; but I try to slow down the pace, exercise, get as much sleep as possible and increase the amount of relaxation exercises I do. Unfortunately I comfort eat during really anxious times, which doesn't help me manage my weight (I am overweight as a result), but the amount of comfort eating I do has reduced a bit over the years. I no longer feel guilty about cutting back on social invitations when I am unwell; to be really busy socially when I am anxious makes me exhausted.

Having GAD has changed my life in many ways. I cannot burn the candle at both ends. I have to limit alcohol and travel, both of which aggravate my anxiety. I get fatigued easily and must get enough sleep. My husband is very supportive and understanding, although the anxiety has put a strain on our marriage. I can be very clingy, needy and antisocial when I am in a bad bout and we can argue quite a bit at these times. The arguing fuels the anxiety so it is a vicious cycle. My parents do not accept that I am ill; they think I am highly strung and self-indulgent and that I should pull myself together, so they do not support me much. On a positive note, having GAD and panic attacks has made me take care of myself and I have learned to nurture myself a bit more. In some ways the anxiety pushed me to achieve standards of excellence in school and college and in my career by pushing me to work harder and be smarter.

I now regard anxiety like an old friend who has been with me for over 40 years. My anxiety is part of me and I have learned through counselling to work with the anxiety, not to ignore it. In that way I get better more quickly.

4.2.3   Personal account B

I was diagnosed with generalised anxiety disorder in November 2008 when I was 22, although I believe I suffered from it for around 3 years prior to being officially diagnosed.

It's difficult to pinpoint precisely when it began, although I have a vague idea. After spending a gap year working between 2004 and 2005, I moved to London to pursue a degree. It was a huge change – from earning a wage, I was now relying on my parents and by going to what is considered a prestigious university, I felt that I needed to justify my place there. Coming from a comprehensive school and a working-class family, it was as if I had to prove I was somehow better than students from more privileged backgrounds.

While in London, my mental state began to deteriorate quickly; I spent large periods not interacting with people because I was tied to my work and naturally suspicious, and every element of my day was dictated by the feeling that university work came first before anything else. This meant that while I was doing something enjoyable, whether in a pub, watching television or listening to music, I would be in a constant anxious state.

Over the course of my year in London my anxiety worsened to the point that during exams I broke down entirely. I passed my exams and did attempt to return to London, but because of my anxiety and concerns around finances, I decided not to. This led to the breakdown of my relationship with my then girlfriend who was moving to London to pursue a postgraduate course. This only exacerbated my anxiety further and led to a prolonged period of being single, as I was afraid to approach women and believed that my anxiety prevented me from entering relationships.

Months later I started a fresh degree course at another university and now I felt I had to prove my change of course was the right decision. This meant work could take a lot longer compared with other students and resulted in me being given a week's extension to use if necessary.

My anxiety began to affect my social life more widely; because I was suspicious of people I had met in London, I now found social interaction with new people difficult and frustrating. This meant I spent large parts of my university life alone and relied on the friendship base that I've had for several years through secondary school and sixth form college.

As I entered my final year of university, I had had enough. The anxiety was preventing me from pursuing personal writing projects and fulfilling my ambition to be a journalist. I had previously visited my GP practice on two occasions and got nonchalant responses; firstly I was given self-help sheets and another time was ignored altogether: the disorder was not diagnosed.

It was not until I visited my GP for a third time in October 2008 and explicitly told the practice I did not want to see those previous two GPs that things began to improve. I was seen by a trainee GP who was well aware of the services offered and was empathetic about my condition and fully understanding. Importantly, she finally diagnosed my GAD.

While suffering from anxiety I was also diagnosed with depression. I vowed to never take antidepressants as I did not want my parents to find them and consequently find out about my GAD, and I was uncertain about the possible side effects. Yet eventually through discussion with my new GP I decided it was time to pursue the option and was prescribed citalopram.

I found the antidepressants the most difficult out of all therapies to keep up with; the initial side effects left me feeling highly nauseous and shaky, and almost left me housebound for a small period.

I began talking about my GAD and depression to a tutor of mine, who explained his problems with depression. I realised two things: firstly, there was no need to feel there was a stigma attached to anxiety and depression; and secondly, it made me determined to keep up with the medication and find a long-term solution.

From there I made every effort to combine medication with additional longer-term therapies. Fortunately I gained access to my university's counselling service and was also offered CCBT through my GP and local PCT within a few weeks of beginning antidepressants. I was pleasantly surprised by this, yet somewhat guilty; patients on the NHS occasionally have to wait months to access either service, while I managed to access both quickly.

Since the beginning of this year, I have noticed a real improvement in my condition. The CCBT allowed me to recognise and control thinking errors, meaning I can distinguish between my own thoughts and ones that are triggered by the anxiety. The counselling also let me speak to someone confidentially and to work out an organised plan of action since my GAD meant I had trouble planning and organising.

I also began talking to my family about my problems with anxiety and depression, which was particularly difficult at first. They were concerned about why I hadn't raised this sooner and why I was not able to confide in them. I explained that I felt this was something I had to deal with on my own because of stigma and because I wanted to gain independence on my own instead of relying on the help of others. In the end my family understood my point of view, yet I also felt rather stupid: family are there to help you in whichever way they can and whatever situation you are in. I now feel I can be more open with my family and get support when I need it most.

I now feel more comfortable in social circumstances, can balance work and my social life better and feel much more confident in pursuing my writing and journalistic ambitions. I am now off antidepressants and, thanks to therapy, I can manage independently and confidently.

Importantly, I feel gaining treatment at the beginning of my final year of university helped me secure a first-class honours degree and employment. I am also in a relationship and have been for almost 6 months. There is the odd period of anxiety and depression, but these are far less common and less debilitating then previously. I feel so much better.

4.2.4   Personal account C

About 18 years ago I began experiencing panic attacks which initially occurred occasionally but over time became more frequent and worrying. These attacks followed several close family bereavements. Initially I was prescribed antidepressants which I took for a few weeks – I was reluctant to take medication and instead learned more about panic attacks and how to manage them from self-help books. Several years later I returned to my GP on two or three occasions because I was experiencing acute and debilitating anxiety around revision and exam times while doing a part-time psychology degree. Despite doing very well in exams my confidence did not grow and instead I became more anxious. My doctor was dismissive and offered me no advice other than to say it was normal to feel anxious at these times.

About 5 years ago I felt under a lot of pressure with work, family and my final exams. At this time my anxiety became more chronic; I experienced it quite severely and almost constantly. I felt I could not cope and had to take time off work and defer my final exams. I returned to my doctor (a different doctor than previously), who recommended antidepressants. I explained I would like to avoid this as I thought therapy would be more helpful to me. It was a battle to convince him to refer me to the practice's person-centred counsellor. At this time my GP and counsellor believed that my difficulties were due to depression. I found this very frustrating because my overriding experience was of daily, debilitating anxiety and chronic worry.

I was allowed about six sessions of counselling after which I continued seeing my counsellor on a private basis. Although in some respects the counselling was helpful in terms of support and having someone to discuss my concerns with, it did not provide me with any strategies with which to manage my anxiety. Over several months and while receiving weekly counselling sessions my anxiety worsened and I had to take further time off work. I believe my anxiety worsened because I felt unable to control my anxiety and I felt less able to cope. This time I agreed to take an anti-depressant (Seroxat). This did help to a degree and I was able to return to work and my studies. At the same time I continued to see my counsellor privately. However, while taking Seroxat, I never felt quite myself and I felt the range of emotions available to me had become limited. After about 12 months I decided to come off the anti-depressants and I gradually reduced them over 7 or 8 months under the supervision of my counsellor. A few months later I had a relapse, which led to me taking sick leave. At this time I began taking St John's wort and although I took it for a year or so, I could not say with any certainty if it helped or not.

As I was unable to give an indication of when I might return to work and my employer felt unable to continue running his business without a manager for an indefinite period of time, my contract was terminated on health grounds. Around this time I stopped seeing my counsellor as I felt the therapy was not helping. On a number of occasions I raised the possibility of having CBT but for reasons I did not fully understand this was not offered. I then contacted Mind who assessed me but because of limited resources, and because I had just had a course of therapy, they were unable to offer me further therapy. They did offer me a relaxation course, which I attended and found very helpful – I still practise this daily. I was also able to do an assertiveness and self-esteem course, which helped me enormously as it enabled me to see that I was not assertive in some of my relationships. It also gave me skills for managing aggressive and passive-aggressive people, which I found especially helpful.

At this time I also started going to the gym on a regular basis; again this was very helpful and I continue to exercise regularly in order to maintain my mental wellbeing. I also started voluntary work in a school and this led to me being offered a job, which I agreed to take on a part-time basis. Although I explained to the head of the school I wanted to do this work on a part-time basis because I was still struggling with my anxiety it soon became clear the job required a full-time administrator. With a reduction in staff my workload increased and after a few months I felt unable to cope and my anxiety worsened. I discussed this with the head but to no avail and again I had to take time off. My contract was not renewed.

Around this time I contacted my doctor again and asked if I could be referred to a cognitive behavioural therapist; he gave me the telephone number for the community mental health team and asked me to phone them myself. After waiting several weeks I was assessed and told I would be contacted when my case had been before a panel who would decide if I was suitable to access their services. Several weeks later I was told my condition was not severe enough, but if I deteriorated further I should contact them again. It was also suggested that I contact Anxiety UK. I was quite devastated by this response; I felt there was no help available to me on the NHS and I was now unemployed and on benefits and was not in a position to pay for further therapy.

Experience of care

I contacted Anxiety UK and they arranged for me to see a cognitive behavioural therapist and although I had to pay for this I was only asked to pay a small amount because I was on benefits. One of the advantages of seeing a therapist through Anxiety UK was there were no limits on the number of sessions I could have – I felt at the time that this took a lot of pressure off me because a time limit was not being placed on how quickly I should get better. By this time my self-belief was rock bottom and I probably had around 40 sessions of CBT.

My recovery was somewhat up and down but on the whole CBT helped me a great deal – I began to feel I was able to manage my anxiety. Also for the first time in 3 years I began to feel more hopeful for the future. I also attended a self-help group (provided by Self Help Services, Anxiety UK's sister organisation), which I found very useful. It was a relief to meet other people who understood how I felt. It was also great seeing other people who were further along the path of recovery – I met some very inspiring people. While attending the self-help group I learned about the possibility of training to become a volunteer helpline worker with Anxiety UK. With a great deal of encouragement from some members of the group who were already doing this I decided to apply. Following my training I began to work as a volunteer even though my anxiety was still a major problem. At Anxiety UK there is a strong belief that you can still make a contribution in terms of work/volunteering while learning to overcome your own anxiety and this was indeed the case for me.

It was while I was working at Anxiety UK that it became apparent that I was suffering from GAD with depression – it was a relief to know this because it helped me to understand what I was dealing with and what I needed to do to get better.

As my confidence grew and my anxiety became more manageable I started volunteering for Self Help Services as a CCBT support worker. I did this for several months and then I was offered the opportunity to co-ordinate a CCBT service, which I have done for almost 2 years on a part-time basis alongside my volunteer helpline work. My volunteering work has been very rewarding – it also provided me with the opportunity to work in a positive and supportive environment where there is no stigma attached to having a mental health problem.

In early 2008 I started taking steps to return to full-time work and went to an organisation that helps people on incapacity benefit return to work. Looking back I realise that I was probably not ready but I felt under some pressure to try (my incapacity benefit review was due in a several months). This led to a worsening of my anxiety and I started to fear another relapse. I returned to my doctors who referred me to the primary care mental health team. After a few weeks I was contacted and an assessment was carried out over the phone. I was offered CCBT, which I felt was inappropriate given my history and the duration of my GAD (4 years), or person-centred counselling – no other options were offered. Although I reluctantly decided to have counselling I did find it beneficial because the therapist was able to help me increase my self-belief – a problem that had become almost as troublesome as the GAD. Over time my anxiety/self-belief improved and this was further helped by the realisation, following two major life events, that I am able to cope with such events.

54

I also found doing a few courses (maths and IT) helped increase my confidence and by doing these alongside my other commitments enabled me to believe that I could cope with returning to full-time work, which I will be doing shortly.

4.2.5   Personal account D

I was diagnosed with GAD around 2000 when I was 15. I was already having CBT after being referred by my doctor for depression. My therapist recognised that my anxiety did not attach itself to one particular thing or event, but was generalised. She informed my doctor, who agreed and was very supportive. I was quite mature for my age, so was mostly just relieved to have a name for the fact that I am on edge all the time. I thought there must be something much worse wrong with me. I found that GAD meant I was never relaxed and found it very hard to enjoy social situations, school work and any type of relationship with friends and family. I still did all these things but with a constant feeling of anxiety and stress. I was always determined to do everything in spite of my anxiety, so I don't feel it affected me that much – I just didn't enjoy things the way others did.

I feel that my GAD may have been brought on by my Mum having a very stressful pregnancy and the fact that until I was 8 I lived with a very unpredictable and mentally ill father, who changed from minute to minute. Maybe I never learnt to relax properly. I did not ever feel secure and relaxed and that has translated to my adult life.

I first went to my doctor for help when I was about 14 and was diagnosed with severe depression. Obviously at that age my mum was involved in asking me to go to the doctor but I remember that I did go by myself and I recognised I wasn't well. The doctor discussed therapy (eventually I contacted a private CBT therapist due to long NHS waiting lists) and I was prescribed venlafaxine (I was not offered any other treatments). I found both very helpful and still use CBT regularly today for both depression and anxiety, although my main problem is with anxiety. My doctor was very helpful and supportive, but I did have a bad experience when I had to get my prescription from another doctor who was very unsupportive and indicated that I was just lazy and could easily get over my problems by myself. The problem really is that stigma is so ingrained, it needs to change for healthcare professionals first before the public will have more understanding.

Since then, I have constantly been on medication. I went onto Prozac and then onto citalopram, which I am still taking. I am also currently having private counselling to sort out issues from my childhood and my relationship with my father. CBT remains the most helpful thing I have ever done and I always recommend it to anyone who may need it. I have also been supported by friends and family, although I am careful who I talk to about my feelings and diagnosis as I know how people may react due to the stigma of mental health issues! No one at my work knows anything about it. I would really love to be able to talk about it more freely, but am really worried about being judged.

I have got better over time. I think I function really well – I have a good job, social life, act in my spare time and I don't think anyone would guess that I have an anxiety disorder. I'm not sure how well I would function without medication but I am much more accepting of who I am and how I am. I have also seen a nutritionist and have found changes in diet very beneficial for anxiety. I am still on edge most of the time, and don't really ever relax properly, but I feel better about it now and enjoy my life. It makes me really enjoy things when I can and appreciate things more. I stay well using CBT techniques day to day, taking citalopram and doing exercise (swimming helps me a lot, as does dancing). I have found 'usual' relaxation techniques difficult, as it is hard for me to relax and be still, but I do try to meditate sometimes.

I feel that GAD affects my everyday life in that I have to be aware of what my limitations are and how to deal with them. I have to watch myself to check I am not becoming too stressed – but I think everyone could do with being a bit more self-aware and I don't feel like this is an issue for me. I do not let it affect my work, but it has led me to choose a less stressful work environment that I know I can handle and enjoy. I find that it does not affect personal relationships too much, as I know myself and how to control it, and only tell people about it if I trust them and know they will be understanding. I would say that the experience of GAD has made me more empathetic and self-aware, and while I find the condition hard sometimes, I would not want to lose these traits.

4.2.6   Personal account E

As far as I was aware, my childhood was a happy one. I was a confident little girl, quite bright and sociable at primary school and went to ballet, Sunday school and Brownies where I was keen to do my best. Secondary school was also not a problem for me. Having passed my 11 plus, I went to a small selective school where I was often top of the class. I worked hard, had a Saturday job which I stuck at despite hating it for a while, and eventually got to university and teaching training college, both of which I loved. I then began a career in teaching.

It was in 1990 at the age of 25 that I began to suffer with anxiety. I thought I felt sick and took a day off work. I became very distressed and asked my mother to travel 50 miles by train to be with me. I had never done this before. She came and found me weepy and overly worried and scared of being sick. I had always had 'a thing' about being sick and had not vomited since the age of about 12, however, this terror was something new. We went to the doctors and explained my difficulties and the doctor gave me medication (Buspar). I am not really sure that the medication helped. There was certainly no immediate effect – as I now know would be expected with medication of this type. He recorded 'anxiety state' on my sick note which I was hurt by as I felt this was his way of saying I was not ill, just worrying and making an unnecessary fuss. There was little explanation or reassurance. He told me to walk round the streets drinking from cans and to go and sit in A&E to see people with real problems!

I went back to work after a while as I have high standards and it is highly unusual for me to be off sick, but I had lost my confidence. At the age of 29 I had a serious relapse, which led to me being off work for about 8 months. This time I had a different GP. He was one of the least helpful professionals that I have dealt with in my life. He prescribed drugs and referred me to a psychiatrist, who referred me to a day hospital which I attended for several months. This was all to his credit. However, he seemed to have no idea how to talk to anxious people, scolding me for not recovering sooner, and explaining that his budget was finite and he had targets to meet. He told me lies and caused me to feel angry – which is not how I am. (I made a formal complaint about him.) I also met with a clinical psychologist for several years. We talked through whatever I wanted to talk through, with his role seeming to be to challenge my thinking and perspective on things. I felt that he understood and that he knew I was trying to dig myself out of the hole I was in. I knew he was an expert in the field of post-traumatic stress and trusted his judgements. It was not easy to share the 'inner me' with him – but I never missed an appointment. I feel that this therapy did help.

I didn't know why I had to go to the day hospital but did, religiously, never missing an appointment. I was allocated a key worker and attended group and individual sessions. I was terrified at times and would shake from head to foot. I met people from all walks of life – people who self-harmed and were suicidal, and violent people – but I got to know them all and we tried to support each other, respecting each other's problems. We did relaxation exercises, groups where we talked about our worries, 'lessons' about fight and flight, and so on. I also had to attend gym and art classes. In individual lessons, we did some behavioural work, such as trying to fight the fear I felt regarding vomit. I had to hold a sick bucket, clear up imitation sick and watch a video of actors pretending to vomit. The practical help was good, although I felt pathetic that I was being asked to nurse a bucket and would despair about what my next challenge might be. I was embarrassed when receiving praise for 'managing' the tasks that I felt 'normal' people would do easily. It was not easy but it did give me more self-belief and confidence that, in the real world, I might cope and not cry like a baby if faced with a vomit situation! I felt I needed more of this type of support, but my time at the hospital was terminated.

Two things were not great about the experience at the day hospital. I was given a student as a key worker for a while and I did not feel confident that she knew what she was doing. Then, when her placement was over, I had to establish a relationship with a new key worker. We worked well together until she left. Amazingly, the powers that be decided I had recovered enough to leave the day hospital at the same time my key worker left. I am not sure that that decision was based on medical diagnosis – more convenience, I believe. Anyhow, I coped!

I think that being brave enough to confide and trust in others and understanding the feelings of panic and dread were key to being able to control the wish to run away. The medication was changed by the hospital psychiatrist to imipramine (150 mg), which I think also helped. Talking to people who were not judgemental was great, as was having my thoughts challenged by professionals in a kindly manner. I don't think the art and gym helped, nor the relaxation! My mother and father took it in turns to live with me for several months as I was terrified of being alone. My mother rang the Phobics Society who offered support – it was great to realise there were many more like me and that it was not the end of the world.

I do feel that life experiences have contributed to my condition. I knew nothing of my father's mental illness until a dreadful day when I was 16 and learned that he had held a carving knife to my mother's throat. He had apparently been ill for many years with bipolar affective disorder but the truth had been masked from me. His mood swings, temper and strange behaviours had all been hidden or disguised so that I would not be hurt by them – but I guess the stresses in the house were there. I am an only child and had no one to talk to. Indeed, talking is not something that is done well in the family. You just get on and work hard and take your mind off any problems, which is perhaps not always the best option. I think being the only child also put a lot of pressure on me to do well. I am now a perfectionist in all that I do, and if I am not confident in something, I do not do it. I work, work, work, and give little time to myself. I have no hobbies. I like to be in control.

It is embarrassing and makes me angry with myself when worrying prevents me from joining in with what most people would call 'a treat' or 'an adventure', but I imagine too many problems that may arise. I can worry for England and build my life in such a way as to avoid as much anxiety as possible (apart from going to work, which is a very stressful environment). There is a famous children's poem called 'Whatif', and that's how I think! I know that I am missing out on so much but cannot muster the courage to do many things such as travel on trains or buses, go abroad, learn new skills, socialise with new acquaintances, or look for promotion. I had a phase when I could not eat in front of others so never ate out. I have phases where I cannot drink in the company of others. I could not travel and still dislike travelling in strange cars. I will not go on public transport for more than about 3 miles. I worry about decisions so take a long time to make them. I worried that a child of mine might turn out like me, so have chosen to not have children.

I have very low self-esteem, despite being quite successful and highly respected in my career. Indeed, my employer sees improving my confidence as being a target for me and cannot understand why everyone else's perception of me as being highly skilled and competent fails to give me the reassurance that I need. Confidence never used to be an issue. I believe that the GAD and putting limitations on my life has made me feel worthless and useless at times. As my friends have moved forwards and 'grown', I have become stationary and shrunken.

My friends know what I am like. Whenever there is a social occasion, I apologise profusely and rarely attend if alcohol and potential over indulging may occur. I feel ridiculous about this and spend the day of the occasion wishing I dare go, but this is not enough. I somehow feel not good enough to go and that I'll spoil the occasion because people will have to look after me. I also have a thing of not looking 'right' – not wearing the 'in' clothes, having the right hair style, make-up and so on.

I now live with my partner of 13 years. He does not understand my phobia but lives with the limitations it puts on my life. Indeed, we do not discuss my 'condition' as previous discussions were not helpful. Following 12 years of being supported by medication, I have been off it for a year and a half. I am working full time as a teacher where the 'threat' of a child vomiting is with me each day. However, I do not panic as much as I used to when a child says they feel ill and my colleagues know that I may need their support should the event occur. I keep rubber gloves nearby and also carry an opaque carrier bag with me at all times just in case I am ill.

I think that society in general does not understand mental issues and often sees them as a way for people to shirk away from their responsibilities. Television and the media are not helpful as most of their coverage of mental illness is about where 'care in the community' has gone seriously wrong, rather than trying to explain and educate the community it serves.

4.2.7   Personal account F

I began suffering with GAD 5 years ago. I am now 52. At the time I had dreadful problems with my periods, which were very heavy and frequent. I then began to have bladder problems. Hospital tests revealed that my bladder wall was prone to bleeding owing to a deep infection. I was told by my consultant that most sufferers needed group support as the constant pain and discomfort was very wearing. The support group for the bladder infection was 10 miles away, and in my current state I couldn't face the journey or the socialising. I could not cope at all, so I was visiting my GP two or three times a week, desperate for help, however I was given no such help. I was already suffering from depression, which was diagnosed about 10 years ago.

I was on escitalopram, but it really didn't help the depression or the GAD. My doctor believed I was OK. He said, 'When the weather improves, so will you!' But the feeling of pure panic was overwhelming. My family was at a loss what to do. My mother lives just down the street from us and I would visit her every day. When I became ill I would walk down to see her, but I couldn't settle there. I would go home and go around all the rooms, and feel so afraid and low that I would just go to bed. This became a pattern. The only thing I wanted to do was turn myself off.

After much pleading for help, my doctor gave me a low dose of diazepam, but only for 1 week. Even that didn't do anything, and my doctor wouldn't give me any more. I did a lot of crying and pleading, and as I was desperate at the time I couldn't understand why he wouldn't prescribe me any more diazepam. But now I understand – I think he was worried I might get addicted to them.

I visited the doctor again in a suicidal state. He sent the mental health team and they gave me an action plan which consisted of things we 'could do' including CBT. I had no faith in it, but I would consider anything. I had an appointment for CBT, but when I went I was told that No Panic was doing everything the CBT would achieve anyway, that is, telephone counselling. On the back of my action plan were various phone numbers, including for the Samaritans, Mind, SANE and No Panic. I rang them all again and again. Although very sympathetic, the Samaritans, Mind and SANE left me feeling no better nor worse than if I hadn't rung them. No Panic was the only organisation that really helped. By this time I could hardly leave the house, and could only spend a limited time out of bed; it was my only escape. I was later told that I had been failed by the mental health system. I agree. The thought of travelling backwards and forwards for CBT only added to the anxiety.

I also rang NHS Direct and asked how I could be committed. The reply was harsh and unkind. I knew that the person I spoke to didn't know how I felt, but it just made things worse.

I visited A&E numerous times. During one visit a mental health nurse was on duty and he said that my antidepressants were not strong enough and to visit my GP again and discuss it. My doctor wouldn't hear of it. 'I am your doctor' he said. 'I decide. Not a nurse. I will only listen to another doctor.' That was that. He then said, 'I don't know what to do for you now!' I was in a terrible state. I got so bad I took an overdose of venlafaxine, which I had been prescribed years before. Although it made me sick, I woke up as early the next morning as I always do, about 3 o'clock.

It was after this that I asked for one-to-one mentoring over the phone from No Panic. It helped. They were understanding and kind and I didn't feel stupid!

I wanted to know what I was suffering with, so I looked on the internet. GAD was the first explanation for exactly how I felt. Not wanting to self diagnose, I visited my GP and asked him if I had GAD. 'Yes, I think you do', he replied. I asked him about seeing a psychiatrist, but this never materialised. The mental health team told me about beta blockers and another doctor I saw had no problem prescribing them. I think they help, although she now says she wants to take me off them in the next few months. I am so afraid. All in all I am still struggling.

4.3   PERSONAL ACCOUNTS – CARERS

4.3.1   Introduction

The methods used for obtaining the carers' accounts were the same as outlined in section 4.2.1, but the questions also included:
● How long have you been a carer of someone with GAD?
● How involved are/were you in the treatment plans of the person with GAD?
● Were you offered support by the person's practitioners?
● Do you yourself have any mental health problems? If so, were you offered an assessment and treatment by a healthcare professional?
● How would you describe your relationship with the person's practitioner(s)? (GP/community psychiatric nurse/psychiatrist, and so on.)
● Did you attend a support group and was this helpful? Did any people close to you help and support you in your role as a carer?
● In what ways has being a carer affected your everyday life (such as schooling, employment and making relationships) and the lives of those close to you?
Two personal accounts from carers of people with anxiety were received, which offer very different perspectives of being a carer.

4.3.2   Carer account A

My grandparents live near us and have been very involved in my growing up and helped my mother a lot. However, 2 years ago, my competent and energetic grandmother suddenly changed. She became anxious, was scared to go out without my grandfather, and occasionally panicked that she was close to death. This change occurred following an incident when a friend from church, who had only been slightly ill, called one day for help and within a few hours had died. After this my grandmother's health declined. She complained of feeling cold all the time, and became anxious about her heart. She was in her late 70s, but her health had not been giving cause for concern. She looked after herself well, ate sensibly, and had regular check-ups. Now she was anxious all the time and sometimes, especially at night, thought she was going to die (we now know she was experiencing panic attacks). On one occasion she believed that her heart was failing, and asked my grandfather to ring 999. The hospital carried out all the usual tests for suspected heart problems and kept her in overnight. This happened more than once until the only place she felt safe was the hospital – a place she had always wanted to avoid up till now!

At the time we thought we would lose her. Nobody realised that the problem was psychological rather than physical. At her age, it was necessary to put her through quite arduous tests before the healthcare professionals could be sure that she was suffering with anxiety. I think the fact that my grandmother had private health insurance compounded this difficulty, as many tests were made available to her, and she could choose between two healthcare systems. One doctor at the local A&E, where she was always treated with great kindness, finally made it clear that tests revealed no major heart or other problems and she was experiencing anxiety.

However it was hard for my grandmother to accept this diagnosis because she felt so physically unwell and was not of a generation likely to admit to mental health problems. More tests were offered by the private sector, and I question the validity of this, as the extensive tests were an ordeal that both weakened my grandmother and prolonged the period before she was ready to accept the anxiety diagnosis. I imagine this may often be a difficulty with older patients, as it is necessary to establish that their symptoms do not have a physical basis, but medical staff need to be alert to the possibility that there may be a psychological component to their presentation, and be able to put this possibility to the patient without pushing them into denial. The net effect otherwise is to delay the introduction of treatments for the anxiety while testing for non-existent physical problems.

My mother and I were quicker to accept the suggestion that anxiety might be at the root of the problem. I thought that the sudden death of her friend, which had been so traumatic for my grandmother, might have stirred up earlier experiences of her childhood growing up during the second world war, and also of the premature death of a loved younger brother in the late 1980s. I asked a friend, who works on a telephone helpline and has personally suffered with anxiety, if she could help. While not pushing my grandmother too much, she was able to secure her agreement to send her information about some simple techniques to help manage the anxious feelings. I used this as a cue to buy a book that explained anxiety and outlined cognitive behavioural therapy as a Christmas present. Being provided with written information and guidance and finding that it did indeed apply to her – but not feeling railroaded into deeper interpretations that failed to acknowledge her physical symptoms – was the most helpful thing at this time. It also opened the door to an exploration of alternative approaches.

My grandmother saw a homeopath for a while, and was given helpful advice about her sleep patterns. She also saw a person-centred counsellor privately for a short time, which helped her gain insight into the meaning of what had happened and realise that she could not always be the strong person that she had tried to be up till now. She was prescribed antidepressants and other medications by her GP, but has a tendency to give up taking medicines, as she is quite slight and they often seem to have a disproportionate effect. At first, she was quite unwilling to persevere with medication and would describe having a distressing reaction in the first few days. However at one point an opportune combination of painkillers for her back pain, a cough suppressant for sinus problems and antidepressants for the anxiety finally resolved long-standing insomnia problems dating back to her brother's death. The restoration of her ability to sleep through the night was a significant factor in aiding her recovery. She continues now to take a low dose of citalopram and finds it helpful.

My grandmother is not wholly over her anxiety, but is learning to adjust her life and goals, and live with the condition. She still doesn't go out without my grandfather, and doesn't like to travel too far. But she sleeps and eats quite well, and is able to let others look after her more after years of being the strong one. For all the close family, including myself, it has been a relief to know that her life is not threatened and her condition is manageable. However we have had to adjust to a significant change in her and therefore in the family system as a whole. It is hard when someone goes from being very competent to suddenly lacking in confidence and needing a lot of support. She used to travel the world and now just getting on a bus feels difficult. She has become very reliant on my grandfather, whose own health is not good, so my mother and I do everything we can to support them both emotionally and practically. We are aware that they need more help, even though it's hard to ask for it, and offer what we can while trying not to give offence. I think we have also seen a different, more vulnerable, side of my grandmother – part of her we didn't get to know before because of her confident and strong approach to life. I am glad to be able to offer her some support now in the way that she has always tried to support me. I am also grateful to the NHS for the help they have given her, and the perseverance of medical staff in establishing a diagnosis and seeking effective treatment.

Finally, I think it is helpful if professionals can find ways of talking about psychological distress that patients are able to accept. It was hard for my grandmother to come to terms with something like this happening to her, and subsequently to tell family and friends that she had been diagnosed with anxiety rather than a physical health problem. There is still a stigma about mental health, especially for the older generation. However the stresses of older age – coping with worsening health and seeing people you care about die – are very likely to bring about a resurgence of anxiety that people may have experienced earlier in their lives, but had been able to control with the greater resilience of youth.

4.3.3   Carer account B

My son is almost 21 years old and has recently been diagnosed with generalised anxiety disorder. He has had problems with anxiety and panic attacks from around the age

Experience of care

of 16 following a summer when he and some friends were smoking cannabis on a regular basis for about 2 weeks. He had previously been quite an anxious child and labelled 'hyper' at school. There had been a question as to whether he was dyspraxic or just a 'clumsy child' but it was never investigated. Otherwise he was fit and well, having had no physical problems other than recurrent tonsillitis as a toddler and a tonsillectomy aged 6.

The symptoms of anxiety led his father (my ex-husband who had trained as a registered mental health nurse years before) to arrange CBT with a former colleague. Our son had CBT as a private arrangement (our GP and the NHS were not involved) over a 3-month period, which eventually helped.

At the age of 17 following the death of a college friend and being mugged, he became anxious again but coped to a certain extent until he was 18 when finally after much persuasion he went to our GP who gave him 'self-help' leaflets. His anxiety at the time was not debilitating enough to affect his usual life style.

In the past 5 months my son's GAD has become acute and my caring role has increased. He has been unable to work, eat or carry out 'normal activities' (for example, travel on public transport) without me being present. His father suggested that our son should see his colleague again for CBT, which he agreed to until the NHS appointment materialised.

I have visited my son's GP with him on many occasions regarding his anxiety. The second GP referred him for CBT in November 2009 and he was offered a first appointment in January 2010 – this was 'online' not person to person. After two events that led to visits to the A&E department at the local hospital, a fourth GP agreed to refer him to a CPN [community psychiatric nurse]. On both occasions, the casualty doctors explained they could not refer him to the psychiatric team as he was not 'a danger to himself or others'. They recommended a GP referral to psychiatry.

The GP who referred my son prescribed citalopram (10 mg daily) as a short-term measure to alleviate his anxiety not knowing how soon he would be offered an appointment with a psychiatrist. After 2 weeks my son's anxiety had reached such a peak that I had to leave work to come home having had three panicky phone calls from him in an hour. I phoned the CPN's office to enquire about his referral as we felt desperate that we hadn't heard anything. They had not received the GP's referral and suggested I contacted the GP. The GP apologised that he had 'forgotten' and faxed a referral as 'urgent'.

I requested involvement in my son's first hospital visit with the CPN for his assessment and I was invited in for 10 minutes after his hour with her. When I enquired what the plan was for his care, she replied that he was going to be referred for psychological treatment and see a psychiatrist regarding further medication as my son had developed a fear of eating/choking. I asked what I should be doing to help him, where he could go on a daily basis, where there were support groups, day centres, and so on. I was told I would know more after his psychological appointment. I was not offered help.

I have had reactive depression in the past and recognise when I am 'going down the slippery slope'. I know the triggers (for example, sleep deprivation, which I was having constantly with my son waking me regularly during the night, afraid that he was going to die.) My son's healthcare professionals did not ask me about my mental health but I believe they may have asked my son when taking a history. I made it clear that I had taken time off from work to look after him as I had no family in the area or partner and his father had never provided support or care. On one occasion when I had to contact a CPN on the phone I was told it was my right to have compassionate leave from work. I had been off a total of 6 weeks by then and my allowance from work is 5 days. I was totally exhausted at the time and had phoned to ask about respite care and advice regarding the side effects of quetiapine (recently prescribed to my son) that were very worrying.

Generally speaking my relationship with my son's practitioners is unsatisfactory. I lost some trust when the GP forgot to refer my son and I am made to feel I am almost a nuisance when I have been in touch with the GP for advice regarding my son's medication even though he had many side effects and I needed help. The CPN in the day unit who I contacted for the same reason was not helpful and only phoned back with a relayed message from the consultant after my son had made a complaint with the help of an advocate from Mind. This was 6 days after my initial plea for help. When I contacted the consultant psychiatrist's secretary regarding the same problem I was told that he did not speak to patients or their carers on the phone. She also told me that if I was worried about my son I should take him to A&E. It was then that my son and I went to see the staff at our local Mind, who were very helpful. Due to the relationship with my son's practitioners I feel he has little confidence in them, which in turn adds to his anxiety.

My son and I have not been offered information regarding support groups from the hospital staff or GP. I have searched the internet and have found a few voluntary organisations that offer support and activities for my son and a carers group for me. I have had moral support from a handful of friends including two work colleagues. A close friend offered practical help in terms of 'son sitting' for a couple of hours when he was at his worst. My son's friends have been extremely supportive, calling at the house and staying in with him, which enables me to go out for an hour or two.

My whole life has been 'put on hold' since my son's GAD. I cannot plan holidays or weekends, which I did find frustrating at first as I am usually a very active person. Leaving my son alone for more than an hour to go to the shops can be traumatic for him. I am not yet able to return to full-time work as he is too anxious to be left for such a long time alone. At present I am working mornings only, returning home at 2 pm and he has arranged his sleeping pattern so that he goes to bed at 3 to 4 am and sleeps until midday. He is just coping with that. When I arrive home I usually cook him a meal or encourage him to make toast or whatever he fancies. He will not eat without me being there but will drink a Complan whilst alone if I prepare it for him and leave it in the fridge.

I feel constantly tired, have developed eczema, my arthritis, which is usually under control when I have the chance to exercise, has flared up and my relationships are suffering. My true friends, however, have shown their worth and I am very grateful.

My son is due to begin psychotherapy in March 2010, 5 months after the start of the problem. He has improved and I feel cautiously optimistic that he will continue to do so, be it a long and winding road. Sadly, his progress is not, I feel, due to the input of the NHS as a whole, but he is getting by 'with a little help from his friends' (and his mother!).

4.4 REVIEW OF THE LITERATURE

4.4.1 Introduction

A systematic search for published reviews of relevant qualitative studies of people with GAD was undertaken. The aim of the review was to explore the experience of care for people with GAD and their families and carers in terms of the broad topics of receiving the diagnosis, accessing services and having treatment.

4.4.2 Review question

For people who have GAD and their carers, what are their experiences of having problems with GAD, of access to services and of treatment?

4.4.3 Evidence search

Reviews were sought of qualitative studies that used relevant first-hand experiences of people with GAD and families/carers. For more information about the databases searched see Table 3.

The GDG decided that quantitative studies picked up in this search should also be included in this review, if they looked at the experience of GAD. A total of 7,961 references were identified by the electronic search. Of these references, 7,909 were excluded at the screening stage on the basis of reading the title and/or abstract. The remaining 52 references were assessed for eligibility on the basis of the full text.

The search found one systematic review that explored the experience of care for people with anxiety and depression (Prins *et al.*, 2008), however, the results focused

Table 3: Databases searched and inclusion/exclusion criteria for clinical evidence

Electronic databases	MEDLINE, EMBASE, CINAHL, PSYCINFO, IBSS
Date searched	01.01.1994 to 09.05.2010
Study design	Systematic reviews of qualitative studies, surveys, observational studies, primary studies
Population	People with anxiety and depression and families/carers
Outcomes	None specified

mainly on people with depression alone. Therefore, a decision was made to look at the studies identified in the review for this guideline that met the following inclusion criteria: qualitative or quantitative studies looking at the experience of people with either a primary diagnosis of GAD, mixed anxiety or mixed anxiety with depression, in which at least 20% of the population were diagnosed with GAD or mixed anxiety. Overall, six qualitative studies, 20 quantitative studies and two non-systematic reviews met these inclusion criteria, the characteristics of which have been summarised in Appendix 15a. Twenty-five studies were considered for the review but they did not meet the inclusion criteria so were excluded (see Appendix 15a). The most common reason for exclusion was that at least 20% of the population did not have a diagnosis of anxiety disorder.

4.4.4   Experience of generalised anxiety disorder

This section summarises quantitative and qualitative studies that have looked at the experience of GAD, in terms of thoughts and feelings, worry content and comorbid depression.

Thoughts, feelings and worry content in people with GAD
The following experiences of thoughts, feelings and worry content are drawn from people who have pure GAD. Craske and colleagues (1989) were among the first to examine worry content in GAD and found that, in general, people with GAD have long-lasting and uncontrollable worries that are likely to occur without a precipitant. Compared with controls, they worried more about 'illness, health or injury' and less about financial matters, but no significant differences were found regarding family, work or school. Diefenbach and colleagues (2001a) also found no differences between those with GAD and controls regarding worries about family or work, and no differences on finances, health and other miscellaneous topics (in people 60 years and over). They did find that compared with another study that looked at a younger population, older adults with GAD had more health worries than younger adults with GAD, an effect which was not found to be as strong in the control comparison (Roemer *et al.*, 1997). More recently, Becker and colleagues (2003) found that compared with controls with no mental health problems, as well as people with other anxiety, somatoform, mood and eating disorders and substance-related problems, women with GAD had significantly higher levels of worry about work, family, finances and social factors.

Breitholtz and Westling (1998) interviewed 43 people with GAD and found that 'inability to cope' was reported as the most 'important' thought, followed by thoughts of loss of self-control, injury to self/others and ill-health. In addition 44 people with panic disorder were interviewed in the comparison group and were found, in general, to have more thoughts focusing on physical, as opposed to mental, catastrophes than those with GAD. Diefenbach and colleagues (2001b) compared worry content in people with GAD to people with depression and found the latter population reported a higher frequency of worries relating to relationships, finances, lack of confidence and having an aimless future, whereas people with GAD reported slightly more physical threats and loss of control. Hoyer and colleagues (2002) found that young women with GAD experienced a higher intensity and frequency of worry episodes compared with women with other anxiety disorders or depression and healthy controls.

Borkovec and Roemer (1995) examined reasons behind their worry in a population sample of college students and found that, compared with non-anxious controls, people with GAD saw worry as a distraction from other emotional concerns and an effective problem-solving solution, and they also held superstitious beliefs that worrying about a certain event would reduce the likelihood of it happening. Decker and colleagues (2008) used questionnaires and daily diaries to investigate emotional experiences and found that people with GAD experienced negative emotions more intensely compared with controls without the disorder. Those with GAD reported higher use of emotion regulation strategies, including: situation selection (avoidance to manage emotions), distraction, rumination, masking/hiding emotions and soothing one's emotions. Overall, people with GAD had to work harder to regulate emotions; however this was based on a student population, so findings could differ in a treatment-seeking population.

More recent findings by Ruscio & Borkovec (2004) looked at the differences between highly worried individuals without GAD and worriers with GAD. Subjects were matched on their trait level of worry and completed an attention-focused task after which they were assessed. Results showed that people with GAD experience less control over negative intrusive thoughts following worry and report stronger negative beliefs than their worry matched controls. The quantity, frequency and intensity of worries, however, did not differ between the two groups. GAD is therefore associated with some unique experiences compared with equally worried individuals without the condition.

GAD and depression

There were a few studies that looked at differences between 'pure' GAD and GAD comorbid with depression or another anxiety disorder. Porensky and colleagues (2009) used a range of tools to investigate experience of disability, health-related quality of life, anxiety, depression and cognition in older adults. People with GAD reported significantly less participation and more difficulty in carrying out everyday activities than controls with no mental health problems. The largest differences in functional limitations between GAD and the controls were found in mental and emotional health, social functioning and vitality. People with GAD also used more healthcare resources than the controls, although this was not linked to severity. This study was in a population aged 60 years or above, so findings may not be wholly applicable to younger age groups.

Wittchen and colleagues (2000) found people with 'pure' GAD or GAD comorbid with depression rated their general health, mental health, physical functioning, physical and emotional roles, bodily pain, social functioning and vitality, significantly lower than non-affected controls.

4.4.5   Access and engagement

In a review of the under recognition of anxiety and mood disorders, Tylee & Walters (2007) highlighted that 70% of patients with depression and anxiety have a somatic presentation. People with GAD do not often associate their symptoms with a psychological disorder and those who normalise or minimise their symptoms are less likely to be identified. Recognition of depression and anxiety is usually determined by the knowledge, skills and attitudes of primary care practitioners. Factors that improve recognition from primary care practitioners include empathy, interest in psychiatry and asking about family and problems at home.

Mojtabai and colleagues (2002) found that participants with comorbid problems were three times more likely than participants with anxiety disorders alone to perceive a need for professional help. Of 648 people with anxiety, 21% perceived a need for professional help and of these only 14% sought professional help.

Haslam and colleagues (2004) found that people often do not realise that their symptoms, which are sometimes physical, are indicative of anxiety or depression and can be treated, until either someone (a friend family or colleague) advises them of this, or a crisis occurs. Once people are aware they have a mental health problem, they may feel more motivated to seek help. In a study by Lang (2005) one barrier to seeking treatment included people feeling that they could deal with their problems themselves. Other barriers included problems with locating a therapist, lack of time, transportation and cost.

Kadam and colleagues (2001), interviewing 27 patients in four UK general practices, reported that people with depression with or without anxiety, who had sought help through a range of self-help and alternative therapies, found that having someone to talk to was very important, particularly someone outside their family situation such as a counsellor, who would listen, understand and offer advice. However, finding someone to talk to could be a problem. Some saw their GP as being willing to listen and refer on; others had reservations about approaching their GP, thinking that they would be 'too busy' to spend time on what they might consider to be trivial matters and some felt that they were not encouraged to disclose their emotions or psychological problems. There were some preconceptions that a GP would do nothing but prescribe drugs (although some people did find drug treatment useful, the majority did not want to take medication). People would have liked to have had more information provided by their GP and better access to preferred treatments. People also felt that waiting times were a barrier to accessing help – when they felt anxious they wanted to speak to someone immediately and not wait days or weeks for an appointment.

Boardman and colleagues (2004) looked at the prevalence of unmet need among patients attending primary care services in Cheshire for mental health problems and found that there was a high level of unmet need especially among people with anxiety disorders. Needs were assessed by the practitioner rather than the patient, who may not have accepted the treatments offered.

In a non-systematic review, Blair and Ramones (1996) highlighted that anxiety can severely affect all aspects of a person's life and can lead to physical diseases or stress-related disorders if it is left untreated. The author suggests that untreated anxiety can also lead to poor treatment adherence and therefore a negative outcome, which can cause resentment towards healthcare professionals. This review mentions misconceptions by nurses and highlights that people who have had untreated symptoms for a long time are more likely to become irritable and demand medication.

Ironically, if a person were seen as being demanding or difficult, the accuracy of their self-report of anxiety symptoms might be doubted.

Gender and ethnicity

Alvidrez and Azocar (1999) highlighted the practical barriers for women with depression (66%) and anxiety (15% with GAD and 9% with panic) in accessing effective treatments, such as financial problems, lack of transport and childcare. These were pressing issues for women rather than stigma-related barriers such as embarrassment, being afraid of what others may think and lack of approval from family. Ninety-two percent of those surveyed identified at least one barrier to treatment; the average number of barriers identified was 2.2. Fewer women with a college education identified a stigma-based barrier to treatment than those who did not attend college; college-educated women were also less interested in medication. Thirty-four percent of people with common mental health disorders (such as a current mood or anxiety disorder) anticipated a stigma-based barrier to services, compared with 13% of people without a common mental health disorder. There was high interest in individual and group therapy, depression prevention and mood management classes, and a low interest in medication. There was no ethnic difference in whether a person preferred medication or therapy.

South Asian people with common mental health disorders, including GAD, were found to be less likely to have problems identified in primary care and have lower rates of uptake for treatment, and were more likely to incorporate physical symptoms into their presentation (Commander *et al.*, 2004). Commander and colleagues also found that South Asian people did not seek support from lay or traditional healers and were more likely to consult a GP regarding their problem rather than a friend or relative. However, only half of both sets of participants (South Asians and Caucasians) who saw their GP disclosed their problem. There was no difference between South Asian and white populations in terms of what they understood to be their psychological problem, and what they perceived to be the cause.

4.4.6   Beliefs about and experiences of treatment

Beliefs about and preferences for treatment

Prins and colleagues (2009) found that there is a high level of need for care, as perceived by primary care patients with anxiety and/or depression. The majority expressed a need for information (58%) and counselling (61%) as opposed to medication (41.5%). Older people are less likely to perceive a need for services, with the exception of medication.

In the study by Boardman and colleagues (2004) medication and CBT were the two treatment options most often thought appropriate for anxiety.

Wagner and colleagues (2005) found that patients' beliefs about psychotropic medication and psychotherapy did not depend on any specific anxiety disorder they were experiencing. However, people who also had depression had more favourable views of medication than those with anxiety alone.

Experience of care

Bystritsky and colleagues (2005) found that people with anxiety disorders from a white ethnic background had more favourable views about medication and psychotherapy than non-whites. People who had strong beliefs in medication were more likely to adhere to treatment; however, a strong belief in either medication or psychotherapy could not predict adherence to the use of psychotherapy. Older people had more favourable views of medication than younger people.

A study of older people with depression (with and without anxiety) by Gum and colleagues (2006) showed that experiences of previous treatments play a strong role in treatment preference. People with previous experience of counselling or those who had visited a mental health professional before had more favourable views about counselling than people who had not. Similarly, people who had used antidepressants in the past and found them helpful had more favourable views about medication. It was felt that access to preferred treatment is better provided in collaborative care rather than usual care. Although some factors could help to predict a treatment preference, once that treatment is received it does not predict patient satisfaction or outcomes.

Lang (2005) found that primary care patients (45% with distress, 35% somatisation, 30% depression and 20% anxiety) expressed a need for help in understanding the cause of their feelings, learning skills to manage their mood and having someone to talk to. Seventy percent of people expressed a preference for individual treatment over a group mode of treatment and medication. People said that if such interventions were offered in their clinic they would be more likely to attend fitness programmes and classes about healthy living and stress management than counselling. People who had taken antidepressants in the past, compared with those who had not, appreciated that the response was not immediate and could take time. People of Caucasian origin received more mental health treatment, believed medication to be more helpful and thought that they could work their problems out for themselves compared with non-Caucasians. Of the people who had individual counselling, the majority were non-Caucasian.

Experiences of drug and psychological treatment
In a study by Haslam and colleagues (2004) side effects of medication for depression and anxiety were described by participants as being similar to symptoms of anxiety, such as confusion, dizziness, nausea and inability to make decisions. Others reported side effects such as shaking, severe weight loss, speech impairment, and feeling unsteady, disorientated and generally ill. For this reason, non-adherence to medication for anxiety and depression was common – people took less medication than prescribed, and discontinued it because of side effects or because symptoms had not improved. People were generally not positive about taking medication but for those who found it beneficial, there was a common fear of dependency or addiction, which could also lead to stopping medication too soon. There was some confusion among people with anxiety and depression about how long it took for antidepressants to work and about why, at the start of treatment, their symptoms could become worse before they improved at the beginning of treatment (where there were high rates of discontinuation). Regular reviews of medication could help people maintain treatment long

enough to prevent relapse. Moreover people felt that if they were given more information about their medication they would be more able to comply with their course of treatment.

The study by Haslam and colleagues (2004) was a focus group study involving people with anxiety and depression, as well as some of the staff involved in their care, and the authors recommended the provision of information leaflets in primary care to help people know what to expect in terms of side effects of medication, worsening of symptoms at the outset of treatment and withdrawal effects on discontinuation. People reported finding pharmaceutical drug company leaflets unhelpful and alarming. Given the time pressures on GPs, information leaflets would help the patient to improve take-up and maintenance of treatment. GPs could be supported by practice nurses and mental health professionals (such as primary care mental health workers) in the provision of information.

In a non-systematic review of issues around the under treatment of anxiety, Blair and Ramones (1996) highlighted that if people do not receive appropriate treatment from their GP, they may repeatedly present with a range of complaints or self-medicate with over the counter agents, alcohol or other substances. As well as inadequate assessment, often people do not seek help at an early stage and wait until their anxiety becomes overwhelming.

Deacon and Abramowitz (2005) found that CBT was an effective and acceptable long-term intervention compared with medication for people with mixed anxiety disorders (11% GAD), and that patients would choose CBT as a first choice of treatment, even if they had a recent history of taking medication. Some people thought that medication was acceptable and effective in the long-term but this depended on whether they were currently taking it – their attitudes were more favourable if they were taking medication.

4.4.7   GP perspectives

The primary care consultation is a two-person process in which the role and action of the GP can influence the patient's involvement in the dialogue and the outcome of the consultation. Rijswijk and colleagues (2009) conducted a qualitative study using loosely structured interviews in focus groups comprising 23 family physicians from the Netherlands and identified barriers in recognising, diagnosing and managing depression and anxiety in general practice. This study found that there may be difficulties in agreeing a diagnosis with the patient, who may be more inclined to view their symptoms as having a physical cause. Without agreement as to the cause of the problem it was hard for effective treatment to proceed. Reaching a diagnosis was experienced as more problematic in relation to certain groups: the elderly, those with a different cultural background and those with limited verbal skills.

Rijswijk and colleagues (2009) also found that over long periods of time, symptoms of anxiety and depression may fluctuate, which makes it difficult to classify these disorders as distinct diagnostic entities. Assessment tools can be seen as useful aids to diagnosis, especially in determining the severity and burden of the illness.

They could also help with monitoring progress and could be used by practice nurses as well as doctors. The time constraints of GPs' work made it difficult to give adequate time talking to anxious patients. Patient education was felt to be empowering and follow-up by practice nurses was supported.

Patients could be resistant towards drug treatment due to fear of side effects and dependency, and there was often an inclination to discontinue treatment too soon. Finally, Rijswijk and colleagues (2009) reported that GPs found it difficult to balance recommendations in guidelines of a specific, often drug-based approach to treatment, with meeting patient preferences.

Bjorner and Kjolsrod (2002) described the pressures on GPs to be active in consultations and find solutions for their patients (who had a range of physical conditions, some of which were comorbid with anxiety, and who had been prescribed benzodiazepines and minor opiates), rather than adopting a 'wait and see' approach. As a result there was an over-emphasis on prescribing, especially in the face of people's chronic difficulties. The study also found that doctors could feel embattled by patients' needs and demands, resorting to high or medium levels of prescribing.

It should be noted that both studies reviewed in this section are non-UK. There has not been much comparable work done on GP perspectives in a UK population and the GDG concluded that this is clearly needed to explore the potential barriers to the accurate detection and effective treatment of anxiety disorders in the UK.

4.5 FROM EVIDENCE TO RECOMMENDATIONS

4.5.1 Experience of generalised anxiety disorder

The literature highlights that people with GAD have long-standing and often uncontrollable worries and negative thoughts, and that the worries are likely to occur without a specific reason, although people with anxiety tend to also worry about health concerns or their family and feel an inability to cope. Older people were more likely to worry about their health than younger people. The anecdotal evidence from the personal accounts also reveals that people with GAD experience long-standing symptoms. Most reported that GAD affected many areas of their lives, particularly relationships, self-esteem, daily activities, employment, work life and education.

4.5.2 Access and engagement

The literature suggested that few people with GAD perceive the need for professional help and even fewer seek it. When people with GAD do present to primary care the disorder is under-recognised, for a variety of reasons. Firstly, people with GAD may not associate their symptoms with a psychological disorder and may 'minimise' such symptoms in their presentation and they may not realise that their somatic symptoms are related to anxiety; second, primary care practitioners may not be skilled in recognising GAD; and third, healthcare professionals and the wider society may collude in the tendency for people with GAD to minimise or trivialise their symptoms. The personal accounts also suggest that GAD may not be recognised initially, or the symptoms may not be taken seriously. Again, this may be because the person with anxiety minimises the symptoms, or that professionals do not recognise the seriousness of the presentation.

It was agreed by the GDG that appropriate training of primary care practitioners should help to improve the recognition of GAD and reduce the tendency to misrecognise or minimise symptoms. Healthcare professionals should be aware that people with anxiety may exhibit reassurance seeking behaviours and that trust, a non-judgemental approach, collaborative working, and engaging the person from the outset are important in establishing a therapeutic relationship.

There was an expressed need for information about GAD and its treatments in both the reviewed literature and the personal accounts. Lack of accessible information may be a particular issue for people from black and Asian minority ethnic groups. Both the literature and the personal accounts also highlight the importance of self-help, support groups and help lines for people with GAD so that they can talk to people with similar experiences.

4.5.3 Experience of treatment

The literature indicated that patients' experience of previous treatments (both psychological and pharmacological) played a strong role in treatment preference. People's experiences of drug treatments were mixed; some reported side effects that were similar to their anxiety symptoms and non-adherence to medication was common. People felt that if they were given more information about their medication they would be more able to comply with their course of treatment. Some people with GAD found medication helpful and relied on it to function in important parts of their life. They did, however, worry about side effects and long-term dependency on drugs and attempted to either reduce their dose or stop taking the medication altogether. Most people, however, felt that they could not do this for fear of relapse – discontinuation symptoms could be interpreted as a return of their original anxiety. In three studies, there was an expressed patient preference for psychological treatment such as CBT, individual or group treatment and counselling over medication. Regardless of whether a person with anxiety has a history of taking medication, most found CBT an acceptable long-term intervention compared with drug treatment. Medication was also considered effective as a long-term intervention but this was more favoured by people who were currently taking medication.

The personal accounts highlighted a range of helpful approaches to managing anxiety, including both NHS and non-NHS prescribed treatments (psychological and pharmacological), but there was dissatisfaction about the lack of treatment options: antidepressants were frequently offered first leaving people to seek psychological therapy independently and/or privately.

4.5.4   GP perspectives

GPs felt that a diagnosis should not be made prematurely and that people should be given time to overcome their problems. Some thought that an accurate diagnosis was helpful for symptom-specific treatment. It could be difficult to reach agreement with a patient that the underlying cause of their physical problems might be psychological, which could make it challenging to agree on a treatment strategy, particularly in the elderly, those with limited verbal skills and ethnic minorities.

4.5.5   Families and carers

Issues for families and carers of people with GAD did not emerge from the literature and common themes could not be identified in the personal accounts, which offer different perspectives of being a carer. However, common principles about working with families and carers of people with common mental health disorders apply, such as providing accessible information, helping people to access support groups, and offering a carer's assessment of the carer's caring, physical and mental health needs.

4.5.6   Recommendations

Information and support for people with GAD, their families and carers
4.5.6.1   When working with people with GAD:
- build a relationship and work in an open, engaging and non-judgemental manner
- explore the person's worries in order to jointly understand the impact of GAD
- explore treatment options collaboratively with the person, indicating that decision making is a shared process
- ensure that discussion takes place in settings in which confidentiality, privacy and dignity are respected.

4.5.6.2   When working with people with GAD:
- provide information appropriate to the person's level of understanding about the nature of GAD and the range of treatments available
- if possible, ensure that comprehensive written information is available in the person's preferred language and in audio format
- offer independent interpreters if needed.

4.5.6.3   When families and carers are involved in supporting a person with GAD, consider:
- offering a carer's assessment of their caring, physical and mental health needs
- providing information, including contact details, about family and carer support groups and voluntary organisations, and helping families or carers to access these

- negotiating between the person with GAD and their family or carers about confidentiality and the sharing of information
- providing written and verbal information on GAD and its management, including how families and carers can support the person
- providing contact numbers and information about what to do and who to contact in a crisis.

4.5.6.4 Inform people with GAD about local and national self-help organisations and support groups, in particular where they can talk to others with similar experiences.

4.5.6.5 For people with GAD who have a mild learning disability or mild acquired cognitive impairment, offer the same interventions as for other people with GAD, adjusting the method of delivery or duration of the intervention if necessary to take account of the disability or impairment.

4.5.6.6 When assessing or offering an intervention to people with GAD and a moderate to severe learning disability or moderate to severe acquired cognitive impairment, consider consulting with a relevant specialist.

Identification

4.5.6.7 Identify and communicate the diagnosis of GAD as early as possible to help people understand the disorder and start effective treatment promptly.

4.5.6.8 Consider the diagnosis of GAD in people presenting with anxiety or significant worry, and in people who attend primary care frequently who:
- have a chronic physical health problem or
- do not have a physical health problem but are seeking reassurance about somatic symptoms (particularly older people and people from minority ethnic groups) or
- are repeatedly worrying about a wide range of different issues.

4.5.6.9 When a person with known or suspected GAD attends primary care seeking reassurance about a chronic physical health problem or somatic symptoms and/or repeated worrying, consider with the person whether some of their symptoms may be due to GAD.

5   ASSESSMENT AND SERVICE DELIVERY

5.1   INTRODUCTION

The first section of this chapter describes key issues in the recognition and assessment of suspected and confirmed GAD. The second section sets out a stepped-care approach for the treatment and management of GAD. Unlike other chapters in this guideline, this chapter is not based on a systematic review of evidence but represents the consensus of the GDG drawing on the available literature.

5.2   RECOGNITION AND ASSESSMENT

5.2.1   Introduction

Recognition of GAD is necessary for effective treatment. Untreated GAD most commonly runs a chronic course (Yonkers *et al.*, 2000) with significant disability (Kessler, 2000; Wittchen, 2002). However, recognition of GAD in primary care is poor with the result that the majority of people with GAD do not receive treatment or they have inappropriate treatment (Roy-Byrne & Wagner, 2004; Wittchen, 2002; Wittchen & Jacobi, 2005). In the most recent UK *Adult Psychiatric Morbidity in England* survey (McManus *et al.*, 2009), only 33% of patients with GAD reported receiving any treatment.

Assessment is an important part of the process of the recognition of GAD, and also to identify factors that impact on course of the disorder and its treatment.

5.2.2   Narrative review

People with GAD often do not present to services complaining of symptoms of anxiety. The central 'multiple excessive worries' component of GAD may present as 'concerns' or 'fears', which in medical settings may be a concern about the person's health or about the health of a family member (Dugas & Robichaud, 2007). People with GAD may mention these apologetically or as an aside, and it is only after a succession of consultations that it is apparent that the person has multiple worries and that reassurance has only had a temporary impact on the worries.

People with GAD, particularly older age groups and people from minority ethnic groups, often just present with the physical or somatic symptoms of GAD, which are not recognised as anxiety symptoms (Arroll & Kendrick, 2009) or lead to lengthy and costly investigations (Hales *et al.*, 1997). For this reason, GAD is common in hospital medical settings (Culpepper, 2009; Kennedy & Schwab, 1997) as well as in primary care.

A number of symptoms are common to both GAD and depression – fatigue, sleep disturbance, irritability and concentration difficulties (APA, 2000). This symptom overlap, together with the high comorbidity between GAD and depressive disorders (Kessler *et al.*, 2008) complicates recognition and diagnosis.

To compound the difficulties, GAD is also commonly comorbid with other anxiety disorders (especially panic disorder, social phobia, and specific phobias) (Bitran *et al.*, 2009; Carter *et al.*, 2001; Hunt *et al.*, 2002; Grant *et al.*, 2005; Kessler *et al.*, 2005b). In addition, worry, as well as being the central feature of GAD, also occurs in other anxiety disorders (panic disorder, social phobia, PTSD, OCD and hypochondriasis). In these other anxiety disorders, the focus of the worry is on a single area (having a panic attack, social embarrassment, a traumatic event, being contaminated or having a serious illness), whereas in GAD people's worries are about a range of different areas of their life (APA, 2000). As the criterion of anxiety and worry being 'excessive' is dependent on whether it is appropriate to the person's life circumstances (for example, worry about a family member's health may be appropriate if the family member has been recently diagnosed with a life-threatening illness), assessment of the individual's life circumstances is necessary.

Groups with a higher prevalence of GAD and for whom there should be a higher index of suspicion are:
- people with a chronic physical health problem (Culpepper, 2009; Gili *et al.*, 2010; Roy-Byrne *et al.*, 2008; Sareen *et al.*, 2006).
- people with other anxiety and depressive disorders (Bitran *et al.*, 2009; Carter *et al.*, 2001; Hunt *et al.*, 2002; Grant *et al.*, 2005; Kessler *et al.*, 2005b).
- people who misuse alcohol (Grant *et al.*, 2005; Kessler *et al.*, 2005b).

A number of case identification measures exist for GAD. These are reviewed in the NICE guideline on referral and identification of common mental health disorders (NCCMH, 2011 forthcoming).

Evidence of factors that influence the course of GAD is limited. Factors that have been found to be associated with reduced likelihood of remission include the duration and severity of GAD, comorbid major depressive disorder and other anxiety disorders, comorbid personality disorder, and poorer spousal and family relationships (Yonkers *et al.*, 2000). However, for a number of these factors the relationships with outcome are inconsistent between studies or have not been replicated in other samples.

5.3   FROM EVIDENCE TO RECOMMENDATIONS

On the basis of this narrative review of the literature and evidence from the personal accounts and literature review in Chapter 4, the GDG highlighted a number of areas as important in the recognition and assessment of GAD.

Early detection of GAD was identified as important, given the evidence above that untreated GAD is likely to run a chronic and often disabling course. The personal accounts of GAD contained several examples of long delay in identifying the condition and obtaining a diagnosis. Receiving the diagnosis of GAD was experienced by several people as a relief and the first step in making progress with their GAD.

The review of how GAD presents in primary care and information about groups with high prevalence gives pointers to practitioners in identifying GAD and what should alert them to the possibility of GAD. Repeated presentation with worries about different issues is the most central feature of GAD. Presentation of different physical symptoms of anxiety and the high prevalence of GAD in people with a chronic physical health problem suggest these factors should raise the index of suspicion.

Although good evidence of factors predictive of the course of GAD to determine treatment choice is lacking, from the evidence available and from consensus of the GDG, a variety of factors was considered to be important when assessing GAD and relevant for treatment choices in the guideline. These included duration of GAD, degree of distress, functional impairment, diagnostic comorbidities and past mental health history and response to treatment. The key comorbidities to assess, as identified from the literature and consensus of the GDG, are other anxiety and depressive disorders, alcohol and drug misuse and chronic physical health problems.

With the high comorbidity between GAD and both depressive and other anxiety disorders, a key consideration in treatment is which disorder to treat first. The first NICE guideline on depression recommended treating depression first where there is a comorbid depressive and anxiety disorder (NICE, 2004b). The updated depression guideline (NICE, 2009b), in contrast, recommends consulting the NICE guideline for the relevant anxiety disorder and considering treating the anxiety disorder first (since effective treatment of the anxiety disorder will often improve the depression or the depressive symptoms). In line with the updated depression guideline, the GDG for this guideline considered that healthcare professionals need to make a clinical judgement where the GAD is comorbid with other anxiety disorders or a depressive disorder and treat first the disorder that is primary in terms of severity and likelihood that treatment will impact on overall functioning.

With the high comorbidity between GAD and alcohol misuse, the GDG considered a recommendation about when to first treat the GAD and when first to manage the alcohol misuse to be important for healthcare professionals. With this issue also being considered at the same time by the GDG for the guideline on harmful drinking and alcohol dependence, the recommendations from that guideline (NICE, 2011a) were adapted by the GDG and included in the GAD guideline.

5.3.1   Recommendations

Assessment and education

5.3.1.1   For people who may have GAD, conduct a comprehensive assessment that does not rely solely on the number, severity and duration of symptoms, but also considers the degree of distress and functional impairment.

5.3.1.2   As part of the comprehensive assessment, consider how the following factors might have affected the development, course and severity of the person's GAD:
- any comorbid depressive disorder or other anxiety disorder
- any comorbid substance misuse
- any comorbid medical condition
- a history of mental health disorders
- past experience of, and response to, treatments.

5.3.1.3   For people with GAD and a comorbid depressive or other anxiety disorder, treat the primary disorder first (that is, the one that is more severe and in which it is more likely that treatment will improve overall functioning).[8,9]

5.3.1.4   For people with GAD who misuse substances, be aware that:
- substance misuse can be a complication of GAD
- non-harmful substance use should not be a contraindication to the treatment of GAD
- harmful and dependent substance misuse should be treated first as this may lead to significant improvement in the symptoms of GAD.[10]

5.3.1.5   Following assessment and diagnosis of GAD:
- provide education about the nature of GAD and the options for treatment, including the 'Understanding NICE guidance' booklet[11]
- monitor the person's symptoms and functioning (known as active monitoring).

This is because education and active monitoring may improve less severe presentations and avoid the need for further interventions.

5.3.1.6   Discuss the use of over-the-counter medications and preparations with people with GAD. Explain the potential for interactions with other prescribed and over-the-counter medications and the lack of evidence to support their safe use.

5.4   STEPPED CARE

5.4.1   Introduction

Stepped care is a framework of organisation of pathways of care designed to reduce burden to patients while maximising health gain (Davison, 2000; Scogin *et al.*, 2003).

---

[8]For NICE guidance on depression, obsessive–compulsive disorder and post-traumatic stress disorder see NICE, 2009b; 2009c; 2005a; 2005b.

[9]NICE is developing a guideline on identification and pathways to care for common mental health disorders (NICE, 2011b, forthcoming).

[10]For NICE guidance on drug misuse and alcohol-use disorders see NICE, 2007a; 2007b; 2010a; 2010b; 2011a.

[11]Available from www.nice.org.uk/CG113

It is based on two core principles: first, that interventions offered should be the 'least restrictive' that will be effective for the problems with which an individual presents; second, that there should be 'self-correcting' monitoring and feedback systems to ensure individuals are stepped up to more intensive interventions if they are not obtaining sufficient benefit from the initially offered treatments. In treatment of common mental health problems, the most often used less intensive interventions are those less dependent on the availability of professional staff and focus on patient-initiated use of evidence-based 'health technologies' (Richards *et al.*, 2002) including books (Marrs, 1995), video- and audiotapes (Blenkiron, 2001), computer programmes (Proudfoot *et al.*, 2004) and internet sites (Spek *et al.*, 2007). The use of these materials may be entirely managed by the patient (referred to as 'non-facilitated self-help' in this guideline but also known as 'pure self-help') or involve some limited input from a professional or paraprofessional (referred to as guided self-help) (Gellatly *et al.*, 2007). More intensive interventions include psychological therapies that are dependent on highly-trained staff and pharmacological interventions, which require medically trained staff to prescribe and monitor and can have negative side effects as well as benefits.

5.4.2   Narrative review

Stepped-care models, as a basis for care pathways, have been incorporated into previous NICE guidelines for depression and anxiety disorders (NICE, 2005b; 2009b; 2009c), although they were not part of the previous NICE guideline on anxiety (NICE, 2004a). A stepped-care framework is also central to the IAPT programme in the UK.

Evidence for stepped care in depression was recently systematically reviewed for the update of the NICE guideline on depression (NICE, 2009b; NCCMH, 2010a). This review updated an earlier review (Bower & Gilbody, 2005) on stepped care in the provision of psychological therapies, to which can be added an Australian review of mental health services organisation (Andrews & Tolkein II Team, 2006). Both these earlier reviews concluded that, although of inherently good sense, there was a lack of specific empirical evidence for stepped care in either provision of psychological therapies or of high prevalence mental health disorders. Although the literature search of the systematic review for the depression guideline (NCCMH, 2010a) was limited to studies of depression, the one RCT that evaluated stepped care included people with both depression and anxiety disorders (van Straten *et al.*, 2006). This found no clinical benefit of stepped care over care where therapists could determine choice of intervention without any clinical protocol, although it was possible that stepped care was more cost effective (Hakkart-van Roijen *et al.*, 2006). The review for the guideline on depression (NCCMH, 2010a) also considered the evaluation of the two IAPT demonstration sites (Clark *et al.*, 2008; 2009) both of which provided a stepped psychological care programme and included people with anxiety disorders as well as depression. In the demonstration projects there was good evidence for increased patient flows through the system and the outcomes obtained were broadly in line with those reported in RCTs for depression and anxiety disorders.

The review for the update of the guideline on depression (NCCMH, 2010a) concluded that 'there is limited evidence from direct studies in common mental health problems which provide evidence for the effectiveness of the stepped-care model.' It added that beyond the area of common mental health problems, in fields such as addiction (Davison, 2000), there is some evidence for the effectiveness of stepped care and that the adoption of stepped-care models in non-mental healthcare has been associated with better physical health outcomes.

Stepped-care models vary in the extent to which they are sequential stepped models or stratified models with initial matching of patients to treatment steps (Bower & Gilbody, 2005). In sequential stepped models, all people regardless of severity, need or choice move through the steps in a systematic way, starting at the initial step and only 'stepping up' when the initial intervention has failed. In stratified models patients with more severe difficulties or greater needs, however defined, may be allocated directly to a higher, more intensive step without initially receiving a less intensive intervention (Lovell & Richards, 2000). Stratification may be based on the severity of the disorder (see NICE, 2009b) or on degree of functional impairment (see NICE, 2005b). Currently there is no evidence to choose between sequential or stratified models.

Patient choice is an important principle in care. Stepped-care models may appear to constrain choice by prescribing care pathways and the sequencing of interventions. In stepped-care models, patient preference has an important part to play in choice of intervention within a step but is generally not sufficient to influence choice between steps. How this is viewed by people receiving treatment in stepped-care systems and the acceptability of stepped-care models are only beginning to be explored (Richards *et al.*, 2010).

As well as patient choice, stepped-care systems also constrain healthcare professionals' choice of intervention. Practitioners may be unsure about the effectiveness of low-intensity interventions and ambivalent about recommending them. There is considerable evidence in other areas that practitioner confidence in treatment offered is a factor in its effectiveness. Accordingly it is likely that how practitioners discuss intervention options in stepped care will influence their effectiveness, and a communication that the practitioner has little faith in a low-intensity intervention will undermine its effectiveness.

5.4.3 From evidence to recommendations

On the basis of the evidence for stepped care reviewed in the update of the depression guideline (NCCMH, 2010a) and the incorporation of stepped-care models in other NICE guidelines for common mental health disorders, the GDG developed a stepped-care model for GAD (see Figure 3). This is based on that used in the NICE depression guideline (NICE, 2009b). It incorporates a stratification based on functional impairment, although most people, other than those with marked functional impairment, would be expected to start at step one or step two, only progressing to higher steps if their symptoms do not improve with less intensive interventions. A key difference from the stepped-care model for depression is that there is no category for subthreshold

Figure 3: The stepped-care model

Focus of the intervention	**Nature of the intervention**
STEP 4: Complex treatment-refractory GAD and very marked functional impairment, such as self-neglect or a high risk of self-harm	Highly specialist treatment, such as complex drug and/or psychological treatment regimens; input from multi-agency teams, crisis services, day hospitals or inpatient care
STEP 3: GAD with an inadequate response to step 2 interventions or marked functional impairment	Choice of a high-intensity psychological intervention (CBT/applied relaxation) or a drug treatment
STEP 2: Diagnosed GAD that has not improved after education and active monitoring in primary care	Low-intensity psychological interventions: individual non-facilitated self-help*, individual guided self-help and psychoeducational groups
STEP 1: All known and suspected presentations of GAD	Identification and assessment; education about GAD and treatment options; active monitoring

*A self-administered intervention intended to treat GAD involving written or electronic self-help materials (usually a book or workbook). It is similar to individual guided self-help but usually with minimal therapist contact, for example an occasional short telephone call of no more than 5 minutes.

GAD symptoms. While subthreshold GAD symptoms are the subject of increased attention (Kessler *et al.*, 2005a; Ruscio *et al.*, 2007), they are as yet not generally recognised by clinicians and there is no comparable research literature as in depression regarding treatment of subthreshold disorder. The model in Figure 3 represents the consensus of the GDG drawing on the principles of stepped care as best applied to GAD.

Step 1

This step covers initial identification and assessment of GAD and basic education about the condition and information about treatment options. The focus is all suspected and known cases of GAD. GPs are the most common practitioners carrying out step 1 interventions, but as GAD may be missed by GPs and also present in other settings, they may be delivered by other primary care practitioners (practice nurses, district nurses, primary care mental health practitioners) and by practitioners in some acute medical settings (A&E staff, hospital medical and nursing staff). They include:

- identification and assessment of GAD
- education about the nature of GAD
- information about treatment options
- active monitoring.

Some people with GAD may want to take some time to consider the treatment options and to read about the nature of GAD. Others, on the other hand, may want to move on to treatments identified in step 2 straight away. Healthcare professionals should be guided by patient choice, the severity of symptoms and levels of impairment.

Step 2

Interventions in this step are the least restrictive first-line active treatment options for which there is evidence. They are appropriate for all people with GAD who have not improved with education and active monitoring in primary care. In many cases step 2 interventions may be offered immediately after diagnosis given that the diagnosis of GAD requires symptoms for at least 6 months. Psychological wellbeing practitioners and primary care mental health workers are the most common healthcare professionals delivering step 2 interventions, but non-facilitated self-help may be delivered by GPs (for example, if there is a local self-help book prescription scheme) and guided self-help and psychoeducational groups may be conducted by a variety of trained mental health and other healthcare professionals. Step 2 interventions recommended in this guideline (see Chapter 6) are:

- non-facilitated self-help (defined as a self-administered intervention involving self-help materials, similar to guided self-help but without any contact from a healthcare professional)
- guided self-help
- psychoeducational groups.

Step 3

Interventions in this step are active treatment options that are relatively more restrictive in terms of personal inconvenience to patients, potential for negative side effects and cost. They are appropriate for all people with GAD who do not respond to step 2 interventions. They are also appropriate first-line treatments for people with GAD with marked functional impairment, for whom the personal inconvenience and potential for negative side effects of the treatments are balanced by need for rapid alleviation of their impairment. Step 3 interventions recommended in this guideline are:

- high-intensity psychological interventions – CBT and applied relaxation (see Chapter 7)
- pharmacological interventions (see Chapter 8).

Referral for specialist assessment and further treatment in secondary care should be considered when there has been an inadequate response to treatments at step 3 or when the person with GAD has severe anxiety with marked functional impairment and there is a risk of self-harm or suicide, significant comorbidity or self-neglect.

Step 4

This covers interventions in specialist secondary and tertiary settings such as multiagency community, day and inpatient services and in some highly specialist treatment teams. They are appropriate for a small number of people with treatment refractory GAD and very marked functional impairment (for example, self-neglect) or high risk of self-harm. Interventions at step 4 may include psychological and phar-macological treatments offered at step 3, but also specialist psychological regimes, pharmacological augmentation with combinations of drugs, and specialist combina-tions of pharmacological and psychological treatment for which evidence is currently lacking as to their effectiveness. These should only be undertaken by healthcare professionals with expertise in the pharmacological and psychological treatment of severe and complex anxiety. Step 4 interventions will also include care coordination to assist people with GAD manage self-care needs they cannot meet on their own and to manage risk. The two broad categories of step 4 interventions are thus:

● specialist psychological, pharmacological and combination regimes
● care coordination to assist managing basic self-care needs and monitoring risk.

It should be noted that the same healthcare professional may deliver interventions at different steps: for example, a GP may assess and provide education about GAD (step 1), then prescribe a non-facilitated self-help book for GAD (step 2), then later prescribe an SSRI (step 3).

5.4.4   Recommendations

Stepped care for people with GAD

5.4.4.1   Follow the stepped-care model [see Figure 3], offering the least intrusive, most effective intervention first.

Step 4[12]: Complex, treatment-refractory GAD and very marked functional impairment or high risk of self-harm

Assessment

5.4.4.2   Offer the person with GAD a specialist assessment of needs and risks, including:
   ● duration and severity of symptoms, functional impairment, comorbidi-ties, risk to self and self-neglect
   ● a formal review of current and past treatments, including adherence to previously prescribed drug treatments and the fidelity of prior psycho-logical interventions, and their impact on symptoms and functional impairment
   ● home environment
   ● support in the community
   ● relationships with and impact on families and carers.

5.4.4.3   Review the needs of families and carers and offer an assessment of their caring, physical and mental health needs if one has not been offered previously.

---

[12]Step 4 normally refers to community mental health teams but may include specialist services and special-ist practitioners in primary care.

5.4.4.4   Develop a comprehensive care plan in collaboration with the person with GAD that addresses needs, risks and functional impairment and has a clear treatment plan.

Treatment
5.4.4.5   Inform people with GAD who have not been offered or have refused the interventions in steps 1–3 about the potential benefits of these interventions, and offer them any they have not tried.
5.4.4.6   Consider offering combinations of psychological and drug treatments, combinations of antidepressants or augmentation of antidepressants with other drugs, but exercise caution and be aware that:
● evidence for the effectiveness of combination treatments is lacking and
● side effects and interactions are more likely when combining and augmenting antidepressants.
5.4.4.7   Combination treatments should be undertaken only by practitioners with expertise in the psychological and drug treatment of complex, treatment-refractory anxiety disorders and after full discussion with the person about the likely advantages and disadvantages of the treatments suggested.
5.4.4.8   When treating people with complex and treatment-refractory GAD, inform them of relevant clinical research in which they may wish to participate, working within local and national ethical guidelines at all times.

5.5   COLLABORATIVE CARE

5.5.1   Introduction

Collaborative care has been described by researchers (Gunn *et al.*, 2006) as a 'system level' intervention with four key elements:
● Collaboration between a GP and at least one other healthcare professional (for example, a psychiatrist, clinical psychologist, social worker, or nurse) in a person's care.
● The use of a structured management protocol or guidelines. The intervention may include pharmacological and/or psychological/psychosocial interventions.
● Scheduling regular follow-up appointments to provide specific interventions, facilitate treatment adherence, and monitor symptoms or adverse effects.
● A system or mechanism to facilitate and enhance inter-professional communication regarding the care plan. This could include team meetings, case reviews, shared electronic patient records, and professional supervision of the care manager.

The healthcare professional collaborating with the GP in a person's care is sometimes described as a 'case manager', where a key element of the role involves coordinating care with the GP including referral on to secondary care. Case managers may not always be from traditional healthcare professional backgrounds; they may be specifically trained to undertake this and/or related roles (for example graduate mental health workers). Where the healthcare professional or case manager is not a mental health professional, there is commonly supervision of the individual by a senior mental health professional and there is some evidence from reviews of collaborative care for depression that this supervision may be important in the effectiveness of these approaches (Bower *et al.*, 2006).

The purpose of collaborative care approaches is to improve the uptake of evidence-based treatments in primary care. These approaches were developed in the US with a focus on depression in the context of the publication of the American Agency for Health Care Policy and Research (1993) *Depression in Primary Care* clinical guideline and evidence that few people with depression in primary care received an evidence-based pharmacological and psychological treatment for their depression. Reflecting this origin, most studies of collaborative care have been on depression and have been conducted in the US (Gilbody *et al.*, 2006; NCCMH, 2010b). However, a few studies have begun to explore the potential of collaborative care approaches for anxiety disorders.

5.5.2   Narrative review

Two trials (Rollman *et al.*, 2005; Roy-Byrne *et al.*, 2010) examined the effectiveness of collaborative care trials in primary care settings for a mixed anxiety population in the US. Collaborative care is a complex intervention that differs in terms of its treatment modalities, service delivery and monitoring, and relations between patients, physicians and care workers. Given that the two trials had different mixes of population, and that there is uncertainty attached to the comparability of complex service-level interventions, the trials have not been meta-analysed. The study characteristics and the results are presented in Table 4 and Table 5.

Mode of delivery
Care workers delivered services to patients in both trials. In the study by Roy-Byrne and colleagues (2010), the majority of care workers were social workers and nurses, with a few master's level psychologists. Half had prior experience in mental health, half had some pharmacotherapy experience, while only a few had prior experience in CBT. They received six half-day training sessions in CBT and one session on medication management. Rollman and colleagues (2005) had two non-behavioural health specialists who were not specially trained in CBT or pharmacotherapy. Details of training were not specified.

The care workers in both trials collaborated with patients and their primary care physicians. At the beginning of the trial, the care workers assessed the patients, and allowed them to choose a treatment modality. Care workers facilitated the patient's access to CBT treatments via a computer (Roy-Byrne *et al.*, 2010) or a self-help booklet (Rollman *et al.*, 2005). Thereafter, care workers were responsible for monitoring patients' progress and adherence to treatment. They were also responsible for reporting progress to patient's physicians. Where necessary, the care workers discussed the treatment regimen and recommended modifications to the physicians.

Table 4: Study information table for trials comparing collaborative care with treatment as usual

	Roy-Byrne *et al.*, 2010	Rollman *et al.*, 2005
Study design	RCT	RCT
Total participants/ % female	1004 (71%)	191 (81%)
Mean age (years)	43	44
Diagnosis	Panic disorder, GAD, social anxiety disorder and/or PTSD (DSM-IV)	Panic disorder and/or GAD (DSM-IV)
Population mix (%)	Panic disorder: N = 475 (47%) GAD: N = 756 (75%) Social anxiety disorder: N = 405 (40%) PTSD: N = 181 (18%) Co-occurring depression: N = 648 (64.5%) One or more chronic physical health problem: N = 801 (80%)	Panic disorder: N = 20 (10%) GAD: N = 80 (42%) Panic disorder or GAD: N = 91 (48%) Co-occurring depression: N = 108 (57%)
Baseline severity (clinician-rated)	Scored at least 8 (moderate anxiety symptoms on scale of 20) on the Overall Anxiety Severity and Impairment Scale (OASIS)	Baseline HAM-A score 20.3 (6.4)
Comparator	Treatment as usual – with medication, counselling (limited mental health resources), or referral to mental health specialist	Treatment as usual
Treatment length	10-12 weeks	Not specified
Follow-up	6, 12 and 18 months	Accessed at 2, 4, 8 and 12 months

Table 5: Evidence summary table for trials of collaborative care

	Roy-Byrne *et al.*, 2010	Rollman *et al.*, 2005
Treatment length	10-12 weeks	Not specified
Frequency of care manager contact	*Frequency of CBT visits at 12 months:* Mean 7 (SD 4.1), median 8 visits *Frequency of medication/ care management visits at 12 months*: Mean 2.24 (SD 3.57), median 1 visit *Percentage of service uptake at 12 months:* 34% CBT visits only 9% Medication/care management visits only 57% Some of both CBT and medication visits	*Median care manager contacts at 6 months:* Median 7 (range 0–25) *Median care manager contacts at 12 months:* Median 12 (range 0–41) *Three or more care manager contacts in first 6 months:* 79.3% (92 out of 116)
Results for GAD only population	<u>*Adjusted mean Brief Symptom Inventory Score (BSI-12)*</u> *At 6 months:* Difference score −2.52 (−3.76 to −1.27) Effect size −0.32 (p value .002) *At 12 months:* Difference scores −2.67 (−3.89 to −1.45) Effect size −0.32 (p value <.001) *At 18 months:* Difference scores −1.71 (−2.92 to −0.49) Effect size −0.19 (p value .05)	<u>*Structured Interview Guide for the Hamilton Anxiety Rating Scale (SIGH-A):*</u> *At 12 months:* Difference score −1.1 (−5 to 2.7) Effect size 0.25 (−0.21 to 0.7) (p value .57) <u>*SF-12 – Mental component score*</u> *At 12 months:* Difference score 3.8 (−3.4 to 11) Effect size 0.24 (−0.21 to 0.69) (p value .3)
Results for full population (mixed anxiety disorders)	<u>*Non-response (response defined by at least 50% reduction on BSI-12):*</u> *At 6 months:* RR 0.67 (0.60, 0.76)	<u>*Dropouts due to any reason:*</u> RR 2.07 (0.79, 5.41)

	At 12 months: RR 0.66 (0.57, 0.76) *At 18 months:* RR 0.73 (0.63, 0.85) *Non-remission (remission* *defined by score less than* *5 on OASIS):* *At 6 months:* RR 0.78 (0.71, 0.86) *At 12 months:* RR 0.73 (0.65, 0.81) *At 18 months:* RR 0.77 (0.69, 0.86) *Dropouts due to any reason:* *At 6 months:* RR 0.80 (0.58, 1.11) *At 12 months:* RR 0.95 (0.73, 1.22) *At 18 months:* RR 0.88 (0.69, 1.13) *Mean BSI-12 score:* *At 6 months:* Effect size −0.3 (−0.43 to −0.17) *At 12 months:* Effect size −0.31 (−0.44 to −0.18) *At 18 months:* Effect size −0.18 (−0.3 to −0.06) *Depression score (PHQ-9):* *At 6 months:* Effect size −0.25 (−0.37 to −0.12)	*SIGH-A:* Effect size 0.38 (0.09 to 0.67) (p value .01) *Panic Disorder Severity* *Scale (PDSS):* Effect size 0.33 (0.04 to 0.62) (p value .02) *Depression score* *(Hamilton Depression* *Rating Scale [HDRS]):* Effect size 0.35 (0.25 to 0.46) (p value .03) *Quality of life (SF-12* *Mental health composite):* Effect size 0.39 (0.1 to 0.68) (p value .01) *Quality of life (SF-12* *Physical health composite):* Effect size 0.01 (−0.28 to 0.3) (p value .96)

Table 5: (***Continued***)

	Roy-Byrne *et al.*, 2010	Rollman *et al.*, 2005
	At 12 months: Effect size −0.37 (−0.51 to −0.23) *At 18 months:* Effect size −0.24 (−0.37 to −0.11) *Quality of life (SF-12 Mental health composite)* *At 6 months:* Effect size 0.34 (0.21 to 0.47) *At 12 months:* Effect size 0.47 (0.33 to 0.61) *At 18 months:* Effect size 0.39 (0.24 to 0.54) *Quality of life (SF-12 Physical health composite)* *At 6 months:* Effect size 0.05 (−0.07 to 0.17) *At 12 months:* Effect size −0.01 (−0.16 to 0.14) *At 18 months:* Effect size 0.08 (−0.05 to 0.22)	
Statistically significant differences in care processes (intervention versus treatment as usual)	*Medication change during first 6 months (calculations based on those responding at 6 months, weighted for non-response):* Intervention 25.4% (21.3–29.4) Treatment as usual 17.1% (13.5–20.7) p-value .05	*Months on pharmacotherapy for a mental health problem:* *At 2 months:* Intervention 65.4% (53/81) Treatment as usual 41.5% (22/53) p-value .006

	Receive any counselling *At 6 months:* Intervention 88.1% (84.2–92) Treatment as usual 51% (47.1–55) p value <.001 *At 12 months:* Intervention 58.4% (53.7–63.2) Treatment as usual 46.3% (41.5–51.1) p value .01 _Receive counselling with_ _more than three CBT elements_ _(six in total)_ *At 6 months:* Intervention 82.1% (78.2–86.1) Treatment as usual 33.6% (29.6–37.7) p value <.001 *At 12 months*: Intervention 49.1% (44.5–53.6) Treatment as usual 26.6% (22.1–31.2) p value <.001 _Receive counselling with_ _more than three CBT elements_ _delivered consistently_ *At 6 months*: Intervention 54.8% (51–58.7) Treatment as usual 9.98% (6.08–13.88) p value <.001 *At 12 months:* Intervention 21.6% (18.2–25.1) Treatment as usual 9.31% (5.83–12.79) p value <.001	

The final decision on prescriptions was still made by the physicians. The care workers received weekly supervision from a psychologist and psychiatrist in the Roy-Byrne and colleagues' trial (2010), and weekly case review sessions were conducted with the principal investigators in the Rollman and colleagues' trial (2005).

Treatment modality

There were three main treatment modalities in the two trials: pharmacotherapy, assisted CBT or both. The pharmacotherapy treatment was primarily an SSRI or SNRI. In the case of non-response, an additional antidepressant or a benzodiazepine could be used. The Roy-Byrne and colleagues' trial (2010) included a computer-assisted CBT treatment with five basic modules (education, self-monitoring, hierarchy development, breathing training and relapse prevention) and three modules (cognitive restructuring and exposure to internal and external stimuli) tailored to four specific disorders. In the Rollman colleagues' trial (2005), a guided CBT booklet for managing panic disorder or GAD was used to review lesson plans with a care worker.

In the case of non-response, patients could receive more of the same treatment (that is, increased dosage or CBT sessions with extra modules), switch to a different treatment modality, or receive both modalities simultaneously.

5.5.3   Clinical evidence summary

Care process analysis

Both studies reported differences in uptake of drug treatment and CBT between collaborative care and treatment as usual during the trial. The percentages of uptake can be found in Table 5.

Rollman and colleagues (2005) reported an overall 80% uptake of guided self-help CBT booklets in the collaborative care group. At 2 months' assessment, there was a statistically significant difference between collaborative care (65.4%) and treatment as usual (41.5%) in terms of their self-report usage of drug treatment. The percentage did not differ at other assessment points. In addition, the self-report visits to a mental health specialist did not differ between the collaborative care and treatment as usual groups.

Roy-Byrne and colleagues (2010) reported that the collaborative care group received significantly more counselling with CBT components at 6 and 12 months than the treatment as usual group, but the groups no longer differed at 18 months. In terms of drug treatment, the collaborative care group (25.4%) changed medication significantly more than the treatment as usual group (17.1%) during the first 6 months of the trial, but the groups no longer differed at 12 months. There were no between-group differences in receiving any psychotropic medication at any time point.

Results

GAD-only population

When the collaborative care group was compared with treatment as usual, Roy-Byrne and colleagues (2010) reported a small effect favouring collaborative care on anxiety symptoms for the population with GAD at assessment at 6 and 12 months. The small effect was lost at the 18-month assessment. However, Rollman and colleagues (2005) did not find statistically significant differences on anxiety outcomes for the GAD-only population.

Mixed anxiety population

Similar results were observed for the mixed anxiety population. In Roy-Byrne and colleagues (2010), there was a 27 to 34% reduction in non-response in the collaborative care group at 6, 12 and 18-month assessments. There was a 22 to 27% reduction in non-remission in the collaborative care group at 6, 12 and 18 month assessments. There were significant small effects favouring collaborative care on anxiety, depression and quality of life (mental health scores) outcomes compared with treatment as usual at 6 and 12 months. However, although effect sizes were statistically significant, they dropped at 18 months on anxiety and depression outcomes. Findings were similar in Rollman and colleagues' (2005) study, in which small effects favouring collaborative care were found on anxiety, panic severity, depression and quality of life (mental health scores) outcomes at a 12-month assessment.

5.5.4   From evidence to recommendations

The results from the two trials implied that collaborative care had a small effect on outcome measures compared with treatment as usual. Roy-Byrne and colleagues (2010) and Rollman and colleagues (2005) are good quality RCTs, with a reasonably large sample size. However, the GDG considered they were unable to make a clinical recommendation on the basis of the evidence reviewed for a number of reasons.

Both trials reported small clinical benefits for a mixed anxiety population. However, the two trials had different conclusions for the population with GAD only. Roy-Byrne and colleagues (2010) reported a small clinical benefit on anxiety symptoms. However, they did not report other outcomes (depression, quality of life, response and remission) for the GAD-only population. Rollman and colleagues (2005) did not find a differential effect on anxiety or quality of life outcomes for those with GAD only. With Roy-Byrne and colleagues (2010) being published just a few weeks before finalising and submitting the guideline to NICE, it was not possible to undertake health economic analyses of the two trials. Collaborative care interventions are complex in nature and can be difficult to cost (van Steenbergen-Weijenburg *et al.*, 2010). A robust health economic analysis is necessary in order to make a firm clinical recommendation.

In addition, collaborative care is a complex service-level intervention, which is embedded in a service context. Given the variation in nature of usual care between the US and UK, it may not be possible to extrapolate results from US studies to the UK. Adapting collaborative care to the UK context and replicating results would be advisable. However, while no clinical recommendation for collaborative care was made, the intervention shows some promise for the GAD population, therefore the GDG made a research recommendation.

5.5.5   Research recommendation

5.5.5.1   The clinical and cost effectiveness of a primary care-based collaborative care approach to improving the treatment of GAD compared with usual care

What are the benefits of a primary care-based collaborative care approach to improving the treatment of GAD compared with usual care?

This question should be addressed using a cluster randomised controlled design in which the clusters are GP practices and people with GAD are recruited following screening of consecutive attenders at participating GP practices. GPs in intervention practices should receive training in recognising GAD and providing both drug treatment and GP-delivered low-intensity psychological interventions (psychoeducation and non-facilitated self-help). Psychological wellbeing practitioners[13] (PWPs) in intervention practices should provide these low-intensity psychological interventions and support GP-prescribed drug treatment by providing information about side effects, monitoring medication use and liaising about any changes to medication. They should also support the referral for CBT of participants whose symptoms have not improved following low-intensity interventions. Structured, practice-based protocols should define care pathways, the interventions to be provided by practitioners at each point in the care pathway and the mechanisms they should use to liaise about individual patients. In control practices, participants should receive care as usual from the GP, including referral for primary and secondary care psychological interventions or mental health services.

Outcomes should be evaluated at 6 months with follow-up assessments continuing for up to 2 years to establish whether short-term benefits are maintained in the longer term. The outcomes chosen should include both observer- and participant-rated measures of clinical symptoms and functioning specific to GAD, and of quality of life. An economic analysis should also be carried out alongside the trial. The trial needs to be large enough to determine the presence or absence of clinically important effects and of any differences in costs between collaborative care and usual care.

Why this is important

Most people with GAD in the UK do not receive evidence-based management and poor recognition of GAD by GPs contributes to a lack of appropriate interventions being offered. There is some evidence that complex interventions involving the training of primary care practitioners, together with a collaborative care approach involving GPs, other primary care practitioners and mental health professionals, can improve the uptake of evidence-based interventions and clinical and functional outcomes for people with GAD. However, these approaches have not been evaluated in primary care in the UK. Given the differences between the organisation of primary care in different countries, such as the US, it is important to demonstrate whether these approaches can also be effective in the UK.

---

[13]Also known as graduate mental health workers.

6   LOW-INTENSITY PSYCHOLOGICAL INTERVENTIONS

6.1   INTRODUCTION

This chapter reviews the evidence for the clinical efficacy and cost effectiveness of low-intensity interventions including CCBT, guided self-help, non-facilitated self-help, psychoeducational groups and relaxation training in the treatment of GAD.

Low-intensity interventions have become firmly embedded into service provision as a way of increasing access to psychological treatments for people experiencing mild to moderate anxiety and depressive disorders. Although low-intensity interventions have been used as a precursor or adjunct to conventional face-to-face CBT this review will focus on them as a primary treatment. Low-intensity interventions are integral to stepped-care models and provide many of the least restrictive treatments in step 2. Most low-intensity interventions are based on the principles of CBT and vary according to whether their delivery involves support from a healthcare professional (guided self-help) or not (non-facilitated self-help). Low-intensity interventions differ in delivery style, amount of input from the healthcare professional, content and degree of complexity. The delivery of low-intensity psychological treatments is rapidly changing with innovations being adopted that have the potential to enhance the accessibility, availability, and cost effectiveness of mental health services

The healthcare professional's role in delivering low-intensity interventions (both non-facilitated and guided self-help) is to engage people to choose the mode of delivery of CBT materials and provide sufficient information about the materials to be used and know the material sufficiently well to enable the person to choose the most appropriate materials for their needs. They also need to ensure that progress is appropriately monitored and reviewed. In the case of guided self-help, healthcare professionals should provide additional support and guidance during the course of the intervention and address barriers that impede progress in collaboration with the person. Self-help materials need to be user friendly and of an appropriate reading age (Richardson *et al.*, 2008) and translated into languages that reflect the needs of the local community.

6.1.1   Definitions of low-intensity interventions

Although there is no agreed definition on exactly what constitutes a low-intensity intervention they share several common characteristics. Low-intensity interventions use fewer resources (virtually none in the case of non-facilitated self-help) in terms of healthcare professional time than conventional psychological therapies. However the interventions are not necessarily less intensive (for example, the time taken to go through the self-help materials) for the individuals using them. These interventions are often delivered and/or supported by mental health workers without formal mental health professional training, who have been specifically trained to deliver low-intensity interventions (including primary care graduate mental health workers and psychological wellbeing practitioners). Most but not all interventions utilise a health technology (Richards *et al.*, 2003) such as CDs, books (Marrs, 1995), video- and audiotapes (Blenkiron, 2001), the internet (Christensen *et al.*, 2004), or CCBT (Proudfoot *et al.*, 2004; Kaltenthaler *et al.*, 2006). In this review CCBT has been categorised as either 'guided self-help' or 'non-facilitated self-help', depending on how it was delivered, rather than analysing it separately. The majority of low-intensity interventions are based on the principles of CBT to enable individuals to learn specific techniques (for example, thought challenging and behavioural activation) with the aim of relieving distress and improving daily functioning. Low-intensity interventions are often supported by a healthcare professional and use remote methods including the telephone or email. Remote delivery of low-intensity CBT has the ability to overcome many of the social, physical and economic barriers that can prevent access to mental health services, and is increasingly being used as a means to support treatment provision (Bee *et al.*, 2008).

Guided self-help
Guided self-help is defined as a self-administered intervention intended to treat GAD and usually involves a CBT-based self-help resource (such as a book, self-help workbook or multimedia) with limited support from a healthcare professional. The role of the healthcare professional or paraprofessional (for example, a psychological wellbeing practitioner) is to guide and support use of the self-help resource and monitor and review the process and outcome of treatment. Guidance from the healthcare professional ranges from three to ten sessions with between 3 and 6 hours' total healthcare professional time and is usually delivered face-to-face or by telephone. However, there remains ambiguity concerning the best way to deliver guided self-help, such as the most appropriate health technology for the delivery of the self-help materials (written materials or multimedia), the level and nature of the guidance required, and the skills and expertise required to deliver this guidance (Gellatly *et al.*, 2007; Lovell *et al.*, 2008). There are limitations to written self-help resources in that a level of literacy is required and few self-help resources have been translated into other languages.

Non-facilitated self-help
Non-facilitated self-help is defined as a self-administered intervention intended to treat GAD and involves a self-help resource (usually a book or workbook) and is similar to guided self-help but usually with minimal therapist contact, for example an occasional short telephone call of no more than 5 minutes.

Psychoeducational groups
Group psychoeducation is usually delivered in large groups (between 20 and 24 patients) and is similar to an evening class (White, 1998). Psychoeducational groups

use a didactic approach and focus on educating people about the nature of anxiety and ways of managing anxiety using CBT techniques. The 'classes' are delivered weekly for 2 hours over a 6-week period and usually include presentations and self-help materials. Groups are conducted by appropriately trained practitioners and usually have a therapist-participant ratio of 1 to 12.

6.1.2 Review question

In the treatment of GAD, do any of the following improve outcomes compared with other interventions (including treatment as usual): non-facilitated bibliotherapy, non-facilitated audiotherapy, non-facilitated computer therapy, guided bibliotherapy, guided computer therapy, psychoeducational groups and helplines.

6.1.3 Databases searched and inclusion/exclusion criteria

Information about the databases searched and the inclusion/exclusion criteria used for this section of the guideline can be found in Table 6 (further information about the search for health economic evidence can be found in Section 3.6).

Trials of low-intensity interventions have only rarely been restricted to people with GAD. This is partly because the interventions have commonly been designed to

Table 6: Databases searched and inclusion/exclusion criteria for clinical evidence

Electronic databases	MEDLINE, EMBASE, CINAHL, PsycINFO, Cochrane Library
Date searched	Database inception to 09.05.2010
Study design	RCT, quasi-RCTs
Patient population	People with a primary diagnosis of GAD or any anxiety disorders
Interventions	Guided or non-facilitated self-help (bibliotherapy; audiotherapy; computer-delivered therapy); psycho-educational groups; helplines; physical activity
Outcomes	Non-remission, non-response, dropouts Mean rating scale scores for anxiety, depression, worry, somatic symptoms, quality of life

target a wider range of anxiety disorders and partly because the studies have often been of pragmatic trials in primary care and other settings where differentiation between the anxiety disorders is not common practice. Accordingly, for this review of low-intensity psychological interventions, broader inclusion criteria were used than for the reviews of high-intensity psychological interventions (see Chapter 7) and of pharmacological interventions (see Chapter 8). Specifically, the meta-analysis for this review included:

● Quasi-RCTs as well as true RCTs. Quasi-RCTs are trials where the method of randomisation is based on some not truly random factors; for example, in recruiting for trials of psychoeducational groups it is common to recruit a batch of successive participants into the intervention group and then a further batch into the control group (alternating batches until the recruitment target has been met) in order to recruit sufficient people in a timely manner to start each psychoeducational group.

● Trials of people with a diagnosis of GAD under DSM-III criteria, rather than restricting diagnosis of GAD as defined by DSM-III-R, DSM-IV or ICD-10.

● Trials of people with mixed anxiety disorders where these were likely to include a significant number of people with GAD, where the intervention was relevant for people with GAD and where the primary outcome measure was a measure of anxiety appropriate to GAD, for example, the Hamilton Anxiety Rating Scale (HAM-A). From epidemiological data, between one quarter and two thirds of a mixed anxiety disorder population would be expected to have GAD – either GAD only or comorbid with another anxiety disorder (Alonso *et al.*, 2004b; Kessler *et al.*, 2005c; McManus *et al.*, 2009).

6.1.4   Studies considered

The review team conducted a new systematic search for RCTs (including quasi-RCTs) that assessed the effectiveness of psychological interventions for the treatment of people with GAD, or mixed anxiety disorder in general as defined by DSM-IIII, DSM-III-R or DSM-IV.

A total of 7,182 references were identified by the electronic search relating to clinical evidence; none were identified from other reviews, unpublished trials and websites. Of these references, 7,103 were excluded at the screening stage on the basis of reading the title and/or abstract. The remaining 79 references were assessed for eligibility on the basis of the full text. Twelve trials met the eligibility criteria set by the GDG providing data on 690 participants. Of these, all were published in peer-reviewed journals between 1992 and 2009. Sixty-seven studies were excluded from the analysis: 20 studies did not provide an acceptable diagnosis of GAD; 18 were not RCTs; five had fewer than ten participants per group; in nine studies the outcomes were not extractable or not valid; in two the participants were aged under 18 years; two studies were non-English language; and 11 did not use a relevant intervention. Further information about both included and excluded studies can be found in Appendix 15b.

A total of twelve RCTs were included, of which four targeted people with a GAD-only diagnosis and eight targeted a population with mixed anxiety disorder. Six studies used non-facilitated self-help, four used guided self-help and two used psychoeducational groups. There were no trials on helplines or physical activity. Data were available to compare treatments with waitlist control and treatment as usual. Treatment as usual typically consisted of continually receiving a mixture of conventional treatments, whereas the waitlist control group received no active treatments.

All of the participants had a diagnosis of one or more anxiety disorders, most of which (if not otherwise stated) included a diagnosis of GAD and panic disorder. The severity of disorder was unknown as this were not reported in the studies.

A range of self-rated and clinician-rated outcomes were reported in the included studies. The most commonly reported were the HAM-A, Beck Depression Inventory (BDI), Hamilton Rating Scale for Depression (HRSD), Beck Anxiety Inventory (BAI) and Penn State Worry Questionnaire (PSWQ) (see Appendix 15b for outcomes reported in each study).

The included studies were analysed based on the nature of support offered to patients. These are presented as follows:
● Non-facilitated self-help (which includes bibliotherapy or computerised therapy) (see Section 6.2). This is characterised by:
  – no therapist support
  – zero or one session used to explain instructions.
● Guided self-help (which includes bibliotherapy or computerised therapy) (see Section 6.3). This is characterised by:
  – five to seven sessions lasting 10 to 20 minutes each.
● Psychoeducational groups (see Section 6.4). This includes:
  – six sessions lasting 120 minutes each
  – delivered by paraprofessionals.

6.2   NON-FACILITATED SELF-HELP

6.2.1   Studies considered

There were six RCTs that compared non-facilitated self-help with waitlist control or treatment as usual. Four targeted mixed anxiety populations and two targeted people with GAD only. A summary of study characteristics can be found in Table 7, with full details in Appendix 15b which also includes details of excluded studies.

Table 7: Study information table for trials comparing non-facilitated self-help with control

	Non-facilitated bibliotherapy versus non-active control in mixed anxiety populations	Non-facilitated bibliotherapy versus waitlist control in a GAD-only population	Non-facilitated computer therapy versus waitlist control in a GAD-only population
No. trials (total participants)	4 RCTs (159)	1 RCT (38)	1 RCT (100)
Study ID	(1) KASSINOVE1980 (2) MAUNDER2009 (3) TARRIER1986 (4) WHITE1995	BOWMAN1997	HOUGHTON2008
N/% female	(1) 34/64% (2) 38/0% (3) 50/60% (4) 62/58%	38/74%	231/100%
Mean age (years)	(1) No information (2) 35 (3) 41 (4) 38	43	43
Diagnosis	(1) Previously diagnosed with an anxiety disorder (2) All diagnosed with an anxiety disorder with a minimum cut-off score of 8 on HADS-A (3) Previously diagnosed with an anxiety disorder (4) All diagnosed with an anxiety disorder by DSM-III-R	All diagnosed with GAD as a primary diagnosis by DSM-III-R	All previously diagnosed with GAD
Baseline severity (clinician-rated)	(1) Not reported (2) Cut-off scores for HADS is 8 (3) Not reported (4) Baseline ADIS score 5.65–6.05	Baseline HAM-A score 27.9-29.1	Not reported
Treatment	(1) Rational emotive bibliotherapy and audiotherapy (2) CBT	Problem solving	Mindfulness

	(3) Relaxation training (4) CBT		
Comparator	(1) Waitlist control (2) Treatment as usual (3) Waitlist control (4) Waitlist control and information control	Waitlist control	Waitlist control
Treatment length	(1) 8 weeks (2) 4 weeks (3) 3 weeks (4) 13 weeks	4 weeks	8 weeks
No. of sessions	(1) 16 sessions (2) No sessions (3) 1 session (4) Unclear	4 sessions	8 sessions

6.2.2   Clinical evidence for non-facilitated self-help

Evidence from the important outcomes and overall quality of evidence are presented in Table 8. The full GRADE profiles and associated forest plots can be found in Appendix 18a and Appendix 16a, respectively.

6.2.3   Evidence summary (non-facilitated self-help)

When non-facilitated self-help was compared with a non-active control in a mixed anxiety population, the results indicate a statistically significant moderate effect size for anxiety scores and a moderate effect size for depression scores, favouring non-facilitated self-help for a mixed anxiety population. It also indicates a statistically significant improvement in non-remission. None of these studies provided follow-up data.

When studies targeting both GAD-only and mixed anxiety populations were combined, the results indicate a very similar and statistically significant moderate effect size for anxiety scores and a moderate effect size for depression scores, favouring non-facilitated self-help for both populations. There were significantly more dropouts in the comparison group. The above evidence suggests that non-facilitated self-help is effective for both populations.

Table 8: Evidence summary table for trials of non-facilitated self-help

	Mixed anxiety population – non-facilitated bibliotherapy versus non-active control	GAD-only population – non-facilitated bibliotherapy versus waitlist control	GAD-only population – non-facilitated computer therapy versus waitlist control	Combined population – non-facilitated self-help versus non-active control (waitlist control or treatment as usual)	Combined population – non-facilitated self-help versus waitlist control	Combined population – non-facilitated self-help versus treatment as usual	Mixed anxiety population – non-facilitated bibliotherapy versus non-facilitated audiotherapy
No. trials (total participants)	4 RCTs (164)	1 RCT (38)	1 RCT (231)	6 RCTs (433)	5 RCTs (202)	1 RCT (38)	1 RCT (22)
Study ID	(1) KASSINOVE1980 (2) MAUNDER2009* (3) TARRIER1986 (4) WHITE1995	BOWMAN1997	HOUGHTON2008	(1) BOWMAN1997 (2) HOUGHTON2008 (3) KASSINOVE1980 (4) MAUNDER2009* (5) TARRIER1986 (6) WHITE1995	(1) BOWMAN1997 (2) HOUGHTON2008 (3) KASSINOVE1980 (4) TARRIER1986 (5) WHITE1995	MAUNDER2009*	KASSINOVE1980
Length of follow-up	(1) None (2) 4 weeks (not reportable) (3)–(4) None	3 months	None	(1) 3 months (2)–(3) None (4) 4 weeks (not reportable) (5)–(6) None	(1) 3 months (2)–(5) None	4 weeks (not reportable)	None
Benefits							
Anxiety (self-rated)	SMD −0.76 (−1.12, −0.40) K = 4, N = 142 Quality: moderate	SMD −1.06 (−1.77, −0.35) K = 1, N = 35 Quality: high	SMD −0.61 (−1.01, −0.21) K = 1, N = 100 Quality: high	SMD −0.74 (−0.99, −0.49) K = 6, N = 277 Quality: moderate	SMD −0.74 (−1.01, −0.48) K = 5, N = 243 Quality: moderate	SMD −0.70 (−1.40, −0.01) K = 1, N = 34 Quality: moderate	SMD −0.55 (−1.40, 0.31) K = 1, N = 22 Quality: moderate

Anxiety (self-rated) at follow-up	-	SMD -1.06 (-1.83, -0.29) K = 1, N = 30	-	SMD -1.06 (-1.83, -0.29) K = 1, N = 30	SMD -1.06 (-1.83, -0.29) K = 1, N = 30	-	-
Depression (self-rated)	SMD -0.78 (-1.27, -0.30) K = 2, N = 85 Quality: moderate	-	-	SMD -0.78 (-1.27, -0.30) K = 2, N = 85 Quality: moderate	-	-	-
Non-remission	RR 0.68 (0.53, 0.87) K = 2, N = 76 Quality: moderate	-	-	RR 0.68 (0.53, 0.87) K = 2, N = 76 Quality: moderate	RR 0.65 (0.46, 0.92) K = 1, N = 42 Quality: high	RR 0.71 (0.50, 1.01) K = 1, N = 34 Quality: high	-
Harm							
Discontinuation due to any reason	RR 0.50 (0.09, 2.84) K = 2, N = 80 Quality: low	RR 2.00 (0.20, 20.24) K = 1, N = 38 Quality: moderate	RR 0.55 (0.39, 0.77) K = 1, N = 231 Quality: moderate	RR 0.56 (0.40, 0.78) K = 4, N = 349 Quality: low	RR 0.55 (0.37, 0.82) K = 3, N = 311 Quality: moderate	RR 0.90 (0.14, 5.74) K = 1, N = 38 Quality: low	Did not provide dropout data

*Treatment as usual.

103

There was limited evidence comparing modes of delivery. One study (KASSINOVE1980) compared non-facilitated bibliotherapy with audiotherapy. Bibliotherapy appeared to be more effective than audiotherapy but it was not statistically significant.

The overall quality of evidence was low. The detailed reasons for downgrading quality can be found in Appendix 18a. The main reason for downgrading was the combined populations of people with mixed anxiety and people with GAD only. The studies targeting people with GAD only were generally of higher quality than those targeting mixed anxiety populations.

Specific interventions for treating populations with GAD only
Two of the studies of non-facilitated self-help included only people with GAD rather than people with a variety of anxiety disorders including GAD. The non-facilitated self-help interventions in these two studies were delivered using different approaches. One study delivered a mindfulness-based stress reduction computer programme (HOUGHTON2008) and the other used a problem solving-based bibliotherapy booklet (BOWMAN1997). When each of these interventions was compared with a non-active control, the results indicated a statistically significant moderate effect (mindfulness-based stress reduction) and large effect (problem solving-based bibliotherapy) for anxiety scores, favouring the treatments. None of these studies provided follow-up data.

6.3   GUIDED SELF-HELP

6.3.1   Studies considered

There were four RCTs comparing guided self-help with waitlist control or treatment as usual. Three targeted mixed anxiety populations and one was aimed at people with GAD only. A summary of study characteristics can be found in Table 9, with full details in Appendix 15b which also includes details of excluded studies.

6.3.2   Clinical evidence for guided self-help

Evidence from the important outcomes and overall quality of evidence are presented in Table 10. The full GRADE profiles and associated forest plots can be found in Appendix 18a and Appendix 16a, respectively.

Table 9: Study information table for trials of guided self-help

	Guided bibliotherapy versus waitlist control in a mixed anxiety population	Guided bibliotherapy versus treatment as usual in mixed anxiety populations	Guided computer therapy versus waitlist control in a GAD-only population
No. trials (total participants)	1 Quasi-RCT (96)	2 RCTs (139)	1 RCT (48)
Study ID	LUCOCK2008	(1) SORBY1991 (2) VANBOEIJEN2005	TITOV2009A
N/% female	96/65%	(1) 60/82% (2) 142/63%	48/71%
Mean age (years)	40	(1) No information (2) 38	44
Diagnosis	Previously diagnosed with an anxiety disorder: 54% had GAD and 46% had panic disorder	(1) All diagnosed with an anxiety disorder by DSM-III (20–30% panic disorder; 14% GAD) (2) All diagnosed with an anxiety disorder by DSM-IV (31% primary diagnosis of GAD; 28% dual diagnosis of GAD and panic disorder)	All diagnosed with GAD as a primary diagnosis by DSM-III-R
Baseline severity (clinician-rated)	Not reported	(1)–(2) Not reported	Cut-off score of 10 on GAD-7 (ranges from 13.62 to 14.33)
Treatment	CBT	(1) Anxiety management training (2) CBT (low-intensity in secondary care)	CBT
Comparator	Waitlist control	(1) Treatment as usual (2) Treatment as usual (in primary care)	Waitlist control
Treatment length	8 weeks	(1) 8 weeks (2) 12 weeks	9 weeks
Follow-up	None	(1) None (2) 3 and 9 months	None

Table 10: Evidence summary table for trials of guided self-help

	Mixed anxiety population – guided bibliotherapy versus waitlist control	Mixed anxiety populations – guided bibliotherapy versus treatment as usual	GAD-only population – guided computer therapy versus waitlist control	Combined populations – guided self-help versus non-active control (waitlist control or treatment as usual)	Combined populations – guided self-help versus waitlist control	Combined populations – guided self-help versus treatment as usual	Mixed anxiety population – guided CBT bibliotherapy versus high-intensity CBT
No. trials (total participants)	1 Quasi-RCT (96)	2 RCTs (139)	1 RCT (48)	3 RCTs 1 Quasi-RCT (283)	1 RCT 1 Quasi RCT (144)	2 RCTS (139)	1 RCT (142)
Study ID	LUCOCK2008	(1) SORBY1991 (2) VANBOEIJEN2005	TITOV2009A	(1) LUCOCK2008 (2) SORBY1991 (3) TITOV2009A (4) VANBOEIJEN2005	(1) TITOV2009A (2) LUCOCK2008	(1) SORBY1991 (2) VANBOEIJEN2005	VANBOEIJEN 2005
Follow-up	None	(1) None (2) 3 and 9 months	None	(1)–(3) None (4) 3 and 9 months	(1)–(2) None	(1) None (2) 3 and 9 months	3 and 9 months
Benefit							
Anxiety (self-rated)	SMD −0.62 (−1.14, −0.10) K = 1, N = 60 Quality: moderate	SMD 0.15 (−0.22, 0.51) K = 2, N = 124 Quality: low	SMD −1.22 (−1.86, −0.57) K = 1, N = 45 Quality: high	SMD −0.38 (−0.99, 0.24) K = 4, N = 229 Quality: very low	SMD −0.89 (−1.47, −0.31) K = 2, N = 105 Quality: low	SMD 0.15 (−0.22, 0.51) K = 2, N = 124 Quality: low	SMD 0.30 (−0.07, 0.67) K = 1, N = 116 Quality: moderate
Anxiety (self-rated) at follow-up	-	*At 3 months:* SMD 0.11 (−0.36, 0.58) K = 1, N = 79	-	-	-	-	*At 3 months:* SMD 0.28 (−0.08, 0.65) K = 1, N = 116

Depression (self-rated)	SMD -0.44 (-0.95, 0.08) K = 1, N = 60 Quality: low	*At 9 months:* SMD 0.29 (-0.19, 0.76) K = 1, N = 79	SMD -0.85 (-1.46, 0.23) K = 1, N = 45 Quality: high	SMD -0.31 (-0.86, 0.25) K = 4, N = 227 Quality: very low	SMD -0.63 (-1.02, -0.23) K = 2, N = 105 Quality: low	SMD 0.03 (-0.78, 0.84) K = 2, N = 122 Quality: very low	SMD 0.25 (-0.11, 0.62) K = 1, N = 116 Quality: moderate; *At 9 months:* SMD 0.15 (-0.22, 0.52) K = 1, N = 116
Depression (self-rated) at follow-up	-	*At 3 months:* SMD 0.29 (-0.18, 0.77) K = 1, N = 79; *At 9 months:* SMD 0.43 (-0.04, 0.91) K = 1, N = 79	-	-	-	-	*At 3 months:* SMD 0.17 (-0.19, 0.54) K = 1, N = 116; *At 9 months:* SMD 0.12 (-0.24, 0.49) K = 1, N = 116
Worry (self-rated)	-	SMD 0.17 (-0.30, 0.64) K = 1, N = 79 Quality: moderate	SMD -0.93 (-1.55, -0.32) K = 1, N = 45 Quality: high	SMD -0.36 (-1.44, 0.71) K = 2, N = 124 Quality: very low	SMD -0.93 (-1.55, -0.32) K = 1, N = 45 Quality: high	SMD 0.17 (-0.30, 0.64) K = 1, N = 79 Quality: moderate	SMD 0.28 (-0.09, 0.64) K = 1, N = 116 Quality: moderate
Worry (self-rated) at follow-up	-	*At 3 months:* SMD 0.24 (-0.23, 0.71) K = 1, N = 79; *At 9 months:* SMD 0.42 (-0.05, 0.90) K = 1, N = 79	-	-	-	-	*At 3 months:* SMD 0.35 (-0.02, 0.72) K = 1, N = 116; *At 9 months:* SMD 0.34 (-0.03, 0.71) K = 1, N = 116

Continued

Table 10: *(Continued)*

	Mixed anxiety population – guided bibliotherapy versus waitlist control	Mixed anxiety populations – guided bibliotherapy versus treatment as usual	GAD-only population – guided computer therapy versus waitlist control	Combined populations – guided self-help versus non-active control (waitlist control or treatment as usual)	Combined populations – guided self-help versus waitlist control	Combined populations – guided self-help versus treatment as usual	Mixed anxiety population – guided CBT bibliotherapy versus high-intensity CBT
Non-remission	RR 1.00 (0.86, 1.16) K = 1, N = 96 Quality: moderate	-	RR 0.48 (0.31, 0.75) K = 1, N = 45	RR 0.71 (0.32, 1.59) K = 2, N = 141 Quality: very low	-	-	-
Non-response	-	-	RR 0.63 (0.46, 0.87) K = 1, N = 45 Quality: high	-			-
Harm							
Discontinuation due to any reason	RR 1.40 (0.83, 2.37) K = 1, N = 96 Quality: low	RR 0.57 (0.03, 9.99) K = 2, N = 153 Quality: very low	RR 2.63 (0.59, 11.64) K = 1, N = 45 Quality: high	RR 1.42 (0.70, 2.91) K = 4, N = 294 Quality: low	RR 1.50 (0.91, 2.47) K = 2, N = 141 Quality: very low	RR 0.57 (0.03, 9.99) K = 2, N = 153 Quality: very low	RR 0.79 (0.30, 2.08) K = 1, N = 116 Quality: moderate

6.3.3   Evidence summary (guided self-help)

Three studies (LUCOCK2008; SORBY1991; VANBOEIJEN2005) compared guided bibliotherapy with a non-active control group. These studies were too heterogeneous to be analysed together. LUCOCK2008 compared guided bibliotherapy with waitlist control. The treatment group showed a statistically significant moderate effect on anxiety scores. A small, yet not statistically significant effect was found on depression scores. There was no statistically significant difference in terms of improving non-remission. These results are based on one study and given the wide confidence intervals, it is difficult to make any firm conclusions from this evidence.

VANBOEIJEN2005 and SORBY1991 both compared guided bibliotherapy with treatment as usual and therefore were analysed together. However, SORBY1991 regarded guided bibliotherapy as an augmentation to treatment as usual and compared it with standard care with no bibliotherapy. Results indicate that there were no statistically significant effects on either anxiety, depression or worry outcomes at post-treatment. However, a small, yet insignificant improvement in anxiety at 9 months and depression at 3 and 9 months was found in standard care (VANBOEIJEN2005). However, it is difficult to make firm conclusions from this limited evidence.

One study directly compared low-intensity CBT bibliotherapy with high-intensity CBT (VANBOEIJEN2005). There was no statistically significant difference in the risk of discontinuation between low-intensity and high-intensity treatments. Although not significant, there was a small trend favouring high-intensity treatment on anxiety, depression and worry outcomes. At 3 and 9 months' follow-up, the effects remained statistically insignificant. These results are based on data from one study and therefore it is difficult to draw firm conclusions about the relative effectiveness of low or high-intensity CBT treatments.

The overall quality of evidence was low. The main reason for downgrading the quality was the difference in target population (people with mixed anxiety and people with a GAD-only diagnosis), as well as difference in comparator group (waitlist control and treatment as usual). It was observed that the studies targeting mixed anxiety populations were of lower quality than the study treating a GAD-only population.

Specific interventions for treating GAD only population
Only one study of guided self-help included people with GAD only (rather than a variety of anxiety disorders including GAD) (TITOV2009A). This study compared CCBT treatment with waitlist control and showed a statistically significant large effect on anxiety, depression and worry outcomes. There was also a statistically significant improvement in non-remission and non-response. These results are based on one study, therefore it is difficult to make any firm conclusions from this evidence.

6.4   PSYCHOEDUCATIONAL GROUPS

6.4.1   Studies considered

There were two studies comparing psychoeducational groups with waitlist control. One targeted a mixed anxiety population and the other people with GAD only. A summary of study characteristics can be found in Table 11 with full details in Appendix 15b which also includes details of excluded studies.

6.4.2   Clinical evidence for psychoeducational groups

Evidence from the important outcomes and overall quality of evidence are presented in Table 12. The full GRADE profiles and associated forest plots can be found in Appendix 18a and Appendix 16a, respectively.

Table 11: Study information table for trials comparing psychoeducational groups with waitlist

	Psychoeducational groups versus waitlist control in a mixed anxiety population	Psychoeducational groups versus waitlist control in a GAD-only population
No. trials (total participants)	1 RCT (73)	1 Quasi-RCT (37)
Study ID	KITCHINER2009	WHITE1992
N/% female	73/48%	109/72%
Mean age (years)	40	38
Diagnosis	All diagnosed with an anxiety disorder by DSM-IV (29% GAD; 55% panic disorder with/without agoraphobia)	All diagnosed with GAD as a primary diagnosis by DSM-III-R
Baseline severity (clinician-rated)	Not reported	Not reported
Treatment	CBT (in secondary care); anxiety management training (in secondary care)	CBT
Comparator	Waitlist control	Waitlist control
Treatment length	6 weeks	6 weeks
Follow-up	1 month	6 months

Table 12: Evidence summary table for trials of psychoeducational groups

	Psychoeducational group (CBT) versus waitlist control in a mixed anxiety population	Psychoeducational group (CBT) versus waitlist control in a GAD-only population	Psychoeducational group versus waitlist control in combined populations	Psychoeducational group (CBT) versus group anxiety management psychoeducation in a mixed anxiety population
No. trials (total participants)	1 RCT (73)	1 Quasi-RCT (37)	1 RCT 1 Quasi-RCT (110)	1 RCT (73)
Study ID	KITCHINER2009	WHITE1992	(1) KITCHINER2009 (2) WHITE1992	KITCHINER2009
Follow-up	1 month	6 months	(1) 1 month (2) 6 months	1 month
Benefits				
Anxiety (self-rated)	SMD −0.34 (−0.90, 0.23) K = 1, N = 49 Quality: moderate	SMD −0.70 (−1.45, 0.04) K = 1, N = 33 Quality: low	SMD −0.47 (−0.92, −0.02) K = 2, N = 82 Quality: low	SMD 0.16 (−0.40, 0.72) K = 1, N = 49 Quality: moderate
Anxiety (self-rated) at follow-up	*At 1 month:* SMD −0.04 (−0.60, 0.52) K = 1, N = 49	-	-	*At 1 month:* SMD 0.02 (−0.54, 0.58) K = 1, N = 49 *At 3 months:* SMD 0.22 (−0.34, 0.79) K = 1, N = 49

Continued

Table 12: *(Continued)*

	Psychoeducational group (CBT) versus waitlist control in a mixed anxiety population	Psychoeducational group (CBT) versus waitlist control in a GAD-only population	Psychoeducational group versus waitlist control in combined populations	Psychoeducational group (CBT) versus group anxiety management psychoeducation in a mixed anxiety population
				At 6 months: SMD −0.05 (−0.61, 0.51) K = 1, N = 49
Depression (self-rated)	SMD −0.49 (−1.06, 0.08) K = 1, N = 49 Quality: high	SMD −0.51 (−1.25, 0.22) K = 1, N = 33 Quality: low	SMD −0.50 (−0.95, −0.05) K = 2, N = 82 Quality: low	SMD 0.10 (−0.46, 0.66) K = 1, N = 49 Quality: moderate
Depression (self-rated) at follow-up	*At 1 month:* SMD −0.18 (−0.75, 0.38) K = 1, N = 49	-	-	*At 1 month:* SMD −0.10 (−0.66, 0.46) K = 1, N = 49 *At 3 months:* SMD 0.07 (−0.49, 0.64) K = 1, N = 49 *At 6 months:* SMD 0.07 (−0.49, 0.63) K = 1, N = 49

Worry (self-rated)	SMD −0.36 (−0.93, 0.20) K = 1, N = 49 Quality: moderate	-	SMD −0.28 (−0.84, 0.29) K = 1, N = 49 Quality: moderate
Worry (self-rated) at follow-up	*At 1 month:* SMD −0.17 (−0.73, 0.39) K = 1, N = 49	-	*At 1 month:* SMD −0.42 (−0.99, 0.15) K = 1, N = 49 *At 3 months:* SMD −0.26 (−0.83, 0.30) K = 1, N = 49 *At 6 months:* SMD −0.36 (−0.93, 0.20) K = 1, N = 49
Harm			
Dropouts	9/25 dropped out from treatment group; no data reported from comparison K = 1, N = 49	RR 4.00 (0.23, 68.57) K = 1, N = 37 Quality: very low	-

6.4.3   Evidence summary (psychoeducational groups)

One study (WHITE1992) targeted a GAD-only population and the other (KITCHINER2009) a mixed anxiety population. WHITE1992 was based in a primary care setting and KITCHINER2009 was based in a secondary care setting. When the two studies were analysed together, the results indicate a small and statistically significant effect for anxiety and depression scores. However, conclusions should be subject to cautious interpretation due to the limited number of studies available.

The overall quality of the two studies was low to moderate. The main reason for downgrading was due to the limitations in study design.

KITCHINER2009 compared two psychoeducational groups; mental health nurses delivered group CBT in one group while occupational therapists delivered a more interactive anxiety management psychoeducational group in the other. When group CBT was compared with waitlist control, there appeared to be a small, yet not significant effect on anxiety and depression scores. The effect size decreased at 1 month's follow-up.

When the two treatment groups (group CBT versus group anxiety management) were compared, there was no statistically significant difference in the risk of discontinuation or anxiety, depression and worry scores. Follow-up data at 1, 3 and 6 months remained insignificant and varied widely. Therefore, due to limited evidence and wide confidence intervals in the results, no definitive conclusion can be drawn as to which treatment principle is better.

Specific interventions for treating a GAD-only population
One study (WHITE1992) specifically targeted a GAD-only population. Due to the small sample size, the only statistically significant finding was a marginal significant moderate effect on self-rated anxiety scores, favouring psychoeducational groups compared with waitlist control.

6.5   MODES OF DELIVERY

Guided bibliotherapy
Three studies (LUCOCK2008; SORBY1991; VANBOEIJEN2005) looked at the effectiveness of guided bibliotherapy on anxiety. Two of the booklets were based on CBT principles (LUCOCK2008; VANBOEIJEN2005) and one on anxiety management training (SORBY1991). The average duration of treatment was 9 weeks with seven guided weekly sessions that lasted approximately 20 minutes each. Therapist support was delivered by a trained GP (SORBY1991; VANBOEIJEN2005) or a trained assistant psychologist who had a first degree in psychology (LUCOCK2008). Support included reinforcing the participant's achievements and motivating them to continue (VANBOEIJEN2005), monitoring their progress and giving advice (LUCOCK2008; SORBY1991) and administering treatment as usual (SORBY1991). Training generally involved educational sessions about the diagnosis and treatment of anxiety and regular supervision or modules on guided self-help for anxiety. At the

beginning of the programme participants were generally given an introductory talk by the therapist about the contents of the booklet and how to use it. Homework assignments were used to consolidate learning and comprised practical exercises to do at home or worksheets relevant to a particular section of the booklet.

Non-facilitated bibliotherapy

Five studies examined the effectiveness of non-facilitated bibliotherapy on anxiety (BOWMAN1997; WHITE1995; MAUNDER2009; KASSINOVE1980; TARRIER1986). The majority of booklets were based on CBT (WHITE1995; MAUNDER2009; KASSINOVE1980) or related principles such as relaxation training (TARRIER1986), but one was based on problem solving therapy (BOWMAN1997). The number of pages in the booklets used ranged from 45 to 79 pages and the average duration of treatment was 6 weeks. No therapist support or contact was provided for these treatments; however, it was often suggested that participants could call the therapist to clarify any questions regarding the therapy itself (for example, BOWMAN1997). These calls, however, were restricted to a maximum of 5 minutes per week and no therapy was provided. Moreover, for some studies (for example, WHITE1995) some time was allocated at the beginning of the programme to describe the booklet, its rationale and an explanation of how to use it. No advice on dealing with specific problems was offered. All of the studies but one (WHITE1995) required participants to complete homework or conduct exercises at home to consolidate learning. For example, participants were required to complete worksheets (BOWMAN1997), questions (KASSINOVE1980) or to practice relaxation techniques (TARRIER1986).

Non-facilitated audiotherapy

There was one trial that examined the effectiveness of rational emotional therapy in the form of audiotherapy (KASSINOVE1980). This involved 16 sessions lasting 1 hour over a period of 8 weeks. The central aim of the therapy was to reduce the endorsement of irrational beliefs and to aid the development of a more objective and empirically-based attitude to life. A group of people given audiotherapy were asked to listen to a tape developed by rational emotive experts, with an aim to encourage rational thinking and develop a more suitable philosophy of life. No homework assignment or therapist support was provided.

Non-facilitated computer-delivered therapy

Only one study delivered non-facilitated computer-delivered self-help (HOUGHTON2008), which was based on the principles of mindfulness. The course consisted of eight modules that provided self-help instructions over a period of 8 weeks. The self-help instructions were accessed via the internet on a weekly basis in the participants' own homes. At the start of the treatment an introduction to the internet programme was provided via a web page. This briefly discussed the aims of the programme, what it would entail and listed additional information resources. Participants were asked to practice the exercises for a minimum of 10 minutes per day, 6 days per week. All participants completed the entire 8 weeks of the mindfulness stress reduction programme. The central components were: focusing on the mindfulness of breathing; formal sitting meditation; body scan meditation; and yoga. Focusing on the mindfulness of breathing involved paying attention to the inflow and outflow of breath on a regular basis. Formal sitting meditation entailed adopting an erect and dignified posture, with the head, neck and back aligned vertically. During body scan meditation, the person focused on and sensed each area of the body thoroughly, envisaging the strain and fatigue pouring out with each breath. Similarly, yoga involved slow stretching and strengthening movements performed with consciousness of breath and body sensations. There were no homework assignments to consolidate learning and no therapist contact or support.

Guided computer-delivered therapy
There was only one study examining the effectiveness of a guided CBT-based computer-delivered programme (TITOV2009A). The Worry Programme is a clinician-assisted CCBT course of six sessions conducted over a 9-week period. Participants were encouraged to complete one session per week. Eighteen (75%) treatment group participants completed all six sessions within the required time frame (that is, 9 weeks). The course consisted of the following components: weekly homework assignments, weekly email contact from a clinical psychologist and a moderated online discussion forum with other participants. Participants also had access to a number of other resources including guidelines about assertiveness, health anxiety, and answers to frequently asked questions about the application of particular skills described in the course. The first two sessions provided education about the symptoms and treatment of GAD and an introduction to the basic principles of cognitive therapy. Subsequent sessions gave advice about challenging positive and negative beliefs and offered guidance about practicing graded exposure, challenging core beliefs and relapse prevention. A clinical psychologist provided all clinical contact with participants. The mean therapist time given per treatment group was 130 minutes including monitoring of the discussion forum, instant email messages and telephone calls. During the programme the clinician sent 132 personal instant messages in total (mean = 5.5 per participant), made a total of 98 telephone calls (mean = 4.1 telephone calls per participant) and made 26 forum postings to the entire group.

Psychoeducational groups
Two studies examined the effectiveness of group psychoeducation on anxiety (KITCHINER2009; WHITE1992). There were two main packages: 'Stress Control', a CBT package that used a robustly educational approach, including lectures or presentation and a self-help manual (KITCHINER2009; WHITE1992) and an anxiety management training group (KITCHINER2009), which also used CBT principles but was designed to be more interactive and had a stronger emphasis on activity scheduling and relaxation techniques. Furthermore, group processes were utilised by the therapists to engender a self-help ethos, whereby participants could share and learn from one another's experiences in a 'safe' environment. Each group was run by two therapists who placed a greater emphasis on their role as educators and organisers of self-help services than on their role as individual therapists. Therapist support was

delivered by either experienced mental health nurses with extensive experience of treating outpatients with CBT under supervision or by two occupational therapists with 15 to 20 years' experience in anxiety management groups. The average size of the groups was 20 to 24 participants with a total of two therapists per group. Thus, the therapist to participant ratio was approximately one therapist to 10 to 12 participants. The discussion of personal problems was prohibited on the basis that the motivation of attendance was for participants to become their own therapist. The average number of sessions was six weekly 2-hour sessions. Homework assignments were also distributed at the end of each session to consolidate learning.

6.6   HEALTH ECONOMIC EVIDENCE

6.6.1   Research question

What is the cost effectiveness of low-intensity interventions (non-facilitated bibliotherapy, non-facilitated audiotherapy, non-facilitated computer therapy, guided bibliotherapy, guided computer therapy, psychoeducational groups, and helplines) compared with other interventions in the treatment of GAD?

6.6.2   Systematic literature review

No studies assessing the cost effectiveness of low-intensity psychological interventions compared with other available interventions (including treatment as usual) for people with GAD only or mixed anxiety disorders were identified by the systematic search of the economic literature undertaken for this guideline. Details on the methods used for the systematic search of the economic literature are described in Chapter 3.

6.6.3   Cost analysis: low-intensity psychological interventions

The cost effectiveness of low-intensity psychological interventions relative to other available treatments for people with GAD was considered by the GDG as an area with likely significant resource implications. The GDG was particularly interested in the cost effectiveness of low-intensity psychological interventions compared with high-intensity psychological interventions and pharmacological interventions, as well as the relative cost effectiveness of different low-intensity psychological interventions. Comparison of low-intensity psychological interventions with non-active treatments was not deemed a priority by the GDG and thus was not considered as an area for economic modelling. Nevertheless, an exception was made in the case of CCBT: since this guideline also updates the NICE Technology Appraisal 97 on *Computerised Cognitive Behaviour Therapy for Depression and Anxiety* (NICE, 2006), it was decided to develop an economic model to assess the cost effectiveness of CCBT compared with waitlist for people with GAD, using data from the only RCT on CCBT in people with GAD included in the clinical review for this guideline (TITOV2009A). The economic analysis for CCBT is presented in the next section.

The development of an economic model comparing low-intensity psychological interventions with high-intensity psychological interventions and/or pharmacological treatments using clinical effectiveness data from the guideline systematic review was not possible: first of all, no RCTs directly comparing low-intensity psychological interventions with other active treatments (high-intensity psychological interventions or pharmacological treatments) were identified in the systematic clinical literature review. Indirect comparisons between low-intensity psychological interventions and other active treatments using a common, 'baseline' comparator, were problematic due to important differences in study designs, specifically:

- Comparators: studies of psychological interventions used mainly waitlist or standard care as a comparator, while studies of pharmacological treatments used placebo as control (but never a waitlist control or standard care); therefore, it was not possible to make indirect comparisons between low-intensity psychological therapies with pharmacological treatments.
- Study population: a number of studies of low-intensity psychological interventions were conducted in people with mixed anxiety rather than GAD only; in contrast, only studies of people with GAD were included in the systematic literature review of pharmacological and high-intensity psychological interventions.
- Reported clinical outcomes: psychological studies tended to report mainly continuous outcomes. Few psychological studies reported rates of response or remission, which were commonly used as outcome measures in pharmacological studies; even then, the definition of response/remission in psychological studies was not the same as the respective definitions in pharmacological studies. In fact, there was inconsistency in the definition of response and remission across psychological studies, which made indirect comparisons between different psychological interventions difficult.

The above differences across studies were evident even within the set of studies on low-intensity psychological interventions, thus not allowing the development of an economic model assessing their relative (in-between) cost effectiveness. Instead, simple cost analyses were undertaken to estimate the intervention costs associated with their provision within the NHS.

In order to estimate intervention costs of the low-intensity psychological interventions reviewed in this guideline, relevant healthcare resource use estimates associated with their provision were combined with appropriate national unit costs. The resource use estimates were based on the descriptions of resources used in the RCTs included in the guideline systematic review, supported by the expert opinion of the GDG in order to reflect optimal clinical practice within the NHS context. It was assumed that low-intensity psychological interventions were generally provided by mental health workers in the UK; nevertheless, it is recognised that other trained healthcare professionals of similar qualifications may also provide such interventions. As unit costs of mental health workers were not available, those of mental health nurses were used as a proxy instead. These were based on the median full-time equivalent basic salary for Agenda for Change band 5, of the January to March 2009 NHS staff earnings estimates for qualified nurses. Estimation of unit costs considered wages or salary, salary oncosts, qualification costs and overheads (Curtis, 2009).

Table 13 provides an overview of the low-intensity psychological interventions considered in the cost analysis, the resource use estimates, the respective unit costs and the estimated total cost of each intervention. According to this table, non-facilitated self-help is the least costly low-intensity psychological intervention for people with GAD, costing roughly £15 per person treated. Guided bibliotherapy is estimated to cost between £83 and £150 per person treated, depending on the number of

Table 13: Cost analysis of low-intensity psychological interventions for people with GAD

Intervention	Resource use estimate (based on descriptions in RCTs and the expert opinion of the GDG)	Unit cost	Total intervention per person (2009 prices)
Non-facilitated self-help	One 15-minute session with a mental health nurse (band 5)	£45 per hour of face-to-face contact (Curtis, 2009)	£11
	Booklet	£4 per item (assumption)	£4
			TOTAL £15
Guided bibliotherapy	Three to six sessions with a mental health nurse (band 5), lasting 45 minutes for the first session and 30 minutes for the rest	£45 per hour of face-to-face contact (Curtis, 2009)	£79 – £146
	Booklet	£4 per item (assumption)	£4
			TOTAL £83 – £150
Psychoeducational groups	Six sessions of 2 hours each, provided by two mental health nurses (band 5) to groups of 10 to 30 people	£45 per hour of face-to-face contact (Curtis, 2009)	TOTAL £36 – £108

sessions provided by the therapist. Finally, the intervention cost of psychoeducational groups lies between the costs of the other two low-intensity interventions, ranging from £36 to £108, depending on the number of people with GAD participating in the group (estimated between 10 and 30 people). These estimates of intervention costs were considered by the GDG alongside the findings of the clinical effectiveness review, in order to make a judgement regarding the cost effectiveness of low-intensity psychological treatments.

6.6.4   Economic modelling: computerised cognitive behavioural therapy

An economic model in the form of a decision-tree was developed to assess the cost effectiveness of CCBT for the treatment of people with GAD. The economic analysis was undertaken as part of updating NICE Technology Appraisal 97, *Computerised Cognitive Behaviour Therapy for Depression and Anxiety* (NICE, 2006).

Interventions assessed
The only study examining CCBT for people with GAD included in the guideline systematic review was TITOV2009A. The study examined the effectiveness of the Worry Programme a clinician-assisted CCBT course, versus waitlist. Thus, based on the availability of clinical data, the economic model compared CCBT (the Worry Programme) versus waitlist. However, it must be noted that the Worry Programme is not available for use by people with GAD, and therefore is only used as a case-study in order to explore the cost effectiveness of a CCBT programme for this population, relative to a do-nothing option.

Model structure
A decision-tree was constructed in order to estimate the costs and benefits of a hypothetical cohort of people with GAD presenting to primary care who were either started on CCBT or were assigned to waitlist for a period of 9 weeks, that is, the duration of treatment in TITOV2009A. At the end of this period, people either responded to treatment (or demonstrated an equivalent spontaneous clinical improvement if assigned to waitlist) or did not respond. People who responded to treatment (or improved spontaneously) at the end of the 9-week period might relapse over the next 6 months following treatment, otherwise they would remain improved. The duration of 6 months (26 weeks) reflects the mean duration of studies examining relapse prevention following pharmacological treatment or placebo that provided the relapse data for the model. Thus the time horizon of the analysis was 35 weeks in total. A schematic diagram of the decision-tree is presented in Figure 4.

Costs and outcomes considered in the analysis
The economic analysis adopted the perspective of the NHS and personal social services, as recommended by NICE (2009a). Costs consisted of intervention costs and other health and social care costs incurred by people with GAD, including contacts with healthcare professionals such as GPs, psychiatrists, psychologists, mental health

Figure 4: Schematic diagram of the economic model structure

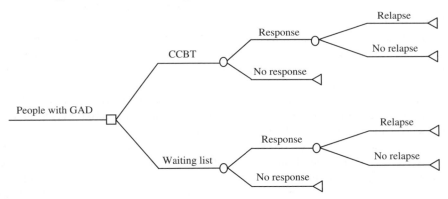

nurses and social workers, community care, and inpatient and outpatient secondary care. The measure of outcome was the quality-adjusted life year (QALY).

Clinical input parameters of the economic model
Clinical input parameters included response rates for the two interventions assessed as well as relapse rates following response to treatment or spontaneous improvement. Response data were derived from TITOV2009A. The study reported response rates for CCBT and waitlist, with response defined as a 50% reduction in the pre-treatment Generalised Anxiety Disorder Assessment 7-item (GAD-7) score. The relapse rate following response was conservatively assumed to be the same for both interventions, and was derived from the guideline meta-analysis of studies on pharmacological relapse prevention, after pooling the data from all placebo arms in the trials considered in the guideline meta-analysis (see Chapter 8). Clinical input parameters of the economic analysis are provided in Table 17.

Utility data and estimation of quality-adjusted life years
In order to express outcomes in the form of QALYs, the health states of the economic model needed to be linked to appropriate utility scores. Utility scores represent the health-related quality of life (HRQoL) associated with specific health states on a scale from 0 (death) to 1 (perfect health); they are estimated using preference-based measures that capture people's preferences on the HRQoL experienced in the health states under consideration.

The systematic search of the literature identified two studies that reported utility scores for specific health states associated with GAD (Allgulander *et al.*, 2007; Revicki *et al.*, 2008).

Allgulander and colleagues (2007) generated utility scores using SF-36 data (Ware *et al.*, 1993) derived from 273 people with GAD participating in a double-blind, placebo-controlled, relapse prevention, multinational clinical trial of escitalopram (Allgulander *et al.*, 2006). Participants (who were included in the trial if they had a HAM-A total score of 20 or more) first received 12 weeks of open-label treatment with escitalopram. Those responding to treatment were then randomised to double-blind treatment with escitalopram or placebo aiming at relapse prevention. Response to treatment was defined as a HAM-A score of 10 or less; relapse was defined as a HAM-A total score 15 or more or lack of efficacy, as judged by the investigator. SF-36 data were taken from participants at the end of the open-label period, and at the end of, or at last assessment during, the double-blind period. SF-36 scores were converted into utility scores using the SF-6D algorithm (Brazier *et al.*, 2002). The SF-6D algorithm has been generated using the standard gamble (SG) technique in a representative sample of the UK general population.

Revicki and colleagues (2008) generated utility scores using SF-12 data from 297 people with GAD recruited from an integrated healthcare delivery system in the US. The SF-12 is a shorter form of SF-36 (Ware *et al.*, 1995). Participants in the study were categorised into different levels of GAD symptom severity, according to their HAM-A scores; 297 people with GAD provided SF-12 data, which were translated into SF-6D profiles; symptom severity was measured using HAM-A. Asymptomatic anxiety was defined as a HAM-A score of 9 or less; mild anxiety as a HAM-A score between 10 and 15; moderate anxiety as a HAM-A score between 16 and 24; and severe anxiety as a HAM-A score of 25 or more. SF-12 scores were transformed into utility scores using the SF-6D algorithm (Brazier & Roberts, 2004).

Table 14 summarises the methods used to derive and value health states associated with GAD in the literature and presents the respective utility scores reported in the two utility studies of GAD identified by the systematic search of the literature.

According to NICE guidance on the selection of utility values for use in cost-utility analysis, the measurement of changes in HRQoL should be reported directly from people with the condition examined, and the valuation of health states should be based on public preferences elicited using a choice-based method, such as the time trade-off (TTO) or SG, in a representative sample of the UK population. NICE recommends the European Quality of Life - 5 Dimensions (EQ-5D; Brooks, 1996) as the preferred measure of HRQoL in adults for use in cost-utility analysis. When EQ-5D scores are not available or are inappropriate for the condition or effects of treatment, NICE recommends that the valuation methods be fully described and comparable to those used for the EQ-5D (NICE, 2008a).

No study generating utility scores from EQ-5D for people with GAD was identified by the systematic search of the literature. However, both studies included in the review used SF-6D for the estimation of utility scores in this population. The SF-36 (and SF-12) is a validated generic measure of HRQoL. The SF-6D algorithm can generate utility scores for all health states described in SF-36 (Brazier *et al.*, 2002) and SF-12 (Brazier & Roberts, 2004), which have been elicited by a representative sample of the UK general population using SG; thus, the valuation method meets NICE criteria.

The utility data reported in Allgulander and colleagues (2006) corresponds to the respective health states described in the economic model (that is, response, non-response, relapse following response, and response not followed by relapse), although it should be noted that the definition of response in Allgulander and colleagues (2006)

Table 14: Summary of studies reporting utility scores for health states of GAD

Study	Definition of health states	Valuation method	Population valuing	Results	
Allgulander *et al.*, 2006	SF-36 scores of 273 people with GAD transformed into SF-6D profiles Definition of GAD health states: Response to treatment: HAM-A score $\leq$ 10 Relapse: HAM-A score $\geq$ 15	SG	UK general population	Baseline: Response: No response: Relapse following response: Response and no relapse:	0.64 (SD 0.10) 0.76 (SD 0.10) 0.63 (SD 0.10) 0.73 (SD 0.12) 0.79 (SD 0.12)
Revicki *et al.*, 2008	SF-12 scores of 297 people with GAD transformed into SF-6D profiles Definition of GAD health states: Asymptomatic anxiety: HAM-A score $\leq$ 9 Mild anxiety: 10 $\leq$ HAM-A score $\leq$ 15 Moderate anxiety: 16 $\leq$ HAM-A score $\leq$ 24 Severe anxiety: HAM-A score $\geq$ 25	SG	UK general population	Asymptomatic anxiety: Mild anxiety: Moderate anxiety: Severe anxiety:	0.72 (SD 0.1) 0.64 (SD 0.1) 0.60 (SD 0.1) 0.53 (SD 0.1)

is different from that in TITOV2009A, which provided the clinical data utilised in the model. In contrast, the health states described in Revicki and colleagues (2008) could not be linked to the model health states. Therefore, it was decided to use the utility data reported in Allgulander and colleagues (2006) in the economic analysis.

It was assumed that the improvement in utility for people with GAD responding to treatment (or spontaneously improving if they were on a waitlist) occurred linearly over the 9 weeks of treatment, starting from the utility value of non-response and reaching the utility value of response.

People responding and not relapsing were assumed to experience a linear increase in their utility over the remaining 6 months of the time horizon, starting from the utility value of response and reaching the utility value of response and no relapse. In contrast, people relapsing following response were assumed to experience a linear reduction in their utility over the remaining 6 months of the time horizon, starting from the utility value of response and reaching the utility value of relapse following response.

Cost data

Intervention costs as well as other health and social care costs incurred by people with GAD were calculated by combining resource use estimates with respective national unit costs. Intervention costs for the CCBT programme consisted of therapists' time (spent on telephone calls, emails and 'live' contacts as reported in TITOV2009A), hardware (personal computers – PCs) and capital overheads. The Worry Programme is available for research purposes only; therefore no licence fee was considered at the estimation of the intervention cost, although this cost component, which may be considerable, needs to be taken into account in the assessment of cost effectiveness of other CCBT packages available in the future for the management of people with GAD. Alternatively, for a CCBT programme that is freely available via the internet, a server or website hosting cost may be relevant (for example if the programme is provided by the NHS) and should be considered at the estimation of the intervention cost. The intervention cost of waitlist was zero.

The cost of a therapist's time for CCBT was estimated by combining the mean total therapist's time per person treated, as reported in TITOV2009A, with the national unit cost of a clinical psychologist (Curtis, 2009). The latter was selected because the Worry Programme in TITOV2009A was provided by clinical psychologists. However, it is acknowledged that CCBT could be provided by other healthcare professionals with appropriate qualifications/training. The unit cost of a clinical psychologist per hour of client contact has been estimated based on the median full-time equivalent basic salary for Agenda for Change Band 7, including salary, salary oncosts and overheads, but no qualification costs as the latter are not available for clinical psychologists. The unit cost of other types of healthcare professionals who have the qualifications and skills to provide CCBT is expected to be similar.

The annual costs of hardware and capital overheads (space around the PC) were taken from the economic analysis undertaken to inform the NICE Technology Appraisal on CCBT for depression and anxiety (Kaltenthaler *et al.*, 2006). In the same report it is estimated that one PC can serve around 100 people treated with

CCBT per year. For this economic analysis, and in order to estimate the cost of hardware and capital overheads per person with GAD treated with CCBT, it was conservatively assumed that one PC can serve 75 people per year. It was also assumed that a PC is used under full capacity (that is, it serves no less than 75 people annually), considering that the PC is available for use not only by people with GAD, but also by people with other mental health conditions, such as depression, who may use other CCBT packages on the PC. The annual cost of hardware and capital overheads, as estimated in Kaltenthaler and colleagues (2006), was therefore divided by 75 and adjusted to reflect a 35-week cost, corresponding to the time horizon of the analysis. It should be noted that if people with GAD can access the CCBT package from home or a public library, then the cost of hardware and capital overheads to the NHS is zero.

The server or website hosting cost per person with GAD treated with an internet-based CCBT package provided by the NHS was estimated to be negligible and was omitted from the analysis. Estimation of this cost was based on the price of a ten-page website, which was found to range between £550 and £800 annually (prices based on internet search). According to the most recent *Adult Psychiatric Morbidity in England* survey (McManus *et al.*, 2009), 4.7% of people aged between 16 and 64 years are expected to have GAD at any point in time. This translates to an estimate of 1.7 million people with GAD in England and Wales, given that the population aged 16 to 64 years was approximately 35.3 million people in 2008 (Office for National Statistics [ONS], 2009). Assuming that 5% of them are treated with CCBT (a deliberately conservative low percentage), this would result in 85,000 people. Spreading the annual server/website cost to this population would result in a cost of less than one penny per person treated; meaning that if the NHS wanted to maintain a website with a CCBT programme for GAD, the website cost per person treated would be negligible. Table 15 presents the cost elements of the intervention cost.

The extra health and social care costs incurred by people with GAD were estimated based on data reported in the *Adult Psychiatric Morbidity in England* survey (McManus *et al.*, 2009), supported by the expert opinion of the GDG. Data reported in the survey included the percentages of people with GAD who sought various types of health and social services over a period of time ranging from 'over the past 2 weeks' to 'over the past year'. These services included inpatient care, outpatient services, contacts with GPs, psychiatrists, psychologists, community psychiatric nurses, social and outreach workers, other nursing services, home help and home care, participation in self-help and support groups, and services provided by community day care centres. The reported percentages were extrapolated in order to estimate the percentage of people with GAD using each service on an annual basis. The GDG determined which of these services were likely to be sought specifically for the condition of GAD within the NHS, and made estimates on the number of visits and the time spent on each visit where relevant, in order to provide a total resource use estimate for each type of service. The average length of stay for people with GAD receiving inpatient care was taken from national hospital episode statistics (NHS, The Information Centre, 2009). The resource use estimates were then combined with appropriate unit costs taken from national sources (Curtis, 2009; DH, 2010) in order to estimate an overall annual health and social care cost incurred by people with GAD. Using this

Table 15: Intervention cost of CCBT

Cost element	Resource use estimate and respective unit cost (2009 prices)	Total cost per person (2009 prices)
Therapist's time	130 minutes per person (TITOV2009A) £75 per hour of client contact (clinical psychologist; Curtis, 2009)	£162.5
Hardware	£309 per PC per year (Kaltenthaler *et al.*, 2006) Cost divided by 75 people treated with CCBT and adjusted for 35 weeks (time horizon of analysis)	£2.8
Capital overheads	£2,053 per PC per year (Kaltenthaler *et al.*, 2006) Cost divided by 75 people treated with CCBT and adjusted for 35 weeks (time horizon of analysis)	£18.4
Licence fee	0 (Worry Programme not available in clinical practice)	0
Server/website hosting cost	£550–£800 for a ten-page website annually Cost divided by 85,000 people, representing 5% of the estimated 1.7 million people with GAD in England and Wales; latter estimate based on a 4.7% prevalence of GAD (McManus *et al.*, 2009) and a population of 35.3 million people aged 16–64 years in England and Wales (ONS, 2009).	Negligible
		TOTAL: £183.7

figure, a monthly health and social care cost was then estimated, which was assumed to be incurred by people not responding to treatment (or not improving spontaneously if they were on a waitlist) and by people relapsing following response. People responding to treatment and remaining improved over the 6 months post-treatment were estimated to incur zero health and social care costs, apart from the intervention cost, according to the expert opinion of the GDG.

People not responding to treatment were assumed to incur the additional health and social care cost starting from the end of treatment and for the remaining time horizon of the analysis, that is, over 6 months post-treatment. People relapsing following response were assumed, for costing purposes, to experience relapse in the middle of the 6-month post-treatment period, that is, at 3 months post-treatment. These people were assumed to incur zero costs over the first 3 months post-treatment, and the extra health and social care cost over the next 3 months.

Table 16 presents the published data and the expert opinion of the GDG estimates used for the calculation of the annual health and social care cost incurred by people with GAD. All costs were expressed in 2009 prices, uplifted, where necessary, using the Hospital and Community Health Services (HCHS) Pay and Prices Index (Curtis, 2009). Discounting of costs was not necessary since the time horizon of the analysis was shorter than 1 year.

Table 17 presents the values of all input parameters utilised in the economic model.

Data analysis and presentation of the results
Two methods were employed to analyse the input parameter data and present the results of the economic analysis.

First, a *deterministic* analysis was undertaken, where data were analysed as point estimates. The output of the analysis was the incremental cost-effectiveness ratio (ICER) of CCBT versus waitlist, expressing the additional cost per QALY gained associated with provision of CCBT instead of waitlist.

One-way sensitivity analysis explored the impact of the uncertainty characterising the monthly health and social care cost incurred by people with GAD not responding to treatment or relapsing following response on the results of the deterministic analysis. Since the estimation of this cost was based on a number of assumptions and data extrapolations, a scenario of a 70% change in this cost was tested to investigate whether the conclusions of the analysis would alter.

Second, in addition to deterministic analysis, a *probabilistic* analysis was also conducted. In this case, all model input parameters were assigned probability distributions (rather than being expressed as point estimates), to reflect the uncertainty characterising the available clinical and cost data. Subsequently, 10,000 iterations were performed, each drawing random values out of the distributions fitted onto the model input parameters. This exercise provided more accurate estimates of mean costs and benefits for each intervention assessed (averaging results from the 10,000 iterations), by capturing the non-linearity characterising the economic model structure (Briggs *et al.*, 2006).

The probability of non-response for waitlist and the probability of relapse following response were given a beta distribution. Beta distributions were also assigned to utility values, using the method of moments. The relative risk of non-response of CCBT versus waitlist was assigned a log-normal distribution. The estimation of distribution ranges was based on available data in the published sources of evidence.

Costs were assigned a gamma distribution; in order to define the distribution, wide standard errors around the mean costs (equalling 40% of the mean CCBT intervention cost and 60% of the mean monthly health and social care cost incurred by people with GAD) were assumed. Table 17 provides details of the types of distributions assigned to each input parameter and the methods employed to define their range.

Table 16: Annual health and social care cost incurred by people with GAD

Cost component	% of people with GAD receiving care annually	Time spent on each service annually	Unit cost (2009 prices)		Annual weighted cost per person (2009 prices)
Inpatient care	4%	22.4 days	£290/day in mental health unit	DH, 2010	£259.84
Outpatient visit	32%	2 visits	1st visit: £244; follow-up visit: £155	DH, 2010	£127.68
Psychiatrist	6%	2 visits: 1 hour + 20 minutes each	£322/hour of client contact	Curtis, 2009	£25.76
Psychologist	4%	8 visits × 45 minutes each	£75/hour of client contact	Curtis, 2009	£18.00
Mental health nurse	5%	6 visits × 1 hour each	£53/hour of face-to-face contact	Curtis, 2009	£15.90
Other nursing services	0	-	-	-	-
Social worker	5%	6 visits × 1 hour each	£140/hour of face-to-face contact	Curtis, 2009	£42.00
Self-help/support group	3%	Not an NHS cost	-	-	-
Home help/home care	2%	Not directly relevant	-	-	-
Outreach worker	2%	Not directly relevant	-	-	-
Community day care centre	9%	100 sessions	£33 per user session	Curtis, 2009	£297.00
GP	52%	1 visit	£35 per surgery consultation	Curtis, 2009	£18.20

% of people column note: McManus *et al.*, 2009; extrapolated to 1 year where necessary

Unit cost column note: Length of inpatient stay for GAD from hospital episode statistics (NHS, The Information Centre, 2009); all other estimates based on the expert opinion of the GDG

Total annual health and social care cost incurred per person with GAD					**£804.38**

Table 17: Input parameters utilised in the economic model of CCBT versus waitlist for people with GAD

Input parameter	Deterministic value	Probabilistic distribution	Source of data – comments
Clinical data			
Probability of non-response to treatment – waitlist	0.905	Beta distribution $\alpha = 19$, $\beta = 2$	TITOV2009A
Probability of relapse (both interventions)	0.491	$\alpha = 422$, $\beta = 437$	Guideline meta-analysis – pharmacological relapse prevention, pooling of placebo arms
Relative risk of non-response, CCBT versus waitlist	0.41	Log-normal distribution 95% CIs: 0.24 to 0.71	TITOV2009A
Utility values		Beta distribution	
Response	0.76	$\alpha = 177.84$, $\beta = 56.16$	Allgulander *et al.*, 2006; distribution estimated based on data reported in the study using the method of moments
Non-response	0.63	$\alpha = 24.57$, $\beta = 14.43$	
Relapse following response	0.73	$\alpha = 51.83$, $\beta = 19.17$	
Non-relapse following response	0.79	$\alpha = 97.96$, $\beta = 26.04$	
Cost data		Gamma distribution	
CCBT intervention cost	£184	$\alpha = 6.25$, $\beta = 29.44$	See Table 15
Monthly health and social care cost	£67	$\alpha = 2.78$, $\beta = 24.13$	See Table 16
			Standard error of CCBT intervention cost assumed to be 40% of its mean estimate; standard error of monthly health and social care cost assumed to be 60% of its mean estimate

Results of probabilistic analysis are presented in the form of a cost-effectiveness acceptability curve (CEAC), which demonstrates the probability of CCBT being cost effective relative to waitlist at different levels of willingness-to-pay per QALY (that is, at different cost-effectiveness thresholds the decision-maker may set).

Results

The results of deterministic analysis are presented in Table 18. It can be seen that CCBT is associated with a higher total cost but also produces a higher number of QALYs compared with waitlist. The ICER of CCBT versus waitlist is only £541 per QALY gained, which is well below the NICE cost-effectiveness threshold of £20,000–£30,000/QALY (NICE, 2008b), meaning that CCBT is a cost-effective option when compared with waitlist (practically with a 'do-nothing' option).

According to one-way sensitivity analysis, changing the monthly health and social care cost incurred by people not responding to treatment and people relapsing following response by 70% did not affect the conclusions of the analysis: CCBT remained the cost-effective option with an ICER of £3,322 per QALY gained when the cost was reduced by 70%; CCBT became dominant (that is, less costly and more effective than waitlist) when the cost was increased by 70%.

Probabilistic analysis demonstrated that the probability of CCBT being cost effective at the NICE lower cost-effectiveness threshold of £20,000/QALY gained reached 93%.

Figure 5 provides the CEAC for CCBT, which shows the probability of CCBT being cost effective relative to waitlist for different levels of willingness-to-pay per extra QALY gained.

Discussion of findings – limitations of the analysis

The results of the economic analysis indicate that CCBT is probably a cost-effective treatment option compared with waitlist. However, the analysis was based on the only study of CCBT for people with GAD that was included in the guideline systematic clinical literature review (TITOV2009A). Moreover, this study had a small sample size (n = 45). The CCBT package evaluated, the Worry Programme, has been designed for research purposes and is not available in clinical practice. For this reason, the model did not consider a licence fee at the estimation of the intervention cost. However, alternative CCBT packages designed for the treatment of people with GAD in the future may

Table 18: Results of deterministic analysis – mean costs and QALYs of each intervention assessed per 100 people assigned to intervention and ICER of CCBT versus waitlist

Intervention	Mean total cost	Mean total QALYs	ICER
CCBT	£39,534	47.177	
Waitlist	£37,329	43.101	
Difference	£2,205	4.076	£541/QALY

Figure 5: CEAC of CCBT versus waitlist. X axis shows the level of willingness-to-pay per extra QALY gained and Y axis shows the probability of CCBT being cost effective at different levels of willingness-to-pay

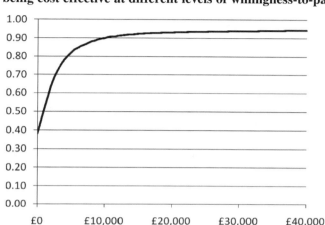

not be freely available. A licence fee would need to be added to the intervention cost in such cases, which, if significant, may affect the cost effectiveness of CCBT.

CCBT was found to be cost effective compared with waitlist. However, the latter does not represent routine practice for people with GAD within the NHS. Other active treatments, such as high-intensity and other low-intensity psychological interventions as well as pharmacological interventions are available treatment options for people with GAD. Ideally, CCBT needs to be assessed against other active treatment options in order to establish its relative cost effectiveness. CCBT is likely to reduce therapists' time per person treated and therefore to result in cost savings if it replaces clinician-led therapy. However, its effectiveness relative to clinician-led treatments needs to be evaluated first, in order to explore its relative cost effectiveness. If CCBT has a similar effectiveness to that of clinician-led therapies, or if the loss in effectiveness is small compared with the magnitude of produced cost savings, then provision of CCBT is going to be, most probably, a cost-effective strategy. Treatment of people with GAD with CCBT can free up resources that could be used in a different way. Alternatively, CCBT could be made available in areas where there is a shortage of therapists providing psychological treatments for people with GAD. In any case, currently no CCBT packages are available in clinical practice for the treatment of this population.

6.7   FROM EVIDENCE TO RECOMMENDATIONS

Non-facilitated self-help was found to have a moderate effect on relevant outcome measures against the inactive control. Also, there was no apparent harm associated with the treatment. Although the evidence came from relatively small trials of low to moderate quality, the cost of non-facilitated self-help interventions was low relative to other treatment options. Therefore, clinicians should consider offering non-facilitated self-help as an initial low-intensity intervention.

Guided self-help had a moderate effect on relevant outcome measures against wait-list control. There were no apparent harms associated with treatment. The evidence base for guided self-help against waitlist control was smaller and of lower quality for the mixed anxiety population. In terms of cost, guided self-help is the most costly intervention (depending on the number of sessions) in comparison with other low-intensity interventions. On the other hand, a trial comparing CCBT with waitlist control in a GAD-only population (TITOV2009A) showed a statistically significant large effect on anxiety, worry and depression, and a statistically significant improvement in remission and response. The economic analysis undertaken for this guideline using data from TITOV2009A demonstrated that the CCBT package described in this study is likely to be cost effective in the treatment of GAD compared with waitlist control within the NHS. However, it should be emphasised that this finding is based exclusively on one trial; moreover, the CCBT package evaluated in TITOV2009A is unavailable within the UK. For these reasons, a clinical recommendation for CCBT for people with GAD cannot be made. A research recommendation has been made instead, comparing CCBT to CBT. Should a CCBT package be researched and developed within the NHS, it would involve no licence fees, which is in accordance with the guideline economic analysis described in Section 6.6.4, which assumed no licence fees in the estimation of the cost of CCBT. In conclusion, clinicians may consider offering forms of individual guided self-help, other than CCBT, as an initial low-intensity intervention.

For psychoeducational groups, there was a small effect on relevant outcome measures when targeted at the mixed anxiety population. There is a general lack of evidence with regard to harmful outcomes and it is unclear whether psychoeducational groups are associated with an increased risk of discontinuation compared with controls. Moreover, the results have come from two small studies and the quality of the outcome data for psychoeducational groups is low. The cost effectiveness of psychoeducational groups lies between the non-facilitated self-help and guided self-help interventions. Because of the limited evidence, clinicians may consider psychoeducational groups as an initial low-intensity intervention.

Moderate quality evidence would normally lead to a moderately worded recommendation. However in this case, recommendation 6.7.1.1 is more strongly worded ('offer' rather than 'consider offer') because individual non-facilitated self-help, individual guided self-help and psychoeducational groups are the only interventions available in step 2, and the GDG considered it important that people with GAD are offered these low-intensity interventions as a first-line treatment.

6.7.1   Recommendations

Low-intensity psychological interventions for GAD
6.7.1.1   For people with GAD whose symptoms have not improved after education and active monitoring in step 1, offer one or more of the following as a first-line intervention, guided by the person's preference:

- individual non-facilitated self-help
- individual guided self-help
- psychoeducational groups.

6.7.1.2 Individual non-facilitated self-help for people with GAD should:

- include written or electronic materials of a suitable reading age (or alternative media)
- be based on the treatment principles of cognitive behavioural therapy (CBT)
- include instructions for the person to work systematically through the materials over a period of at least 6 weeks
- usually involve minimal therapist contact, for example an occasional short telephone call of no more than 5 minutes.

6.7.1.3 Individual guided self-help for people with GAD should:

- include written or electronic materials of a suitable reading age (or alternative media)
- be supported by a trained practitioner, who facilitates the self-help programme and reviews progress and outcome
- usually consist of five to seven weekly or fortnightly face-to-face or telephone sessions, each lasting 20–30 minutes.

6.7.1.4 Psychoeducational groups for people with GAD should:

- be based on CBT principles, have an interactive design and encourage observational learning
- include presentations and self-help manuals
- be conducted by trained practitioners
- have a ratio of one therapist to about 12 participants
- usually consist of six weekly sessions, each lasting 2 hours.

6.7.1.5 Practitioners providing guided self-help and/or psychoeducational groups should:

- receive regular high-quality supervision
- use routine outcome measures and ensure that the person with GAD is involved in reviewing the efficacy of the treatment.

6.7.2 Research recommendations

6.7.2.1 The clinical and cost effectiveness of two CBT-based low-intensity interventions (CCBT and guided bibliotherapy) compared with a waiting-list control for the treatment of GAD.

In well-defined GAD, what is the clinical and cost effectiveness of two CBT-based low-intensity interventions (CCBT and guided bibliotherapy) compared with a waiting-list control?

This question should be answered using a three-armed randomised controlled design using both short- and medium-term outcomes (including cost-effectiveness outcomes). Particular attention should be paid to the reproducibility of the treatment model with regard to content, duration and the training and supervision of those delivering interventions to ensure that the results are both robust and generalisable. The outcomes chosen should include both observer- and participant-rated measures of clinical symptoms and functioning specific to GAD, and an assessment of the acceptability and accessibility of the treatment options.

Why this is important
Psychological treatments are a recommended therapeutic option for people with GAD. CCBT is a promising low-intensity intervention for GAD that does not yet have a substantial evidence base. It is therefore important to establish whether CCBT is an effective and cost-effective treatment that should be provided for GAD, and how it compares with other low-intensity interventions such as guided bibliotherapy. The results of this trial will have important implications for the provision, accessibility and acceptability of psychological treatment in the NHS.

6.7.2.2   The effectiveness of physical activity compared with waiting-list control for the treatment of GAD

For people with GAD who are ready to start a low-intensity intervention, what is the clinical effectiveness of physical activity compared with waiting-list control?
This question should be answered using a randomised controlled design for people with GAD who have been educated about the disorder (as described in step 1) and are stepping up to a low-intensity intervention. The period of waiting-list control should be 12 weeks. The outcomes chosen should include both observer- and participant-rated measures of clinical symptoms and functioning specific to GAD, and of quality of life.

Why this is important
The evidence base for the effectiveness of physical activity in reducing anxiety symptoms is substantially smaller than that for depression. However, where evidence exists there are signs that physical activity could help to reduce anxiety. As GAD is a commonly experienced mental health disorder the results of this study will have important implications in widening the range of treatment options available in the NHS.

7   HIGH-INTENSITY PSYCHOLOGICAL INTERVENTIONS

7.1   INTRODUCTION

This chapter reviews the evidence for the clinical efficacy and cost effectiveness of high-intensity psychological interventions for the treatment of GAD, including CBT, applied relaxation, psychodynamic therapy, non-directive therapies and combined psychological and pharmacological treatments.

High-intensity psychological interventions are commonly used for people with moderate and severe anxiety or depressive disorders, and people with these disorders typically prefer such treatments to medication (Prins *et al.*, 2008). The updated NICE guideline on depression recommended a stepped-care approach (NICE, 2009b) and the use of high-intensity psychological interventions for people who have not responded to initial low-intensity interventions or for those who first present with moderate to severe depression; a similar stepped-care approach is recommended in Chapter 5 for GAD. The IAPT programme specifically supports the implementation of NICE guidelines on anxiety disorders and depression by training staff in the delivery of both low- and high-intensity interventions. High-intensity psychological interventions can be delivered by a range of practitioners appropriately trained in their delivery including CBT and other psychological therapists, clinical psychologists, nurses, occupational therapists and counsellors.

The effectiveness of psychological therapies for GAD was the subject of a recent Cochrane review (Hunot *et al.*, 2007), which concluded that therapy based on CBT principles was effective in reducing anxiety symptoms for short-term treatment of GAD. All studies included in the Cochrane review were considered for inclusion in the review for this guideline. When studies did not meet the inclusion criteria for this guideline, this was generally because participants were diagnosed using earlier DSM-III criteria.

7.1.1   Definitions of high-intensity interventions

Cognitive behavioural therapy
CBT encompasses a range of therapies derived from cognitive behavioural models of disorders, where the person works collaboratively with a therapist using a shared formulation to achieve specific treatment goals. Such goals may include recognising the impact of behavioural and/or thinking patterns on feeling states and encouraging alternative cognitive and/or behavioural coping skills to reduce the severity of target symptoms and problems.

As set out in Chapter 2, CBT for GAD has developed over the years with earlier CBT treatments involving multicomponent cognitive behavioural packages often under the

135

rubric of 'anxiety management', while later versions focus more on worry, the symptom now considered central to GAD, and on processes thought to underlie the disorder.

In this review, cognitive behavioural therapies were defined as discrete, time-limited, structured psychological interventions, derived from cognitive behavioural models of anxiety disorders and where the person:

- works collaboratively with the therapist to identify the types and effects of thoughts, beliefs and interpretations on current symptoms, feelings states and/or problem areas
- develops skills to identify, monitor and then counteract problematic thoughts, beliefs and interpretations related to the target symptoms or problems
- learns a repertoire of coping skills appropriate to the target thoughts, beliefs, behaviours and/or problem areas.

Applied relaxation

Applied relaxation was originally developed by Lars-Göran Öst in the 1980s (Öst, 1987) for the treatment of phobias but has wider application to other anxiety disorders, as well as to the management of physical pain and nausea. Applied relaxation focuses on applying muscular relaxation in situations and occasions where the person is or might be anxious and allows people to intervene early in response to anxiety and worry. The elements of applied relaxation as described by Davis and colleagues (1995) include:

- Progressive muscle relaxation: focusing attention onto particular muscle groups and understanding the differences between tensing and relaxing the muscles.
- Release-only relaxation: allows the patient to go directly into relaxation without having to switch between tension and relaxation of the muscles.
- Cue-controlled relaxation: reduces the time needed to relax (2 to 3 minutes) by making an association between a cue (for example, the word 'relax') and the relaxation of the muscles.
- Rapid relaxation: further reduces the time needed to relax by selecting specific cues that are encountered regularly and practised frequently every day until a state of deep relaxation can be reached in less than 30 seconds.
- Applied relaxation: application of relaxation skills acquired through exposure to anxiety-provoking situations.

The final of these components is critical and distinguishes applied relaxation from other forms of relaxation training and practice that do not have the applied component. Applied relaxation follows a clear protocol, takes place over 12 to 15 sessions and is carried out by practitioners trained in CBT. Studies included as applied relaxation in this review needed to follow the applied relaxation protocol and for applied relaxation to be the only intervention. Studies of anxiety management that included relaxation training and elements of applied relaxation as one component of a multicomponent package were classified under the definition of CBT.

Psychodynamic therapy

Psychodynamic therapy was defined as a psychological intervention derived from a psychodynamic/psychoanalytic model, and where:

- Therapist and patient explore and gain insight into conflicts and how these are represented in current situations and relationships including the therapy relationship (for example, transference and counter-transference). This leads to patients being given an opportunity to explore feelings, and conscious and unconscious conflicts, originating in the past, with a technical focus on interpreting and working though conflicts.

- Therapy is non-directive and recipients are not taught specific skills (for example, thought monitoring, re-evaluating or problem-solving).

Non-directive therapies

Non-directive therapies and counselling were developed by Carl Rogers (1957) who believed that people had the means for self-healing, problem resolution and growth if the right conditions could be created. These conditions include the provision of positive regard, genuineness and empathy. Roger's original model was developed into structured counselling approaches by Truax and Carkhuff (1967) and, independently, by Egan (1990) who devised the three stage model: exploration, personalising and action. Voluntary sector counselling training (for example, Relate) tends to draw on these models. However, although many other therapies now use the basic ingredients of client-centred counselling (Roth & Fonagy, 1996), there are differences in how they are used (Kahn, 1985; Rogers, 1986) and counselling has become a generic term used to describe a broad range of interventions delivered by counsellors usually working in primary care. The content of these various approaches may include psychodynamic, systemic or cognitive behavioural elements (Bower *et al.*, 2003).

The British Association for Counselling and Psychotherapy defines counselling as 'a systematic process which gives individuals an opportunity to explore, discover and clarify ways of living more resourcefully, with a greater sense of wellbeing'.

7.1.2   Review question

In the treatment of GAD, what are the risks and benefits associated with high-intensity psychological interventions compared with other interventions (including wait-list control and treatment as usual)? For example: CBT, applied relaxation, psychodynamic therapy and non-directive therapies (see Table 19 for more interventions).

7.2   REVIEW OF HIGH-INTENSITY INTERVENTIONS FOR GENERALISED ANXIETY DISORDER

7.2.1   Databases searched and inclusion/exclusion criteria

Information about the databases searched and the inclusion/exclusion criteria used for this section of the guideline can be found in Table 19 (further information about the search for health economic evidence can be found in Section 3.6).

Table 19: Databases searched and inclusion/exclusion criteria for clinical evidence

Electronic databases	MEDLINE, EMBASE, CINAHL, PsycINFO, Cochrane Library
Date searched	Database inception to 09.05.2010
Study design	RCT
Patient population	People with a primary diagnosis of GAD
Interventions	CBT, cognitive therapy, behavioural therapy/activation, systemic interventions, applied relaxation, psychodynamic therapy, non-directive therapies/person-centred therapy, counselling, problem solving therapy, interpersonal therapy, performance art therapies, mindfulness-based cognitive therapy, physical activity, cognitive analytic therapy, dialectical behaviour therapy, family or couples therapy, humanistic therapy
Outcomes	Non-remission, non-response, dropouts, mean rating scale scores for anxiety, depression, worry, quality of life

7.2.2   Studies considered[14]

The review team conducted a new systematic search for RCTs that assessed the effectiveness of high-intensity psychological interventions for the treatment of GAD as defined by DSM-III-R or DSM-IV.

A total of 5,761 references were identified by the electronic search relating to clinical evidence. Of these, 5,707 were excluded at the screening stage on the basis of reading the title and/or abstract. The remaining 54 references were assessed for eligibility on the basis of the full text. Twenty-seven trials met the eligibility criteria set by the GDG, providing data on 1,473 participants. Of these, all were published in peer-reviewed journals between 1992 and 2009. In addition, 27 studies were excluded from the analysis: nine studies did not provide an acceptable diagnosis of GAD, four were not RCTs, four had less than ten participants per group, in two studies participants were aged under 18 years, two studies did not provide valid or relevant outcomes, one study was non-English language and five studies did not use a relevant intervention. Further information about both included and excluded studies can be found in Appendix 15c.

---

[14]Here and elsewhere in the guideline, each study considered for review is referred to by a study ID in capital letters (primary author and date of study publication, except where a study is in press or only submitted for publication, then a date is not used).

7.2.3   Clinical evidence for high-intensity psychological interventions

The 27 included RCTs explored the effect of three main different treatment types. Data were available to compare treatments with waitlist control, active control or other active treatments. For all of the included studies, participants had a primary diagnosis of GAD by DSM-III-R or DSM-IV.

The included studies were analysed based on three types of treatments:
● Section 7.3: cognitive behavioural therapy
● Section 7.4: applied relaxation
● Section 7.5: psychodynamic therapy.

7.3   COGNITIVE BEHAVIOURAL THERAPY

7.3.1   Studies considered

A total of 21 trials compared CBT with waitlist control and other active treatments or comparators. Twelve trials compared CBT with waitlist control; eight trials with applied relaxation; two trials with psychodynamic therapy; two trials with non-directive therapy; and three trials with three other active comparators. One trial looked at the dose-response relationship of CBT, which has been narratively reviewed. The 21 trials mainly targeted adults, but some were aimed at older adults. For most of the CBT comparisons, there was no evidence of publication bias at the study level as assessed by visual inspection of funnel plots and formally by the Egger's test (Egger *et al.*, 2003). Only one outcome (worry) was downgraded on the basis of publication bias (see Appendix 18b for further details).

A summary of study characteristics can be found in Table 20 with full details in Appendix 15c, which also includes details of excluded studies.

7.3.2   Clinical evidence for cognitive behavioural therapies

Evidence from the important outcomes and overall quality of evidence are presented in Table 21. The full GRADE profiles and associated forest plots can be found in Appendix 18b and Appendix 16b, respectively.

7.3.3   Clinical evidence summary

CBT versus waitlist control
When CBT was compared with waitlist control, the data showed a statistically significant improvement in non-remission and non-response. Unlike pharmacological studies, the definitions of remission and response varied across studies. Most studies defined remission as 'free of GAD' using diagnostic tools such as DSM criteria, and response as 75% improvement on the reported anxiety measure. The difference in definitions should be noted when interpreting results. The long-term effect is unknown because no follow-up data could be extracted for analysis.

Table 20: Study information tables for trials of cognitive behavioural therapy

	CBT versus waitlist control	CBT versus applied relaxation	CBT versus short-term psychodynamic psychotherapy	CBT versus non-directive therapy	CBT versus other active comparisons
No. trials (total participants)	12 RCTs (659)	8 RCTs (439)	2 RCTs (167)	2 RCTs (114)	3 RCTs (319)
Study ID	(1) BARLOW1992 (2) BUTLER1991* (CT) (3) DUGAS2003* (group CBT) (4) DUGAS2009A (5) HOYER2009* (worry exposure) (6) LADOUCEUR2000 (7) LINDEN2005 (8) MOHLMAN2003A (9) REZVAN2008* (CBT only) (10) ROEMER2008* (acceptance-based behaviour therapy) (11) STANLEY2003B (12) WETHERELL2003* (group CBT)	(1) ARNTZ2003* (CT) (2) BARLOW1992 (3) BORKOVEC1993 (4) BORKOVEC2002 (5) DUGAS2009A (6) HOYER2009* (worry exposure) (7) ÖST2000 (8) WELLS2010* (metacognitive therapy)	(1) DURHAM1994* (CT) (2) LEICHSENRING2009	(1) BORKOVEC1993 (2) STANLEY1996	(1) DURHAM1994* (CT) (2) STANLEY2009 (3) WETHERELL2003 (group CBT)

N/% female	(1) 65/no information (2) 57/86% (3) 52/71% (4) 65/66% (5) 73/71% (6) 26/77% (7) 72/83% (8) 27/70% (9) 36/100% (10) 31/71% (11) 80/75% (12) 75/80%	(1) 45/67% (2) 65/no information (3) 66/65% (4) 69/no information (5) 65/66% (6) 73/71% (7) 36/72% (8) 20/60%	(1) 110/68% (2) 57/81%	(1) 66/65% (2) 48/71%	(1) 110/68% (2) 134/78% (3) 75/80%
Mean age (years)	(1) 40 (2) 35 (3) 41 (4) 39 (5) 45 (6) 40 (7) 43 (8) 66 (9) 20 (10) 34 (11) 66 (12) 67	(1) 36 (2) 40 (3) 38 (4) 37 (5) –(6) 39 (7) 40 (8) 49	(1) 39 (2) 42	(1) 38 (2) 68	(1) 39 (2) 70 (3) 67
Diagnosis	(1)–(2) GAD by DSM-III-R (3)–(12) GAD by DSM-IV	(1)–(4) GAD by DSM-III-R (5)–(8) GAD by DSM-IV	(1) GAD by DSM-III-R (2) GAD by DSM-IV	(1)–(2) GAD by DSM-III-R	(1) GAD by DSM-III-R (2)–(3) GAD by DSM-IV-R

Continued

141

Table 20: *(Continued)*

	CBT versus waitlist control	CBT versus applied relaxation	CBT versus short-term psychodynamic psychotherapy	CBT versus non-directive therapy	CBT versus other active comparisons
Baseline severity (clinician-rated)	(1) ADIS score: 5.3–5.5 (2) HAM-A score: 5.1–5.4 (3) ADIS score: 5.8–6.4 (4) ADIS score: 5.7 (5) HAM-A score: 21.6–23.3 (6) ADIS score: 5.92–6.36 (7) HAM-A score: 24–26.8 (8) Not reported (9) Scored more than 5.7 on GAD-Q-IV (10) ADIS score: 5.69–5.73 (11) ADIS score: 5.2–5.3 (12) ADIS score: 4.9–5	(1) STAI-T score: 53.7–57.5 (2) ADIS score: 5.3–5.5 (3) ADIS score: 4.7–4.8 (4) ADIS score: 5.4–5.61 (5) ADIS score: 5.7 (6) HAM-A score: 21.6–23.3 (7) ADIS score:5.33–5.47 (8) BAI score: 22.2–30.5	(1) ADIS score: 6.1–6.6 (2) HAM-A score: 25–25.9	(1) ADIS score: 4.7–4.8 (2) ADIS score 5.11–5.46	(1) ADIS score: 6.1–6.6 (2) Not reported (3) ADIS score: 4.9–5.1
Comparator	(1)–(12) Waitlist control	(1)–(8) Applied relaxation	(1) Analytic psychotherapy (low and high-intensity) (2) Short-term psycho-dynamic psychotherapy	(1)–(2) Non-directive therapy	(1) Anxiety management training (2) Enhanced usual care (3) Discussion group
Treatment length	(1) 15 weeks (2) 8 weeks (3) 14 weeks (4) 12 weeks (5) 15 weeks (6) 16 weeks	(1) 12 weeks (2) 15 weeks (3) 12 weeks (4) 8 weeks (5) 12 weeks (6) 15 weeks	(1) 14 weeks (2) 30 weeks	(1) 12 weeks (2) 14 weeks	(1) 14 weeks (2) 13 weeks (3) 12 weeks

	(7) 25 weeks (8) 13 weeks (9) 8 weeks (10) 14 weeks (11) 15 weeks (12) 12 weeks	(7) 12 weeks (8) 8–12 weeks			
Follow-up	(1) 24 months (data not extractable) (2) 6 months (3) 24 months (data not extractable) (4) 6, 12 and 24 months (data not extractable) (5) 6 and 12 months (6) 12 months (data not extractable) (7) 8 months (data not extractable) (8) 6 months (data not extractable) (9) 12 months (10) 3 and 9 months (data not extractable) (11) 3, 6 and 12 months (data not extractable) (12) 6 months	(1) 1 and 6 months (2) 24 months (data not extractable) (3) 6 and 12 months (4) 6, 12 and 24 months (5) 6, 12 and 24 months (data not extractable) (6) 6 and 12 months (7) 12 months (8) 6 and 12 months	(1) 6 and 12 months (2) 6 months	(1) 6 and 12 months (2) 1 and 6 months	(1) 6 and 12 months (2) 6, 9, 12 and 15 months (3) 6 months

*Indicates studies that have interventions approximating to CBT.

Table 21: Evidence summary table for trials of CBT

	CBT versus waitlist control	CBT versus applied relaxation	CBT versus short-term psychodynamic therapy	CBT versus non-directive therapy	CBT versus other active comparisons
No. trials (total participants)	12 RCTs (N = 659)	8 RCTs (N = 439)	2 RCTs (N = 167)	2 RCTs (N = 114)	3 RCTs (N = 319)
Study ID	(1) BARLOW1992 (2) BUTLER1991 (3) DUGAS2003 (4) DUGAS2009A (5) HOYER2009 (6) LADOUCEUR2000 (7) LINDEN2005 (8) MOHLMAN2003A (9) REZVAN2008 (10) ROEMER2008 (11) STANLEY2003B (12) WETHERELL2003	(1) ARNTZ2003 (2) BARLOW1992 (3) BORKOVEC1993 (4) BORKOVEC2002 (5) DUGAS2009A (6) HOYER2009 (7) ÖST2000 (8) WELLS2010	(1) DURHAM1994 (2) LEICHSENRING2009	(1) BORKOVEC1993 (2) STANLEY1996	(1) DURHAM1994 (2) STANLEY2009 (3) WETHERELL2003
Benefits					
Anxiety (self-rated)	SMD = −0.63 (−0.83, −0.42) K = 10, N = 398 Quality: high	SMD = 0.01 (−0.22, 0.23) K = 8, N = 303 Quality: moderate	SMD = −0.45 (−0.81, −0.08) K = 2, N = 121 Quality: moderate	(1) SMD = −0.69 (−1.35, −0.02) K = 1, N = 37 Quality: moderate (2) SMD = −0.25 (−0.97, 0.46) K = 1, N = 31 Quality: moderate	(1) SMD = −0.59 (−1.19, 0.01) K = 1, N = 51 Quality: low (3) SMD = −0.13 (−0.78, 0.53) K = 1, N = 36 Quality: low

Anxiety (self-rated) at follow-up	–	At 6 months: SMD = −0.03 (−0.38, 0.32) K = 4, N = 128 At 12 months: SMD = −0.03 (−0.39, 0.32) K = 4, N = 124	At 6 months: SMD = −0.81 (−1.64, 0.02) K = 2, N = 121 At 12 months: SMD = −1.28 (−1.82, −0.74) K = 1, N = 64	At 6 months: (1) SMD = −0.21 (−0.89, 0.46) K = 1, N = 34 (2) SMD = −0.15 (−0.87, 0.56) K = 1, N = 31 At 12 months: (1) SMD = −0.18 (−0.85, 0.50) K = 1, N = 34	At 6 months: (1) SMD = −0.28 (−0.88, 0.31) K = 1, N = 51 (3) SMD = −0.15 (−0.80, 0.51) K = 1, N = 36 At 12 months: (1) SMD = −0.33 (−0.92, 0.27) K = 1, N = 51
Anxiety (clinician-rated) at follow-up	SMD = −1.09 (−1.33, −0.84) K = 11, N = 474 Quality: moderate	SMD = −0.15 (−0.40, 0.10) K = 6, N = 249 Quality: low	SMD = −0.46 (−0.90, −0.02) K = 2, N = 121 Quality: high	(1) SMD = −0.93 (−1.61, −0.25) K = 1, N = 37 Quality: moderate (2) SMD = −0.01 (−0.72, 0.70) K = 1, N = 31 Quality: moderate	(1) SMD = −0.59 (−1.19, 0.01) K = 1, N = 51 Quality: moderate (3) SMD = −0.06 (−0.72, 0.59) K = 1, N = 36 Quality: low
Anxiety (clinician-rated) at follow-up	–	At 6 months: SMD = −0.09 (−0.69, 0.51) K = 2, N = 72 At 12 months: SMD = −0.06 (−0.45, 0.33) K = 3, N = 105 At 24 months: SMD = 0.19 (−0.28, 0.65) K = 2, N = 72	At 6 months: SMD = −0.35 (−0.87, 0.18) K = 1, N = 57	At 6 months: (1) SMD = −0.45 (−1.13, 0.24) K = 1, N = 34 (2) SMD = −0.07 (−0.79, 0.64) K = 1, N = 31 At 12 months: (1) SMD = −0.57 (−1.26, 0.12) K = 1, N = 34	At 6 months: (3) SMD = −0.32 (−0.98, 0.33) K = 1, N = 36

Continued

Table 21: *(Continued)*

	CBT versus waitlist control	CBT versus applied relaxation	CBT versus short-term psychodynamic therapy	CBT versus non-directive therapy	CBT versus other active comparisons
Depression (self-rated)	SMD = −0.81 (−1.11, −0.51) K = 10, N = 401 Quality: high	SMD = −0.18 (−0.5, 0.13) K = 7, N = 270 Quality: moderate	SMD = −0.76 (−1.21, −0.31) K = 2, N = 121 Quality: moderate	(1) SMD = −0.90 (−1.58, −0.22) K = 1, N = 37 Quality: moderate (2) SMD = 0.24 (−0.48, 0.95) K = 1, N = 31 Quality: moderate	(1) SMD = −0.76 (−1.37, −0.15) K = 1, N = 51 Quality: high (2) SMD = −0.34 (−0.71, 0.03) K = 1, N = 116 Quality: moderate (3) SMD = −0.27 (−0.93, 0.39) K = 1, N = 36 Quality: low
Depression (self-rated) at follow-up	–	*At 6 months:* SMD = 0.09 (−0.22, 0.4) K = 4, N = 159 *At 12 months:* SMD = 0.03 (−0.25, 0.32) K = 5, N = 192	*At 6 months:* SMD = −0.33 (−0.85, 0.19) K = 1, N = 57	*At 6 months:* (1) SMD = −0.24 (−0.92, 0.43) K = 1, N = 37 (2) SMD = −0.12 (−0.83, 0.59) K = 1, N = 31	*At 6 months:* (2) SMD = −0.21 (−0.61, 0.20) K = 1, N = 95
Depression (clinician-rated)	SMD = −0.74 (−1.11, −0.36) K = 4, N = 191 Quality: high	SMD = −0.08 (−0.4, 0.25) K = 3, N = 146 Quality: low	–	(1) SMD = −0.71 (−1.38, −0.05) K = 1, N = 37 Quality: moderate	(3) SMD = −0.33 (−0.98, 0.33) Quality: low K = 1, N = 36

Depression (clinician-rated) at follow-up	–	At 6 months: SMD = -0.26 (-0.91, 0.39) K = 1, N = 37 At 12 months: SMD = 0.46 (-0.01, 0.94) K = 2, N = 70 At 24 months: SMD = 0.42 (-0.23, 1.08) K = 1, N = 37	–	At 6 months: (1) SMD = -0.49 (-1.18, 0.19) K = 1, N = 34 At 12 months: (1) SMD = -0.30 (-0.98, 0.38) K = 1, N = 34	At 6 months: (3) SMD = -0.24 (-0.89, 0.42) K = 1, N = 36
Worry	SMD = -1.13 (-1.58, -0.68) K = 9, N = 366 Quality: very low	SMD = -0.02 (-0.27, 0.23) K = 6, N = 249 Quality: moderate	SMD = -0.32 (-0.84, 0.21) (change score) K = 1, N = 57 Quality: moderate	(1) SMD = -0.97 (-1.65, -0.28) K = 1, N = 37 Quality: moderate (2) SMD = -0.06 (-0.78, 0.65) K = 1, N = 31 Quality: moderate	(2) SMD = -0.90 (-1.29, -0.52) K = 1, N = 116 Quality: high (3) SMD = -0.17 (-0.82, 0.49) K = 1, N = 36 Quality: low
Worry at follow-up	–	At 6 months: SMD = -0.07 (-0.38, 0.24) K = 4, N = 159 At 12 months: SMD = -0.05 (-0.34, 0.23) K = 5, N = 192	At 6 months: SMD = -0.39 (-0.91, 0.14) K = 1, N = 57	At 6 months: (1) SMD = -0.39 (-1.07, 0.29) K = 1, N = 37 (2) SMD = 0.04 (-0.67, 0.76) K = 1, N = 31	At 6 months: (2) SMD = -0.85 (-1.28, -0.43) K = 1, N = 95 (3) SMD = -0.13 (-0.79, 0.52) K = 1, N = 36

Continued

147

Table 21: *(Continued)*

	CBT versus waitlist control	CBT versus applied relaxation	CBT versus short-term psychodynamic therapy	CBT versus non-directive therapy	CBT versus other active comparisons
Quality of life	SMD = −1.59 (−3.77, 0.59) K = 2, N = 55 Quality: very low	–	SMD = 0.15 (−0.34, 0.65) K = 1, N = 64 Quality: low	–	*SF-12 Mental:* (2) SMD = −0.47 (−0.84, −0.10) K = 1, N = 116 Quality: high *SF-12 Physical:* (2) SMD = 0.02 (−0.34, 0.39) K = 1, N = 116 Quality: moderate *Energy scores:* (3) SMD = −0.18 (−0.84, 0.47) K = 1, N = 36 Quality: low *(3) Role functioning scores:* SMD = −0.59 (−1.26, 0.08) K = 1, N = 36 Quality: low *(3) Social role scores:* SMD = −0.11 (−0.76, 0.54) K = 1, N = 36 Quality: low

Continued

Quality of life at follow-up	SF-12 Mental at 6 months: (2) SMD = –0.4 (–0.81, 0.01) K = 1, N = 95 SF-12 Physical at 6 months: (2) SMD = –0.21 (–0.62, 0.19) K = 1, N = 95 Energy scores at 6 months: (3) SMD = 0.08 (–0.57, 0.74) K = 1, N = 36 Role functioning scores at 6 months: (3) SMD = –0.11 (–0.77, 0.54) K = 1, N = 36 Social role scores at 6 months: (3) SMD = 0.31 (–0.35, 0.97) K = 1, N = 36 SF-12 Mental at 12 Months: (2) SMD = –0.3 (–0.71, 0.12) K = 1, N = 92	–	–	–

Table 21: *(Continued)*

	CBT versus waitlist control	CBT versus applied relaxation	CBT versus short-term psychodynamic therapy	CBT versus non-directive therapy	CBT versus other active comparisons
					SF-12 Physical at 12 months: (2) SMD = 0.03 (−0.38, 0.43) K = 1, N = 94 *SF-12 Mental at 15 months:* (2) SMD = −0.35 (−0.76, 0.06) K = 1, N = 94 *SF-12 Physical at 15 months:* (2) SMD = −0.04 (−0.45, 0.37) K = 1, N = 92
Non-response	RR = 0.67 (0.53, 0.84) K = 5, N = 219 Quality: low	RR = 1.11 (0.86, 1.44) K = 4, N = 178 Quality: very low	–	(1) RR = 0.65 (0.42, 1.02) K = 1, N = 43 Quality: low (2) RR = 1.24 (0.86, 1.80) K = 1, N = 46 Quality: moderate	(2) RR = 0.89 (0.63, 1.26) K = 1, N = 134 Quality: moderate (3) RR = 1.05 (0.77, 1.44) K = 1, N = 52 Quality: low
Non-response at follow-up	–	*At 12 months:* RR = 0.96 (0.35, 2.61) K = 2, N = 79	–	*At 6 months:* (2) RR = 1.31 (0.78, 2.20) K = 1, N = 46	*At 15 months:* (2) RR = 0.94 (0.71, 1.23) K = 1, N = 134

Non-remission	RR = 0.62 (0.51, 0.75) K = 5, N = 259 Quality: high	–	–		(1) RR = 0.92 (0.52, 1.63) K = 1, N = 52 Quality: low
Non-remission at follow-up	–	RR = 0.94 (0.63, 1.41) K = 4, N = 156 Quality: low *At 6 months:* RR = 1.15 (0.8, 1.65) K = 2, N = 91 *At 12 months:* RR = 0.53 (0.07, 4.01) K = 2, N = 66 *At 24 months:* RR = 1.00 (0.77, 1.30) K = 1, N = 46	–	–	–
Harms					
Discontinuation due to any reason	RR = 1.4 (0.7, 2.79) K = 12, N = 516 Quality: high	RR = 0.75 (0.43, 1.31) K = 8, N = 334 Quality: high	RR = 0.54 (0.21, 1.36) K = 2, N = 142 Quality: moderate	RR = 1.02 (0.49, 2.12) K = 2, N = 89 Quality: very low	(1) RR = 0.42 (0.13, 1.33) K = 1, N = 65 Quality: low (2) RR = 0.26 (0.09, 0.75) K = 1, N = 134 Quality: high (3) RR = 1.00 (0.44, 2.26) K = 1, N = 52 Quality: low

High-intensity psychological interventions

When eleven CBT interventions were compared with waitlist control, there was a statistically significant large improvement in clinician-rated anxiety scores, and a moderate improvement in self-rated anxiety scores post-treatment. No follow-up data was provided and therefore the long-term effect of CBT against waitlist control remains unknown.

In addition to anxiety ratings, trials comparing CBT with waitlist control reported outcomes on depression and worry scores, suggesting a moderate improvement for both clinician- and self-rated depression scores. Despite the wide confidence intervals, CBT had a large improvement on worry symptoms compared with waitlist control. There were no follow-up data on any of the depression or worry measures.

Two trials reported large improvements in quality of life compared with waitlist control. However, these trials displayed large heterogeneity, and therefore this finding must be interpreted with caution. One of these trials (ROEMER2008) was based on acceptance-based behaviour therapy principles and the other trial was CBT-based (REZVAB2008).

The overall quality of the evidence is moderate to high. Some heterogeneity exists for some outcomes, which have been downgraded. The main reason for heterogeneity was due to the variations in CBT treatment principles. Detailed reasons for downgrading can be found in Appendix 18b.

CBT versus applied relaxation
Eight trials directly compared CBT with applied relaxation. CBT was found to be neither inferior nor superior to applied relaxation on the majority of the outcomes. Outcomes included non-remission, non-response, self- and clinician-rated anxiety, self- and clinician-rated depression, worry and dropout rates. There may be a slight trend favouring CBT on clinician-rated anxiety, which had a narrower confidence interval compared with other outcomes. There were no differences between CBT and applied relaxation for those studies that reported follow-up data at 6 and 12 months.

The overall quality of the evidence is low to moderate. The main reason for downgrading the quality was due to the insignificant findings.

CBT versus psychodynamic therapy
Only two trials compared CBT with psychodynamic therapy directly. CBT was found to be better than psychodynamic therapy with a moderate effect on both clinician- and self-rated anxiety and depression scores. However, this significant effect was not sustained at 6 or 12 months' follow-up. Moreover, CBT was not statistically significantly different from psychodynamic therapy in terms of improving worry symptoms. No statistically significant difference in dropout rate was found between the two treatments. The wide confidence intervals were observed as a result of the small sample size; therefore results should be interpreted with caution.

The overall quality of evidence is moderate. Reasons for downgrading the quality of the evidence vary and details can be found in Appendix 18b.

CBT versus non-directive therapy

Two trials compared CBT with non-directive therapy. However, the two trials targeted different populations, which made them too heterogeneous to be analysed together. BORKOVEC1993 examined the efficacy of CBT in a general adult population and found a large improvement on anxiety, depression and worry outcomes relative to non-directive therapy. However, this was not the case for older adults (STAN-LEY1996). CBT was not statistically significantly different from non-directive therapy for older adults on any outcomes.

The overall quality of evidence was low to moderate. In general, the quality of the trial targeting older adults was lower than the trial targeting a general adult population on all outcomes.

CBT versus other active comparisons

Three trials compared CBT with an active comparator that could not be classified under any of the above treatment categories. The trials could not be meta-analysed due to the varying comparisons. These comparisons were anxiety management training delivered by psychiatric registrars following a protocol without any training in CBT (DURHAM1994), enhanced usual care (STANLEY2009) and a discussion group on worry-provoking topics (WETHERELL2003). The latter two studies (STANLEY2009; WETHERELL2003) targeted older adults. CBT was not statistically significantly different compared with anxiety management training and the discussion group on worry-provoking topics on dropout rates individually. However, it was reported that older adults dropped out of the enhanced usual care group significantly more than those receiving CBT. One study reported remission rates and found no statistically significant difference between group CBT and discussion groups on worry-provoking topics for older adults. Two trials reported response data and, again, found no statistically significant difference between CBT and enhanced usual care or the discussion group on worry-provoking topics for older adults. As dichotomous data such as remission and response are defined differently in each study these findings should be interpreted with caution. Moreover, there were no statistically significant differences when comparing CBT with enhanced usual care or a discussion group on worry-provoking topics on all clinician- and self-rated anxiety and depression scores for older adults. CBT had a large effect compared with enhanced usual care on worry outcomes, which was sustained at 6 months' follow-up. CBT also had a small effect on the mental subscale of the Quality of Life over enhanced usual care.

In the case of CBT versus anxiety management training for adults, there were trends of a moderate effect on clinician- and self-rated anxiety scores favouring CBT. The findings were marginally significant due to the small sample size. CBT was found to be moderately effective against anxiety management training on self-rated depression scores.

Cautious interpretation should be noted for all of the above outcomes as these findings are based on single trials and warrant further investigation.

7.3.4 Sensitivity analysis for type of CBT and type of applied relaxation

Type of CBT

A sensitivity analysis was conducted because of the different types of CBT available, which may have different effects on outcomes. The classification of types of CBT was: the Beckian CBT model, Dugas CBT model and other models of CBT.

The sensitivity analysis results did not reveal significant difference in effect compared with the combined CBT model (presented in the previous section). The only difference in effect was found on three outcomes presented below.

Clinician-rated anxiety

The combined CBT model had a large effect on this outcome compared with waitlist control (as presented in the previous section). The Dugas CBT model (DUGAS2003; DUGAS2009A; LADOUCEUR2000) also had a large effect size (SMD –1.46; 95% CI –1.05 to –1.87) compared with waitlist control. However, the Beckian CBT model (BARLOW1992; BUTLER1991; LINDEN2005; MOHLMAN2003; STANLEY2003B; WETHERELL2003) only had a moderate effect size (SMD –0.85; 95% CI –0.59 to –1.11) compared with waitlist control.

Self-rated anxiety

The combined CBT model had a moderate effect on this outcome compared with waitlist control (as presented in the previous section). Both the Dugas model (SMD –0.71; 95% CI –0.25 to –1.16) and the Beckian CBT model (SMD –0.67; 95% CI –0.37 to –0.97) had a moderate effect compared with waitlist control. However, two other models of CBT (HOYER2009; ROEMER2008) only had a small effect size (SMD –0.45; 95% CI –0.03 to –0.86) compared with waitlist control.

Self-rated depression

The combined CBT model was found to be not statistically significantly different from applied relaxation. However, the Beckian CBT model (BARLOW1992; BORKOVEC1993; BORKOVEC2002) was marginally more effective than applied relaxation (SMD –0.5; 95% CI 0.09 to –1.09). However, the quality of this comparison is downgraded because of the moderate heterogeneity (52%).

Summary

Based on the results of this sensitivity analysis, taking the quality of studies into account, the results and conclusion from the combined CBT model analysis in the previous section remain robust.

Type of applied relaxation

A sensitivity analysis was conducted for two different applied relaxation models: one developed by Bernstein and Borkovec, and one by Öst. There were seven studies that included applied relaxation as a treatment arm.

The sensitivity analysis did not reveal a significant difference in effect compared with the combined applied relaxation model. The only difference in effect was found on one outcome (self-rated depression).

Self-rated depression
The combined applied relaxation model was no different compared with the combined CBT model (as presented in the previous section) on this outcome. This was still the case for the Öst applied relaxation model (HOYER2009; ÖST2000; WELLS2010) compared with the combined CBT model. However, a moderate effect (marginally significant) was found favouring CBT over the Borkovec applied relaxation model (SMD -0.77; 95% CI -1.57 to 0.02) (BARLOW1992; BORKOVEC1993).

Summary
Based on the results of this sensitivity analysis, and taking into account the limited number of studies, the results and conclusions from the combined applied relaxation model analysed in Section 7.3.3 remain robust.

7.3.5   Subgroup analysis for CBT

A subgroup analysis of the effect of CBT on working-age adults and older adults was conducted (see Table 22). CBT was found to be effective for both populations. There were no statistically significant differences in effect between the two populations on any outcome measures. Therefore, the GDG's general conclusion about the effectiveness of CBT remains robust across age groups.

A subgroup analysis was also conducted to examine whether individual CBT sessions and group CBT sessions were effective against waitlist control. The analysis showed both treatments were effective against waitlist control on anxiety, depression and worry outcomes. However, results from the two trials of group CBT have wide confidence intervals, and each trial targeted different age groups (working-age adults and older adults), therefore findings should be interpreted with caution.

7.3.6   Dose-response relationship of CBT

There was one study (DURHAM2004) that examined the dose-response relationship of CBT (that is, suitable participants were given brief CBT if they had a good prognosis and either standard or intensive CBT if they had a poor prognosis). Since the method of allocation was not randomised, the results favouring brief CBT might be confounded by the better prognosis in the brief treatment group. Therefore it has been narratively reviewed (see Table 23).

Brief versus standard cognitive behavioural therapy
There was a significant difference between brief versus standard CBT in relation to clinician-rated anxiety scores in favour of brief CBT and there appears to be even

Table 22: Subgroup analysis for CBT versus waitlist control

	Working-age adults	Older adults	Individual sessions	Group sessions
No. trials (total participants)	8 RCTs (N = 364)	2 RCTs (N = 129)	8 RCTs (N = 352)	2 RCTs (N = 91)
Study ID	(1) BARLOW1992 (2) BUTLER1991 (3) DUGAS2003 (4) DUGAS2009A (5) HOYER2009 (6) LADOUCEUR2000 (7) LINDEN2005 (8) MOHLMAN2003A	(1) STANLEY2003B (2) WETHERELL2003	(1) BARLOW1992 (2) BUTLER1991 (3) DUGAS2009A (4) HOYER2009 (5) LADOUCEUR2000 (6) LINDEN2005 (7) MOHLMAN2003A (8) STANLEY2003B	(1) DUGAS2003 (2) WETHERELL2003
Benefits				
Anxiety (self-rated)	SMD = −0.59 (−0.85, −0.33) K = 7, N = 264 Quality: high	SMD = −0.72 (−1.12, 0.32) K = 2, N = 103 Quality: high	SMD = −0.56 (−0.80, −0.32) K = 7, N = 276 Quality: high	SMD = −0.83 (−1.26, −0.39) K = 2, N = 91 Quality: moderate
Anxiety (clinician-rated)	SMD = −1.14 (−1.46, −0.83) K = 8, N = 340 Quality: moderate	SMD = −1.09 (−1.58, −0.59) K = 2, N = 103 Quality: high	SMD = −1.08 (−1.38, −0.77) K = 8, N = 352 Quality: moderate	SMD = −1.32 (−1.78, −0.86) K = 2, N = 91 Quality: moderate
Depression (self-rated)	SMD = −0.73 (−1.13, −0.33) K = 7, N = 267 Quality: moderate	SMD = −0.84 (−1.25, −0.44) K = 2, N = 103 Quality: high	SMD = −0.70 (−1.08, −0.32) K = 7, N = 279 Quality: moderate	SMD = −0.96 (−1.40, −0.52) K = 2, N = 91 Quality: moderate
Depression (clinician-rated)	SMD = −0.87 (−1.63, −0.11) K = 2, N = 88 Quality: very low	SMD = −0.59 (−0.99, −0.19) K = 2, N = 103 Quality: moderate	SMD = −0.84 (−1.26, −0.42) K = 3, N = 152 Quality: low	SMD = −0.40 (−1.04, 0.23) K = 1, N = 39 Quality: low
Worry	SMD = −1.15 (−1.81, −0.5) K = 6, N = 232 Quality: low	SMD = 0.89 (−1.33, −0.46) K = 2, N = 103 Quality: high	SMD = −1.16 (−1.81, −0.52) K = 6, N = 244 Quality: low	SMD = −0.85 (−1.28, −0.41) K = 2, N = 91 Quality: moderate
Non-response	RR = 0.6 (0.37, 0.97) K = 3, N = 90 Quality: low	RR = 0.69 (0.49, 0.98) K = 2, N = 129 Quality: moderate	–	–
Non-remission	RR = 0.62 (0.41, 0.94) K = 3, N = 130 Quality: low	RR = 0.62 (0.47, 0.80) K = 2, N = 129 Quality: high	–	–

Table 23: Dose-response relationship of CBT

	Brief versus standard versus intensive CBT
No. trials (total participants)	1 RCT (94)
Study ID	DURHAM2004
N/% female	28/55%
Mean age (years)	39
Diagnosis	GAD as a primary diagnosis by DSM-IV
Baseline severity (clinician-rated)	ADIS score: Brief CBT – 4.7 (good prognosis) Standard CBT – 6 (poor prognosis) Intensive CBT – 5.8 (poor prognosis)
Comparators	Brief CBT (5 sessions) Standard CBT (9 sessions) Intensive CBT (15 sessions)
Treatment length	10 weeks
Follow-up	6 months

greater benefit of brief CBT at 6 months' follow-up. However, there was no significant difference between brief or standard length CBT on self-rated anxiety. At 6 months' follow-up, the results favour brief CBT over standard CBT; however, it should be noted that the confidence just crosses the line of no effect, so this result should be interpreted with caution. Furthermore, remission was similar for both treatment groups at post-treatment and slightly favouring brief CBT at follow-up; however, this difference did not achieve statistical significance. These findings should be interpreted with caution due to the confounding factor of the difference in severity of the two groups (good prognosis and poor prognosis).

Brief versus intensive cognitive behavioural therapy
There was a significant difference between brief versus intensive CBT in relation to clinician-rated anxiety scores at post-treatment in favour of brief CBT. This difference was even greater after 6 months' follow-up. However, despite the results indicating that brief CBT was slightly more effective in reducing self-rated anxiety there were no significant differences between the groups at post-treatment or 6 months' follow-up. Moreover, the evidence suggests that the brief CBT group was

more likely to achieve remission status both at post-treatment and at 6 months' follow-up than those having intensive CBT. However, the results are not significant and the confidence intervals are fairly wide so the evidence remains inconclusive. These findings should be interpreted with caution due to the confounding factor of the difference in severity of the two groups (good prognosis and poor prognosis).

Standard versus intensive cognitive behavioural therapy
There were no significant differences between standard versus intensive CBT in relation to either clinician- or self-rated anxiety scores at post-treatment and 6 months' follow-up. Finally, there was no significant difference between remission rates at post-treatment and 6 months' follow-up. From this evidence it is not possible to draw any clear conclusions about the relative efficacy of the treatments.

7.3.7   Motivational interviewing as a pre-treatment to cognitive behavioural therapy

One study (WESTRA2009) examined whether adding motivational interviewing as a pre-treatment to CBT would improve outcomes. This study could not be meta-analysed and therefore has been narratively reviewed (see Table 24). Participants assigned to the motivational interviewing group received 4 weeks of motivational interviewing as pre-treatment. The other group were put on a waitlist for 4 weeks. After week 4, participants from both groups received CBT for 8 weeks.

Motivational interviewing versus waitlist control
There was no statistically significant difference between participants who had 4 weeks of motivational interviewing and those who did not on any outcome measures. This was not surprising as motivational interviewing was not intended to be a treatment. Instead it was aimed to increase the motivation and homework compliance in further CBT treatment, which may improve outcomes and response.

Motivational interviewing plus cognitive behavioural therapy versus cognitive behavioural therapy only
There was no statistically significant difference between the motivational interviewing plus CBT group and the CBT-only group on anxiety and depression outcomes at post-treatment and 6 months' or 12 months' follow-up. The only statistically significant finding was an improvement of worry scores at post-treatment favouring motivational interviewing plus CBT. However, given the insignificant findings in most outcomes and the wide confidence intervals, the results were inconclusive. Moreover, as these findings are based on a single study, it is difficult to conclude the effect of motivational interviewing as a pre-treatment to CBT. Finally, the study found no statistically significant difference between the two treatment groups for the outcome of self-rated homework compliance.

Table 24: Summary study characteristics and evidence profile for motivational interviewing as a pre-treatment

	Motivational interviewing (MI) plus CBT versus CBT alone	
No. trials (total participants)	1 RCT (90)	
Study ID	WESTRA2009	
N/% female	90/46%	
Mean age (years)	MI-CBT group mean = 42.97, SD = 13.11 CBT only group mean = 40.89, SD = 11.73	
Diagnosis	GAD as a primary diagnosis by DSM-IV	
Baseline severity (clinician-rated)	ADIS score: MI-CBT group 6.03 (0.97) CBT-only group 6.03 (0.75)	
Comparators	CBT-only group (pre-CBT, similar to effect of a waitlist control group) at week 4 CBT-only group (post-CBT) at 12 weeks	
Treatment length	Motivational interviewing (4 weeks) CBT (8 weeks)	
Follow-up	6 and 12 months	
Results	Pre-treatment (MI) versus no pre-treatment (waitlist control) at week 4	MI-CBT versus CBT only at week 12
	Anxiety scores (DASS): −0.12 (−0.57, 0.33) Depression scores (DASS): −2.03 (−6.39, 2.33) Worry scores (PSWQ): −3.84 (−8.36, 0.68)	Anxiety scores (DASS): −0.12 (−0.57, 0.33) Depression scores (DASS): 0.40 (−2.47, 3.27) Worry scores (PSWQ): −6.99 (−12.98, −1.00)
Follow-up results	–	*At 6 months:* Anxiety scores (DASS): −0.08 (−0.53, 0.37) Depression scores (DASS): 1.10 (−1.72, 3.92) Worry scores (PSWQ): −2.93 (−9.66, 3.80) *At 12 months:* Anxiety scores (DASS): 0.05 (−0.40, 0.50) Depression scores (DASS): 1.05 (−2.77, 4.87) Worry scores (PSWQ): −2.90 (−9.54, 3.74) ADIS scores: −0.20 (−0.65, 0.25)

7.4   APPLIED RELAXATION

7.4.1   Studies considered

There were a total of four trials comparing applied relaxation with waitlist control, an active control and other active treatments. Three trials compared applied relaxation with waitlist control and one trial with non-directive therapy. There was no evidence of publication bias at the study level for any of the applied relaxation comparisons as assessed by visual inspection of funnel plots and formally by the Egger's test.

A summary of study characteristics can be found in Table 25 with full details in Appendix 15c, which also includes details of excluded studies.

Table 25: Study information table for trials of applied relaxation

	Applied relaxation versus waitlist control	Applied relaxation versus non-directive therapy
No. trials (total participants)	3 RCTs (127)	1 RCT (43)
Study ID	(1) BARLOW1992 (2) DUGAS2009A (3) HOYER2009	BORKOVEC1993
N/% female	(1) 65/No information (2) 65/66% (3) 73/71%	66/65%
Mean age (years)	(1) 40 (2) 39 (3) 45	38
Diagnosis	(1) GAD by DSM-III-R (2)–(3) GAD by DSM-IV	GAD as a primary diagnosis by DSM-III-R
Baseline severity (clinician-rated)	(1) ADIS score: 5.3–5.5 (2) ADIS score: 5.7 (3) HAM-A score: 21.6–23.3	Baseline ADIS score: 4.7–4.8
Treatment length	(1) 15 weeks (2) 12 weeks (3) 15 weeks	12 weeks
Follow-up	(1) 24 months (not extractable) (2) 6, 12 and 24 months (not extractable) (3) 6 and 12 months	6 and 12 months

7.4.2   Clinical evidence for applied relaxation

Evidence from the important outcomes and overall quality of evidence are presented in Table 26. The full GRADE profiles and associated forest plots can be found in Appendix 18b and Appendix 16b, respectively.

Table 26: Evidence summary table for trials of applied relaxation

	Applied relaxation versus waitlist control	Applied relaxation versus non-directive therapy
No. trials (total participants)	3 RCTs (127)	1 RCT (43)
Study ID	(1) BARLOW1992 (2) DUGAS2009A (3) HOYER2009	BORKOVEC1993
Follow-up	(1) 24 months (not extractable) (2) 6, 12 and 24 months (not extractable) (3) 6 and 12 months	6 and 12 months
Benefits		
Anxiety (self-rated)	SMD = −0.49 (−0.86, −0.13) K = 3, N = 121 Quality: high	SMD = −0.48 (−1.14, 0.19) K = 1, N = 36 Quality: low
Anxiety (self-rated) at follow-up	–	*At 6 months:* SMD = −0.32 (−1.01, 0.36) K = 1, N = 33 *At 12 months:* SMD = −0.08 (−0.76, 0.60) K = 1, N = 33
Anxiety (clinician-rated)	SMD = −1.00 (−1.38, −0.62) K = 3, N = 124 Quality: high	SMD = −0.82 (−1.51, −0.14) K = 1, N = 36 Quality: low
Anxiety (clinician-rated) at follow-up	–	*At 6 months:* SMD = −0.65 (−1.35, 0.06) K = 1, N = 33 *At 12 months:* SMD = −0.20 (−0.89, 0.48) K = 1, N = 33

Continued

Table 26: (*Continued*)

	Applied relaxation versus waitlist control	Applied relaxation versus non-directive therapy
Depression (self-rated)	SMD = −0.54 (−0.98, −0.10) K = 2, N = 82 Quality: high	SMD = −0.36 (−1.02, 0.29) K = 1, N = 36 Quality: low
Depression (self-rated) at follow-up	–	*At 6 months:* SMD = −0.26 (−0.94, 0.43) K = 1, N = 33 *At 12 months:* SMD = 0.04 (−0.64, 0.72) K = 1, N = 33
Depression (clinician-rated)	SMD = −0.47 (−1.14, 0.20) K = 2, N = 104 Quality: low	–
Worry	SMD = −0.70 (−1.10, −0.31) K = 2, N = 104 Quality: high	SMD = −0.61 (−1.28, 0.06) K = 1, N = 36 Quality: low
Worry at follow-up	–	*At 6 months:* SMD = 0.04 (−0.64, 0.72) K = 1, N = 33 *At 12 months:* SMD = −0.08 (−0.77, 0.60) K = 1, N = 33
Non-response	RR = 0.39 (0.21, 0.72) K = 1, N = 36 Quality: moderate	RR = 0.54 (0.32, 0.91) K = 1, N = 43 Quality: moderate
Non-response at follow-up	–	*At 12 months:* RR = 0.8 (0.48, 1.33) K = 1, N = 43
Harm		
Discontinuation due to any reason	RR = 2.20 (0.37, 13.19) K = 3, N = 141 Quality: low	RR = 2.17 (0.47, 10.00) K = 1, N = 43 Quality: low

7.4.3   Clinical evidence summary

Applied relaxation versus waitlist control
There were three trials comparing applied relaxation with waitlist control. One trial found a statistically significant improvement in non-response if participants

were treated with applied relaxation. All three trials suggested a large effect on clinician-rated anxiety and a moderate effect on self-rated anxiety, depression and worry outcomes.

Applied relaxation versus non-directive therapy
One trial compared applied relaxation with non-directive therapy. The results suggested participants receiving applied relaxation were more likely to respond to treatment. Compared with non-directive therapy, applied relaxation had a small to large improvement on clinician-rated anxiety scores. However this effect diminished at 6 and 12 months' follow-up and was no longer statistically significant. Furthermore, there were no statistically significant differences between treatments in terms of dropout rates and depression and worry scores.

7.5   PSYCHODYNAMIC THERAPY

7.5.1   Studies considered

There were two trials comparing psychodynamic therapy with an active control and non-directive therapies. There was no evidence of publication bias at the study level for any of the comparisons of psychodynamic therapy as assessed by visual inspection of funnel plots and formally by the Egger's test.

A summary of study characteristics can be found in Table 27 with full details in Appendix 15c, which also includes details of excluded studies.

Table 27: Study information table for trials of psychodynamic therapy

	Psychodynamic therapy versus active control (anxiety management training)	Psychodynamic therapy versus non-directive/ supportive therapy
No. trials (participants)	1 RCT (n = 70)	1 RCT (N = 31)
Study ID	DURHAM1994	CRITS-CHRISTOPH2005
N/% female	110/68%	31/no information
Mean age (years)	39	No information
Diagnosis	GAD by DSM-III-R	GAD by DSM-IV
Baseline severity (clinician-rated)	ADIS score: 6.1–6.6	Not reported
Treatment length	14 weeks	16 weeks
Follow-up	6 and 12 months	–

7.5.2   Clinical evidence for psychodynamic therapy

Evidence from the important outcomes and overall quality of evidence are presented in Table 28. The full GRADE profiles and associated forest plots can be found in Appendix 18b and Appendix 16b, respectively.

7.5.3   Clinical evidence summary

Psychodynamic therapy versus other active comparisons
One trial compared the effectiveness of psychodynamic therapy with another active comparison (anxiety management training). There was no statistically significant difference in effect on anxiety (clinician- and self-rated), depression and quality of life scores.

Psychodynamic therapy versus non-directive/supportive therapy
One trial compared the effectiveness of psychodynamic therapy with non-directive/supportive therapy. There was no statistically significant difference in dropout rates. Moreover, there were no statistically significant differences found between treatments on anxiety and depression scores.

7.6   OTHER INTERVENTIONS

7.6.1   Studies considered and clinical evidence

Two trials could not be classified with any of the three types of treatment reviewed above; these trials could not be integrated into the meta-analyses, and therefore are narratively reviewed. Study characteristics and evidence from the important outcomes are presented in Table 29.

7.6.2   Clinical evidence summary

Affect-focused body psychotherapy versus treatment as usual
Only one study (BERG2009) included a comparison of affect-focused body psychotherapy versus treatment as usual. Affect-focused body psychotherapy is a novel treatment that integrates bodily techniques and the exploration of emotions into a psychodynamic frame of reference. The focus of therapy is on comprehending the information latent in affects and on increasing the tolerance for affects in general and anxiety in particular. The bodily part of the therapy helps the person to gain a better stability through exercises and massage, which in turn may lead to a reduction in overall anxiety. Also, the therapist aims to gain information regarding the person's emotions by observing their bodily expressions (for example, body posture) and also by being observant of their reactions. The person is then invited to explore their emotions while working directly with the body with massage grips or movements.

164

Table 28: Evidence summary table for trials of psychodynamic therapy

	Psychodynamic therapy versus active control (anxiety management training)	Psychodynamic therapy versus non-directive/ supportive therapy
No. trials (total participants)	1 RCT (70)	1 RCT (31)
Study ID	DURHAM1994	CRITS-CHRISTOPH2005
Follow-up	6 and 12 months	–
Benefits		
Anxiety (clinician-rated)	SMD = 0.08 (−0.41, 0.57) K = 1, N = 64 Quality: low	SMD = −0.25 (−0.95, 0.46) K = 1, N = 31 Quality: moderate
Anxiety (self-rated)	SMD = 0.18 (−0.31, 0.67) K = 1, N = 64 Quality: low	SMD = 0.47 (−0.24, 1.19) K = 1, N = 31 Quality: moderate
Anxiety (self-rated) At follow-up	*At 6 months:* SMD = 1.00 (0.35, 1.65) K = 1, N = 45 *At 12 months:* SMD = 0.95 (0.31, 1.60) K = 1, N = 45	–
Depression (clinician-rated)	–	SMD = −0.08 (−0.78, 0.63) K = 1, N = 31 Quality: moderate
Depression (self-rated)	SMD = 0.24 (−0.38, 0.85) K = 1, N = 45 Quality: low	SMD = 0.12 (−0.58, 0.83) K = 1, N = 31 Quality: moderate
Depression (self-rated) At follow-up	*At 6 months:* SMD = 0.51 (−0.11, 1.13) K = 1, N = 45 *At 12 months:* SMD = 0.46 (−0.16, 1.08) K = 1, N = 45	–
Quality of life	SMD = −0.01 (−0.62, 0.61) K = 1, N = 45 Quality: low	–
Non-remission	–	SMD = 0.61 (0.37, 1.01) K = 1, N = 31 Quality: high

Continued

Table 28: (*Continued*)

	Psychodynamic therapy versus active control (anxiety management training)	Psychodynamic therapy versus non-directive/ supportive therapy
Harm		
Leaving study early for any reason	SMD = 0.83 (0.34, 2.07) K = 1, N = 70 Quality: low	SMD = 0.53 (0.05, 5.29) K = 1, N = 31 Quality: moderate

Cognitive-behavioural techniques, such as formulating self-assertive dialogues, may be used to enhance the person's ability to express feelings satisfactorily. Four female physiotherapists, whose professional experience varied from 10 to 20 years, administered the treatment once weekly during 1 year. All therapists were trained and examined in the provision of affect-focused body psychotherapy before the study commenced and were given regular supervision (twice monthly) to ensure adherence to the manual throughout the study.

The evidence suggests that there is no significant difference between treatments in reduction of anxiety scores after 1-year post-treatment or at 2 years' follow-up. Similarly, despite the results favouring affect-focused body psychotherapy there were no significant differences between treatments in the improvement of quality of life post-treatment or at 2 years' follow-up. Moreover, this limited evidence seems to indicate a high risk of dropout for those receiving affect-focused body psychotherapy when compared with the treatment as usual group, however this difference remains statistically insignificant. These results are based on one small study and given the wide confidence intervals and lack of statistical significance, it is difficult to make any firm conclusions.

Integrative relaxation training versus waitlist
Only one study (JANBOZORGI2009) included a comparison of integrative relaxation training (a combination of CBT approaches with relaxation, lifestyle modification and spiritual exercises) versus waitlist. From this study, it was possible to only extract anxiety scores; the results at post-treatment were significant, favouring integrative relaxation training over waitlist control. However, these results should be interpreted with caution due to the small sample size. Moreover, these results may not be generalisable to the UK because the population was Iranian.

Chinese Taoist cognitive psychotherapy treatment
ZHANG2002 conducted a randomised trial comparing the efficacy of Chinese Taoist cognitive psychotherapy (CTCP), benzodiazepines and combined treatment in people

Table 29: Study information and evidence summary table of trials of other interventions

	Affect-focused body psychotherapy versus treatment as usual	Integrated relaxation therapy versus waitlist	Chinese Taoist cognitive psychotherapy (CTCP) versus benzodiazepine versus combined treatment
No. trials (total participants)	1 RCT (61)	1 RCT (35)	1 RCT (143)
Study ID	BERG2009	JANBOZORGI2009	ZHANG2002
N/% female	61/69%	35/87.5%	143/37%
Mean age (years)	37	25	35
Diagnosis	GAD as a primary diagnosis by DSM-IV	GAD as a primary diagnosis by DSM-IV	CCMD-2-R criteria for GAD is the same as ICD-10 and DSM-IV except that condition has duration of 3 rather than 6 months
Baseline severity (clinician-rated)	Not reported	Not reported	SCL-90: CTCP 90.7, drug 113.8, combined 107.0
Treatment length	1 year	12 weeks	6 months
Follow-up	2 years	Not reported	6 months
Results	*Anxiety score – self-reported BAI* SMD = −0.04 (−0.55, 0.46) (post-treatment) SMD = −0.07 (−0.58, 0.43) (2 years' follow-up) *Quality of Life – self-reported WHO (ten) Well-being index* SMD = −1.90 (−5.42, 1.62) (post-treatment) SMD = −1.40 (−5.02, 2.22) (2 years' follow-up) *Dropout* Treatment: 6/33 Control: 0/28 RR = 11.09 (0.65, 188.55)	*Anxiety score – self-reported STAI-T* SMD = −1.42 (−2.21, −0.63)	*SCL-90 scores (1-month follow-up)* Benzodiazepine versus CTCP SMD = −0.77; 95% CI, −1.19 to −0.35 (favours benzodiazepine group) Combined treatment versus CTCP SMD = −0.53; 95% CI, −0.94 to −0.12 (favours combined treatment group) *SCL-90 scores (6-month follow-up)* CTCP versus benzodiazepine SMD = −0.85; 95% CI, −1.30 to −0.41 (favours CTCP) Combined treatment versus benzodiazepine SMD = −0.88; 95% CI, −1.32 to −0.43 (favours combined treatment group)

diagnosed with GAD according to the *Chinese Classification of Mental Disorders* – 2 (CCMD-2). Participants in the CTCP-only group (n = 46) received cognitive psychotherapy blended with aspects of Chinese culture such as Taoist philosophy. This treatment was carried out by experienced and trained psychiatrists. The drug treatment group (n = 48) received variable doses of diazepam and alprazolam according to patient conditions; however, drug dosage was unaltered in the second of the two phases of the study. The combined treatment group (n = 49) received both CTCP and benzodiazepines. All groups had 1 month of weekly sessions (phase I), each lasting 1 hour (just 10 minutes for the drug-only group) and then 5 months of twice monthly sessions (phase II). Participants were assessed after both phases with the Symptom Checklist (SCL-90), Type A Personality Scale, Coping Style Questionnaire and the Eysenck Personality Questionnaire. After 1 month's follow-up, participants had significantly lower mean SCL-90 scores in the drug only group (SMD = −0.77; 95% CI, −1.19 to −0.35) and combined treatment group (SMD = −0.53; 95% CI, −0.94 to −0.12) than in the CTCP-only group. After 6 months' follow-up, participants had significantly lower mean SCL-90 scores in the CTCP-only group (SMD = −0.85; 95% CI, −1.30 to −0.41) and the combined treatment group (SMD = −0.88; 95% CI, −1.32 to −0.43) compared with the drug-only group. This suggests that CTCP alone or in combination is more effective than medication in the long term.

7.7 COMBINED TREATMENTS

7.7.1 Studies considered and clinical evidence

One trial examined combining pharmacological and psychological interventions; another examined the augmentation of psychological treatment. These trials could not be integrated into the meta-analyses, and therefore are narratively reviewed. Study characteristics and evidence from the important outcomes are presented in Table 30.

7.7.2 Clinical evidence summary

Buspirone and anxiety management training versus active control and anxiety management training
Based on the evidence of one study (BOND2002B), the data favour the combination of buspirone and anxiety management training over the combination of active control and anxiety management training in the reduction of clinician-rated anxiety scores. However, this result is not significant and should be interpreted with caution due to the wide confidence intervals. Similarly, there were no significant differences between the treatment approaches on self-rated anxiety scores, therefore it is not possible to draw any clear conclusions about the relative efficacy of the treatments.

Table 30: Study information and evidence summary tables for trials of combined treatments

	Buspirone and anxiety management training versus active control and anxiety management training	Buspirone and non-directive therapy versus active control and non-directive therapy
No. trials (total participants)	1 RCT (60)	
Study ID	BOND2002B	
N/% female	60/45%	
Mean age (years)	34	
Diagnosis	GAD as a primary diagnosis by DSM-III-R	
Baseline severity (clinician-rated)	HAM-A score: 14.3-15.5	HAM-A score: 14.4-16.3
Treatment length	8 weeks	
Follow-up	None reported	
Results	*Clinician-rated anxiety scores:* SMD = −0.33 (−1.16, 0.49) *Self-rated anxiety scores:* SMD = 0.06 (−0.76, 0.88)	*Clinician-rated anxiety scores:* SMD = −0.18 (−1.09, 0.73) *Self-rated anxiety scores:* SMD = 0.07 (−0.84, 0.97)
	CBT + IPT versus waitlist control	CBT versus CBT + IPT
No. trials (participants in the subgroup)	1 RCT (24)	
Study ID	REZVAN2008	
N/% female	36/100%	
Mean age (years)	20	
Diagnosis	Diagnosed with GAD as a primary diagnosis by DSM-IV	
Treatment length	8 weeks	
Follow-up	12 months	
Results	*Worry score – PSWQ:* SMD = −2.89 (−4.10, −1.69) (post-treatment) SMD = −3.52 (−4.87, −2.17) (12 months' follow-up) *Quality of life – Oxford Happiness Scale:* SMD = −2.40 (−3.49, −1.31) (post-treatment) SMD = −3.62 (−5.00, −2.25) (12 months' follow-up)	*Worry score – PSWQ:* SMD = −0.07 (CI, −0.87, 0.73) (post-treatment) SMD = 0.79 (−0.05, 1.62) (12 months' follow-up) *Quality of life – Oxford Happiness Scale:* SMD = −0.09 (−0.89, 0.71) (post-treatment) SMD = 0.98 (0.13, 1.84) (12 months' follow-up)

Buspirone and non-directive therapy versus active control and non-directive therapy
Based on the evidence of one study (BOND2002B), there was no significant difference found between the combination of buspirone and non-directive therapy over the combination of active control and non-directive therapy in the reduction of clinician-rated anxiety scores. However, the results indicate that the combination of buspirone and non-directive therapy may lead to slightly lower clinician-rated anxiety scores. Similarly, there were no significant differences between the treatment approaches on self-rated anxiety scores. Again, wide confidence intervals, lack of statistical significance and the small sample size, prevent any clear conclusions being drawn.

Cognitive behavioural therapy and interpersonal therapy versus waitlist control
One study looked at the effect of interpersonal therapy augmented with CBT (REZVAN2008). However, the treatment described in the study was not standard CBT and the interpersonal therapy (IPT) described was not derived from standard IPT principles. Results should therefore be interpreted with caution. When augmented with IPT, combined therapy had a statistically significant large effect on worry and quality of life over waitlist control at post-treatment. The effects on both scores were sustained at 12 months' follow-up. However, the augmentation of IPT is not statistically significantly better than CBT alone on both worry and quality of life scores. This result, however, changed at 12 months' follow-up when the data favoured the combined therapy on worry and quality of life over CBT alone. Firm conclusions are subject to cautious interpretation due to the limited evidence available.

7.8   MODE OF DELIVERY

7.8.1   Individual cognitive behavioural therapy

A total of 21 studies examined the effectiveness of individual CBT for GAD (ARNTZ2003; BARLOW1992; BORKOVEC1993; BORKOVEC2002; BUTLER1991; DUGAS2003; DUGAS2009A; DURHAM1994; HOYER2009; LADOUCEUR2000; LEICHSENRING2009; LINDEN2005; MOHLMAN2003A; ÖST2000; REZVAN2008; ROEMER2008; STANLEY1996; STANLEY2003B; STANLEY2009; WETHERELL2003; WELLS2010). The average duration of CBT treatment was approximately 15 weekly sessions (range of 8 to 20 weeks) lasting approximately 70 minutes (range of 50 to 120 minutes). The majority (53%) of these studies required participants to complete homework assignments or practice techniques at home. Homework usually involved the application of reaching alternative perspectives, exposure to worry and various behavioural tasks. The amount of time allocated to homework also varied between studies from twice per day to weekly. Therapist support varied significantly across the studies with the standard amount of therapists per study being three (range of one to nine). Therapists' competence and training also varied widely. In approximately eight studies, the therapists were licensed CBT psychotherapists, eight were doctoral level students and in two others there was a mixture of clinical psychologists, consultant psychotherapists and trainee psychiatrists. Training also varied from little experience in CBT (that is, under 1 year) to 16 years' delivering CBT. Therapist training was provided via a number of diverse methods such as workshops, private practice seminars and by manual.

7.8.2 Group cognitive behavioural therapy

Two studies (DUGAS2003; WETHERELL2003) looked at the efficacy of group CBT on GAD. The duration of treatment for group CBT was around 12 to 14 weekly sessions lasting 90 to 120 minutes per session. DUGAS2003 did not assign homework tasks to participants, while WETHERELL2003 incorporated a 30-minute homework task each day. Therapist support was provided by a licensed psychologist trained in CBT in the DUGAS2003 trial and advanced doctoral students delivered therapy to groups of older adults in the WETHERELL2003 trial. The therapist to client ratio was approximately one therapist per four to six clients. The therapist was provided with a session-by-session treatment manual before starting treatment.

7.8.3 Applied relaxation

A total of eight studies examined the effectiveness of applied relaxation for GAD (ARNTZ2003; BARLOW1992; BORKOVEC1993; BORKOVEC2002; DUGAS2009A; HOYER2009; ÖST2000; WELLS2010). The mean treatment duration was 13 weekly sessions (range of 12 to 15). The average session lasted approximately 80 minutes (range of 60 to 120 minutes). Similar to CBT, homework tasks were allocated to consolidate learning for the majority (71%) of applied relaxation studies. These homework assignments normally required participants to practice applied relaxation techniques at least twice per day or, in one case, at the end of each weekly session. Again, therapist support and competence differed substantially from study to study. Half of the studies were delivered by senior doctoral therapists, three of whom had the additional support of experienced therapists or staff psychologists. Two further studies provided therapy by means of licensed therapists or psychologists with an average of 10 years' clinical experience (range of 5 to 16 years). In another study, therapist support was delivered by a therapist who was trained at an applied relaxation workshop.

7.8.4 Psychodynamic therapy

Three studies examined the efficacy of psychodynamic therapy in improving symptoms of GAD (CRITS-CRISTOPH2005; DURHAM1994; LEICHSENRING2009). The average duration of treatment was 20 weekly sessions (range of 10 to 30) with each session lasting approximately 1 hour. No homework assignments were allocated for these groups. Therapist support was delivered by either a licensed psychotherapist with 15 years' experience in providing psychodynamic therapy (LEICHSEN-RING2009), by a therapist with a PhD or Master's degree in social work who had a minimum of 10 years' experience of providing psychodynamic therapy (CRITS-CRISTOPH2005), or by a clinical psychologist, consultant psychotherapist or trained psychotherapist (DURHAM1994).

7.8.5   Non-directive therapy

Three studies examined the efficacy of non-directive therapy in improving the symptoms of GAD (BORKOVEC1993; CRITS-CRISTOPH2005; STANLEY1996). The average duration of treatment was 14 weekly sessions (range of 12 to 16) with each session lasting approximately 90 minutes. Only one of the studies (BORKOVEC1993) required participants to carry out a daily homework assignment as part of the therapy. Therapist support was delivered by an experienced and advanced clinical graduate (BORKOVEC1993), by a therapist with a PhD or Master's degree in social work who had a minimum of 10 years' experience of providing therapy (CRITS-CRISTOPH2005), or a therapist specifically trained in non-directive counselling (STANLEY1996).

7.8.6   Other active comparisons

Three studies looked at the efficacy of other active treatments that could not be otherwise classified as applied relaxation, psychodynamic therapy or non directive therapies (DURHAM1994; STANLEY2009; WETHERELL2003). These treatments consisted of anxiety management training delivered by psychiatric registrars (doctors in training) without training in CBT, who followed a written protocol in which coping skills were taught during a structured individual session (DURHAM1994); enhanced usual care, which consisted of biweekly telephone conversations to provide support and ensure the patient's safety (STANLEY2009); and a discussion group in which a different topic relating to common anxieties was discussed each week (WETHERELL2003). The duration of treatment was approximately eleven sessions over a period of 10 weeks with an average of 50 minutes spent per session (range of 15 to 90 minutes). Homework assignments were given to consolidate learning for both the discussion group (WETHERELL2003) and the anxiety management training group (DURHAM1994), but not for the enhanced usual care group (STANLEY2009). Again, therapist support was varied and included clinical psychologists, consultant psychiatrists, a trainee psychiatrist (DURHAM1994), therapists with a Master's degree and 2 years' experience of delivering CBT, a pre-doctoral student with more than 3 years' CBT experience and a post-bachelor level therapist with 5 years' experience of CBT (STANLEY2009) and advanced doctoral students (WETHERELL2003).

7.9   OVERALL CLINICAL SUMMARY

7.9.1   Cognitive behavioural therapy

CBT was found to be an effective treatment compared with waitlist control. Data suggested that CBT is associated with moderate-to-large improvement on anxiety, depression and worry outcomes relative to waitlist control. However, the long-term effects of CBT trials relative to inactive controls are unknown. The quality of this set of evidence is moderate to high. Therefore a rather strong recommendation for CBT as a treatment of GAD can be made.

CBT was not found to be inferior or superior to applied relaxation, with both of these interventions displaying similar effects on the majority of outcomes. The quality of evidence is low to moderate. Despite the lack of statistically significant differences, CBT has a larger magnitude of effect compared with applied relaxation. Thus, clinical evidence for CBT is more robust than applied relaxation due to the larger evidence base and larger effect sizes.

There is some evidence showing that CBT is more effective than psychodynamic therapy in improving anxiety and depression outcomes in the short term. The long-term effects of CBT are unknown, with moderate quality evidence from two trials.

It is not possible to draw conclusions regarding whether CBT is more effective than non-directive therapies because the trials are not comparable.

A subgroup analysis of the effect of CBT on working-age adults and older adults was conducted. CBT was found to be effective for both populations. There were no statistically significant differences in effect between the two populations on any outcome measures. Therefore, the GDG's general conclusion about the effectiveness of CBT remains robust across age groups. Subgroup analysis of individual or group sessions showed both formats are effective against waitlist control on anxiety, depression and worry outcomes. The overall quality of evidence was moderate to high. This suggests CBT can be delivered in an individual or group format.

7.9.2   Applied relaxation

Applied relaxation is an effective treatment compared with waitlist control. It is associated with moderate improvement on anxiety, depression and worry outcomes. The overall quality is moderate, which supports a moderate recommendation in terms of its clinical evidence profile.

There is insufficient evidence comparing the relative effectiveness of applied relaxation and non-directive therapy.

7.9.3   Psychodynamic therapy

The limited evidence shows no statistically significant difference between psychodynamic therapy and an active comparison (anxiety management training). The limited evidence did not show statistically significant differences in relative effectiveness between psychodynamic therapy and non-directive therapies. Therefore no recommendations for psychodynamic therapy in the treatment of GAD can be made.

7.9.4   Non-directive therapy

There is an absence of evidence exploring the effectiveness of non-directive therapy compared with control, and therefore no recommendations for non-directive therapy in the treatment of GAD can be made.

7.10   HEALTH ECONOMIC EVIDENCE

7.10.1   Research question

What is the cost effectiveness of high-intensity psychological interventions (such as CBT, applied relaxation, psychodynamic therapy and non-directive therapies) compared with other interventions in the treatment of GAD?

7.10.2   Systematic literature review

The systematic search of the economic literature undertaken for the guideline identified one eligible study on high-intensity psychological interventions for people with GAD (Heuzenroeder *et al.*, 2004). The study, based on decision-analytic modelling, compared CBT with standard care for the treatment of GAD from the perspective of the healthcare sector in Australia. Standard care was defined as a mixture of care based on evidence-based medicine principles (27%), care according to non-evidence-based medicine principles (28%) and no care (45%). The study population consisted of the total estimated adult population with GAD in Australia, according to national surveys. The outcome measure was the number of disability-adjusted life years (DALYs) saved. The source of clinical effectiveness data was a systematic review and meta-analysis. Resource use estimates were based on assumptions; national unit prices were used. The study estimated the costs of CBT provided by four different types of healthcare professionals: private psychologists, public psychologists, private psychiatrists and public psychiatrists. The analysis estimated that use of CBT for the treatment of the adult population in Australia saved a total of 7,200 DALYs compared with standard care. The incremental cost of providing CBT rather than standard care to all adults with GAD in Australia ranged from $50 million, when CBT was provided by public psychologists, to $170 million, when CBT was provided by private psychiatrists (prices in 2000 Australian dollars). The incremental cost effectiveness ratio (ICER) of CBT versus standard care lay between $12,000/DALY averted (range $7,000 to $25,000/DALY averted in sensitivity analysis) for provision of CBT by public psychologists, to $32,000/DALY averted (range $20,000 to $63,000/DALY averted in sensitivity analysis) for provision of CBT by private psychiatrists. Although the study met the systematic review inclusion criteria, it was considered to be non-applicable to the UK setting for the following reasons: it was conducted in Australia; the measure of outcomes was DALYs saved, which limited the interpretability of the study findings; and standard care, according to its definition, was likely to differ significantly from standard care in the NHS context. For this reason the study was not considered further during the guideline development process.

Details on the methods used for the systematic review of the economic literature are described in Chapter 3; the full reference to the study and the respective evidence table is presented in Appendix 15f. The completed methodology checklist of the study is provided in Appendix 17.

7.10.3   Cost analysis: high-intensity psychological interventions

The cost effectiveness of high-intensity psychological interventions for people with GAD was considered by the GDG as an area with potentially significant resource implications. The GDG was particularly interested in the cost effectiveness of high-intensity psychological interventions compared with low-intensity psychological interventions and pharmacological interventions, as well as in the relative cost effectiveness between different high-intensity psychological interventions. Comparison of high-intensity psychological interventions with non-active treatments was not deemed a priority by the GDG and therefore was not considered as an area for economic modelling.

As already discussed in Chapter 6, it was not possible to construct an economic model in order to compare high-intensity psychological interventions with other active treatments such as low-intensity psychological interventions and/or pharmacological treatments, because no direct (head-to-head) comparisons were available and indirect evidence was problematic because there were significant differences across studies in terms of the study populations, the comparators and the clinical outcome measures used. Even within the clinical literature on high-intensity psychological interventions there were important differences in terms of the population (some studies were conducted on older populations), the comparators, and the definition of response/remission. Moreover, it was not possible to link the outcome measures, such as response and remission, with published utility scores in order to conduct a cost-utility analysis because the definition of response in studies reporting utility scores for GAD-related health states differed significantly from the definition of response in the RCTs included in the guideline systematic literature review. For this reason, it was not possible to assess the relative cost effectiveness between different high-intensity psychological interventions using decision-analytic modelling techniques. Instead, simple cost analyses were undertaken to estimate the intervention costs associated with provision of effective high-intensity psychological interventions in the NHS, as identified by the guideline systematic review and meta-analysis. The resource use estimates were based on the descriptions of resource use in the RCTs included in the guideline systematic review, supported by the expert opinion of the GDG so as to reflect optimal clinical practice within the NHS context. For costing purposes it was assumed that interventions were provided by clinical psychologists; however, it is recognised that other trained healthcare professionals of equivalent qualifications may well provide the interventions assessed. Unit costs of clinical psychologists were based on the median full-time equivalent basic salary for Agenda for Change Band 7, of the January to March 2009 NHS Staff Earnings estimates; estimation of unit costs considered wages/salary, salary oncosts and overheads but did not include qualification costs, as these are not available for clinical psychologists (Curtis, 2009). Subsequently, the GDG considered the intervention costs alongside the findings of the clinical effectiveness review when formulating the recommendations.

The guideline systematic review and meta-analysis indicated that CBT and applied relaxation were effective in the treatment of GAD and were therefore considered in this cost analysis. Both interventions consisted of 12 sessions and three booster sessions, lasting 1 hour each, according to reported overall resource use in the RCTs considered in the systematic clinical review supported by the expert opinion of the GDG. Using a unit cost for clinical psychologists of £75 per hour of patient contact (Curtis, 2009), the total cost of providing either CBT or applied relaxation would reach £1,125 per person treated in 2009 prices. As expected, this cost is significantly higher than the cost of providing any low-intensity psychological intervention such as those considered in the cost analysis described in Chapter 6 where the intervention cost was estimated at £15 per person for non-facilitated self-help; £36 to £108 per person for a psychoeducational group; and £83 to £150 per person for guided bibliotherapy. In addition, the intervention cost of high-intensity psychological interventions is considerably higher than that of pharmacological therapy: the latter was estimated to range from £150 to £700 per person, depending on the drug used. These figures include drug acquisition costs and GP consultations over a period of 8 weeks of initial treatment and 6 months of maintenance treatment (details on intervention costs of pharmacological treatment are provided in the economic section of Chapter 8). Nevertheless, the extra cost associated with provision of high-intensity psychological interventions may be justified, considering the relative clinical benefits and harms across different types of interventions available for people with GAD. Moreover, if high-intensity interventions are delivered in groups, then the intervention cost per person is greatly reduced, as the total cost is spread: for example, if 12 to 14 sessions of group CBT, each lasting 2 hours, are offered to groups of six people (as described in relevant literature considered in this guideline), then the intervention cost per person is estimated to be approximately £300 to £350. It should be noted that the guideline systematic review of clinical evidence indicated that group CBT is likely to be effective against waitlist control on anxiety, depression and worry outcomes; however, the evidence base for group CBT is limited. In addition, no head-to-head trials have assessed the effectiveness of group CBT relative to individual CBT.

7.11 FROM EVIDENCE TO RECOMMENDATIONS

The evidence base for CBT as an effective treatment against an inactive control is quite strong. A reasonably large number of high-quality trials suggested a moderate to large improvement on relevant outcome measures. Also, when CBT was compared with other treatments in a limited number of trials, there appeared to be some moderate quality evidence favouring CBT over psychodynamic therapy. Moreover, the evidence from Chapter 5 suggested people with GAD prefer CBT because it does not have the side effects associated with pharmacological treatments. For this reason, although CBT can be quite costly per person (£1,125), patient preference should be considered and clinicians can offer CBT with the knowledge that it is supported by reasonable evidence.

Furthermore, delivering CBT in groups might be considered as an additional option given the cost per person is substantially lower. However, the clinical evidence for group CBT was from smaller and lower-quality trials. Hence there was not enough statistical power to make any recommendations.

The evidence base for applied relaxation compared with waitlist control is of moderate quality. A smaller number of trials suggested a small to large improvement on relevant outcome measures. However, it was unclear whether there were any adverse side effects for this treatment. The health economic data suggested that CBT and applied relaxation have similar costs if they are provided by fully trained clinical psychologists. In general, applied relaxation can be considered as an option; however clinicians should note the less robust evidence base in support of the intervention.

7.11.1 Recommendations

Treatment options
7.11.1.1 For people with GAD and marked functional impairment, or those whose symptoms have not responded adequately to step 2 interventions:
- Offer either
  - an individual high-intensity psychological intervention (see 7.11.1.2–7.11.1.6) or
  - drug treatment (see 8.10.1.2–8.10.1.12).
- Provide verbal and written information on the likely benefits and disadvantages of each mode of treatment, including the tendency of drug treatments to be associated with side effects and withdrawal syndromes.
- Base the choice of treatment on the person's preference as there is no evidence that either mode of treatment (individual high-intensity psychological intervention or drug treatment) is better.

High-intensity psychological interventions
7.11.1.2 If a person with GAD chooses a high-intensity psychological intervention, offer either CBT or applied relaxation.

High-intensity psychological interventions

7.11.1.3   CBT for people with GAD should:
- be based on the treatment manuals used in the clinical trials of CBT for GAD
- be delivered by trained and competent practitioners
- usually consist of 12–15 weekly sessions (fewer if the person recovers sooner; more if clinically required), each lasting 1 hour.

7.11.1.4   Applied relaxation for people with GAD should:
- be based on the treatment manuals used in the clinical trials of applied relaxation for GAD
- be delivered by trained and competent practitioners
- usually consist of 12–15 weekly sessions (fewer if the person recovers sooner; more if clinically required), each lasting 1 hour.

7.11.1.5   Practitioners providing high-intensity psychological interventions for GAD should:
- have regular supervision to monitor fidelity to the treatment model, using audio or video recording of treatment sessions if possible and if the person consents
- use routine outcome measures and ensure that the person with GAD is involved in reviewing the efficacy of the treatment.

7.11.1.6   Consider providing all interventions in the preferred language of the person with GAD if possible.

Inadequate response

7.11.1.7   If a person's GAD has not responded to a full course of a high-intensity psychological intervention, offer a drug treatment (see 8.10.1.2–8.10.1.12).

7.11.1.8   Consider referral to step 4 if the person with GAD has severe anxiety with marked functional impairment in conjunction with:
- a risk of self-harm or suicide or
- significant comorbidity, such as substance misuse, personality disorder or complex physical health problems or
- self-neglect or
- an inadequate response to step 3 interventions.

8 PHARMACOLOGICAL AND PHYSICAL INTERVENTIONS

8.1 INTRODUCTION

The use of pharmacological interventions to manage anxiety is a far from recent phenomenon; for example, the consumption of alcohol and opiates for this purpose dates back centuries. In the 19th and early 20th century, medicines containing bromides were often prescribed by clinicians to treat what would then have been called 'anxiety neurosis' (Schwartz *et al.*, 2005). The mid-20th century saw the introduction of barbiturates followed by the benzodiazepines, which were widely used for the medical treatment of anxiety between the 1960s and the 1980s. Towards the end of this period the limitations of benzodiazepines in terms of tolerance and dependence became apparent and at the same time the therapeutic benefits of anti-depressants in treating various kinds of anxiety disorders were more widely recognised (Davidson *et al.*, 2010b).

Antidepressants, particularly SSRIs, are now commonly used in the management of anxiety disorders, including GAD. A number of other agents are also licensed for the treatment of GAD, some of which have a long history of use in this area, for example hydroxyzine (an antihistamine) and buspirone (a 5-hydroxytryptamine1A [5-HT$_{1A}$] receptor agonist), while others, such as pregabalin (an anticonvulsant), have been introduced more recently (Baldwin *et al.*, 2005).

The majority of research on pharmacological and physical interventions has concerned the use of interventions such as antidepressants and benzodiazepines. However there are a number of other interventions that are in relatively wide use or of interest in the treatment of GAD and include herbal interventions, acupuncture and hypnotherapy. These are reviewed at the end of this chapter.

8.1.1 Effectiveness of pharmacological interventions

There are currently several different kinds of pharmacological treatment available for the treatment of GAD. Placebo-controlled trials provide the best evidence of efficacy but such studies are not always easy to interpret because of the extent of the placebo response (Baldwin *et al.*, 2005). In addition, in the general population, GAD is commonly comorbid with other anxiety disorders and depression, whereas participants recruited to placebo-controlled trials are more likely to have GAD as a sole diagnosis (Tyrer & Baldwin, 2006). This introduces uncertainty about the generalisability of findings from controlled trials to real-world clinical populations. There is also uncertainty about the length of time for which drug treatment should be continued once an initial response has been obtained. Related to this is the issue of the discontinuation symptomatology that often accompanies medication withdrawal (MHRA, 2004) and how patients may fare subsequently.

8.1.2   Current practice

Current clinical practice, as reflected in previous published guidelines (Baldwin *et al.*, 2005; Davidson *et al.*, 2010a), suggests that pharmacological treatment should be considered only at a certain level of clinical severity when there is evidence of persistent symptomatology that results in occupational and social disability. The presence of a comorbid mental disorder or physical illness may also influence the decision to offer medication (Davidson *et al.*, 2010a).

When medication is recommended, current advice is to consider an antidepressant (either an SSRI or SNRI) as first-line treatment. Benzodiazepines are not advised because of the potential for the development of tolerance and dependence in a condition where treatment may need to be given for several months but they are still in relatively wide use.

8.2   PHARMACOLOGICAL INTERVENTIONS COMPARED WITH PLACEBO

8.2.1   Review question

In the treatment of GAD, which drugs improve outcomes compared with other drugs and with placebo?

8.2.2   Databases searched and inclusion/exclusion criteria

Information about the databases searched and the inclusion/exclusion criteria used for this section of the guideline can be found in Table 31 (further information about the search for health economic evidence can be found in Section 3.6). It should be noted that evidence on quetiapine was searched in order to inform a network meta-analysis of pharmacological treatments for people with GAD. Data on quetiapine were utilised in this meta-analysis to increase inference on other drugs. The results of the network meta-analysis supported the guideline economic analysis on pharmacological treatments for people with GAD. Methods and results of both the network meta-analysis and the guideline economic analysis of pharmacological treatments are reported in Section 8.8.3. The available evidence on quetiapine in the treatment of GAD was not assessed in this guideline as it is the subject of a forthcoming NICE Technology Appraisal.

Table 31: Databases searched and inclusion/exclusion criteria for clinical evidence

Electronic databases	MEDLINE, EMBASE, CINAHL, PsycINFO, Cochrane Library
Date searched	Database inception to 09.05.2010
Study design	RCT
Patient population	People with GAD
Interventions	SSRIs, TCAs, duloxetine, venlafaxine, pregabalin, antipsychotics, benzodiazepines
Outcomes	Mean anxiety rating scale scores, non-response (<50% reduction in anxiety rating scale score), non-remission (still meeting cut-off for caseness on an anxiety rating scale), Sheehan Disability Scale, quality of life

8.2.3   Studies considered[15]

The review team conducted a new systematic search for RCTs that assessed the benefits and harms of pharmacological interventions for the treatment of people with GAD as defined in DSM-III-R or DSM-IV.

A total of 13,356 references were identified by the electronic search relating to clinical evidence; a further seven unpublished trials were identified through pharmaceutical company websites. Of these references, 13,220 were excluded at the screening stage on the basis of reading the title and/or abstract. The remaining 139 references were assessed for eligibility on the basis of the full text. Sixty-two trials met the eligibility criteria set by the GDG, providing data on 20,834 participants. Of these, seven were unpublished and 55 were published in peer-reviewed journals between 1992 and 2009. In addition, 77 studies were excluded from the analysis. Fifty studies did not provide an acceptable diagnosis of GAD; 19 were not RCTs; seven had less than ten participants per group, one was not double blind; and one did not use a relevant intervention. Further information about both included and excluded studies can be found in Appendix 15d.

8.2.4   Antidepressants versus placebo

Studies considered
There were a total of 29 trials comparing various antidepressants with placebo. Most trials were on venlafaxine (all studies used extended release [XL] preparations),

---

[15]Here and elsewhere in the guideline, each study considered for review is referred to by a study ID in capital letters (primary author and date of study publication, except where a study is in press or only submitted for publication, then a date is not used).

duloxetine, escitalopram, sertraline and paroxetine. These trials were all large, high-quality studies funded almost exclusively by drug company sponsorship. There was no evidence of publication bias at the study level for any of the antidepressant comparisons as assessed by visual inspection of funnel plots and formally by the Egger's test.

A summary of study characteristics can be found in Table 32 with full details in Appendix 15d, which also includes details of excluded studies.

Clinical evidence for antidepressants versus placebo
Evidence from the important outcomes and overall quality of evidence are presented in Table 33. The full GRADE profiles and associated forest plots can be found in Appendix 18c and Appendix 16c, respectively.

Clinical evidence summary
There was limited or no data for a number of interventions: there was only one study assessing imipramine; one study assessing citalopram; no data on mirtazapine, bupropion, trazodone, fluvoxamine, fluoxetine and amitriptyline; and no data on most TCAs (for example, clomipramine, doxepin, dosulepin, lofepramine, nortriptyline and trimipramine). A further limitation of the data was the lack of long-term studies (only two studies, one for venlafaxine and one for escitalopram, provided data on use beyond 6 months) and no available follow-up data beyond end of treatment.

The benefits in terms of reducing the risk of non-response, non-remission and the mean anxiety rating score was similar for most antidepressants suggesting a small-to-moderate improvement in anxiety relative to placebo.

The harms were also relatively consistent across drugs. Discontinuation due to adverse events was greater than placebo for most antidepressants but particularly high for paroxetine, duloxetine and venlafaxine. Specific side effects such as nausea and insomnia were more common in people receiving antidepressants compared with placebo. Sexual problems were relatively rare but there was an increased risk associated with antidepressants.

8.2.5   Pregabalin versus placebo

Studies considered
A total of eight trials compared pregabalin with placebo. A summary of study characteristics can be found in Table 34 with full details in Appendix 15d, which also includes details of excluded studies.

Clinical evidence for pregabalin versus placebo
Evidence from the important outcomes and overall quality of evidence are presented in Table 35. The full GRADE profiles and associated forest plots can be found in Appendix 18c and Appendix 16c, respectively.

Table 32: Study information table for trials comparing antidepressants with placebo

	Escitalopram versus placebo	Sertraline versus placebo	Paroxetine versus placebo	Citalopram versus placebo	Duloxetine versus placebo	Venlafaxine versus placebo	Imipramine versus placebo
No. of trials (total participants)	6 RCTs (2136)	2 RCTs (706)	8 RCTs (2784)	1 RCT (34)	4 RCTs (1491)	12 RCTs (3470)	1 RCT (28)
Study ID	(1) ASTRAZENECA2007B (2) BALDWIN2006 (3) BOSE2008 (4) DAVIDSON 2004 (5) GOODMAN 2005 (6) LENZE2009	(1) ALLGULANDER2004 (2) BRAWMANMINTZER2006	(1) ASTRAZENECA2007A (2) BALDWIN 2006 (3) GSK2002 (4) GSK2005 (5) HEWETT2001 (6) POLLACK2001 (7) PFIZER2008 (8) RICKELS2003	LENZE2005	(1) HARTFORD 2007 (2) KOPONEN2007 (3) NICOLINI2009 (4) RYNN2008	(1) ALLGULANDER2001 (2) BOSE2008 (3) DAVIDSON 1999 (4) GELENBERG 2000 (5) HACKETT2003 (6) HARTFORD 2007 (7) KASPER2009 (8) LENOXSMITH 2003 (9) MONTGOMERY2006 (10) NICOLINI2009 (11) NIMATOUDIS 2004 (12) RICKELS 2000A	MCLEOD1992
N/% female (see Appendix 15d for data for individual studies)	2136/range 53–67%	706/range 55–58%	2784/range 55–70%	34/62%	1491/range 62–68%	3470/range 39%–68%	28/not reported
Mean age (years) (see Appendix 15d for data for individual studies)	45	41	41	69	43	42	41

Continued

183

Table 32: *(Continued)*

Diagnosis	(1) GAD by DSM-IV (2) GAD by DSM-IV-TR (3)-(6) GAD by DSM-IV	(1)-(2) GAD by DSM-IV	(1) GAD by DSM-IV (2) GAD by DSM-IV-TR (3)-(8) GAD by DSM-IV	GAD by DSM-IV	(1)-(4) GAD by DSM-IV	(1)-(10) GAD by DSM-IV (11) GAD by DSM-III-R (12) GAD by DSM-IV	GAD by DSM-III-R
Baseline severity (HAM-A): mean (SD)	(1) Not reported (2) Escitalopram 27.06 (4.46); placebo 27.1 (4.6) (3) Escitalopram 24.2 (SE = 0.4); placebo 23.7 (SE = 0.3) (4) Escitalopram 23.40 (4.40); placebo 23.2 (4.2) (5) Escitalopram 23.0 (0.2); placebo 22.7 (0.2) (6) Escitalopram 23.00 (2.30); placebo 23.1 (4.9)	(1) Sertraline 24.6 (4.6); placebo 25.0 (4.9) (2) Sertraline 24.5 (3.1); placebo 24.1 (2.8)	(1) Not reported (2) Paroxetine 27.06 (4.46); placebo 27.1 (4.6) (3) Paroxetine 24.5 (3.71); placebo 24.83 (3.64) (4) Not reported (5) Paroxetine 26.0 (0.4); placebo 25.9 (0.4) (6) Paroxetine 24.2 (0.30); placebo 24.1 (0.30) (7) Paroxetine 23.5 (3.3); placebo 24.0 (4.9) (8) Paroxetine 24.1 (3.6); placebo 24.4 (3.7)	Citalopram 24.1 (4.6); placebo 23.1 (3.8)	(1) Duloxetine 25.6 (5.8); placebo 25.0 (5.8) (2) Duloxetine 25.5 (7.3); placebo 25.8 (7.6) (3) Duloxetine 27.5 (7.3); placebo 27.3 (7.3) (4) Duloxetine 22.6 (7.4); placebo 23.5 (7.9)	(1) Venlafaxine 26.6 (range 20–44); placebo 26.7 (range 20–52) (2) Venlafaxine 23.8 (SE = 0.3); placebo 23.7 (SE = 0.3) (3) Venlafaxine 23.4 (4.1); placebo 23.7 (4.2) (4) Venlafaxine 25.0 (5.0); placebo 25.0 (5.0) (5) Venlafaxine 27.8 (not reported); placebo 27.6 (not reported) (6) Venlafaxine 25 (5.4); placebo 25.0 (5.8) (7) Venlafaxine 27.4 (SE = 0.4); placebo 26.8 (SE = 0.8) (8) Venlafaxine 28 (not reported); placebo 28 (not reported)	Imipramine 25.3 (4.0); placebo 25.1 (2.0)

184

							(9) Venlafaxine 26.8 (4.6); placebo 27.4 (5.5) (10) Venlafaxine 27.3 (7.6); placebo 27.3 (7.3) (11) Venlafaxine 27.8 (4.8); placebo 28.5 (6.4) (12) Venlafaxine 24.7 (4.4); placebo 24.1 (4.2)
Treatment length	Range 8 to 12 weeks	Range 10 to 12 weeks	Range 6 to 8 weeks	8 weeks	Range 9 to 10 weeks	Range 6 to 24 weeks	6 weeks
Follow-up	End of treatment	End of treatment	End of treatment	End of treatment	End of treatment	End of treatment	End of treatment

Table 33: Evidence summary table for trials of antidepressants versus placebo

	Escitalopram versus placebo	Sertraline versus placebo	Paroxetine versus placebo	Citalopram versus placebo	Duloxetine versus placebo	Venlafaxine versus placebo	Imipramine versus placebo
No. trials (total participants)	6 RCTs (N = 2136)	2 RCTs (N = 706)	8 RCTs (N = 2784)	1 RCT (N = 34)	4 RCTs (N = 1908)	12 RCTs (N = 3470)	1 RCT (N = 28)
Study ID	(1) ASTRAZEN-ECA2007B (2) BALDWIN2006 (3) BOSE2008 (4) DAVIDSON2004 (5) GOODMAN2005 (6) LENZE2009	(1) ALLGULAN-DER2004 (2) BRAWMAN-MINTZER2006	(1) ASTRAZEN-ECA 2007A (2) BALDWIN 2006 (3) GSK2002 (4) GSK2005 (5) HEWETT2001 (6) POLLACK2001 (7) PFIZER2008 (8) RICKELS2003	LENZE2005	(1) HARTFORD 2007 (2) KOPONEN2007 (3) NICOLINI2009 (4) RYNN2008	(1) ALLGULANDER 2001 (2) BOSE2008 (3) DAVIDSON1999 (4) GELENBERG 2000 (5) HACKETT2003 (6) HARTFORD 2007 (7) KASPER2009 (8) LENOXSMITH 2003 (9) MONTGOMERY 2006 (10) NICOLINI2009 (11) NIMATOUDIS 2004 (12) RICKELS2000A	MCLEOD1992
Benefits (end of treatment)							
HAM-A	SMD = −0.33 (−0.47, −0.19) MD = −2.36 (−3.28, −1.43) K = 4, N = 1512 Quality: high	SMD = −0.28 (−0.43, −0.13) MD = −2.46 (−4.53, −0.39) K = 2, N = 698 Quality: high	SMD = −0.23 (−0.32, −0.14) MD = −1.46 (−2.23, −0.69) K = 6, N = 1210 Quality: high	–	SMD = −0.41 (−0.56, −0.25) MD = −3.15 (−4.10, −2.21) K = 4, N = 1453 Quality: high	SMD = −0.50 (−0.77, −0.23) MD = −3.16 (−4.81, −1.51) K = 5, N = 1177 Quality: moderate	SMD = −0.49 (−1.24, 0.27) MD = −4.01 (−10.16, 1.96) K = 1, N = 28 Quality: low

Outcome							
Non-response (≤ 50% reduction in HAM-A)	RR = 0.78 (0.63, 0.97) K = 3, N = 1107 Quality: moderate	RR = 0.70 (0.57, 0.86) K = 2, N = 706 Quality: moderate	RR = 0.91 (0.73, 1.13) K = 3, N = 1074 Quality: low	RR = 0.46 (0.23, 0.93) K = 1, N = 34 Quality: moderate	RR = 0.75 (0.62, 0.90) K = 4, N = 1491 Quality: moderate	RR = 0.80 (0.71, 0.92) K = 8, N = 2224 Quality: moderate	–
Non-remission (≥7 on HAM-A)	RR = 0.93 (0.85, 1.02) K = 2, N = 699 Quality: moderate	RR = 0.85 (0.75, 0.95) K = 1, N = 378 Quality: moderate	RR = 0.87 (0.82, 0.92) K = 5, N = 2032 Quality: high	RR = 0.64 (0.39, 1.06) K = 1, N = 34 Quality: moderate	RR = 0.86 (0.75, 0.98) K = 4, N = 1491 Quality: low	RR = 0.83 (0.74, 0.94) K = 6, N = 1441 Quality: moderate	–
Harms (end of treatment)							
Discontinuation due to adverse events	RR = 1.72 (1.16, 2.53) K = 5, N = 1603 Quality: high	RR = 1.10 (0.63, 1.91) K = 2, N = 706 Quality: low	RR = 2.50 (1.81, 3.45) K = 8, N = 2784 Quality: high	RR = 3.00 (0.13, 68.84) K = 1, N = 34 Quality: moderate	RR = 3.12 (1.55, 6.31) K = 4, N = 1491 Quality: moderate	RR = 2.06 (1.59, 2.68) K = 10, N = 3180 Quality: high	–
Nausea	RR = 2.02 (1.45, 2.81) K = 3, N = 986 Quality: high	RR = 1.85 (1.35, 2.55) K = 2, N = 701 Quality: high	RR = 2.98 (2.33, 3.80) K = 7, N = 2304 Quality: moderate		RR = 4.54 (2.91, 7.10) K = 2, N = 840 Quality: high	RR = 2.76 (2.28, 3.34) K = 8, N = 2229 Quality: high	–
Sexual problems	RR = 13.17 (1.83, 94.89) K = 2, N = 723 Quality: moderate	RR = 15.41 (0.89, 267.81) K = 1, N = 373 Quality: moderate	RR = 7.22 (3.77, 13.83) K = 7, N = 2340 Quality: moderate		RR = 2.95 (1.20, 7.29) K = 2, N = 840 Quality: high	RR = 36.32 (7.76, 170.02) K = 3, N = 886 Quality: moderate	–
Insomnia	RR: 1.81 (1.07, 3.08) K = 2, N = 671 Quality: moderate	RR = 1.26 (0.90, 1.76) K = 2, N = 701 Quality: moderate	RR = 2.33 (1.35, 4.00) K = 4, N = 1091 Quality: moderate		RR = 2.46 (1.28, 4.76) K = 2, N = 840 Quality: high	RR = 1.56 (1.16, 2.09) K = 6, N = 1671 Quality: moderate	–

Note: RR <1 favours treatment and RR>1 favours placebo

Table 34: Study information table for trials comparing pregabalin with placebo

	Pregabalin versus placebo
No. trials (participants in the subgroup)	8 RCTs (2079)
Study ID	(1) FELTNER2003 (2) KASPER2009 (3) MONTGOMERY2008 (4) MONTGOMERY2006 (5) PANDE2003 (6) PFIZER2005 (7) POHL2005 (8) RICKELS2005
N/% female (see Appendix 15d for data for individual studies)	2136/range 52% to 76%
Mean age (years) (see Appendix 15d for data for individual studies)	45
Diagnosis	(1)-(8) GAD by DSM-IV
Baseline severity: mean (SD)	(1) HAM-A 24.9 (3.9) 50 mg; 25.4 (4.6) 200 mg; placebo 24.8 (4.1) (2) HAM-A 27.6 (SE = 0.4); placebo 26.8 (SE = 0.8) (3) HAM-A 27 (4.8); placebo 26 (4.1) (4) HAM-A 26.3 (4.4) 400 mg/day; 26.5 (4.6) 600 mg/day; placebo 27.4 (5.5) (5) HAM-A 22.35 (2.68) 150 mg; 23.16 (2.73) 600 mg; placebo 22.90 (3.88) (6) HAM-A 25.5, 150 mg; 24.4, 600 mg; placebo 23.9 (7) Not reported (8) HAM-A 25.0 (SE = 0.4) 300 mg; 24.6 (SE = 0.4) 450 mg; 25.2 (SE = 0.4) 600 mg; placebo 24.6 (SE = 0.4)
Treatment length	(1) 4 weeks (2)-(3) 8 weeks (4) 6 weeks (5)-(6) 4 weeks (7) 6 weeks (8) 4 weeks
Follow-up	End of treatment

Table 35: Evidence summary table for trials of pregabalin versus placebo

	Pregabalin versus placebo
No. trials (total participants)	8 RCTs (N = 2145)
Study ID	(1) FELTNER2003 (2) KASPER2009 (3) MONTGOMERY2008 (4) MONTGOMERY2006 (5) PANDE2003 (6) PFIZER2005 (7) POHL2005 (8) RICKELS2005
Benefits (end of treatment)	
HAM-A	SMD = −0.42 (−0.55, −0.29) MD = −2.97 (−3.70, −2.24) K = 5, N = 1296 Quality: high
Non-response (≤50% reduction in HAM-A)	RR = 0.79 (0.73, 0.85) K = 8, N = 2145 Quality: high
Non-remission (≥7 on HAM-A)	RR = 0.91 (0.87, 0.96) K = 6, N = 1896 Quality: high
Harms (end of treatment)	
Discontinuation due to adverse events	RR = 1.31 (0.99, 1.74) K = 8, N = 1145 Quality: high
Nausea	RR = 1.19 (0.85, 1.66) K = 6, N = 1532 Quality: moderate
Insomnia	RR = 0.70 (0.32, 1.54) K = 3, N = 765 Quality: moderate
Dizziness	RR = 3.36 (2.46, 4.58) K = 6, N = 1532 Quality: high
Fatigue	RR = 2.54 (0.92, 6.99) K = 1, N = 249 Quality: moderate

Clinical evidence summary
Pregabalin was associated with a moderate benefit in terms of mean anxiety rating scores and non-response. However, although there was statistically significant evidence of benefit in relation to non-remission, the effect size was small.

In terms of harms, there was a small borderline statistically significant increase in the risk of discontinuation due to adverse events. For specific side effects, there was a different pattern from that found for antidepressants. There was no statistically significant increase in risk of experiencing nausea or insomnia. In addition, sexual problems were not reported as frequent side effects in any of the studies. However, there were large increases in risk of dizziness and fatigue (although for the latter this was not statistically significant).

8.2.6 Benzodiazepines versus placebo

Study characteristics
A total of four trials compared benzodiazepines with placebo. A summary of study characteristics can be found in Table 36 with full details in Appendix 15d, which also includes details of excluded studies.

Clinical evidence for benzodiazepines versus placebo
Evidence from the important outcomes and overall quality of evidence are presented in Table 37. The full GRADE profiles and associated forest plots can be found in Appendix 18c and Appendix 16c, respectively.

Clinical evidence summary
The evidence base for benzodiazepines was much smaller than for antidepressants and pregabalin reported above. There were inconsistent effects for most outcomes. On the mean anxiety rating score there were small-to-moderate benefits found but the effect for diazepam was not statistically significant. On non-response there was a moderate reduction for diazepam but no statistically significant effects were identified for lorazepam and alprazolam. For non-remission, no data was found for diazepam and there were no statistically significant effects for lorazepam or alprazolam.

There was inconsistent reporting of harms, therefore the data on side effects is relatively limited. There was no statistically significant increase in risk of discontinuation for diazepam and alprazolam but there was a higher risk in lorazepam. Increased risk of experiencing sexual problems was found for diazepam but this was not reported for the other drugs. There was an increased risk of dizziness for diazepam, lorazepam and alprazolam.

8.2.7 Buspirone versus placebo

Studies considered
There were a total of five trials comparing buspirone with placebo. A summary of study characteristics can be found in Table 38 with full details in Appendix 15d which also includes details of excluded studies.

Table 36: Study information table for trials comparing benzodiazepines with placebo

	Diazepam versus placebo	Alprazolam versus placebo	Lorazepam versus placebo
No. trials (total participants)	4 RCTs (529)	4 RCTs (544)	4 RCTs (515)
Study ID	(1) ANDREATINI2002 (2) ANSSEAU1991 (3) HACKETT2003 (4) RICKELS2000B	(1) LYDIARD1997 (2) MCLEOD1992 (3) MOLLER2001 (4) RICKELS2005	(1) FELTNER2003 (2) FRESQUET2000 (3) PANDE2003 (4) PFIZER2008
N/ (% of female) (see Appendix 15d for data for individual studies)	529/range 53–68%	544/range 54–67%	515/ range 53 - 59%
Mean age (years) (see Appendix 15d for data for individual studies)	42	43	37
Diagnosis	(1)-(2) GAD by DSM-III-R (3) GAD by DSM-IV (4) GAD by DSM-III-R	(1) GAD by DSM-III-R (2) GAD by DSM-IV (3) GAD by ICD-10 (4) GAD by DSM-IV	(1)-(4) GAD by DSM-IV

Continued

191

Table 36: (*Continued*)

	Diazepam versus placebo	Alprazolam versus placebo	Lorazepam versus placebo
Baseline severity: HAM-A: mean (SD)	(1) Diazepam 25.2 (4.5); placebo 25.1 (7.5) (2) Diazepam 29.9 (5.2); placebo 29.4 (5.7) (3) Diazepam 28.4 (not reported); placebo 27.9 (not reported) (4) Diazepam 24.0 (not reported); placebo 24.9 (not reported)	(1) Alprazolam 24.1 (not reported); placebo 24.8 (not reported) (2) Alprazolam 28.1 (4.3); placebo 25.1 (2.0) (3) Alprazolam 29.7 (7.6); placebo 29.3 (7.0) (4) Alprazolam 24.9 (SE 0.4); placebo 24.6 (SE 0.4)	(1) Lorazepam 24.7 (3.7); placebo 24.8 (4.1) (2) Lorazepam 21.5 (3.2); placebo 20.3 (1.7) (3) Lorazepam 23.85 (3.24); Placebo 22.90 (3.88) (4) Lorazepam 24.2 (3.6); placebo 24.0 (4.9)
Treatment length	(1)-(2) 4 weeks (3) 8 weeks (4) 6 weeks	(1) 4 weeks (2) 6 weeks (3)-(4) 4 weeks	(1) 4 weeks (2) 6 weeks (3)-(4) 4 weeks
Follow-up	End of treatment	End of treatment	End of treatment

Table 37: Evidence summary table for trials of benzodiazepines versus placebo

	Diazepam versus placebo	Alprazolam versus placebo	Lorazepam versus placebo
No. trials (total participants)	4 RCTs (N = 529)	4 RCTs (N = 544)	4 RCTs (N = 515)
Study ID	(1) ANDREATINI2002 (2) ANSSEAU2001 (3) HACKETT2003 (4) RICKELS2000B	(1) LYDIARD1997 (2) MCLEOD1992 (3) MOLLER2001 (4) RICKELS2005	(1) FELTNER2003 (2) FRESQUET2000 (3) PANDE2003 (4) PFIZER2008
Benefits (end of treatment)			
HAM-A	SMD = −0.21 (−1.01, 0.59) MD = −1.90 (−8.94, 5.14) K = 1, N = 24 Quality: moderate	SMD = −0.33 (−0.53, −0.14) MD = −2.53 (−3.90, −1.17) K = 3, N = 419 Quality: high	SMD = −0.53 (−0.83, −0.24) MD = −2.49 (−3.78, −1.20) K = 2, N = 185 Quality: high
Non-response (≤50% reduction in HAM-A)	RR = 0.67 (0.54, 0.84) K = 3, N = 505 Quality: high	RR = 0.87 (0.70, 1.08) K = 1, N = 184 Quality: moderate	RR = 0.84 (0.66, 1.07) K = 4, N = 453 Quality: low
Non-remission (≥7 on HAM-A)	-	RR = 0.89 (0.76, 1.03) K = 1, N = 184 Quality: moderate	RR = 0.90 (0.77, 1.05) K = 3, N = 406 Quality: low

Table 37: Evidence summary table for trials of benzodiazepines versus placebo

Harms (end of treatment)	Diazepam versus placebo	Alprazolam versus placebo	Lorazepam versus placebo
Discontinuation due to adverse events	RR = 1.67 (0.82, 3.39) K = 4, N = 529 Quality: moderate	RR = 1.30 (0.58, 2.95) K = 1, N = 184 Quality: moderate	RR = 4.04 (2.55, 6.38) K = 4, N = 515 Quality: high
Nausea	RR = 0.50 (0.20, 1.28) K = 1, N = 208 Quality: moderate	RR = 0.74 (0.36, 1.52) K = 3, N = 516 Quality: moderate	RR = 1.42 (0.82, 2.46) K = 4, N = 435 Quality: moderate
Sexual problems	RR = 11.00 (0.62, 196.43) K = 1, N = 208 Quality: moderate	–	–
Insomnia	–	RR = 0.59 (0.15, 2.37) K = 1, N = 125 Quality: moderate	RR = 2.21 (0.3, 16.32) K = 3, N = 300 Quality: very low
Fatigue	RR = 2.83 (1.16, 6.90) K = 1, N = 208 Quality: moderate	RR = 0.74 (0.17, 3.16) K = 1, N = 125 Quality: moderate	–
Dizziness	RR = 3.26 (1.22, 8.70) K = 2, N = 319 Quality: high	RR = 1.65 (0.95, 2.85) K = 3, N = 516 Quality: moderate	RR = 2.76 (1.54, 4.93) K = 4, N = 435 Quality: high

Note: RR <1 favours treatment and RR >1 favours placebo

Table 38: Study information table for trials comparing buspirone with placebo

	Buspirone versus placebo
No. trials (total participants)	5 RCTs (806)
Study ID	(1) DAVIDSON1999 (2) LADER1998 (3) MAJERCSIK2003 (4) POLLACK1997 (5) SRAMEK1996
N/% female (see Appendix 15d for data for individual studies)	806/range 0–70%
Mean age (years) (see Appendix 15d for data for individual studies)	39
Diagnosis	(1)-(3) GAD by DSM-IV (4)-(5) GAD by DSM-III-R
Baseline severity: HAM-A: mean (SD)	(1) Buspirone 23.8 (4.6); placebo 23.7 (4.2) (2) Buspirone 26.7 (4.1); placebo 26.2 (4.2) (3) Buspirone 19.45 (SE = 0.46); placebo 21.48 (SE = 0.47) (4) Buspirone 24.4; placebo 25.1 (5) Buspirone 24.9 (4.2); placebo 25.6 (4.4)
Treatment length	(1) 8 weeks (2) 4 weeks (3)-(5) 6 weeks
Follow-up	End of treatment

Clinical evidence for buspirone versus placebo
Evidence from the important outcomes and overall quality of evidence are presented in Table 39. The full GRADE profiles and associated forest plots can be found in Appendix 18c and Appendix 16c, respectively.

Clinical evidence summary
There was a small benefit associated with buspirone on both the mean anxiety rating score and non-response. However, no data was reported on non-remission therefore it is not possible to draw conclusions on this outcome.

There was greater risk of discontinuation due to adverse events associated with buspirone. There was a higher risk of experiencing nausea and dizziness compared with placebo.

Table 39: Evidence summary table for trials of buspirone versus placebo

	Buspirone versus placebo
No. trials (total participants)	5 RCTs (N = 806)
Study ID	(1) DAVIDSON1999 (2) LADER1998 (3) MAJERCSIK2003 (4) POLLACK1997 (5) SRAMEK1996
Benefits (end of treatment)	
HAM-A	SMD = −0.27 (−0.48, −0.06) MD = −1.93 (−3.04, −0.82) K = 4, N = 519 Quality: high
Non-response (≤ 50% reduction in HAM-A)	RR = 0.87 (0.74, 1.01) K = 2, N = 365 Quality: moderate
Non-remission (≥7 on HAM-A)	–
Harms (end of treatment)	
Discontinuation due to adverse events	RR = 2.02 (1.12, 3.67) K = 3, N = 591 Quality: high
Nausea	RR = 2.34 (1.53, 3.58) K = 2, N = 364 Quality: high
Insomnia	RR = 1.46 (0.59, 3.66) K = 1, N = 162 Quality: moderate
Dizziness	RR = 3.68 (2.66, 5.08) K = 4, N = 754 Quality: high

8.2.8   Hydroxyzine versus placebo

Studies considered
A total of three trials compared hydroxyzine with placebo. A summary of study characteristics can be found in Table 40 with full details in Appendix 15d, which also includes details of excluded studies.

Clinical evidence for hydroxyzine versus placebo
Evidence from the important outcomes and overall quality of evidence are presented in Table 41. The full GRADE profiles and associated forest plots can be found in Appendix 18c and Appendix 16c, respectively.

Clinical evidence summary
There was inconsistent reporting of data on hydroxyzine therefore it is difficult to draw conclusions concerning the harms and benefits of this drug. The mean anxiety rating score suggested a moderate reduction in anxiety. However, most studies did not

Table 40: Study information table for trials comparing hydroxyzine with placebo

	Hydroxyzine versus placebo
No. trials (total participants)	3 RCTs (482)
Study ID	(1) DARCIS1995 (2) LADER1998 (3) LLORCA2002
N/% female (see Appendix 15d for data for individual studies)	482/range 56–70%
Mean age (years) (see Appendix 15d for data for individual studies)	43
Diagnosis	(1) GAD by DSM-III-R (2)-(3) GAD by DSM-IV
Baseline severity (HAM-A): mean (SD)	(1) Hydroxyzine 25.9 (4.2); placebo 24.1 (2) Hydroxyzine 26.6 (4.3); placebo 26.2 (4.2) (3) Hydroxyzine 25.49 (3.61); placebo 25.73 (4.14)
Treatment length	(1)-(2) 4 weeks (3) 12 weeks
Follow-up	End of treatment

Table 41: Evidence summary table for trials of hydroxyzine versus placebo

	Hydroxyzine versus placebo
No. trials (total participants)	3 RCTs (N = 482)
Study ID	(1) DARCIS1995 (2) LADER1998 (3) LLORCA2002
Benefits (end of treatment)	
HAM-A	SMD = −0.45 (−0.64, −0.27) MD = −3.51 (−4.91, −2.11) K = 3, N = 482 Quality: high
Non-response (≤ 50% reduction in HAM-A)	RR = 0.81 (0.64, 1.02) K = 1, N = 162 Quality: moderate
Harms (end of treatment)	
Discontinuation due to adverse events	RR = 1.48 (0.48, 4.60) K = 2, N = 328 Quality: moderate

report data in sufficient detail on non-response and non-remission. There were also very little data on discontinuation or reporting of specific side effects.

8.2.9   Quetiapine versus placebo

Studies considered
A total of four trials compared quetiapine with placebo. A summary of study characteristics can be found in Table 42 with full details in Appendix 15d, which also includes details of excluded studies.

Clinical evidence for quetiapine versus placebo
Evidence from the important outcomes and overall quality of evidence are presented in Table 43. The full GRADE profiles and associated forest plots can be found in Appendix 18c and Appendix 16c respectively.

Table 42: Study information table for trials comparing quetiapine with placebo

	Quetiapine (50 mg) versus placebo	Quetiapine (150 mg) versus placebo	Quetiapine (300 mg) versus placebo	Quetiapine (flexible dose) versus placebo
No. trials (total participants)	2 RCTs (907)	3 RCTs (1345)	2 RCTs (898)	1 RCT (450)
Study ID	(1) ASTRAZENECA 2007A (2) ASTRAZENECA 2007C	(1) ASTRAZENECA 2007A (2) ASTRAZENECA 2007B (3) ASTRAZENECA 2007C	(1) ASTRAZENECA 2007B (2) ASTRAZENECA 2007C	ASTRAZENECA 2008
N/% of female	(1) 873/65% (2) Not reported	(1) 873/65% (2)–(3) Not reported	(1)–(2) Not reported	450/57%
Mean age (years) (see Appendix 15d for data for individual studies)	41	40	39	70
Diagnosis	(1)-(2) GAD by DSM-IV	(1)-(3) GAD by DSM-IV	(1)-(2) GAD by DSM-IV	GAD by DSM-IV
Baseline severity	Not reported	Not reported	Not reported	Not reported
Treatment length	8 weeks	8 weeks	8 weeks	9 weeks
Follow-up	End of treatment	End of treatment	End of treatment	End of treatment

Table 43: Evidence summary table for trials of quetiapine versus placebo

	Quetiapine (50 mg) versus placebo	Quetiapine (150 mg) versus placebo	Quetiapine (300 mg) versus placebo	Quetiapine (flexible dose) versus placebo
No. trials (total participants)	2 RCTs (N = 907)	3 RCTs (N = 1345)	2 RCTs (N = 898)	1 RCT (N = 450)
Study ID	(1) ASTRAZENECA2007A (2) ASTRAZENECA2007C	(1) ASTRAZENECA2007A (2) ASTRAZENECA2007B (3) ASTRAZENECA2007C	(1) ASTRAZENECA2007B (2) ASTRAZENECA2007C	ASTRAZENECA2008
Benefits (end of treatment)				
Non-response (<50% reduction in HAM-A)	RR 0.82 (0.71, 0.95) K = 2, N = 907 Quality: high	RR 0.73 (0.62, 0.85) K = 3, N = 1345 Quality: high	RR 0.92 (0.81, 1.05) K = 2, N = 898 Quality: moderate	RR 0.42 (0.34, 0.51) K = 1, N = 450 Quality: high
Non-remission (<7 on HAM-A)	RR 0.92 (0.84, 1.00) K = 2, N = 907 Quality: moderate	RR 0.86 (0.79, 0.92) K = 3, N = 1345 Quality: high	RR 1.00 (0.92, 1.08) K = 2, N = 898 Quality: moderate	RR 0.69 (0.61, 0.78) K = 1, N = 450 Quality: high
Harms (end of treatment)				
Discontinuation due to adverse events	RR 2.62 (1.68, 4.07) K = 2, N = 907 Quality: high	RR 2.97 (2.11, 4.18) K = 3, N = 1345 Quality: high	RR 3.69 (2.54, 5.37) K = 2, N = 898 Quality: moderate	RR 4.07 (1.16, 14.23) K = 1, N = 450 Quality: moderate

Clinical evidence summary
A review of the clinical efficacy of quetiapine is included in a forthcoming NICE Technology Appraisal and therefore is not assessed in this guideline. The data is to inform the network-analysis only (see section 8.8.3).

8.3 HEAD-TO-HEAD TRIALS OF PHARMACOLOGICAL INTERVENTIONS

8.3.1 Antidepressants versus other antidepressants

Studies considered
There were a total of six trials comparing antidepressants with other antidepressants. A summary of study characteristics can be found in Table 44 with full details in Appendix 15d, which also includes details of excluded studies.

Clinical evidence for antidepressants versus other antidepressants
Evidence from the important outcomes and overall quality of evidence are presented in Table 45. The full GRADE profiles and associated forest plots can be found in Appendix 18c and Appendix 16c, respectively.

Clinical evidence summary
There was a small statistically significant effect in favour of escitalopram compared with paroxetine based on a reduction in HAM-A scores. In addition, there was a 40% reduction in risk of non-response for escitalopram compared with paroxetine. Moreover, there was greater risk (although not statistically significant) of discontinuation of treatment due to adverse events associated with paroxetine.

There were no differences found on reduction of anxiety symptoms between escitalopram and venlafaxine. However, venlafaxine was associated with a greater risk of discontinuation (although this was not statistically significant).

No difference was found between duloxetine and venlafaxine for reduction in anxiety but there was a greater risk of discontinuation for venlafaxine (although again this was not statistically significant)

There were no statistically significant differences found between paroxetine and sertraline on any outcomes. However, this was based on a small trial that was unlikely to have sufficient power to identify any differences.

8.3.2 Antidepressants versus other pharmacological interventions

Studies considered
There were a total of six trials comparing antidepressants with other pharmacological interventions. A summary of study characteristics can be found in Table 46 with full details in Appendix 15d, which also includes details of excluded studies.

Table 44: Study information table for trials comparing antidepressants with other antidepressants

	Escitalopram versus paroxetine	Sertraline versus paroxetine	Escitalopram versus venlafaxine	Duloxetine versus venlafaxine
No. trials (total participants)	2 RCTs (523)	1 RCT (55)	1 RCT (264)	2 RCTs (653)
Study ID	(1) BALDWIN2006 (2) BIELSKI2005	BALL2005	BOSE2008	(1) HARTFORD2007 (2) NICOLINI2009
N/% female (see Appendix 15d for data for individual studies)	523/range 37 to 64%	55/75%	264/62%	653/63%
Mean age (years) (see Appendix 15d for data for individual studies)	39	39	38	42
Diagnosis	GAD by DSM-IV	GAD by DSM-IV	GAD by DSM-IV	GAD by DSM-IV
Baseline severity (HAM-A); mean (SD)	(1) Escitalopram 27.04 (4.46); paroxetine 27.3 (4.2) (2) Escitalopram 23.7 (SE = 0.5); paroxetine 23.4 (SE = 0.4)	Paroxetine 20.8 (2.3); sertraline 21.4 (3.4)	Escitalopram 24.2 (SE = 0.4); venlafaxine 23.8 (SE = 0.3)	(1) Duloxetine 25.6 (5.8); venlafaxine 24.9 (5.4) (2) Duloxetine 27.74 (7.32); venlafaxine 27.36 (7.57)
Treatment length	(1) 12 weeks (2) 24 weeks	8 weeks	8 weeks	(1)–(2) 10 weeks
Follow-up	End of treatment	End of treatment	End of treatment	End of treatment

Table 45: Evidence summary table for trials of antidepressants versus other antidepressants

	Escitalopram versus paroxetine	Sertraline versus paroxetine	Escitalopram versus venlafaxine	Duloxetine versus venlafaxine
No. trials (total participants)	2 RCTs (N = 523)	1 RCT (N = 55)	1 RCT (N = 404)	2 RCTs (N = 653)
Study ID	(1) BALDWIN2006 (2) BIELSKI2005	BALL2005	BOSE2008	(1) HARTFORD2007 (2) NICOLINI2009
Benefits (end of treatment)				
HAM-A	SMD −0.32 (−0.50, −0.14) MD −1.66 (−2.59, −0.73) K = 2, N = 523 Quality: high	–	–	SMD 0.03 (−0.13, 0.18) MD 0.20 (−0.92, 1.32) K = 2, N = 653 Quality: moderate
Non-response	RR 0.60 (0.45, 0.81) K = 1, N = 409 Quality: high	RR 0.81 (0.39, 1.70) K = 1, N = 53 Quality: moderate	RR 0.98 (0.77, 1.26) K = 1, N = 264 Quality: moderate	RR 1.04 (0.78, 1.39) K = 2, N = 653 Quality: low
Non-remission	–	RR 1.12 (0.70, 1.79) K = 1, N = 53 Quality: moderate	RR 0.99 (0.85, 1.16) K = 1, N = 264 Quality: moderate	RR 1.07 (0.94, 1.21) K = 2, N = 653 Quality: moderate
Quality of life	–	–	–	SMD 0.02 (−0.13, 0.18) MD 0.18 (−0.83, 1.20) K = 2, N = 653 Quality: moderate
Harms (end of treatment)				
Discontinuation due to adverse events	RR 0.88 (0.46, 1.69) K = 1, N = 409 Quality: moderate	–	RR 0.54 (0.25, 1.16) K = 1, N = 264 Quality: moderate	RR 1.18 (0.78, 1.77) K = 2, N = 653 Quality: moderate
Diarrhoea	RR 1.13 (0.59, 2.17) K = 1, N = 409 Quality: moderate	–	–	RR 1.86 (0.95, 3.62) K = 1, N = 326 Quality: moderate
Sexual problems	RR 0.57 (0.25, 1.32) K = 1, N = 409 Quality: moderate	–	–	–
Anxiety	RR 0.52 (0.19, 1.45) K = 1, N = 409 Quality: moderate	–	–	–

Table 46: Study information table for trials comparing antidepressants with other pharmacological interventions

	Venlafaxine versus pregabalin	Venlafaxine versus buspirone	Venlafaxine versus diazepam	Quetiapine (50 mg and 150 mg) versus paroxetine	Quetiapine (150 mg and 300 mg) versus escitalopram
No. trials (total participants)	2 RCTs (566)	1 RCT (301)	1 RCT (459)	1 RCT (441)	1 RCT (432)
Study ID	(1) KASPER2009 (2) MONTGOMERY2006	DAVIDSON1999	HACKETT2003	ASTRAZENECA2007A	ASTRAZENECA2007B
N/female % (see Appendix 15d for data for individual studies)	566/Range 61–62%	301/39%	459/68%	441/65%	432/not reported
Mean age (years) (see Appendix 15d for data for individual studies)	43	38	44	41	38
Diagnosis	(1)–(2) GAD by DSM-IV	GAD by DSM-IV	GAD by DSM-IV	GAD by DSM-IV	GAD by DSM-IV
Baseline severity (HAM-A): mean (SD)	(1) Venlafaxine 27.4 (SE = 0.4); pregabalin 27.6 (SE = 0.4) (2) Venlafaxine 26.0 (4.6); pregabalin 26.3 (4.4)	Venlafaxine 23.6 (4.1); buspirone 23.8 (4.6)	Venlafaxine 27.9 (not reported); diazepam28.4 (not reported)	Not reported	Not reported
Treatment length	(1) 8 weeks (2) 6 weeks	8 weeks	10 weeks	8 weeks	8 weeks
Follow-up	End of treatment	End of treatment	End of treatment	End of treatment	End of treatment

Clinical evidence for antidepressants versus other pharmacological interventions
Evidence from the important outcomes and overall quality of evidence are presented
in Table 47. Data for quetiapine, which is considered in the network meta-analysis,
are reported in the same table. The full GRADE profiles and associated forest plots
can be found in Appendix 18c and Appendix 16c, respectively.

Clinical evidence summary
Similar to the data in Section 8.3.1, there was limited data concerning comparisons
between active interventions. There were no statistically significant differences in
reduction in anxiety for venlafaxine in comparison with pregabalin, buspirone or
diazepam. However there was an increased risk of discontinuation due to adverse
events for venlafaxine compared with these drugs.

**8.3.3   Head-to-head comparisons of pharmacological interventions other
than antidepressants**

Studies considered
There were a total of six head-to-head trials of pharmacological interventions
other than antidepressants. A summary of study characteristics can be found in
Table 48 with full details in Appendix 15d, which also includes details of excluded
studies.

*Clinical evidence for head-to-head trials of pharmacological interventions other than
antidepressants*
Evidence from the important outcomes and overall quality of evidence are presented
in Table 49. The full GRADE profiles and associated forest plots can be found in
Appendix 18c and Appendix 16c, respectively.

Clinical evidence summary
As above, there was a lack of head-to-head comparisons. There were borderline
statistically significant effects favouring pregabalin over lorazepam and alprazolam in
reduction of anxiety. In addition, pregabalin was associated with a reduced risk of
discontinuation due to adverse events compared with lorazepam. However, both
lorazepam and alprazolam were less likely to be associated with reporting dizziness
as a side effect.

There was a small but not statistically significant difference in favour of hydroxyzine compared with buspirone based on a reduction in HAM-A scores. In addition,
no statistically significant differences were found between buspirone and
lorazepam.

Table 47: Evidence summary table for trials of antidepressants versus other pharmacological interventions

	Venlafaxine versus pregabalin	Venlafaxine versus buspirone	Venlafaxine versus diazepam	Quetiapine versus paroxetine	Quetiapine versus escitalopram
No. trials (total participants)	2 RCTs (N = 566)	1 RCT (N = 301)	1 RCT (N = 459)	1 RCT (N = 441)	1 RCT (N = 432)
Study ID	(1) KASPER2009 (2) MONTGOMERY2006	DAVIDSON1999	HACKETT2003	ASTRAZENECA2007A	ASTRAZENECA2007B
Benefits					
HAM-A	SMD 0.19 (−0.12, 0.50) MD = 1.35 (−0.82, 3.53) K = 2, N = 550 Quality: moderate	–	–	–	–
Non-response	RR 1.12 (0.76, 1.64) K = 2, N = 566 Quality: low	RR 1.02 (0.82, 1.26) K = 1, N = 301 Quality: moderate	RR 1.05 (0.81, 1.36) K = 1, N = 459 Quality: moderate	Quetiapine (50 mg) versus paroxetine: RR 0.92 (0.72, 1.18) K = 1, N = 441 Quality: moderate Quetiapine (150 mg) versus paroxetine: RR 1.17 (0.89, 1.54) K = 1, N = 435 Quality: moderate	Quetiapine (150 mg) versus escitalopram: RR 1.18 (0.94, 1.47) K = 1, N = 432 Quality: moderate Quetiapine (300 mg) versus escitalopram: RR 0.95 (0.77, 1.16) K = 1, N = 420 Quality: moderate
Non-remission	RR 0.99 (0.84, 1.17) K = 1, N = 320 Quality: moderate	–	–	Quetiapine (50 mg) versus paroxetine: RR 0.91 (0.79, 1.04) K = 1, N = 441 Quality: moderate Quetiapine (150 mg) versus paroxetine: RR 0.91 (0.79, 1.04) K = 1, N = 435 Quality: moderate	Quetiapine (150 mg) versus escitalopram: RR 1.09 (0.96, 1.25) K = 1, N = 432 Quality: moderate Quetiapine (300 mg) versus escitalopram: RR 0.97 (0.85, 1.09) K = 1, N = 420 Quality: moderate

Quality of life	SMD = -0.09 (-0.34, 0.16) MD = -1.20 (-4.53, 2.13) K = 1, N = 246 Quality: moderate	-	-	-	-
Harms					
Discontinuation due to adverse events	RR 1.72 (1.15, 2.58) K = 2, N = 566 Quality: high	RR 1.61 (0.95, 2.72) K = 1, N = 301 Quality: moderate	RR 4.81 (1.18, 19.53) K = 1, N = 459 Quality: moderate	Quetiapine (50 mg) versus paroxetine: RR 0.67 (0.37, 1.19) K = 1, N = 441 Quality: moderate Quetiapine (150 mg) versus paroxetine: RR 0.49 (0.28, 0.84) K = 1, N = 435 Quality: high	Quetiapine (150 mg) versus escitalopram: RR 0.55 (0.34, 0.91) K = 1, N = 432 Quality: moderate Quetiapine (300 mg) versus escitalopram: RR 0.39 (0.24, 0.62) K = 1, N = 420 Quality: high
Dizziness	RR 0.49 (0.32, 0.74) K = 2, N = 566 Quality: high	RR 0.40 (0.28, 0.57) K = 1, N = 301 Quality: high	-	-	-
Insomnia	RR 2.80 (1.31, 6.01) K = 2, N = 566 Quality: high	-	-	-	-
Somnolence	RR = 0.36 (0.18, 0.72) K = 2, N = 566 Quality: high	-	-	-	-
Nausea	-	RR 1.30 (0.91, 1.85) K = 1, N = 301 Quality: moderate	-	-	-

Table 48: Study information table for head-to-head comparisons of pharmacological interventions other than antidepressants

	Hydroxyzine versus buspirone	Buspirone versus lorazepam	Pregabalin versus lorazepam	Pregabalin versus alprazolam
No. trials (total participants)	1 RCT (163)	1 RCT (43)	3 RCTs (610)	1 RCT (363)
Study ID	LADER1998	BOURIN1995	(1) FELTNER2003 (2) PANDE2003 (3) PFIZER2005	RICKELS2005
N/% female (see Appendix 15d for data for individual studies)	163/70%	43/68%	610/range 53–59%	363/64%
Mean age (years) (see Appendix 15d for data for individual studies)	41	Not reported	37	39
Diagnosis	GAD by DSM-IV	GAD by DSM-III-R	GAD by DSM-IV	GAD by DSM-IV
Baseline severity (HAM-A): mean (SD)	Hydroxyzine 26.6 (4.3); buspirone 26.7 (4.1)	Buspirone 26.74 (1.89); lorazepam 27.55 (1.84)	(1) Pregabalin 25.2 (4.6); lorazepam 24.7 (3.7) (2) Pregabalin 22.75 (2.68); lorazepam 23.85 (3.24) (3) Pregabalin 25.0 (not reported); lorazepam 24.3 (not reported)	Pregabalin 24.9 (SE = 0.4); alprazolam 24.9 (SE = 0.4)
Treatment length	4 weeks	8 weeks	4 weeks	4 weeks
Follow-up	End of treatment	End of treatment	End of treatment	End of treatment

Table 49: Evidence summary table for head-to-head comparisons of pharmacological interventions other than antidepressants

	Hydroxyzine versus buspirone	Buspirone versus lorazepam	Pregabalin versus lorazepam	Pregabalin versus alprazolam
No. trials (total participants)	1 RCT (N = 163)	1 RCT (N = 43)	3 RCTs (N = 610)	1 RCT (N = 363)
Study ID	LADER1988	BOURIN1995	(1) FELTNER2003 (2) PANDE2003 (3) PFIZER2005	RICKELS2005
Benefits (end of treatment)				
HAM-A	SMD −0.26 (−0.57, 0.05) MD −2.00 (−4.35, 0.35) K = 1, N = 163 Quality: moderate	SMD −0.29 (−0.89, 0.32) MD −2.14 (−6.64, 2.36) K = 1, N = 43 Quality: moderate	SMD −0.31 (−0.65, 0.03) MD −1.55 (−3.22, 0.12) K = 1, N = 134 Quality: moderate	SMD −0.09 (−0.33, 0.15) MD −0.77 (−2.36, 0.82) K = 1, N = 349 Quality: moderate
Non-response	–	–	RR 1.04 (0.76, 1.44) K = 3, N = 610 Quality: low	RR 0.81 (0.66, 1.00) K = 1, N = 363 Quality: moderate
Non-remission	–	–	RR 1.05 (0.95, 1.15) K = 3, N = 610 Quality: high	RR 1.01 (0.88, 1.16) K = 1, N = 363 Quality: high
Harms (end of treatment)				
Discontinuation due to adverse events	–	–	RR 0.42 (0.31, 0.56) K = 3, N = 610 Quality: high	RR 0.63 (0.33, 1.23) K = 1, N = 363 Quality: moderate
At least one side effect	RR 1.05 (0.71, 1.54) K = 1, N = 163 Quality: moderate	–	–	–
Dizziness	–	–	RR 1.85 (1.18, 2.91) K = 2, N = 341 Quality: moderate	RR 2.36 (1.42, 3.93) K = 1, N = 363 Quality: high
Somnolence	–	–	RR 0.62 (0.35, 1.11) K = 2, N = 341 Quality: low	RR 0.86 (0.64, 1.14) K = 1, N = 363 Quality: moderate

8.4 EFFECTS OF DOSE

8.4.1 Venlafaxine

Studies considered
There were four trials on venlafaxine comparing different doses. A summary of study characteristics can be found in Table 50 with full details in Appendix 15d, which also includes details of excluded studies.

Doses used in studies of venlafaxine ranged from a mean of 37.5 mg to 225 mg but there was limited data for most comparisons. The most common comparison was of 75 mg versus 150 mg.

Clinical evidence for venlafaxine comparing different doses
Evidence from the important outcomes and overall quality of evidence are presented in Table 51. The full GRADE profiles and associated forest plots can be found in Appendix 18c and Appendix 16c, respectively.

Clinical evidence summary
There were no statistically significant differences between 37.5 mg and 75 mg of venlafaxine for discontinuation due to adverse events and dizziness. However, with 37.5 mg compared with 75 mg, there was a 35% reduction in the risk of nausea. There was a borderline statistically significant difference on mean HAM-A score in favour of 75 mg in comparison with 150 mg of venlafaxine based on a reduction in HAM-A scores (SMD -0.27; CI -0.57 to 0.03) and a reduction in the risk of side effects such as nausea (RR $= 0.82$; CI 0.68 to 0.98) and insomnia (RR $= 0.59$; CI 0.34 to 1.01). There were no statistically significant differences in regards to a reduction in the risk of non-response, in discontinuation for any reason and side effects such as nervousness, dizziness and asthenia.

There were no statistically significant differences between 150 mg and 255 mg for risk of side effects such as insomnia, nervousness, asthenia and dizziness.

8.4.2 Selective serotonin reuptake inhibitors

Studies considered
There were limited studies (only two trials) comparing doses for SSRIs. Comparisons could only be made for escitalopram and paroxetine, with just one study found for each drug. A summary of study characteristics can be found in Table 52 with full details in Appendix 15d, which also includes details of excluded studies.

Clinical evidence for selective serotonin reuptake inhibitors comparing different doses
Evidence from the important outcomes and overall quality of evidence are presented in Table 53. The full GRADE profiles and associated forest plots can be found in Appendix 18c and Appendix 16c, respectively.

Table 50: Study information table for trials of venlafaxine comparing different doses

	Venlafaxine 37.5 mg versus 75 mg	Venlafaxine 75 mg versus 150 mg	Venlafaxine 150 mg versus 225 mg
No. trials (participants)	1 RCT (n = 268)	4 RCTs (N = 1027)	1 RCT (N = 181)
Study ID	ALLGULANDER2001	(1) ALLGULANDER2001 (2) DAVIDSON1999 (3) HACKETT2003 (4) RICKELS2000A	RICKELS2000A
N/female% (see Appendix 15d for data for individual studies)	275/65%	1027/range 38–67%	181/53%
Mean age (years) (see Appendix 15d for data for individual studies)	45	41	41
Diagnosis	GAD by DSM-IV	(1)–(4) GAD by DSM-IV	GAD by DSM-IV
Baseline severity (HAM-A): mean (SD)	HAM-A: Venlafaxine 37.5 mg 26.6 (range 20–44); 75 mg 26.3 (range 20–43)	(1) HRS-A: Venlafaxine 75 mg 26.3 (range 20–43); 150 mg 26.3 (range 17–38) (2) Venlafaxine 75 mg 23.7 (4.1); 150 mg 23.0 (4.6) (3) Venlafaxine 75 mg 27.9 (not reported); 150 mg 27.9 (not reported) (4) Venlafaxine 75 mg 24.7 (4.4); 150 mg 24.5 (4.1)	Venlafaxine 150 mg 24.5 (4.1); 225 mg 23.6 (3.7)
Treatment length	24 weeks	(1) 24 weeks (2)–(4) 8 weeks	8 weeks
Follow-up	End of treatment	End of treatment	End of treatment

Continued

211

Table 51: Evidence summary table for trials of venlafaxine comparing different doses

	Venlafaxine 37.5 mg versus 75 mg	Venlafaxine 75 mg versus 150 mg	Venlafaxine 150 mg versus 225 mg
No. trials (total participants)	1 RCT (268)	4 RCTs (1,027)	1 RCT (181)
Study ID	ALLGULANDER2001	(1) ALLGULANDER2001 (2) DAVIDSON1999 (3) HACKETT2003 (4) RICKELS2000A	RICKELS2000A
Benefits (end of treatment)			
HAM-A	–	SMD = −0.27 (−0.57, 0.03) MD = −1.50 (−3.15, 0.15) K = 1, N = 174 Quality: moderate	–
Non-response (≤50% reduction in HAM-A)	–	RR = 0.93 (0.78, 1.12) K = 2, N = 546 Quality: moderate	–
Harms (end of treatment)			
Discontinuation due to adverse events	RR = 0.61 (0.30, 1.26) K = 1, N = 275 Quality: moderate	RR = 0.85 (0.55, 1.32) K = 2, N = 641 Quality: moderate	–
Nausea	RR = 0.65 (0.44, 0.95) K = 1, N = 274 Quality: high	RR = 0.82 (0.68, 0.98) K = 3, N = 657 Quality: high	RR = 1.08 (0.80, 1.46) K = 1, N = 181 Quality: moderate
Insomnia	–	RR = 0.59 (0.34, 1.01) K = 1, N = 183 Quality: high	RR = 0.95 (0.61, 1.48) K = 1, N = 181 Quality: moderate
Nervousness	–	RR = 0.62 (0.30, 1.29) K = 1, N = 183 Quality: moderate	RR = 1.76 (0.82, 3.77) K = 1, N = 181 Quality: moderate
Dizziness	RR = 0.69 (0.42, 1.15) K = 1, N = 274 Quality: moderate	RR = 0.82 (0.56, 1.20) K = 3, N = 657 Quality: moderate	RR = 1.16 (0.65-2.07) K = 1, N = 181 Quality: high
Asthenia	–	RR = 0.70 (0.43, 1.13) K = 2, N = 386 Quality: moderate	RR = 0.62 (0.32, 1.21) K = 1, N = 181 Quality: moderate

Clinical evidence summary

There were borderline statistically significant effects in the reduction of anxiety in favour of 10 mg of escitalopram compared with 5 mg based on mean HAM-A scores. There was no significant difference between the two groups regarding side effects

Table 52: Study information table for trials of SSRIs comparing different doses

	Escitalopram 5 mg versus 10 mg	Escitalopram 10 mg versus 20 mg	Paroxetine 20 mg versus 40 mg
No. trials (total participants)	1 RCT (N = 270)	1 RCT (N = 269)	1 RCT (N = 386)
Study ID	BALDWIN2006	BALDWIN2006	RICKELS2003
N/% female	270/64%	269/64%	386/55%
Mean age (years)	41	41	40
Diagnosis	GAD by DSM-IV-TR	GAD by DSM-IV-TR	GAD by DSM-IV
Baseline severity (HAM-A): mean (SD)	Escitalopram 5 mg 27.1 (4.5); 10 mg 26.0 (4.1)	Escitalopram 10 mg 26.0 (4.1); 20 mg 27.7 (4.9)	Paroxetine 20 mg 24.1 (3.6); 40 mg 23.8 (3.4)
Treatment length	12 weeks	12 weeks	9 weeks
Follow-up	End of treatment	End of treatment	End of treatment

with the exception of a reduction in the risk of reported headache with 5 mg compared with 10 mg of escitalopram. There was a reduced risk of reported headaches in the 20 mg group compared with the 10 mg escitalopram group.

There were no clear differences on outcomes between 20 mg and 40 mg of paroxetine.

8.4.3   Duloxetine

Studies considered
There were two trials on duloxetine comparing different doses. A summary of study characteristics can be found in Table 54 with full details in Appendix 15d, which also includes details of excluded studies.

Doses used in the studies ranged from a mean of 20 mg to a mean of 120 mg. Results were similar as those reported above – there was limited evidence of differences between doses.

Clinical evidence for duloxetine comparing different doses
Evidence from the important outcomes and overall quality of evidence are presented in Table 55. The full GRADE profiles and associated forest plots can be found in Appendix 18c and Appendix 16c, respectively.

Table 53: Evidence summary table for trials of SSRIs comparing different doses

	Escitalopram 5 mg versus 10 mg	Escitalopram 10 mg versus 20 mg	Paroxetine 20 mg versus 40 mg
No. trials (total participants)	1 RCT (N = 270)	1 RCT (N = 269)	1 RCT (N = 386)
Study ID	BALDWIN2006	BALDWIN2006	RICKELS2003
Benefits (end of treatment)			
HAM-A	SMD = 0.23 (−0.01, 0.47) MD = 1.27 (−0.06, 2.60) K = 1, N = 268 Quality: moderate	SMD = −0.07 (−0.31, 0.17) MD = −0.41 (−1.75, 0.93) K = 1, N = 266 Quality: moderate	SMD = −0.03 (−0.23, 0.17) MD = −0.30 (−2.02, 1.42) K = 1, N = 386 Quality: moderate
HADS-A	–	–	SMD = −0.03 (−0.23, 0.17) MD = −0.30 (−2.02, 1.42) K = 1, N = 386 Quality: moderate
Non-response (≤50% reduction in HAM-A)	–	–	RR = 1.19 (0.91, 1.57) K = 1, N = 386 Quality: moderate
Non-remission (≥7 on HAM-A)	–	–	RR = 1.09 (0.95, 1.26) K = 1, N = 386 Quality: moderate
Harms (end of treatment)			
Discontinuation due to adverse events	RR = 0.89 (0.33, 2.38) K = 1, N = 270 Quality: moderate	RR = 0.56 (0.24, 1.29) K = 1, N = 269 Quality: moderate	RR = 0.83 (0.47, 1.46) K = 1, N = 386 Quality: moderate

Nausea	RR = 0.72 (0.43, 1.22) K = 1, N = 270 Quality: moderate	RR = 0.98 (0.61, 1.56) K = 1, N = 269 Quality: moderate	RR = 1.14 (0.74, 1.74) K = 1, N = 386 Quality: moderate
Fatigue	RR = 0.80 (0.38, 1.69) K = 1, N = 270 Quality: moderate	RR = 0.62 (0.33, 1.16) K = 1, N = 269 Quality: moderate	–
Headache	RR = 0.63 (0.38, 1.02) K = 1, N = 270 Quality: moderate	RR = 1.58 (0.97, 2.58) K = 1, N = 269 Quality: moderate	–
Insomnia	RR = 0.72 (0.36, 1.44) K = 1, N = 270 Quality: moderate	RR = 1.19 (0.61, 2.31) K = 1, N = 269 Quality: moderate	–
Somnolence	RR = 2.03 (0.71, 5.78) K = 1, N = 270 Quality: moderate	RR = 0.49 (0.17, 1.39) K = 1, N = 269 Quality: moderate	RR = 1.13 (0.75, 1.71) K = 1, N = 386 Quality: moderate
Anxiety	RR = 3.04 (0.84, 11.00) K = 1, N = 270 Quality: moderate	RR = 0.73 (0.17, 3.21) K = 1, N = 269 Quality: moderate	–
Dizziness	RR = 0.43 (0.17, 1.10) K = 1, N = 270 Quality: moderate	RR = 1.14 (0.55, 2.37) K = 1, N = 269 Quality: moderate	–
Decreased libido	–	–	RR = 1.19 (0.91, 1.57) K = 1, N = 386 Quality: moderate
Decreased appetite	–	–	RR = 1.13 (0.53, 2.41) K = 1, N = 386 Quality: moderate

Table 54: Study information table for trials of duloxetine comparing different doses

	Duloxetine 20 mg versus 60–120 mg	Duloxetine 60 mg versus 120 mg
No. trials (participants)	1 RCT (n = 242)	1 RCT (N = 338)
Study ID	NICOLINI2009	KOPONEN2007
N/% female	581/57%	338/68%
Mean age (years)	43	44
Diagnosis	GAD by DSM-IV	GAD by DSM-IV
Baseline severity (HAM-A): mean (SD)	Duloxetine 20 mg 27.7 (8.0); 60–120 mg 27.7 (7.3)	Duloxetine 60 mg 25.0 (7.1); 120 mg 25.2 (7.3)
Treatment length	10 weeks	9 weeks
Follow-up	End of treatment	End of treatment

Table 55: Evidence summary table for trials of duloxetine comparing different doses

	Duloxetine 20 mg versus 60–120 mg	Duloxetine 60 mg versus 120 mg
No. trials (participants)	1 RCT (n = 242)	1 RCT (N = 338)
Study ID	NICOLINI2009	KOPONEN2007
Benefits (end of treatment)		
HAM-A	SMD = 0.10 (−0.17, 0.36) MD = 0.60 (−1.09, 2.29) K = 1, N = 234 Quality: moderate	SMD = −0.03 (−0.25, 0.18) MD = −0.34 (−2.47, 1.79) K = 1, N = 334 Quality: moderate
HADS-A	SMD = 0.21 (−0.06, 0.47) MD = 0.70 (−0.19, 1.59) K = 1, N = 234 Quality: moderate	SMD = −0.04 (−0.26, 0.18) MD = −0.18 (−1.20, 0.84) K = 1, N = 323 Quality: moderate

Non-response (≤50% reduction in HAM-A)	RR = 1.07 (0.77, 1.48) K = 1, N = 242 Quality: moderate	RR = 0.96 (0.75, 1.22) K = 1, N = 338 Quality: moderate
Non-remission (≥7 on HAM-A)	–	RR = 1.12 (0.96, 1.31) K = 1, N = 338 Quality: moderate
Sheehan Disability Scale	–	SMD = −0.11 (−0.33, 0.11) MD = −0.99 (−2.90, 0.92) K = 1, N = 316 Quality: moderate
Q-LES-Q-SF	–	SMD = 0.02 (−0.22, 0.26) MD = 0.18 (−2.21, 2.57) K = 1, N = 265 Quality: moderate
Harms (end of treatment)		
Discontinuation due to adverse events	RR = 0.38 (0.13, 1.06) K = 1, N = 242 Quality: moderate	RR = 0.74 (0.43, 1.28) K = 1, N = 338 Quality: moderate
Discontinuation for any reason	–	RR = 0.73 (0.49, 1.08) K = 1, N = 338 Quality: moderate

Clinical evidence summary
There was a reduction in anxiety in favour of 60 to 120 mg of duloxetine compared with 20 mg based on HADS-A scores. However, this did not reach statistical significance. There were no clear differences between 60 mg and 120 mg found on any outcomes.

8.4.4   Pregabalin

Studies considered
There were five trials on pregabalin comparing different doses. A summary of study characteristics can be found in Table 56 with full details in Appendix 15d, which also includes details of excluded studies. Dosages used in the studies ranged from a mean of 150 mg to a mean of 600 mg.

Clinical evidence for pregabalin comparing different doses
Evidence from the important outcomes and overall quality of evidence are presented in Table 57. The full GRADE profiles and associated forest plots can be found in Appendix 18c and Appendix 16c, respectively.

Table 56: Study information table for trials of pregabalin comparing different dosages

	Pregabalin 150 mg versus 600 mg	Pregabalin 200 mg versus 400 mg	Pregabalin 300 mg versus 450 mg	Pregabalin 400 mg versus 450 mg	Pregabalin 400 mg versus 600 mg	Pregabalin 450 mg versus 600 mg
No. trials (total participants)	2 RCTs (269)	1 RCT (167)	1 RCT (181)	1 RCT (177)	1 RCT (207)	1 RCT (179)
Study ID	(1) FELTNER2003 (2) PANDE2003	POHL2005	RICKELS2005	POHL2005	MONTGOMERY2006	RICKELS2005
N/% female (see Appendix 15d for data for individual studies)	269/range 53–59%	167/Not reported	181/64%	177/Not reported	207/62%	179/64%
Mean age (years) (see Appendix 15d for data for individual studies)	40	44	44	44	44	44
Diagnosis	GAD by DSM-IV	GAD by DSM-IV	GAD by DSM-IV	GAD by DSM-IV	GAD by DSM-IV	GAD by DSM-IV
Baseline severity: HAM-A: mean (SD)	*150 mg:* (1) 24.9 (3.9); placebo: 24.8 (4.1); (2) 22.35 (2.68); placebo: 22.90 (3.88) *600 mg:* (1) 25.4 (4.6); placebo: 24.8 (4.1); (2) 23.16 (2.73); placebo: 22.90 (3.88)	Not reported	*300 mg:* 25.0 (3.82); placebo: 24.6 (3.82) *450 mg:* 24.6 (3.79); placebo: 24.6 (3.82)	Not reported	*400 mg:* 26.3 (4.4); placebo: 27.4 (5.5) *600 mg:* 26.5 (4.6); placebo: 27.4 (5.5)	*450 mg:* 24.6 (3.79); placebo: 24.6 (3.82) *600 mg:* 25.2 (3.77); placebo: 24.6 (3.82)
Treatment length	4 weeks	6 weeks	4 weeks	6 weeks	6 weeks	4 weeks
Follow-up	End of treatment	End of treatment	End of treatment	End of treatment	End of treatment	End of treatment

Table 57: Evidence summary table for trials of pregabalin comparing different dosages

	Pregabalin 150 mg versus 600 mg	Pregabalin 200 mg versus 400 mg	Pregabalin 300 mg versus 450 mg	Pregabalin 400 mg versus 450 mg	Pregabalin 400 mg versus 600 mg	Pregabalin 450 mg versus 600 mg
No. trials (total participants)	2 RCTs (269)	1 RCT (167)	1 RCT (181)	1 RCT (177)	1 RCT (207)	1 RCT (179)
Study ID	(1) FELTNER2003 (2) PANDE2003	POHL2005	RICKELS2005	POHL2005	MONTGOMERY2006	RICKELS2005
Benefits (end of treatment)						
HAM-A	SMD = 0.46 (0.11, 0.81) MD = 2.28 (0.58, 3.98) K = 1, N = 130 Quality: high	SMD = 0.10 (−0.21, 0.40) MD = 0.50 (−1.07, 2.07) K = 1, N = 167 Quality: moderate	SMD = −0.22 (−0.52, 0.07) MD = −1.20 (−2.77, 0.37) K = 1, N = 176 Quality: moderate	SMD = −0.09 (−0.39, 0.20) MD = −0.50 (−2.07, 1.07) K = 1, N = 177 Quality: moderate	SMD = −0.54 (−0.83, −0.26) MD = 0.80 (−0.77, 2.37) K = 1, N = 172 Quality: high	SMD = 0.15 (−0.15, 0.45) MD = 0.80 (−0.77, 2.37) K = 1, N = 172 Quality: moderate
HADS-A	–	–	–	–	SMD = −0.11 (−0.39, 0.17) MD = −0.40 (−1.41, 0.61) K = 1, N = 198 Quality: moderate	
Non-response (≤50% reduction in HAM-A)	–	–	RR = 0.72 (0.52, 1.00) K = 1, N = 181 Quality: high	–	–	RR = 1.13 (0.84, 1.51) K = 1, N = 179 Quality: moderate
Harms (end of treatment)						
Discontinuation due to adverse events	RR = 0.36 (0.16, 0.79) K = 1, N = 139 Quality: high	–	RR = 0.42 (0.11, 1.59) K = 1, N = 181 Quality: moderate	–	RR = 0.45 (0.18, 1.12) K = 1, N = 207 Quality: moderate	RR = 0.53 (0.22, 1.27) K = 1, N = 179 Quality: moderate

Continued

Table 57: (*Continued*)

	Pregabalin 150 mg versus 600 mg	Pregabalin 200 mg versus 400 mg	Pregabalin 300 mg versus 450 mg	Pregabalin 400 mg versus 450 mg	Pregabalin 400 mg versus 600 mg	Pregabalin 450 mg versus 600 mg
Discontinuation due to any reason	–	–	–	–	RR = 0.63 (0.36, 1.08) K = 1, N = 207 Quality: moderate	–
Somnolence	RR = 0.41 (0.21, 0.78) K = 1, N = 139 Quality: high	RR = 0.83 (0.54, 1.27) K = 1, N = 167 Quality: moderate	RR = 0.96 (0.67, 1.38) K = 1, N = 181 Quality: moderate	RR = 1.55 (0.98, 2.46) K = 1, N = 177 Quality: high	RR = 0.98 (0.49, 1.96) K = 1, N = 207 Quality: moderate	RR = 0.96 (0.68, 1.37) K = 1, N = 179 Quality: moderate
Dizziness	RR = 0.60 (0.36, 1.01) K = 1, N = 139 Quality: moderate	RR = 0.70 (0.48, 1.01) K = 1, N = 167 Quality: moderate	RR = 1.08 (0.75, 1.55) K = 1, N = 181 Quality: moderate	RR = 1.18 (0.85, 1.62) K = 1, N = 177 Quality: moderate	RR = 0.86 (0.53, 1.39) K = 1, N = 207 Quality: moderate	RR = 0.96 (0.66, 1.39) K = 1, N = 179 Quality: moderate
Nausea	RR = 0.85 (0.27, 2.64) K = 1, N = 139 Quality: moderate	–	RR = 0.76 (0.35, 1.65) K = 1, N = 181 Quality: moderate	–	RR = 0.73 (0.33, 1.61) K = 1, N = 207 Quality: moderate	RR = 1.29 (0.59, 2.78) K = 1, N = 179 Quality: moderate
Headache	RR = 0.88 (0.45, 1.71) K = 1, N = 139 Quality: moderate	–	–	–	RR = 0.88 (0.34, 2.28) K = 1, N = 207 Quality: moderate	–
Insomnia	–	–	–	–	RR = 0.38 (0.04, 3.57) K = 1, N = 207 Quality: moderate	–

Clinical evidence summary

There were few differences found between doses of pregabalin. However, there was some evidence that a mean of 600 mg was associated with greater reduction in anxiety compared with 150 mg. But 150 mg was associated with fewer reported side effects (particularly somnolence and dizziness). In addition, 400 mg was associated with greater benefits in reduction of anxiety compared with 600 mg.

8.4.5   Overall clinical evidence summary

The evidence from controlled trials indicates that SSRIs (sertraline, escitalopram and paroxetine) and SNRIs (duloxetine and venlafaxine) are efficacious in the treatment of GAD in that relative to placebo they produce greater reductions in HAM-A ratings and increase the probability of response to treatment. Generally, effect sizes are in the low to moderate range and do not seem to differ between the different antidepressants to a clinically significant extent, although there are much more data available for some drugs than others. There is no clear indication of a dose-response relationship where this has been specifically assessed. Nausea and insomnia are commonly experienced side effects. Discontinuation due to adverse events was more common in people receiving antidepressant treatment. There were few direct comparisons between antidepressants but there were indications that escitalopram may be slightly more effective than paroxetine.

Other drugs (particularly pregabalin) were also efficacious in GAD with effect sizes generally in the range of those seen with antidepressants. Again, comparative data did not yield evidence of consistent differences in efficacy, although the side-effect profile of the non-antidepressant agents differed from that of the SSRIs and SNRIs, consisting mainly of somnolence and dizziness.

8.5   MAINTENANCE TREATMENT

In many people GAD runs a chronic course and even where patients improve with treatment, relapse is common, particularly in those who remain symptomatic to some extent (Yonkers *et al.*, 1996). Stopping treatment after a few weeks can lead to relapses in 60 to 80% of patients over the next year (Rickels & Schweizer, 1990). For this reason current guidelines (Baldwin *et al.*, 2005; Davidson *et al.*, 2010) suggest that where drug treatment is helpful it should be continued over the next 6 to 12 months if tolerance and efficacy are satisfactory. Establishing the efficacy of this practice is therefore important. How long treatment should be continued subsequently is unclear and guidelines suggest adapting an individualised approach depending on the needs and preferences of the patient (Davidson *et al.*, 2010).

8.5.1   Databases searched and inclusion/exclusion criteria

Information about the databases searched and the inclusion/exclusion criteria used for this section of the guideline can be found in Table 58 (further information about the search for health economic evidence can be found in Section 3.6).

8.5.2   Studies considered

The review team conducted a new systematic search for RCTs that assessed the benefits and downsides of pharmacological interventions for the maintenance treatment of people with GAD. Maintenance treatment was defined as interventions for participants who had already responded to treatment in order to maintain reductions in anxiety. While all other antipsychotics were reviewed, quetiapine was not examined in this review as it will be formally evaluated in a forthcoming NICE Technology Appraisal.

A total of four trials met the eligibility criteria of the review, with one trial each comparing pregabalin, paroxetine, escitalopram and duloxetine with placebo.

A summary of study characteristics can be found in Table 59 with full details in Appendix 15d, which also includes details of excluded studies.

Table 58: Databases searched and inclusion/exclusion criteria for clinical evidence

Electronic databases	MEDLINE, EMBASE, CINAHL, PsycINFO, Cochrane Library
Date searched	Database inception to 09.05.2010
Study design	RCT
Patient population	People with GAD
Interventions	SSRIs, TCAs, duloxetine, venlafaxine, pregabalin, antipsychotics
Outcomes	Relapse, mean anxiety rating scale scores, non-response ($<$50% reduction in anxiety rating scale score), non-remission (still meeting cut-off for caseness on an anxiety rating scale), Sheehan Disability Scale, quality of life

Table 59: Study information table for trials of maintenance treatment

	Pregabalin versus placebo	Duloxetine versus placebo	Paroxetine versus placebo	Escitalopram versus placebo
No. trials (total participants)	1 RCT (338)	1 RCT (429)	1 RCT (566)	1 RCT (375)
Study ID	FELTNER2008	DAVIDSON2008	STOCCHI2003	ALLGULANDER2006
N/% female	338/57%	429/Not reported	566/64%	375/32%
Mean age (years)	39	43	43	41
Diagnosis	GAD by DSM-IV	GAD by DSM-IV	GAD by DSM-IV	GAD by DSM-IV
Baseline severity (HAM-A): mean (SD)	Pregabalin 5.9 (3.2); placebo 5.5 (3.4)	Not reported	Not reported	Escitalopram 5.7 (3.9); placebo 5.0 (3.1)
Treatment length	Open label: 8 weeks Randomised: 24 weeks	Open label: 26 weeks Randomised: 26 weeks	Open label: 8 weeks Randomised: 24 weeks	Open label: 12 weeks Randomised: 24–76 weeks
Follow-up	End of treatment	End of treatment	End of treatment	End of treatment

8.5.3   Clinical evidence for maintenance treatment

Evidence from the important outcomes and overall quality of evidence are presented in Table 60. The full GRADE profiles and associated forest plots can be found in Appendix 18c and Appendix 16c, respectively.

8.5.4   Clinical evidence summary

There was only one trial each examining pregabalin, duloxetine, escitalopram, and paroxetine. The findings suggest that where people have responded to pharmacological treatment in the short-term, continuing treatment over the next 6 months resulted in fewer relapses than switching to placebo. These findings support current guidelines that drug treatment should be continued for at least 6 months in people who respond in the short-term (Baldwin, *et al.*, 2005; Davidson *et al.*, 2010). In addition, there was no difference between the drugs and placebo for reported side effects.

However, the main limitation of this review is the very high dropout reported in most studies particularly in the placebo groups. For example, 49% dropped out of the placebo group in the paroxetine trial and 45.5% dropped out in the placebo group in the duloxetine trial. In addition, there was some variability in the length of follow-up.

Table 60: Evidence summary table for trials of maintenance treatment

	Pregabalin versus placebo	Duloxetine versus placebo	Paroxetine versus placebo	Escitalopram versus placebo
No. trials (total participants)	1 RCT (N = 338)	1 RCT (N = 429)	1 RCT (N = 566)	1 RCT (N = 375)
Study ID	FELTNER2008	DAVIDSON2008	STOCCHI2003	ALLGULANDER2006
Benefit (end of treatment)				
Relapse	RR 0.65 (0.53, 0.80) K = 1, N = 338 Quality: moderate	RR 0.33 (0.22, 0.48) K = 1, N = 405 Quality: moderate	RR 0.27 (0.19, 0.39) K = 1, N = 561 Quality: moderate	RR 0.36 (0.26, 0.49) K = 1, N = 375 Quality: moderate
Non-remission	–	RR 0.53 (0.42, 0.66) K = 1, N = 424 Quality: moderate	RR 0.41 (0.33, 0.51) K = 1, N = 561 Quality: moderate	–
HAM-A	SMD −0.52 (−0.73, −0.30) MD −5.00 (−7.06, −2.94) K = 1, N = 338 Quality: moderate	SMD −0.70 (−0.90, −0.51) MD −5.89 (−7.48, −4.30) K = 1, N = 424 Quality: moderate	SMD −1.03 (−1.20, −0.85) MD −6.70 (−7.78, −5.62) K = 1, N = 561 Quality: moderate	–
Quality of life	–	SMD −0.74 (−0.94, −0.53) MD -12.24 (−15.47, −9.01) K = 1, N = 407 Quality: moderate	–	–
Harm (end of treatment)				
Discontinuation for any reason	Pregabalin: 61/168 (36.3%) Placebo: 38/170 (22.4%) RR 1.62 (1.15, 2.29) K = 1, N = 338 Quality: moderate	Duloxetine: 49/216 (22.7%) Placebo: 97/213 (45.5%) RR 0.50 (0.37, 0.68) K = 1, N = 429 Quality: moderate	Paroxetine: 62/278 (22.6%) Placebo: 141/288 (49.0%) RR 0.46 (0.36, 0.58) K = 1, N = 566 Quality: moderate	Escitalopram: 71/187 (37.97%) Placebo: 136/188 (72.3%) RR 0.52 (.43, 0.64) K = 1, N = 375 Quality: moderate
Discontinuation due to adverse events	RR 2.53 (0.81, 7.91) K = 1, N = 338 Quality: moderate	RR 1.97 (0.37, 10.65) K = 1, N = 429 Quality: moderate	RR 1.27 (0.53, 3.01) K = 1, N = 566 Quality: moderate	RR 0.82 (0.40, 1.65) K = 1, N = 375 Quality: moderate

The high dropout raises questions concerning whether differences between groups is due to the benefit of continuing to receive pharmacological treatment or due to the effects of withdrawing the medication. In addition, there is a lack of controlled data to guide management of pharmacological treatment in the longer-term.

8.6   MANAGEMENT OF NON-RESPONSE
TO PHARMACOLOGICAL INTERVENTIONS

8.6.1   Introduction

For many people, symptomatic remission is not achieved during pharmacological treatment for GAD. Guidelines emphasise the importance of giving initial drug treatment sufficient time to exert its effect because clinical improvement in GAD may be slow with both response and remission rates increasing beyond 2 months of drug treatment (Bielski & Bose, 2005; Davidson *et al.*, 2010). Where clinician and service user agree that pharmacological treatment should be modified, there are three possible strategies: (i) increase the dose of the current treatment (if the maximum dose has not been reached); (ii) augment with another agent from a different pharmacological class; (iii) switch to an alternative agent. In general (i) and (ii) are favoured when there has been a partial response to initial treatment.

Conventional antipsychotic drugs such as trifluoperazine were previously used to treat anxiety where clinicians wished to avoid the use of benzodiazepines. There is currently interest in the possible role of a typical antipsychotic drugs in GAD because relative to conventional agents these drugs have a reduced propensity to cause serious movement disorders such as tardive dyskinesia (Correll *et al.*, 2004). Some guidelines have advocated the use of atypical antipsychotic drugs such as olanzapine, risperidone and quetiapine to augment antidepressants in people who do not have a satisfactory response to antidepressant treatment alone (Davidson *et al.*, 2010).

8.6.2   Databases searched and inclusion/exclusion criteria

Information about the databases searched and the inclusion/exclusion criteria used for this section of the guideline can be found in Table 61 (further information about the search for health economic evidence can be found in section 3.6).

8.6.3   Studies considered

The review team conducted a new systematic search for RCTs that assessed the benefits and downsides of pharmacological interventions for the treatment of people with GAD.

A total of four trials met the eligibility criteria for the review. Two trials compared risperidone with placebo, one trial compared olanzapine with placebo and one trial

Table 61: Databases searched and inclusion/exclusion criteria for clinical evidence

Electronic databases	MEDLINE, EMBASE, CINAHL, PsycINFO, Cochrane Library
Date searched	Database inception to 09.05.2010
Study design	RCT
Patient population	People with GAD
Interventions	Pharmacological intervention for GAD in combination with another pharmacological intervention Switching and sequencing strategies of pharmacological interventions
Outcomes	Mean anxiety rating scale scores, non-response (<50% reduction in anxiety rating scale score), non-remission (still meeting cut-off for caseness on an anxiety rating scale), Sheehan Disability Scale, quality of life

compared ziprasidone with placebo, as augmentation strategies in combination with pharmacological interventions for GAD.

No trials were identified on switching or sequencing pharmacological interventions.

8.6.4 Augmentation strategies

Studies considered
There were four trials on augmentation strategies. A summary of study characteristics can be found in Table 62 with full details in Appendix 15d, which also includes details of excluded studies.

Clinical evidence for augmentation strategies
Evidence from the important outcomes and overall quality of evidence are presented in Table 63. The full GRADE profiles and associated forest plots can be found in Appendix 18c and Appendix 16c, respectively.

Clinical evidence summary
There was limited evidence because three of the four trials were small and there was high heterogeneity in HAM-A scores ($I^2 = 73\%$) for risperidone. There was no statistically significant evidence of benefit for any of the antipsychotic drugs assessed individually. When combining the antipsychotic data there was still limited evidence of benefit.

Table 62: Study information table for trials of augmentation strategies

	Pharmacological treatment for GAD + olanzapine	Pharmacological treatment for GAD + risperidone	Pharmacological treatment for GAD + ziprasidone	Pharmacological treatment for GAD + antipsychotics
No. trials (total participants)	1 RCT (24)	2 RCTs (429)	1 RCT (17)	4 RCTs (470)
Study ID	POLLACK2006	(1) BRAWMAN-MINTZER2005 (2) PANDINA2007	LOHOFF2010	(1) BRAWMAN-MINTZER2005 (2) LOHOFF2010 (3) PANDINA 2007 (4) POLLACK2006
N/% female (see Appendix 15d for data for individual studies)	24/54%	429/range 71–83%	17/Not reported	470/range 54–83%
Mean age (years) (see Appendix 15d for data for individual studies)	40	49	42	See section on each specific drug to the left
Diagnosis	GAD by DSM-IV	GAD by DSM-IV	GAD by DSM-IV	GAD by DSM-IV
Baseline severity (HAM-A): mean (SD)	Olanzapine 17.4 (6.5); placebo 22.6 (5.2)	Risperidone 22.1 (3.8); placebo 20.4 (1.7)	Not reported	See section on each specific drug to the left
Treatment length	Open label: 6 weeks of fluoxetine treatment without responding to treatment Randomised: 4 weeks of augmentation with olanzapine or placebo	Anxiolytic medication: at least 4 weeks without sufficient reduction in anxiety Randomised: 5 weeks of augmentation with risperidone or placebo	Open label: not reported Randomised: 8 weeks of augmentation with ziprasidone or placebo	See section on each specific drug to the left
Follow-up	End of treatment	End of treatment	End of treatment	End of treatment

Table 63: Evidence summary table for trials of augmentation strategies

	Pharmacological treatment for GAD + olanzapine	Pharmacological treatment for GAD + risperidone	Pharmacological treatment for GAD + ziprasidone	Pharmacological treatment for GAD + antipsychotics
No. trials (total participants)	1 RCT (24)	2 RCTs (429)	1 RCT (17)	4 RCTs (470)
Study ID	POLLACK2006	(1) BRAWMAN-MINTZER2005 (2) PANDINA2007	LOHOFF2010	(1) BRAWMAN-MINTZER2005 (2) LOHOFF2010 (3) PANDINA 2007 (4) POLLACK2006
Benefits (end of treatment)				
HAM-A/anxiety symptoms	SMD −0.30 (−1.17, 0.57) MD −3.10 (−11.54, 5.34) K = 1, N = 21 Quality: low	SMD −0.27 (−0.90, 0.36) MD −1.56 (−4.90, 1.77) K = 2, N = 429 Quality: moderate	SMD −0.33 (−1.31, 0.64) MD −2.80 (−10.71, 5.11) K = 1, N = 17 Quality: low	SMD −0.20 (−0.53, 0.12) MD −1.46 (−3.56, 0.64) K = 4, N = 467 Quality: moderate
Non-remission	RR 0.73 (0.47, 1.12) K = 1, N = 24 Quality: low	RR = 0.98 (0.89–1.08) K = 1, N = 390 Quality: high	–	RR 0.91 (0.71, 1.18) K = 2, N = 414 Quality: moderate
Non-response	RR 0.64 (0.38, 1.06) K = 1, N = 24 Quality: moderate	RR = 0.99 (0.84, 1.16) K = 1, N = 390 Quality: moderate	–	RR 0.85 (0.56, 1.28) K = 2, N = 414 Quality: moderate
Harms (end of treatment)				
Discontinuation due to adverse events	RR 4.00 (0.52, 30.76) K = 1, N = 24 Quality: low	RR = 2.17 (1.09, 4.32) K = 2, N = 429 Quality: moderate	–	RR 2.31 (1.20, 4.43) K = 4, N = 453 Quality: high

8.6.5 Overall clinical summary of non-response to pharmacological interventions

There was no data identified on increasing the dose or switching pharmacological treatments. There was only data available on atypical antipsychotics (olanzapine, risperidone and ziprasidone) for augmentation treatment. It appears such interventions were associated with limited benefit and greater risk of discontinuation due to adverse events.

8.7 SIDE EFFECTS OF PHARMACOLOGICAL INTERVENTIONS

8.7.1 Introduction

The purpose of this review is to assess the side effects and adverse events of pharmacological interventions for the treatment of GAD. However given the lack of data specifically focused on this disorder, data were examined for common mental health problems (that is, depression and anxiety disorders). Pharmacological interventions were limited to those most commonly used in clinical practice including antidepressants, pregabalin, benzodiazepines, hydroxyzine and buspirone.

8.7.2 Databases searched and inclusion/exclusion criteria

Information about the databases searched and the inclusion/exclusion criteria used for this section of the guideline can be found in Table 64 (further information about the search for health economic evidence can be found in section 3.6).

8.7.3 Studies considered

The review team conducted a new systematic search for systematic reviews that assessed the efficacy and safety of antidepressants.

Twenty systematic reviews relating to clinical evidence met the eligibility criteria set by the GDG. All were published in peer-reviewed journals between 1999 and 2009.

8.7.4 Clinical evidence for side effects and adverse events of antidepressants

The side effects and adverse events of antidepressants have already been reviewed in detail in the NICE guideline for depression in people with a chronic physical health problem (NCCMH, 2010b). The key characteristics of the included systematic reviews discussed in that guideline and relevant to the present guideline are summarised in Table 65.

The main adverse events associated with antidepressants are cardiovascular symptoms, bleeding, gastrointestinal symptoms, sexual dysfunction, weight change, and suicidal ideation and behaviour.

Table 64: Databases searched and inclusion/exclusion criteria for clinical evidence

Electronic databases	MEDLINE, EMBASE, CINAHL, PsycINFO, Cochrane Library
Date searched	Database inception to 09.05.2010
Study design	Systematic reviews
Patient population	People with common mental health problems (that is, depression and anxiety disorders)
Interventions	SSRIs, venlafaxine, duloxetine, TCAs, benzodiazepines, buspirone, pregabalin, hydroxyzine
Outcomes	Side effects and adverse events of pharmacological interventions: weight change, sexual functioning, gastrointestinal symptoms, cardiotoxicity, mortality

Cardiovascular symptoms

SSRIs do not appear to be associated with an increase risk in cardiovascular adverse events (for example, Swenson *et al.*, 2006; Taylor, 2008) and are associated with a relatively low fatal toxicity index (number of poisoning deaths per million prescriptions). However, TCAs are associated with a higher risk of cardiovascular adverse events and have found to be cardiotoxic in overdose (Taylor, 2008).

Duloxetine was associated with small increases in diastolic blood pressure, tachycardia and cholesterol compared with placebo (Duggan & Fuller, 2004; Wernicke *et al.*, 2007). In addition, there is evidence of moderate acute toxicity associated with venlafaxine (Taylor, 2008).

Bleeding

Several observational studies utilising data from national prescribing databases have found a relatively strong association (approximately a three-fold increase) between SSRIs and increased risk of gastrointestinal bleeding (Weinrieb *et al.*, 2003; Yuan *et al.*, 2006). However, it should be noted that the outcome was relatively rare with approximately four to five events per 1000 person years. This effect was particularly strong (approximately a 15-fold increase of bleeding) in people concurrently using non-steroidal anti-inflammatory drugs (NSAIDs) and SSRIs.

Gastrointestinal symptoms

There is consistent evidence both in depression and anxiety populations of the increased risk of gastrointestinal (GI) symptoms such as nausea, vomiting and diarrhoea associated with SSRI use (Brambilla *et al.*, 2005; Beasley *et al.*, 2000). This has been confirmed in the current systematic review of SSRIs for GAD (see section 8.2.3). TCAs also appear to be associated with higher risk of constipation when compared with fluoxetine (Beasley *et al.*, 2000).

Table 65: Study information table of included systematic reviews on side effects and adverse events

Study	Focus of review	Method of synthesis	Inclusion criteria	Results
Taylor, 2008	Cardiovascular	Narrative	Design: no restriction (focus on meta-analyses) Population: people with cardiovascular diseases Intervention: most antidepressants	TCAs: highly cardiotoxic in overdose and may induce cardiovascular disease Reboxetine, duloxetine, venlafaxine increase blood pressure Other antidepressants: neutral or beneficial in various cardiovascular diseases
Swenson *et al.*, 2006	Cardiovascular	Meta-analysis	Design: RCT Population: people with chronic physical health problems, substance misuse, and older adults Interventions: SSRIs and TCAs	SSRIs versus placebo: reduced risk of serious adverse events (not statistically significant) SSRIs versus TCAs: reduced risk of non-serious adverse events
Ramasubbu, 2004	Cerebrovascular	Narrative	Design: RCTs, controlled studies, WHO data monitoring programme, case studies Interventions: SSRIs	Controlled studies: no association between SSRIs and increased adverse cerebrovascular effects WHO data on SSRI-induced cardiovascular effects: fluoxetine (122 cases), paroxetine

Continued

231

Table 65: *(Continued)*

Study	Focus of review	Method of synthesis	Inclusion criteria	Results
				(51), sertraline (47), citalopram (13), fluvoxamine (7)
				Case studies: 4 cases of vasoconstrictive stroke related to SSRIs
Weinrieb *et al.*, 2003	Bleeding	Narrative	Design: controlled studies, national prescribing databases, case studies	Increased risk of bleeding associated with SSRIs and SSRI/NSAID use
			Intervention: SSRIs	
Yuan *et al.*, 2006	Bleeding	Narrative	Design: controlled studies, national prescribing databases, case studies	Increased risk of bleeding associated with SSRIs and SSRI + NSAID use
			Intervention: SSRIs	
Werneke *et al.*, (2006)	Sexual dysfunction	Narrative	Design: primarily RCTs, meta-analyses, supplemented with controlled studies, case studies where data limited	SSRIs: paroxetine highest prevalence
				Third generation antidepressants: venlafaxine highest prevalence; reboxetine, bupropion less risk
			Intervention: SSRIs, third generation antidepressants, TCAs, monoamine oxidase inhibitors (MAOIs)	TCAs: clomipramine highest prevalence; amitriptyline, doxepin lowest prevalence

Gregorian et al., (2002)	Sexual dysfunction	Narrative	Design: no limitations Interventions: SSRIs, third generation antidepressants	MAOIs: high prevalence but less in moclobemide SSRIs: consistent evidence of high prevalence of sexual adverse events compared with placebo; bupropion and nefazodone have fewer sexual adverse events compared with SSRIs
Stone et al., 2009	Suicidal ideation and behaviour	Meta-analysis	Design: RCTs Interventions: antidepressants	SSRIs: for those aged under 25 years there was an increased risk of suicidal ideation and behaviour
Beasley et al., 2000	Fluoxetine	Meta-analysis	Design: RCTs Intervention: fluoxetine	Increased risk of GI symptoms and sexual dysfunction compared with placebo Increased risk of GI symptoms (except constipation) but less risk of postural hypotension compared with TCAs
Wernicke, 2004	Fluoxetine	Narrative	Design: no limitations Intervention: fluoxetine	Acceptable tolerability in a range of populations (diabetes, stroke, cancer, cardiovascular disease) Increased risk of GI symptoms One case report of loss of hypoglaecemic awareness in diabetes

Continued

Table 65: (*Continued*)

Study	Focus of review	Method of synthesis	Inclusion criteria	Results
Brambilla *et al.*, 2005	Fluoxetine	Meta-analysis	Design: RCT Intervention: fluoxetine	GI symptoms (nausea, vomiting, diarrhoea) higher prevalence in fluoxetine Weight: loss greater in fluoxetine compared with TCAs and other SSRIs
Dhillon *et al.*, 2008	Bupropion	Narrative	Design: no limitation Intervention: bupropion	Risk of seizures with an incidence ~0.4% but increases 10-fold with higher doses (450–600 mg) Less risk of sexual dysfunction compared with SSRIs Risk of weight loss compared with placebo Risk of increase in blood pressure
Demyttenaere & Jaspers, 2008	SSRIs	Narrative	Design: no limitation	Greater risk of adverse sexual effects in SSRIs compared with bupropion Risk of weight loss for some SSRIs early in treatment but risk of weight gain later on in treatment
Duggan & Fuller, 2004	Duloxetine	Narrative	Design: no limitation	Increase in blood pressure

Study	Intervention	Design	Criteria	Findings
			Intervention: duloxetine	Possible risk of weight loss / Higher risk of sexual dysfunction compared with placebo
Wernicke et al., 2007	Duloxetine	Narrative	Design: no limitation / Intervention: duloxetine	Increase in palpitations, tachycardia, orthostatic hypotension, cholesterol compared with placebo / Sexual dysfunction higher than placebo
Hansen et al., 2005	Second and third generation antidepressants	Narrative	Design: no limitation / Intervention: duloxetine	Venlafaxine higher risk of nausea and vomiting than SSRIs
Machado et al., 2006	Antidepressants	Meta-analysis	Design: RCTs / Intervention: most antidepressants	TCAs the highest overall adverse-effects profile, followed by SNRIs
Wade & Rosenberg, 2001	Citalopram	Narrative	Design: no limitations / Intervention: citalopram	Fewer adverse events than TCAs (constipation, tachycardia) / No differences found between citalopram and other SSRIs
Keller, 2000	Citalopram	Narrative	Design: no limitations	Greater risk of nausea than placebo but less than fluvoxamine / Risk of small increase in heartbeat rate

Continued

235

Table 65: *(Continued)*

Study	Focus of review	Method of synthesis	Inclusion criteria	Results
Edwards & Anderson, 1999	SSRIs	Meta-analysis and narrative	Design: minor limitation – a number of included studies also included a percentage of people with psychosis	CSM and prescription-event monitoring data: greater risk of adverse events, including discontinuation reaction to paroxetine and greater risk of GI adverse events with fluvoxamine and paroxetine compared with other SSRIs Controlled studies: more patients discontinued fluvoxamine because of adverse events; fewer patients discontinued sertraline

Sexual dysfunction

There was consistent evidence of sexual adverse events associated with SSRIs, duloxetine and venlafaxine in people with depression (Werneke *et al.*, 2006; Gregorian *et al.*, 2002; Beasley *et al.*, 2000; Keller, 2000). These results have been replicated in people with GAD in the current systematic review (see section 8.2.3).

Weight change

Fluoxetine appears to be associated with greater loss in weight compared with placebo (Beasley *et al.*, 2000), TCAs and other SSRIs (Brambilla *et al.*, 2005). However, as noted by Demyttenaere and Jaspers (2008), these effects are reported early on in treatment. When assessing continuation studies there is a possibility that paroxetine and fluoxetine may actually be associated with weight gain but this needs further research to establish this finding.

In addition, there is some evidence that duloxetine was associated with weight loss with a mean reduction of 2.2 kg compared with 1 kg for placebo (Duggan & Fuller, 2004).

Suicidal ideation and behaviour

One systematic review was identified on the association between antidepressant use and suicidal ideation and/behaviour (Stone *et al.*, 2009). For those aged under 25 years there was an increased odds of suicidal behaviour (OR 2.30; 95% CI 1.04, 5.09) for people taking antidepressants compared with placebo. There was a borderline statistically significant increase in odds of suicidal ideation and suicidal behaviour (OR 1.62; 95% CI 0.97, 2.71).

8.7.5   Clinical evidence for side effects for pregabalin

The included reviews are summarised in Table 66. Three reviews were included; however there are a number of limitations to their quality. The methods of identifying the included studies, data extraction and so on were not reported. In addition, the results were almost exclusively concerned with the results of short-term RCTs therefore no long-term evidence of the safety and side effects of pregabalin was examined.

Pregabalin appeared to be well tolerated by most participants but was associated with greater risk of headaches, dizziness and somnolence.

8.7.6   Clinical evidence for side effects for buspirone

No systematic reviews were identified that specifically assessed the side effects of buspirone.

Table 66: Study information table of included systematic reviews of pregabalin

Study	Focus of review	Method of synthesis	Inclusion criteria	Results
Baldwin & Ajel, 2007	Pregabalin	Narrative	Efficacy and tolerability of pregabalin for GAD Mostly reviewed benefits and side effects reported in RCTs	Pregabalin is better tolerated than venlafaxine, alprazolam and lorazepam in the short term
Kavoussi, 2006	Pregabalin	Narrative	Efficacy and tolerability of pregabalin for GAD Mostly reviewed benefits and side effects reported in RCTs	Dizziness and somnolence reported in association with pregabalin
Tassone *et al.*, 2007	Pregabalin	Narrative	Efficacy and tolerability of pregabalin Mostly reviewed benefits and side effects reported in RCTs	Most common side effects were headache, dizziness, somnolence

8.7.7 Clinical evidence for side effects for hydroxyzine

No systematic reviews were identified that specifically assessed the side effects of hydroxyzine.

8.7.8 Clinical evidence for side effects for benzodiazepines

The three included reviews are summarised in Table 67. As above there were no high-quality systematic reviews available. Very few, if any, details are reported on inclusion criteria, search strategies, data extraction, and so on. The most common reported problem with benzodiazepine use was risk of dependence. This suggests only short-term use of this treatment is appropriate and that particular caution should be exercised for people with comorbid alcohol or drug misuse.

Table 67: Study information table of included systematic reviews of benzodiazepines

Study	Focus of review	Method of synthesis	Inclusion criteria	Results
Ashton, 2005	Benzodiazepines	Narrative	Benzodiazepine dependence Inclusion criteria not clear	Benzodiazepine meets the criteria currently defining 'substance dependence' Long-term use can aggravate anxiety and cause deficits in learning, memory, attention and visuospatial ability Escalation of dosage and chronic use can cause depression and sedation (causing accidents).
Chouinard (2004)	Benzodiazepines	Narrative	Anxiety disorders	Can experience recurrent symptoms (gradual return of original symptoms with same intensity) Rebound symptoms (rapid return of original symptoms but worse than before treatment), for example, anxiety and insomnia; greater with benzodiazepines that have short to intermediate half-lives

Table 67: Study information table of included systematic reviews of benzodiazepines

Study	Focus of review	Method of synthesis	Inclusion criteria	Results
				New CNS withdrawal symptoms that were not part of original illness; minor in nature are, for example, insomnia, gastric problems and tremors; major in nature, but rare new symptoms, are seizures and psychosis Memory impairments can be increased by the following factors: absorption rates (high lipid solubility), high potency, high dose, short-intermediate half-life and route of administration (Healey *et al.*, 1983); affects delayed, not immediate word recall; triazolam and lorazepam mostly associated with amnesia
Cloos & Ferreira, 2009	Benzodiazepines	Narrative	Anxiety disorders	Sedation, fatigue, ataxia, slurred speech, memory impairment and weakness Higher risk of adverse events and dependency in older people

There were a number of cognitive side effects reported, including impairment of speech and memory. In addition, sedation, fatigue and ataxia were commonly associated with benzodiazepine use.

8.7.9   Overall clinical summary for side effects of pharmacological interventions

The systematic review confirms the characteristic side-effect profile of the various drugs used in pharmacological interventions in GAD. Many of the studies of antidepressants concern the use of these agents in conditions other than GAD; however, there do not seem to be important differences in the nature and frequency of the side effects experienced across diagnoses. SSRIs are well known to be associated with nausea, insomnia and sexual dysfunction and a similar profile of effect is seen with SNRIs. Discontinuation symptoms are common after antidepressant drug withdrawal and appear to be more frequent after withdrawal of agents with relatively short half-lives such as paroxetine and venlafaxine. SSRIs can also be associated with serious bleeding problems such as gastrointestinal haemorrhage, a risk that is significantly increased by co-administration of NSAIDs. Although it should be acknowledged that these events are relatively rare. SSRIs are generally safe in patients with cardiovascular problems though SNRIs carry a risk of increasing blood pressure. Venlafaxine appears more toxic in overdose than SSRIs.

In contrast to the SSRIs and SNRIs, pregabalin and benzodiazepines cause more sedation and dizziness but are less likely to be associated with nausea and sexual problems. Benzodiazepines are well known to be associated with tolerance and dependence and cause a withdrawal syndrome upon discontinuation. Withdrawal effects after pregabalin have not yet been well characterised. In keeping with its action at central 5-HT receptors, buspirone causes nausea and dizziness while the antihistamine, hydroxyzine, is associated with sedation.

8.8   HEALTH ECONOMIC EVIDENCE

8.8.1   Research question

What is the cost effectiveness of pharmacological treatments compared with other interventions in the treatment of GAD?

8.8.2   Systematic literature review

The systematic search of the economic literature undertaken for the guideline identified five eligible studies on pharmacological treatments for people with GAD (Guest *et al.*, 2005; Heuzenroeder *et al.*, 2004; Iskedjian *et al.*, 2008; Jørgensen *et al.*, 2006; Vera-Llonch *et al.*, 2010). Two studies were conducted in the UK

241

(Guest *et al.*, 2005; Jørgensen *et al.*, 2006), one in Spain (Vera-Llonch *et al.*, 2010), one in Canada (Iskedjian *et al.*, 2008) and one in Australia (Heuzenroeder *et al.*, 2004). Details on the methods used for the systematic review of the economic literature are described in Chapter 3; references to included studies and evidence tables for all economic evaluations included in the systematic literature review are provided in Appendix 15f. Completed methodology checklists of the studies are provided in Appendix 17. Economic evidence profiles of studies considered during guideline development (that is, studies that fully or partly met the applicability and quality criteria) are presented in Appendix 18c, accompanying the respective GRADE clinical evidence profiles.

Jørgensen and colleagues (2006) evaluated the cost effectiveness of escitalopram versus paroxetine in the treatment of people with GAD in the UK. A decision-analytic model was constructed for this purpose. The study population consisted of newly diagnosed people with GAD with a HAM-A score of 18 or more, who were treated in a primary care setting. The primary measure of outcome in the analysis was the rate of initial response as well as the rate of maintained response (that is, initial response and no relapse until the end of the time horizon). Initial response was defined by a Clinical Global Impressions (CGI) Improvement score of 1 or 2. Relapse was defined as a HAM-A total score of 15 or more, a CGI-S score of 4 or more, or discontinuation due to lack of efficacy. Response and discontinuation rates were taken from Bielski and Bose (2005); relapse data and other clinical input parameters were based on published literature and further assumptions. The study adopted a societal perspective but an analysis using NHS costs only was also provided. Estimates of resource use (medication, GP and/or psychiatrist visits as well as productivity losses) were based on recommendations from the previous NICE guideline on anxiety (NICE, 2004a) and the expert opinion of the GDG; UK national unit costs were used. The time horizon of the analysis was 9 months.

According to the results of the analysis, escitalopram dominated paroxetine in both the NHS and societal perspectives considered. Escitalopram demonstrated a higher rate of initial response (14.4% more responders) and a higher rate of maintained response (7.7% more responders) than paroxetine. The mean total costs of escitalopram and paroxetine over 9 months, estimated from an NHS perspective, were £447 and £486 per person treated, respectively (2005 prices). Results were robust to changes in response rates, tolerance and acquisition costs.

The study is directly applicable to the review question and the NHS setting. The methods appear to be rigorous overall; however, the study has been funded by the pharmaceutical industry, which raises issues about potential conflicts of interest.

Guest and colleagues (2005) examined the cost effectiveness of venlafaxine XL compared with diazepam in the treatment of people with GAD in primary care in the UK, from the perspective of the NHS. The study was based on decision-analytic modelling. The primary outcome measure was the percentage of successful treatment, defined as the percentage of people in remission at 6 months, with remission defined as a CGI score of 1. The source of clinical effectiveness data was Hackett and colleagues (2003). Resource use estimates were based on expert opinion; national prices were used. The time horizon of the analysis was 6 months.

Venlafaxine XL was shown to be more effective and more costly than diazepam. The percentage of successful treatment was 27.6% with venlafaxine XL, versus 16.8% with diazepam. The mean total costs of venlafaxine XL and diazepam were £352 and £310 per person treated, respectively (2001 prices). Venlafaxine XL incurred an extra £381 per successfully treated person compared with diazepam. Results were sensitive to changes in rates of response, remission, relapse and discontinuation, as well as to changes in resource use estimates. Probabilistic analysis revealed that venlafaxine XL dominated diazepam in at least 25% of iterations. The authors concluded that venlafaxine XL was more cost effective than diazepam for the treatment of people with GAD. However, the results are difficult to interpret due to lack of use of QALYs as the measure of outcome. In addition, the study is at risk of bias as it was funded by the pharmaceutical industry.

Vera-Llonch and colleagues (2010) examined the cost effectiveness of pregabalin compared with venlafaxine XL in the treatment of people with GAD in Spain, from the perspective of a third-party payer. The study was based on decision-analytic modelling. The measure of outcome was the number of QALYs gained. Clinical data were taken from Kasper and colleagues (2009). Resource use estimates were based on published and unpublished data; national unit costs were used. The time horizon of the analysis was 12 months.

Pregabalin was found to be more effective and more costly than venlafaxine XL. The ICER of pregabalin versus venlafaxine was estimated at €23,909 per QALY, ranging from €19,829 to €35,993 per QALY in sensitivity analysis (2007 prices). Converted and uplifted to 2009 UK pounds, the ICER of pregabalin versus venlafaxine becomes £17,565 per QALY, ranging from £14,567 to £26,442 per QALY in sensitivity analysis. Results were sensitive to changes in utility values, the time horizon, and whether discontinuation was assumed. The probability of pregabalin being cost effective at a threshold of roughly €25,000/QALY (£20,000/QALY) was approximately 95% (as read from a graph). Based on these results, the authors concluded that paroxetine was likely to be more cost effective than venlafaxine XL for the treatment of people with GAD in a Spanish healthcare setting. However, the study was conducted in Spain and therefore is not directly applicable to the UK setting. In addition, a major limitation of the analysis is that it was assumed that the treatment effect lasted for 44 weeks following end of treatment (that is, from 8 weeks until 12 months). Over this period it was assumed that all people retained the level of clinical improvement achieved by the end of treatment and no relapse was observed. Finally, the study is at risk of bias as it was funded by the pharmaceutical industry.

Iskedjian and colleagues (2008) undertook a modelling study to compare the costs and benefits of escitalopram versus paroxetine over 24 weeks, for the treatment of people with GAD in Canada. The study used both a Ministry of Health and a societal perspective. The primary measure of outcome was the number of symptom-free days, defined by a score of 1 or 2 on the CGI-I. Response and discontinuation rates were taken from Bielski and Bose (2005); other clinical input parameters were based on published literature and expert opinion. Resource use estimates were also based on expert opinion; national unit prices were used.

From a Ministry of Health perspective, escitalopram was shown to be more effective than paroxetine at an extra cost of $6.56 per symptom-free day, or $2,362 per symptom-free year (2005 Canadian dollars); converted and uplifted to 2009 UK pounds, this makes £3.4 per symptom-free day or £1,240 per symptom-free year. When a societal perspective was considered, escitalopram dominated paroxetine, that is, escitalopram was more effective, and at the same time was associated with lower total costs, compared with paroxetine. These results were robust to changes in rates of response, tolerance and adherence. Based on their results, the authors concluded that escitalopram was more cost effective than paroxetine for the treatment of GAD. However, the results are difficult to interpret due to lack of use of QALYs as the outcome measure. In addition, the study was conducted in Canada and therefore is not directly applicable to the UK setting. Finally, the study is at risk of bias as it was funded by the pharmaceutical industry.

The fifth study included in the systematic economic literature review was a modelling study that compared venlafaxine XL versus standard care for the treatment of GAD from the perspective of the healthcare sector in Australia (Heuzenroeder *et al.*, 2004). Standard care was defined as a mixture of care based on evidence-based medicine principles (27%), non-evidence-based medicine principles (28%) and no care (45%). The study population was the total estimated adult population with GAD in Australia, according to national surveys. The measure of outcome was the number of DALYs saved. The source of clinical effectiveness data was a meta-analysis of two RCTs (Allgulander *et al.*, 2001; Davidson *et al.*, 1999). Resource use estimates were based on assumptions; national unit prices were used. The study reported that use of venlafaxine XL for the treatment of the adult population in Australia incurred an extra Aus$77 million and saved 3,300 DALYs compared with standard care, resulting in an incremental cost of $30,000/DALY saved, which ranged between $20,000 and $51,000/DALY saved in sensitivity analysis. The study, although meeting the systematic review inclusion criteria, was considered to be non-applicable to the UK setting for the following reasons: it was conducted in Australia, the outcome measure was DALYs saved, which limited the interpretability of the study findings, and standard care, according to its definition, was likely to differ significantly from standard care in the NHS. For these reasons the study was not considered further during the guideline development process.

8.8.3   Economic modelling

Introduction – objective of economic modelling
The cost effectiveness of pharmacological interventions relative to other available treatments for people with GAD was considered by the GDG as an area with likely significant resource implications. The GDG was particularly interested in the cost effectiveness of pharmacological interventions compared with low- and high-intensity psychological interventions, as well as in the relative cost effectiveness between different pharmacological interventions, including no treatment (placebo).

The development of an economic model comparing pharmacological interventions with low- and high-intensity psychological interventions using clinical effectiveness data from the guideline systematic review was not possible: no RCTs directly comparing pharmacological with psychological interventions were identified in the systematic clinical literature review. Indirect (clinical) comparisons between pharmacological and psychological interventions using a common 'baseline' comparator were problematic because of important differences in study designs in terms of the following:

- Comparators: psychological studies used mainly waitlist or standard care as a comparator, while studies on pharmacological treatments used placebo as control (but never waitlist or standard care); therefore, it was not possible to make indirect comparisons between pharmacological and psychological interventions using a common 'baseline' comparator.
- Reported clinical outcomes: psychological studies tended to report mainly continuous outcomes. Few psychological studies reported rates of response or remission, which were often used as outcome measures in pharmacological studies; even then, the definitions of response and remission in psychological studies were not the same as the respective definitions in pharmacological studies.
- Study population: a number of studies on low-intensity psychological interventions were conducted on people with mixed anxiety rather than GAD only; in contrast, only studies on people with GAD were included in the systematic literature review of pharmacological interventions.

Due to the above limitations, which did not allow consideration of both psychological and pharmacological treatments in one economic analysis, an economic model was developed to assess the relative cost effectiveness between different pharmacological interventions for people with GAD in the UK. This analysis was considered as a priority by the GDG, because of the likely significant resource implications associated with the choice of drug in the treatment of people with GAD. Moreover, existing economic evidence in the area of pharmacological treatment for people with GAD is rather limited and not directly applicable to the UK setting, since only two of the five studies were conducted in the UK. The economic studies included in the systematic review were characterised by a number of limitations; besides, they did not assess the whole range of drugs available in the UK for the treatment of people with GAD.

Economic modelling methods
Interventions assessed

The choice of drugs assessed in the economic analysis was determined by the availability of respective clinical data included in the guideline systematic literature review. The economic analysis considered all drugs with an acceptable risk-to-benefit ratio, as demonstrated by the systematic review of clinical evidence, that were deemed appropriate as first-line pharmacological treatment options for people with GAD. Based on the findings of the clinical systematic review, the following drugs were assessed in the economic analysis: duloxetine, escitalopram, paroxetine, pregabalin, sertraline and venlafaxine XL. It must be noted that sertraline was included in the economic analysis, despite the fact that it is not licensed for the treatment of people with GAD, because available evidence suggested that this is an effective drug in the treatment of GAD, with an acceptable risk-to-benefit ratio. Sertraline is widely used in the UK for the treatment of depression and mixed depression and anxiety; the

GDG acknowledged that it is likely to be less commonly used in the treatment of GAD, but that this is probably because people presenting with anxiety in primary care are not often diagnosed with GAD. The model also considered no pharmacological treatment (placebo), consisting of GP visits only, as one of the treatment options.

Model structure

A decision-analytic model in the form of a decision-tree was constructed using Microsoft Office Excel 2007. The structure of the model was determined by the availability of clinical data. According to the model structure, hypothetical cohorts of people with GAD were initiated on each of the six drugs assessed (first-line drug) or no pharmacological treatment. People initiated on the first-line drug could either continue treatment for 8 weeks, or discontinue due to intolerable side effects during this 8-week period. For modelling purposes, it was assumed that drug discontinuation because of intolerable side effects occurred at 2 weeks following initiation of treatment; this was based on the GDG's estimate that the majority of people discontinuing treatment because of intolerable side effects do so within 2 weeks from starting treatment. People who continued on the first-line drug either responded to treatment or did not respond. Those who responded were given maintenance treatment (consisting of the same drug) for 6 months. During this period, they either experienced a relapse or did not relapse. In each cohort, people discontinuing the first-line drug due to intolerable side effects and those not responding to the first-line drug were switched to a second-line drug, which was a mixture of all drugs assessed in the economic analysis, except the first-line drug administered to this cohort. People taking the second-line drug were all assumed to continue treatment with this drug. From that point onwards they followed the same pathways as people who continued the first-line drug (that is, no response or response and maintenance treatment, during which they could relapse or not relapse). People receiving no pharmacological treatment were assumed to either discontinue treatment, in which case they did not clinically improve ('no response'), or continue their treatment and follow a similar pathway to that experienced by people continuing pharmacological treatment (that is, no response or response followed by relapse or no relapse). The time horizon of the analysis was 42 weeks, based on the optimal duration of initial pharmacological treatment (8 weeks) and maintenance treatment (26 weeks), and in order to allow for switching to second-line treatment in case the 8-week first-line treatment did not lead to response. A schematic diagram of the decision-tree is presented in Figure 6.

Costs and outcomes considered in the analysis

The economic analysis adopted the perspective of the NHS and personal social services, as recommended by NICE (2009a). Costs consisted of intervention costs (drug acquisition and GP visit costs) and other health and social care costs incurred by people with GAD not responding to treatment or experiencing a relapse following response (including contacts with healthcare professionals such as GPs, psychiatrists, psychologists, mental health nurses and social workers, community care, inpatient and outpatient secondary care). The measure of outcome was the QALY.

Figure 6. Schematic diagram of the decision-tree constructed for the assessment of the relative cost effectiveness of pharmacological interventions for people with GAD

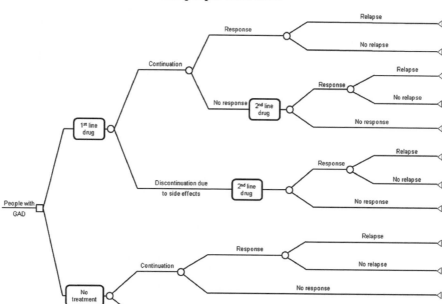

Clinical input parameters and overview of methods employed for evidence synthesis
Clinical input parameters consisted of the probability of drug discontinuation due to intolerable side effects, the probability of response for those not discontinuing treatment due to side effects (conditional response), and the probability of relapse following response to treatment.

The guideline systematic review of the clinical literature on pharmacological treatments identified two dichotomous outcomes that could be utilised in economic modelling: response (defined in the vast majority of studies as 50% reduction in HAM-A scores) and remission (defined in the vast majority of studies as a HAM-A score below 7). Utilisation of both types of data was not possible because not all studies provided data on both outcomes; therefore, it was not possible to estimate the numbers of people with GAD who responded to treatment but did not meet criteria for remission, and of those who responded to treatment and remitted for the whole dataset. For the economic model, it was decided to utilise response (rather than remission) data for the following reasons:

- response data were available from a larger number of studies including a higher number of participants, compared with data on remission
- available relapse data referred to people who had responded to treatment; no relapse data following remission were available in the guideline systematic review

● utility data were available for the health state of 'response' but not for the health state of 'remission'; in addition, there were utility data available for 'relapse following response' but not for 'relapse following remission'.

The availability of clinical and utility data, and the subsequent selection of response data in order to populate the model, determined the economic model structure.

To take all trial information into consideration, network (mixed treatment comparison) meta-analytic techniques were employed to synthesise evidence on discontinuation due to intolerable side effects, as well as evidence on conditional response (the methods used can be found in Appendix 13). Network meta-analysis is a generalisation of standard pair-wise meta-analysis for A versus B trials to data structures that include, for example, A versus B, B versus C and A versus C trials (Lu & Ades, 2004). A basic assumption of network meta-analysis is that direct and indirect evidence estimate the same parameter; in other words, the relative effect between A and B measured directly from an A versus B trial is the same with the relative effect between A and B estimated indirectly from A versus C and B versus C trials. Network meta-analytic techniques strengthen inference concerning the relative effect of two treatments by including both direct and indirect comparisons between treatments and, at the same time, allow simultaneous inference on all treatments examined in the pair-wise trial comparisons while respecting randomisation (Lu & Ades, 2004; Caldwell *et al.*, 2005). Simultaneous inference on the relative effect of a number of treatments is possible provided that treatments participate in a single 'network of evidence', that is, every treatment is linked to at least one of the other treatments under assessment through direct or indirect comparisons.

Details on the methods and clinical data utilised in the two network meta-analyses that were undertaken to estimate the probability of discontinuation due to intolerable side effects and the probability of conditional response for each treatment option considered in the economic analysis (that is, each first-line drug or no pharmacological treatment) are presented in Appendix 13. The findings of the two network meta-analyses are discussed in the next sub-section. The probability of response for the second-line drug in each decision node of the model was calculated as the average probability of conditional response of all drugs except the one that was used as a first-line treatment in this particular node of the model.

The probability of relapse following response to treatment was estimated based on relevant data included in the guideline systematic review. Four placebo-controlled trials assessed the efficacy of pharmacological treatments in preventing relapse in people with GAD: two of them assessed an SSRI (ALLGULANDER2006 – escitalopram; STOCCHI2003 – paroxetine), one assessed an SNRI (DAVIDSON2008 – duloxetine) and one assessed pregabalin (FELTNER2008). According to the expert opinion of the GDG, pregabalin is not a drug routinely used in the maintenance treatment of people with GAD. Moreover, the relative risk of relapse of pharmacological treatment versus placebo was higher in FELTNER2008 compared with the respective relative risk estimated for each of the other three studies, indicating that pregabalin may be potentially less effective than the other three drugs in preventing relapse in people with GAD that has responded to initial treatment. Inclusion of data from FELTNER2008 in a meta-analysis of the above four trials increased the heterogeneity of the analysis considerably (87% when data from all four studies were pooled together versus 0% when data from FELTNER2008 were excluded). For the above reasons, the estimation of the relative risk of relapse of pharmacological treatment versus placebo was based on meta-analysis of the remaining three studies (ALLGU-LANDER2006, DAVIDSON2008, STOCCHI2003). This estimate was utilised in all decision nodes of the model that involved pharmacological treatment, including the pregabalin node. Nevertheless, the probability of relapse following response in the 'no treatment' node of the model was estimated by pooling data from the placebo arms of all four studies.

Table 71 provides all the clinical input parameters utilised in the economic model.

Findings of the network meta-analyses undertaken to inform the economic analysis
The summary statistics of a number of parameters of the two network meta-analyses undertaken to inform the economic analysis, including the log hazard ratios of all drugs considered in the economic analysis versus placebo and the between-trial variation, are reported in Appendix 13.

Table 68 provides the results of the network meta-analysis of data on drug discontinuation due to side effects, as well as the findings of classical pair-wise comparisons of each drug versus placebo on the same outcome. Results of the network meta-analysis are reported as mean values with 95% credible intervals, which are analogous to confidence intervals in frequentist statistics. Only results on options considered in the economic analysis are presented. The table shows the probability of each option leading to discontinuation side effects over 8 weeks of treatment, the probability of each option being the 'best' among available options in averting discontinuation due to side effects, as well as the hazard ratio of each drug versus placebo in this outcome. In addition to these three parameters examined in the network meta-analysis, the table shows the relative risk of each drug versus placebo for discontinuation due to side effects (mean and 95% confidence intervals), as estimated in the guideline classical, pair-wise meta-analysis. Treatment options have been ranked from 'best' to 'worst' in terms of their ability to minimise discontinuation due to side effects, according to the results of the network meta-analysis.

The results of the network meta-analysis indicated that placebo had the lowest probability of discontinuation due to side effects (mean 5.8% over 8 weeks). Among drugs, sertraline had the lowest probability of leading to discontinuation due to side effects (mean 7.2% over 8 weeks), followed by pregabalin, escitalopram, paroxetine, venlafaxine XL and, finally, duloxetine (mean 17.5% over 8 weeks). The probability of sertraline being the best drug in limiting discontinuation due to side effects reached 61%. All drugs showed a significantly higher hazard of discontinuation compared with placebo, except sertraline. The results of the guideline classical meta-analysis of placebo-controlled trials were consistent overall with the findings of the network meta-analysis: it can be seen that the ranking of relative risks of each drug versus placebo with respect to discontinuation due to side effects (classical, pair-wise meta-analysis) was the same with the ranking of the hazard ratios (network meta-analysis), with the exception of venlafaxine XL. The relative effect of sertraline versus placebo was found to be non-significant in the classical pair-wise meta-analysis, in accordance with the finding in the network meta-analysis. However, it must be noted that

Table 68: **Pharmacological treatment discontinuation due to side effects: findings of the network meta-analysis and of classical pair-wise comparisons versus placebo**

Drug	Network meta-analysis (results for 8 weeks)				Classical pair-wise meta-analysis
	Probability (Pr) of discontinuation due to side effects (95% credible interval - CrI)	Pr that drug is best in averting discontinuation due to side effects	Pr that drug is best in averting discontinuation due to side effects (excluding placebo)	Hazard ratio (HR) versus placebo (95% CrI)	RR versus placebo (95% CI)
Placebo	0.058 (0.014, 0.161)	0.549			
Sertraline	0.072 (0.013, 0.237)	0.338	0.606	1.24 (0.60, 2.35)	1.10 (0.63, 1.91)
Pregabalin	0.086 (0.017, 0.256)	0.062	0.223	1.48 (1.06, 2.01)	1.31 (0.99, 1.74)
Escitalopram	0.094 (0.018, 0.275)	0.047	0.145	1.62 (1.09, 2.36)	1.72 (1.16, 2.53)
Paroxetine	0.135 (0.029, 0.381)	0.003	0.015	2.41 (1.72, 3.37)	2.50 (1.81, 3.45)
Venlafaxine XL	0.142 (0.031, 0.395)	0.001	0.008	2.55 (1.97, 3.32)	2.06 (1.59, 2.68)
Duloxetine	0.175 (0.037, 0.475)	0.000	0.003	3.26 (2.15, 4.84)	3.12 (1.55, 6.31)

data on sertraline were taken from a small number of studies relative to other drugs (two placebo-controlled studies with 706 participants). On the other hand, in contrast to pair-wise comparisons, which failed to demonstrate a significant effect of pregabalin compared with placebo in terms of discontinuation due to side effects, data combined in the network meta-analysis had sufficient strength to demonstrate that pregabalin significantly increases the risk of discontinuation due to side effects compared with placebo.

Table 69 provides the results of the network meta-analysis of data on conditional response (that is, response in people who have not discontinued the drug due to side effects), as well as the findings of classical pair-wise comparisons of each drug versus placebo on non-response. It must be noted that the classical meta-analysis was based on an intention-to-treat (ITT) approach, and therefore considered all trial participants, without excluding those who discontinued due to side effects (exclusion of people discontinuing due to side effects in the network meta-analysis was dictated by the economic model structure). The table shows the probability of conditional response of each option considered in the economic analysis over 8 weeks of treatment, the probability of each option being the 'best' in leading to conditional response among available options, as well as the hazard ratio of each drug versus placebo with respect

Table 69: Response to pharmacological treatment: findings of the network meta-analysis and of classical pair-wise comparisons versus placebo

Drug	Network meta-analysis (results for 8 weeks) Conditional response			Classical pair-wise meta-analysis – non-response
	Pr of conditional response (95% CrI)	Pr that drug is best in achieving response (in those who have not discontinued the drug due to side effects)	HR versus placebo (95% CrI) – conditional response	RR versus placebo (95% CI) – non-response
Duloxetine	0.651 (0.357, 0.919)	0.366	1.971 (1.549, 2.473)	0.75 (0.62, 0.90)
Sertraline	0.629 (0.329, 0.910)	0.277	1.859 (1.302, 2.591)	0.70 (0.57, 0.86)
Venlafaxine XL	0.616 (0.337, 0.892)	0.166	1.777 (1.482, 2.120)	0.80 (0.71, 0.92)
Pregabalin	0.590 (0.315, 0.872)	0.090	1.643 (1.349, 1.978)	0.79 (0.73, 0.85)
Escitalopram	0.579 (0.305, 0.870)	0.083	1.596 (1.237, 2.020)	0.78 (0.63, 0.97)
Paroxetine	0.519 (0.261, 0.822)	0.018	1.330 (1.059, 1.660)	0.91 (0.73, 1.13)
Placebo	0.428 (0.223, 0.684)	0.000		

to conditional response. In addition to these three parameters examined in the network meta-analysis, the table shows the relative risk of each drug versus placebo regarding non-response (mean and 95% confidence intervals), as estimated in the guideline classical, pair-wise meta-analysis. Treatment options have been ranked from 'best' to 'worst' in terms of their ability to achieve conditional response, according to the results of the network meta-analysis.

The results of the network meta-analysis indicated that duloxetine had the highest probability of conditional response (mean 65.1% over 8 weeks), followed by sertraline, venlafaxine XL, pregabalin, escitalopram and paroxetine (mean 51.9% over 8 weeks). Placebo had the lowest probability of conditional response among options assessed (mean 42.8% over 8 weeks). The probability of duloxetine being the best drug in terms of response in people who have not discontinued their drug treatment was approximately 37%. Hazard ratios demonstrated that all drugs were significantly better than placebo in the outcome of conditional response. On the other hand, the relative risks derived from the guideline classical meta-analysis of placebo-controlled trials showed that all drugs significantly reduced the risk of non-response compared with placebo, with the exception of paroxetine; the latter demonstrated a positive effect which, nevertheless, did not reach statistical significance. However, it must be noted that since the data in the classical meta-analyses were based on ITT, cases of discontinuation due to side effects were counted as non-responders. This means that the classical meta-analysis considered both people who discontinued due to side effects, as well as people who did not discontinue due to side effects but did not respond to treatment either, as non-responders. This difference between network and classical meta-analysis may explain the discrepancies observed between the results: for example, duloxetine was shown to have the highest probability of conditional response (that is, the highest probability of response in those not discontinuing due to side effects) in the network meta-analysis, but not the lowest relative risk versus placebo in terms of non-response in the classical meta-analysis. The latter finding may be attributed to the fact that duloxetine is characterised by a high rate of discontinuation due to side effects, which reduces the response rate measured using an ITT approach. The lowest relative risk versus placebo in terms of non-response in the classical meta-analysis was that of sertraline. This is consistent with the fact that sertraline had the lowest probability of discontinuation due to side effects among the drugs considered, and, at the same time, the second highest probability of response in people who did not discontinue treatment due to side effects (that is, of conditional response).

The probability of discontinuation due to intolerable side effects and the probability of conditional response of each treatment option comprised the outcomes of the network meta-analyses that were utilised in the economic model. These data are also provided in Table 71.

Utility data and estimation of quality-adjusted life years
In order to express outcomes in the form of QALYs, the health states of the economic model needed to be linked to appropriate utility scores. Utility scores represent the HRQoL associated with specific health states on a scale from 0 (death) to 1 (perfect

health); they are estimated using preference-based measures that capture people's preferences on the HRQoL experienced in the health states under consideration. The systematic search of the literature identified two studies that reported utility scores for specific health states associated with GAD (Allgulander *et al.*, 2007; Revicki *et al.*, 2008). Details on the studies, their methods and reported utility data are provided in the respective section of the economic model described in Section 6.6.4.

According to NICE guidance regarding the selection of utility scores for use in cost-utility analysis, the measurement of changes in HRQoL should be reported directly from people with the condition examined, and the valuation of health states should be based on public preferences elicited using a choice-based method, such as TTO or SG, in a representative sample of the UK population. NICE recommends the EQ-5D (Brooks, 1996) as the preferred measure of HRQoL in adults for use in cost-utility analysis. When EQ-5D scores are not available or are inappropriate for the condition or effects of treatment, NICE recommends that the valuation methods be fully described and comparable to those used for the EQ-5D (NICE, 2008a).

Available utility data for people with GAD were not generated using EQ-5D. However, both studies included in the respective review used SF-6D for the estimation of utility scores in this population. SF-36 (and its shorter form SF-12) is a validated generic measure of HRQoL. The SF-6D algorithm can generate utility scores for all health states described from SF-36 (Brazier *et al.*, 2002) and SF-12 (Brazier & Roberts, 2004), which have been elicited from a representative sample of the UK general population using SG; thus the valuation method meets NICE criteria.

The utility data reported in Allgulander and colleagues (2006) corresponded to the health states described in the economic model (that is, response, non-response, relapse following response, and no relapse following response); moreover, the definition of response in Allgulander and colleagues (2006) was the same as that used in all RCTs considered in the network meta-analysis that provided data on conditional response for the economic model. In contrast, the utility data reported in Revicki and colleagues (2008) corresponded to the health states of mild, moderate and severe anxiety, which could not be directly linked to the model health states of response, no response, relapse following response and no relapse following response. Therefore, it was decided to use the utility data reported in Allgulander and colleagues (2006) in the economic analysis.

It was assumed that the improvement in utility for people with GAD responding to treatment occurred linearly over the 8 weeks of treatment, starting from the utility value of non-response and reaching the utility value of response. People responding and not relapsing were assumed to experience a linear increase in their utility during the 6 months of maintenance treatment, starting from the utility value of response and reaching the utility value of response and no relapse. In contrast, people relapsing following response were assumed to experience a linear reduction in their utility during maintenance treatment, starting from the utility value of response and reaching the utility value of relapse following response.

Side effects of medication are expected to result in a reduction in utility scores corresponding to GAD-related health states. However, no studies on people with GAD reporting such 'disutility' due to side effects were identified in the literature. On the other hand, Revicki and Wood (1998) examined the effect of the presence of side effects associated with antidepressants in the HRQoL of people with depression. According to the study, people with a side effect reported lower utility scores compared with those not experiencing side effects. The observed mean disutility ranged from 0.01 for dry mouth and nausea to 0.12 for nervousness and light-headedness. However, except for light-headedness and dizziness, the reduction in utility caused by side effects did not reach statistical significance.

Clinical evidence on people with GAD suggests that side effects from drugs considered in the economic analysis consist mainly of nausea, insomnia and sexual problems (SSRIs and SNRIs), as well as dizziness, fatigue and headaches (pregabalin). Less common side effects include palpitations, tachycardia and orthostatic hypotension associated with duloxetine; SNRIs may increase blood pressure. Both SSRIs and SNRIs may result in suicidal thinking and self-harming behaviour in a minority of young people. Finally, SSRIs can cause gastrointestinal bleeding, especially if they are administered alongside NSAIDs.

Data on the risk for common, tolerable side effects have not been consistently collected and reported across RCTs included in the guideline systematic review, but available evidence indicates that all drugs are associated with such side effects in a similar degree. Data on less common but more severe side effects were sparser. On the other hand, discontinuation due to intolerable side effects was consistently reported in clinical trials. Development of intolerable side effects is expected to reduce more significantly the HRQoL of people with GAD compared with tolerable side effects.

Based on the above facts, data availability and limitations of available evidence, the economic analysis did consider the reduction in utility caused by intolerable side effects, given that data on discontinuation due to side effects were consistently reported for all drugs and analysed using network meta-analysis. The disutility caused by intolerable side effects was assumed to equal 0.12, which was the highest reduction in utility caused by the presence of side effects reported by people with depression taking antidepressants (Revicki & Wood, 1998). This reduction in utility due to intolerable side effects was assumed to last only 2 weeks, as discontinuation of drug treatment due to intolerable side effects was estimated to occur usually within 2 weeks from initiation of the particular drug. However, the reduction in utility caused by tolerable side effects was not considered in the economic analysis for two reasons: (i) inconsistent reporting of clinical data on tolerable side effects in RCTs might introduce bias in the economic analysis, should such data be included in the economic model, and (ii) available evidence on people with depression indicated that the majority of common side effects of antidepressants do not significantly reduce the HRQoL. Regarding less common and more severe side effects, such as gastrointestinal bleeding and suicidal thinking, these are likely to have a stronger negative impact on the HRQoL, but, given their low frequency, the implications of their omission (in terms of utility losses) are deemed to be less substantial at a study population level. Nevertheless, the lack of full consideration of the impact of side effects on the HRQoL of people with GAD treated with medication is acknowledged as a limitation of the economic analysis.

Cost data

Costs associated with the pharmacological treatment of people with GAD were calculated by combining resource-use estimates with respective national unit costs. Costs consisted of intervention costs and other health and social care costs incurred by people with GAD not responding to treatment or relapsing following response. Intervention costs of pharmacological treatment consisted of drug acquisition costs and GP visit costs. Intervention costs of no pharmacological treatment related to GP visit costs only. All costs were expressed in 2009 prices, uplifted, where necessary, using the HCHS Pay and Prices Index (Curtis, 2009). Discounting of costs was not necessary since the time horizon of the analysis was shorter than 1 year.

Drug acquisition costs were taken from the *British National Formulary* (BNF) 59 (British Medical Association and the Royal Pharmaceutical Society of Great Britain, March 2010). For each drug the lowest reported price was selected and used in the analysis; where available, costs of generic forms were considered. The average daily dosage of each drug was determined according to optimal clinical practice (the expert opinion of the GDG) and was consistent with the respective average daily dosage reported in the RCTs considered in the economic model. People discontinuing treatment due to intolerable side effects were assumed to have been already prescribed 1 month's drug supply for their initiated drug, and therefore incurred the initiated drug cost over 4 weeks before switching to second-line treatment. The average daily dosages and acquisition costs as well as the total ingredient costs over 8 weeks of initial treatment and 6 months of maintenance treatment for all drugs are presented in Table 70. The ingredient cost of the second-line drug in each arm of the model was assumed to equal the average ingredient cost of all drugs except the one that was used as first-line treatment in this particular arm.

Regarding GP visits, these included one visit at initiation, two visits over the first 8 weeks of treatment, and another visit during maintenance treatment. People who discontinued their first-line treatment due to intolerable side effects were assumed to pay one extra visit to their GP, and then were initiated on second-line drug treatment following the same pattern of GP visits as that estimated for the first-line drug treatment. This pattern of GP visits was also assumed to apply to the cohort of people under no pharmacological treatment.

Costs of managing tolerable side effects were not considered separately in the analysis, partly due to inconsistent reporting of side-effect data in the RCTs included in the guideline systematic review of clinical evidence. Nevertheless, the GDG estimated that the majority of common tolerable side effects, such as nausea, insomnia, sexual problems (associated with SSRIs and SNRIs), dizziness, fatigue and headaches (associated with pregabalin), as well as the less commonly observed suicidal thinking (associated with antidepressants administered to younger people), palpitations and tachycardia (associated with duloxetine), would be discussed during monitoring GP visits which were considered at the estimation of intervention costs relating to initial and maintenance pharmacological treatment. It was the GDG's view that even if the presence of these common side effects led to extra GP visits and incurred additional costs, these were unlikely to be considerable compared with total intervention costs. Regarding less common side effects, such as hypertension

**Table 70: Average daily dosage, acquisition costs and estimated 8-week and
6-month ingredient costs of drugs used in the treatment of people with
GAD included in the economic model**

Drug	Average daily dosage	Unit cost (BNF 59, March 2010)	8-week ingredient cost	6-month ingredient cost
Duloxetine	60 mg	Cymbalta 60 mg, 28-cap pack = £27.72	£55.44	£180.18
Escitalopram	10 mg	Cipralex 10 mg, 28-tab pack = £14.91	£29.82	£96.92
Paroxetine	20 mg	Generic 20 mg, 30-tab pack = £2.58	£4.82	£15.65
Pregabalin	300 mg divided in two doses of 150 mg	Lyrica 150 mg, 56-cap pack = £64.40	£128.80	£418.60
Sertraline	100 mg	Generic 100 mg, 28-tab pack = £1.59	£3.18	£10.34
Venlafaxine XL	75 mg	Venaxx XL 75 mg, 28-cap pack = £10.40	£20.80	£67.60

(associated with SNRIs) and gastrointestinal bleeding (associated with SSRIs), these
were thought to result in higher management costs at an individual level, but given
their low frequency they were deemed to entail smaller economic implications at a
study population level. Therefore, although omission of costs associated with
management of tolerable side effects is acknowledged as a limitation of the analysis,
it is not considered to have substantially affected the economic modelling results.

The extra health and social care costs incurred by people with GAD not responding to treatment or relapsing following response to treatment were estimated based on
data reported in the *Adult Psychiatric Morbidity in England* survey (McManus *et al.*,
2009), supported by the expert opinion of the GDG. Data on resources used by people
with GAD (including inpatient care, outpatient services, contacts with GPs, psychiatrists, psychologists, community psychiatric nurses, social workers and services
provided by community day care centres) were combined with appropriate national
unit costs (Curtis, 2009; DH, 2010) in order to estimate a total weekly cost incurred
by people with GAD. The average length of stay for people with GAD receiving inpatient care was taken from national hospital episode statistics (NHS, The Information
Centre, 2009). Based on the above data, the health and social care cost incurred by
people with GAD not responding to treatment or relapse following response was

approximately £804 per year or £15 per week. Details on the methods of estimation of this cost are provided in the economic analysis described in Section 6.6.4. People who did not respond to second-line pharmacological treatment and those who did not respond to no pharmacological treatment were assumed to incur this weekly health and social care GAD-related cost for the remaining time horizon of the analysis following no response. People who relapsed following response to treatment were assumed to incur maintenance treatment costs over 3 months and this health and social care GAD-related cost over the remaining 3 months of the 6-month mainte-nance treatment period that led to relapse.

Costs of treating tolerable side effects were not considered in the economic analy-sis due to lack of consistency in reporting appropriate side-effect data across all drugs.

Table 71 reports the mean (deterministic) values of all input parameters utilised in the economic model and provides information on the distributions assigned to specific parameters in probabilistic sensitivity analysis.

Data analysis and presentation of the results
Two methods were employed to analyse the input parameter data and present the results of the economic analysis.

First, a *deterministic* analysis was undertaken, where data are analysed as point estimates; results are presented as mean total costs and QALYs associated with each treatment option are assessed. Relative cost effectiveness between alternative treat-ment options is estimated using incremental analysis: all options are initially ranked from most to least effective; options that are dominated (they are more expensive and less effective than other options) are excluded from further analysis. Subsequently, ICERs are calculated for all pairs of consecutive options. ICERs express the addi-tional cost per additional unit of benefit associated with one treatment option relative to its comparator. Estimation of such a ratio allows consideration of whether the addi-tional benefit is worth the additional cost when choosing one treatment option over another.

After excluding cases of extended dominance (which occur when an intervention is less effective and more costly than a linear combination of two other options), ICERs are recalculated. The treatment option with the highest ICER below the cost-effectiveness threshold is the most cost-effective option.

One-way sensitivity analyses explored the following:
- The impact of the uncertainty characterising the monthly health and social care cost incurred by people with GAD not responding to treatment or relapsing following response on the results of the deterministic analysis. Since the estima-tion of this cost was based on a number of assumptions and data extrapolations, a scenario of a 70% change in this cost was tested to investigate whether the conclu-sions of the analysis would change.
- The impact of an increase in the extra GP visits following discontinuation of the first-line treatment due to intolerable side effects. The impact of three extra GP visits on the results was tested (in base-case analysis one extra visit was assumed).
- The uncertainty around the probability of response achieved by second-line drug treatment. In the base-case analysis, this probability was calculated as the average

Table 71: Input parameters utilised in the economic model of pharmacological treatments for people with GAD

Input parameter	Deterministic value	Probabilistic distribution	Source of data - comments
Probability of discontinuation because of intolerable side effects		**Distribution based on 10,000 iterations**	Network meta-analysis of data included in the guideline systematic review; data refer to a period of 8 weeks; distribution based on 10,000 iterations
		95% credible intervals	
Duloxetine	0.1750	0.0374 to 0.4749	
Escitalopram	0.0935	0.0182 to 0.2750	
Paroxetine	0.1348	0.0291 to 0.3808	
Pregabalin	0.0858	0.0172 to 0.2560	
Sertraline	0.0725	0.0127 to 0.2368	
Venlafaxine XL	0.1423	0.0312 to 0.3953	
No treatment	0.0583	0.0136 to 0.1614	
Probability of conditional response (in people who did not discontinue because of intolerable side effects)		**Distribution based on 10,000 iterations**	Network meta-analysis of data included in the guideline systematic review; data refer to a period of 8 weeks; distribution based on 10,000 iterations
		95% credible intervals	
Duloxetine	0.6509	0.3571 to 0.9194	
Escitalopram	0.5788	0.3051 to 0.8699	
Paroxetine	0.5190	0.2611 to 0.8219	
Pregabalin	0.5904	0.3147 to 0.8719	
Sertraline	0.6287	0.3290 to 0.9101	
Venlafaxine XL	0.6160	0.3371 to 0.8917	
No treatment	0.4277	0.2231 to 0.6838	
Probability of relapse – no treatment	0.4917	**Beta distribution** $\alpha = 416$; $\beta = 430$	Pooled data from 4 RCTs included in the guideline systematic review
Relative risk of relapse – drugs versus no treatment	0.32	**Log-norm distribution** 95% CIs: 0.26 to 0.40	Guideline meta-analysis excluding FELTNER2008

	Value	Distribution	Source / notes
Utilities		**Beta distribution**	Estimated using method of moments, based on data reported in Allgulander *et al.*, 2007
Response	0.760	α = 177.84; β = 56.16	
Non-response	0.630	α = 24.57; β = 14.43	
Relapse	0.730	α = 51.83; β = 19.17	
No relapse following response	0.790	α = 97.96; β = 26.04	
Disutility due to intolerable side effects	−0.120	α = 8.40; β = 61.60	Estimated using method of moments, based on data reported in Revicki & Wood, 1998
Drug acquisition costs (8 weeks)		**No distribution assigned**	BNF 59 (British Medical Association and the Royal Pharmaceutical Society of Great Britain, March 2010) – see Table 70 for more details
Duloxetine	£55.44		
Escitalopram	£29.82		
Paroxetine	£4.82		
Pregabalin	£128.80		
Sertraline	£3.18		
Venlafaxine XL	£20.80		
GP visit costs (common in drug treatment and no pharmacological treatment)		**Gamma distribution** SE: 30% of mean value (assumption)	Using an estimate of 3 visits over the 8 weeks of initial treatment, 1 visit during the 6 months of maintenance treatment and 1 extra visit in case of discontinuation (the expert opinion of the GDG); combined with national unit costs (Curtis, 2009)
Initial 8-week treatment	£105		
Maintenance 6-month treatment	£35		
Discontinuation of treatment	£35		
Weekly health and social care cost incurred by people with GAD	£15.47	**Gamma distribution** SE: 30% of mean value (assumption)	Based on resource use data from a national psychiatric morbidity survey (McManus *et al.*, 2009) and the expert opinion of the GDG, combined with national unit costs (Curtis, 2009; DH, 2010); average length of inpatient stay for people with GAD based on national sources (NHS, The Information Centre, 2009)

probability of conditional response of all drugs considered in the analysis except the one that was used as first-line treatment in each particular decision node of the model. However, it is possible that responsiveness to a drug used as second-line is lower than that observed when the drug is used as first-line. Therefore a scenario in which the responsiveness of the second-line drug was reduced by 15% was tested.

In addition to deterministic analysis, a *probabilistic* analysis was also conducted. In this case, all model input parameters were assigned probability distributions (rather than being expressed as point estimates), to reflect the uncertainty character-ising the available clinical and cost data. Subsequently, 10,000 iterations were performed, each drawing random values out of the distributions fitted onto the model input parameters. This exercise provided more accurate estimates of mean costs and benefits for each intervention assessed (averaging results from the 10,000 iterations), by capturing the non-linearity characterising the economic model structure (Briggs *et al.*, 2006).

The distributions of the probability of discontinuation due to intolerable side effects and the probability of conditional response for each drug, which were obtained using mixed treatment comparison techniques, were defined directly from values recorded in each of the 10,000 iterations performed in WinBUGS, as described in Appendix 13.

The probability of relapse for no pharmacological treatment was given a beta distribution. Beta distributions were also assigned to utility values, using the method of moments. The relative risk of relapse of drug treatment versus no treatment was assigned a log-normal distribution. The estimation of distribution ranges was based on available data in the guideline meta-analysis (relapse data) and the published sources of evidence (utility data). Costs (with the exception of drug acquisition costs) were assigned a gamma distribution; in order to define the distribution, a 30% stan-dard error around the mean costs was assumed.

Table 71 provides details on the types of distributions assigned to each input parameter and the methods employed to define their range.

Results of probabilistic analysis are presented in the form of CEACs, which demonstrate the probability of each treatment option being the most cost effective among the strategies assessed at different levels of willingness-to-pay per unit of effectiveness (that is, at different cost-effectiveness thresholds the decision maker may set). In addition, the cost-effectiveness acceptability frontier is provided along-side CEACs, showing which treatment option among those examined offers the high-est average net monetary benefit (NMB) at each level of willingness-to-pay (Fenwick *et al.*, 2001). The NMB of a treatment option at different levels of willingness-to-pay is defined by the following formula:

$$NMB = E \cdot \lambda - C$$

Where E is effectiveness (number of QALYs), C is the costs associated with the treatment, and λ is the level of the willingness-to-pay per unit of effectiveness.

8.8.4   Economic modelling results

Results of deterministic analysis

According to deterministic analysis, sertraline was the most cost-effective option among those assessed because it produced the highest number of QALYs and was associated with the lowest costs (dominant option). 'No pharmacological treatment' was dominated by all drugs except pregabalin; the latter was more effective than placebo at an extra cost of £3,768 per QALY.

Table 72 provides mean costs and QALYs for every treatment option assessed in the economic analysis. The seven options have been ranked from the most to the least effective in terms of number of QALYs gained. It can be seen that sertraline is associated with lowest costs and highest benefits (QALYs) and consequently dominates all other drugs as well as no treatment. Figure 7 provides the cost-effectiveness plane showing the incremental costs and QALYs of all drugs versus paroxetine. It can be seen that sertraline is in the southeast quadrant and has the highest number of QALYs and the lowest costs relative to all other drugs assessed (no treatment is not shown in this graph).

Results were robust under all scenarios examined in one-way sensitivity analyses: sertraline remained dominant when the health and social care costs incurred by people with GAD not responding to treatment or relapsing following response increased by 70%, when three extra GP visits (instead of one) were assumed in the case of discontinuation of first-line treatment, and when conditional response for the second-line drug was reduced by 15%. Sertraline dominated all options except no treatment when the health and social costs incurred by people with GAD not responding to treatment or relapsing following response decreased by 70%. In this case, the ICER of sertraline versus no treatment was £946 per QALY gained, which is well

Table 72: Mean costs and QALYs for each pharmacological treatment option for people with GAD assessed in the economic analysis - results per 1,000 people

Treatment option	Mean total QALYs	Mean total costs	Cost effectiveness
Sertraline	589.49	£347,372	Dominant
Duloxetine	587.65	£481,213	Dominated
Pregabalin	587.48	£652,467	Dominated
Venlafaxine XL	587.16	£405,013	Dominated
Escitalopram	586.81	£426,541	Dominated
Paroxetine	583.59	£393,755	Dominated
No treatment	547.19	£500,674	Dominated

Figure 7: Cost-effectiveness plane of all drugs assessed in the economic analysis plotted against paroxetine – incremental costs and QALYs per 1,000 people with GAD

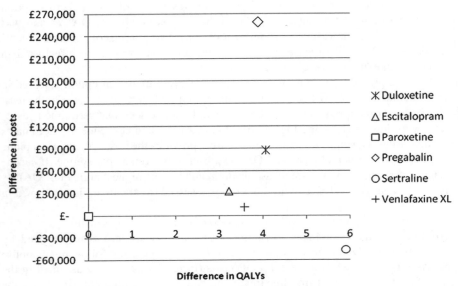

below the lower cost-effectiveness threshold of £20,000 per QALY set by NICE (NICE, 2008b).

Results of probabilistic analysis
Results of probabilistic analysis were very similar to those of deterministic analysis: sertraline dominated all other treatment options when mean costs and QALYs derived from 10,000 iterations were estimated. Sertraline had also the highest probability of being the most cost-effective treatment option, at any level of willingness-to-pay per additional QALY gained. At the lower NICE cost-effectiveness threshold of £20,000/QALY (NICE, 2008b) the probability of sertraline being cost effective was 0.70, whereas venlafaxine XL, which was the second most cost-effective option, had a probability of only 0.13. The cost-effectiveness acceptability frontier coincided with the CEAC for sertraline, because sertraline produced the highest average net benefit at any level of willingness to pay.

Figure 8 shows the CEACs generated for each pharmacological treatment option assessed in the economic model. Table 73 shows the probability of each treatment option being cost effective at various cost-effectiveness thresholds, that is, at various levels of willingness-to-pay per QALY gained.

Discussion – limitations of the analysis
The results of the economic analysis suggest that sertraline is likely to be the most cost-effective pharmacological treatment for people with GAD. Sertraline dominated

Figure 8: CEACs of all pharmacological treatment options for people with GAD assessed in the economic analysis

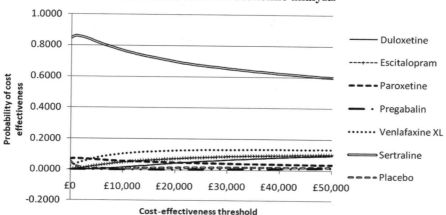

all other treatment options and had the highest probability of being the most cost-effective option at any level of willingness-to-pay per QALY gained, which reached 0.70 at the lower NICE cost-effectiveness threshold of £20,000 per QALY. The cost effectiveness of sertraline is attributed to a number of factors: sertraline had the lowest average probability of discontinuation due to intolerable side effects among all drugs assessed, and the second best probability of conditional response; in addition, sertraline had the lowest acquisition cost among all drugs, as it is available in generic form. It must be noted that sertraline is currently not licensed for the treatment of people with GAD.

Clinical data on discontinuation due to intolerable side effects as well as response for those who did not discontinue due to intolerable side effects (conditional response) were synthesised using network meta-analytic techniques. Such methods enable evidence synthesis from both direct and indirect comparisons between treatments, and allow simultaneous inference on all treatments examined in pair-wise trial comparisons while respecting randomisation (Lu & Ades, 2004; Caldwell *et al.*, 2005).

One limitation of the economic analysis was that data on conditional response for first-line drug treatment were also used to estimate the probability of response for second-line drug treatment, which, in every decision node of the model, was calculated as the average probability of conditional response of all drugs except the one that was used as first-line treatment in this particular node. This assumption was necessary in order to populate the model due to lack of response data on people with GAD switched to a second-line drug. However, it is possible that responsiveness to a drug used as second-line is lower than that observed when the drug is used as first-line. Nevertheless, one-way sensitivity analysis, in which the responsiveness of the second-line drug was assumed to be reduced by 15%, demonstrated that the results of the economic analysis were robust to this assumption.

Table 73: Probability of each pharmacological treatment option being cost effective at various levels of willingness-to-pay per QALY gained (WTP)

WTP	Duloxetine	Escitalopram	Paroxetine	Pregabalin	Sertraline	Venlafaxine XL	Placebo
£0	0.0000	0.0039	0.0685	0.0000	0.8481	0.0233	0.0562
£5,000	0.0045	0.0263	0.0639	0.0000	0.8199	0.0785	0.0069
£10,000	0.0154	0.0493	0.0556	0.0000	0.7662	0.1045	0.0090
£15,000	0.0291	0.0625	0.0508	0.0002	0.7280	0.1181	0.0113
£20,000	0.0439	0.0725	0.0466	0.0009	0.6966	0.1258	0.0137
£25,000	0.0558	0.0808	0.0440	0.0021	0.6724	0.1301	0.0148
£30,000	0.0661	0.0884	0.0412	0.0040	0.6529	0.1315	0.0159
£35,000	0.0747	0.0936	0.0392	0.0063	0.6356	0.1337	0.0169
£40,000	0.0830	0.0961	0.0378	0.0088	0.6212	0.1354	0.0177
£45,000	0.0902	0.0993	0.0363	0.0121	0.6087	0.1350	0.0184
£50,000	0.0963	0.1021	0.035	0.0148	0.5972	0.1359	0.0187

Another limitation of the economic analysis is that it did not take into account the reduction in HRQoL and the costs associated with the management of tolerable side effects, which do not lead to treatment discontinuation. Consideration of these factors was not possible as there was no consistent reporting of side effects across trials included in the systematic review. Moreover, there is limited evidence on the reduction in HRQoL caused by the presence of side effects from drugs considered in the analysis and no such evidence in people with GAD. Regarding the reduction in HRQoL associated with the presence of side effects from antidepressants, available evidence has demonstrated that this is largely insignificant in people with depression (Revicki & Wood, 1998). Regarding costs associated with the management of tolerable side effects, these were considered to be non-substantial, as most side effects are expected to be managed during GP monitoring visits, which have already been considered at the estimation of intervention costs of pharmacological treatment. It should be noted that the economic analysis did consider the impact of the development of intolerable side effects, which lead to treatment discontinuation, on costs and HRQoL associated with pharmacological treatment of people with GAD.

The economic analysis revealed that drug acquisition costs may be an important factor in determining the relative cost effectiveness of pharmacological treatments for GAD: sertraline, which was found to be the most cost-effective option resulting also in lowest total costs, has currently the lowest acquisition cost, as it is available in generic form. Paroxetine, which is also available in generic form and has the second lowest acquisition cost among the drugs assessed, was ranked the second least costly drug and fourth most cost-effective option at a cost-effectiveness threshold of £20,000 per QALY (with probability of being cost effective about 0.05), despite the fact that it had one of the highest probabilities of discontinuation due to side effects and the lowest probability of conditional response among drugs. Venlafaxine XL, which has the lowest acquisition cost among patented drugs included in the analysis, was ranked the third least costly drug and second most cost-effective option at a cost-effectiveness threshold of £20,000 per QALY (with probability of being cost effective about 0.13). Based on these findings, it is expected that the relative cost effectiveness of drugs for the treatment of GAD is likely to change in the future, as eventually drugs will become available in generic form, resulting in a considerable reduction in their acquisition costs.

8.8.5   Overall conclusions from economic evidence

Existing economic evidence is limited in the area of pharmacological treatment for people with GAD. Of the five studies meeting the inclusion criteria, one was considered as non-applicable to the UK setting (Heuzenroeder *et al.*, 2004) and was therefore not considered at formulation of recommendations. One study conducted in Canada (Iskedjian *et al.*, 2008) concluded that escitalopram was more cost effective than paroxetine. Another modelling study conducted in Spain concluded that paroxetine might be more cost effective than venlafaxine XL. Both studies are partially applicable to the UK context. Two other modelling studies that were conducted in the

UK and were thus directly applicable to the guideline development process concluded that escitalopram was more cost effective than paroxetine (Jørgensen *et al.*, 2006) and that venlafaxine XL was more cost effective than diazepam (Guest *et al.*, 2005). All four studies, considered at the development of guideline recommendations, were funded by the pharmaceutical industry, which may have introduced bias in the analyses. Overall, the choice of drugs evaluated in previously published economic literature is very limited. Therefore, it is difficult to draw conclusions on the cost effectiveness of particular pharmacological interventions for the treatment of people with GAD based on existing evidence.

The economic analysis undertaken for this guideline concluded that sertraline was the most cost-effective drug in the treatment of people with GAD, as it was associated with the highest number of QALYs and lowest total costs among all treatments assessed, including no treatment. Sertraline had the highest probability of being cost effective at any cost-effectiveness threshold, which reached 0.70 at the lower NICE cost-effectiveness threshold of £20,000/QALY.

8.9   FROM EVIDENCE TO RECOMMENDATIONS

Acute treatment

Short-term efficacy studies suggested that a range of pharmacological interventions were associated with a small to moderate benefit in reducing anxiety symptoms and reducing the risk of non-response and non-remission. Head-to-head studies were limited in number but suggested little difference between treatments. There was also consistent evidence of a higher probability of experiencing side effects for people receiving pharmacological treatment and a greater risk of discontinuation due to these side effects. In addition, it was noted that benzodiazepines appeared to be associated with risk of dependence therefore did not appear to be an appropriate medication for routine use for people with GAD who often require long-term treatment. Clinical data on quetiapine, although collected to increase inference in the network meta-analysis undertaken to support the guideline economic analysis, were not assessed, as this is the subject of a future NICE Technology Appraisal.

The GDG weighed up the evidence for benefit and harm for each of the acute treatments and identified interventions with sufficient clinical effectiveness data to be considered for further cost-effectiveness analysis. The following drugs were considered to have sufficient clinical effectiveness data and an acceptable harm-to-benefit ratio, and were thus considered as potentially suitable first-line pharmacological treatments: escitalopram, duloxetine, paroxetine, pregabalin, sertraline and venlafaxine XL. It must be noted that sertraline was included in the economic analysis, despite the fact that it is not licensed for the treatment of people with GAD, because available evidence suggested that this is an effective drug in the treatment of GAD, with an acceptable risk-to-benefit ratio. Sertraline is widely used in the UK for the treatment of depression and mixed depression and anxiety; the GDG acknowledged that it is likely to be less commonly used in the treatment of GAD, but that this is probably because people presenting with anxiety in primary care are not often diagnosed with GAD.

Several drugs that were assessed in the guideline systematic review and meta-analysis were not considered in the economic analysis. Lorazepam, alprazolam and diazepam were excluded from further consideration because of the well documented withdrawal syndrome associated with them. The GDG considered it would not be appropriate to recommend these drugs as first-line pharmacological treatments for GAD as it is a chronic disorder often requiring long-term treatment. Hydroxyzine and buspirone did not have sufficient evidence of clinical effectiveness as both were found to have no statistically significant difference from placebo in terms of non-response. Finally, citalopram and imipramine were not included in the economic model because for both drugs there was only one small trial, which was not sufficient to draw conclusions on their clinical effectiveness.

The network meta-analysis that was undertaken to inform the guideline economic analysis demonstrated that sertraline had the lowest probability of discontinuation due to intolerable side effects, followed by pregabalin, escitalopram, paroxetine, venlafaxine XL and duloxetine. Duloxetine had the highest probability of conditional response (that is, response in people not discontinuing pharmacological treatment due to intolerable side effects), followed by sertraline, venlafaxine XL, pregabalin, escitalopram and paroxetine. Network meta-analysis demonstrated that sertraline was the best drug in limiting discontinuation due to side effects, and the second best drug (following duloxetine) in achieving conditional response (that is, based on a completer analysis). Although duloxetine was the drug with the highest probability of conditional response, it was also associated with the highest risk of discontinuation due to side effects, indicating that its overall probability of response (in an ITT rather than a completer analysis) will be lower than the respective probability for sertraline. This is reinforced by a review of the relative risks of non-response of all drugs versus placebo in the classical meta-analysis, where an ITT approach was adopted, which shows that the relative risk of non-response versus placebo was lowest for sertraline, indicating that sertraline is likely to have the highest probability of overall response.

The guideline economic analysis demonstrated that sertraline dominated all other treatment options (that is, it was associated with lowest total costs and higher number of QALYs) and had the highest probability of being cost effective, which reached 0.70 at a willingness-to-pay of £20,000/QALY. All drugs were shown to be more effective and less costly than placebo, with the exception of pregabalin, which was more effective at an additional cost of roughly £3,800 per QALY, which is well below the NICE lower cost-effectiveness threshold of £20,000 per QALY (NICE, 2008b).

However, given the consistent evidence of a greater risk of side effects and discontinuation from treatment compared with placebo the GDG concluded that pharmacological interventions should only be routinely offered to people who have not benefited from low- or high-intensity psychological interventions.

Relapse prevention
There was a lack of data for most medications with only one trial each on paroxetine, escitalopram, pregabalin and duloxetine. In all of the four studies, continuing the treatment was more effective than being randomised to placebo and was not associated with greater risk of side effects.

Augmentation

There were limited data on the effectiveness of antipsychotics (olanzapine, risperidone and ziprasidone) as an augmentation treatment. There was no evidence to conclude that antipsychotics were effective as an augmentation treatment for reducing anxiety. In addition, there was evidence of an increase in discontinuation due to adverse events. The GDG therefore concluded, given the current evidence, that the benefits did not appear to justify the harms associated with antipsychotic augmentation. Therefore the GDG judged that such treatment should not be routinely used and should only be provided in specialist settings.

In addition, it was the judgment of the GDG that antipsychotics should not be offered in primary care as stand-alone or augmentation treatment, as this would require specialist expertise.

Side effects

There was consistent evidence that SSRIs were associated with an increased risk of gastrointestinal bleeding particularly in elderly people. Although such events were relatively rare, the GDG considered this was still important to take into account when considering prescribing an SSRI.

In addition, there was evidence that antidepressant use was associated with an increased probability of suicidal behaviour in participants under 25 years of age. The GDG also took into account related advice on risk of suicide from both the Medicines and Healthcare products Regulatory Agency (MHRA, 2004) and the NICE guideline on depression (NICE, 2009a) which suggested a cut-off of under 30 years of age. Therefore the GDG judged that it would be important for prescribers to inform this group of the potential risk and to monitor the risk early on in treatment.

8.10   RECOMMENDATIONS

Drug treatment

8.10.1.1   For people with GAD and marked functional impairment, or those whose symptoms have not responded adequately to step 2 interventions:
- Offer either
  - an individual high-intensity psychological intervention (see 7.11.1.2–7.11.1.6) or
  - drug treatment (see 8.10.1.2–8.10.1.12).
- Provide verbal and written information on the likely benefits and disadvantages of each mode of treatment, including the tendency of drug treatments to be associated with side effects and withdrawal syndromes.
- Base the choice of treatment on the person's preference as there is no evidence that either mode of treatment (individual high-intensity psychological intervention or drug treatment) is better. [16]

---

[16]This recommendation also appears in section 7.7.1.1 where the psychological data is presented.

8.10.1.2   If a person with GAD chooses drug treatment, offer a selective serotonin reuptake inhibitor (SSRI). Consider offering sertraline first because it is the most cost-effective drug, but note that at the time of publication (January 2011)[17] sertraline did not have UK marketing authorisation for this indication. Informed consent should be obtained and documented. Monitor the person carefully for adverse reactions.

8.10.1.3   If sertraline is ineffective, offer an alternative SSRI or a serotonin–noradrenaline reuptake inhibitor (SNRI), taking into account the following factors:

- tendency to produce a withdrawal syndrome (especially with paroxetine and venlafaxine)
- the side-effect profile and the potential for drug interactions
- the risk of suicide and likelihood of toxicity in overdose (especially with venlafaxine)
- the person's prior experience of treatment with individual drugs (particularly adherence, effectiveness, side effects, experience of withdrawal syndrome and the person's preference).

8.10.1.4   If the person cannot tolerate SSRIs or SNRIs, consider offering pregabalin.

8.10.1.5   Do not offer a benzodiazepine for the treatment of GAD in primary or secondary care except as a short-term measure during crises. Follow the advice in the 'British national formulary' on the use of a benzodiazepine in this context.

8.10.1.6   Do not offer an antipsychotic for the treatment of GAD in primary care.

8.10.1.7   Before prescribing any medication, discuss the treatment options and any concerns the person with GAD has about taking medication. Explain fully the reasons for prescribing and provide written and verbal information on:

- the likely benefits of different treatments
- the different propensities of each drug for side effects, withdrawal syndromes and drug interactions
- the risk of activation with SSRIs and SNRIs, with symptoms such as increased anxiety, agitation and problems sleeping
- the gradual development, over 1 week or more, of the full anxiolytic effect
- the importance of taking medication as prescribed and the need to continue treatment after remission to avoid relapse.

8.10.1.8   Take into account the increased risk of bleeding associated with SSRIs, particularly for older people or people taking other drugs that can damage the gastrointestinal mucosa or interfere with clotting (for example, NSAIDS or aspirin). Consider prescribing a gastroprotective drug in these circumstances.

8.10.1.9   For people aged under 30 who are offered an SSRI or SNRI:

- warn them that these drugs are associated with an increased risk of suicidal thinking and self-harm in a minority of people under 30 and
- see them within 1 week of first prescribing and
- monitor the risk of suicidal thinking and self-harm weekly for the first month.

---

[17]The date of publication of the NICE guideline containing the recommendations only on the NICE website: http://guidance.nice.org.uk/CG113

8.10.1.10 For people who develop side effects soon after starting drug treatment, provide information and consider one of the following strategies:
- monitoring the person's symptoms closely (if the side effects are mild and acceptable to the person) or
- reducing the dose of the drug or
- stopping the drug and, according to the person's preference, offering either
  - an alternative drug (see 8.10.1.13–8.10.1.4) or
  - a high-intensity psychological intervention (see 7.11.1.2–7.11.1.6).

8.10.1.11 Review the effectiveness and side effects of the drug every 2–4 weeks during the first 3 months of treatment and every 3 months thereafter.

8.10.1.12 If the drug is effective, advise the person to continue taking it for at least a year as the likelihood of relapse is high.

Inadequate response

8.10.1.13 If a person's GAD has not responded to drug treatment, offer either a high-intensity psychological intervention (see 7.11.1.2–7.11.1.6) or an alternative drug treatment (see 8.10.1.13–8.10.1.4)).

8.10.1.14 If a person's GAD has partially responded to drug treatment, consider offering a high-intensity psychological intervention in addition to drug treatment.

8.10.2   Research recommendations

8.10.2.1   A comparison of the clinical and cost effectiveness of sertraline and CBT in people with GAD that has not responded to guided self-help and psychoeducation

What is the relative effectiveness of sertraline compared with CBT in people with GAD that has not responded to guided self-help and psychoeducation in a stepped-care model?

This question should be addressed using a randomised controlled design in which people with GAD that has not responded to step 2 interventions are allocated openly to treatment with sertraline, CBT or waiting-list control for 12–16 weeks. The control group is important to demonstrate that the two active treatments produce effects greater than those of natural remission. The period of waiting-list control is the standard length of CBT treatment for GAD and is also commonly the length of time that it would take for specialist CBT to become available in routine practice. After 12–16 weeks all participants should receive further treatment chosen in collaboration with their treating clinicians.

The outcomes chosen at 12–16 weeks should include both observer- and participant-rated measures of clinical symptoms and functioning specific to GAD, and of quality of life. An economic analysis should also be carried out alongside the trial.

The trial needs to be large enough to determine the presence or absence of clinically important effects and of any differences in costs between the treatment options using a non-inferiority design. Mediators and moderators of response should be investigated. Follow-up assessments should continue over the next 2 years to ascertain whether short-term benefits are maintained and, in particular, whether CBT produces a better long-term outcome.

Why is this important?

Both sertraline and CBT are efficacious in the treatment of GAD but their relative efficacy has not been compared. In a stepped-care model both CBT and sertraline are treatment options if step 2 interventions (guided self-help and/or psychoeducation) have not resulted in a satisfactory clinical response. At present, however, there are no randomised trial data to help prioritise next-step treatments and no information on how individuals with GAD may be matched to particular therapies. Clarification of the relative short- and longer-term benefits of sertraline and CBT would be helpful in guiding treatment.

8.11 OTHER INTERVENTIONS

8.11.1 Introduction

There are a variety of herbal interventions that have been considered as possible treatments for GAD; these include chamomile, ginkgo biloba, combined plant extracts, valerian extract, galphimia glauca, lavender and passion flower. Chamomile is a common name for several daisy-like plants, which are best known for their ability to be made into a tea. It is not licensed as a medicine in the UK but can be bought 'over the counter' from health food shops, herbalists, supermarkets and community pharmacies. Many different branded preparations are available (Mann & Staba, 1986). Ginkgo biloba is one of the oldest living tree species and has been used in the past to treat circulatory disorders and to enhance memory. Similarly, gingko biloba is not licensed in the UK but can be bought 'over the counter'. Moreover, various preparations are available such as capsules, tablets, liquid extracts and dried leaves for teas (Johne & Roots, 2005). Combined plant extracts (that is, Sympathyl) consists of hawthorn berry extract, California poppy extract and magnesium. This particular combination of plant extracts is not licensed as a medicine in the UK but can be bought online (Hanus *et al.*, 2004). Valerian is an extract of the roots of the *Valeriana officinalis* plant. Many different branded preparations are available and it is most commonly found in capsule form, but can also be consumed as a tea. Valerian is used for insomnia and other disorders as an alternative to benzodiazepines. Oral forms are available in both standardised and unstandardised forms. However, standardised products may be preferable considering the wide variation of chemicals in the dried root. Standardisation is a percentage of valerenic or valeric acid (Johne & Roots, 2005). Galphimia glauca is an extract from the *Thryallis* shrub and, again, is available in various preparations but is not licensed as a medicine in the UK. This herb is not widely available but can be bought online (Herrera-Arellano, 2007). There are a number of different species of lavender that are available in several forms, such as drops, capsules and oils among others. Similar to the other herbal remedies, it is not licensed in the UK but can be bought 'over the counter' (Woelk & Schalke, 2010). Passion flower is derived from the family of plants called *Passifloraceae* and has been used for medicinal purposes for many years including the treatment of anxiety-related disorders. It is not as widely available as other herbal remedies but may be bought online. Similar to the other herbal interventions, this remedy is not licensed in the UK (Akhondzadeh *et al.*, 2001).

Acupuncture has received much public interest and has widely been applied in different medical conditions including GAD. Generally acupuncture is regarded as having a more acceptable safety profile than conventional medications for GAD and therefore the literature has been reviewed on the efficacy and safety of acupuncture as an alternative or combinational treatment for this indication. Guizhen and colleagues (1998) state that, according to traditional Chinese medicine, a causative factor for disease (such as anxiety disorders) is an excess or decline in yin or yang, which can lead to an imbalance and disorders of the 'qi' (energy flow) and blood, leading to dysfunction of internal organs. By correctly selecting and needling acupuncture points it is argued there can be a removal of obstructions of qi and blood, which normalises the yin-yang balance and effectively cures the disease. Zhang and colleagues (2003) suggest that because the characteristic symptoms of 'anxiety neurosis' include anxiety, restlessness and constant fear, people should receive treatment designed to regulate the heart qi, although in practice acupuncture points can vary according to different treatment approaches.

8.11.2   Databases searched and inclusion/exclusion criteria

Information about the databases searched and the inclusion/exclusion criteria used for this section of the guideline can be found in Table 74 (further information about the search for health economic evidence can be found in Section 3.6).

8.11.3   Studies considered

The review team conducted a new systematic search for RCTs that assessed the benefits and harms of herbal interventions for the treatment of people with GAD as defined in DSM-III-R or DSM-IV.

A total of 3,397 references were identified by the electronic search relating to clinical evidence. Of these references, 3,353 were excluded at the screening stage on the basis of reading the title and/or abstract. The remaining 44 references were assessed for eligibility on the basis of the full text and 30 studies were excluded from the analysis. Five studies did not meet the criteria for GAD, nine studies did not provide an acceptable diagnosis of GAD, nine studies did not use a relevant intervention, five

Table 74: Databases searched and inclusion/exclusion criteria for clinical evidence

Electronic databases	MEDLINE, EMBASE, CINAHL, PsycINFO, AMED, BNI, Cochrane Library
Date searched	Database inception to 09.05.2010
Study design	RCT
Patient population	People with GAD or anxiety disorders
Interventions	Acupuncture, hypnosis, meditation and other mind body therapies, plant extracts (including ginkgo, valerian, kava and St John's wort)
Outcomes	Mean anxiety rating scale scores, non-response (<50% reduction in anxiety rating scale score), non-remission (a score of below 10 on the HAM-A)

studies did not have a suitable study design, one study had fewer than 10 participants, and one other was not written in the English language. Further information about both included and excluded studies can be found in Appendix 15d.

Fourteen trials met the eligibility criteria set by the GDG, providing data on 1,627 participants. All were published in peer-reviewed journals between 1998 and 2010.

8.11.4 Herbal interventions versus placebo

Studies considered
There were a total of four trials comparing various herbal interventions with placebo. These were all small- to medium-sized trials, all of which were high quality. For two of the studies funding was provided by drug company sponsorship and one other from a national grant. One study failed to declare any funding. These trials could not be meta-analysed and therefore they are narratively reviewed below.

A summary of study characteristics can be found in Table 75 with full details in Appendix 15d, which also includes details of excluded studies. An evidence summary is provided in Table 76.

Narrative review of herbal interventions versus placebo
AMSTERDAM2009 conducted a randomised, double-blind efficacy trial in an outpatient clinic in the US comparing chamomile (n = 28) with placebo (n = 29) in participants with GAD. Participants met the DSM-IV diagnostic criteria for GAD and had a HAM-A score of greater than nine. Participants in the treatment group received one to five 220 mg capsules daily depending on tolerability levels. The placebo group received up to five capsules containing lactose monohydrate per day depending on their tolerability levels. Both treatment courses lasted for 8 weeks. Based on the evidence of this study, there is a moderate effect for chamomile over placebo in the

Table 75: Study information table for trials comparing herbal interventions with placebo

	Chamomile versus placebo	Ginkgo biloba versus placebo	Combined plant extracts versus placebo	Valerian extract versus placebo
No. trials (total participants)	1 RCT (57)	1 RCT (107)	1 RCT (264)	1 RCT (24)
Study ID	AMSTERDAM2009	WOELK2007	HANUS2004	ANDREATINI2002
N/% female	57/Not reported	107/62%	264/81%	24/53%
Mean age (years)	46	47	45	41
Diagnosis	GAD by DSM-IV	GAD by DSM-III-R Adjustment disorder with anxious mood by DSM-III-R	GAD by DSM-III-R	GAD by DSM-III-R
Baseline severity (HAM-A): mean (SD)	Chamomile 15.4 (SD = 4.2); placebo 14.3 (SD = 2.8)	Ginkgo biloba 30.2 (SD = 5.35); placebo 29.5 (SD = 5.5)	Plant extracts 22.7 (SD = 2.57); placebo 22.4 (SD = 2.56)	Valerian extract 22.8 (SD = 7.6); placebo 25.1 (SD = 7.50)
Treatment length	8 weeks	4 weeks	13 weeks	4 weeks
Follow-up	End of treatment	End of treatment	End of treatment	End of treatment

Table 76: Evidence summary table for trials of herbal interventions versus placebo

	Chamomile versus placebo	Ginkgo biloba versus placebo	Combined plant extracts versus placebo	Valerian extract versus placebo
No. trials (total participants)	1 RCT (57)	1 RCT (107)	1 RCT (264)	1 RCT (24)
Study ID	AMSTERDAM2009	WOELK2007	HANUS2004	ANDREATINI2002
Benefits (end of treatment)				
HAM-A	SMD -0.54 (-1.07, -0.01) K = 1, N = 57 Quality: moderate	SMD -0.58 (-1.01, -0.15) K = 1, N = 107 Quality: high	SMD -0.35 (-0.59, -0.11) K = 1, N = 264 Quality: high	SMD 0.09 (-0.71, 0.89) K = 1, N = 24 Quality: moderate
Non-response (50% reduction in HAM-A)	RR 0.69 (0.41, 1.15) K = 1, N = 57 Quality: moderate	RR 0.75 (0.58, 0.97) K = 1, N = 107 Quality: moderate	RR 0.80 (0.66, 0.98) K = 1, N = 264 Quality: moderate	–
Non-remission	–	RR 0.97 (0.87, 1.07) K = 1, N = 107 Quality: moderate		–
Harms (end of treatment)				
Discontinuation due to adverse events	RR 1.04 (0.07, 15.77) K = 1, N = 57 Quality: moderate	–	RR 1.03 (0.21, 5.01) K = 1, N = 264 Quality: moderate	–
Discontinuation due to any reason	–	RR 3.75 (0.20, 70.65) K = 1, N = 24 Quality: moderate	–	RR 1.00 (0.17, 5.98) K = 1, N = 24 Quality: moderate

reduction of clinician-rated anxiety scores. However, as this result has wide confidence intervals that just include the line of non-significance it should be interpreted with caution. This study also examined the difference in response rates as measured by a 50% reduction in HAM-A scores between the two groups. No statistically significant differences between the two groups were found. However, there was a 29% reduction in the level of non-response in favour of chamomile. With regards to discontinuation due to adverse events, there was no difference between the groups, suggesting that neither group was more likely to discontinue due to adverse events. Due to the limited evidence, it is difficult to draw any clear conclusions regarding the relative efficacy of chamomile to placebo.

WOELK2007 conducted a double-blind RCT in multiple outpatient centres in Germany, evaluating the therapeutic efficacy of gingko biloba (n = 70) versus placebo (n = 37) in participants with GAD. Some participants met the DSM-III-R diagnostic criteria for GAD (n = 82) and others met the diagnostic criteria for adjustment disorder with anxious mood by DSM-III-R (n = 25). Participants in the active treatment group received either a mean dose of 240 mg (n = 36) or a mean dose of 480 mg (n = 34) over 4 weeks. The placebo group took two film-coated drugs per day that were of the same appearance as the gingko biloba pills. Based on this limited evidence, there was a statistically significant moderate effect in favour of gingko biloba in the reduction of clinician-rated anxiety scores. For non-response, which was measured by a 50% reduction in HAM-A scores, there was a 25% reduction in non-response, which was statistically significant suggesting that those in the active treatment group were more likely to respond than those in the placebo group. In contrast, there were no significant differences in relation to non-remission between the two conditions. Finally, there were no significant differences in relation to dropout due to any reason. However, these results should be interpreted with caution as they are based on one medium-scale study, and given the wide confidence intervals it is difficult to make any firm conclusions from this evidence about the relative efficacy of ginkgo biloba to placebo.

HANUS2004 conducted a double-blind RCT in multiple outpatient centres in Paris, evaluating the therapeutic efficacy of combined plant extracts (n = 130) in comparison with placebo (n = 134) in participants with GAD. Participants met the DSM-IV diagnostic criteria for GAD and had a HAM-A score of between 16 and 28. Participants in the active treatment group received a mean dose of 375 mg (two tablets per day) of combined plant extracts (that is, *Crataegus oxyacantha*, *Eschscholzia californica* and magnesium) over a period of 3 months. The placebo group were given an indistinguishable tablet that was made from the same ingredients as the study drug except for the active ingredients. Firstly, in relation to HAM-A scores, there was a statistically significant small effect between treatments in favour of the combined plant extracts. Secondly, in relation to non-response (again measured as a 50% reduction in HAM-A scores), there was a 20% reduction in non-response for those taking the active treatment, which was statistically significant. Finally, there was no statistically significant difference between treatments in relation to dropout due to adverse events. Once more, firm conclusions are subject to cautious interpretation due to the limited evidence available and the small sample size.

ANDREATINI2002 conducted a double-blind RCT in Brazil, evaluating the therapeutic efficacy of valerian extract (n = 12) in comparison with placebo (n = 12) in participants with GAD. All participants met the DSM-III-R diagnostic criteria for GAD. Participants in the active treatment group received a mean dosage of 81.3 mg per day of valerian extract over 4 weeks. The placebo group were given identical capsules, which were administered three times per day. Firstly, in relation to HAM-A scores, there was no statistically significant differences between valerian extract versus placebo. There was no data reported for either non-response or non-remission. Finally, there was no statistically significant difference between treatments in relation to dropout due to any reason. Again, conclusions are subject to cautious interpretation because of the limited evidence available.

8.11.5 Herbal interventions versus benzodiazepines

Studies considered
There were a total of four trials comparing various herbal interventions with benzodiazepines, including lorazepam, diazepam and oxazepam. These trials were all small to medium sized and of high quality. One study was funded by drug company sponsorship and the other three studies failed to declare any funding. These trials could not be meta-analysed therefore they are narratively reviewed below. A summary of study characteristics can be found in Table 77 with full details in Appendix 15d, which also includes details of excluded studies. An evidence summary is provided in Table 78.

Narrative review of herbal interventions versus benzodiazepines
Only one study (HERRERA-ARELLANO2007) examined the effectiveness of galphimia glauca (n = 72) in comparison with lorazepam (n = 80) for treating the symptoms of GAD. This was a medium-scale, high-quality RCT in an outpatient setting in Mexico. With regard to the comparative beneficial effects of these two treatments in reducing clinician-rated anxiety scores, there was no statistically significant difference at post-treatment. Also, there was no statistically significant difference in dropout for any reason between the two groups. However, there was a statistically significant difference in favour of the herbal intervention with regard to dropout due to adverse events, with only 7% dropping out due to adverse events in the herbal intervention compared with 20% in the lorazepam group. However, the results as a whole should be interpreted with caution due to the lack of placebo group, wide confidence intervals, and lack of statistical significance.

WOELK2010 conducted a double-blind RCT in multiple outpatient centres in Germany, comparing lavender capsules (n = 40) with lorazepam treatment (n = 37) in participants with GAD as diagnosed by DSM-IV criteria. Participants in the herbal treatment group received one capsule (80 mg) of silexan (an oil-produced form of lavender) and one capsule of lorazepam placebo. Participants in the drug condition received one capsule (0.5mg) of lorazepam and one capsule of silexan placebo. Both treatment courses lasted 6 weeks. In terms of reducing clinician-rated anxiety scores, there was a non-significant difference between the two treatments.

Table 77: Study information table for trials comparing herbal interventions with benzodiazepines

	Galphimia glauca versus lorazepam	Lavender versus lorazepam	Valerian versus diazepam	Passion flower extract versus oxazepam
No. trials (total participants)	1 RCT (152)	1 RCT (77)	1 RCT (24)	1 RCT (36)
Study ID	HERRERA-ARELLANO2007	WOELK2010	ANDREATINI2002	AKHONDZADEH2001
N/% female	152/77%	77/77%	24/53%	36/56%
Mean age (years)	38	43	36	36
Diagnosis	GAD by DSM-IV	GAD by DSM-IV	GAD by DSM-III-R	GAD by DSM-IV
Baseline severity (HAM-A): mean (SD)	Not reported	Lavender 25.0; lorazepam 25.0	Valerian 22.8 (7.6); diazepam 25.2 (4.5)	Not reported
Treatment length	4 weeks	4 weeks	4 weeks	4 weeks
Follow-up	End of treatment	End of treatment	End of treatment	End of treatment

Table 78: Evidence summary table for trials of herbal interventions versus benzodiazepines

	Galphimia glauca versus lorazepam	Lavender versus lorazepam	Valerian versus diazepam	Passion flower extract versus oxazepam
No. trials (total participants)	1 RCT (N = 152)	1 RCT (N = 77)	1 RCT (N = 24)	1 RCT (N = 36)
Study ID	HERRERA-ARELLANO2007	WOELK2010	ANDREATINI2002	AKHONDZADEH2001
Benefits (end of treatment)				
HAM-A	SMD = −0.1 (−0.41, 0.21) MD = −0.1 (−0.41, 0.21) K = 1, N = 152 Quality: low	SMD = 0.04 (−0.41, 0.49) MD = 0.04 (−0.41, 0.49) K = 1, N = 77 Quality: moderate	SMD = 0.31 (−0.49, 1.11) MD = 0.31 (−0.49, 1.11) K = 1, N = 24 Quality: moderate	–
Non-response (≤50% reduction in HAM-A)	–	RR = 0.80 (0.52, 1.22) K = 1, N = 77 Quality: moderate	–	–
Non-remission (>10 on HAM-A)	–	RR = 0.82 (0.60, 1.13) K = 1, N = 77 Quality: moderate	–	–
Harms (end of treatment)				
Discontinuation due to adverse events	RR = 0.35 (0.13, 0.90) K = 1, N = 152 Quality: moderate	–	–	–
Discontinuation due to any reason	RR = 0.90 (0.52, 1.57) K = 1, N = 152 Quality: low	RR = 1.85 (0.17, 19.56) K = 1, N = 77 Quality: moderate	RR = 2.00 (0.21, 19.23) K = 1, N = 24 Quality: moderate	–

Note: RR <1 favours treatment and RR >1 favours placebo

In addition, there was a 20% reduction in the risk of non-response in favour of lavender, however, this was not statistically significant. Moreover, there was an 18% reduction in the risk of non-remission in favour of lavender, which again was not statistically significant. Finally, there were no statistically significant differences between treatments in the risk of dropout for any reason. Due to the limited evidence, it is difficult to come to any firm conclusions about the relative efficacy of these two treatments.

ANDREATINI2002 is a double-blind RCT in Brazil, comparing diazepam (n = 12) with valerian extract (n = 12) in participants with GAD as diagnosed by DSM-III-R criteria. Participants in the active treatment group received a mean dosage of 81.3 mg per day of valerian extract over 4 weeks. Participants in the diazepam condition received a dosage of 6.5 mg per day in capsule form. The capsules were administered three times a day with the lowest dose consisting of two placebo pills and one active capsule based on response. In terms of reducing clinician-rated anxiety scores, there was a small but statistically insignificant effect in favour of diazepam treatment. There was no data available for either response or remission. Finally, there was no statistically significant difference between the two conditions on the outcome of dropout for any reason. It is difficult to come to any clear conclusions about the relative efficacy of these two treatments due to the small sample size, lack of statistical significance and large confidence intervals.

Only one study examined the effectiveness of passion flower extract (n = 18) versus oxazepam (n = 18) for the treatment of GAD (AKHONDZADEH 2001A). The study consisted of a double-blind RCT conducted in an outpatient setting in Iran. Both passion flower extract and oxazepam were found to be effective in reducing clinician-rated anxiety scores from baseline severity. In both groups, post-hoc comparisons of the baseline HAM-A scores at post-treatment revealed a significant reduction from baseline (p < .001). The differences between the two treatments were significant at day four (t = 2.84, df = 30, p = .008), however, after the fourth day the differences were no longer significant. Moreover, significantly more problems relating to impairment of job performance were encountered with people taking oxazepam (p = .049). However, there was no significant differences between the two treatments in terms of total side-effect profile (p = .83). These results are based on one small-scale study and thus it is difficult to make any firm conclusions from this evidence.

8.11.6   Acupuncture

Narrative review of acupuncture
There were no studies concerning people with GAD who had received a diagnosis that met the eligibility criteria of the GDG. However, this partly reflected the fact that all identified studies were conducted in China and used the *Chinese Classification of Mental Disorders* (CCMD) criteria.

Zhiling and colleagues (2006) conducted a RCT in China, comparing acupuncture treatment (n = 35) with a medication control group (n = 30) in participants with GAD. Participants met the CCMD-3 criteria and had Self-rating Anxiety Scale (SAS) scores of 50 or more. Acupuncture treatment (which consisted of six acupuncture points) was given once daily. The control group were administered 0.5 to 2 mg of lorazepam (two or three times a day) with 20 mg of oryzanol, which is a mixture of plant chemicals (three times a day), or 10 to 20 mg of propanolol. Both treatment courses lasted for 30 days. The therapeutic effects between the groups looked at a measure of remission (disappearance of symptoms with stable emotions). No statistically significant difference between groups was found (RR = 0.90; CI, 0.65 to 1.24). Of participants in the treatment group, 65.7% did not achieve remission compared with 73.3% in the control group. For response (apparent improvement of symptoms with occasional anxious state) no statistical difference was found (RR = 0.90; CI, 0.59 to 1.38). Of participants in the treatment group, 54.3% did not respond compared to 60% in the control group.

Yuan and colleagues (2007) conducted a quasi-randomised trial, also in China, comparing the therapeutic efficacy of needling therapy with Western medication and a combination treatment. Participants were diagnosed with GAD using the CCMD-3-R criteria and had a HAM-A score of 15 or more. Participants in the Western medication group (n = 29) were treated with 20 mg of fluoxetine or paroxetine. In addition, 0.4 to 1.6 mg of alprazolam was given according to the participant's condition. All drugs were administered once daily for 6 weeks. There were nine to ten acupuncture points selected in the needling therapy group (n = 29) and the treatment was given once daily, 6 times a week for 6 weeks. The same method for both Western medication and needling therapy groups was used for participants in the combination treatment group (n = 28). Clinical efficacy was scored using the CGI which includes a general index subscale. A high general index score indicates an inferior therapeutic effect. There was no statistically significant difference between the Western medication and needling therapy groups (SMD = 0.09; 95% CI, -0.44 to 0.63) or between the needling therapy and combination treatment groups (SMD = −0.16; 95% CI, −0.70 to 0.38).

Ruan (2003) conducted an RCT in China, comparing combined treatment of Chinese medicine with acupuncture (COM) with Western medication. Participants were diagnosed with 'anxiety neurosis' using CCMD-2 and the self-rated Anxiety Neurosis Scale. Those scoring more than 50 were eligible to participate. They were randomised into the COM group (n = 86) or the Western medication group (n = 83). The COM group were treated with Chinese medicine, taken twice each day, and received acupuncture daily for 30 to 60 minutes. The Western medication group were given the TCA doxepin (an average of 150 mg per day). Treatment lasted for 30 days. Thirty-nine out of 86 in the COM group and 30 out of 83 in the Western medication group remitted. There was no statistically significant difference between the COM and Western medication group. Clinical efficacy was scored using SAS-CR and there was no statistically significant difference between the COM and Western medication group (SMD = −0.14; 95% CI, −0.45 to 0.16).

Zhou and colleagues (2003) conducted a randomised trial comparing the combined effect (n = 50) of acupuncture and flupentixol (an antipsychotic drug) with flupentixol only (n = 50). Participants were diagnosed with 'anxiety neurosis' using CCMD-2-R. Participants were given acupuncture once per day for 10 days. They took 5 days' rest before the second wave of treatment. There were three waves of treatment in total. They also took 20 mg of flupentixol three times daily continuously for 40 days. According to remission rates, combined treatment was statistically significantly better than treatment with a single drug (RR = 0.71; CI, 0.57 to 0.89). Of participants in the treatment group, 64% did not achieve remission compared with 90% in the control group. Participants also reported side effects. One person experienced dry mouth in the combined treatment group, and one person experienced insomnia in the drug-only group. One from each group had dizziness.

Zhang and colleagues (2003) conducted a randomised trial comparing the clinical efficacy of acupuncture (n = 157) and doxepin (n = 139). They selected people with 'anxiety neurosis' according to CCMD-2 and an SAS score of more than 50. The acupuncture group had treatment once a day, with a 1-day interval after six consecutive treatments; there were 30 sessions in total. They used any two of four methods (varying in methodology), one of which included giving an injection at an acupuncture point. Participants in the comparison group were given 25 mg of doxepin three times a day for 4 weeks, which was modified according to therapeutic or adverse events. The therapeutic effects between the groups looked at a measure of remission (disappearance of symptoms with stable emotions). No statistical difference was found (RR = 0.86; CI, 0.71 to 1.03). Of participants in the treatment group, 56.1% did not achieve remission compared with 65.5% in the control group. For response (clinical symptoms relieved with occasional emotional fluctuation) no statistical difference was found (RR = 1.04; CI, 0.90 to 1.21). Of participants in the treatment group, 72.1% did not respond compared with 69.1% in the control group.

Guizhen and colleagues (1998) conducted a randomised trial comparing the clinical efficacy of acupuncture (n = 80) with behavioural desensitisation (n = 80) and a combination of both treatments (n = 80) on people with 'anxiety neurosis' (with SAS scores of 50 or more). The acupuncture-only group were treated once every other day for ten sessions (this comprised one course). Each participant received between one and three courses. Behavioural desensitisation involved self-relaxation techniques (twice daily) and psychotherapy that incorporated desensitisation therapy (twice weekly for ten sessions). For acupuncture combined with behavioural desensitisation, each participant received both treatments in the same day and between one and four courses of treatment with 3 to 7 day intervals between courses. Physical examination and SAS evaluation measured remission (disappearance of symptoms – SAS score of less than 45). The results for the combined treatment group were significantly better than the acupuncture-only (RR = 0.59; CI, 0.46 to 0.77) or the behavioural desensitisation-only (RR = 0.64; CI, 0.49 to 0.84) groups. Of participants in the acupuncture-only group, 80% did not remit; in the behavioural desensitisation-only group, 73.8% did not remit; 47.5% in the combined treatment group did not remit. For response (marked improvement in symptoms and significant decrease in SAS scores, that is, more than 20 points) combined treatment was significantly higher than the acupuncture-only (RR = 1.30; CI, 1.02 to 1.65) and behavioural desensitisation-only (RR = 1.24; CI, 0.98 to 1.57) groups. Of participants in the combined treatment group, 72.3% did not respond compared with 55% and 57.5% in the acupuncture-only and behavioural desensitisation-only groups, respectively.

8.11.7   Hypnotherapy

Zhao and colleagues (2005) conducted a randomised trial, comparing clinical efficacy of hypnotherapy and alprazolam. Participants were diagnosed with GAD using CCMD-3, with a HAM-A score of over 14. Participants were randomly assigned into the hypnotherapy group (n = 32) and a comparison group (n = 30). The hypnotherapy group received treatment twice each week for 30 to 40 minutes each session. The comparison group received 0.8 mg of alprazolam twice each day and met with a doctor twice a week. The total length of treatment was 4 weeks. When looking at response (defined as 50% or more reduction in HAM-A scores), there was no statistically significant difference between groups (SMD = 0.10; 95% CI, -0.40 to 0.60). Evidence appeared to suggest no difference in effect between hypnotherapy and alprazolam.

8.11.8   Overall clinical summary of other interventions

Most of the herbal interventions were more effective than placebo in reducing anxiety-related symptoms with the exception of valerian extract. Moreover, no significant differences were found between herbal interventions and benzodiazepines in relation to anxiety-related outcomes. This evidence must be interpreted with caution, however, due to the small evidence base and the quality of the studies.

The results indicate that acupuncture may be of equivalent effectiveness to medication in the treatment of GAD or 'anxiety neurosis'. It is important to note, however, that these trials use a range of medications as comparison conditions, many of which have uncertain effectiveness in the treatment of GAD. In addition, there are differences between the CCMD diagnoses of GAD and 'anxiety neuroses' and the DSM or ICD classification systems, for example, in duration of symptoms required to meet diagnostic criteria. Therefore this is an important limitation of the review. Furthermore, the trials are only medium sized and also of low to moderate quality, which makes it difficult to arrive at a confident conclusion.

There was very limited evidence for hypnotherapy, which proved inconclusive.

8.11.9   From evidence to recommendations

Due to the limited evidence base for most interventions reviewed in this section, the GDG concluded that it was not yet possible to generate recommendations on the use of any of these interventions for the treatment of GAD.

Existing research shows initial evidence for herbal interventions to be effective when compared with placebo, however, due to the small number of studies and small sample sizes, larger RCTs examining the effectiveness of these herbal interventions, any possible side effects and potential herb-drug interactions are necessary to increase confidence in these initial findings.

8.11.10 Research recommendation

8.11.10.1 The effectiveness of chamomile and ginkgo biloba in the treatment of GAD

Is chamomile/ginkgo biloba more effective than placebo in increasing response and remission rates and decreasing anxiety ratings for people with GAD?
This question should be addressed using a placebo-controlled, double-blind randomised design to compare the effects of a standardised dose of chamomile (220–1100 mg) or ginkgo biloba (30–500 mg) in a readily available form, for example a capsule, with placebo. This should assess outcomes at the end of the trial and at 12-month post-trial follow-up. The outcomes chosen should include both observer- and participant-rated measures of clinical symptoms and functioning specific to GAD, and of side effects. There should be a health economic evaluation included and an assessment of quality of life. The trial should be large enough to determine the presence or absence of clinically important effects using a non-inferiority design. Mediators and moderators of response should be investigated.

Why this is important
GAD is a common mental health disorder and the results of this study will be generalisable to a large number of people. There is evidence for the efficacy of chamomile and ginkgo biloba in reducing anxiety in people with GAD but the evidence base is small (one study). However, the scarce literature on the effectiveness of other herbal interventions for treating GAD points to chamomile and ginkgo biloba as two of the more effective herbal interventions. Moreover, both these herbal remedies are widely available and relatively inexpensive. Furthermore, at present there is no scientific evidence of side effects or drug–herbal interactions in relation to chamomile or ginkgo biloba. As both these herbal interventions are readily available and have no known side effects, they could be used at an early stage as a means of preventing progression to drug treatments, which are associated with a number of undesirable side effects and dependency.

9   COMPUTERISED COGNITIVE BEHAVIOURAL THERAPY FOR PANIC DISORDER

9.1   INTRODUCTION

This chapter reviews the evidence for the clinical efficacy and cost effectiveness of CCBT in the treatment of panic disorder. This review work was undertaken as a partial update of NICE technology appraisal 97 *Computerised Cognitive Behaviour Therapy for Depression and Anxiety* (NICE, 2006).

Panic disorder

Panic disorder is characterised by the presence of recurrent unexpected panic attacks associated with persistent worry and anticipatory anxiety about future panic attacks and their consequences. Fear of attacks is often complicated by avoidance of certain situations or the need to be accompanied by someone else when venturing into settings that the person associates with the likelihood of attacks. Diagnostic criteria usually define panic disorder as the occurrence of four or more 'uncued' panic attacks (and its associated symptoms) over a 1-month period, but it is well-recognised that panic attacks that do not meet these diagnostic criteria are very common and almost equally disabling (Weissman *et al.*, 1997; Kessler *et al.*, 2006; Goodwin *et al.*, 2005).

Epidemiological data on panic disorder from cross-national (Weissman *et al.*, 1997) and American (Kessler *et al.*, 2006) community studies, alongside comprehensive reviews of community and clinical studies from across Europe (Goodwin *et al.*, 2005), reveal relatively consistent findings, with the prevalence of panic disorder estimated at about 2% (1 to 4%); with the median prevalence among primary care attendees being about 4% (range 3 to 8%). Rates are twice as high in females as compared with males in all countries. Age of onset of first symptoms of panic disorder is often adolescence or early adulthood, with peak rates for panic disorder in the age range of 25 to 35 years.

As well as the strong association of panic disorder with agoraphobia, panic disorder is also frequently comorbid with affective disorders (both unipolar depression and bipolar disorder), other anxiety disorders, substance use disorders and a range of somatoform disorders (Wittchen & Essau, 1993; Grant *et al.*, 2004). A review by Roy-Byrne and colleagues (2005) suggested that the median prevalence of panic disorder is also higher among certain medical populations, such as those with cardiac (20 to 50%) or gastrointestinal presentations (28 to 40%).

However, panic disorder is often recurrent or persistent so people experience substantial long-term disability and are heavily represented among people classified as 'high utilisers' of healthcare (Roy-Byrne *et al.*, 2005).

Panic disorder has repeatedly been shown to be associated with decreased quality of life and impaired social and work functioning, with unemployment rates of approximately 25% (Ettigi *et al.*, 1997). Greenberg and colleagues (1999) reported that people with panic disorder were over three times more likely to be receiving disability payments than those without the disorder.

Batelaan and colleagues (2007) reported that the annual per capita costs of panic disorder were €10,269, while subthreshold panic disorder generated €6,384. About a quarter of these costs could be attributed to comorbidities, but both forms of panic disorder were associated with substantial costs due to excessive healthcare uptake, lost productivity and service user and carer burden.

Current practice

Despite its frequency in primary care settings, panic disorder is significantly under-recognised and people may have many investigations to exclude significant physical disorders before the correct diagnosis is made (Bystritsky *et al.*, 2010). Others present for the first time to emergency services, and again there may be a delay before the true nature of the presenting problem is discovered. When panic disorder or panic attacks are recognised, there are a number of specific treatments, such as SSRIs and CBT, which have been shown to be effective in producing response or remission. Response to treatment is usually defined as being 'panic free', and remission as being asymptomatic for at least 3 months.

The majority of people with panic disorder will be offered treatment in primary care, although some will be referred to an expert therapist and fewer still will be referred to other specialist mental health services. Most clinical providers advocate a collaborative care approach, although it should be noted that the use of this has been studied less frequently for panic or other anxiety disorders than other conditions (Rollman *et al.*, 2005). Roy-Byrne and colleagues (2005) have argued that people with anxiety and panic disorders are less likely to seek, and/or may find it harder to engage with, treatment. As such, it is important to assess a person's expectations of and preferences regarding treatment and to spend time preparing the person for the treatment programme in order to facilitate the uptake of and adherence to potentially effective interventions (Hazlett-Stevens *et al.*, 2002).

The acute treatment of panic disorder with medication usually involves the use of an SSRI; some TCAs (imipramine or clomipramine) may also be effective and there may be benefits from the brief use of benzodiazepines (Baldwin *et al.*, 2005). However, the use of the latter must be balanced against the risks of developing dependency and most first-line pharmacological interventions focus on the use of medications also used as antidepressants. The use of SSRIs beyond 12 to 52 weeks is associated with increased treatment response rates, but the overall level of medication adherence often decreases with time. Hazlett-Stevens and colleagues (2002) argue that individuals with panic disorder show a strong preference for psychological treatment and that CBT may have advantages over pharmacological interventions in terms of maintaining clinical improvements over time (Nadiga *et al.*, 2003). The use of combined CBT and medication is sometimes beneficial in cases of very severe, complex or treatment-refractory panic disorder, but in the majority of people the choice is either medication or CBT. The evidence for the benefits of CBT delivered in a number of formats (group or individual) in the short term and long term is, however, undermined by the fact that as few as 20% of people with panic disorder treated in primary care receive CBT, and in the US it is reported that only 12% have 'adequate' psychotherapy (Grant *et al.*, 2004; Bandelow *et al.*, 1995). Not surprisingly the need to increase access to CBT has led to developments of CBT packages that require less input from therapists.

CBT is well recognised as an effective treatment for most commonly occurring mental disorders (such as depression and anxiety), and is an especially useful treatment in panic disorder. However, the public health impact of CBT is attenuated because of the relative lack of availability of trained therapists (Lovell & Richards, 2000).

To increase access to CBT, and reduce dependence on face-to-face therapy, self-administered CBT packages were developed. These were initially presented in a written format, but written programmes have increasingly been replaced by digitalised or electronic packages that can be accessed via computers, other media or the internet.

Historically, the written versions of self-help or guided self-help interventions were referred to as 'bibliotherapy', but this description is increasingly inappropriate as it fails to convey the differences in the approaches subsumed under the self-help or guided self-help 'umbrella'. The more recently employed term is 'computerised cognitive behavioural therapy' (CCBT). However, CCBT needs further definition as programmes may differ significantly in:

- the media used for delivery
- the content and duration of therapy modules
- whether the programme is used alone or as an adjunct to a briefer course of face–to-face therapy (for example, personal digital assistants [PDAs] to deliver additional therapy interventions or to allow users to record homework tasks)
- the degree to which the therapy is directed by the therapist or the client
- the duration and nature of additional support offered from professionals (in person or via telephone or email contact) or from peers (for example, via 'patient support' chatrooms, and so on).

It is therefore important to clarify these issues in any description of a CCBT package in order to truly examine its benefits in the context of duration (number of sessions or hours), time commitment (by therapist or client), and degree to which the programme will be used independently by clients.

The use of virtual reality headsets or other media has been reported recently, but these strategies employ technology as a 'live aid' to the therapy process as they are used under the direction of a therapist within face-to-face sessions (the virtual reality headsets and so on are employed within traditional CBT sessions, rather than being used independently by people outside the clinical setting). As such, these approaches do not fit within the models of CCBT being considered in this chapter and will not be discussed further.

9.2 CLINICAL EVIDENCE FOR COMPUTERISED COGNITIVE BEHAVIOURAL THERAPY FOR PANIC DISORDER

9.2.1 Review question

In the treatment of panic disorder does CCBT improve outcomes?

9.2.2   Clinical review protocol

Information about the databases searched and the inclusion/exclusion criteria used for this section of the guideline can be found in Table 79 (further information about the search for health economic evidence can be found in Section 3.6).

9.2.3   Studies considered[18]

The review team conducted a new systematic search for RCTs that assessed the effectiveness of CCBT for people with 100% diagnosis of panic disorder as defined by DSM-III, DSM-III-R or DSM-IV.

A total of 1,670 references were identified by the electronic search relating to clinical evidence. Of these, 1,635 were excluded at the screening stage on the basis of reading the title and/or abstract. The remaining 35 references were assessed for eligibility on the basis of the full text. Trials that involved the applied use of technology within traditional CBT sessions or trials that used technology as an adjunct to traditional CBT sessions were excluded. Other computerised self-help programmes with or without therapist support were considered. Eight trials met the eligibility criteria set by the GDG, providing data on 367 participants. All of these CCBT trials were

Table 79: Databases searched and inclusion/exclusion criteria for clinical evidence

Electronic databases	MEDLINE, EMBASE, CINAHL, PsycINFO, Cochrane Library
Date searched	Database inception to 09.05.2010 [excluded HTA search results up to the end of 2004]
Study design	RCT
Patient population	People with a diagnosis of panic disorder with or without agoraphobia according to DSM-III-R or DSM-IV criteria
Interventions	CCBT
Outcomes	Anxiety (self- and clinician-rated), panic severity (self- and clinician-rated), depression, quality of life, number of panic attacks per week, dropout rate

---

[18]Here and elsewhere in the guideline, each study considered for review is referred to by a study ID in capital letters (primary author and date of study publication, except where a study is in press or only submitted for publication, then a date is not used).

guided self-help computerised programmes with some therapist support. Of these, all were published in peer-reviewed journals between 1992 and 2009. Twenty-seven studies were excluded from the analysis. Five studies did not provide an acceptable diagnosis of panic disorder, eight studies were not RCTs, four studies had fewer than ten participants per group, in two studies the data were not extractable, and six studies did not use a relevant intervention.

Six studies provided data for inclusion in the meta-analysis; two of these (CARLBRING2001; CARLBRING2005) were also included in the original Technology Appraisal. The six studies compared CCBT with traditional CBT, information control and waitlist control. There were two other relevant studies that were not meta-analysed due to incomparable comparators (CARLBRING2003, KLEIN2009), which were narratively reviewed (see Section 9.2.6).

Two studies (MARKS2004; SCHNEIDER2005), which reviewed Fear Fighter, were both excluded as the population was primarily people with phobic disorders (about 67%). This did not meet the inclusion criteria for this guideline. KENARDY2003A was excluded because the GDG considered that the intervention used in the trial (a traditional CBT intervention augmented with a palm-top computer) did not meet the definition of CCBT.

A summary of study characteristics can be found in Table 80 with full details in Appendix 15e, which also includes details of excluded studies.

9.2.4   Clinical evidence for computerised cognitive behavioural therapy for a population with panic disorder only

Evidence from the important outcomes and overall quality of evidence are presented in Table 81. The full evidence profiles and associated forest plots can be found in Appendix 18d and Appendix 16d, respectively.

9.2.5   Clinical evidence summary

CCBT versus waitlist control
CCBT was largely effective compared with waitlist for self-rated anxiety and depression outcomes. It was moderately effective for quality-of-life outcomes. The overall quality of the aforementioned outcomes was high. However, no conclusion about 'panic-free' status could be drawn due to the inconsistent definition in the studies. There was no difference in terms of dropout rates.

CCBT versus information control
CCBT had a significant improvement on 'panic-free' status relative to information control. It reported a large improvement in self-rated panic severity and a moderate improvement in self-rated depression. However, effects on anxiety and quality of life were not statistically significant. There was no difference in dropout rates.

Table 80: Study information table for trials of CCBT for a population with panic disorder only

	CCBT versus waitlist control	CCBT versus information control	CCBT versus any control (waitlist and information control)	CCBT versus face-to-face therapy
No. trials (total participants)	2 RCTs (101)	2 RCTs (58)	4 RCTs (159)	2 RCTS (135)
Study ID	(1) CARLBRING2001** (2) CARLBRING2006	(1) KLEIN2006 (2) RICHARDS2006A	(1) CARLBRING2001** (2) CARLBRING2006 (3) KLEIN2006 (4) RICHARDS2006A	(1) CARLBRING2005** (2) KIROPOULOS2008
N/% female	(1) 41/71 (2) 60/60	(1) 37/80 (2) 21/31	(1) 41/71 (2) 60/60 (3) 37/80 (4) 21/31	(1) 49/71 (2) 80/72
Mean age (years)	(1) 34 (2) 37	(1) age range 18–70 (2) 36.59	1) 34 (2) 37 (3) age range 18–70 (4) 36.59	(1) 35 (2) 38.96
Diagnosis	(1)–(2) 100% panic disorder (>1 year) by DSM-IV	(1) 100% panic disorder with (82%) or without (18%) agoraphobia (2) 100% panic disorder (with or	(1)–(2) 100% panic disorder (>1 year) by DSM-IV (3) 100% panic disorder with (82%) or without (18%)	(1) 100% panic disorder (>1 year) by DSM-IV (2) 100% panic disorder with (58%) or without (42%) agoraphobia

Continued

		without agoraphobia)	agoraphobia (4) 100% panic disorder (with or without agoraphobia)	
Baseline severity: mean (SD)	(1) BAI: CCBT = 19.3 (6.2), control = 21.5 (10) (2) BAI: CCBT = 20.8 (10), control = 19.5 (9.4)	(1) Clinician-rated panic severity*: CCBT = 6.40 (1.0), control = 6.28 (1.1) (2) Clinician-rated panic severity*: CCBT = 5.61 (1.0), control = 5.57 (0.8)	(1) BAI: CCBT = 19.3 (6.2), control = 21.5 (10) (2) BAI: CCBT = 20.8 (10), control = 19.5 (9.4) (3) Clinician-rated panic severity*: CCBT = 6.40 (1.0), control = 6.28 (1.1) (4) Clinician-rated panic severity*: CCBT = 5.61 (1.0), control = 5.57 (0.8)	(1) BAI: CCBT = 18.7 (10.3), CBT = 24.5 (10.4) (2) Clinician-rated panic severity*: CCBT = 5.51 (1.11), CBT = 5.90 (1.16)
CCBT package	(1)–(2) Internet Psykiatri: the programme includes 10 modules and is designed to help the user understand and alleviate panic symptoms using the principles of CBT	(1)–(2) Panic Online: based on CBT principles. It is designed to assist the user to understand and master strategies effective in reducing	(1)–(2) Internet Psykiatri: the programme includes 10 modules and is designed to help the user understand and alleviate panic	(1) Internet Psykiatri: the programme includes 10 modules and is designed to help the user understand and alleviate panic symptoms using the principles

Table 80: *(Continued)*

	CCBT versus waitlist control	CCBT versus information control	CCBT versus any control (waitlist and information control)	CCBT versus face-to-face therapy
		the impact of panic disorder	symptoms using the principles of CBT (3)–(4) Panic Online: based on CBT principles. It is designed to assist the user to understand and master strategies effective in reducing the impact of panic disorder	of CBT (2) Panic Online: based on CBT principles. It is designed to assist the user to understand and master strategies effective in reducing the impact of panic disorder
Comparator	(1)–(2) Waitlist control	(1)–(2) Information control	(1)–(2) Waitlist control (3)–(4) Information control	(1)–(2) Face-to-face therapy
Type of CCBT and support	(1)–(2) Internet delivered self-help programme plus some therapist contact and feedback within 24 hours (1) Email (2) Email plus	(1)–(2) Internet delivered self-help programme plus some therapist contact via email within 24 hours	(1)–(2) Internet delivered self-help programme plus some therapist contact and feedback within 24 hours (1) Email (2) Email plus	(1) Internet delivered self-help programme plus minimal therapist contact via email (2) Same as (1) only email response within 24 hours

	phone calls		phone calls (3)–(4) Internet delivered self-help programme plus some therapist contact via email within 24 hours	
Amount of therapist time in CCBT group (approximately)	(1) 55 minutes per week (2) 47 minutes per week	(1) 12 minutes per week (2) 24 minutes per week	(1) 12 minutes per week (2) 24 minutes per week (3) 55 minutes per week (4) 47 minutes per week	(1) 15 minutes per week (2) 29 minutes per week
Amount of therapist time in comparison group: mean (SD)	(1) Total number of phone calls made: 4.23 (1.5) (2) Not reported	(1) N/A (2) N/A	(1) N/A (2) N/A (3) Total number of phone calls made: 4.23 (1.5) (4) Not reported	(1) Approximately 45–60 minutes per week (2) Approximately 52 minutes per week
Completion rate	(1)–(2) Unclear	(1) CCBT:100% (2) CCBT: 80%	(1) CCBT:100% (2) CCBT: 80% (3)–(4) Unclear	(1) CCBT: 28%; face-to-face: 88% (2) CCBT: no data available; face-to-face: completed mean of 11/12 weeks' treatment
Treatment length	(1) 6 weeks (2) 8 weeks	(1)–(2) 10 weeks	(1)–(2) 10 weeks (3) 6 weeks (4) 8 weeks	(1) 10 weeks (2) 12 weeks

*Note: Clinician-rated PDSS scale ranging from 0–8 (the higher the score the higher the severity); ** Included in original Technology Appraisal.

Table 81: Evidence summary table for trials of CCBT for a population with panic disorder only

	CCBT versus waitlist control	CCBT versus info control	CCBT versus any control (waitlist + info control)	CCBT versus face-to-face therapy
No. trials (total participants)	2 RCTs (101)	2 RCTs (58)	4 RCTs (159)	2 RCTS (135)
Study ID	(1) CARLBRING2001 (2) CARLBRING2006	(1) KLEIN2006 (2) RICHARDS2006A	(1) CARLBRING2001 (2) CARLBRING2006 (3) KLEIN2006 (4) RICHARDS2006A	(1) CARLBRING2005 (2) KIROPOULOS2008
Benefits				
Self-rated anxiety	SMD −1.29 (−1.72, −0.86) K = 2, N = 101 Quality: high	SMD −0.10 (−0.77, 0.58) K = 2, N = 58 Quality: moderate	SMD −0.70 (−1.41, 0.01) K = 4, N = 159 Quality: low	SMD 0.11 (−0.41, 0.62) K = 2, N = 129 Quality: low
Self-rated anxiety at follow-up	–	–	–	At 12 months: SMD −0.17 (−0.74, 0.39) K = 1, N = 49
Self-rated panic severity	–	SMD −1.90 (−3.04, −0.76) K = 2, N = 58 Quality: moderate	SMD −1.90 (−3.04, −0.76) K = 2, N = 58 Quality: moderate	–
Self-rated depression	SMD −0.84 (−1.39, −0.29) K = 2, N = 105 Quality: high	SMD −0.57 (−1.10, −0.04) K = 2, N = 58 Quality: high	SMD −0.72 (−1.05, −0.40) K = 4, N = 159 Quality: moderate	SMD 0.13 (−0.22, 0.47) K = 2, N = 133 Quality: moderate

Self-rated depression at follow-up	–	–	–	*At 12 months:* SMD 0.14 (−0.42, 0.70) K = 1, N = 49
Quality of life	SMD −0.55 (−0.95, −0.15) K = 2, N = 101 Quality: high	SMD −0.25 (−1.12, 0.61) K = 1, N = 21 Quality: moderate	SMD −0.50 (−0.86, −0.14) K = 3, N = 122 Quality: high	SMD 0.09 (−0.26, 0.44) K = 2, N = 127 Quality: moderate
Quality of life at follow-up	–	–	–	*At 12 months:* SMD 0.14 (−0.42, 0.70) K = 1, N = 49
Non-panic free status	RR 0.44 (0.12, 1.55) (1) Treatment: 7/30; control: 30/30 (2) Treatment 14/21; control: 19/21 K = 2, N = 101 Quality: very low	RR 0.32 (0.18, 0.56) K = 2, N = 58 Quality: high	RR 0.38 (0.19, 0.78) K = 4, N = 160 Quality: low	RR 0.95 (0.61, 1.46) K = 2, N = 135 Quality: moderate
Harm				
Discontinuation due to any reason	RR 1.48 (0.20, 10.79) K = 2, N = 101 Quality: moderate	RR 0.42 (0.11, 1.63) K = 2, N = 58 Quality: moderate	RR 0.72 (0.22, 2.40) K = 4, N = 159 Quality: low	RR 1.41 (0.48, 4.20) K = 2, N = 135 Quality: moderate

CCBT versus any control
A comparison of CCBT versus 'any control' (that is, waitlist and information control combined) was carried out to see if CCBT still had a beneficial outcome. CCBT was found to be largely effective relative to waitlist or information control on reducing panic severity and moderately effective on depression symptoms and improving quality of life. The overall quality for these outcomes was above moderate. It should be noted that the improvement in anxiety measures is not consistent for waitlist control and information control. It appears that CCBT is effective in improving anxiety scores against waitlist control but not information control.

CCBT versus face-to-face therapy
There were no statistically significant differences between CCBT and face-to-face CBT on any outcomes. This continued to be the case for follow-up data at 12 months. Although the data was insignificant, CCBT had higher dropout rates than face-to-face CBT. This might suggest that there may be a reduced adherence rate to CCBT treatment. It is difficult to draw any firm conclusions about the relative efficacy of the two treatments due to the limited number of studies.

9.2.6 Narrative review of studies on CCBT for a population with panic disorder only

Two studies that were not meta-analysed in the review above due to incomparable comparators (CARLBRING2003, KLEIN2009) are narratively reviewed below. RICHARDS2006A and KLEIN2006 were studies with three treatment arms. They each compared CCBT with the third comparator arm, which was deemed not to be comparable with other studies in the meta-analysis. Hence, these comparisons were not included in the meta-analysis, and they were reviewed in a narrative manner below. Study characteristics are summarised in Table 82 with full details in Appendix 15e, which also includes details of excluded studies.

CCBT versus bibliotherapy
When CCBT is compared with bibliotherapy, no statistically significant differences were found on any relevant outcomes. The clinician-rated non-remission ratio was 7 out of 19 in the CCBT group and 10 out of 18 in the bibliotherapy group. The dropout rate was 1 out of 19 in the CCBT group and 3 out of 18 in the bibliotherapy group. The ratings on anxiety and panic severity were moderately to largely effective with wide confidence intervals, and the result is not statistically significant. Since there was only one small trial comparing CCBT and bibliotherapy, no conclusions can be made.

CCBT in conjunction with a stress management programme versus information control
The CCBT programme that incorporated stress management was associated with a better non-remission status compared with information control. Two out of 11 participants did not remit in the CCBT (plus stress management) group, whereas eight out of nine did not remit in the information control group. One out of 11 participants dropped out from the CCBT (plus stress management) group and two out of nine dropped out

Table 82: Summary of study characteristics for narratively reviewed studies of CCBT

	CCBT versus bibliotherapy	CCBT + stress management versus information control	CCBT versus computerised applied relaxation	CCBT (frequent versus infrequent)
No. trials (total participants)	1 RCT	1 RCT	1 RCT	1 RCT
Study ID	KLEIN2006	RICHARDS2006A	CARLBRING2003	KLEIN2009
N/% female	37/80	20/31	22/68	57/82
Diagnosis	100% panic disorder with (82%) or without (18%) agoraphobia	100% panic disorder (with or without agoraphobia)	100% panic disorder by DSM-IV	100% panic disorder by DSM-IV
Baseline severity: mean (SD)	Clinician-rated panic severity*: CCBT = 6.40 (1.0), bibliotherapy = 6.57 (1.3)	Clinician-rated panic severity*: treatment = 6.26 (0.90), control = 5.57 (0.80)	BAI: CCBT = 19.6 (12.4), applied relaxation = 19.2 (4.1)	Clinician-rated panic severity*: frequent = 5.96 (1.14), infrequent = 5.76 (1.21)
Treatment length	6 weeks	8 weeks	2 weeks	8 weeks
Follow-up	3 months	3 months	End of treatment	End of treatment
Mean age (years)	Range 18–70	36.59	38	39
Type of CCBT and support	Internet delivered self-help programme plus some therapist contact via email	Internet delivered self-help programme plus some therapist contact via email	Internet delivered self-help programme plus some therapist contact and feedback	Internet delivered self-help programme plus some therapist contact via email

Table 82: Summary of study characteristics for narratively reviewed studies of CCBT

	CCBT versus bibliotherapy	CCBT + stress management versus information control	CCBT versus computerised applied relaxation	CCBT (frequent versus infrequent)
	within 24 hours	within 24 hours. Also provided a stress management programme that included six learning modules on coping with daily stresses, time and anger management.	within 24 hours via email	within 24 hours
Amount of therapist time in CCBT group (approximately)	55 minutes per week	47 minutes per week	15 minutes per week	Frequent CCBT = 38.5 minutes per week
Comparator and brief description	CBT bibliotherapy: participants were given a copy of a manual that provides a variety of CBT strategies. Information regarding	Information control	Computerised applied relaxation: participants were given a CD with relaxation instructions, as well as access for self-help use via the	Infrequent CCBT

	CBT is the same but organised and presented differently from the CCBT condition		internet. They were sent text message reminders to relax twice a day	
Amount of therapist time in comparison group: mean (SD)	Total number of phone calls made: 4.23 (1.5)	Not reported	Unclear	Infrequent CCBT = approximately 25.6 minutes per week
Completion rate	Unclear	Unclear	56% (3.4/6 modules)	Compliance with treatment for frequent CCBT = 6.74 (2.32), Infrequent CCBT = 6.04 (2.58)
CCBT programme	Panic Online	Panic Online	Internet Psykiatri	Panic Online

*Note: Clinician-rated PDSS ranging from 0–8 (the higher the score the higher the severity).

from the information control group. The CCBT (plus stress management) group had a large statistically significant effect on improving panic severity and depression scores. The effect on anxiety and quality of life is large but not statistically significant.

CCBT versus applied relaxation
When the CCBT programme is compared head to head with a computerised applied relaxation programme, out of the 11 participants in each group, five did not remit in the CCBT group and seven did not remit in the computerised applied relaxation group. Three dropped out from the CCBT group and two dropped out from the computerised applied relaxation group. With regards to continuous outcomes, there are no statistically significant differences between groups on any outcome measures including anxiety, panic severity, depression and quality of life. This small single trial did not reveal any difference between the two treatment principles.

CCBT frequent versus infrequent CCBT
At post-treatment, there were no significant differences in non-remission and dropout rates between the two groups. Six out of 28 participants dropped out in the frequent contact group and eight out of 29 dropped out in the infrequent contact group. Seventeen out of 28 and 19 out of 28 did not remit from the frequent contact and infrequent contact groups, respectively. With regards to continuous outcomes, there are no statistically significant differences between the frequent and infrequent contact groups on clinician- and self-rated panic severity and quality-of-life measures. Moreover, therapist alliance, treatment credibility and satisfaction did not differ between groups, despite significantly greater therapist time invested in the frequent contact condition.

9.3   HEALTH ECONOMIC EVIDENCE

9.3.1   Systematic literature review

The systematic search of the economic literature undertaken for the guideline identified two eligible studies on CCBT for people with panic disorder (Klein *et al.*, 2006; Michalopoulos *et al.*, 2005). Both studies evaluated the cost effectiveness of the Panic Online package in Australia. Details on the methods used for the systematic review of the economic literature are described in Chapter 3; references to included studies and evidence tables of economic evidence considered in the systematic literature review are provided in Appendix 15f. Completed methodology checklists of the studies are provided in Appendix 17. Economic evidence profiles of studies considered during guideline development (that is, studies that fully or partly met the applicability and quality criteria) are presented in Appendix 18d, accompanying the respective GRADE clinical evidence profiles.

Klein and colleagues (2006) conducted a simple cost analysis alongside an RCT comparing the Panic Online CCBT package versus therapist-assisted, self-administered CBT and information control for the treatment of people with panic disorder in Australia (KLEIN2006). The authors estimated the costs of providing each intervention from the perspective of the health service. Estimation of intervention costs considered therapists' time, server and website hosting costs for the CCBT package, cost of the self-administered CBT manual, post and telephone calls, calculated presumably in local prices. The RCT used several measures of outcome, such as the Panic Disorder Severity Scale (PDSS), panic frequency, the Agoraphobic Cognitions Questionnaire, the Anxiety Sensitivity Profile, the Depression Anxiety Stress Scale as well as the Body Vigilance Scale. Panic Online was found to be significantly more effective than information control in all panic parameter measures, cognitive variables, and anxiety and stress variables. Panic Online was significantly better that self-administered CBT only in terms of clinician-rated agoraphobia. The estimated average intervention cost per person was $350 for Panic Online, $379 for self-administered CBT and $55 for information control. The difference in cost between Panic Online and self-administered CBT was not statistically significant; no statistical analysis was performed between the costs of Panic Online and information control. The authors reported that Panic Online also reduced the number of GP visits post-treatment relative to self-administered CBT. These preliminary findings indicate that Panic Online might be a cost-effective option in Australia, but a formal economic analysis is required to establish the cost effectiveness of the CCBT programme.

Michalopoulos and colleagues (2005) assessed the cost effectiveness of Panic Online versus standard care for the treatment of people with panic disorder from the perspective of the healthcare sector in Australia. Standard care was defined as a mixture of care based on evidence-based medicine principles (27%), non-evidence-based medicine principles (28%) and no care (45%). The study population was the total estimated adult population with panic disorder in Australia, according to national surveys. The measure of outcome was the number of DALYs saved. Clinical data were taken from a literature review, while resource use estimates were based on assumptions; national unit prices were used. The study, based on decision-analytic modelling, reported that use of Panic Online for the treatment of the whole adult population with panic disorder in Australia would incur an extra $3.8 million (if it were provided by a clinical psychologist) or $2.8 million (if it were provided by a GP), and would save 870 DALYs compared with standard care. The estimated ICER of Panic Online versus standard care was $4,300/DALY averted when delivered by a clinical psychologist (range $3,500-$5,400/DALY averted in sensitivity analysis) or $3,200/DALY averted when delivered by a GP (range $2,700-$3,900/DALY averted in sensitivity analysis). The study was considered to be non-applicable to the UK setting for the following reasons: it was conducted in Australia, the outcome measure was DALYs saved, which limited the interpretability of the study findings, and standard care, according to its definition, was likely to differ significantly from standard care in the NHS. For this reason the study was not considered at the formulation of guideline recommendations.

9.3.2   Economic modelling

A number of economic models were developed for this guideline, as part of updating the NICE Technology Appraisal 97, *Computerised Cognitive Behaviour Therapy for*

Depression and Anxiety (NICE, 2006), to assess the cost effectiveness of CCBT for people with panic disorder, using clinical data from the RCTs included in the guideline systematic review.

Overview of interventions assessed in economic modelling

The CCBT packages examined in economic modelling included the Panic Online package (assessed in KIROPOULOS2008, KLEIN2006, KLEIN2009 and RICHARDS2006A) and the Internet Psykiatri package (assessed in CARLBRING2001, CARLBRING2005 and CARLBRING2006). The clinical evidence on the Panic Online and Internet Psykiatri packages is fairly limited. Both packages have been evaluated against inactive treatments: Panic Online against information control in KLEIN2006 and RICHARDS2006A and Internet Psykiatri against waitlist in CARLBRING2001 and CARLBRING2006. Both packages have also been evaluated against clinician-led CBT (Panic Online in KIROPOULOS2008 and Internet Psykiatri in CARLBRING2005). The clinical evidence from all these RCTs has been considered in economic modelling. Given the limited number of studies and the small number of participants in each study it was decided not to synthesise evidence using network meta-analytic techniques, as the outcome was expected to be highly uncertain. Instead, each CCBT package was assessed, in two separate models, against an inactive treatment and clinician-led CBT, respectively, resulting in four separate economic models:

- Model 1: Panic Online versus information control
- Model 2: Panic Online versus clinician-led CBT
- Model 3: Internet Psykiatri versus waitlist
- Model 4: Internet Psykiatri versus clinician-led CBT

KLEIN2009, which assessed the provision of Panic Online under different frequency of therapists' contact with participants, was not considered in economic modelling.

It must be noted that the Panic Online package has been developed for research purposes only and is not available in clinical practice for use by people with panic disorder. On the other hand, Internet Psykiatri is freely available on the internet for treatment of this population; however the package is available only in Swedish and therefore cannot be used within the NHS. The two packages have been considered in economic modelling only as case studies in order to explore the cost effectiveness of CCBT for people with panic disorder in the UK clinical setting.

Structure of the economic models

A simple decision-tree was constructed in order to estimate the cost effectiveness of Panic Online and Internet Psykiatri in the four separate models developed for this purpose. According to the common structure of the four models, hypothetical cohorts of people with panic disorder presenting to primary care were initiated on each of the interventions considered in the analyses. At completion of treatment, the panic status of the cohorts was assessed. People achieving panic-free status could remain panic-free or could return to a panic health state. People with a panic status following treatment could remain in this condition or could move to a panic-free health state. A second evaluation of the panic status was undertaken at follow-up. The time horizon of all four models was 1 year. A schematic diagram of the decision-tree used at the construction of the four models is presented in Figure 9.

Costs and outcomes considered in the economic models
The economic analyses adopted the perspective of the NHS and personal social services, as recommended by NICE (2009a). Costs consisted of intervention costs and other health and social care costs incurred by people with panic disorder, including contacts with healthcare professionals such as GPs, psychiatrists, psychologists, mental health nurses and social workers, community care, and inpatient and outpatient secondary care. The measure of outcome was the QALY.

Clinical input parameters of the economic models
In each model, clinical input parameters consisted of the probability of not achieving a panic-free status with the baseline treatment (that is, inactive treatment or clinician-led CBT), and of the relative risk of not achieving a panic-free status of CCBT versus its comparator (baseline treatment), at end of treatment and at 1-year follow-up. Clinical input parameters (both comparator probabilities and relative risks of CCBT versus its comparator) at end of treatment were estimated using the following data:
- Data for model 1 (Panic Online versus information control) were based on the guideline meta-analysis of KLEIN2006 and RICHARDS2006A. Both studies reported the rates of people who were panic-free, defined by clinician-rated panic severity of 2 or below on the PDSS. Assessment was carried out 1 week before the end of treatment in both studies, that is, at 5 weeks in KLEIN2006 and at 7 weeks

Figure 9: Schematic diagram of the structure of the economic models evaluating the Panic Online and the Internet Psykiatri CCBT packages

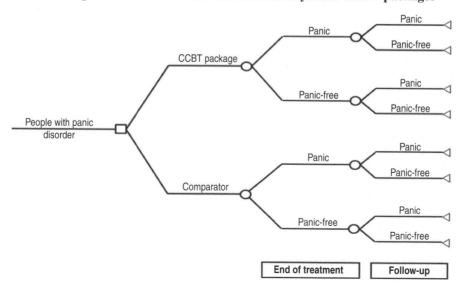

in RICHARDS2006A. Assessment of panic status in the model occurred at 6 weeks, which is the average time point of assessment between the two trials.

- Data for model 2 (Panic Online versus clinician-led CBT) were derived from KIROPOULOS2008, which reported the rate of people who were panic-free, defined by clinician-rated panic severity of 2 or below on the PDSS. Assessment was undertaken at the end of treatment, which lasted 12 weeks.

- Data for model 3 (Internet Psykiatri versus waitlist) were taken from the guideline meta-analysis of CARLBRING2001 and CARLBRING2006. CARLBRING2001 reported rates of people with a clinically significant improvement post-treatment, defined as no occurrence of either full-blown or limited-symptom panic attacks. CARLBRING2006 reported rates of people not fulfilling criteria for panic disorder according to the Structured Clinical Interview for DSM (SCID) at end of treatment. Treatment in both studies had a duration of 10 weeks; assessment of panic status was undertaken at 2 weeks' post-treatment in CARLBRING2001 (that is, at 12 weeks) and at 1 month's post-treatment in CARLBRING2006 (that is, at 14 weeks). Assessment in the model was assumed to be carried out at 13 weeks, which is the average assessment time between the two studies.

- Data for model 4 (Internet Psykiatri versus clinician-led CBT) were derived from CARLBRING2005, which reported rates of people no longer meeting criteria for panic disorder according to SCID; assessment of panic disorder occurred at 1 month after the 10-week treatment (that is, at 14 weeks).

One-year follow-up probabilities on panic-free status were estimated using data from CARLBRING2005, which was the only study on CCBT for panic disorder that reported follow-up data. This study compared Internet Psykiatri with clinician-led CCBT. For each intervention a post-treatment weekly probability of no panic was estimated using post-treatment data (obtained at 14 weeks) and follow-up data (obtained at 52 weeks) reported in CARLBRING2005. The weekly probability of no panic was then used to estimate the proportion of panic-free people at follow-up in each arm of the four models, after taking into account the proportion of people who were panic-free in each arm at the end of treatment.

The estimated post-treatment weekly probability of no panic for CCBT was conservatively applied in both arms of models assessing CCBT versus an inactive treatment (that is, models 1 and 3). Use of the same probability in both arms may have underestimated the future impact of CCBT on panic status, if CCBT retains a better clinical effect relative to inactive treatment after the end of treatment.

The estimated post-treatment weekly probability of no panic for clinician-led CBT was used in both arms of model 2, which assessed Panic Online versus clinician-led CBT. This was decided because the long-term effectiveness of Internet Psykiatri after the end of treatment, which was observed in CARLBRING2005, might be specific to this CCBT package; therefore it should not be attached to the Panic Online package in model 2. However, if there is indeed a long-term clinical effect of CCBT versus clinician-led CBT (as indicated in CARLBRING2005) in general, regardless of the specific package, then use of the clinician-led CBT data in both arms of model 2 has only underestimated the cost effectiveness of Panic Online relative to CBT.

Model 4, which evaluated the two treatments assessed in CARLBRING2005, utilised data from both arms of the study. More specifically, model 4 utilised the 1-year probability of non-panic-free status of clinician-led CBT and the relative risk of non-panic-free status of Internet Psykiatri versus clinician-led CBT at 1 year.

Clinical input parameters utilised in the four models are provided in Table 8.

Utility data for panic disorder

The systematic search of the literature identified no studies reporting utility scores for specific health states associated with panic disorder. However, two studies reported utility data for people with panic disorder in general, without differentiating between distinct health states of the condition (Alonso *et al.*, 2004a; Rubin *et al.*, 2000).

Alonso and colleagues (2004a) reported EQ-5D and SF-36 data for people participating in a large, community-based mental health European survey, the European Study of the Epidemiology of Mental Disorders (ESEMeD). Participants were members of the general population who underwent psychiatric assessments and completed various HRQoL instruments. The authors conducted additional analyses to those reported in their publication and generated EQ-5D and SF-36 utility scores that were subsequently provided to the research team that conducted the economic analysis for the NICE Technology Appraisal on the use of CCBT for depression and anxiety (Kaltenthaler *et al.*, 2006). Thus, EQ-5D utility scores for people with panic disorder who participated in the ESEMeD are available in that publication. Utility scores from EQ-5D have been elicited from the UK general population using TTO (Dolan *et al.*, 1996; Dolan, 1997). The EQ-5D utility scores from ESEMeD were derived from a sample of 186 people who had experienced panic disorder over 12 months and of 19,334 people who had no mental disorder over this period.

Rubin and colleagues (2000) provided utility scores derived from 56 people with panic disorder and matched historical population controls in the US. Utility scores were generated from participants' responses on the Quality of Well Being Scale (QWB), a generic HRQoL scale measuring mobility, physical and social activity, which has been valued by a sample of the general population in the US using scaling methods (Kaplan & Anderson, 1988).

Table 83 summarises the methods used to derive utility scores associated with panic disorder as well as the results reported in the two relevant studies identified by the systematic search of the literature.

No study reported utility data for specific health states in panic disorder. Both sets of data refer to an overall state of panic disorder, which may include a wide range of symptoms, from very mild to very severe. However, no other utility data that could be used in order to generate QALYs for people with panic disorder were identified. The utility data by Alonso and colleagues (2004a) refer to people who experienced panic disorder over 12 months, thus may not be fully applicable to the study population in the economic analyses conducted for this guideline. On the other hand, these data were generated using EQ-5D profiles, as recommended by NICE. The utility data by Rubin and colleagues (2000) were generated based on another generic measure of HRQoL, the QWB, which has been valued by a sample of the general population in the US, using scaling methods. Therefore, it is apparently less relevant to the UK population and less consistent with NICE criteria on the use of utility scores, which require the use of EQ-5D scores, or, when these are unavailable or inappropriate, the use of utility scores derived from patient-based, generic measures of HRQoL, valued by a sample of the general UK population using TTO or SG (NICE, 2008a). Based on the above, it was decided to use the data by Alonso and colleagues (2004a) in the guideline economic analyses for CCBT packages for panic disorders, and also because these data were used in the cost-utility analysis conducted for the NICE Technology Appraisal on the use of CCBT for depression and anxiety (Kaltenthaler *et al.*, 2006).

It was assumed that the change in utility between panic and panic-free health states occurred linearly over the time period between consecutive assessments of panic status.

Cost data
Intervention costs as well as other health and social care costs incurred by people with panic disorder were calculated by combining resource use estimates with respective national unit costs. Intervention costs for the CCBT packages consisted of therapists'

Table 83: Summary of studies reporting utility scores for panic disorder

Study	Definition of health states	Valuation method	Population valuing	Results
Alonso *et al.*, 2004a	EQ-5D profiles from 186 people with panic disorder over the last 12 months and 19, 334 people with no mental disorder over the last 12 months participating in a large community-based mental health European survey	TTO	UK general population	12-month panic disorder: 0.76 (95% CI, 0.70–0.82) No 12-month mental disorder: 0.91 (95% CI, 0.90–0.91)
Rubin *et al.*, 2000	QWB profiles from 56 people with panic disorder and matched population controls in the US	Scaling method	US general population	Panic disorder: 0.721 (SD 0.122) No panic disorder: 0.820 (SD 0.054)

time (spent on telephone calls, emails and 'live' contacts as reported in the RCTs considered in economic analyses), hardware (personal computers [PCs]) and capital overheads. Panic Online is available for research purposes only; Internet Psykiatri, on the other hand, is freely available on the internet. Therefore no licence fee was considered at the estimation of the CCBT intervention cost, although this cost component, which may be considerable, needs to be taken into account in the assessment of the cost effectiveness of CCBT packages available in the future for the management of people with panic disorder in the NHS. Alternatively, for a CCBT programme that is freely available via the internet, a server and website hosting cost may be relevant (for example if the programme is provided by the NHS) and should be considered at the estimation of the intervention cost.

The cost of therapist's time for CCBT was estimated by combining the mean total therapist's time per person treated, as reported in KLEIN2006 and RICHARDS2006A (model 1), KIROPOULOS2008 (model 2), CARLBRING2001 and CARLBRING2006 (model 3), and CARLBRING2005 (model 4), with the national unit cost of a clinical psychologist (Curtis, 2009). The latter may be a conservative estimate—in some of the RCTs, CCBT was provided by therapists with a lower salary or level of qualifications. It is acknowledged, though, that CCBT may be provided by other healthcare professionals with appropriate qualifications and training. The unit cost of a clinical psychologist per hour of client contact has been estimated based on the median full-time equivalent basic salary for Agenda for Change Band 7, including salary, salary oncosts and overheads, but no qualification costs because the latter are not available for clinical psychologists (Curtis, 2009).

The annual costs of hardware and capital overheads (space around the PC) were taken from the economic analysis undertaken to inform the NICE Technology Appraisal on CCBT for depression and anxiety (Kaltenthaler *et al.*, 2006). In the same report it is estimated that one PC can serve around 100 people treated with CCBT per year. For this economic exercise, and in order to estimate the cost of hardware and capital overheads per person with panic disorder treated with CCBT, it was conservatively assumed that one PC can serve 75 people per year. It was also assumed that a PC is used under full capacity (that is, it serves no fewer than 75 people annually), considering that the PC is available for use not only by people with panic disorder, but also by people with other mental health conditions, such as depression, who may use other CCBT packages on the PC. The annual cost of hardware and capital overheads, as estimated in Kaltenthaler and colleagues (2006), was therefore divided by 75. It should be noted that if people with panic disorder can access the CCBT package from home or a public library, then the cost of hardware and capital overheads to the NHS is zero.

Regarding the server and website hosting cost per person with panic disorder treated with a CCBT package provided by the NHS via the internet, this was estimated to be negligible and was omitted from analysis. Estimation of this cost was based on the price of a ten-page website, which was found to range between £550 and £800 annually (prices based on an internet search). According to the most recent *Adult Psychiatric Morbidity in England* survey (McManus *et al.*, 2009), 1.2% of people aged 16 to 64 years are expected to have panic disorder at any point in time.

This translates to an estimate of 425,000 people with panic disorder in England and Wales, given that the population aged 16–64 years was approximately 35.3 million people in 2008 (ONS, 2009). Assuming that 5% of them are treated with CCBT (a deliberately conservative low percentage), this would result in 21,000 people. Spreading the annual server and website cost to this population would result in a cost of approximately 3 to 4 pence per person treated; meaning that if the NHS wanted to maintain a website with a CCBT programme for panic disorder, the website cost per person treated would be negligible.

Intervention costs of clinician-led CBT were calculated by combining the mean total therapist's time per person treated, estimated from the number of CBT sessions and the duration of each session as reported in KIROPOULOS2008 (model 2) and CARLBRING2005 (model 4), with the national unit cost of a clinical psychologist (Curtis, 2009). Intervention costs of inactive treatments (waitlist and information control) were estimated to be zero.

Table 84 presents the cost elements of the intervention costs in each of the economic models developed for the economic assessment of CCBT for the treatment of people with panic disorder.

Table 84: Intervention costs of CCBT packages and clinician-led CBT considered in the economic models evaluating CCBT for the treatment of people with panic disorder

Cost element	Resource use estimates and respective unit cost (2009 prices)	Total cost per person (2009 prices)
CCBT	(Unit cost: £75 per hour of client contact; clinical psychologist; Curtis, 2009)	
Therapist's time per person treated	Model 1 (Panic Online): 355 minutes (average time between KLEIN2006 and RICHARDS2006A)	£443
	Model 2 (Panic Online): 352 minutes (KIROPOULOS2008)	£440
	Model 3 (Internet Psykiatri): 162 minutes (average time between CARLBRING2001 and CARLBRING2006)	£203
	Model 4 (Internet Psykiatri): 150 minutes (CARLBRING2005)	£188
Hardware	£309 per PC per year (Kaltenthaler *et al.*, 2006) Cost divided by 75 people treated with CCBT	£4.1

Capital overheads	£2,053 per PC per year (Kaltenthaler *et al.*, 2006) Cost divided by 75 people treated with CCBT	£27.4
Licence fee	0 (Panic Online not available in clinical practice; Internet Psykiatri freely available)	0
Server/website hosting cost	£550-£800 for a ten-page website annually Cost divided by 21,000 people, representing 5% of the estimated 420,000 people with panic disorder in England and Wales; latter estimate based on a 1.2% prevalence of panic disorder (McManus *et al.*, 2009) and a population of 35.3 million people aged 16 to 64 years in England and Wales (ONS, 2009)	Negligible
	TOTAL COST	**TOTAL COST**
	Model 1 (Panic Online)	£475
	Model 2 (Panic Online)	£472
	Model 3 (Internet Psykiatri)	£234
	Model 4 (Internet Psykiatri)	£219
Clinician-led CBT	(Unit cost £75 per hour of client contact; clinical psychologist; Curtis, 2009)	
Number of sessions and duration	Model 2: 12 sessions × 52 minutes each (KIROPOULOS2008)	**£780**
	Model 4: 10 sessions × 50 minutes each (CARLBRING2005)	**£625**

The extra health and social care costs incurred by people with panic disorder were estimated based on data reported in the *Adult Psychiatric Morbidity in England* survey (McManus *et al.*, 2009), supported by the expert opinion of the GDG. Data reported in the survey included the percentages of people with panic disorder who sought various types of health and social services over a period of time ranging from 'over the past 2 weeks' to 'over the past year'. These services included inpatient care, outpatient services, contacts with GPs, psychiatrists, psychologists, community psychiatric nurses, social and outreach workers, other nursing services, home help and home care, participation in self-help and support groups, and services provided by community day care centres. The reported percentages were extrapolated in order to estimate the percentage of people with panic disorder using each service on an annual basis. The GDG determined which of these services were likely to be sought specifically for the condition of panic disorder within the NHS, and made estimates on the number of visits and the time spent on each visit where relevant, in order to provide a total resource use estimate for each type of service. The average length of stay for people with panic disorder receiving inpatient care was taken from national hospital episode statistics (NHS, The Information Centre, 2009). The resource use estimates were then combined with appropriate unit costs taken from national sources (Curtis, 2009; DH, 2010) in order to estimate an overall annual health and social care cost incurred by people with panic disorder. Using this figure, a weekly health and social care cost was then estimated, which was assumed to be incurred by people in a non-panic-free status. People remaining in a non-panic-free status over the whole time horizon of the analyses were assumed to incur this weekly cost from a point in time starting at the end of treatment and up to 1 year. People who switched between a panic status and a panic-free status over the time period between end of treatment and end of the time horizon were assumed to incur this weekly health and social care cost for half of the period between the endpoint of treatment and the end of the time horizon.

Table 85 presents the published data and the expert opinion of the GDG estimates used for the calculation of the annual health and social care cost incurred by people with panic disorder.

All costs were expressed in 2009 prices, uplifted, where necessary, using the HCHS Pay and Prices Index (Curtis, 2009). As the time horizon of the four analyses was 1 year, discounting of costs was not necessary.

Table 86 presents the values of all input parameters utilised in the four economic models.

Data analysis and presentation of the results

Two methods were employed to analyse the input parameter data and present the results of the four economic models.

First, a *deterministic* analysis was undertaken for each model, where data are analysed as point estimates. The output of each analysis was the ICER of CCBT versus its comparator, expressing the additional cost per QALY gained associated with provision of CCBT instead of its comparator.

Second, a *probabilistic* analysis was also conducted for each model. In this case, all model input parameters were assigned probability distributions (rather than being expressed as point estimates), to reflect the uncertainty characterising the available clinical and cost data. Subsequently, 10,000 iterations were performed, each drawing random values out of the distributions fitted onto the model input parameters. This exercise provided more accurate estimates of mean costs and benefits for each intervention assessed (averaging results from the 10,000 iterations), by capturing the non-linearity characterising the economic model structure (Briggs *et al.*, 2006).

Table 85: Annual health and social care cost incurred by people with panic disorder

Cost component	% of people with panic disorder receiving care annually	Time spent on each service annually	Unit cost (2009 prices)		Annual weighted cost per person (2009 prices)
Inpatient care	4%	2.5 days	£290/day in mental health unit	DH, 2009	£29.00
Outpatient visit	8%	2 visits	1st visit: £244; follow-up visit: £155	DH, 2009	£31.92
Psychiatrist	2%	2 visits: 1 hour + 20 minutes	£322/hour of patient contact	Curtis, 2009	£8.59
Psychologist	4%	8 visits × 45 minutes each	£75/hour of client contact	Curtis, 2009	£18.00
Mental health nurse	4%	6 visits × 1 hour each	£53/hour of face-to-face contact	Curtis, 2009	£12.72
Other nursing services	1%	–	–	–	
Social worker	5%	6 visits × 1 hour each	£140/hour of face-to-face contact	Curtis, 2009	£42.00
Self-help – support group	1%	Not an NHS cost	–	–	
Home help – home care	1%	Not directly relevant	–	–	
Outreach worker	5%	Not directly relevant	–	–	
Community day care centre	8%	100 sessions	£33 per user session	Curtis, 2009	£264.00
GP	45%	1 visit	£35 per surgery consultation	Curtis, 2009	£15.75

McManus *et al.*, 2009; extrapolated to 1 year where necessary

Length of inpatient stay for panic disorder from hospital episode statistics (NHS, The information centre, 2009); all other estimates based on the expert opinion of the GDG

Total annual health and social care cost incurred per person with panic disorder £421.98

Table 86: Input parameters utilised in the economic models of CCBT for the treatment of people with panic disorder

Input parameter	Deterministic value	Probabilistic distribution	Source of data - comments
Clinical data			
END OF TREATMENT			
Probability of non-panic-free status		**Beta distribution**	
Model 1 – information control – 6 weeks	0.964	$\alpha = 27$, $\beta = 1$	Meta-analysis of KLEIN2006 and RICHARDS2006A KIROPOULOS2008
Model 2 – clinician-led CBT	0.625	$\alpha = 25$, $\beta = 15$	Meta-analysis of CARLBRING2001 and CARLBRING2006
Model 3 – waitlist	0.961	$\alpha = 49$, $\beta = 2$	CARLBRING2005
Model 4 – clinician-led CBT	0.333	$\alpha = 8$, $\beta = 16$	
Relative risk of non-panic-free status, CCBT versus comparator		**Log-normal distribution**	
Model 1 – Panic Online versus information control – 6 weeks	0.50	95% CIs: 0.32 to 0.79	Meta-analysis of KLEIN2006 and RICHARDS2006A KIROPOULOS2008
Model 2 – Panic Online versus clinician-led CBT	1.04	95% CIs: 0.76 to 1.44	Meta-analysis of CARLBRING2001 and CARLBRING2006
Model 3 – Internet Psykiatri versus waitlist	0.44	95% CIs: 0.12 to 1.55	CARLBRING2005
Model 4 – Internet Psykiatri versus clinician-led CBT	0.60	95% CIs: 0.23 to 1.58	
1 YEAR'S FOLLOW-UP – selected data used in all 4 models		**Beta distribution**	
Probability of non-panic free status – clinician-led CBT	0.125	$\alpha = 3$, $\beta = 21$	All follow-up data from CARLBRING2005
Weekly post-treatment probability of non-panic-free status – clinician-led CBT	0.026	Determined by linked distributions	
Probability of non-panic-free status – CCBT (Internet Psykiatri)	0.080	$\alpha = 2$, $\beta = 23$	
Weekly post-treatment probability of non-panic-free status – CCBT (Internet Psykiatri)	0.024	Determined by linked distributions	
Relative risk of non-panic-free status, CCBT versus clinician-led CBT	0.64	**Log-normal distribution** 95% CIs: 0.12 to 3.50	

Utility values		**Beta distribution**	
Panic-free status	0.91	$\alpha = 17{,}594,\ \beta = 1{,}740$	Alonso *et al.*, 2004a; data available in Kaltenthaler *et al.*, 2006; distribution estimated from reported data using the method of moments
Panic status	0.76	$\alpha = 141.36,\ \beta = 44.64$	
Cost data		**Gamma distribution**	
CCBT intervention cost - model 1	£475	$\alpha = 6.25,\ \beta = 75.94$	See Table 15 in Chapter 6; standard error of CCBT intervention cost assumed to be 40% of its mean estimate
– model 2	£472	$\alpha = 6.25,\ \beta = 75.44$	
– model 3	£234	$\alpha = 6.25,\ \beta = 37.44$	
– model 4	£219	$\alpha = 6.25,\ \beta = 35.04$	
Clinician-led CBT intervention cost - model 2	£780	$\alpha = 6.25,\ \beta = 124.80$	See Table 15 in Chapter 6; standard error of clinician-led CBT intervention cost assumed to be 40% of its mean estimate
– model 4	£625	$\alpha = 6.25,\ \beta = 100.00$	
Weekly health and social care cost	£8	$\alpha = 2.78,\ \beta = 2.92$	See Table 16 in Chapter 6; standard error of weekly health and social care cost assumed to be 60% of its mean estimate

The baseline probabilities of non-panic-free status at end of treatment and at 1-year follow-up (for inactive treatments and clinician-led CBT) were given a beta distribution. Beta distributions were also assigned to utility values, using the method of moments. The relative risks of non-panic free status of CCBT versus its comparator were assigned a log-normal distribution. The estimation of distribution ranges was based on available data in the published sources of evidence.

Costs were assigned a gamma distribution; in order to define the distribution, wide standard errors around the mean costs (equalling 40% of the mean CCBT intervention cost and 60% of the mean monthly health and social care cost incurred by people with panic disorder) were assumed.

Table 17 in Chapter 6 provides details on the types of distributions assigned to each input parameter and the methods employed to define their range.

Results of probabilistic analysis are presented in the form of a CEAC, which demonstrates the probability of CCBT being cost effective relative to its comparator at different levels of willingness-to-pay per QALY (that is, at different cost effectiveness thresholds the decision-maker may set).

Results
Model 1: Panic Online versus information control
Deterministic results are presented in Table 87. Panic Online was associated with a higher total cost and a higher number of QALYs compared with information control. The ICER of Panic Online versus information control was £7,599 per QALY gained.

Probabilistic analysis demonstrated that the probability of Panic Online being cost effective at the NICE lower cost-effectiveness threshold of £20,000/QALY reached 92%. Figure 10 provides the CEAC showing the probability of Panic Online being cost effective relative to information control at different levels of willingness-to-pay per extra QALY gained.

Model 2: Panic Online versus clinician-led CBT
Deterministic results are presented in Table 88. Panic Online was associated with a significantly lower cost and a slight loss in QALYs compared with clinician-led CBT. The ICER of Panic Online versus clinician-led CBT was a saving of £126, 849 per QALY lost.

Table 87: Deterministic results of model 1 – mean costs and QALYs per 100 people and ICER of Panic Online versus information control

Intervention	Mean total cost	Mean total QALYs	ICER
Panic Online	£59,429	85.463	
Information control	£23,933	80.792	£7,599/QALY
Difference	£35,496	4.671	

Figure 10: CEAC of Panic Online versus information control. X axis shows the level of willingness-to-pay per extra QALY gained and Y axis shows the probability of Panic Online being cost effective at different levels of willingness-to-pay

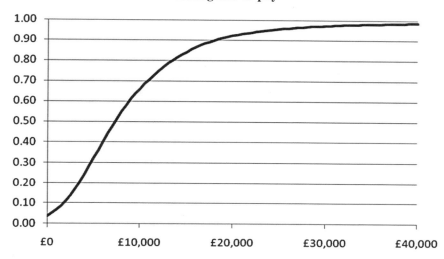

Table 88: Deterministic results of model 2 – mean costs and QALYs per 100 people and ICER of Panic Online versus clinician-led CBT

Intervention	Mean total cost	Mean total QALYs	ICER
Panic Online	£61,456	83.059	
Clinician-led CBT	£91,756	83.298	£126,849/QALY
Difference	-£30,300	−0.239	

According to probabilistic analysis, the probability of Panic Online being cost effective at the NICE lower cost-effectiveness threshold of £20,000/QALY gained was 71%. Figure 11 provides the CEAC showing the probability of Panic Online being cost effective relative to clinician-led CBT at different levels of willingness-to-pay per extra QALY gained.

Model 3: Internet Psykiatri versus waitlist
Deterministic results are presented in Table 89. Internet Psykiatri resulted in a higher total cost and a higher number of QALYs compared with waitlist. The ICER of Internet Psykiatri versus waitlist was £2,216 per QALY gained.

Figure 11: CEAC of Panic Online versus clinician-led CBT. X axis shows the level of willingness-to-pay per extra QALY gained and Y axis shows the probability of Panic Online being cost effective at different levels of willingness-to-pay.

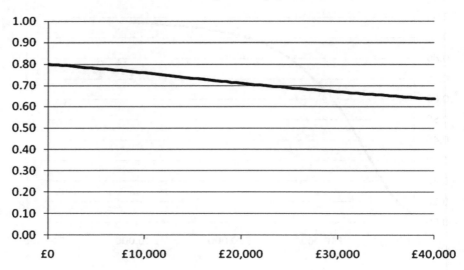

Table 89: Deterministic results of model 3 – mean costs and QALYs per 100 people and ICER of Internet Psykiatri versus waitlist

Intervention	Mean total cost	Mean total QALYs	ICER
Internet Psykiatri	£32,702	85.026	
Waitlist	£21,140	79.809	£2,216/QALY
Difference	£11,562	5.217	

Probabilistic analysis showed that the probability of Internet Psykiatri being cost effective at the NICE lower cost-effectiveness threshold of £20,000/QALY reached 85.3%. Figure 12 provides the CEAC showing the probability of Internet Psykiatri being cost effective relative to waitlist at different levels of willingness-to-pay per extra QALY gained.

Model 4: Internet Psykiatri versus clinician-led CBT
Deterministic results are presented in Table 90. Internet Psykiatri resulted in a significantly lower cost and at the same time it provided a higher number of QALYs compared with clinician-led CBT. Thus Internet Psykiatri was the dominant option in this comparison.

Figure 12: CEAC of Internet Psykiatri versus waitlist. X axis shows the level of willingness-to-pay per extra QALY gained and Y axis shows the probability of Internet Psykiatri being cost effective at different levels of willingness-to-pay

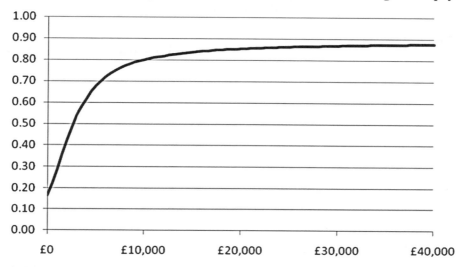

Table 90: Deterministic results of model 4 – mean costs and QALYs per 100 people and ICER of Internet Psykiatri versus clinician-led CBT

Intervention	Mean total cost	Mean total QALYs	ICER
Internet Psykiatri	£26,217	87.042	Internet Psykiatri dominant
Clinician-led CBT	£69,567	85.796	
Difference	−£43,350	1.247	

According to probabilistic analysis, the probability of Internet Psykiatri being cost effective at the NICE lower cost-effectiveness threshold of £20,000/QALY gained was 95%.

Figure 13 provides the CEAC showing the probability of Internet Psykiatri being cost effective relative to clinician-led CBT at different levels of willingness-to-pay per extra QALY gained.

Discussion of findings - limitations of the models

The results of the four economic models indicate that CCBT (represented by two different packages, Panic Online and Internet Psykiatri) is likely to be a cost-effective treatment option for people with panic disorder compared with inactive treatment and clinician-led CBT. However, analyses were based on clinical data derived from a

317

Figure 13: CEAC of Internet Psykiatri versus clinician-led CBT. X axis shows the level of willingness-to-pay per extra QALY gained and Y axis shows the probability of Internet Psykiatri being cost effective at different levels of willingness-to-pay

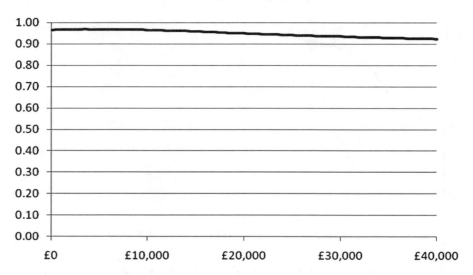

small number of studies (six studies utilised in four models). Moreover, the total number of participants in the six studies was rather low (N = 294). The studies were characterised by important limitations, as discussed in the clinical evidence section of this chapter. The definition of panic-free status was not consistent across studies, a fact that was potentially the cause of the substantial heterogeneity observed in the guideline meta-analyses. Follow-up data were available in only one study (CARLBRING2005); the other five studies had very short time horizons ranging from 5 to 14 weeks.

Panic Online is a CCBT package designed for research purposes only and is not available in clinical practice. Internet Psykiatri is freely available on the internet for the treatment of people with panic disorder, but in Swedish. Therefore, the models did not consider a licence fee at the estimation of the CCBT intervention cost. However, alternative CCBT packages designed for the treatment of people with panic disorder in the future may not be freely available. A licence fee would need to be added to the intervention cost in such cases, which, if significant, may affect the cost effectiveness of CCBT.

CCBT packages were found to be cost effective compared with inactive treatments. Nevertheless, the latter do not represent routine practice for people with panic disorder within the NHS. On the other hand, both packages were found to be cost effective when compared with clinician-led CBT. If this is confirmed by future research, it will have significant resource implications, as availability of CCBT packages in English for the treatment of people with panic disorder will free up a large amount of therapists' time that could be used for provision of psychological therapies in other areas of mental health within NHS. Alternatively, CCBT may be effectively used in areas where there is a shortage of therapists providing psychological treatments, to cover the local needs of people with panic disorder. In any case, currently there are no CCBT packages available for the treatment of this population in the NHS.

9.4   FROM EVIDENCE TO RECOMMENDATIONS

In the clinical evidence review, there was some evidence favouring CCBT when compared with control for improving panic severity and depression scores. Furthermore, there was initial evidence showing CCBT is comparable with traditional face-to-face CBT. The evidence was of moderate to high quality for most outcomes.

Economic analyses using the available (limited) clinical evidence showed that CCBT is likely to be cost effective relative to inactive treatments and also compared with clinician-led CBT. Currently no CCBT package is available for the treatment of people with panic disorder in the NHS. It must be noted that the cost effectiveness of a new CCBT package depends also on its (potential) licence fee – the economic models undertaken for this guideline assumed no licence fee, since this was not relevant to the two CCBT packages assessed. However, licence fees need to be considered when evaluating the cost effectiveness of CCBT packages developed in the future.

Because CCBT packages specifically for the treatment of people with panic disorders are not available in the NHS, and due to the limited evidence, it was not possible to make a recommendation for people with panic disorder only; therefore a research recommendation was made instead.

9.4.1   Research recommendation

9.4.1.1   The clinical and cost effectiveness of two CBT-based low-intensity interventions (CCBT and guided bibliotherapy) compared with a waiting-list control for the treatment of panic disorder

In well-defined panic disorder, what is the clinical and cost effectiveness of two CBT-based low-intensity interventions (CCBT and guided bibliotherapy) compared with a waiting-list control?

This question should be answered using a three-armed randomised controlled design using both short- and medium-term outcomes (including cost-effectiveness outcomes). Particular attention should be paid to the reproducibility of the treatment model with regard to content, duration and the training and supervision of those delivering interventions to ensure that the results are both robust and generalisable. The outcomes chosen should include both observer- and participant-rated measures of clinical

319

symptoms and functioning specific to panic disorder, and an assessment of the acceptability and accessibility of the treatment options.

Why this is important

Psychological treatments are a recommended therapeutic option for people with panic disorder. CCBT is a promising low-intensity intervention for panic disorder that does not yet have a substantial evidence base. It is therefore important to establish whether CCBT is an effective and cost-effective treatment that should be provided for panic disorder, and how it compares with other low-intensity interventions such as guided bibliotherapy. The results of this trial will have important implications for the provision, accessibility and acceptability of psychological treatment in the NHS.

10   SUMMARY OF RECOMMENDATIONS

10.1   PRINCIPLES OF CARE FOR PEOPLE WITH GENERALISED ANXIETY DISORDER (GAD)

10.1.1   Information and support for people with GAD, their families and carers

10.1.1.1   When working with people with GAD:
- build a relationship and work in an open, engaging and non-judgemental manner
- explore the person's worries in order to jointly understand the impact of GAD
- explore treatment options collaboratively with the person, indicating that decision making is a shared process
- ensure that discussion takes place in settings in which confidentiality, privacy and dignity are respected.

10.1.1.2   When working with people with GAD:
- provide information appropriate to the person's level of understanding about the nature of GAD and the range of treatments available
- if possible, ensure that comprehensive written information is available in the person's preferred language and in audio format
- offer independent interpreters if needed.

10.1.1.3   When families and carers are involved in supporting a person with GAD, consider:
- offering a carer's assessment of their caring, physical and mental health needs
- providing information, including contact details, about family and carer support groups and voluntary organisations, and helping families or carers to access these
- negotiating between the person with GAD and their family or carers about confidentiality and the sharing of information
- providing written and verbal information on GAD and its management, including how families and carers can support the person
- providing contact numbers and information about what to do and who to contact in a crisis.

10.1.1.4   Inform people with GAD about local and national self-help organisations and support groups, in particular where they can talk to others with similar experiences.

10.1.1.5   For people with GAD who have a mild learning disability or mild acquired cognitive impairment, offer the same interventions as for other people with

GAD, adjusting the method of delivery or duration of the intervention if necessary to take account of the disability or impairment.

10.1.1.6 When assessing or offering an intervention to people with GAD and a moderate to severe learning disability or moderate to severe acquired cognitive impairment, consider consulting with a relevant specialist.

10.2 STEPPED CARE FOR PEOPLE WITH GENERALISED ANXIETY DISORDER

A stepped-care model (see Figure 14) is used to organise the provision of services and to help people with GAD, their families, carers and practitioners to choose the most effective interventions.

10.2.1.1 Follow the stepped-care model, offering the least intrusive, most effective intervention first.

Figure 14. The stepped-care model

Focus of the intervention	Nature of the intervention
STEP 4: Complex treatment-refractory GAD and very marked functional impairment, such as self-neglect or a high risk of self-harm	Highly specialist treatment, such as complex drug and/or psychological treatment regimens; input from multi-agency teams, crisis services, day hospitals or inpatient care
STEP 3: GAD with an inadequate response to step 2 interventions or marked functional impairment	Choice of a high-intensity psychological intervention (CBT/applied relaxation) or a drug treatment
STEP 2: Diagnosed GAD that has not improved after education and active monitoring in primary care	Low-intensity psychological interventions: individual non-facilitated self-help*, individual guided self-help and psychoeducational groups
STEP 1: All known and suspected presentations of GAD	Identification and assessment; education about GAD and treatment options; active monitoring

*A self-administered intervention intended to treat GAD involving written or electronic self-help materials (usually a book or workbook). It is similar to individual guided self-help but usually with minimal therapist contact, for example an occasional short telephone call of no more than 5 minutes.

322

Step 1: All known and suspected presentations of GAD

Identification

10.2.1.2   Identify and communicate the diagnosis of GAD as early as possible to help people understand the disorder and start effective treatment promptly.

10.2.1.3   Consider the diagnosis of GAD in people presenting with anxiety or significant worry, and in people who attend primary care frequently who:
- have a chronic physical health problem **or**
- do not have a physical health problem but are seeking reassurance about somatic symptoms (particularly older people and people from minority ethnic groups) **or**
- are repeatedly worrying about a wide range of different issues.

10.2.1.4   When a person with known or suspected GAD attends primary care seeking reassurance about a chronic physical health problem or somatic symptoms and/or repeated worrying, consider with the person whether some of their symptoms may be due to GAD.

Assessment and education

10.2.1.5   For people who may have GAD, conduct a comprehensive assessment that does not rely solely on the number, severity and duration of symptoms, but also considers the degree of distress and functional impairment.

10.2.1.6   As part of the comprehensive assessment, consider how the following factors might have affected the development, course and severity of the person's GAD:
- any comorbid depressive disorder or other anxiety disorder
- any comorbid substance misuse
- any comorbid medical condition
- a history of mental health disorders
- past experience of, and response to, treatments.

10.2.1.7   For people with GAD and a comorbid depressive or other anxiety disorder, treat the primary disorder first (that is, the one that is more severe and in which it is more likely that treatment will improve overall functioning)[19,20].

10.2.1.8   For people with GAD who misuse substances, be aware that:
- substance misuse can be a complication of GAD
- non-harmful substance use should not be a contraindication to the treatment of GAD
- harmful and dependent substance misuse should be treated first as this may lead to significant improvement in the symptoms of GAD[21].

---

[19]For NICE guidance on depression, obsessive–compulsive disorder and post-traumatic stress disorder see NICE (2009c; 2009b; 2005a; 2005b).

[20]NICE is developing a guideline on identification and pathways to care for common mental health disorders. Publication expected Summer 2011.

[21]For NICE guidance on drug misuse and alcohol-use disorders see NICE (2007a; 2007b; 2010a; 2010b; 2011a).

10.2.1.9 Following assessment and diagnosis of GAD:
- provide education about the nature of GAD and the options for treatment, including the 'Understanding NICE guidance' booklet
- monitor the person's symptoms and functioning (known as active monitoring).

  This is because education and active monitoring may improve less severe presentations and avoid the need for further interventions.

10.2.1.10 Discuss the use of over-the-counter medications and preparations with people with GAD. Explain the potential for interactions with other prescribed and over-the-counter medications and the lack of evidence to support their safe use.

Step 2:   Diagnosed GAD that has not improved after step 1 interventions

Low-intensity psychological interventions for GAD

10.2.1.11 For people with GAD whose symptoms have not improved after education and active monitoring in step 1, offer one or more of the following as a first-line intervention, guided by the person's preference:
- individual non-facilitated self-help
- individual guided self-help
- psychoeducational groups.

10.2.1.12 Individual non-facilitated self-help for people with GAD should:
- include written or electronic materials of a suitable reading age (or alternative media)
- be based on the treatment principles of cognitive behavioural therapy (CBT)
- include instructions for the person to work systematically through the materials over a period of at least 6 weeks
- usually involve minimal therapist contact, for example an occasional short telephone call of no more than 5 minutes.

10.2.1.13 Individual guided self-help for people with GAD should:
- include written or electronic materials of a suitable reading age (or alternative media)
- be supported by a trained practitioner, who facilitates the self-help programme and reviews progress and outcome
- usually consist of five to seven weekly or fortnightly face-to-face or telephone sessions, each lasting 20–30 minutes.

10.2.1.14 Psychoeducational groups for people with GAD should:
- be based on CBT principles, have an interactive design and encourage observational learning
- include presentations and self-help manuals
- be conducted by trained practitioners
- have a ratio of one therapist to about 12 participants
- usually consist of six weekly sessions, each lasting 2 hours.

10.2.1.15 Practitioners providing guided self-help and/or psychoeducational groups should:
- receive regular high-quality supervision
- use routine outcome measures and ensure that the person with GAD is involved in reviewing the efficacy of the treatment.

Step 3: GAD with marked functional impairment or that has not improved after step 2 interventions

Treatment options

10.2.1.16 For people with GAD and marked functional impairment, or those whose symptoms have not responded adequately to step 2 interventions:
- Offer either
  - an individual high-intensity psychological intervention (see 10.2.1.17–10.2.1.21) **or**
  - drug treatment (see 10.2.1.22–10.2.1.32).
- Provide verbal and written information on the likely benefits and disadvantages of each mode of treatment, including the tendency of drug treatments to be associated with side effects and withdrawal syndromes.
- Base the choice of treatment on the person's preference as there is no evidence that either mode of treatment (individual high-intensity psychological intervention or drug treatment) is better.

High-intensity psychological interventions

10.2.1.17 If a person with GAD chooses a high-intensity psychological intervention, offer either CBT or applied relaxation.

10.2.1.18 CBT for people with GAD should:
- be based on the treatment manuals used in the clinical trials of CBT for GAD
- be delivered by trained and competent practitioners
- usually consist of 12–15 weekly sessions (fewer if the person recovers sooner; more if clinically required), each lasting 1 hour.

10.2.1.19 Applied relaxation for people with GAD should:
- be based on the treatment manuals used in the clinical trials of applied relaxation for GAD
- be delivered by trained and competent practitioners
- usually consist of 12–15 weekly sessions (fewer if the person recovers sooner; more if clinically required), each lasting 1 hour.

10.2.1.20 Practitioners providing high-intensity psychological interventions for GAD should:
- have regular supervision to monitor fidelity to the treatment model, using audio or video recording of treatment sessions if possible and if the person consents

- use routine outcome measures and ensure that the person with GAD is involved in reviewing the efficacy of the treatment.

10.2.1.21 Consider providing all interventions in the preferred language of the person with GAD if possible.

Drug treatment

10.2.1.22 If a person with GAD chooses drug treatment, offer a selective serotonin reuptake inhibitor (SSRI). Consider offering sertraline first because it is the most cost-effective drug, but note that at the time of publication (January 2011)[22] sertraline did not have UK marketing authorisation for this indication. Informed consent should be obtained and documented. Monitor the person carefully for adverse reactions.

10.2.1.23 If sertraline is ineffective, offer an alternative SSRI or a serotonin–noradrenaline reuptake inhibitor (SNRI), taking into account the following factors:

- tendency to produce a withdrawal syndrome (especially with paroxetine and venlafaxine)
- the side-effect profile and the potential for drug interactions
- the risk of suicide and likelihood of toxicity in overdose (especially with venlafaxine)
- the person's prior experience of treatment with individual drugs (particularly adherence, effectiveness, side effects, experience of withdrawal syndrome and the person's preference).

10.2.1.24 If the person cannot tolerate SSRIs or SNRIs, consider offering pregabalin.

10.2.1.25 Do not offer a benzodiazepine for the treatment of GAD in primary or secondary care except as a short-term measure during crises. Follow the advice in the 'British national formulary' on the use of a benzodiazepine in this context.

10.2.1.26 Do not offer an antipsychotic for the treatment of GAD in primary care.

10.2.1.27 Before prescribing any medication, discuss the treatment options and any concerns the person with GAD has about taking medication. Explain fully the reasons for prescribing and provide written and verbal information on:

- the likely benefits of different treatments
- the different propensities of each drug for side effects, withdrawal syndromes and drug interactions
- the risk of activation with SSRIs and SNRIs, with symptoms such as increased anxiety, agitation and problems sleeping
- the gradual development, over 1 week or more, of the full anxiolytic effect
- the importance of taking medication as prescribed and the need to continue treatment after remission to avoid relapse.

---

[22]The date of publication of the NICE guideline containing the recommendations only on the NICE website: http://guidance.nice.org.uk/CG113

10.2.1.28 Take into account the increased risk of bleeding associated with SSRIs, particularly for older people or people taking other drugs that can damage the gastrointestinal mucosa or interfere with clotting (for example, NSAIDS or aspirin). Consider prescribing a gastroprotective drug in these circumstances.

10.2.1.29 For people aged under 30 who are offered an SSRI or SNRI:
- warn them that these drugs are associated with an increased risk of suicidal thinking and self-harm in a minority of people under 30 **and**
- see them within 1 week of first prescribing **and**
- monitor the risk of suicidal thinking and self-harm weekly for the first month.

10.2.1.30 For people who develop side effects soon after starting drug treatment, provide information and consider one of the following strategies:
- monitoring the person's symptoms closely (if the side effects are mild and acceptable to the person) **or**
- reducing the dose of the drug **or**
- stopping the drug and, according to the person's preference, offering either
  - an alternative drug (see 10.2.1.23–10.2.1.24) **or**
  - a high-intensity psychological intervention (see 10.2.1.17–10.2.1.21).

10.2.1.31 Review the effectiveness and side effects of the drug every 2–4 weeks during the first 3 months of treatment and every 3 months thereafter.

10.2.1.32 If the drug is effective, advise the person to continue taking it for at least a year as the likelihood of relapse is high.

Inadequate response to step 3 interventions

10.2.1.33 If a person's GAD has not responded to a full course of a high-intensity psychological intervention, offer a drug treatment (see 10.2.1.22–10.2.1.32).

10.2.1.34 If a person's GAD has not responded to drug treatment, offer either a high-intensity psychological intervention (see 10.2.1.17–10.2.1.21) or an alternative drug treatment (see 10.2.1.23–10.2.1.24).

10.2.1.35 If a person's GAD has partially responded to drug treatment, consider offering a high-intensity psychological intervention in addition to drug treatment.

10.2.1.36 Consider referral to step 4 if the person with GAD has severe anxiety with marked functional impairment in conjunction with:
- a risk of self-harm or suicide or
- significant comorbidity, such as substance misuse, personality disorder or complex physical health problems or
- self-neglect or
- an inadequate response to step 3 interventions.

Summary of recommendations

Step 4[23]:   Complex, treatment-refractory GAD and very marked functional impairment or high risk of self-harm

Assessment

10.2.1.37 Offer the person with GAD a specialist assessment of needs and risks, including:
- duration and severity of symptoms, functional impairment, comorbidities, risk to self and self-neglect
- a formal review of current and past treatments, including adherence to previously prescribed drug treatments and the fidelity of prior psychological interventions, and their impact on symptoms and functional impairment
- home environment
- support in the community
- relationships with and impact on families and carers.

10.2.1.38 Review the needs of families and carers and offer an assessment of their caring, physical and mental health needs if one has not been offered previously.

10.2.1.39 Develop a comprehensive care plan in collaboration with the person with GAD that addresses needs, risks and functional impairment and has a clear treatment plan.

Treatment

10.2.1.40 Inform people with GAD who have not been offered or have refused the interventions in steps 1–3 about the potential benefits of these interventions, and offer them any they have not tried.

10.2.1.41 Consider offering combinations of psychological and drug treatments, combinations of antidepressants or augmentation of antidepressants with other drugs, but exercise caution and be aware that:
- evidence for the effectiveness of combination treatments is lacking
  and
- side effects and interactions are more likely when combining and augmenting antidepressants.

10.2.1.42 Combination treatments should be undertaken only by practitioners with expertise in the psychological and drug treatment of complex, treatment-refractory anxiety disorders and after full discussion with the person about the likely advantages and disadvantages of the treatments suggested.

10.2.1.43 When treating people with complex and treatment-refractory GAD, inform them of relevant clinical research in which they may wish to participate, working within local and national ethical guidelines at all times.

---

[23]Step 4 normally refers to community mental health teams but may include specialist services and specialist practitioners in primary care.

10.2.2   Research recommendations

10.2.2.1   A comparison of the clinical and cost effectiveness of sertraline and CBT in people with GAD that has not responded to guided self-help and psychoeducation

What is the relative effectiveness of sertraline compared with CBT in people with GAD that has not responded to guided self-help and psychoeducation in a stepped-care model?

This question should be addressed using a randomised controlled design in which people with GAD that has not responded to step 2 interventions are allocated openly to treatment with sertraline, CBT or waiting-list control for 12–16 weeks. The control group is important to demonstrate that the two active treatments produce effects greater than those of natural remission. The period of waiting-list control is the standard length of CBT treatment for GAD and is also commonly the length of time that it would take for specialist CBT to become available in routine practice. After 12–16 weeks all participants should receive further treatment chosen in collaboration with their treating clinicians.

The outcomes chosen at 12–16 weeks should include both observer- and participant-rated measures of clinical symptoms and functioning specific to GAD, and of quality of life. An economic analysis should also be carried out alongside the trial. The trial needs to be large enough to determine the presence or absence of clinically important effects and of any differences in costs between the treatment options using a non-inferiority design. Mediators and moderators of response should be investigated. Follow-up assessments should continue over the next 2 years to ascertain whether short-term benefits are maintained and, in particular, whether CBT produces a better long-term outcome.

Why this is important
Both sertraline and CBT are efficacious in the treatment of GAD but their relative efficacy has not been compared. In a stepped-care model both CBT and sertraline are treatment options if step 2 interventions (guided self-help and/or psychoeducation) have not resulted in a satisfactory clinical response. At present, however, there are no randomised trial data to help prioritise next-step treatments and no information on how individuals with GAD may be matched to particular therapies. Clarification of the relative short- and longer-term benefits of sertraline and CBT would be helpful in guiding treatment.

10.2.2.2   The clinical and cost effectiveness of two CBT-based low-intensity interventions (CCBT and guided bibliotherapy) compared with a waiting-list control for the treatment of GAD

In well-defined GAD, what is the clinical and cost effectiveness of two CBT-based low-intensity interventions (CCBT and guided bibliotherapy) compared with a waiting-list control?

Summary of recommendations

This question should be answered using a three-armed randomised controlled design using both short- and medium-term outcomes (including cost-effectiveness outcomes). Particular attention should be paid to the reproducibility of the treatment model with regard to content, duration and the training and supervision of those delivering interventions to ensure that the results are both robust and generalisable. The outcomes chosen should include both observer- and participant-rated measures of clinical symptoms and functioning specific to GAD, and an assessment of the acceptability and accessibility of the treatment options.

Why this is important
Psychological treatments are a recommended therapeutic option for people with GAD. CCBT is a promising low-intensity intervention for GAD that does not yet have a substantial evidence base. It is therefore important to establish whether CCBT is an effective and cost-effective treatment that should be provided for GAD, and how it compares with other low-intensity interventions such as guided bibliotherapy. The results of this trial will have important implications for the provision, accessibility and acceptability of psychological treatment in the NHS.

10.2.2.3   The effectiveness of physical activity compared with waiting-list control for the treatment of GAD

For people with GAD who are ready to start a low-intensity intervention, what is the clinical effectiveness of physical activity compared with waiting-list control?
This question should be answered using a randomised controlled design for people with GAD who have been educated about the disorder (as described in step 1) and are stepping up to a low-intensity intervention. The period of waiting-list control should be 12 weeks. The outcomes chosen should include both observer- and participant-rated measures of clinical symptoms and functioning specific to GAD, and of quality of life.

Why this is important
The evidence base for the effectiveness of physical activity in reducing anxiety symptoms is substantially smaller than that for depression. However, where evidence exists there are signs that physical activity could help to reduce anxiety. As GAD is a commonly experienced mental health disorder the results of this study will have important implications in widening the range of treatment options available in the NHS.

10.2.2.4   The effectiveness of chamomile and ginkgo biloba in the treatment of GAD

Is chamomile/ginkgo biloba more effective than placebo in increasing response and remission rates and decreasing anxiety ratings for people with GAD?
This question should be addressed using a placebo-controlled, double-blind randomised design to compare the effects of a standardised dose of chamomile (220–1100 mg) or ginkgo biloba (30–500 mg) in a readily available form, for example a capsule, with placebo. This should assess outcomes at the end of the trial and at 12-month post-trial follow-up. The outcomes chosen should include both observer- and

participant-rated measures of clinical symptoms and functioning specific to GAD, and of side effects. There should be a health economic evaluation included and an assessment of quality of life. The trial should be large enough to determine the presence or absence of clinically important effects using a non-inferiority design. Mediators and moderators of response should be investigated.

Why this is important

GAD is a common mental health disorder and the results of this study will be generalisable to a large number of people. There is evidence for the efficacy of chamomile and ginkgo biloba in reducing anxiety in people with GAD but the evidence base is small (one study). However, the scarce literature on the effectiveness of other herbal interventions for treating GAD points to chamomile and ginkgo biloba as two of the more effective herbal interventions. Moreover, both these herbal remedies are widely available and relatively inexpensive. Furthermore, at present there is no scientific evidence of side effects or drug–herbal interactions in relation to chamomile or ginkgo biloba. As both these herbal interventions are readily available and have no known side effects, they could be used at an early stage as a means of preventing progression to drug treatments, which are associated with a number of undesirable side effects and dependency.

10.2.2.5   The clinical and cost effectiveness of a primary care-based collaborative care approach to improving the treatment of GAD compared with usual care

What are the benefits of a primary care-based collaborative care approach to improving the treatment of GAD compared with usual care?

This question should be addressed using a cluster randomised controlled design in which the clusters are GP practices and people with GAD are recruited following screening of consecutive attenders at participating GP practices. GPs in intervention practices should receive training in recognising GAD and providing both drug treatment and GP-delivered low-intensity psychological interventions (psychoeducation and non-facilitated self-help). Psychological wellbeing practitioners[24] (PWPs) in intervention practices should provide these low-intensity psychological interventions and support GP-prescribed drug treatment by providing information about side effects, monitoring medication use and liaising about any changes to medication. They should also support the referral for CBT of participants whose symptoms have not improved following low-intensity interventions. Structured, practice-based protocols should define care pathways, the interventions to be provided by practitioners at each point in the care pathway and the mechanisms they should use to liaise about individual patients. In control practices, participants should receive care as usual from the GP, including referral for primary and secondary care psychological interventions or mental health services.

---

[24]Also known as graduate mental health workers.

Outcomes should be evaluated at 6 months with follow-up assessments continuing for up to 2 years to establish whether short-term benefits are maintained in the longer term. The outcomes chosen should include both observer- and participant-rated measures of clinical symptoms and functioning specific to GAD, and of quality of life. An economic analysis should also be carried out alongside the trial. The trial needs to be large enough to determine the presence or absence of clinically important effects and of any differences in costs between collaborative care and usual care.

Why this is important
Most people with GAD in the UK do not receive evidence-based management and poor recognition of GAD by GPs contributes to a lack of appropriate interventions being offered. There is some evidence that complex interventions involving the training of primary care practitioners, together with a collaborative care approach involving GPs, other primary care practitioners and mental health professionals, can improve the uptake of evidence-based interventions and clinical and functional outcomes for people with GAD. However, these approaches have not been evaluated in primary care in the UK. Given the differences between the organisation of primary care in different countries, such as the US, it is important to demonstrate whether these approaches can also be effective in the UK.

10.2.2.6   The clinical and cost effectiveness of two CBT-based low-intensity interventions (CCBT and guided bibliotherapy) compared with a waiting-list control for the treatment of panic disorder

In well-defined panic disorder, what is the clinical and cost effectiveness of two CBT-based low-intensity interventions (CCBT and guided bibliotherapy) compared with a waiting-list control?
This question should be answered using a three-armed randomised controlled design using both short- and medium-term outcomes (including cost-effectiveness outcomes). Particular attention should be paid to the reproducibility of the treatment model with regard to content, duration and the training and supervision of those delivering interventions to ensure that the results are both robust and generalisable. The outcomes chosen should include both observer- and participant-rated measures of clinical symptoms and functioning specific to panic disorder, and an assessment of the acceptability and accessibility of the treatment options.

Why this is important
Psychological treatments are a recommended therapeutic option for people with panic disorder. CCBT is a promising low-intensity intervention for panic disorder that does not yet have a substantial evidence base. It is therefore important to establish whether CCBT is an effective and cost-effective treatment that should be provided for panic disorder, and how it compares with other low-intensity interventions such as guided bibliotherapy. The results of this trial will have important implications for the provision, accessibility and acceptability of psychological treatment in the NHS.

11   APPENDICES

Appendices

APPENDIX 1:

SCOPE FOR THE DEVELOPMENT OF THE

CLINICAL GUIDELINE

FINAL VERSION

Date: July 2009

1   GUIDELINE TITLE

Anxiety: management of generalised anxiety disorder in adults in primary, secondary and community care (update)[25]

1.1   SHORT TITLE

Anxiety (update)

2   BACKGROUND

This is a partial update of NICE clinical guideline 22 (2004): 'Anxiety: management of generalised anxiety disorder and panic disorder (with or without agoraphobia) in adults in primary, secondary and community care'. In the original remit, the Department of Health asked NICE to 'prepare a clinical guideline for the NHS in England and Wales for "talking" therapies, drug treatments and prescribing for anxiety and related common mental disorders, including generalised anxiety disorder (GAD) and panic disorder (with or without agoraphobia).'[26] Following informal consultation with a number of experts and the assessment of recent high-quality systematic reviews, substantial new trial evidence has been identified for adults with GAD therefore the management of this disorder has been prioritised for updating. Other areas of the original scope will be considered for review at a later date.

---

[25]The title changed to 'Generalised anxiety disorder and panic disorder (with or without agoraphobia) in adults: management in primary, secondary and community care (partial update)' during the course of development.

[26] See Appendix 2 for the scope to the original anxiety guideline.

In December 2008 the technology appraisal team put forward an update proposal for the anxiety section of 'Technology Appraisal TA97: computerised cognitive behaviour therapy for depression and anxiety' to be updated within the clinical guideline on anxiety. After consideration of all of the consultation comments the Institute's Guidance Executive agreed to proceed with the proposal.

3   CLINICAL NEED FOR THE GUIDELINE

3.1   EPIDEMIOLOGY

(a) Generalised anxiety disorder is a relatively common condition. It often has a chronic course, which can lead to significant distress and impairment to the person with the disorder.

(b) A recent US household survey reported prevalence for a range of psychiatric disorders. For anxiety disorders as a whole there was a 12-month prevalence of 18.1% and a lifetime prevalence of 28.8%. For generalised anxiety disorder specifically, there was a 12-month prevalence of 3.1% and a lifetime prevalence of 5.7%. However, a European study (Belgium, France, Germany, Italy, Netherlands, and Spain) reported a much lower 12-month prevalence of 4.6% for anxiety disorders as a whole.

3.2   CURRENT PRACTICE

(a) GAD, along with other anxiety disorders, is most commonly treated in primary care, although some with more severe impairment are also treated in secondary care. Treatments include psychological interventions (computerised and face-to-face), pharmacological interventions (for example, SSRIs, venlafaxine, duloxetine, TCAs, benzodiazepines) and self-help.

(b) The Department of Health initiative 'Improving Access to Psychological Therapies' started in 2008, and is currently increasing the capacity to deliver psychological interventions for common mental health disorders in primary care, including interventions for anxiety disorders.

4   THE GUIDELINE

The guideline development process is described in detail on the NICE website (see section 6, 'Further information').

This scope defines what the guideline will (and will not) examine, and what the guideline developers will consider. The scope is based on the referral from the Department of Health.

The areas that will be addressed by the guideline are described in the following sections.

4.1 POPULATION

4.1.1 Groups that will be covered

(a) Adults (aged 18 years or older) with a working diagnosis of generalised anxiety disorder

4.1.2 Groups that will not be covered

(a) Children and young people (younger than 18)
(b) This guideline update may be relevant to adults with the following conditions, but will not specifically address: panic disorder, major depression, bipolar depression, seasonal affective disorder, combat disorder, phobic disorders, obsessive-compulsive disorder, post-traumatic stress disorder and anxiety disorders associated with dementia.

4.2 HEALTHCARE SETTING

(a) The guideline will cover care received from primary, secondary and community healthcare professionals who have direct contact with and make decisions concerning care of people with generalised anxiety disorder.

4.3 CLINICAL MANAGEMENT

4.3.1 Topics that will be updated

(a) Pharmacological interventions compared with: placebo, other pharmacological interventions (those available in the UK according to the British National Formulary), psychological interventions, or combined psychological and pharmacological treatment for generalised anxiety disorder. This will include selective serotonin reuptake inhibitors (SSRIs) (and related drugs), duloxetine, venlafaxine, tricyclic antidepressants, benzodiazepines, azapirones, antihistamines, beta-blockers, antipsychotics.
(b) When referring to pharmacological interventions, the guideline will normally recommend use within licensed indications. Exceptionally, and only where the evidence supports it, the guideline may recommend use outside a treatment's licensed indications. The guideline will expect that prescribers will use the Summary of Product Characteristics to inform their prescribing decisions for individual patients.
(c) Psychological interventions compared with: control groups (such as treatment as usual), other psychological interventions, pharmacological interventions, or combined psychological and pharmacological treatment for generalised anxiety

disorder. This will include cognitive behavioural therapy (CBT), guided self-help, counselling, and short-term psychodynamic psychotherapy.

(d) The Guideline Development Group will also review the structure of recommendations of the original guideline and care pathways on which it is based to ensure fit with other NICE guidelines for common mental health disorders.

(e) The delivery of computerised cognitive behavioural therapy (CCBT) for panic disorder and generalised anxiety disorder.

4.3.1   Topics that will not be updated

(a) Diagnosis
(b) Pharmacological and psychological interventions for panic disorder (with or without agoraphobia)

4.4   MAIN OUTCOMES

(a) Anxiety symptoms (mean anxiety rating scale score, response [>50% reduction in mean anxiety rating scale score], remission) at end of treatment and follow-up
(b) Quality of life (for example, SF-36, EQ-5D) at end of treatment and follow-up
(c) Tolerability (leaving the study early for any reason, leaving the study early due to lack of efficacy, leaving the study early due to adverse events)
(d) Adverse effects (for example gastrointestinal symptoms, weight gain/loss, mortality)

4.5   ECONOMIC ASPECTS

Developers will take into account both clinical and cost effectiveness when making recommendations involving a choice between alternative interventions. A review of the economic evidence will be conducted and further economic analyses will be carried out as appropriate. Outcomes of economic analyses will be expressed in terms of the quality-adjusted life year (QALY), depending on availability of appropriate clinical and utility data. Costs will be considered from an NHS and personal social services (PSS) perspective. Further detail on the methods can be found in 'The guidelines manual' (see 'Further information').

4.6   STATUS

4.6.1   Scope

This is the final scope. There will be no consultation as no new key areas have been identified that need updating in this guideline (see appendix 2 for the scope of the original guideline).

4.6.2   Timing

The development of the guideline recommendations will begin in June 2009.

5   RELATED NICE GUIDANCE

5.1   PUBLISHED GUIDANCE

5.1.1   NICE guidance to be updated

This guideline will update and partially replace the following NICE guidance.
- Anxiety. NICE Clinical Guideline 22 (2004). Available from www.nice.org.uk/CG22
- Computerised cognitive behaviour therapy for depression and anxiety. NICE Technology Appraisal guidance 97 (2006). Available from www.nice.org.uk/TA97. (Anxiety indications only)

5.1.2   Other related NICE guidance

- Obsessive-compulsive disorder. NICE Clinical Guideline 31 (2005). Available from www.nice.org.uk/CG31
- Post-traumatic stress disorder. NICE Clinical Guideline 26 (2005). Available from www.nice.org.uk/CG26
- Guidance on the use of zaleplon, zolpidem and zopiclone for the short-term management of insomnia. NICE Technology Appraisal guidance 77 (2007). Available from www.nice.org.uk/TA77.

5.2   GUIDANCE UNDER DEVELOPMENT

NICE is currently developing the following related guidance (details available from the NICE website).
- Depression in adults (update). NICE clinical guideline. Publication expected September 2009.[27]
- Depression in chronic health problems. NICE clinical guideline. Publication expected September 2009.[28]
- Depression and anxiety – identification and referral in primary care. NICE clinical guideline. Publication expected April 2011.[29]

---

[27]Since the scope was developed, this guideline has been published as *Depression: the Treatment and Management of Depression in Adults*. Clinical Guideline 90 (2009) (NICE, 2009b).

[28]Since the scope was developed, this guideline has been published as *Depression in Adults with a Chronic Physical Health Problem: Treatment and Management*. Clinical Guideline 91. (2009) (NICE, 2009c).

[29]Since the scope was developed, this guideline's title has changed to 'Common mental health disorders: identification and pathways to care' (publication expected Summer 2011) (NICE, 2011b).

6   FURTHER INFORMATION

Information on the guideline development process is provided in:
- 'How NICE clinical guidelines are developed: an overview for stakeholders' the public and the NHS'
- 'The guidelines manual'.

These are available from the NICE website (www.nice.org.uk/guidelinesmanual). Information on the progress of the guideline will also be available from the NICE website (www.nice.org.uk).

APPENDIX 2:

SCOPE FOR THE ORIGINAL ANXIETY GUIDELINE

1   GUIDELINE TITLE

Anxiety: management of generalised anxiety disorder and panic disorder (with or without agoraphobia) in adults in primary, secondary and community care[30]

1.1   SHORT TITLE

Anxiety

2   BACKGROUND

(a) The National Institute for Clinical Excellence ('NICE' or 'the Institute') has commissioned the National Collaborating Centre for Primary Care to develop a clinical guideline on the management of generalised anxiety disorder and panic disorder (with or without agoraphobia) in adults in primary and secondary care and in the community for use in the NHS in England and Wales. This follows referral of the topic by the Department of Health and Welsh Assembly Government (included in the Appendix [to the scope]). Post-traumatic stress disorder and obsessive-compulsive disorder are excluded from this scope, but will be the subject of another guideline being prepared by the National Collaborating Centre for Mental Health. The guideline will provide recommendations for good practice that are based on the best available evidence of clinical and cost effectiveness.

(b) The Institute's clinical guidelines will support the implementation of National Service Frameworks (NSFs) in those aspects of care where a Framework has been published. The statements in each NSF reflect the evidence that was used at the time the Framework was prepared. The clinical guidelines and technology appraisals published by the Institute after an NSF has been issued will have the effect of updating the Framework.

3   CLINICAL NEED FOR THE GUIDELINE

(a) Generalised anxiety disorder is a relatively common condition. It can often have a chronic course, leading to significant distress and impairment to the individual.

---

[30]The title changed to 'Anxiety: management of anxiety (panic disorder, with or without agoraphobia, and generalised anxiety disorder) in adults in primary, secondary and community care' during the course of development.

(b) Precise and accurate statistics for the incidence and prevalence of generalised anxiety disorder and related disorders are difficult to find. In a recent survey, the overall findings suggested that one in six adults living in private households in Great Britain had a neurotic disorder (Office of National Statistics, 2000). Of these, about 4% were assessed as having generalised anxiety disorder. Less than 2% had other related disorders such as phobias, obsessive-compulsive disorder and panic disorder. Whilst these findings indicate that women have a higher overall rate of anxiety disorders than men, for generalised anxiety disorder and panic disorder the rates are similar.

4   THE GUIDELINE

(a) The guideline development process is described in detail in three booklets that are available from the NICE website (see 'Further information'). The Guideline Development Process - Information for Stakeholders describes how organisations can become involved in the development of a guideline.
(b) This document is the scope. It defines exactly what this guideline will (and will not) examine, and what the guideline developers will consider. The scope is based on the referral from the Department of Health and Welsh Assembly Government (see Appendix [to the scope]).
(c) The areas that will be addressed by the guideline are described in the following sections.

4.1   POPULATION

4.1.1   Group that will be covered

The recommendations made in the guideline will cover management of the following group.
(a) Adults (aged 16 years or older) with a working diagnosis of generalised anxiety disorder or panic disorder (with or without agoraphobia).

4.1.2   Groups that will not be covered

The following groups will not be covered by this guideline.
(a) Children (younger than 16 years).
(b) People with major depression.
(c) People with bipolar depression.
(d) People with seasonal affective disorder (SAD).
(e) People with combat disorder.
(f) People with anxiety disorders associated with dementia.
(g) People with phobic disorders other than panic disorder with agoraphobia.
(h) People with organic brain disorders.

4.2   HEALTHCARE SETTING

(a) The guideline will cover the care received from primary, secondary and community healthcare professionals who have direct contact with and make decisions concerning the care of people with generalised anxiety disorder and panic disorder (with or without agoraphobia).

(b) The guideline will also be relevant to the work, but will not cover the practice, of those in:

● the occupational health services
● social services
● the voluntary sector.

4.3   CLINICAL MANAGEMENT - AREAS THAT WILL BE COVERED

The guideline will cover the following areas of clinical practice.

(a) Diagnosis of generalised anxiety disorder and panic disorder (with or without agoraphobia).

(b) Pharmacological interventions for generalised anxiety disorder and panic disorder (with or without agoraphobia) (those available in the UK according to the British National Formulary). When referring to pharmacological treatments, the guideline will normally recommend use within licensed indications. Exceptionally, and only where the evidence supports it, the guideline may recommend use outside a treatment's licensed indications. The guideline will expect that prescribers will use the Summary of Product Characteristics to inform their prescribing decisions for individual patients.

(c) Non-pharmacological interventions for generalised anxiety disorder and panic disorder (with or without agoraphobia) - the 'talking' therapies, including counselling.

(d) Self-care.

**4.4   CLINICAL MANAGEMENT - AREAS THAT WILL
          NOT BE COVERED**

The following areas will not be covered in this guideline.

(a) Complementary medicine approaches and interventions for generalised anxiety disorder, except where high-quality syntheses of evidence exist (for example, Cochrane reviews).

(b) Management of the related anxiety disorder post-traumatic stress disorder (anxiety disorder manifested by the development of characteristic symptoms following a psychologically traumatic event that is outside the normal range of human experience).

(c) Management of the related anxiety disorder obsessive-compulsive disorder (an anxiety disorder characterised by recurrent, persistent obsessions or compulsions).

4.5   AUDIT SUPPORT WITHIN GUIDELINE

The guideline will be accompanied by level 2 audit review criteria and advice.

4.6   STATUS

4.6.1   Scope

This is the final version of the scope.

4.6.2   Guideline

The development of the guideline recommendations will begin in April 2002.

5   FURTHER INFORMATION

Information on the guideline development process is provided in:
- The Guideline Development Process – Information for the Public and the NHS
- The Guideline Development Process – Information for Stakeholders
- The Guideline Development Process – Information for National Collaborating Centres and Guideline Development Groups.

These booklets are available as PDF files from the NICE website (www.nice.org.uk). Information on the progress of the guideline will also be available from the website.

6   REFERENCE

Office of National Statistics (2000) First Release: Psychiatric Morbidity Among Adults, 2000. www.statistics.gov.uk/pdfdir/psymorb0701.pdf

APPENDIX: REFERRAL FROM THE DEPARTMENT OF HEALTH AND WELSH ASSEMBLY GOVERNMENT

The Department of Health and Welsh Assembly Government asked the Institute:

'To prepare a clinical guideline and audit tool for the NHS in England and Wales for 'talking' therapies, drug treatments and prescribing for anxiety and related common mental disorders, including generalised anxiety disorder (GAD), panic disorder (with or without agoraphobia), post-traumatic stress disorder, and obsessive-compulsive disorder (OCD). The audit tool should include a dataset, database and audit methodology.'

APPENDIX 3:

DECLARATIONS OF INTERESTS BY GUIDELINE DEVELOPMENT GROUP MEMBERS

With a range of practical experience relevant to GAD in the GDG, members were appointed because of their understanding and expertise in healthcare for people with generalised anxiety disorder and support for their families and carers, including: scientific issues; health research; the delivery and receipt of healthcare, along with the work of the healthcare industry; and the role of professional organisations and organisations for people with generalised anxiety disorder, and their families and carers.

To minimise and manage any potential conflicts of interest, and to avoid any public concern that commercial or other financial interests have affected the work of the GDG and influenced guidance, members of the GDG must declare as a matter of public record any interests held by themselves or their families which fall under specified categories (see below). These categories include any relationships they have with the healthcare industries, professional organisations and organisations for people with GAD, and their families and carers.

Individuals invited to join the GDG were asked to declare their interests before being appointed. To allow the management of any potential conflicts of interest that might arise during the development of the guideline, GDG members were also asked to declare their interests at each GDG meeting throughout the guideline development process. The interests of all the members of the GDG are listed below, including interests declared prior to appointment and during the guideline development process.

Categories of interest

- Paid employment
- Personal pecuniary interest: financial payments or other benefits from either the manufacturer or the owner of the product or service under consideration in this guideline, or the industry or sector from which the product or service comes. This includes holding a directorship, or other paid position; carrying out consultancy or fee paid work; having shareholdings or other beneficial interests; receiving expenses and hospitality over and above what would be reasonably expected to attend meetings and conferences.
- Personal family interest: financial payments or other benefits from the healthcare industry that were received by a member of your family.
- Non-personal pecuniary interest: financial payments or other benefits received by the GDG member's organisation or department, but where the GDG member has not personally received payment, including fellowships and other support provided by the healthcare industry. This includes a grant or fellowship or other

payment to sponsor a post, or contribute to the running costs of the department; commissioning of research or other work; contracts with, or grants from, NICE.
- Personal non-pecuniary interest: these include, but are not limited to, clear opinions or public statements you have made about GAD, holding office in a professional organisation or advocacy group with a direct interest in GAD, other reputational risks relevant to GAD.

Declarations of interest	
Professor John Cape - Chair, GDG	
Employment	Head of Psychological Therapies, Camden and Islington NHS Foundation Trust, London and Visiting Professor, University College London
Personal pecuniary interest	None
Personal family interest	None
Non-personal pecuniary interest	None
Personal non-pecuniary interest	Member of Mental Health Research Network Clinical Research Group on the topic of 'Improving the Detection and Management of Anxiety Disorders in Primary Care'. (October 2010) Member of the British Association of Behaviour and Cognitive Psychotherapy. (October 2010)
Dr Marta Buszewicz	
Employment	Senior Lecturer, Research Department of Primary Care and Population Health, University College London
Personal pecuniary interest	None
Personal family interest	None
Non-personal pecuniary interest	None
Personal non-pecuniary interest	I have been asked to lead a Mental Health Research Network Clinical Research Group on the topic of 'Improving the Detection and Management of Anxiety Disorders in Primary

	Care', and as such will be involved in writing research proposals on this topic. (April 2009)
	Involved in research proposal to the HTA using pregabalin as augmentation to SSRIs in people with refractory anxiety. (April 2010)
Professor Carolyn Chew-Graham	
Employment	Professor of Primary Care, University of Manchester
Personal pecuniary interest	Clinical Advisor Joint Commissioning Team, Manchester (June 2009)
	Invited speaker at 'Neurology and mental health conference'; honorarium will be paid. Organised by Haymarket conferences.
Personal family interest	None
Non-personal pecuniary interest	*Research grants:* A Research and Development programme to increase equity of access to high quality mental health services in primary care. 2007-2012 NIHR 1071 Programme Grant £1,924,231. (AMP [Improving Access to Mental Health in Primary Care] programme). (June 2009)
	Multi-centre RCT of Collaborative Care for Depression. (CADET study) £2,295,000 Medical Research Council 2008-2010. (June 2009)
	Short-term research fellowship with Manchester PCT to support grant writing. £25,000. February - October 2008. (June 2009)
	Co-investigator on the successful Greater Manchester CLAHRC award. £10million from NIHR plus £10million in matched funds from Greater Manchester Association of PCTs. October 2008 - October 2013. (June 2009)
	Developing effective strategies to reduce unscheduled care in chronic disease. £190,000. January 2009 – 2014. (June 2009)
	Development and evaluation of a communication training package for primary care practitioners to

	reduce inappropriate antibiotic prescribing for respiratory tract infections. British Society for Antimicrobial Therapy. EDG/07/02. £30,000 January 2009 - December 2010. (June 2009)
Personal non-pecuniary interest	Royal College of General Practitioners Clinical Champion, Mental Health and Co-lead of Primary Care Mental Health Forum. (June 2009) Member of steering group, Anxiety UK (third sector organisation in Manchester). (June 2009)
Professor Phillip Cowen	
Employment	Professor of Psychopharmacology, University of Oxford
Personal pecuniary interest	I have acted as a paid member of advisory boards and given paid lectures for companies that market medicines relevant to the treatment of anxiety. Eli Lilly (£6,000 over the last 2 years for lectures on depression - not product related). Lundbeck (£1,000 for a lecture on depression this year - not product related). Servier (£3,000 over the last 2 years for advisory boards concerning agomelatine). Wyeth (£1,000 over the last 2 years for an advisory board on desvenlafaxine). (April 2009) I have provided expert advice to solicitors representing GlaxoSmithKline in claims over paroxetine (Seroxat) (payment of £3,000 over the last year). (April 2009) AstraZeneca (£250 for chairing a meeting on bipolar disorder. (November 2009)
Personal family interest	None
Non-personal pecuniary interest	None
Personal non-pecuniary interest	I am one of the authors of the *Oxford Textbook of Psychiatry*, which provides advice about the treatment of psychiatric disorders. (April 2009)

	I have been a member of guideline development groups for the British Association for Psychopharmacology, which issues advice on the appropriate use of psychotropic medicines in the treatment of a range of psychiatric disorders. (April 2009).
Ms Joanna Hackman	
Employment	Service user member
Personal pecuniary interest	None
Personal family interest	None
Non-personal pecuniary interest	None
Personal non-pecuniary interest	None
Ms Jill Keegan	
Employment	Carer member, Islington Carers Centre
Personal pecuniary interest	None
Personal family interest	None
Non-personal pecuniary interest	None
Personal non-pecuniary interest	None
Dr Judy Leibowitz	
Employment	Consultant Clinical Psychologist and Clinical Lead, Camden Psychological Therapies Service, London
Personal pecuniary interest	None
Personal family interest	None
Non-personal pecuniary interest	None
Personal non-pecuniary interest	None
Professor Karina Lovell	
Employment	Professor in Mental Health, University of Manchester
Personal pecuniary interest	None

Personal family interest	I receive £6000 a year in my role as a Non-Executive Director, and earn approximately £1000 a year running various workshops for NHS Trusts and British Association of Behavioural and Cognitive Psychotherapy. I also received £1000 to be editor of the CSIP [Care Services Improvement Partnership] publication of CCBT in 2008. (April 2009)
Non-personal pecuniary interest	I am an applicant on a number of NIHR research grants and therefore the University of Manchester employ research assistants and therapists, but all funding goes to the university. The PCT pay the University of Manchester for 2 hours a week of my time to conduct clinical supervision but this is not paid to me. (April 2009)
Personal non-pecuniary interest	I am a patron of Anxiety UK and part of the steering group for 'Self Help Services' both 3rd sector organisations. (April 2009)
Ms Catherine O'Neill	
Employment	Service User Member and Services Manager at Anxiety UK
Personal pecuniary interest	None
Personal family interest	None
Non-personal pecuniary interest	I was approached in my role at Anxiety UK to be part of the working group for the mental health providers' forum, which has an agenda of campaigning for different types of evidence to be accepted by NICE. (July 2009) Delivered training to East Sussex Partnership Trust on phone CBT. (Feb 2010) Delivered training to Pfizer pharmaceuticals, the cost of which was £800 for half a day. I declare a non-personal pecuniary interest as the money went to Anxiety UK and was part of my role as Services Manager there. (Sept 2010)
Personal non-pecuniary interest	I do work for an anxiety disorders charity that provides support, advice and therapy services to individuals suffering with a range of anxiety disorders. We do not provide CCBT or medication advice however. (April 2009)

Professor Paul Salkovskis	
Employment	Professor of Clinical Psychology and Applied Science, University of Bath
	Clinical Director, Centre for Anxiety Disorders and Trauma, Maudsley Hospital
	Editor, *Behavioural and Cognitive Psychotherapy*
Personal pecuniary interest	None
Personal family interest	None
Non-personal pecuniary interest	Will receive £2154.10 from Meiji Seika Kaisha, Ltd (http://www.meiji.co.jp/en/) for flights from London to Tokyo and Hong Kong to London for teaching in Japan and Hong Kong in October 2009. There are no conditions attached to this funding, which was actually awarded to the conference which I had agreed to speak at and I was unaware of any industry links at that time. I am not aware of the products that this company manufactures. (July 2009)
	My group has been contracted to provide 'top-up' training in CBT for the London IAPT services. This funding is awarded to King's College and does not benefit me personally. (July 2009)
Personal non-pecuniary interest	I have conducted and been involved in a number of research projects on the treatment of panic disorder with and without agoraphobia. I have been a co-author on a paper in which it was concluded that cognitive behavioural treatment performed better than antidepressant medication. (May 2009)
	I edit the journal of the British Association for Behavioural and Cognitive Psychotherapy; this organisation is a special interest group for people working in cognitive behavioural treatment. (May 2009)
	I am the patron of four charities (No Panic, Anxiety UK, OCD Action and OCD-UK) involved in advocacy for anxiety disorders. (May 2009)
Professor Jan Scott	
Employment	Professor of Psychological Medicine, University of Newcastle

Personal pecuniary interest	I have attended some advisory boards for the following: AstraZeneca, Janssen-Cilag, 4SK, BSM Otsuka, Eli Lilly, Sanofi Aventus. My work is on psychosocial aspects of bipolar disorder and medication adherence. (April 2009)
Personal family interest	None
Non-personal pecuniary interest	In the past I have had an unrestricted educational award: 1) to teach multidisciplinary teams about engagement and enhancing adherence, 2) for a catchment art study on met and unmet requirements in bipolar, and 3) have had an independent investigator award from Janssen-Cilag on medication adherence. (April 2009)
Personal non-pecuniary interest	When asked my views (following lectures) on CCBT I have pointed out that is not always feasible, for example, no computer at home, and some patients, for example, older females, may not take up such treatments. (April 09)
NCCMH	
Professor Tim Kendall	
Employment	Joint Director, NCCMH; Medical Director and Consultant Psychiatrist, Sheffield Health and Social Care NHS Foundation Trust
Personal pecuniary interest	None
Personal family interest	None
Non-personal pecuniary interest	The NCCMH received a grant of £78,000 in January 2010 to carry out a systematic review of the mental health impact of induced abortion in unwanted pregnancies. This project will be completed by March 2011.
	Grant holder for £1.44 million per year (approximately) from NICE for guidelines work. Work with NICE International.
	Undertake some research into mental health and the mental health workforce for Department of Health, Royal College of Psychiatrists and the Academy of Medical Royal Colleges.
Personal non-pecuniary interest	None

Ms Henna Bhatti	
Employment	Research Assistant, NCCMH
Personal pecuniary interest	None
Personal family interest	None
Non-personal pecuniary interest	None
Personal non-pecuniary interest	None

Ms Melissa Chan	
Employment	Systematic Reviewer, NCCMH
Personal pecuniary interest	None
Personal family interest	None
Non-personal pecuniary interest	None
Personal non-pecuniary interest	None

Ms Esther Flanagan	
Employment	Project Manager, NCCMH (until 2010)
Personal pecuniary interest	None
Personal family interest	None
Non-personal pecuniary interest	None
Personal non-pecuniary interestNone	None

Ms Laura Gibbon	
Employment	Project Manager, NCCMH (from 2010)
Personal pecuniary interest	None
Personal family interest	None
Non-personal pecuniary interest	None
Personal non-pecuniary interest	None

Appendix 3

Ms Marie Halton	
Employment	Research Assistant, NCCMH
Personal pecuniary interest	None
Personal family interest	None
Non-personal pecuniary interest	None
Personal non-pecuniary interest	None
Dr Ifigeneia Mavranezouli	
Employment	Senior Health Economist, NCCMH
Personal pecuniary interest	None
Personal family interest	None
Non-personal pecuniary interest	None
Personal non-pecuniary interest	None
Dr Nick Meader	
Employment	Systematic Reviewer, NCCMH
Personal pecuniary interest	None
Personal family interest	None
Non-personal pecuniary interest	None
Personal non-pecuniary interest	None
Ms Sarah Stockton	
Employment	Senior Information Scientist, NCCMH
Personal pecuniary interest	None
Personal family interest	None
Non-personal pecuniary interest	None
Personal non-pecuniary interest	None

Dr Clare Taylor	
Employment	Senior Editor, NCCMH
Personal pecuniary interest	None
Personal family interest	None
Non-personal pecuniary interest	None
Personal non-pecuniary interest	None

APPENDIX 4:
STAKEHOLDERS AND EXPERTS WHO
SUBMITTED COMMENTS IN RESPONSE
TO THE CONSULTATION DRAFT OF
THE GUIDELINE

STAKEHOLDERS

Anxiety UK
Association for Family Therapy and Systemic Practice
Association of Psychoanalytic Psychotherapy in the NHS and Tavistock and Portman NHS Foundation Trust
British Association for Counselling and Psychotherapy
CCBT Ltd
College of Mental Health Pharmacy
Department of Health
Lundbeck
National Institute for Health Research Evaluation, Trials and Studies Coordinating Centre, Health Technology Assessment
National Treatment Agency for Substance Misuse
NHS Direct
Nottinghamshire Healthcare NHS Trust
Pfizer Ltd
Royal College of General Practitioners, Wales
Royal College of Nursing
Royal Pharmaceutical Society of Great Britain
Sheffield Health and Social Care Trust
Welsh Assembly Government

EXPERTS

Professor Ian Anderson
Dr David Baldwin
Professor Malcolm Lader
Professor Adrian Wells

APPENDIX 5:
RESEARCHERS CONTACTED TO REQUEST INFORMATION ABOUT UNPUBLISHED OR SOON-TO-BE PUBLISHED STUDIES

Professor Per Carlbring
Dr Michelle Craske
Professor Paul Crits-Christoph
Professor Michel J. Dugas
Dr Alessandra Gorini
Professor Jurgen Hoyer
Professor Justin Kenardy
Dr Litza Kiropoulos
Professor Britt Klein
Dr Julie Williams

APPENDIX 6:
REVIEW QUESTIONS

1. For people who have GAD and their carers, what are their experiences of having problems with GAD, of access to services and of treatment? (see Chapter 4)
2. In the treatment of GAD, do any of the following improve outcomes compared with other interventions (including treatment as usual): non-facilitated bibliotherapy, non-facilitated audiotherapy, non-facilitated computer therapy, guided bibliotherapy, guided computer therapy, psychoeducational groups and helplines? (see Chapter 6)
3. In the treatment of GAD, what are the risks and benefits associated with high-intensity psychological interventions compared with other interventions (including treatment as usual)? For example: CBT, applied relaxation, psychodynamic therapy and non-directive therapies. (see Chapter 7)
4. In the treatment of GAD, which drugs improve outcomes compared with other drugs and with placebo? (see Chapter 8)
5. In the treatment of panic disorder does CCBT improve outcomes? (see Chapter 9)

APPENDIX 7:
REVIEW PROTOCOLS

The completed forms can be found on the CD accompanying this guideline.

APPENDIX 8:

SEARCH STRATEGIES FOR THE IDENTIFICATION

OF CLINICAL STUDIES

1   SEARCH STRATEGIES

The search strategies should be referred to in conjunction with information set out in Chapter 3 (Section 3.5). Each search was constructed using the groups of terms as set out in Text Box 3. The full set of search terms is documented in sections 1.1 to 1.3. The selections of terms were kept broad to maximise retrieval of evidence in a wide range of areas of interest to the GDG. Some of the interventions searched are not documented in the main body of the guideline due to a lack of evidence.

Text Box 3: Summary of systematic search strategies: Search strategy construction

---

GAD:
Psychological interventions (high- or low-intensity)
i)   [(GAD terms) AND (general psychological terms) AND (SR filter OR RCT
     Filter)] OR
ii) [(GAD terms) AND (high-intensity terms) AND (SR filter OR RCT filter)] OR
iii) [(GAD terms) AND (low-intensity terms) AND (SR filter OR RCT filter)]

Pharmacological interventions
i)   (GAD terms) AND (pharmacological terms) AND (SR filter OR RCT Filter)
Alternative interventions
i)   (GAD terms) AND (alternative intervention terms) AND (SR filter OR RCT
     filter)

Experience of care
i)   [(GAD terms) AND (qualitative filter) AND (SR filter)] OR
ii) [(GAD terms) AND (experience of care terms) AND (qualitative filter)] OR
iii) [(GAD terms – modified to be more precise) AND (experience of care terms)]

Panic disorder:
CCBT for panic disorder
i)   (Panic terms) AND (CCBT terms) AND (SR filter OR RCT filter)

1.1 POPULATION SEARCH TERMS

GAD – population search terms

MEDLINE – Ovid SP interface

1. (anxiety or anxiety disorders).sh.
2. (anxiet$ or anxious$ or ((chronic$ or excessiv$ or intens$ or (long$ adj2 last$) or neuros$ or neurotic$ or ongoing or persist$ or serious$ or sever$ or uncontrol$ or un control$ or unrelent$ or un relent$) adj2 worry)).ti,ab.
3. or/1-2

Panic – population search terms

MEDLINE – Ovid SP interface

1. (panic or panic disorder).sh.
2. panic$.ti,ab.
3. or/1-2

1.2 QUESTION-SPECIFIC SEARCH STRATEGIES

Psychological interventions – high- and low-intensity

MEDLINE – Ovid SP interface

General psychological terms
1. psychotherapy/ or adaption, psychological/
2. (psychotherap$ or psycho therap$ or psychotherapeutic or ((humanistic or non pharmacological or psychologic$) adj3 (approach$ or assist$ or coach$ or educat$ or instruct$ or interven$ or manag$ or module$ or program$ or rehab$ or strateg$ or support$ or technique$ or therap$ or train$ or treat$ or workshop$ or work shop$)) or ((integrated or multimodal or multi modal) adj2 therap$)).ti,ab.
3. or/1-2
4. psychotherapy, brief.sh.
5. ((brief or short term or time limited) adj2 (intervention$ or program$ or psycho-analy$ or psychotherap$ or solution$ or therap$ or treat$)).ti,ab.
6. or/4-5
7. or/1-6

High-intensity psychological interventions

1. exp counseling/
2. (counsel$ or (((((client$ or person) adj2 (centred or centered or focus?ed)) or non directive$ or nondirective$ or rogerian) adj5 (approach$ or assist$ or coach$ or communicat$ or counsel$ or educat$ or help$ or instruct$ or interven$ or learn$ or manag$ or module$ or network$ or program$ or psychoanaly$ or psychotherap$ or rehab$ or skill$ or strateg$ or support$ or teach$ or technique$ or therap$ or train$ or treat$ or workshop$ or work shop$)) or pastoral care or ((individual or personal or talk$) adj (psycho$ or therap$))).ti,ab.
3. or/1-2
4. interpersonal relations/ and (th.fs. or (psychotherap$ or therap$ or treatment).hw.)
5. (((interpersonal$ or inter personal$ or interrelation$ or relation$) adj5 (analy$ or approach$ or assist$ or coach$ or communicat$ or counsel$ or educat$ or help$ or instruct$ or interven$ or learn$ or manag$ or module$ or network$ or program$ or psychoanaly$ or psychotherap$ or rehab$ or skill$ or strateg$ or support$ or teach$ or technique$ or therap$ or train$ or treat$ or workshop$ or work shop$)) or ((interpersonal$ or inter personal$ or interrelation$ or relation$) adj5 (deficit$ or difficult$ or instab$ or issue$ or problem$ or unstab$) adj5 (analy$ or approach$ or assist$ or coach$ or communicat$ or counsel$ or educat$ or help$ or instruct$ or interven$ or learn$ or manag$ or module$ or network$ or program$ or psychoanaly$ or psychotherap$ or rehab$ or skill$ or strateg$ or support$ or teach$ or technique$ or therap$ or train$ or treat$ or workshop$ or work shop$)) or ipsst or ipsrt or (ipt not ipth) or (intermittent preventive adj (therap$ or treatment$)) or ((interpersonal$ or inter personal$) adj2 social rhythm$)).ti,ab.
6. or/4-5
7. (patient acceptance of health care/ or patient compliance.sh.) and (th.fs. or (psychotherap$ or therap$ or treatment).hw.)
8. ((acceptance adj (based or centered or centred)) or (acceptance adj2 (commitment or mindfulness)) or (act adj (psychotherap$ or therap$)) or (contextual adj2 (analy$ or approach$ or assist$ or coach$ or engag$ or help$ or instruct$ or interven$ or learn$ or manag$ or module$ or network$ or program$ or psychoanaly$ or psychotherap$ or rehab$ or skill$ or strateg$ or support$ or teach$ or technique$ or therap$ or train$ or treat$ or workshop$ or work shop$)) or comprehensive distancing).ti,ab.
9. or/7-8
10. exp behavior therapy/ or psychotherapy, rational emotive.sh.
11. (((cognit$ or behavio?r$ or metacognit$) adj5 (analy$ or interven$ or modif$ or program$ or psychoanaly$ or psychotherap$ or restructur$ or retrain$ or technique$ or therap$ or train$ or treat$)) or (behav$ and cognit$ and (analy$ or interven$ or modif$ or program$ or psychoanaly$ or psychotherap$ or restructur$ or retrain$ or technique$ or therap$ or train$ or treat$)) or behavio?r$ activat$cbt).ti,ab.

12. (self care.sh. and (cognit$ or behavio?r$ or metacognit$ or recover$).tw,hw.) or (selfinstruct$ or selfmanag$ or selfattribut$ or (self$ adj (instruct$ or manag$ or attribution$)) or (rational$ adj3 emotiv$) or (rational adj (living or psychotherap$ or therap$)) or (ret adj (psychotherap$ or therap$)) or rebt or (active directive adj (psychotherap$ or therap$))).ti,ab.
13. or/10-12
14. biofeedback (psychology)/
15. (biofeed$ or bio feed$ or neurofeed$ or neuro feed$ or psychophysiolog$ or psycho physiolog$ or ((alpha or brainwave$ or electromyography or emg or physiological) adj2 feed$)).ti,ab.
16. or/14-15
17. (vret$1 or (expos$ adj3 fear) or ((exposure or fear) adj3 (interven$ or psycho-analy$ or psychotherap$ or therap$ or treat$)) or (fear$ adj5 (decreas$ or dimin-ish$ or extinct$ or lessen$ or prevent$ or reduc$) adj5 (analy$ or approach$ or assist$ or coach$ or educat$ or help$ or interven$ or instruct$ or learn$ or manag$ or modif$ or module$ or network$ or program$ or psychoanaly$ or psychotherap$ or rehab$ or skill$ or strateg$ or support$ or teach$ or technique$ or therap$ or train$ or treat$ or workshop$ or work shop$))).ti,ab.
18. 17
19. exp leisure activities/ or relaxation therapy/ or (breathing exercises or meditation or relaxation or yoga).sh.
20. (relaxation or ((autogen$ or relax$) adj5 (applied or approach$ or assist$ or coach$ or educat$ or excercis$ or help$ or imagery or instruct$ or interven$ or learn$ or manag$ or modif$ or module$ or network$ or program$ or psycho-analy$ or psychotherap$ or rehab$ or skill$ or strateg$ or support$ or teach$ or technique$ or therap$ or train$ or treat$ or workshop$ or work shop$)) or ((control$ or deep) adj breathing) or ((breath$ or respirat$) adj5 (exercis$ or physiotherap$ or technique$ or therap$ or train$)) or chi kung or chundosunbup or kriya or kundalini or meditat$ or mindfulness or pranayama or qi gong or qigong or reiki or sudarshan or tai chi or vipassana or yoga or yogic or zen or jacobsonian or ((jacobson$ or neuromuscular or neuro muscular or progressive) adj2 relax$) or chest physiotherap$ or inter receptor exposure or respiratory musc$ train$ or holiday$ or leisure or life skill$ or meditat$ or mind body or pastime$ or restful$ or tranquil$1 or vacation$).ti,ab.
21. or/19-20
22. exp psychoanalytic therapy/ or psychoanalysis.sh.
23. (free association or psychoanal$ or psycho anal$ or psychodynamic$ or psycho dynamic$ or transference or ((analytic or dynamic$) adj3 (approach$ or assist$ or coach$ or educat$ or help$ or instruct$ or interven$ or learn$ or manag$ or modif$ or module$ or network$ or program$ or psychoanaly$ or psychotherap$ or rehab$ or short term or skill$ or strateg$ or support$ or teach$ or technique$ or therap$ or time limited or train$ or treat$ or workshop$ or work shop$)) or ((dream or psychologic or self transactional) adj anal$) or b app$1).ti,ab.
24. or/22-23

25. socioenvironmental therapy.sh.
26. ((psychosocial or social) adj3 (care or caring or approach$ or club$ or class$ or coach$ or educat$ or group$ or help$ or instruct$ or interven$ or learn$ or manag$ or modif$ or module$ or program$ or psychotherap$ or rehab$ or skill$ or support$ or teach$ or technique$ or therap$ or train$ or treat$ or workshop$ or work shop$)) .ti,ab.
27. or/25-26
28. exp group processes/ or exp psychotherapy, group/ or self help groups/ or (community networks or peer group or social support).sh.
29. (conjoint therap$ or family responsive or family relation$ or ((couples or family or group$1 or marital or marriage$ or support$) adj (based or cent$ or focus?ed)) or ((couples or famil$ or marital or marriage$) adj3 (advocacy or approach$ or assist$ or coach$ or educat$ or help$ or instruct$ or learn$ or module$ or network$ or participat$ or program$ or psychoanaly$ or psychotherap$ or skill$ or strateg$ or support$ or teach$ or train$ or workshop$ or work shop$)) or (group$1 adj3 (advocacy or approach$ or assist$ or coach$ or educat$ or help$ or instruct$ or learn$ or module$ or network$ or participat$ or program$ or psychoanaly$ or psychotherap$ or skill$ or strateg$ or support$ or teach$ or train$ or workshop$ or work shop$)) or (support$ adj3 (approach$ or educat$ or instruct$ or interven$ or learn$ or module$ or network$ or program$ or psychoanaly$ or psychotherap$ or strateg$ or technique$ or therap$ or train$ or treat$ or workshop$ or work shop$)) or (groupwork or (group adj2 work)) or ((emotion$ or network$ or organi?ation$ or peer$) adj2 support$) or ((couples or famil$ or group or marital or marriage$) adj therap$) or ((group$ or network$ or peer$1) adj2 (discuss$ or exchang$ or interact$ or meeting$))).ti,ab.
30. or/28-29
31. ((anxiet$ or fear or stress$ or worry$) adj3 (control$ or manag$)).ti,ab.
32. 31
33. ((multisystemic or systemic) adj2 (interven$ or therap$ or treat$)).ti,ab.
34. 33
35. dialectic$.ti,ab.
36. 35
37. (signpost$ or sign post$).ti,ab.
38. 37
39. (problem based learning or problem solving).sh.
40. (((identif$ or deal$ or resolv$ or solution$ or solv$) adj3 (difficult$ or problem$)) or ((educat$ or learn$ or module$ or teach$) adj5 skill$ adj5 (difficult$ or problem$)) or (skill$ adj3 problem$) or (problem adj (focus$ or orientat$))).ti,ab.
41. or/39-40
42. solution focused therapy.sh.
43. (solution$ adj2 (build$ or focus$)).ti,ab.
44. or/42-43
45. exp milieu therapy/ or exp psychodrama/ or exp sensory art therapies/ or acoustic stimulation/ or creativeness/ or poetry as topic/ or recreational therapy/

46. (chromotherap$ or chromo therap$ or craft$ or creativ$ or dance or dancing or drama or expressive or improvi?ation or milieu or music$ or paint$ or (performance adj2 art$) or play or poetry or psychodrama$ or recreation$ or role-play or story or stories or theatre or theatrical or ((acoustic$ or art$ or auditor$ or colo?r$) adj5 (activit$ or educat$ or help$ or instruct$ or interven$ or learn$ or module$ or network$ or opportunit$ or program$ or psychoanaly$ or psychotherap$ or rehab$ or skill$ or support$ or teach$ or technique$ or therap$ or train$ or treat$ or work or workshop$ or work shop$))).ti,ab.
47. or/45-46
48. or/1-47

Evidence of high-intensity physical activity was retrieved as part of the search for low-intensity psychological interventions (see below).

Low-intensity psychological interventions
1. bibliotherapy.sh.
2. (bibliotherap$ or biblio therap$ or ((audio$ or book$1 or booklet$ or brochure$ or cd$1 or cd rom$ cdrom$ or computer$ or cyber$ or dvd$1 or electronic$ or floppy or handheld or hand held or interactive or internet$ or leaflet$ or manual$1 or material$ or mobile or multimedia or multi media or online or palm-top or palm top or pamphlet$ or pc$1 or phone$ or poster$ or read$1 or reading or sms$1 or telephone$ or text or texts or texting or video$ or virtual or web$ or workbook$ or written or www) adj5 (approach$ or assist$ or coach$ or club$ or class$ or educat$ or empower$ or help$ or instruct$ or interven$ or learn$ or module$ or program$ or psychoanaly$ or psychotherap$ or rehab$ or skill$ or strateg$ or support$ or teach$ or technique$ or therap$ or train$ or treat$ or workshop$ or work shop$)) or ((listen$ or read$1 or reading or watch$) adj4 (audio$ or book$1 or booklet$ or brochure$ or cd$1 or cd rom$ or computer$ or dvd$1 or floppy or internet$ or leaflet$ or manual$1 or material$ or multimedia or multi media or pamphlet$ or poster$ or read$1 or reading or video$ or virtual or workbook$ or written or www))).ti,ab.
3. ((self adj (administer$ or care or change or directed or help$ or instruct$ or manag$ or monitor$ or regulat$ or reinforc$ or re inforc$)) or selfhelp$ or smart recover$ or (minimal adj (contact or guidance)) or helpseek$ or (help$ adj2 seek$) or (mutual adj (help or aid or support$))).ti,ab.
4. or/1-3
5. exp health education/ or exp health promotion/ or patient education as topic.sh.
6. (((adult$ or client$ or consumer$ or inpatient$ or outpatient$ or participant$ or patient$ or service user$) adj4 (educat$ or empower$ or knowledge or informa-tion$ or instruct$ or promot$ or teach$ or train$)) or ((anxiet$ or anxious$ or worry or worrying) adj4 (educat$ or empower$ or knowledge or information$ or instruct$ or promot$ or teach$ or train$)) or (education$ adj3 (interven$ or program$ or strateg$ or therap$ or treat$)) or booklet$ or brochure$ or leaflet$ or pamphlet$ or poster$ or workbook$ or psychoeducat$ or psycho educat$ or ((oral or printed or written) adj3 inform$) or ((adult$ or client$1 or consumer$ or

365

inpatient$ or outpatient$ or participant$ or patient$ or service user$) adj5 (book$1 or manual$1 or material$ or multimedia or multi media or video$)) or ((book$1 or manual$1 or material$ or multimedia or multi media or video$) adj5 (intervention$ or program$ or therap$ or treat$))).ti,ab.

7. or/5-6
8. hotlines.sh. or (call in or callline$ or call line$ or help line$ or helpline$ or hotline$ or hot line$ or phone in or phonein or (caller$1 adj3 (interven$ or program$ or therap$ or treat$))).ti,ab.
9. 8
10. exp exercise/ or exp physical therapy modalities/ or exp sports/
11. (active living or a?robic$ or bicycling or cycling or exercis$ or (physical$ adj3 (activit$ or agil$ or educat$ or fitness$)) or kinesiotherap$ or kinesitherap$ or movement therap$ or running or sport$ or swimming or walking or yoga).ti,ab.
12. or/10-11
13. (caccbt or ccbt or c cbt).tw,id.
14. ((beating adj2 blues) or fearfighter or ffeducation or ff education or internet psykiatri or internet psychiatri or moodgym or netcope or netff or net ff or (living life adj2 full) or oc fighter or ocfighter or odin or overcoming depression or panic online or (restoring adj2 balance) or standaloneff or standalone ff or therapeutic learning program$).ti,ab.
15. (bt step$ or calipso$ or climate or climategp$ or climateschool$ or climatemh$ or climateclinic$ or climatetv$ or crufad$ or gpcare$ or ultrasis or ((anxiety or anxious$) adj3 package$)).ti,ab.
16. telemedicine/ or therapy, computer assisted/
17. ((anxiety or stress$ or worry) adj3 (package$ or program$)).ti,ab.
18. (etherap$ or e therap$ or telehealth or tele health).ti,ab.
19. (e communication$ or ecommunication$ or e consult$ or econsult$ or e visit$ or evisit$ or e therap$ or etherap$ or telehealth or tele health).ti,ab.
20. ((audio$ or cd$1 or cd rom or cdrom or computer$ or cyber$ or digital assistant$ or dvd or electronic$ or floppy or handheld or hand held or information or interactiv$ or internet or mobile or multimedia or multi media or online or palmtop or palm top or pc$1 or pda or pdas or personal digital or phone$ or sms$1 or telephone$ or text or texts or texting or video$ or virtual or web$ or www) adj5 (advocacy or approach$ or coach$ or discussion or educat$ or exchang$ or guide$1 or help$ or instruct$ or interact$ or interven$ or learn$ or manag$ or meeting$ or module$ or network$ or online or participat$ or program$ or psychoanaly$ or psychotherap$ or rehab$ or retrain$ or re train$ or self guide$ or self help or self-guide$ or selfhelp or skill$ or strateg$ or support$ or teach$ or technique$ or telephone$ or therap$ or train$ or treat$ or work shop$ or workshop$)).ti,ab.
21. ((audio$ or cd$1 or cd rom or cdrom or computer$ or cyber$ or digital assistant$ or dvd or electronic$ or floppy or handheld or hand held or information or interactiv$ or internet or mobile or multimedia or multi media or online or palmtop or palm top or pc$1 or pda or pdas or personal digital or phone$ or sms$1 or telephone$ or text or texts or texting or video$ or virtual or web$ or www) adj2 (assist$ or based)).ti,ab.

22. ((audio$ or cd$1 or cd rom or cdrom or computer$ or cyber$ or digital assis-
    tant$ or dvd or electronic$ or floppy or handheld or hand held or interactiv$
    or internet or mobile or multimedia or multi media or online or palmtop or
    palm top or pc$1 or pda or pdas or personal digital or phone$ or sms$1 or tele-
    phone$ or text or texts or texting or video$ or virtual or web$ or www) adj5
    (aid or aided or appointment$ or booking$ or communicat$ or consult$ or
    deliver$ or feedback or forum or guided or input$ or interactiv$ or letter$ or
    messag$ or referral$ or remind$ or send$ or transfer$ or transmi$ or visit$)).
    ti,ab.
23. ((audio$ or cd$1 or cd rom or cdrom or computer$ or cyber$ or digital assistant$
    or dvd or electronic$ or floppy or handheld or hand held or information or inter-
    activ$ or internet or mobile or multimedia or multi media or online or palmtop or
    palm top or pc$1 or pda or pdas or personal digital or phone$ or sms$1 or tele-
    phone$ or text or texts or texting or video$ or virtual or web$ or www) adj5
    group$).ti,ab.
24. ((client$ or consumer$ or inpatient$ or outpatient$ or patient$) adj5 (audio$ or
    cd$1 or cd rom or cdrom or computer$ or cyber$ or digital assistant$ or dvd or
    electronic$ or floppy or handheld or hand held or interactiv$ or internet or mobile
    or multimedia or multi media or online or palmtop or palm top or pc$1 or pda or
    pdas or personal digital or phone$ or sms$1 or telephone$ or text or texts or
    texting or video$ or virtual or web$ or www)).ti,ab.
25. ((client$ or consumer$ or inpatient$ or outpatient$ or patient$ or health or infor-
    mation or web or internet) adj3 portal$).ti,ab.
26. or/13-25
27. exp psychotherapy/
28. attitude to computers/ or audiovisual aids/ or computer literacy/ or computer user
    training/ or computer-assisted instruction/ or computing methodologies/ or deci-
    sion support systems, clinical/ or hotlines/ or information systems/ or medical
    informatics computing/ or medical informatics/ or multimedia/ or telemedicine/
    or exp audiovisual aids/ or exp computer systems/ or exp decision making,
    computer assisted/ or exp optical storage devices/ or exp software/ or exp
    telecommunications/ or comput$.hw.
29. (audio$ or cd$1 or cd rom or cdrom or computer$ or cyber$ or dvd or electronic$
    or floppy or handheld or hand held or interactiv$ or internet or mobile or multi-
    media or multi media or online or palmtop or palm top or pc$1 or pda or personal
    digital assistant$ or phone$ or portal$1 or sms$1 or telephone$ or text or texts or
    texting or video$ or virtual or web$ or www).ti,ab.
30. interactive voice response.ti,ab.
31. 27 and or/28-30
32. or/26,31
33. or/1-12,32

The high-intensity search for CBT was sifted for any additional evidence relating to
CCBT.

Pharmacotherapy – includes marketing names and different forms of drugs on the advice of the GDG

MEDLINE – Ovid SP interface

Antidepressants - all

1. exp antidepressive agents, tricyclic/
2. (tricyclic$ or tca$1).ti,ab.
3. amitriptyline.sh. or (amitriptyl$1 or amitryptil$1 or amitryptin$1 or amit-ryptylin$1 or amytriptil$1 or amytryptyl$1 or amytryptil$1 or adepress or adepril$1 or ambivalon$1 or amineurin$1 or amitid$1 or amitril$1 or amitrip or amitrol$1 or anapsique or antitriptylin$1 or apoamitriptylin$1 or damilen$1 or damylen$1 or domical$1 or elatrol$1 or elavil$1 or endep or enovil$1 or etafon$1 or etafron$1 or euplit$1 or lantron$1 or laroxal$1 or laroxyl$1 or lenti-zol$1 or novoprotect or proheptadien$1 or redomex or sarboten retard 75 or saroten$1 or sarotex or stelminal$1 or sylvemid$1 or syneudon$1 or teperin$1 or terepin$1 or triptafen$1 or triptanol$1 or triptizol$1 or triptyl or triptylin$1 or tryptanol$1 or tryptin$1 or tryptizol$1).ti,ab.
4. chlomipramine.sh. or (chlomipramin$1 or chlorimipramin$1 or chloroimipramin$1 or clomipramin$1 or anafranil$1 or anafranilin$1 or anafranyl or domipramin$1 or hydiphen$1 or monochlor imipramin$1 or monochlorimipramin$1 or mono-chloroimipramin$1).ti,ab.
5. dothiepin.sh. or (dothiepin$1 or dosulepin$1 or altapin$1 or depresym$1 or dopress or dothep or idom or prothiaden$1 or prothiadien$1 or prothiadin$1 or protiaden$1 or thaden).ti,ab.
6. doxepin.sh. or (doxepin$1 or adapin$1 or apodoxepin$1 or aponal$1 or co dox or curatin$1 or deptran$1 or desidox or doneurin$1 or doxepia or espadox or mareen or prudoxin$1 or quitaxon$1 or silenor or sinepin or sinequan$1 or sinquan$1 or xepin$1 or zonalon$1).ti,ab.
7. imipramine.sh. or (imipramin$1 or antideprin$1 or berkomin$1 or chrytemin$1 or deprimin or deprinol$1 or depsonil or dynaprin or eupramin or ia pram or imavate or imidobenzyl$1 or imidol$1 or imipramid$1 or imipramil or imiprex or imiprin$1 or imizin$1 or irmin or janimin$1 or melipramin$1 or norchlorim-ipramin$1 or norpramin$1 or novopramin$1 or presamin$1 or pryleugan$1 or psychoforin$1 or psychoforin$1 or servipramin$1 or sk pramin$1 or surplix or tofranil$1 or trofanil$1).ti,ab.
8. lofepramine.sh. or (lofepramin$1 or lopramin$1 or amplit$1 or deftan$1 or fepra-pax or gamanil$1 or gamonil$1 or lomont or lopramin$1 or tymelyt).ti,ab.
9. mianserin.sh. or (mianserin$1 or athymil$1 or bolvidon$1 or investig or lantanon$1 or lanthanon$1 or lerivon$1 or miaxan$1 or norval or serelan$1 or tetramid$1 or tolvin$1 or tolvon$1).ti,ab.
10. nortriptyline.sh. or (nortriptylin$1 or acetexa or allegron$1 or altilev or atilev or avantyl or aventyl or desitriptylin$1 or desmethylamitriptylin$1 or martimil$1 or noramitriptylin$1 or norfenazin$1 or noritren$1 or norpress or nortrilen$1 or

nortryptilin$1 or nortryptylin$1 or pamelor or paxtibi or propylamin$1 or psychostyl or sens?val).ti,ab.

11. opipramol.sh. or (opipramol$1 or dinsidon$1 or ensidon$1 or eusidon$1 or insidon$1 or nisidan$1 or oprimol or pramolan$1).ti,ab.

12. trazodone.sh. or (trazodon$1 or beneficat or deprax or desirel or desyrel$1 or molipaxin$1 or pesyrel$1 or rpragazon$1 or pragmarel$1 or pragmazon$1 or thombran$1 or thrombin$1 or thrombran$1 or tombran$1 or trasodon$1 or trazolan$1 or trazorel or trazon$1 or trialodine or trittico).ti,ab.

13. trimepramine.sh. or (trimepramin$1 or trimeprimin$1 or trimepropimin$1 or trimidura or trimineurin$1 maleate or trimipramin$1 or trimoprimin$1 or eldoral$1 or herphonal$1 or trimineurin$1 or novo tripramin$1 or novotripramin$1 or nutrimipramin$1 or rhotrimin$1 or stangyl or surmontil$1 or apo trimip or apotrimip or herphonal$1 or stangyl or surmontil$1).ti,ab.

14. or/1-13

15. exp serotonin uptake inhibitors/

16. (ssri$ or ((serotonin or 5 ht or 5 hydroxytryptamine) adj (uptake or reuptake or re uptake) adj inhibit$)).ti,ab.

17. citalopram.sh. or (celexa or cipramil$1 or cytalopram or elopram or escitalopram or lexapro or nitalapram or sepram or seropram).ti,ab.

18. (escitalopram or cipralex or lexapro or seroplex).ti,ab.

19. fluoxetine.sh. or (fluoxetin$1 or fluctin$1 or flunirin$1 or fluoxifar or prosac or prozac or prozamin or sarafem or symbyax).ti,ab.

20. fluvoxamine.sh. or (fluvoxamin$1 or depromel$1 or desiflu or dumirox or faverin$1 or fevarin$1 or floxyfral$1 or fluoxamin$1 or fluroxamin$1 or fluvoxadura or luvox).ti,ab.

21. (nefazadon$1 or dutonin or nefadar or reseril$1 or serzon$1).ti,ab.

22. paroxetine.sh. or (paroxetin$1 or aropax or deroxat or motivan$1 or paxil or pexeva or seroxat or tagonis).ti,ab.

23. sertraline.sh. or (sertralin$1 or altrulin$1 or aremis or besitran$1 or gladem or lustral$1 or naphthylamin$1 or sealdin$1 or serad or serlain$1 or tresleen or zoloft).ti,ab.

24. or/15-23

25. exp antidepressive agents/ or exp monoamine oxidase inhibitors/

26. (antidepress$ or anti depress$ or maoi$1 or ((adrenaline or amine or mao or mono amin$ or monoamin$ or tyramin$) adj2 inhibit$)).ti,ab.

27. (agomelatin$1 or melitor or thymanax or valdoxan$1).ti,ab.

28. chlorprothixene.sh. or (chlorprothixen$1 or aminasin$1 or aminasin$1 or aminazin$1 or aminazin$1 or ampliactil$1 or amplictil$1 or ancholactil$1 or chlopromazin$1 or chlor pz or chlorbromasin$1 or chlordelazin$1 or chlorderazin$1 or chloropromazin$1 or chlorpromanyl or chlorpromazin$1 or chlorprotixen$1 or clordelazin$1 or clorpromazin$1 or cloxan or contomin$1 or elmarin$1 or fenactil$1 or hibanil$1 or hibernal$1 or hibernol$1 or klorpromex or largactil$1 or largactyl or megaphen$1 or neurazin$1 or novomazin$1 or phenathyl$1 or plegomazin$1 or plegomazin$1 or proma or promacid$1 or

promactil$1 or promapar or promazil$1 or propaphen$1 or propaphenin$1 or prozil$1 or psychozin$1 or sanopron$1 or solidon$1 or sonazin$1 or taractan$1 or taroctil$1 or thor prom or thorazen$1 or thorazin$1 or torazina or truxal or vegetamin a or vegetamin b or wintamin$1 or wintermin$1 or zuledin$1).ti,ab.

29. desvenlafaxine.sh. or (desvenlafaxin$1 or o desmethylvenlafaxin$1 or o norven-lafaxin$1 or pristiq).ti,ab.
30. (duloxetin$1 or ariclaim or cymbalta or xeristar or yentreve).ti,ab.
31. fezolamin$1 .ti,ab.
32. (isocarboxacid$1 or bmih or enerzer or isocarboazid$1 or isocarboxazid$1 or marplan$1 or marplon).ti,ab.
33. (mirtazapin$1 or avanza or 6 azamianserin$1 or lerivon$1 or remergil$1 or remergon$1 or remeron$1 or tolvon$1 or zispin).ti,ab.
34. moclobemide.sh. or (moclobemid$1 or arima or aurorex or aurorix or deprenorm or feraken$1 or manerix or moclamin$1 or moclix or moclobamid$1 or moclo-beta or moclodura or moclonorm or novomoclobemid$1 or numoclobemid$1 or rimoc).ti,ab.
35. phenelzine.sh. or (phenelzin$1 or 2 phenethylhydrazin$1 or 2 phenylethylhy-drazin$1 or benzylmethylhydrazin$1 or beta phenethylhydrazin$1 or beta phenylethylhydrazine or fenelzin or fenizin$1 or mao rem or nardelzin$1 or nardil$1 or phenalzin$1 or phenethylhydrazin$1 or phenylethylhydrazin$1 or stinerval$1).sh,tw.
36. (reboxetin$1 or davedax or edronax or norebox or prolift or solvex or vestra).sh,tw.
37. tranylcypromine.sh. or (tranylcypromin$1 or phenylcyclopropylamin$1 or dl trans 2 phenylcyclopropylamin$1 or jatrosom$1 or parmodalin$1 or parnate or parniten$1 or parnitin$1 or trancilpromin$1 or trancylpromin$1 or trancylpromi-nesulfate or tranilacipromin$1 or trans 2 phenylcyclopropylamin$1 or transamin$1 or tylciprin$1).ti,ab.
38. (venlafaxin$1 or efexor or effexor or foraven or tifaxin or trevilor or venaxx or venlalic or winfex).sh,tw.
39. or/25-38
40. exp serotonin uptake inhibitors/
41. (snri$ or ssnri$ or ((noradrenalin or norepinephrine) adj serotonin adj (uptake or reuptake or re uptake) adj inhibitor$) or (serotonin adj (noradrenalin or norepi-nephrine) adj (uptake or reuptake or re uptake) adj inhibitor$)).ti,ab.
42. or/40-41
43. tetracyclic$.ti,ab.
44. 1-43

Antipsychotics, antihistamines, azapirones
1. exp antipsychotic agents/
2. (antipsychotic$ or anti psychotic$ or (major adj2 (butyrophenon$ or phenoth-iazin$ or tranquil$)) or neuroleptic$).ti,ab.
3. (amisulprid$1 or aminosultoprid$1 or amisulpirid$1 or sertol$1 or socian or solian).ti,ab.

4. (aripiprazol$1 or abilify or abilitat).ti,ab.
5. (benperidol$1 or anquil or benperidon$1 or benzoperidol$1 or benzperidol$1 or frenactil$1 or frenactyl or glianimon$1 or phenactil$1).ti,ab.
6. chlorpromazine.sh. or (chlorpromazin$1 or aminazin$1 or chlorazin$1 or chlordelazin$1 or contomin$1 or fenactil$1 or largactil$1 or propaphenin$1 or thorazin$1).ti,ab.
7. chlorprothixene.sh. or (chlorprothixen$1 or aminasin$1 or aminasin$1 or aminazin$1 or aminazin$1 or ampliactil$1 or amplictil$1 or ancholactil$1 or chlopromazin$1 or chlor pz or chlorbromasin$1 or chlordelazin$1 or chlorderazin$1 or chloropromazin$1 or chlorpromanyl or chlorpromazin$1 or chlorprotixen$1 or clordelazin$1 or clorpromazin$1 or cloxan or contomin$1 or elmarin$1 or fenactil$1 or hibanil$1 or hibernal$1 or hibernol$1 or klorpromex or largactil$1 or largactyl or megaphen$1 or neurazin$1 or novomazin$1 or phenathyl or plegomazin$1 or plegomazin$1 or proma or promacid$1 or promactil$1 or promapar or promazil$1 or propaphen$1 or propaphenin$1 or prozil or psychozin$1 or sanopron$1 or solidon$1 or sonazin$1 or taractan$1 or taroctil$1 or thor prom or thorazen$1 or thorazin$1 or torazin$1 or truxal or vegetamin a or vegetamin b or wintamin$1 or wintermin$1 or zuledin$1).ti,ab.
8. clozapine.sh. or (clozapin$1 or alemoxan$1 or azaleptin$1 or clopine or clozaril$1 or denzapin$1 or dorval or dozapin$1 or fazaclo or froidir or klozapol or lapenax or leponex or wander compound or zaponex).ti,ab.
9. flupenthixol.sh. or (flupentixol$1 or flupenthixol$1 or depixol$1 or emergil$1 or fluanxol$1 or flupentixol$1 or emergil$1 or fluanxol$1 or piperazineethanol$1 or viscoleo).ti,ab.
10. fluspirilene.sh. or (fluspirilen$1 or fluspi or imap or kivat or redeptin$1 or spirodiflamin$1).ti,ab.
11. haloperidol.sh. or (haloperidol$1 or aloperidin$1 or bioperidolo or brotopon or celenase or cerenace or dozic or duraperidol or einalon s or eukystol or fortunan$1 or haldol or halidol or haloneural$1 or haloperitol$1 or halosten or keselan or linton or peluces or serenace or serenase or siegoperidol$1 or sigaperidol$1).ti,ab.
12. methotrimeprazine.sh. or (levomepromazin$1 or 2 methoxytrimeprazin$1 or hirnamin$1 or levo promazin$1 or levomeprazin$1 or levopromazin$1 or levoprom$1 or mepromazin$1 or methotrimeprazin$1 or methotrimperazin$1 or milezin$1 or minozinan$1 or neozin$1 or neuractil$1 or neurocil$1 or nirvan or nosinan$1 or nozinan$1 or sinogan or tisercin$1 or tizercin$1 or tizertsin$1 or veractil$1).ti,ab.
13. (olanzapin$1 or lanzac or midax or olansek or olzapin or rexapin or zalasta or zolafren or zydis or zypadhera or zyprex$1).ti,ab.
14. (paliperidon$1 or 9 hydroxyrisperidon$1 or invega).ti,ab.
15. paroxetine.sh. or (paroxetin$1 or aropax or deroxat or motivan or paxil$1 or pexeva or seroxat or tagonis).ti,ab.
16. (pericyazin$1 or aolept or neulactil$1 or neuleptil$1 or periciazin$1 or properciazin$1 or propericiazin$1).ti,ab.
17. perphenazine.sh. or (perphenazin$1 or chlorperphenazin$1 or chlorpiprazin$1 or chlorpiprozin$1 or decentan$1 or etaperazin$1 or ethaperazin$1 or etrafon or

fentazin$1 or perfenazin$1 or perfenazin$1 or perferazin$1 or perphenan$1 or perphenezin$1 or thilatazin$1 or tranquisan$1 or triavail or trifalon$1 or trilafan$1 or trilafon$1 or trilifan$1 or triliphan$1).ti,ab.

18. pimozide.sh. or (pimozid$1 or antalon$1 or opiran$1 or orap or pimocid$1 or pimorid$1 or pinozid$1).ti,ab.

19. prochlorperazine.sh. or (prochlorperazin$1 or buccastem or capazin$1 or chlormeprazin$1 or chlorpeazin$1 or chlorperazin$1 or compazin$1 or dicopal$1 or emelent or kronocin$1 or meterazin$1 or metherazin$1 or nipodal$1 or phenotil or prochlor perazin$1 or prochlorpemazin$1 or prochlorperacin$1 or prochlorperzin$1 or prochlorpromazin$1 or proclorperazin$1 or stemetil or stemzine or tementil$1 or temetil$1).ti,ab.

20. promazine.sh. or (promazin$1 or alofen$1 or alophen$1 or ampazin$1 or amprazim$1 or centractyl or delazin$1 or esparin$1 or lete or liranol$1 or neo hibernex or neuroplegil$1 or piarin$1 or prazin$1 or pro tan or promantin$1 or promanyl$1 or promilen$1 or promwill or protactil$1 or protactyl$1 or romthiazin$1 or romtiazin$1 or sediston$1 or sinophenin$1 or sparin$1 or tomil or varophen$1 or verophen$1).ti,ab.

21. (quetiapin$1 or ketipinor or quepin or seroquel or tienapin$1).ti,ab.

22. risperidone.sh. or (risperidon$1 or belivon$1 or ridal or riscalin or risolept or rispen or risperdal$1 or sizodon).ti,ab.

23. (sertindol$1 or indole or serdolect or serlect).ti,ab.

24. sulpiride.sh. or (sulpirid$1 or abilit or aiglonyl$1 or arminol$1 or bosnyl or deponerton$1 or desisulpid$1 or digton or dobren or dogmatil$1 or dogmatyl or dolmatil$1 or eglonyl or ekilid or equilid or guastil$1 or isnamid$1 or leboprid$1 or levopraid or levosulpirid$1 or meresa or miradol$1 or modal or neogama or pontirid$1 or psicocen$1 or sulfirid$1 or sulp$1 or sulperid$1 or sulpitil$1 or sulpivert or sulpor or sulpyride or synedil$1 or tepavil$1 or vertigo meresa or vertigo neogama or vipral).sh,tw.

25. trifluoperazine.sh. or (trifluoperazin$1 or apotrifluoperazine$1 or calmazin$1 or dihydrochlorid$1 or eskazin$1 or eskazin$1 or eskazinyl or fluoperazin$1 or flupazin$1 or jatroneural$1 or modalina or stelazin$1 or terfluzin$1 or terfluzin$1 or trifluoperazid$1 or trifluoperazin$1 or trifluoperzin$1 or trifluoroperazin$1 or trifluorperacin$1 or trifluperazin$1 or triflurin$1 or triftazin$1 or triftazinum or triphtazin$1 or triphthasin$1 or triphthazin$1).ti,ab.

26. (zotepin$1 or lodopin$1 or losizopilon or nipolept or setous or zoleptil).ti,ab.

27. clopenthixol.sh. or (zuclopenthixol$1 or acuphase or clopenthixol$1 or clopixol or cisordinol$1 or sedanxol$1).ti,ab.

28. or/1-27

29. a?apiron$.ti,ab.

30. (gepiron$2 or ariza or variza).ti,ab.

31. (ipsapiron$2 or isapiron$2).ti,ab.

32. lesopitron$2.ti,ab.

33. (tandospiron$2 or dihydrogen citrate or metanopirone or sediel).ti,ab.

34. umespiron$2.ti,ab.

35. zalospiron$2.ti,ab.

36. or/29-35
37. exp histamine antagonists/
38. (antihistamin$ or anti histamin$ or (histamin$ adj2 (antagonist$ or block$))).ti,ab.
39. cetirizine.sh. or (cetirizin$1 or alerlisin$1 or cetalerg or ceterifug or ceti tad or cetiderm or cetidura or cetil von ct or cetilich or ceti puren or cetirigamma or cetirlan or cetzine or reactin$1 or virlix or voltric or zetir or zirtec or zirtek or zyrtec or zyrtek).ti,ab.
40. chlorphenamine.sh. or (chlorphenamin$1 or alermine$1 or aller chlor or aller-gisan$1 or alunex or antihistaminico llorens or chlo amine or chlor trimeton or chlortrimeton or chlor tripolon or chlor tripolon or chloramate unicelles or chlorophenamin$1 or chloroton$1 or chlorpheniramin$1 or chlorpro or chlor-prophenpyridamin$1 or chlortab 4 or chlortrimeton$1 or chlor trimeton$1 or chlortripolon$1 or chlor tripolon$1 or cloro trimeton$1 or efidac 24 or histadur or hista 12 or histaspan$1 or kloromin$1 or noscosed or piriton or teldrin).ti,ab.
41. (clemastin$1 or meclastin$1 or mecloprodin$1 or neclastin$1 or tavegil$1 or tavegyl or tavist).ti,ab.
42. cyproheptadine.sh. or (cyproheptadin$1 or antergan$1 or astonin or cipractin$1 or ciproeptadin$1 or cryoheptidin$1 or crypoheptadin$1 or cypraheptidin$1 or cyprohaptadin$1 or cyproheptadien$1 or dihexazin$1 or nuran or periactin$1 or periactinol$1 or peritol$1 or viternum).ti,ab.
43. (desloratadin$1 or aerius or allex or azomyr or clarinex or claramax or clarinex or decarbethoxyloratadin$1 or delot or descarboethoxyloratadin$1 or neoclari-tyn$1 or opulis).ti,ab.
44. (fexofenadin$1 or allegra or fastofen or methylpropionic acid or telfast or tilfur or vifas).ti,ab.
45. hydroxyzine.sh. or (hydroxyzin$1 or arcanax or alamon or atarax or attarax or aterax or durrax or equipose or hydroxizin$1 or idroxizin$1 or masmoran$1 or orgatrax or otarex or paxistil or quiess or tran q or tranquizine or ucerax or vistaril$1).ti,ab.
46. ketotifen.sh. or (ketotifen$1 or ketotiphen$1 or zaditen).ti,ab.
47. (levocetirizin$1 or xozal or xusal or xuzal or xyzal).ti,ab.
48. loratadine.sh. or (loratadin$1 or alavert or civeran$1 or claratyn$1 or claritin$1 or clarityn$1 or clarium or flonidan or fristamin or lisino or lisono or loratazin$1 or loratidin$1 or lomilan or lorfast or rinolan or roletra or symphoral or tidilor or versal).ti,ab.
49. (mizolastin$1 or mizolen$1 or mizollen$1 or zolim).ti,ab.
50. promethazine.sh. or (promethazin$1 or allergan or anergan or antiallersin$1 or atosil$1 or avomine or baymethazine or dimapp or diphergan$1 or diprazin$1 or diprazin$1 or diprazin$1 or diprozin$1 or fargan$1 or fellozin$1 or fenazil$1 or fenergan$1 or ganphen$1 or hiberna or isopromethazin$1 or lercigan$1 or lergi-gan$1 or phargan$1 or phenargan$1 or phenergan$1 or phensedyl$1 or pipolfen$1 or pipolphen$1 or proazamin$1 or procit or promazinamid$1 or promet or prometazin$1 or promethacin$1 or promethegan or promethazon$1 or prothiazine or protazin$1 or prothazin$1 or provigan$1 or pyrethia or receptozine

or remsed or romergan$1 or rumergan$1 or sayomol$1 or tanidil$1 or thiergan$1 or vallergin$1).ti,ab.
51. trimeprazine.sh. or (alimemazin$1 or isobutrazin$1 or methylpromazin$1 or nedeltran$1 or panectyl or repeltin$1 or spansul$1 or temaril$1 or temaryl or teralen$1 or therafene or theralen$1 or theraligene or trimeprazin$1 or valergan$1 or vallergan$1 or vanectyl$1 or variargil$1).ti,ab.
52. or/37-51
53. or/1-52

Anxiolytics
1. exp benzodiazepines/
2. (benzo$1 or benzodiazepin$).ti,ab.
3. alprazolam.sh. or (alprazolam or alprox or apo alpraz or apoalpraz or aprazolam$1 or cassadan$1 or esparon$1 or helex or kalma or novo alprazol$1 or novoalprazol$1 or nu alpraz or nualpraz or ralozam or solanax or tafil$1 or trankimazin$1 or valeans or xanax or xanor).ti,ab.
4. bromazepam.sh. or (bromazepam or anxyrex or bartul or bromalich or bromaz 1a pharma or bromazanil$1 or bromazep von ct or durazanil$1 or lectopam$1 or lexamil$1 or lexatin$1 or lexaurin$1 or lexilium or lexomil$1 or lexotan$1 or lexotanil$1 or lexotanil$1 or normoc or sintrogel$1).ti,ab.
5. chlordiazepoxide.sh. or (chlordiazepoxid$1 or methaminodiazepoxid$1 or elenium$1 or librium$1 or chlozepid$1 or ansiacal$1 or benzodiapin$1 or cebrum$1 or chlordiazepoxyd$1 or chlorodiazepoxid$1 or clopoxid$1 or contol$1 or decacil$1 or defobin$1 or disarim$1 or dizepin$1 or dopoxid$1 or droxol$1 or eden psich or elenium$1 or elenum$1 or equibral$1 or kalmocaps or labican$1 or librelease or libritabs or librium or lipoxide or mesural$1 or metaminodiazepoxid$1 or methaminodiazepoxid$1 or mildmen$1 or mitran$1 or multum$1 or murcil$1 or napoton$1 or napoton$1 or novosed$1 or psichial$1 or psicosan$1 or psicoterin$1 or radepur or reliberan$1 or reposans 10 or risolid or seren vita or servium or silibrin$1 or sk lygen or sonimen$1 or timosin$1 or viansin$1 or viopsicol$1).ti,ab.
6. (clobazam or chlorepin$1 or clobazepam or clorepin$1 or frisium or noiafren$1 or urbadan$1 or urbanil$1 or urbanyl).ti,ab.
7. clonazepam.sh. or (clonazepam or antelepsin$1 or clonopin$1 or iktorivil$1 or klonazepam or klonopin$1 or landsen$1 or rivotril$1).ti,ab.
8. clorazepate dipotassium.sh. or (clorazepat$1 or carboxylic acid or chlorazepat$1 or chloroazepat$1 or clorazepic acid or tranxen$1 or tranxilium).ti,ab.
9. (delorazepam or briantum$1 or chlordemethyldiazepam or chlordesmethyldiazepam or chloro n demethyldiazepam or chlorodemethyldiazepam or chlorodesmethyldiazepam or chloronordiazepam).ti,ab.
10. diazepam.sh. or (diazepam or alupram or ansiolin$1 or antenex or apaurin$1 or apaurin$1 or apozepam or assival$1 or audium$1 or bialzepam or bialzepan$1 or calmpos$1 or cercin$1 or cersin$1 or chlordiazepam or dialar or diastat or diazelium or diazemuls or diazidem or ducen$1 or duxen$1 or eridan or eurosan$1 or evacalm$1 or fanstan$1 or faustan$1 or gewacalm$1 or lamra or

lembrol$1 or lipodiazepam or lorinon$1 or methyldiazepinon$1 or methyl-
diazepinon$1 or morosan$1 or neocalm$1 or neurolytril$1 or noan or novazam
or paceum or plidan or psychopax or relanium or rimapam or sedapam or
seduxen$1 or serendin$1 or setonil$1 or sibazon$1 or sonacon$1 or stesolid$1 or
stesolin$1 or tanquo tablinen$1 or tensium or tranimul$1 or tranquo puren or
umbrium$1 or valaxon$1 or valclair or valiquid$1 or valium or valpam or valre-
leas$1 or vatran$1 or vival$1 or vivol4 or zetran$1).ti,ab.

11. flunitrazepam.sh. or (flunitrazepam or flurazepam or fluridrazepam or darken$1
    or fluni 1a pharma or flunibeta or flunimerck or fluninoc or flunipam or flunita
    or flunitrax or flunizep von ct or hypnodorm$1 or hypnosedon$1 or inervon$1 or
    narcozep or parnox or rohipnol$1 or rohypnol$1 or roipnol$1 or silece or
    valsera).ti,ab.

12. flurazepam.sh. or (flurazepam or benozil$1 or dalmadorm$1 or dalman$1 or
    dalmate or dormodor$1 or lunipax or staurodorm$1 or dalman$1 or dormodor$1
    or dalmadorm$1).ti,ab.

13. (flutoprazepam or restas).ti,ab.

14. loprazolam .ti,ab.

15. lorazepam.sh. or (lorazepam or almazin$1 or alzapam or apolorazepam or ativan
    or bonatranquan$1 or donix or duralozam or durazolam or idalprem or kendol$1
    or laubeel or lorabenz or loranas$1 or loranaz$1 or lorans or lorax or lorazep von
    ct or loridem$1 or lorivan$1 or mesmerin$1 or novo lorazem$1 or
    novolorazem$1 or novo lorazem$1 or nu loraz or nuloraz or orfidal or orifadal$1
    or pro dorm or quait or securit or sedicepan$1 or sinestron$1 or somagerol$1 or
    tavor or temesta or tolid or wypax).ti,ab.

16. (lormetazepam or loramet or (lorazepam adj2 methyl) or methyllorazepam or
    minians or minias or noctamid$1 or pronoctan$1).ti,ab.

17. (mexazolam or melex or sedoxil$1).ti,ab.

18. midazolam.sh. or (midazolam or dormicum or dormonid$1 or hypnoval$1 or
    hypnovel$1 or hypnoyvel$1 or versed).ti,ab.

19. nitrazepam.sh. or (nitrazepam or alodorm or atempol$1 or benzalin$1 or
    dormalon$1 or dormo puren or dumolid or eatan or eunoctin$1 or hypnotex or
    imadorm or imeson$1 or insomin$1 or mogadan$1 or mogadon$1 or nelbon$1 or
    nirven$1 or nitra zepam or nitrados or nitravet or nitrazadon$1 or nitrazep or
    nitrodiazepam or novanox or pacisyn or radedorm$1 or remnos or restorem$1 or
    sedamon$1 or serenade or somnased$1 or somnibel$1 n or somnit$1).ti,ab.

20. oxazepam.sh. or (oxazepam or abboxapam or adumbran$1 or alopam or anxi-
    olit$1 or azutranquil$1 or durazepam or expidet$1 or hilong or isodin$1 or
    linbial$1 or noctazepam or oxapuren$1 or oxepam or praxiten$1 or serax or
    serenid$1 or serepax or seresta or serpax or sigacalm$1 or sobril$1 or tazepam$1
    or uskan).ti,ab.

21. prazepam.sh. or (prazepam or centrax or demetrin$1 or lysanxia or mono
    demetrin$1 or monodemetrin$1 or reapam or sedapran$1 or verstran).ti,ab.

22. temazepam.sh. or (temazepam or apo temazepam or dasuen or euhypnos or
    hydroxydiazepam or levanxol$1 or methyloxazepam or nocturne$1 or norkotral
    tema or normison$1 or normitab or nortem or oxydiazepam or planum or

pronervon t or remestan$1 or restoril$1 or signopam or temaz$1 or temazep von ct or temazepax or temtabs or tenox or texapam).ti,ab.

23. or/1-22
24. exp antianxiety agents/
25. (((antianxiety or anti anxiety or ataractic) adj2 (agent$ or drug$ or treat$)) or anxiolytic$ or ((medium or minor) adj2 tranquil$) or (serotonergic adj (agent$ or drug$ or preparation$))).ti,ab.
26. buspiron.sh. or (buspiron$1 or anxut or axoren or bespar or busp or buspar or buspin$1 or neurosin$1).ti,ab.
27. chlormezanone.sh. or (chlormezanon$1 or alinam$1 or banabin sintyal or chlormethazanon$1 or chlormethazan$1 or dichloromethazanon$1 or fenarol$1 or lobak or mio sed or rexan$1 or rilansyl or rilaquil$1 or rilassol$1 or supotran$1 or suprotan$1 or tanafol$1 or trancopal$1).ti,ab.
28. estazolam.sh. or (estazolam or domnamid$1 or eurodin$1 or kainever or nuctalon$1 or prosom or tasedan$1).ti,ab.
29. medazepam.sh. or (medazepam or anxitol$1 or diepin$1 or mezepam or nobrium or resmit or rudotel$1 or rusedal$1 or siman).ti,ab.
30. meprobamate.sh. or (meprobamat$1 or anastress or andaxin$1 or aneural$1 or aneurol$1 or aneuxral$1 or apascil$1 or apasil$1 or appetrol$1 or arpon$1 or artolon$1 or atraxin$1 or aycramat$1 or biobamat$1 or biobamat$1 or calmax or calmiren$1 or cirpon$1 or cirponyl or cyrpon$1 or dapaz or ecuanil$1 or edenal$1 or epikur or equanil$1 or equinil$1 or gadexyl$1 or gagexyl$1 or harmonin$1 or hartrol$1 or holbamat$1 or klort or laitren$1 or lepetown$1 or mepantin$1 or mepavlon$1 or meposed$1 or meprindon$1 or meproban$1 or meprobomat$1 or meprocompren$1 or meprodil$1 or meprol$1 or meprosan$1 or meprosin$1 or meprospan$1 or meprotab$1 or meprotan$1 or meprotap$1 or meptran$1 or mesmar or miltann$1 or miltaun$1 or miltown or misedant or morbam or muprobamat$1 or nervonus or oasil or panediol$1 or panquil$1 or pathibamat$1 or perequil$1 or perquietil$1 or pertranquil$1 or placidon$1 or probamat$1 or probamyl or procalinadiol$1 or procalmadiol$1 or procalmidol$1 or quanam$1 or quanil$1 or reostral$1 or restenil$1 or restinal$1 or restinil$1 or sedanyl$1 or sedazil$1 or sedoquil$1 or seril$1 or setran$1 or shalvaton$1 or sowell or tamate or trankvilan$1 or tranlisant or tranmep or tranquila$1 or tranquilax or urbil or visano).ti,ab.
31. nordazepam.sh. or (nordazepam or 1 demethyldiazepam or 1 desmethyldiazepam or 1 nordiazepam or calmday or dealkylhalazepam or dealkylprazepam or decyclopropylmethylprazepam or demethyldiazepam or deoxydemoxepam or desalkylhalazepam or desmethyldiazepam or madar or n dealkylhalazepam or n demethyl diazepam or n demethyldiazepam or n desalkylhalazepam or n descyclopropylmethyl prazepam or n descyclopropylmethylprazepam or n desmethyl diazepam or n desmethyldiazepam or n destrifluoroethylhalazepam or n nordiazepam or nordaz or nordiazepam or norprazepam or stilny or tranxilium n or vegesan$1).ti,ab.
32. (pregabalin$1 or 3 aminomethyl 5 methylhexanoic acid or 3 isobutyl 4 aminobutyric acid or 3 isobutylgaba or 4 amino 3 isobutylbutyric acid or lyrica).ti,ab.

33. (tiagabin$1 or gabitril$1 or tiabex).ti,ab.
34. triazolam.sh. or (triazolam or apo triazo or halcyon$1 or somniton$1 or songar or triazolam or trilam).ti,ab.
35. zolazepam.sh. or (zolazepam or zolasepam or flupyrazopon$1 or flupyraza-pon$1).ti,ab.
36. or/24-35
37. or/1-36

Beta blockers
1. exp adrenergic betaantagonists/
2. ((beta adj3 (antagonist$ or block$)) or betaantagonis$ or betablock$ or (beta adj2 (adrenolytic$ or antagonist$ or antiadrenergic or sympathicolytic$ or sympa-tholytic)) or betasympatholytic$).ti,ab.
3. acebutolol.sh. or (acebutolol$1 or acetobutolol$1 or apoacebutolol$1 or espesil$1 or monitan$1 or neptal$1 or neptall$1 or novoacebutolol$1 or prent or rhotral$1 or sectral$1).ti,ab.
4. alprenolol.sh. or (alprenol$1 or alfeprol$1 or alloprenalol$1 or alpheprol$1 or alprendol$1 or alprenololum or apliobal$1 or apllobal or aprenolol$1 or aptia or aptin or aptine or aptindurile$1 or aptondurile$1 or aptin or aptol or astra or betacard or betapin$1 or gubernal$1 or patina or regletin or yobir).ti,ab.
5. atenolol.sh. or (atenol$1 or atenigron$1 or beta adalat or blokium or co tenidon$1 or diube or kalten or neotenol$1 or normiten$1 or ormidol$1 or teneretic or tenif or tenoblock or tenolol$1 or tenorectic or tenoret or tenoretic or tenormin$1 or tensinor$1).ti,ab.
6. betaxolol.sh. or (betaxolol$1 or betaxon$1 or betoptic or betoptim$1 or kerlon$1 or lokren or oxodal$1).ti,ab.
7. bisoprolol.sh. or (bisoprolol$1 or cardicor or concor or emcor).ti,ab.
8. bupranolol.sh. or (bupranolol$1 or betadrenol$1 or ophtorenin$1 or panimit).ti,ab.
9. butoxamine.sh or (butoxamin$1 or butaxamin$1 or butaxamin$1 or butox-amid$1).ti,ab.
10. carteolol.sh. or (carteol$1 or arteolol$1 or arteoptic or arteoptik or carbonolol$1 or cartrol$1 or endak or endak mite or mikelan$1 or ocupress teoptic).ti,ab.
11. (carvedilol$1 or carloc or coreg or dilatrend or dilbloc or dimiton$1 or eucardic or eucardic or kredex or querto).ti,ab.
12. celiprolol.sh. or (celiprolol$1 or abecor or cardem or celectol$1 or celipres or celipro or celol or cordiax or diethylurea or dilanorm or selecor or selectol$1).ti,ab.
13. dihydroalprenolol$1.sh,tw.
14. (esmolol$1 or brevibloc).ti,ab.
15. iodocyanopindolol.sh. or (iodocyanopindolol$1 or icyp or i cyanopindolol$1 or cyanoiodopindolol$1).ti,ab.
16. labetalol.sh. or (labetalol$1 or albetol$1 or apolabetalol$1 or dilevalol$1 or labetolol$1 or normodyn$1 or presolol$1 or trandate).ti,ab.

17. levobunolol.sh. or (levobunolol$1 or ak beta or akbeta or albetol$1 or apolevobunolol$1 or betagan$1 or bunolol$1 or ibidomid$1 or lamitol$1 or liquifilm or normodyn$1 or novo levobunolol$1 or novolevobunolol$1 or pmslevobunolol$1 or presdate or trandate or ultracortenol$1 or vistagan$1).ti,ab.

18. metipranolol.sh. or (metipranolol$1 or beta ophtiol$1 or betaman$1 or betamet or betanol$1 or betanolol$1 or disorat or glaulin$1 or methypranol$1 or minims or ophtiol$1 or optipranolol$1 or trimepranol$1).ti,ab.

19. metoprolol.sh. or (metoprolol$1 or beloc durile$1 or belocdurile$1 or belok zok or betaloc or betalocastra or betalok or corvitol or lopres?or or metropolol$1 or minax or metrol or neobloc or presolol or seloke?n$1 or spesicor or spesikor or toprolxl).ti,ab.

20. nadolol.sh. or (nadolol$1 or altinadolol or anabet or aponadol or betadol$1 or corgard or corzide or novonadolol or propanol$1 or solgol$1).ti,ab.

21. (nebivolol$1 or bystolic or lobivon$1 or narbivolol$1 or nebilet or nebilong or nebicard or nebilet or nebilox or nodon or nubeta or symbian).ti,ab.

22. oxprenolol.sh. or (oxprenol$1 or captol or corbeton or cordexol$1 or coretal$1 or koretal$1 or laracor or oxtrenolol$1 or oxyprenolol$1 or slowpren or tevacor or tras?cor or trasidex or trasitensin).ti,ab.

23. penbutolol.sh. or (penbutolol$1 or betapressin$1 or betapressin$1 or blocotin$1 or hostabloc or levatol$1 or lobeta or paginol$1 or penbutalol$1).ti,ab.

24. pindolol.sh. or (pindolol$1 or betapindol$1 or blockin 1 or blocklin 1 or calvisken$1 or cardilate or carvisken$1 or decreten$1 or durapindol$1 or glauco visken or hydroxypropylaminopropoxyindol$1 or pectobloc or pectoblock or pinbetol or pinolol lb 46 or prindolol$1 or prindolol$1 or prinodolol$1 or pynastin or viskeen or visken$1).ti,ab.

25. practolol.sh. or (practolol$1 or cardiol or cordialina or dalzic or dl practolol$1 or eraldin$1 or practalol$1 or praktol or praktolol$1 or pralon or proctalol$1 or teranol).ti,ab.

26. propranolol.sh. or (propranolol$1 or anaprilin$1 or anaprilin$1 or anaprylin$1 or arcablock or authus or avlocardyl or bedranol$1 or bepran$1 or bercolol$1 or beta neg or beta tablinen$1 or beta timelet$1 or betadipresan$1 or betadren$1 or betaneg or betaprol$1 or betares or betaryl$1 or cardinol$1 or ciplar or corbeta or deralin$1 or dexpropranolol$1 or dideral$1 or dociton$1 or durabeton$1 or efektolol$1 or elbrol$1 or frekven$1 or ikopal$1 or inderal$1 or inderex or indobloc or innopran$1 or ipran or l propranolol$1 or lederpronol$1 or levopropranolol$1 or naprilin$1 or obsidian$1 or obsin or obzidan or prandol$1 or prano puren or pranopuren$1 or prolol$1 or pronovan$1 or propabloc or propal$1 or propercuten$1 or prophylux or propra ratiopharm or propral$1 or propranur$1 or proprasylyt or proprasylyt$1 or rexigen or sagittol$1 or stapranolol$1 or sumial$1).ti,ab.

27. sotalol.sh. or (sotalol$1 or darob or beta cardon$1 or betacardon$1 or betade$1 or betapace or bonpro or corsotalol$1 or darob or dexsotalol$1 or dextrosotalol$1 or gilucor$1 or isotalol$1 or levosotalol$1 or l sotalol$1 or rentibloc or rotalol$1 or satalol$1 or satolol$1 or sotabeta or sotacol$1 or sotacor or sotahexal$1 or sotalex or sotalol or sotapor$1 or sota saar or sotastad or tachytalol$1).ti,ab.

28. timolol.sh. or (timolol$1 or betim or betimol$1 or blocadren$1 or istalol$1 or moducren$1 or optimal$1 or prestim or propanol$1 or timacar or timoptic or timoptol$1).sh,tw.
29. or/1-28

Lithium
1. lithium$.sh. or (lithium$1 or camcolit or candamid$1 or carbolith or carbolitium or cibalith s or contemnol$1 or dilithium or eskalith or hypnorex or li salt or limas or linthane or liskonium or liskonum or litarex or lithane or lithiofor or lithionit or lithiophor or lithobid or lithocarb or lithonate or lithotabs or maniprex or mesin or micalith or neurolepsin or neurolithium or plenur or priadel or quilinormretard or quilonorm or quilonum or teralithe or theralite or theralithe).ti,ab.

Alternative interventions

MEDLINE - Ovid SP interface

1. exp complementary therapies/or ((alternative or complement$ or traditional) adj2 (medicine$ or interven$ or therap$ or treat$)).ti,ab.
2. acupuncture.sh. or exp acupuncture therapy/ or electroacupuncture/ or medicine, chinese traditional/
3. (acu point$ or acupoint$ or acu pressure or acupressure or acu puntur$ or acupunctur$ or (ching adj2 lo) or cizhen or dianzhen or electroacupunc$ or (jing adj2 luo) or jingluo or zhenjiu or zhenci or electroacupunctur$ or needle therap$).ti,ab.
4. (meridian or moxa$ or moxibustion).ti,ab.
5. or/1-4
6. (reflexotherapy or therapeutic touch).sh. or exp musculoskeletal manipulations/
7. (acupressure or acu pressure or acu touch or acutouch or alexander technique or jin shin or massage or myofascial release or myotherapy or polarity therapy or reflexology or rolfing or shiatsu or therapeutic touch or trager psychophysical or ((craniosacral or neuromuscular or neuro muscular or reflex) adj2 therapy) or ((feldenkrais or hakomi or mitchell) adj method) or (pfrimmer adj25 therapy)).ti,ab.
8. or/6-7
9. (holistic health or homeopathy).sh.
10. (homeop$ or homoeop$ or homoop$ or omeop$).ti,ab.
11. or/9-10
12. exp balneology/ or (health resorts or hydrotherapy).sh.
13. (balneotherapy or balneology or crenotherapy or hydrotherapy or spa or (water adj (exercis$ or therap$)) or thalassotherapy).ti,ab.
14. or/12-13
15. (relaxation or relaxation therapy).sh.
16. (relaxation or ((autogen$ or relax$) adj5 (apply or applied or analy$ or approach$ or assist$ or coach$ or educat$ or help$ or imagery or instruct$ or interven$ or

learn$ or manag$ or modif$ or program$ or psychoanaly$ or psychotherap$ or seminar$ or strateg$ or support$ or teach$ or technique$ or therap$ or train$ or treat$ or workshop$ or work shop$)) or relaxed state or ((breath$ or movement or respirat$ or relax$) adj2 (exercis$ or interven$ or physiotherap$ or technique$ or therap$ or train$)) or ((control?ed or deep) adj breathing)).ti,ab.

17. or/15-16
18. (breathing exercises or buddhism or mind body therapies or tai ji or therapeutic touch or meditation or yoga).sh.
19. (chikung or chi kung or chundosunbup or kriya or kundalini or qigong or qi gong or meditat$ or mindfulness or mind body or pranayama or reiki or sudarshan or taichi or tai chi or tai ji or tai ji quan or taiji or taijiquan or t ai chi or vipassana or yoga or yogic or zen).ti,ab.
20. or/18-19
21. exp hypnosis/ or exp hypnosis, anesthetic/ or imagery (psychotherapy)/
22. (autohypnosis or (autogenic adj (ormesmer$ or train$)) or hypnos$ or hypnotherap$ or imagery or mesmerism or suggestion or visuali?ation).ti,ab.
23. or/21-22
24. ginkgo biloba.sh.
25. (gingko$ or ginkgo$ or ginkgold or ginko$ or kaveri$ or rokan or superg-ingko$ or superginkgo$ or superginko$ or tanakan$ or tanaken$ or tebonin$).ti,ab.
26. or/24-25
27. (valerian or valerianaceae).sh.
28. (valerian$ or valepotriat$).ti,ab.
29. or/27-28
30. galphimia.sh,ti,ab.
31. 30
32. kava.sh.
33. (kava or kawa or piper methysticum).ti,ab.
34. or/32-33
35. hypericum.sh.
36. (hyperic$ or johanniskraut or john$ wort or johnswort).ti,ab.
37. or/35-36
38. (drugs, chinese herbal or medicine, chinese traditional or medicine, east asian traditional or plant extracts or plants, medicinal).sh.
39. ((chinese adj2 medic$) or herb$ or plant$1).ti,ab.
40. or/38-39
41. or/1-40

Experience of care

An initial broad search was conducted for systematic reviews of qualitative research for anxiety. Further to analysis of the results, the GDG requested a more specific search for primary studies as follows. Given the diversity of qualitative approaches, and the difficulties of retrieving such evidence from the bibliographic databases, search requests #2–3,6 were generated without the use of a qualitative filter.

MEDLINE – Ovid SP interface

1. (anxiety or anxiety disorders).sh. and (anxiet$ or anxious$ or ((chronic$ or exces-siv$ or intens$ or (long$ adj2 last$) or neuros$ or neurotic$ or ongoing or persist$ or serious$ or sever$ or uncontrol$ or un control$ or unrelent$ or un relent$) adj2 worry)).ti,ab. and (consumer participation or consumer satisfaction or health behavior or hospital patient relations or medication adherence or nurse patient relations or patient acceptance of health care or patient advocacy or patient compliance or patient participation or patient preference or patient satisfaction or physician patient relations or professional patient relations or public opinion or treatment refusal).sh.

2. ((anxiet$ or anxious$ or (gad$1 not (glutamic acid decarboxylase or glutamic decarboxylase or gad saad)) or ((chronic$ or excessiv$ or incessant$ or intens$ or neuros$ or neurotic$ or ongoing or persist$ or serious$ or sever$ or uncontrol$ or un control$ or unrelent$ or un relent$) adj2 worr$)) and (acceptance or account$1 or adher$ or aspiration$ or attitude$ or aversion$ or awareness or barrier$ or belief$ or centredness or choice$ or cognitions or complianc$ or conception$1 or concern$1 or confus$ or content$ or diary or diaries or demand$ or disatisf$ or disclos$ or discontent$ or disgruntle$ or engaging or engage$1 or experienc$ or feeling or happy or help$ or incentive$ or involv$ or need or needs or obstacle$ or opinion$ or participa$ or perception$ or perceived or perspective$ or position$ or prefer or preferred or preference$ or persistence or refus$ or satisf$ or scepticism or selfobservat$ or self observat$ or (service$ adj2 use$) or stigma$ or story or stories or support$ or tolerance or understand$ or unhappy or utili?ation or view$ or willing$ or voice$) and (adult$1 or attendee$ or attender$ or client$ or consumer$ or individuals or inpatient$ or men or minorities or outpatient$ or participant$ or patient$ or people or population or public or respondent$ or subjects or survivor$ or women or user$ or care giver$ or care-giver$ or carer$ or (care adj (manager$ or worker$)) or family or families)).ti.

3. (((mental$ or psychological or psychiatric) adj2 (disease$ or disorder$ or distress or health or ill or problem$)) and (acceptance or account$1 or adher$ or aspiration$ or attitude$ or aversion$ or awareness or barrier$ or belief$ or centredness or choice$ or cognitions or complianc$ or conception$ or concern$1 or confus$ or content$ or diary or diaries or demand$ or disatisf$ or disclos$ or discontent$ or disgruntle$ or engaging or engage$1 or experienc$ or feeling or happy or help$ or incentive$ or involv$ or need or needs or obstacle$ or opinion$ or participa$ or perception$ or perceived or perspective$ or position$ or prefer or preferred or preference$ or persistence or refus$ or satisf$ or scepticism or selfobservat$ or self observat$ or (service$ adj2 use$) or stigma$ or story or stories or support$ or tolerance or under-stand$ or unhappy or utili?ation or view$ or willing$ or voice$) and (adult$1 or attendee$ or attender$ or client$ or consumer$ or individuals or inpatient$ or men or minorities or outpatient$ or participant$ or patient$ or people or population or public respondents or subjects or survivor$ or women or user$ or care giver$ or care-giver$ or carer$ or (care adj (manager$ or worker$)) or family or families)).ti.

4. ((anxiet$ or anxious$ or (gad$1 not (glutamic acid decarboxylase or glutamic decarboxylase or gad saad)) or ((chronic$ or excessiv$ or incessant$ or intens$ or neuros$ or neurotic$ or ongoing or persist$ or serious$ or sever$ or uncontrol$

or un control$ or unrelent$ or un relent$) adj2 worr$)) adj8 (acceptance or account$1 or adher$ or aspiration$ or attitude$ or aversion$ or awareness or barrier$ or belief$ or centredness or choice$ or cognitions or complianc$ or conception$ or concern$1 or confus$ or content$ or diary or diaries or demand$ or disatisf$ or disclos$ or discontent$ or disgruntle$ or engaging or engage$1 or experienc$ or feeling or happy or help$ or incentive$ or involv$ or need or needs or obstacle$ or opinion$ or participa$ or perception$ or perceived or perspective$ or position$ or prefer or preferred or preference$ or persistence or refus$ or satisf$ or scepticism or selfobservat$ or self observat$ or (service$ adj2 use$) or stigma$ or story or stories or support$ or tolerance or understand$ or unhappy or utili?ation or view$ or willing$ or voice$) adj8 (adult$1 or attendee$ or attender$ or client$ or consumer$ or individuals or inpatient$ or men or minorities or outpatient$ or participant$ or patient$ or people or population or public or respondents or subjects or survivor$ or women or user$ or care giver$ or care-giver$ or carer$ or (care adj (manager$ or worker$)) or family or families)).ab.

5. (((adult$ or attendee$ or client$ or consumer$ or inpatient$ or minorities or outpa-tient$ or patient$ or people or public or survivor$ or user$) adj2 (acceptance or account$1 or adher$ or aspiration$ or attitude$ or aversion$ or awareness or barrier$ or belief$ or centredness or choice$ or cognitions or complianc$ or conception$ or concern$1 or confus$ or content$ or diary or diaries or demand$ or disatisf$ or disc-los$ or discontent$ or disgruntle$ or engaging or engage$1 or experienc$ or feeling or happy or help$ or incentive$ or involv$ or need or needs or obstacle$ or opinion$ or participa$ or perception$ or perceived or perspective$ or position$ or prefer or preferred or preference$ or persistence or refus$ or satisf$ or scepticism or selfob-servat$ or self observat$ or (service$ adj2 use$) or stigma$ or story or stories or support$ or tolerance or understand$ or unhappy or utili?ation or view$ or willing$ or voice$)) adj15 (anxiet$ or anxious$ or (gad$1 not (glutamic acid decarboxylase or glutamic decarboxylase or gad saad)) or ((chronic$ or excessiv$ or incessant$ or intens$ or neuros$ or neurotic$ or ongoing or persist$ or serious$ or sever$ or uncontrol$ or un control$ or unrelent$ or un relent$) adj2 worr$))).ti,ab.

6. (anxiety or anxiety disorders).sh. and (anxiet$ or anxious$ or ((chronic$ or exces-siv$ or intens$ or (long$ adj2 last$) or neuros$ or neurotic$ or ongoing or persist$ or serious$ or sever$ or uncontrol$ or un control$ or unrelent$ or un relent$) adj2 worry)).ti,ab. and (attitude or attitude to health or knowledge, atti-tudes, practice or patient satisfaction).sh.

7. or/1-6

CCBT for panic disorder

MEDLINE – Ovid SP interface

1. exp psychotherapy/
2. (((cognit$ or behavio?r$ or metacognit$) adj5 (analy$ or interven$ or modif$ or program$ or psychoanaly$ or psychotherap$ or restructur$ or retrain$ or technique$ or therap$ or train$ or treat$)) or (behav$ and cognit$ and (analy$ or

interven$ or modif$ or program$ or psychoanaly$ or psychotherap$ or restruc-
tur$ or retrain$ or technique$ or therap$ or train$ or treat$)) or cbt).ti,ab.
3. (self care.sh. and (cognit$ or behavio?r$ or metacognit$ or recover$).tw,hw.) or
    (selfinstruct$ or selfmanag$ or selfattribut$ or (self$ adj (instruct$ or manag$ or
    attribution$)) or (rational$ adj3 emotiv$) or (rational adj (living or psychotherap$
    or therap$)) or (ret adj (psychotherap$ or therap$)) or rebt or (active directive adj
    (psychotherap$ or therap$))).ti,ab.
4. or/1-3
5. attitude to computers/ or audiovisual aids/ or computer literacy/ or computer user
    training/ or computer-assisted instruction/ or computing methodologies/ or deci-
    sion support systems, clinical/ or hotlines/ or information systems/ or medical
    informatics computing/ or medical informatics/ or multimedia/ or telemedicine/
    or exp audiovisual aids/ or exp computer systems/ or exp decision making,
    computer assisted/ or exp optical storage devices/ or exp software/ or exp
    telecommunications/ or comput$.hw.
6. (audio$ or cd$1 or cd rom or cdrom or computer$ or cyber$ or digital assistant$
    or dvd or electronic$ or floppy or handheld or hand held or interactiv$ or inter-
    net or mobile or multimedia or multi media or online or palmtop or palm top or
    pc$1 or pda or personal digital r phone$ or portal$1 or sms$1 or telephone$ or
    text or texts or texting or video$ or virtual or web$ or www).ti,ab.
7. interactive voice response.ti,ab.
8. or/5-7
9. 4 and 8
10. (caccbt or ccbt or c cbt).ti,ab.
11. ((beating adj2 blues) or fearfighter or ffeducation or ff education or internet
    psykiatri or internet psychiatri or moodgym or netcope or netff or net ff or (living
    life adj2 full) or oc fighter or ocfighter or odin or overcoming depression or panic
    online or (restoring adj2 balance) or standaloneff or standalone ff or therapeutic
    learning program$).ti,ab.
12. (bt step$ or calipso$ or climate or climategp$ or climateschool$ or climatemh$
    or climateclinic$ or climatetv$ or crufad$ or gpcare$ or ultrasis).ti,ab.
13. telemedicine/ or therapy, computer assisted/
14. (panic$ adj3 (package$ or program$)).ti,ab.
15. (etherap$ or e therap$ or telehealth or tele health).ti,ab.
16. (e communication$ or ecommunication$ or e consult$ or econsult$ or e visit$ or
    evisit$ or e therap$ or etherap$ or telehealth or tele health).ti,ab.
17. ((audio$ or cd$1 or cd rom or cdrom or computer$ or cyber$ or digital assistant$
    or dvd or electronic$ or floppy or handheld or hand held or information or inter-
    activ$ or internet or mobile or multimedia or multi media or online or palmtop or
    palm top or pc$1 or pda or pdas or personal digital or phone$ or sms$1 or tele-
    phone$ or text or texts or texting or video$ or virtual or web$ or www) adj5
    (advocacy or approach$ or coach$ or discussion or educat$ or exchang$ or
    guide$1 or help$ or instruct$ or interact$ or interven$ or learn$ or manag$ or
    meeting$ or module$ or network$ or online or participat$ or program$ or
    psychoanaly$ or psychotherap$ or rehab$ or retrain$ or re train$ or self guide$

or self help or selfguide$ or selfhelp or skill$ or strateg$ or support$ or teach$ or technique$ or telephone$ or therap$ or train$ or treat$ or work shop$ or work-shop$)).ti,ab.

18. ((audio$ or cd$1 or cd rom or cdrom or computer$ or cyber$ or digital assistant$ or dvd or electronic$ or floppy or handheld or hand held or information or inter-activ$ or internet or mobile or multimedia or multi media or online or palmtop or palm top or pc$1 or pda or pdas or personal digital or phone$ or sms$1 or tele-phone$ or text or texts or texting or video$ or virtual or web$ or www) adj2 (assist$ or based)).ti,ab.

19. ((audio$ or cd$1 or cd rom or cdrom or computer$ or cyber$ or digital assistant$ or dvd or electronic$ or floppy or handheld or hand held or interactiv$ or inter-net or mobile or multimedia or multi media or online or palmtop or palm top or pc$1 or pda or pdas or personal digital or phone$ or sms$1 or telephone$ or text or texts or texting or video$ or virtual or web$ or www) adj5 (aid or aided or appointment$ or booking$ or communicat$ or consult$ or deliver$ or feedback or forum or guided or input$ or interactiv$ or letter$ or messag$ or referral$ or remind$ or send$ or transfer$ or transmi$ or visit$)).ti,ab.

20. ((audio$ or cd$1 or cd rom or cdrom or computer$ or cyber$ or digital assistant$ or dvd or electronic$ or floppy or handheld or hand held or information or inter-activ$ or internet or mobile or multimedia or multi media or online or palmtop or palm top or pc$1 or personal digital or pda or pdas or personal digital or digital assistant$ or phone$ or sms$1 or telephone$ or text or texts or texting or video$ or virtual or web$ or www) adj5 group$).ti,ab.

21. ((client$ or consumer$ or inpatient$ or outpatient$ or patient$) adj3 (audio$ or cd$1 or cd rom or cdrom or computer$ or cyber$ or digital assistant$ or dvd or electronic$ or floppy or handheld or hand held or information or interactiv$ or internet or mobile or multimedia or multi media or online or palmtop or palm top or pc$1 or pda or pdas or personal digital or phone$ or sms$1 or telephone$ or text or texts or texting or video$ or virtual or web$ or www)).ti,ab.

22. ((client$ or consumer$ or inpatient$ or outpatient$ or patient$ or health or infor-mation or web or internet) adj3 portal$).ti,ab.

23. or/10-22

24. or/9,23

1.3   SEARCH FILTERS

Systematic review search filter – this is an adaptation of a filter designed by the Health Information Research Unit of the McMaster University, Ontario

MEDLINE – Ovid SP interface

1   meta analysis/ or review literature as topic/
2   (((analy$ or evidence$ or methodol$ or quantativ$ or systematic$) adj5 (overview$ or review$)) or (systematic$ adj5 search$)).ti,ab. or ((analy$ or

assessment$ or evidence$ or methodol$ or quantativ$ or qualitativ$ or system-atic$).ti. and review$.ti,pt.)
3   ((electronic database$ or bibliographic database$ or computeri?ed database$ or online database$ or bids or cochrane or embase or index medicus or isi citation or medline or psyclit or psychlit or scisearch or science citation or (web adj2 science)).ti,ab. or databases, bibliographic.sh) and (review$.ti,ab,pt. or systematic$.ti,ab.)
4   (metaanal$ or meta anal$ or metasynthes$ or meta synethes$).ti,ab.
5   (research adj (review$ or integration)).ti,ab.
6   reference list$.ab.
7   bibliograph$.ab.
8   published studies.ab.
9   relevant journals.ab.
10 selection criteria.ab.
11 (data adj (extraction or synthesis)).ab.
12 (handsearch$ or ((hand or manual) adj search$)).ti,ab.
13 (mantel haenszel or peto or dersimonian or der simonian).ti,ab.
14 (fixed effect$ or random effect$).ti,ab.
15 metaanalysis.pt.
16 ((pool$ or combined or combining) adj2 (data or trials or studies or results)).ti,ab.
17 or/1-16

RCT search filter – this is an adaptation of a filter designed by the Health Information Research Unit of the McMaster University, Ontario

MEDLINE – Ovid SP interface

1   exp clinical trial/ or cross over studies/ or double blind method/ or random allo-cation/ or randomized controlled trials as topic/ or single blind method/
2   (clinical adj2 trial$).ti,ab.
3   (crossover or cross over).ti,ab.
4   (((single$ or doubl$ or trebl$ or tripl$) adj5 blind$) or mask$ or dummy or singleblind$ or doubleblind$ or trebleblind$ or tripleblind$).ti,ab.
5   (placebo$ or random$).mp.
6   (clinical trial$ or controlled clinical trial$ or random$).pt.
7   animals/ not (humans/ or human$.tw.)
8   (or/1-6) not 7

Qualitative filter – this is an adaptation of filters designed by the Health Information Research Unit of McMaster University, Ontario, and the University of Alberta

MEDLINE – Ovid SP interface

1. qualitative research/
2. interview/ or personal narratives/ or exp interviews as topic/ or interview, psycho-logical/

3. narration/
4. exp tape recording/ or videodisc recording/
5. sampling studies/ or cluster analysis/
6. anthropology, cultural/
7. nursing methodology research/
8. observation/
9. (qualitative or ethno$ or emic or etic or heuristic or semiotics or phenome-nolog$).ti,ab.
10. interview$.ti,ab.
11. (((audio or tape or video$) adj5 record$) or audiorecord$ or taperecord$ or vide-orecord$ or videotap$).ti,ab.
12. (story or stories or storytell$ or story tell$).ti,ab.
13. testimon$.ti,ab.
14. ((focus adj4 (group$ or sampl$)) or narrat$ or ((life or lived) adj experience$)).ti,ab.
15. ((participant$ or nonparticipant$) adj3 observ$).ti,ab.
16. (constant adj (comparative or comparison)).ti,ab.
17. (content analy$ or (field adj (note$ or record$ or stud$ or research)) or field-note$).ti,ab.
18. (data adj1 saturat$).ti,ab.
19. discourse analys?s.ti,ab.
20. (grounded adj (theor$ or study or studies or research)).ti,ab.
21. (hermeneutic$ or heidegger$ or husserl$ or colaizzi$ or giorgi$ or glaser or spiegelberg$ or strauss).ti,ab.
22. (maximum variation or snowball).ti,ab.
23. (cross case analys$ or metaethno$ or meta ethno$ or metanarrative$ or meta narrative$ or metasynthes$ or meta synthes$ or metasummar$ or meta summar$ or metastud$ or meta stud$ or narrative synthes$ or qualitative synthes$ or qual-itative overview or metaoverview or meta overview).ti,ab.
24. purpos$ sampl$.ti,ab.
25. (structured categor$ or unstructured categor$).ti,ab.
26. ((thematic$ adj3 analys$) or themes).ti,ab.
27. (theoretical sampl$ or ricoeur or spiegelberg$ or merleau).ti,ab.
28. (van kaam$ or van manen or constant compar$).ti,ab.
29. action research.ti,ab.
30. human science.ti,ab.
31. (critical social$ or ethical enquiry or (pilot testing and survey) or shadowing or ((philosophical or social) adj research$)).ti,ab.
32. or/1-31

APPENDIX 9:

CLINICAL STUDY DATA EXTRACTION FORM

Examples of a clinical study data extraction form:

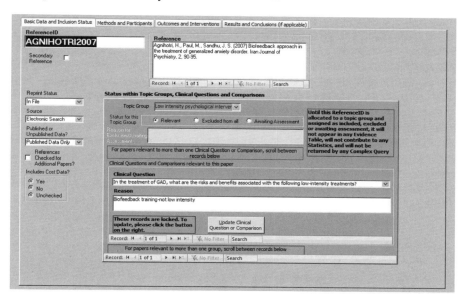

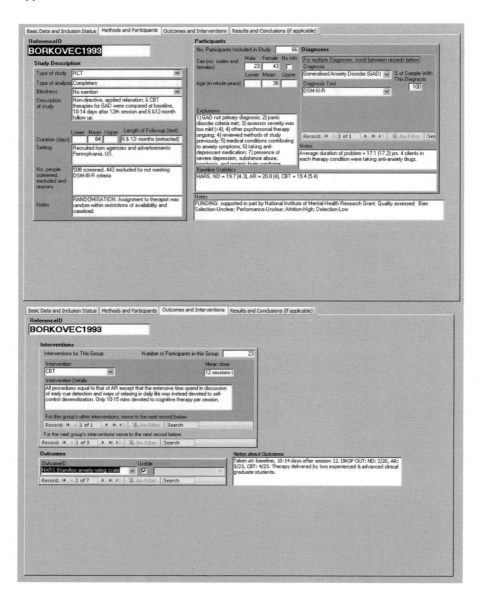

APPENDIX 10:

QUALITY CHECKLISTS FOR CLINICAL STUDIES AND REVIEWS

The methodological quality of each study was evaluated using dimensions adapted from SIGN (SIGN, 2001). SIGN originally adapted its quality criteria from checklists developed in Australia (Liddel *et al.*, 1996). Both groups reportedly undertook extensive development and validation procedures when creating their quality criteria.

Quality checklist for a systematic review or meta-analysis

Quality checklist for a systematic review or meta-analysis	
Study ID:	
Guideline topic:	**Key question no:**
Checklist completed by:	
SECTION 1: INTERNAL VALIDITY	
In a well-conducted systematic review:	In this study this criterion is: *(Circle one option for each question)*
1.1 The study addresses an appropriate and clearly focused question.	Well covered Not addressed Adequately addressed Not reported Poorly addressed Not applicable
1.2 A description of the methodology used is included.	Well covered Not addressed Adequately addressed Not reported Poorly addressed Not applicable
1.3 The literature search is sufficiently rigorous to identify all the relevant studies.	Well covered Not addressed Adequately addressed Not reported Poorly addressed Not applicable
1.4 Study quality is assessed and taken into account.	Well covered Not addressed Adequately addressed Not reported Poorly addressed Not applicable
1.5 There are enough similarities between the studies selected to make combining them reasonable.	Well covered Not addressed Adequately addressed Not reported Poorly addressed Not applicable

SECTION 2: OVERALL ASSESSMENT OF THE STUDY	
2.1	How well was the study done to minimise bias? *Code* $++$, $+$ *or* $-$	

Notes on the use of the methodology checklist: systematic reviews and meta-analyses

Section 1 identifies the study and asks a series of questions aimed at establishing the internal validity of the study under review — that is, making sure that it has been carried out carefully and that the outcomes are likely to be attributable to the intervention being investigated. Each question covers an aspect of methodology that research has shown makes a significant difference to the conclusions of a study.

For each question in this section, one of the following should be used to indicate how well it has been addressed in the review:

- well covered
- adequately addressed
- poorly addressed
- not addressed (that is, not mentioned or indicates that this aspect of study design was ignored)
- not reported (that is, mentioned but insufficient detail to allow assessment to be made)
- not applicable.

1.1   The study addresses an appropriate and clearly focused question

Unless a clear and well-defined question is specified in the report of the review, it will be difficult to assess how well it has met its objectives or how relevant it is to the question to be answered on the basis of the conclusions.

1.2   A description of the methodology used is included

One of the key distinctions between a systematic review and a general review is the systematic methodology used. A systematic review should include a detailed description of the methods used to identify and evaluate individual studies. If this description is not present, it is not possible to make a thorough evaluation of the quality of the review, and it should be rejected as a source of level-1 evidence (though it may be useable as level-4 evidence, if no better evidence can be found).

1.3   The literature search is sufficiently rigorous to identify all the relevant studies

A systematic review based on a limited literature search — for example, one limited to MEDLINE only — is likely to be heavily biased. A well-conducted review should as a minimum look at EMBASE and MEDLINE and, from the late 1990s onward, the Cochrane Library. Any indication that hand searching of key journals, or follow-up of reference lists of included studies, were carried out in addition to electronic database searches can normally be taken as evidence of a well-conducted review.

1.4   Study quality is assessed and taken into account

A well-conducted systematic review should have used clear criteria to assess whether individual studies had been well conducted before deciding whether to include or exclude them. If there is no indication of such an assessment, the review should be rejected as a source of level-1 evidence. If details of the assessment are poor, or the methods are considered to be inadequate, the quality of the review should be downgraded. In either case, it may be worthwhile obtaining and evaluating the individual studies as part of the review being conducted for this guideline.

1.5   There are enough similarities between the studies selected to make combining them reasonable

Studies covered by a systematic review should be selected using clear inclusion criteria (see question 1.4 above). These criteria should include, either implicitly or explicitly, the question of whether the selected studies can legitimately be compared. It should be clearly ascertained, for example, that the populations covered by the studies are comparable, that the methods used in the investigations are the same, that the outcome measures are comparable and the variability in effect sizes between studies is not greater than would be expected by chance alone.

Section 2 relates to the overall assessment of the paper. It starts by rating the methodological quality of the study, based on the responses in Section 1 and using the following coding system:

++	All or most of the criteria have been fulfilled. Where they have not been fulfilled, the conclusions of the study or review are thought **very unlikely** to alter.
+	Some of the criteria have been fulfilled. Those criteria that have not been fulfilled or not adequately described are thought **unlikely** to alter the conclusions.
−	Few or no criteria fulfilled. The conclusions of the study are thought **likely or very likely** to alter.

Quality checklist for an RCT

Quality checklist for an RCT	
Study ID:	
Guideline topic:	**Key question no:**
Checklist completed by:	
SECTION 1: INTERNAL VALIDITY	
In a well-conducted RCT study:	**In this study this criterion is: (Circle one option for each question)**
1.1 The study addresses an appropriate and clearly focused question.	Well covered Not addressed Adequately addressed Not reported Poorly addressed Not applicable
1.2 The assignment of subjects to treatment groups is randomised.	Well covered Not addressed Adequately addressed Not reported Poorly addressed Not applicable
1.3 An adequate concealment method is used.	Well covered Not addressed Adequately addressed Not reported Poorly addressed Not applicable
1.4 Subjects and investigators are kept 'blind' about treatment allocation.	Well covered Not addressed Adequately addressed Not reported Poorly addressed Not applicable
1.5 The treatment and control groups are similar at the start of the trial.	Well covered Not addressed Adequately addressed Not reported Poorly addressed Not applicable
1.6 The only difference between groups is the treatment under investigation.	Well covered Not addressed Adequately addressed Not reported Poorly addressed Not applicable
1.7 All relevant outcomes are measured in a standard, valid and reliable way.	Well covered Not addressed Adequately addressed Not reported Poorly addressed Not applicable
1.8 What percentage of the individuals or clusters recruited into each treatment arm of the study dropped out before the study was completed?	
1.9 All the subjects are analysed in the groups to which they were randomly allocated (often referred to as intention-to-treat analysis).	Well covered Not addressed Adequately addressed Not reported Poorly addressed Not applicable

1.10	Where the study is carried out at more than one site, results are comparable for all sites.	Well covered Adequately addressed Poorly addressed	Not addressed Not reported Not applicable
SECTION 2: OVERALL ASSESSMENT OF THE STUDY			
2.1	How well was the study done to minimise bias? *Code* $++$, $+$ or $-$		

Notes on the use of the methodology checklist: RCTs

Section 1 identifies the study and asks a series of questions aimed at establishing the internal validity of the study under review — that is, making sure that it has been carried out carefully and that the outcomes are likely to be attributable to the intervention being investigated. Each question covers an aspect of methodology that research has shown makes a significant difference to the conclusions of a study.

For each question in this section, one of the following should be used to indicate how well it has been addressed in the review:

● well covered
● adequately addressed
● poorly addressed
● not addressed (that is, not mentioned or indicates that this aspect of study design was ignored)
● not reported (that is, mentioned but insufficient detail to allow assessment to be made)
● not applicable.

1.1   The study addresses an appropriate and clearly focused question

Unless a clear and well-defined question is specified, it will be difficult to assess how well the study has met its objectives or how relevant it is to the question to be answered on the basis of its conclusions.

1.2   The assignment of subjects to treatment groups is randomised

Random allocation of patients to receive one or other of the treatments under investigation, or to receive either treatment or placebo, is fundamental to this type of study. If there is no indication of randomisation, the study should be rejected. If the description of randomisation is poor, or the process used is not truly random (for example, allocation by date or alternating between one group and another) or can otherwise be seen as flawed, the study should be given a lower quality rating.

1.3   An adequate concealment method is used

Research has shown that where allocation concealment is inadequate, investigators can overestimate the effect of interventions by up to 40%. Centralised allocation, computerised allocation systems or the use of coded identical containers would all be regarded as adequate methods of concealment and may be taken as indicators of a well-conducted study. If the method of concealment used is regarded as poor, or relatively easy to subvert, the study must be given a lower quality rating, and can be rejected if the concealment method is seen as inadequate.

1.4   Subjects and investigators are kept 'blind' about treatment allocation

Blinding can be carried out up to three levels. In single-blind studies, patients are unaware of which treatment they are receiving; in double-blind studies, the doctor and the patient are unaware of which treatment the patient is receiving; in triple-blind studies, patients, healthcare providers and those conducting the analysis are unaware of which patients receive which treatment. The higher the level of blinding, the lower the risk of bias in the study.

1.5   The treatment and control groups are similar at the start of the trial

Patients selected for inclusion in a trial should be as similar as possible, in order to eliminate any possible bias. The study should report any significant differences in the composition of the study groups in relation to gender mix, age, stage of disease (if appropriate), social background, ethnic origin or comorbid conditions. These factors may be covered by inclusion and exclusion criteria, rather than being reported directly. Failure to address this question, or the use of inappropriate groups, should lead to the study being downgraded.

1.6   The only difference between groups is the treatment under investigation

If some patients receive additional treatment, even if of a minor nature or consisting of advice and counselling rather than a physical intervention, this treatment is a potential confounding factor that may invalidate the results. If groups are not treated equally, the study should be rejected unless no other evidence is available. If the study is used as evidence, it should be treated with caution and given a low quality rating.

1.7   All relevant outcomes are measured in a standard, valid and reliable way

If some significant clinical outcomes have been ignored, or not adequately taken into account, the study should be downgraded. It should also be downgraded if the measures used are regarded as being doubtful in any way or applied inconsistently.

1.8 **What percentage of the individuals or clusters recruited into each treatment arm of the study dropped out before the study was completed?**

The number of patients that drop out of a study should give concern if the number is very high. Conventionally, a 20% dropout rate is regarded as acceptable, but this may vary. Some regard should be paid to why patients drop out, as well as how many. It should be noted that the dropout rate may be expected to be higher in studies conducted over a long period of time. A higher dropout rate will normally lead to downgrading, rather than rejection, of a study.

1.9 **All the subjects are analysed in the groups to which they were randomly allocated (often referred to as intention-to-treat analysis)**

In practice, it is rarely the case that all patients allocated to the intervention group receive the intervention throughout the trial, or that all those in the comparison group do not. Patients may refuse treatment, or contraindications arise that lead them to be switched to the other group. If the comparability of groups through randomisation is to be maintained, however, patient outcomes must be analysed according to the group to which they were originally allocated, irrespective of the treatment they actually received. (This is known as intention-to-treat analysis.) If it is clear that analysis is not on an intention-to-treat basis, the study may be rejected. If there is little other evidence available, the study may be included but should be evaluated as if it were a non-randomised cohort study.

1.10 **Where the study is carried out at more than one site, results are comparable for all sites**

In multi-site studies, confidence in the results should be increased if it can be shown that similar results have been obtained at the different participating centres.

Section 2 relates to the overall assessment of the paper. It starts by rating the methodological quality of the study, based on the responses in Section 1 and using the following coding system:

++	All or most of the criteria have been fulfilled. Where they have not been fulfilled, the conclusions of the study or review are thought **very unlikely** to alter.
+	Some of the criteria have been fulfilled. Those criteria that have not been fulfilled or not adequately described are thought **unlikely** to alter the conclusions.
−	Few or no criteria fulfilled. The conclusions of the study are thought **likely or very likely** to alter.

Appendix 10

Quality checklist for a cohort study

Quality checklist for a cohort study*	Relevant questions:
Study ID:	
Guideline topic:	
Checklist completed by:	
SECTION 1: INTERNAL VALIDITY	
In a well conducted cohort study:	**In this study the criterion is:** *(Circle one option for each question)*
1.1 The study addresses an appropriate and clearly focused question.	Well covered Not addressed Adequately addressed Not reported Poorly addressed Not applicable
SELECTION OF SUBJECTS	
1.2 The two groups being studied are selected from source populations that are comparable in all respects other than the factor under investigation.	Well covered Not addressed Adequately addressed Not reported Poorly addressed Not applicable
1.3 The study indicates how many of the people asked to take part did so, in each of the groups being studied.	Well covered Not addressed Adequately addressed Not reported Poorly addressed Not reported
1.4 The likelihood that some eligible subjects might have the outcome at the time of enrolment is assessed and taken into account in the analysis.	Well covered Not addressed Adequately addressed Not reported Poorly addressed Not applicable
1.5 What percentage of individuals or clusters recruited into each arm of the study dropped out before the study was completed?	
1.6 Comparison is made between full participants and those lost to follow-up, by exposure status.	Well covered Not addressed Adequately addressed Not reported Poorly addressed Not applicable
ASSESSMENT	
1.7 The outcomes are clearly defined.	Well covered Not addressed Adequately addressed Not reported Poorly addressed Not applicable

1.8	The assessment of outcome is made blind to exposure status.	Well covered Not addressed Adequately addressed Not reported Poorly addressed Not applicable
1.9	Where blinding was not possible, there is some recognition that knowledge of exposure status could have influenced the assessment of outcome.	Well covered Not addressed Adequately addressed Not reported Poorly addressed Not applicable
1.10	The measure of assessment of exposure is reliable.	Well covered Not addressed Adequately addressed Not reported Poorly addressed Not applicable
1.11	Evidence from other sources is used to demonstrate that the method of outcome assessment is valid and reliable.	Well covered Not addressed Adequately addressed Not reported Poorly addressed Not applicable
1.12	Exposure level or prognostic factor is assessed more than once.	Well covered Not addressed Adequately addressed Not reported Poorly addressed Not applicable
CONFOUNDING		
1.13	The main potential confounders are identified and taken into account in the design and analysis.	Well covered Not addressed Adequately addressed Not reported Poorly addressed Not applicable
STATISTICAL ANALYSIS		
1.14	Have confidence intervals been provided?	
SECTION 2: OVERALL ASSESSMENT OF THE STUDY		
2.1	How well was the study done to minimise the risk of bias or confounding, and to establish a causal relationship between exposure and effect? *Code* $++$, $+$ or $-$	

*A cohort study can be defined as a retrospective or prospective follow-up study. Groups of individuals are defined on the basis of the presence or absence of exposure to a suspected risk factor or intervention. This checklist is not appropriate for assessing uncontrolled studies (for example, a case series where there is no comparison [control] group of patients).

Notes on the use of the methodology checklist: cohort studies

The studies covered by this checklist are designed to answer questions of the type 'What are the effects of this exposure?' It relates to studies that compare a group of people with a particular exposure with another group who either have not had the exposure or have a different level of exposure. Cohort studies may be prospective (where the exposure is defined and subjects selected before outcomes occur) or retrospective (where exposure is assessed after the outcome is known, usually by the examination of medical records). Retrospective studies are generally regarded as a weaker design, and should not receive a 2 + + rating.

Section 1 identifies the study and asks a series of questions aimed at establishing the internal validity of the study under review — that is, making sure that it has been carried out carefully, and that the outcomes are likely to be attributable to the intervention being investigated. Each question covers an aspect of methodology that has been shown to make a significant difference to the conclusions of a study.

Because of the potential complexity and subtleties of the design of this type of study, there are comparatively few criteria that automatically rule out use of a study as evidence. It is more a matter of increasing confidence in the likelihood of a causal relationship existing between exposure and outcome by identifying how many aspects of good study design are present and how well they have been tackled. A study that fails to address or report on more than one or two of the questions considered below should almost certainly be rejected.

For each question in this section, one of the following should be used to indicate how well it has been addressed in the review:

● well covered
● adequately addressed
● poorly addressed
● not addressed (that is, not mentioned or indicates that this aspect of study design was ignored)
● not reported (that is, mentioned but insufficient detail to allow assessment to be made)
● not applicable.

1.1   The study addresses an appropriate and clearly focused question

Unless a clear and well-defined question is specified, it will be difficult to assess how well the study has met its objectives or how relevant it is to the question to be answered on the basis of its conclusions.

1.2   The two groups being studied are selected from source populations that are comparable in all respects other than the factor under investigation

Study participants may be selected from the target population (all individuals to which the results of the study could be applied), the source population (a defined subset of the target population from which participants are selected) or from a pool of eligible subjects (a clearly defined and counted group selected from the source population). It is important that the two groups selected for comparison are as similar as possible in all characteristics except for their exposure status or the presence of specific prognostic factors or prognostic markers relevant to the study in question. If the study does not include clear definitions of the source populations and eligibility criteria for participants, it should be rejected.

1.3 The study indicates how many of the people asked to take part did so in each of the groups being studied

This question relates to what is known as the participation rate, defined as the number of study participants divided by the number of eligible subjects. This should be calculated separately for each branch of the study. A large difference in participation rate between the two arms of the study indicates that a significant degree of selection bias may be present, and the study results should be treated with considerable caution.

1.4 The likelihood that some eligible subjects might have the outcome at the time of enrolment is assessed and taken into account in the analysis

If some of the eligible subjects, particularly those in the unexposed group, already have the outcome at the start of the trial, the final result will be biased. A well-conducted study will attempt to estimate the likelihood of this occurring and take it into account in the analysis through the use of sensitivity studies or other methods.

1.5 What percentage of individuals or clusters recruited into each arm of the study dropped out before the study was completed?

The number of patients that drop out of a study should give concern if the number is very high. Conventionally, a 20% dropout rate is regarded as acceptable, but in observational studies conducted over a lengthy period of time a higher dropout rate is to be expected. A decision on whether to downgrade or reject a study because of a high dropout rate is a matter of judgement based on the reasons why people drop out and whether dropout rates are comparable in the exposed and unexposed groups. Reporting of efforts to follow-up participants who drop out may be regarded as an indicator of a well-conducted study.

1.6 Comparison is made between full participants and those lost to follow-up by exposure status

For valid study results, it is essential that the study participants are truly representative of the source population. It is always possible that participants who drop out of the study will differ in some significant way from those who remain part of the study throughout. A well-conducted study will attempt to identify any such differences between full and partial participants in both the exposed and unexposed groups. Any indication that differences exist should lead to the study results being treated with caution.

1.7   The outcomes are clearly defined

Once enrolled in the study, participants should be followed until specified end points or outcomes are reached. In a study of the effect of exercise on the death rates from heart disease in middle-aged men, for example, participants might be followed up until death, reaching a predefined age or until completion of the study. If outcomes and the criteria used for measuring them are not clearly defined, the study should be rejected.

1.8   The assessment of outcome is made blind to exposure status

If the assessor is blinded to which participants received the exposure, and which did not, the prospects of unbiased results are significantly increased. Studies in which this is done should be rated more highly than those where it is not done or not done adequately.

1.9   Where blinding was not possible, there is some recognition that knowledge of exposure status could have influenced the assessment of outcome

Blinding is not possible in many cohort studies. In order to assess the extent of any bias that may be present, it may be helpful to compare process measures used on the participant groups — for example, frequency of observations, who carried out the observations and the degree of detail and completeness of observations. If these process measures are comparable between the groups, the results may be regarded with more confidence.

1.10   The measure of assessment of exposure is reliable

A well-conducted study should indicate how the degree of exposure or presence of prognostic factors or markers was assessed. Whatever measures are used must be sufficient to establish clearly that participants have or have not received the exposure under investigation and the extent of such exposure, or that they do or do not possess a particular prognostic marker or factor. Clearly described, reliable measures should increase the confidence in the quality of the study.

1.11   Evidence from other sources is used to demonstrate that the method of outcome assessment is valid and reliable

The inclusion of evidence from other sources or previous studies that demonstrate the validity and reliability of the assessment methods used should further increase confidence in study quality.

1.12 Exposure level or prognostic factor is assessed more than once

Confidence in data quality should be increased if exposure level or the presence of prognostic factors is measured more than once. Independent assessment by more than one investigator is preferable.

1.13 The main potential confounders are identified and taken into account in the design and analysis

Confounding is the distortion of a link between exposure and outcome by another factor that is associated with both exposure and outcome. The possible presence of confounding factors is one of the principal reasons why observational studies are not more highly rated as a source of evidence. The report of the study should indicate which potential confounders have been considered and how they have been assessed or allowed for in the analysis. Clinical judgement should be applied to consider whether all likely confounders have been considered. If the measures used to address confounding are considered inadequate, the study should be downgraded or rejected, depending on how serious the risk of confounding is considered to be. A study that does not address the possibility of confounding should be rejected.

1.14 Have confidence intervals been provided?

Confidence limits are the preferred method for indicating the precision of statistical results and can be used to differentiate between an inconclusive study and a study that shows no effect. Studies that report a single value with no assessment of precision should be treated with caution.

Section 2 relates to the overall assessment of the paper. It starts by rating the methodological quality of the study, based on the responses in Section 1 and using the following coding system:

+ +	All or most of the criteria have been fulfilled. Where they have not been fulfilled, the conclusions of the study or review are thought **very unlikely** to alter.
+	Some of the criteria have been fulfilled. Those criteria that have not been fulfilled or not adequately described are thought **unlikely** to alter the conclusions.
−	Few or no criteria fulfilled. The conclusions of the study are thought **likely or very likely** to alter.

APPENDIX 11:

SEARCH STRATEGIES FOR THE IDENTIFICATION OF HEALTH ECONOMIC EVIDENCE

1   SEARCH STRATEGIES

The search strategies should be referred to in conjunction with information set out in Chapter 3 (Section 3.6.1). Each search was constructed using the groups of terms as set out in Text Box 4. The selections of terms were kept broad to maximise retrieval of evidence in a wide range of areas of interest to the GDG. Some of the interventions searched are not documented in the main body of the guideline due to a lack of evidence.

Text Box 4: Summary of systematic search strategies for health economic evidence: search strategy construction

---

GAD:
Psychological interventions (high- or low-intensity)
i)   [(GAD terms) AND (general psychological terms) AND (HE filter)] OR
ii) [(GAD terms) AND (high-intensity terms) AND (HE filter)] OR
iii) [(GAD terms) AND (low-intensity terms) AND (HE filter)]

Pharmacological interventions
i)   (GAD terms) AND (pharmacological terms) AND (HE filter)

Alternative interventions
i)   (GAD terms) AND (alternative intervention terms) AND (HE filter)

Panic disorder:
CCBT for panic
i)   (Panic terms) AND (CCBT terms) AND (SR filter OR RCT filter)

1.1   POPULATION SEARCH TERMS

GAD – population search terms

MEDLINE – Ovid SP interface

1.   (anxiety or anxiety disorders).sh.

2. (anxiet$ or anxious$ or ((chronic$ or excessiv$ or intens$ or (long$ adj2 last$) or neuros$ or neurotic$ or ongoing or persist$ or serious$ or sever$ or uncontrol$ or un control$ or unrelent$ or un relent$) adj2 worry)).ti,ab.
3. or/1-2

Panic – population search terms

MEDLINE – Ovid SP interface

1. (panic or panic disorder).sh.
2. panic$.ti,ab.
3. or/1-2

1.2 QUESTION-SPECIFIC SEARCH STRATEGIES

The question-specific searches used in the identification of economic evidence are documented in Section 1.2 of Appendix 8.

1.3 SEARCH FILTERS

Health economics and quality of life search filter – this is an adaptation of a filter designed by the NHS Centre for Reviews and Dissemination (CRD) at the University of York

MEDLINE - Ovid SP interface

1. exp "costs and cost analysis"/ or health priorities/ or health resources/ or exp resource allocation/
2. budgets/ or socioeconomic factors/ or (economi$ or fee or fees or financ$).hw.
3. quality adjusted life years/ or "quality of life"/ or "value of life"/
4. exp models, economic/ or models, statistical/ or monte carlo method/
5. health status indicators/
6. decision trees/
7. (budget$ or cost$ or econom$ or expenditure$ or financ$ or fiscal or funding or pharmacoeconomic$ or socioeconomic$ or price or prices or pricing or (value adj3 money) or (burden adj3 (disease$ or illness$))).ti,ab.
8. (daly or qol or hql or hqol or hrqol or hr ql or hrql or (quality adj2 life) or (adjusted adj2 life) or qaly$ or (health adj2 stat$) or well being or wellbeing or qald$ or qale$ or qtime$ or eq5d or eq 5d or qwb or ((quality or value$) adj3 (life or survival or well$)) or hui$1 or (utilit$ adj1 (health or score$ or weigh$)) or (life adj2 year$) or health year equivalent$ or ((disability or quality) adj adjusted) or utility value$ or (weight$ adj3 preference$) or euroqol or euro qol or visual analog$ or standard gamble or time trade or qtwist or q twist or (valu$ adj2 quality)).tw.

9   decision tree/ or decision trees/

10 (decision analy$ or monte carlo or markov or simulation model$ or rosser or disutili$ or willingness to pay or tto or hye or hyes or (resource adj (allocat$ or use$ or utilit$))).tw.

11 (sf36 or sf 36 or short form 36 or shortform 36 or sf thirtysix or sf thirty six or shortform thirtysix or shortform thirty six or short form thirtysix or short form thirty six).tw.

12 (sf6 or sf 6 or short form 6 or shortform 6 or sf six or sfsix or shortform six or short form six).tw.

13 (sf12 or sf 12 or short form 12 or shortform 12 or sf twelve or sftwelve or short-form twelve or short form twelve).tw.

14 (sf16 or sf 16 or short form 16 or shortform 16 or sf sixteen or sfsixteen or short-form sixteen or short form sixteen).tw.

15 (sf20 or sf 20 or short form 20 or shortform 20 or sf twenty or sftwenty or short-form twenty or short form twenty).tw.

16 ec.fs. *[ANDed with subject heading searches for the main population/topic]*

17 or/1-16

APPENDIX 12:

METHODOLOGY CHECKLIST FOR ECONOMIC STUDIES

Study identification *Including author, title, reference, year of publication*			
Guideline topic:			**Question no:**
Checklist completed by:			
Section 1: Applicability (relevance to specific guideline review question(s) and the NICE reference case). This checklist should be used first to filter out irrelevant studies.		**Yes/ Partly/ No/Unclear/ NA**	**Comments**
1.1	Is the study population appropriate for the guideline?		
1.2	Are the interventions appropriate for the guideline?		
1.3	Is the healthcare system in which the study was conducted sufficiently similar to the current UK NHS context?		
1.4	Are costs measured from the NHS and personal social services (PSS) perspective?		
1.5	Are all direct health effects on individuals included?		
1.6	Are both costs and health effects discounted at an annual rate of 3.5%?		
1.7	Is the value of health effects expressed in terms of QALYs?		
1.8	Are changes in HRQoL reported directly from patients and/or carers?		
1.9	Is the valuation of changes in HRQoL (utilities) obtained from a representative sample of the general public?		

1.10	Overall judgement: Directly applicable/ Partially applicable/Not applicable There is no need to use section 2 of the checklist if the study is considered 'not applicable'.		
Other comments:			

Section 2: Study limitations (the level of methodological quality). This checklist should be used once it has been decided that the study is sufficiently applicable to the context of the clinical guideline.	Yes/ Partly /No/Unclear/ NA	Comments
2.1	Does the model structure adequately reflect the nature of the health condition under evaluation?		
2.2	Is the time horizon sufficiently long to reflect all important differences in costs and outcomes?		
2.3	Are all important and relevant health outcomes included?		
2.4	Are the estimates of baseline health outcomes from the best available source?		
2.5	Are the estimates of relative treatment effects from the best available source?		
2.6	Are all important and relevant costs included?		
2.7	Are the estimates of resource use from the best available source?		
2.8	Are the unit costs of resources from the best available source?		
2.9	Is an appropriate incremental analysis presented or can it be calculated from the data?		
2.10	Are all important parameters whose values are uncertain subjected to appropriate sensitivity analysis?		
2.11	Is there no potential conflict of interest?		

2.12	Overall assessment: Minor limitations/ Potentially serious limitations/Very serious limitations		
Other comments:			

Notes on use of methodology checklist: economic evaluations

For all questions:
- answer 'yes' if the study fully meets the criterion
- answer 'partly' if the study largely meets the criterion but differs in some important respect
- answer 'no' if the study deviates substantively from the criterion
- answer 'unclear' if the report provides insufficient information to judge whether the study complies with the criterion
- answer 'NA (not applicable)' if the criterion is not relevant in a particular instance.

For 'partly' or 'no' responses, use the comments column to explain how the study deviates from the criterion.

SECTION 1:   APPLICABILITY

1.1   Is the study population appropriate for the guideline?

The study population should be defined as precisely as possible and should be in line with that specified in the guideline scope and any related review protocols. This includes consideration of appropriate subgroups that require special attention. For many interventions, the capacity to benefit will differ for participants with differing characteristics. This should be explored separately for each relevant subgroup as part of the base-case analysis by the provision of estimates of clinical and cost effectiveness. The characteristics of participants in each subgroup should be clearly defined and, ideally, should be identified on the basis of an *a priori* expectation of differential clinical or cost effectiveness as a result of biologically plausible known mechanisms, social characteristics or other clearly justified factors.

Answer 'yes' if the study population is fully in line with that in the guideline question(s) and if the study differentiates appropriately between important subgroups. Answer 'partly' if the study population is similar to that in the guideline question(s) but: (a) it differs in some important respects; or (b) the study fails to differentiate between important subgroups. Answer 'no' if the study population is substantively different from that in the guideline question(s).

1.2   Are the interventions appropriate for the guideline?

All relevant alternatives should be included, as specified in the guideline scope and any related review protocols. These should include routine and best practice in the NHS, existing NICE guidance and other feasible options. Answer 'yes' if the analysis includes all options considered relevant for the guideline, even if it also includes other options that are not relevant. Answer 'partly' if the analysis omits one or more relevant options but still contains comparisons likely to be useful for the guideline. Answer 'no' if the analysis does not contain any relevant comparisons.

1.3   Is the healthcare system in which the study was conducted sufficiently similar to the current UK NHS context?

This relates to the overall structure of the healthcare system within which the interventions were delivered. For example, an intervention might be delivered on an inpatient basis in one country whereas in the UK it would be provided in the community. This might significantly influence the use of healthcare resources and costs, thus limiting the applicability of the results to a UK setting. In addition, old UK studies may be severely limited in terms of their relevance to current NHS practice.

Answer 'yes' if the study was conducted within the UK and is sufficiently recent to reflect current NHS practice. For non-UK or older UK studies, answer 'partly' if differences in the healthcare setting are unlikely to substantively change the cost-effectiveness estimates. Answer 'no' if the healthcare setting is so different that the results are unlikely to be applicable in the current NHS.

1.4   Are costs measured from the NHS and personal social services (PSS) perspective?

The decision-making perspective of an economic evaluation determines the range of costs that should be included in the analysis. NICE works in a specific context; in particular, it does not set the budget for the NHS. The objective of NICE is to offer guidance that represents an efficient use of available NHS and PSS resources. For these reasons, the perspective on costs used in the NICE reference case is that of the NHS and PSS. Productivity costs and costs borne by patients and carers that are not reimbursed by the NHS or PSS are not included in the reference case. The reference case also excludes costs to other government bodies, although these may sometimes be presented in additional analyses alongside the reference case.

Answer 'yes' if the study only includes costs for resource items that would be paid for by the NHS and PSS. Also answer 'yes' if other costs have been included in the study, but the results are presented in such a way that the cost effectiveness can be calculated from an NHS and PSS perspective. Answer 'partly' if the study has taken a wider perspective but the other non-NHS/PSS costs are small in relation to the total expected costs and are unlikely to change the cost-effectiveness results. Answer 'no' if non-NHS/PSS costs are significant and are likely to change the cost-effectiveness results. Some interventions may have a substantial impact on non-health outcomes or costs to other government bodies (for example, treatments to reduce illicit drug misuse may have the effect of reducing drug-related crime). In such situations, if the economic study includes non-health costs in such a way that they cannot be separated out from NHS/PSS costs, answer 'no' but consider retaining the study for critical appraisal. If studies containing non-reference case costs are retained, use the comments column to note why.

1.5   Are all direct health effects on individuals included?

In the NICE reference case, the perspective on outcomes should be all direct health effects, whether for patients or, when relevant, other people (principally carers). This is consistent with an objective of maximising health gain from available healthcare resources. Some features of healthcare delivery that are often referred to as 'process characteristics' may ultimately have health consequences; for example, the mode of treatment delivery may have health consequences through its impact on concordance with treatment. Any significant characteristics of healthcare technologies that have a value to people that is independent of any direct effect on health should be noted. These characteristics include the convenience with which healthcare is provided and the level of information available for patients.

This question should be viewed in terms of what is **excluded** in relation to the NICE reference case; that is, non-health effects.

Answer 'yes' if the measure of health outcome used in the analysis excludes non-health effects (or if such effects can be excluded from the results). Answer 'partly' if the analysis includes some non-health effects but these are small and unlikely to change the cost-effectiveness results. Answer 'no' if the analysis includes significant non-health effects that are likely to change the cost-effectiveness results.

1.6   Are both costs and health effects discounted at an annual rate of 3.5%?

The need to discount to a present value is widely accepted in economic evaluation, although the specific rate varies across jurisdictions and over time. NICE considers it appropriate to discount costs and health effects at the same rate. The annual rate of 3.5%, based on the recommendations of the UK Treasury for the discounting of costs, applies to both costs and health effects.

Answer 'yes' if both costs and health effects (for example, QALYs) are discounted at 3.5% per year. Answer 'partly' if costs and effects are discounted at a rate similar to 3.5% (for example, costs and effects are both discounted at 3% per year). Answer 'no' if costs and/or health effects are not discounted, or if they are discounted at a rate (or rates) different from 3.5% (for example, 5% for both costs and effects, or 6% for costs and 1.5% for effects). Note in the comments column what discount rates have been used. If all costs and health effects accrue within a short time (roughly a year), answer 'NA'.

1.7 Is the value of health effects expressed in terms of quality-adjusted life years (QALYs)?

The QALY is a measure of a person's length of life weighted by a valuation of their health-related quality of life (HRQoL) over that period.

Given its widespread use, the QALY is considered by NICE to be the most appropriate generic measure of health benefit that reflects both mortality and effects on HRQoL. It is recognised that alternative measures exist (such as the healthy-year equivalent), but few economic evaluations have used these methods and their strengths and weaknesses are not fully established.

NICE's position is that an additional QALY should be given the same weight regardless of the other characteristics of the patients receiving the health benefit.

Answer 'yes' if the effectiveness of the intervention is measured using QALYs; answer 'no' if not. There may be circumstances when a QALY cannot be obtained or where the assumptions underlying QALYs are considered inappropriate. In such situations answer 'no', but consider retaining the study for appraisal. Similarly, answer 'no' but retain the study for appraisal if it does not include QALYs but it is still thought to be useful for GDG decision-making: for example, if the clinical evidence indicates that an intervention might be dominant, and estimates of the relative costs of the interventions from a cost minimisation study are likely to be useful. When economic evaluations not using QALYs are retained for full critical appraisal, use the comments column to note why.

1.8 Are changes in health-related quality of life (HRQoL) reported directly from patients and/or carers?

In the NICE reference case, information on changes in HRQoL as a result of treatment should be reported directly by patients (and directly by carers when the impact of treatment on the carer's health is also important). When it is not possible to obtain information on changes in patients' HRQoL directly from them, data should be obtained from carers (not from healthcare professionals).

For consistency, the EQ-5D is NICE's preferred measure of HRQoL in adults. However, when EQ-5D data are not available or are inappropriate for the condition or the effects of treatment, other multi-attribute utility questionnaires (for example, SF-6D, QWB or Health Utilities Index [HUI]) or mapping methods from disease-specific questionnaires may be used to estimate QALYs. For studies not reporting QALYs, a variety of generic or disease-specific methods may be used to measure HRQoL.

Answer 'yes' if changes in patients' HRQoL are estimated by the patients themselves. Answer 'partly' if estimates of patients' HRQoL are provided by carers. Answer 'no' if estimates come from healthcare professionals or researchers. Note in the comments column how HRQoL was measured (EQ-5D, QWB, HUI and so on). Answer 'NA' if the cost-effectiveness study does not include estimates of HRQoL (for example, studies reporting 'cost per life year gained' or cost-minimisation studies).

1.9 Is the valuation of changes in HRQoL (utilities) obtained from a representative sample of the general public?

The NICE reference case specifies that the valuation of changes in HRQoL (utilities) reported by patients should be based on public preferences elicited using a choice-based method (such as the time trade-off or standard gamble) in a representative sample of the UK population.

Answer 'yes' if HRQoL valuations were obtained using the EQ-5D UK tariff. Answer 'partly' if the valuation methods were comparable to those used for the EQ-5D. Answer 'no' if other valuation methods were used. Answer 'NA' if the study does not apply valuations to HRQoL (for studies not reporting QALYs). In the comments column note the valuation method used (such as time trade-off or standard gamble) and the source of the preferences (such as patients or healthcare professionals).

1.10 Overall judgement

Classify the applicability of the economic evaluation to the clinical guideline, the current NHS situation and the context for NICE guidance as one of the following:

- **Directly applicable** – the study meets all applicability criteria, or fails to meet one or more applicability criteria but this is unlikely to change the conclusions about cost effectiveness.
- **Partially applicable** – the study fails to meet one or more applicability criteria, and this could change the conclusions about cost effectiveness.
- **Not applicable** – the study fails to meet one or more applicability criteria, and this is likely to change the conclusions about cost effectiveness. Such studies would be excluded from further consideration and there is no need to continue with the rest of the checklist.

SECTION 2: STUDY LIMITATIONS

2.1 Does the model structure adequately reflect the nature of the health condition under evaluation?

This relates to the choice of model and its structural elements (including cycle length in discrete time models, if appropriate). Model type and its structural aspects should be consistent with a coherent theory of the health condition under evaluation. The selection of treatment pathways, whether health states or branches in a decision tree, should be based on the underlying biological processes of the health issue under study and the potential impact (benefits and adverse consequences) of the intervention(s) of interest.

Answer 'yes' if the model design and assumptions appropriately reflect the health condition and intervention(s) of interest. Answer 'partly' if there are aspects of the model design or assumptions that do not fully reflect the health condition or intervention(s) but that are unlikely to change the cost-effectiveness results. Answer 'no' if the model omits some important aspect of the health condition or intervention(s) and this is likely to change the cost-effectiveness results. Answer 'NA' for economic evaluations based on data from a clinical study that do not extrapolate treatment outcomes or costs beyond the study context or follow-up period.

2.2 Is the time horizon sufficiently long to reflect all important differences in costs and outcomes?

The time horizon is the period of analysis of the study: the length of follow-up for participants in a trial-based evaluation, or the period of time over which the costs and outcomes for a cohort are tracked in a modelling study. This time horizon should always be the same for costs and outcomes, and should be long enough to include all relevant costs and outcomes relating to the intervention. A time horizon shorter than lifetime could be justified if there is no differential mortality effect between options, and the differences in costs and HRQoL relate to a relatively short period (for example, in the case of an acute infection).

Answer 'yes' if the time horizon is sufficient to include all relevant costs and outcomes. Answer 'partly' if the time horizon may omit some relevant costs and outcomes but these are unlikely to change the cost-effectiveness results. Answer 'no' if the time horizon omits important costs and outcomes and this is likely to change the cost-effectiveness results.

2.3 Are all important and relevant health outcomes included?

All relevant health outcomes should include direct health effects relating to harms from the intervention (adverse effects) as well as any potential benefits.

Answer 'yes' if the analysis includes all relevant and important harms and benefits. Answer 'partly' if the analysis omits some harms or benefits but these would be unlikely to change the cost-effectiveness results. Answer 'no' if the analysis omits important harms and/or benefits that would be likely to change the cost-effectiveness results.

2.4 Are the estimates of baseline health outcomes from the best available source?

The estimate of the overall net treatment effect of an intervention is determined by the baseline risk of a particular condition or event and/or the relative effects of the intervention compared with the relevant comparator treatment. The overall net treatment effect may also be determined by other features of the people comprising the population of interest.

The process of assembling evidence for economic evaluations should be systematic – evidence must be identified, quality assessed and, when appropriate, pooled, using explicit criteria and justifiable and reproducible methods. These principles apply to all categories of evidence that are used to estimate clinical and cost effectiveness, evidence for which will typically be drawn from a number of different sources.

The sources and methods for eliciting baseline probabilities should be described clearly. These data can be based on 'natural history' (patient outcomes in the absence of treatment or with routine care), sourced from cohort studies. Baseline probabilities may also be derived from the control arms of experimental studies. Sometimes it may be necessary to rely on expert opinion for particular parameters.

Answer 'yes' if the estimates of baseline health outcomes reflect the best available evidence as identified from a recent well-conducted systematic review of the literature. Answer 'partly' if the estimates are not derived from a systematic review but are likely to reflect outcomes for the relevant group of patients in routine NHS practice (for example, if they are derived from a large UK-relevant cohort study). Answer 'no' if the estimates are unlikely to reflect outcomes for the relevant group in routine NHS practice.

2.5 Are the estimates of relative treatment effects from the best available source?

The objective of the analysis of clinical effectiveness is to produce an unbiased estimate of the mean clinical effectiveness of the interventions being compared.

The NICE reference case indicates that evidence on outcomes should be obtained from a systematic review, defined as the systematic location, inclusion, appraisal and synthesis of evidence to obtain a reliable and valid overview of the data relating to a clearly formulated question.

Synthesis of outcome data through meta-analysis is appropriate provided that there are sufficient relevant and valid data obtained using comparable measures of outcome.

Head-to-head RCTs provide the most valid evidence of relative treatment effect. However, such evidence may not always be available. Therefore, data from non-randomised studies may be required to supplement RCT data. Any potential bias arising from the design of the studies used in the assessment should be explored and documented.

Data from head-to-head RCTs should be presented in the base-case analysis, if available. When head-to-head RCTs exist, evidence from indirect or mixed treatment comparison analyses may be presented if it is considered to add information that is not available from the head-to-head comparison. This indirect or mixed treatment comparison must be fully described and presented as additional to the base-case analysis. (A 'mixed treatment comparison' estimates effect sizes using both head-to-head and indirect comparisons.)

If data from head-to-head RCTs are not available, indirect treatment comparison methods should be used. (An 'indirect comparison' is a synthesis of data from a network of trials that compare the interventions of interest with other comparators.)

When multiple interventions are being assessed that have not been compared within a single RCT, data from a series of pairwise head-to-head RCTs should be presented. Consideration should also be given to presenting a combined analysis using a mixed treatment comparison framework if it is considered to add information that is not available from the head-to-head comparison.

Only indirect or mixed treatment comparison methods that preserve randomisation should be used. The principles of good practice for standard meta-analyses should also be followed in mixed and indirect treatment comparisons.

The methods and assumptions that are used to extrapolate short-term results to final outcomes should be clearly presented and there should be documentation of the reasoning underpinning the choice of survival function.

Evidence for the evaluation of diagnostic technologies should normally incorporate evidence on diagnostic accuracy. It is also important to incorporate the predicted changes in health outcomes and costs resulting from treatment decisions based on the test result. The general principles guiding the assessment of the clinical and cost effectiveness of diagnostic interventions should be the same as for other technologies. However, particular consideration of the methods of analysis may be required, particularly in relation to evidence synthesis. Evidence for the effectiveness of diagnostic technologies should include the costs and outcomes for people whose test results lead to an incorrect diagnosis, as well as for those who are diagnosed correctly.

As for other technologies, RCTs have the potential to capture the pathway of care involving diagnostic technologies, but their feasibility and availability may be limited. Other study designs should be assessed on the basis of their fitness for purpose, taking into consideration the aim of the study (for example, to evaluate outcomes, or to evaluate sensitivity and specificity) and the purpose of the diagnostic technology.

Answer 'yes' if the estimates of treatment effect appropriately reflect all relevant studies of the best available quality, as identified through a recent well-conducted systematic review of the literature. Answer 'partly' if the estimates of treatment effect are not derived from a systematic review but are similar in magnitude to the best available estimates (for example, if the economic evaluation is based on a single large study with treatment effects similar to pooled estimates from all relevant studies). Answer 'no' if the estimates of treatment effect are likely to differ substantively from the best available estimates.

2.6   Are all important and relevant costs included?

Costs related to the condition of interest and incurred in additional years of life gained as a result of treatment should be included in the base-case analysis. This should include the costs of handling non-adherence to treatment and treating side effects. Costs that are considered to be unrelated to the condition or intervention of interest should be excluded. If introduction of the intervention requires additional infrastructure to be put in place, consideration should be given to including such costs in the analysis.

Answer 'yes' if all important and relevant resource use and costs are included given the perspective and the research question under consideration. Answer 'partly' if some relevant resource items are omitted but these are unlikely to affect the cost-effectiveness results. Answer 'no' if important resource items are omitted and these are likely to affect the cost-effectiveness results.

2.7   Are the estimates of resource use from the best available source?

It is important to quantify the effect of the interventions on resource use in terms of physical units (for example, days in hospital or visits to a GP) and valuing those effects in monetary terms using appropriate prices and unit costs. Evidence on resource use should be identified systematically. When expert opinion is used as a source of information, any formal methods used to elicit these data should be clearly reported.

Answer 'yes' if the estimates of resource use appropriately reflect all relevant evidence sources of the best available quality, as identified through a recent well-conducted systematic review of the literature. Answer 'partly' if the estimates of resource use are not derived from a systematic review but are similar in magnitude to the best available estimates. Answer 'no' if the estimates of resource use are likely to differ substantively from the best available estimates.

2.8   Are the unit costs of resources from the best available source?

Resources should be valued using the prices relevant to the NHS and PSS. Given the perspective of the NICE reference case, it is appropriate for the financial costs relevant to the NHS/PSS to be used as the basis of costing, although these may not always reflect the full social opportunity cost of a given resource. A first point of reference in identifying costs and prices should be any current official listing published by the Department of Health and/or the Welsh Assembly Government.

When the acquisition price paid for a resource differs from the public list price (for example, pharmaceuticals and medical devices sold at reduced prices to NHS institutions), the public list price should be used in the base-case analysis. Sensitivity analysis should assess the implications of variations from this price. Analyses based on price reductions for the NHS will only be considered when the reduced prices are transparent and can be consistently available across the NHS, and if the period for which the specified price is available is guaranteed.

National data based on healthcare resource groups (HRGs) such as the Payment by Results tariff can be used when they are appropriate and available. However, data based on HRGs may not be appropriate in all circumstances (for example, when the definition of the HRG is broad, or the mean cost probably does not reflect resource use in relation to the intervention(s) under consideration). In such cases, other sources of evidence, such as micro-costing studies, may be more appropriate. When cost data are taken from the literature, the methods used to identify the sources should be defined. When several alternative sources are available, a justification for the costs chosen should be provided and discrepancies between the sources explained. When appropriate, sensitivity analysis should have been undertaken to assess the implications for results of using alternative data sources.

Answer 'yes' if resources are valued using up-to-date prices relevant to the NHS and PSS. Answer 'partly' if the valuations of some resource items differ from current NHS/PSS unit costs but this is unlikely to change the cost-effectiveness results. Answer 'no' if the valuations of some resource items differ substantively from current NHS/PSS unit costs and this is likely to change the cost-effectiveness results.

2.9 Is an appropriate incremental analysis presented or can it be calculated from the data?

An appropriate incremental analysis is one that compares the expected costs and health outcomes of one intervention with the expected costs and health outcomes of the next-best non-dominated alternative.

Standard decision rules should be followed when combining costs and effects, and should reflect any situation where there is dominance or extended dominance. When there is a trade-off between costs and effects, the results should be presented as an ICER: the ratio of the difference in mean costs to the difference in mean outcomes of a technology compared with the next best alternative. In addition to ICERs, expected net monetary or health benefits can be presented using values placed on a QALY gained of £20,000 and £30,000.

For cost-consequence analyses, appropriate incremental analysis can only be done by selecting one of the consequences as the primary measure of effectiveness.

Answer 'yes' if appropriate incremental results are presented, or if data are presented that allow the reader to calculate the incremental results. Answer 'no' if: (a) simple ratios of costs to effects are presented for each alternative compared with a standard intervention; or (b) if options subject to simple or extended dominance are not excluded from the incremental analyses.

2.10 Are all important parameters whose values are uncertain subjected to appropriate sensitivity analysis?

There are a number of potential selection biases and uncertainties in any evaluation (trial- or model-based) and these should be identified and quantified where possible. There are three types of bias or uncertainty to consider:

● Structural uncertainty – for example in relation to the categorisation of different states of health and the representation of different pathways of care. These structural assumptions should be clearly documented and the evidence and rationale to support them provided. The impact of structural uncertainty on estimates of cost effectiveness should be explored by separate analyses of a representative range of plausible scenarios.

- Source of values to inform parameter estimates – the implications of different estimates of key parameters (such as estimates of relative effectiveness) must be reflected in sensitivity analyses (for example, through the inclusion of alternative scenarios). Inputs must be fully justified, and uncertainty explored by sensitivity analysis using alternative input values.
- Parameter precision – uncertainty around the mean health and cost inputs in the model. Distributions should be assigned to characterise the uncertainty associated with the (precision of) mean parameter values. Probabilistic sensitivity analysis is preferred, as this enables the uncertainty associated with parameters to be simultaneously reflected in the results of the model. In non-linear decision models – when there is not a straight-line relationship between inputs and outputs of a model (such as Markov models) – probabilistic methods provide the best estimates of mean costs and outcomes. Simple decision trees are usually linear.

The mean value, distribution around the mean, and the source and rationale for the supporting evidence should be clearly described for each parameter included in the model.

Evidence about the extent of correlation between individual parameters should be considered carefully and reflected in the probabilistic analysis. Assumptions made about the correlations should be clearly presented.

Answer 'yes' if an extensive sensitivity analysis was undertaken that explored all key uncertainties in the economic evaluation. Answer 'partly' if the sensitivity analysis failed to explore some important uncertainties in the economic evaluation. Answer 'no' if the sensitivity analysis was very limited and omitted consideration of a number of important uncertainties, or if the range of values or distributions around parameters considered in the sensitivity analysis were not reported.

2.11   Is there no potential conflict of interest?

The *British Medical Journal* (BMJ) defines competing interests for its authors as follows: 'A competing interest exists when professional judgment concerning a primary interest (such as patients' welfare or the validity of research) may be influenced by a secondary interest (such as financial gain or personal rivalry). It may arise for the authors of a BMJ article when they have a financial interest that may influence—probably without their knowing—their interpretation of their results or those of others.' Whenever a potential financial conflict of interest is possible, this should be declared.

Answer 'yes' if the authors declare that they have no financial conflicts of interest. Answer 'no' if clear financial conflicts of interest are declared or apparent (for example, from the stated affiliation of the authors). Answer 'unclear' if the article does not indicate whether or not there are financial conflicts of interest.

2.12   Overall assessment

The overall methodological study quality of the economic evaluation should be classified as one of the following:

- **Minor limitations** – the study meets all quality criteria, or the study fails to meet one or more quality criteria but this is unlikely to change the conclusions about cost effectiveness.
- **Potentially serious limitations** – the study fails to meet one or more quality criteria and this could change the conclusions about cost effectiveness.
- **Very serious limitations** – the study fails to meet one or more quality criteria and this is highly likely to change the conclusions about cost effectiveness. Such studies should usually be excluded from further consideration.

APPENDIX 13:

NETWORK (MIXED TREATMENT COMPARISON) META-ANALYTIC METHODS USED IN THE ECONOMIC ANALYSIS OF PHARMACOLOGICAL TREATMENTS FOR PEOPLE WITH GAD

Clinical data considered in the network meta-analyses

Clinical data synthesised using network meta-analytic techniques for the economic model on pharmacological treatment for people with GAD consisted of data on treatment discontinuation due to intolerable side effects and data on response for people not discontinuing treatment due to side effects (that is, data on conditional response). All data were derived from trials included in the guideline systematic review of pharmacological interventions for people with GAD. Inspection of the relevant data included in the review indicated that 38 RCTs with 13,298 participants provided direct or indirect evidence on discontinuation due to intolerable side effects between the seven treatment options assessed in the economic analysis (that is, duloxetine, escitalopram, paroxetine, pregabalin, sertraline, venlafaxine XL and no treatment); and 25 RCTs with 9,507 participants provided direct or indirect evidence on conditional response between the seven treatment options assessed. Response, in all 25 trials, was defined as a 50% reduction in HAM-A scores. The rate of conditional response in each arm of a trial was estimated as the number of people in the arm who responded to treatment, divided by the total number of participants in this arm excluding those who discontinued due to intolerable side effects. It must be noted that a small number of trials included in the guideline systematic review reported response data but did not provide data on discontinuation due to intolerable side effects. Consequently, extraction of data on conditional response from these studies was not possible; therefore these studies were not considered in the respective network meta-analysis.

Data on discontinuation due to intolerable side effects that were included in network meta-analysis are presented in Table 91. The evidence network constructed based on these data is shown in Figure 15. Data on conditional response that were considered in network meta-analysis are provided in Table 92. The evidence network constructed from data on conditional response is presented in Figure 16.

Table 91: RCTs reporting data on treatment discontinuation due to intolerable side effects considered in the network meta-analysis

Study	Duration (days)	Placebo 1	Venlafaxine XL 2	Pregabalin 3	Duloxetine 4	Escitalopram 5	Diazepam 6	Buspirone 7	Lorazepam 8	Paroxetine 9	Quetiapine 150mg 10	Sertraline 11
1. ALLGULANDER2001	168	14/130	33/271									
2. RICKELS2000A	56	7/97	49/273									
3. RICKELS2000A	56	7/97	49/273									
4. KASPER2009	60	7/128	22/125	15/121								
5. MONTGOMERY2006	42	10/101	23/113	21/207								
6. HARTFORD2007	70	3/161	18/164		23/162							
7. NICOLINI2009	70	15/170	20/169		20/158							
8. BOSE2008	60	7/140	17/133			9/131						
9. HACKETT2003	60	4/97	40/370				2/89					
10. DAVIDSON1999	56	10/104	50/203					15/98				
11. MONTGOMERY2008	56	9/96		19/177								
12. RICKELS2005	28	9/91		22/270								
13. POHL2005	42	7/86		28/255								
14. PANDE2003	28	7/69		16/139					19/68			
15. PFIZER2005	61	7/67		25/135					26/64			
16. FELTNER2003	28	4/67		18/136					24/68			
17. KOPONEN2007	63	4/175			45/338							
18. RYNN2008	70	13/159	34/168									

Study									
19. DAVIDSON2004	56	8/159		14/158					
20. LENZE2009	84	4/92		3/85					
21. BALDWIN2006	84	4/139		22/269					13/140
22. ASTRAZENECA2007B	56	15/215		25/213					41/219
23. ANSSEAU1991	28	0/57			2/54				
24. RICKELS2000B	60	7/104			15/104				
25. ANDREATINI2002	28	1/12			1/12				
26. SRAMEK1996	42	1/82				9/80			
27. POLLACK1997	42	11/112				22/115			
28. PFIZER2008	28	2/57					14/55	2/55	
29. GSK2005	56	6/182						22/179	
30. POLLACK2001	60	6/163						17/161	
31. RICKELS2003	60	12/180						43/385	
32. GSK2002	56	5/167						9/168	
33. HEWETT2001	56	2/186						18/188	
34. ASTRAZENECA2007A	56	9/217						17/217	35/218
35. ASTRAZENECA2007C	56	16/235							46/241
36. ALLGULANDER2004	84	19/190							
37. BRAWMAN-MINTZER2006	70	3/163							15/188
38. BIELSKI2005	180			4/61				14/62	9/165

Figure 15: Evidence network of data on treatment discontinuation due to intolerable side effects considered in the network meta-analysis. Drugs in grey shading were not considered in the economic analysis but were included in network meta-analysis to strengthen inference on the relative effect of the other treatment options.

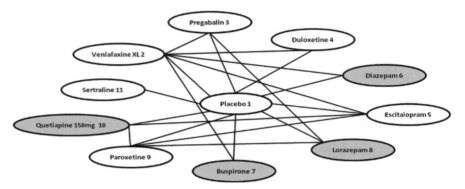

Network meta-analyses of data on discontinuation due to intolerable side effects and data on conditional response – full random effects models

Two separate full random effects models were constructed to estimate the relative effect between k interventions, using data from the 38 RCTs reporting data on discontinuation due to intolerable side effects summarised in Table 91 (model 1a) and the 25 RCTs reporting data on conditional response summarised in Table 92 (model 2a). In each model, the data for each trial j comprised a binomial likelihood:

$$r_{jk} \sim \text{Bin}\,(p_{jk},\, n_{jk})$$

where p_{jk} is the probability of the event of interest (that is, discontinuation due to intolerable side effects in model 1a and conditional response in model 2a) in trial j under treatment k, r_{jk} is the number of people experiencing the event in trial j under treatment k, and n_{jk} is the total number of people at risk of the event in trial j under treatment k.

The duration of the trials considered in the analysis varied from 28 to 196 days in model 1a and from 28 to 84 days in model 2a. Both models assumed constant hazards $\exp(\theta_{jk})$ acting over a period T_j in days. Thus, in each model, the probability of the event of interest by the end of the period T_j for treatment k in trial j was:

$$p_{jk}(T_j) = 1 - \exp\,(-\exp(\theta_{jk})\, T_j)$$

Treatment effects were modelled on the log-hazard rate scale and were assumed to be additive to the baseline treatment b in trial j:

$$\theta_{jk} = \mu_{jb} \qquad\qquad \text{for } k = b;$$
$$\theta_{jk} = \mu_{jb} + \delta_{jkb} \qquad \text{for } k \neq b$$

Table 92: RCTs reporting data on conditional response considered in the network meta-analysis

Study	Duration (days)	Placebo 1	Pregabalin 2	Venlafaxine XL 3	Duloxetine 4	Escitalopram 5	Diazepam 6	Quetiapine 150mg 7	Paroxetine 8	Sertraline 9
1. FELTNER2003	28	29/63	72/118							
2. PANDE2003	28	17/62	51/123							
3. PFIZER2005	61	24/60	55/110							
4. POHL2005	42	28/79	134/227							
5. RICKELS2005	28	29/82	140/248							
6. MONTGOMERY2008	56	39/87	90/158							
7. KASPER2009	60	59/121	71/106	55/103						
8. MONTGOMERY2006	42	45/91	117/186	70/90						
9. DAVIDSON1999	56	35/94		87/153						
10. HARTFORD2007	70	58/158		86/146	70/139					
11. NICOLINI2009	70	69/155		97/149	98/138					
12. BOSE2008	60	57/133		67/116		67/122				
13. HACKETT2003	60	44/93		200/330			50/87			
14. KOPONEN2007	63	53/171			189/293					
15. RYNN2008	70	48/146			67/134					
16. ASTRAZENECA2007B	56	98/200				109/188		133/178		
17. BALDWIN2006	84	83/135				204/247			84/127	
18. ANSSEAU1991	28	19/57					35/52			
19. RICKELS2000B	60	46/97					66/89			
20. ASTRAZENECA2007C	56	114/219						139/195		
21. ASTRAZENECA2007A	56	113/208						153/183	141/200	
22. GSK2005	56	66/176							65/157	
23. POLLACK2001	60	77/157							100/144	
24. ALLGULANDER2004	84	55/171								103/173
25. BRAWMAN-MINTZER2006	70	78/160								97/156

Figure 16: Evidence network of data on conditional response considered in the network meta-analysis. Drugs in grey shading were not considered in the economic analysis but were included in network meta-analysis to strengthen inference on the relative effect of the other treatment options.

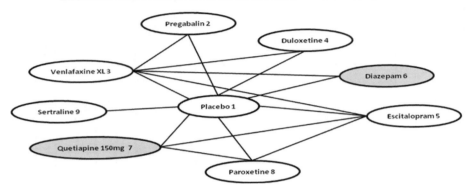

where μ_{jb} is the log hazard of the event (that is, discontinuation due to intolerable side effects in model 1a and conditional response in model 2a) for 'baseline' treatment b in trial j and δ_{jkb} is the trial-specific log-hazard ratio of treatment k relative to treatment b.

The two full random effects models took into account the correlation structure induced by 14 three-arm trials included in the 38 RCTs considered in model 1a and nine three-arm trials included in the 25 RCTs considered in model 2a; this type of model structure relies on the realisation of the bivariate normal distribution as a univariate marginal distribution and a univariate conditional distribution (Higgins & Whitehead, 1996):

In each model, the trial-specific log-hazard ratios for every pair of interventions were assumed to come from a normal random effects distribution:

$$\delta_{jkb} \sim Normal\ (d_{kb},\ \sigma^2)$$

The mean of this distribution (d_{kb}) is the true mean effect size between k and b and σ^2 is the variance of the normal distribution which was assumed to be common in all pairs of treatments, in each of the models.

Vague priors were assigned to trial baselines, mean treatment effects and common variance, separately in each model:

$$\mu_{jb},\ d_{kb} \sim Normal\ (0,\ 100^2); \quad \sigma \sim Uniform\ (0,2)$$

In addition, two separate random effects models (models 1b and 2b) were constructed to estimate the baseline placebo effect on discontinuation due to side effects and on conditional response, using data from 40 trials (model 1b) and 26 trials (model 2b) with a placebo arm, respectively, included in the guideline systematic

**Table 93: Data on discontinuation due to intolerable side effects in all placebo
arms of RCTs included in the guideline systematic review**

Study	Duration (days)	Placebo
1. ALLGULANDER2001	168	14/130
2. GELENBERG2000	196	18/127
3. RICKELS2000A	56	7/97
4. KASPER2009	60	7/128
5. MONTGOMERY2006	42	10/101
6. HARTFORD2007	70	3/161
7. NICOLINI2009	70	15/170
8. BOSE2008	60	7/140
9. HACKETT2003	60	4/97
10. DAVIDSON1999	56	10/104
11. MONTGOMERY2008	56	9/96
12. RICKELS2005	28	9/91
13. POHL2005	42	7/86
14. PANDE2003	28	7/69
15. PFIZER2005	61	7/67
16. FELTNER2003	28	4/67
17. KOPONEN2007	63	4/175
18. RYNN2008	70	13/159
19. DAVIDSON2004	56	8/159
20. LENZE2009	84	4/92
21. BALDWIN2006	84	4/139
22. ASTRAZENECA2007B	56	15/215
23. ANSSEAU1991	28	0/57
24. RICKELS2000B	60	7/104
25. ANDREATINI2002	28	1/12
26. SRAMEK1996	42	1/82
27. POLLACK1997	42	11/112

Continued

Table 93: (*Continued*)

28. PFIZER2008	28	2/57
29. GSK2005	56	6/182
30. POLLACK2001	60	6/163
31. RICKELS2003	60	12/180
32. GSK2002	56	5/167
33. HEWETT2001	56	2/186
34. ASTRAZENECA2007A	56	9/217
35. ASTRAZENECA2007C	56	16/235
36. ALLGULANDER2004	84	19/190
37. BRAWMAN-MINTZER2006	70	3/163
38. ASTRAZENECA2008	64	3/227
39. DARCIS1995	28	1/56
40. LLORCA2002	84	4/113

review. Data for model 1b are shown in Table 93; data for model 2b are shown in Table 94. In model 1b and 2b, the placebo effect (φ_j) was again modelled on a log-hazard scale and was assumed to come from a normal random effects distribution:

$$\varphi_j \sim Normal\ (B,\ \omega^2)$$

$$B \sim Normal\ (0,\ 100^2); \quad \omega \sim Uniform\ (0,2)$$

$$p_j(T_j) = 1 - \exp\ (-\exp(\varphi_j)\ T_j)$$

Subsequently, for each outcome of interest, the absolute log hazard θ_{jk} of each drug k was estimated based on the treatment effect relative to placebo (as estimated in models 1a and 2a for discontinuation due to intolerable side effects and conditional response, respectively) added to a random value of the absolute log hazard of placebo (estimated in models 1b and 2b for discontinuation due to intolerable side effects and conditional response, respectively). The output of each pair of models (that is, models 1a and 1b; models 2a and 2b) used in the economic analysis was the probability of discontinuation due to intolerable side effects (models 1a and 1b) and probability of conditional response (models 2a and 2b) for each intervention by the end of 56 days (8 weeks). The estimated probabilities for placebo were used to populate the 'no treatment' arm of the economic model.

Table 94: Data on conditional response in all placebo arms of RCTs included in the guideline systematic review

Study	Duration (days)	Placebo
1. FELTNER2003	28	29/63
2. PANDE2003	28	17/62
3. PFIZER2005	61	24/60
4. POHL2005	42	28/79
5. RICKELS2005	28	29/82
6. MONTGOMERY2008	56	39/87
7. KASPER2009	60	59/121
8. MONTGOMERY2006	42	45/91
9. DAVIDSON1999	56	35/94
10. HARTFORD2007	70	58/158
11. NICOLINI2009	70	69/155
12. BOSE2008	60	57/133
13. HACKETT2003	60	44/93
14. KOPONEN2007	63	53/171
15. RYNN2008	70	48/146
16. ASTRAZENECA2007B	56	98/200
17. BALDWIN2006	84	83/135
18. ANSSEAU1991	28	19/57
19. RICKELS2000B	60	46/97
20. ASTRAZENECA2007C	56	114/219
21. ASTRAZENECA2007A	56	113/208
22. GSK2005	56	66/176
23. POLLACK2001	60	77/157
24. ALLGULANDER2004	84	55/171
25. BRAWMAN-MINTZER2006	70	78/160
26. ASTRAZENECA2008	64	54/224

Analysis was undertaken following Bayesian statistics principles and conducted using Markov chain Monte Carlo simulation techniques implemented in WinBUGS 1.4 (Lunn *et al.*, 2000; Spiegelhalter *et al.*, 2001). In each pair of models (models 1a and 1b; 2a and 2b) the first 60,000 iterations were discarded, and 300,000 further iterations were run; because of high autocorrelation observed in some model parameters, the model was thinned so that every 30th simulation was retained. Consequently, 10,000 posterior simulations were recorded for each pair of models.

The goodness of fit of the models 1a and 2a was tested using the residual deviance (resdev). The resdev of model 1a was 93.02 (which is acceptable, given that the model has 90 degrees of freedom); the resdev of model 2a was 41.29 (which is, again, satisfactory, since the model has 59 degrees of freedom).

The WinBUGS code used to estimate, separately, the 8-week (56 days) probability of discontinuation due to intolerable side effects and the 8-week (56 days) probability of conditional response is provided in Table 95.

Summary statistics for the treatment options considered in the economic analysis are provided in Table 96 (models 1a and 1b) and Table 97 (models 2a and 2b). Results are reported as mean values with 95% credible intervals, which are analogous to confidence intervals in frequentist statistics.

Table 95: WinBUGS code used to estimate the probability of discontinuation due to intolerable side effects and the probability of conditional response at 56 days of all treatment options considered in the economic analysis

```
model{
sw[1] <- 0
for(i in 1:NA){
r[i] ~ dbin(p[i],n[i])                            #binomial likelihood
theta[i] < -mu[s[i]]+ delta[i]*(1-equals(t[i],b[i]))   #baseline and treatment effects
delta[i] ~ dnorm(md[i],taud[i])                   #trial-specific log-hazard
                                                   distributions

taud[i] <- tau * (1 + equals(m[i],3) /3)          #precisions of log-hazard
                                                   distributions

md[i] <- d[t[i]] - d[b[i]] + equals(m[i],3) * sw[i]   #mean of random effect
p[i] <- (1-exp(-lam[i]*ds[i]/56))                 #prob of event (ds = days; 56
                                                   days = 8 weeks)
log(lam[i]) <- theta[i]                           #log rates for each arm
rhat[i] <- p[i] * n[i]                            #predicted events
dev[i] <- -2 *r[i]*log(rhat[i]/r[i])              #deviance residuals for data i
}
resdev <-sum(dev[])                               #total deviance

for (i in 2:NA) { sw[i] <- (delta[i-1] - d[t[i-1]]
+ d[b[i-1]] ) /2}                                 #adjustment for 3-arm trials
```

```
#priors
for( j in 1:NS){ mu[j] ~ dnorm(0,.0001)}        #vague priors for trial baselines
tau <- 1/(sd*sd)                                #precision
sd ~ dunif(0,2)                                 #vague prior for random effects
                                                standard deviation

d[1] < -0
for (k in 2:NT){d[k] ~ dnorm(0,.0001)           #vague priors for basic parameters
log(hazr[k]) <-d[k]                             #hazard ratios
}


#code for absolute effect on baseline (placebo, treatment 1)
for (i in 1:NSb) {
rb[i] ~ dbin(pb[i],nb[i])                       #binomial likelihood
pb[i] <- (1-exp(-lamb[i]*dsb[i]/56))            #prob of event (dsb = days; 56
                                                days = 8 weeks)
log(lamb[i]) <- mub[sb[i]]                       #log rate
}


for ( j in 1:NSb) {mub[j] ~ dnorm(mb,tab)}      # priors for outcome and
                                                trial-specific events
mb ~ dnorm(0,.001)
tab <- 1/(sdb*sdb)
sdb ~ dunif(0,2)


#code for predicted effect at 56 days, on a probability scale. Baseline risks in new
placebo trial
d.new[1] <-0
for(k in 2:NT)
{d.new[k] ~ dnorm(d[k],tau)}
for (k in 1:NT)
{theta56[k] <-mub[Z] +d.new[k]
log(lam56[k]) <-theta56[k]
p56[k] <- (1-exp(-lam56[k]))
}
}
```

NA = number of arms; NT = number of treatments; NS = number of studies in models 1a and 2a; NSb = number of studies in models 1b and 2b; Z (number of a new placebo trial) is 41 for the 'discontinuation due to side effects' model 1b and 27 for the 'conditional response' model 2b

Table 96: Summary statistics of WinBUGS models 1a and 1b (discontinuation due to intolerable side effects)

Node	Mean	SD	MC error	2.50%	Median	97.50%	Start	Sample
d[2]	0.9254	0.1346	0.003367	0.6768	0.9231	1.1990	60001	10000
d[3]	0.3760	0.1627	0.003669	0.0585	0.3725	0.6991	60001	10000
d[4]	1.1610	0.2022	0.003266	0.7633	1.1550	1.5780	60001	10000
d[5]	0.4657	0.1936	0.004651	0.0829	0.4642	0.8589	60001	10000
d[9]	0.8670	0.1661	0.003578	0.5426	0.8657	1.2160	60001	10000
d[11]	0.1498	0.3523	0.007745	−0.5070	0.1479	0.8550	60001	10000
hazr[2]	2.5460	0.3474	0.008549	1.9680	2.5170	3.3160	60001	10000
hazr[3]	1.4760	0.2433	0.005356	1.0600	1.4510	2.0120	60001	10000
hazr[4]	3.2610	0.6767	0.011020	2.1450	3.1740	4.8440	60001	10000
hazr[5]	1.6230	0.3186	0.007989	1.0860	1.5910	2.3600	60001	10000
hazr[9]	2.4130	0.4094	0.008626	1.7210	2.3770	3.3730	60001	10000
hazr[11]	1.2380	0.4689	0.009258	0.6023	1.1590	2.3510	60001	10000
p56[1]	0.0583	0.0398	3.71E-04	0.0136	0.0483	0.1614	60001	10000
p56[2]	0.1423	0.0963	0.001022	0.0312	0.1183	0.3953	60001	10000
p56[3]	0.0858	0.0624	6.58E-04	0.0172	0.0693	0.2560	60001	10000
p56[4]	0.1750	0.1155	0.001041	0.0373	0.1468	0.4749	60001	10000
p56[5]	0.0935	0.0674	7.27E-04	0.0182	0.0761	0.2750	60001	10000
p56[9]	0.1348	0.0931	9.15E-04	0.0291	0.1113	0.3808	60001	10000
p56[11]	0.0725	0.0599	7.56E-04	0.0127	0.0559	0.2368	60001	10000
resdev	93.02	70.08	0.703200	−45.79	92.84	227	60001	10000
sd	0.2098	0.1193	0.005348	0.0146	0.2103	0.4521	60001	10000
sdb	0.6258	0.1158	0.001069	0.4229	0.6181	0.8742	60001	10000

Table 97: Summary statistics of WinBUGS models 2a and 2b (conditional response)

Node	Mean	SD	MC error	2.50%	Median	97.50%	Start	Sample
d[2]	0.4920	0.0959	0.001203	0.2995	0.4936	0.6820	60001	10000
d[3]	0.5708	0.0899	0.001106	0.3933	0.5716	0.7513	60001	10000
d[4]	0.6713	0.1190	0.001221	0.4375	0.6712	0.9052	60001	10000
d[5]	0.4598	0.1236	0.001228	0.2127	0.4584	0.7029	60001	10000
d[8]	0.2785	0.1140	0.001165	0.0574	0.2769	0.5071	60001	10000
d[9]	0.6048	0.1744	0.001770	0.2640	0.6038	0.9520	60001	10000
hazr[2]	1.6430	0.1577	0.001986	1.3490	1.6380	1.9780	60001	10000
hazr[3]	1.7770	0.1602	0.001955	1.4820	1.7710	2.1200	60001	10000
hazr[4]	1.9710	0.2359	0.002430	1.5490	1.9570	2.4730	60001	10000
hazr[5]	1.5960	0.1981	0.001962	1.2370	1.5810	2.0200	60001	10000
hazr[8]	1.3300	0.1528	0.001561	1.0590	1.3190	1.6600	60001	10000
hazr[9]	1.8590	0.3286	0.003300	1.3020	1.8290	2.5910	60001	10000
p56[1]	0.4277	0.1168	0.001208	0.2231	0.4173	0.6838	60001	10000
p56[2]	0.5904	0.1450	0.001492	0.3147	0.5893	0.8719	60001	10000
p56[3]	0.6160	0.1453	0.001476	0.3371	0.6153	0.8917	60001	10000
p56[4]	0.6509	0.1467	0.001506	0.3571	0.6521	0.9194	60001	10000
p56[5]	0.5788	0.1479	0.001512	0.3051	0.5760	0.8699	60001	10000
p56[8]	0.5190	0.1445	0.001588	0.2611	0.5107	0.8219	60001	10000
p56[9]	0.6287	0.1527	0.001496	0.3290	0.6304	0.9101	60001	10000
resdev	41.29	88.88	0.988100	−129.4	40.48	216.6	60001	10000
sd	0.1782	0.0524	7.35E-04	0.0835	0.1749	0.2904	60001	10000
sdb	0.3719	0.0648	6.81E-04	0.2641	0.3648	0.5192	60001	10000

12   REFERENCES

Agency for Health Care Policy and Research (1993) *Depression in Primary Care: Treatment of Major Depression.* Washington DC: US Department of Health and Human Services.

AGREE Collaboration (2003) Development and validation of an international appraisal instrument for assessing the quality of clinical practice guidelines: the AGREE project. *Quality and Safety in Health Care, 12*, 18–23.

Akhondzadeh, S., Naghavi, H. R., Vazirian, M., *et al.* (2001) Passionflower in the treatment of generalized anxiety: a pilot double-blind randomized controlled trial with oxazepam. *Journal of Clinical Pharmacy and Therapeutics, 26*, 363–367.[31]

Allgulander, C., Hackett, D. & Salinas, E. (2001) Venlafaxine extended release (ER) in the treatment of generalised anxiety disorder. *British Journal of Psychiatry, 179*, 15–22.

Allgulander, C., Dahl, A. A., Austin, C., *et al.* (2004) Efficacy of sertraline in a 12-week trial for generalized anxiety disorder. *American Journal of Psychiatry, 161*, 1624–1649.

Allgulander, C., Florea, I. & Huusom, A. K. T. (2006) Prevention of relapse in generalized anxiety disorder by escitalopram treatment. *International Journal of Neuropsychopharmacology, 9*, 495–505.

Allgulander, C., Jorgensen, T., Wade, A., *et al.* (2007) Health-related quality of life (HRQOL) among patients with generalised anxiety disorder: evaluation conducted alongside an escitalopram relapse prevention trial. *Current Medical Research and Opinion, 23*, 2543–2549.

Alonso, J., Angermeyer, M. C., Bernert, S., *et al.* (2004a) Disability and quality of life impact of mental disorders in Europe: results from the European Study of the Epidemiology of Mental Disorders (ESEMeD) project. *Acta Psychiatrica Scandinavica, 109* (Suppl. 420), 38–46.

Alonso, J., Angermeyer, M.C., Bernet, S., *et al.* (2004b) Prevalence of mental disorders in Europe: results from the European study of the epidemiology of mental disorders (ESEMeD) project. *Acta Psychiatrica Scandinavica, 109*, 21–27.

Alvidrez, J. & Azocar, F. (1999) Distressed women's clinic patients: preferences for mental health treatments and perceived obstacles. *General Hospital Psychiatry, 21*, 340–347.

Amsterdam, J. D., Li, Y., Soeller, I., *et al.* (2009) A randomized, double-blind, placebo-controlled trial of oral matricaria recutita (chamomile) extract therapy for generalized anxiety disorder. *Journal of Clinical Psychopharmacology, 29*, 378–382.

---

[31]This is the reference for study ID AKHONDZADEH2001A.

Andlin-Sobocki, P. & Wittchen, H.-U. (2005) Cost of anxiety disorders in Europe. *European Journal of Neurology, 12* (Suppl. 1), 39–44.

Andlin-Sobocki, P., Jönsson, B., Wittchen, H.-U., *et al.* (2005) Cost of disorders of the brain in Europe. *European Journal of Neurology, 12* (Suppl. 1), 1–27.

Andreatini, R., Sartori, V. A., Seabra, M. L. V., *et al.* (2002) Effect of valepotriates (valerian extract) in generalized anxiety disorder: a randomized placebo-controlled study. *Phytotherapy Research, 16*, 650–654.

Andrews, G. & Tolkein II Team (2006) *A Needs-Based, Costed Stepped-Care Model for Mental Health Services.* Sydney: Clinical Research Unit for Anxiety and Depression, University of New South Wales.

Andrews, G., Issakidis, C., Sanderson, K., *et al.* (2004) Utilising survey data to inform public policy: comparison of the cost-effectiveness of treatment of ten mental disorders. *British Journal of Psychiatry, 184*, 526–533.

Ansseau, M., Olie, J. P., von Frenckell, R., *et al.* (1991) Controlled comparison of the efficacy and safety of four doses of suriclone, diazepam, and placebo in generalized anxiety disorder. *Psychopharmacology, 104*, 439–443.

APA (1980) *Diagnostic and Statistical Manual of Mental Disorders* (3rd edition) (DSM-III). Washington, DC: APA.

APA (1987) *Diagnostic and Statistical Manual of Mental Disorders* (3rd edition – revision) (DSM–III-R). Washington, DC: APA.

APA (1994) *Diagnostic and Statistical Manual of Mental Disorders* (4th edition) (DSM–IV). Washington, DC: APA.

Arntz, A. (2003) Cognitive therapy versus applied relaxation as treatment of generalized anxiety disorder. *Behaviour Research and Therapy, 41*, 633–646.

Arroll, B. & Kendrick, T. (2009) Anxiety. In *Primary Care Mental Health* (eds L. Gask, H. Lester, T. Kendrick & R. Peveler), pp. 147–149. Glasgow: Bell and Bain Ltd.

Ashton, H. (1986) Adverse effects of prolonged benzodiazepine use. *Adverse Drug Reaction Bulletin, 118*, 440–443.

AstraZeneca (2007a) An international, multi-center, randomized, double-blind, parallel-group, placebo-controlled, active-controlled study of the efficacy and safety of sustained-release quetiapine fumarate (Seroquel SR) in the treatment of generalized anxiety disorder (Silver Study). Available from ClinicalTrials.gov (NCT00322595)

AstraZeneca (2007b) A multicenter, randomized, double-blind, parallel-group, placebo-controlled, active-controlled study of the efficacy and safety of sustained-release quetiapine fumarate (Seroquel) compared with placebo in the treatment of generalized anxiety disorder (Gold Study). Available from ClinicalTrials.gov (NCT00329446)

AstraZeneca (2007c) A multi-center, randomized, parallel-group, placebo-controlled study of the efficacy and safety of sustained-release quetiapine fumarate (Seroquel) compared with placebo in the treatment of generalized anxiety disorder (Titanium study). Available from ClinicalTrials.gov (NCT00329264)

AstraZeneca (2008) A multi-center, randomized, parallel-group, placebo-controlled phase III study of the efficacy and safety of quetiapine fumarate extended-release

(Seroquel XR) as monotherapy in the treatment of elderly patients with generalized anxiety disorder (Chromium study). Available from ClinicalTrials.gov (NCT00389064)

Baldwin, D. S. & Ajel, K. (2007) Role of pregabalin in the treatment of generalized anxiety disorder. *Neuropsychiatric Disease and Treatment, 3*, 185–191.

Baldwin, D. S., Anderson, I. M., Nutt, D. J., *et al.* (2005) Evidence-based guidelines for the pharmacological treatment of anxiety disorders: recommendations from the British Association for Psychopharmacology. *Journal of Psychopharmacolgy, 19*, 567–596.

Baldwin, D. S., Huusom, A. K. T. & Maehlum, E. (2006) Escitalopram and paroxetine in the treatment of generalised anxiety disorder: randomised, placebo-controlled, double-blind study. *British Journal of Psychiatry, 189*, 264–272.

Ball, S., Kuhn, A., Wall, D., *et al.* (2005) Selective serotonin reuptake inhibitor treatment for generalized anxiety disorder: a double-blind, prospective comparison between paroxetine and sertraline. *Journal of Clinical Psychiatry, 66*, 94–99.

Bandelow, B., Sievert, K., Röthemeyer, M., *et al.* (1995) What treatments do patients with panic disorder and agoraphobia get? *European Archives of Psychiatry and Clinical Neuroscience, 245*, 165–171.

Barlow, D. H. (2000) Unravelling the mysteries of anxiety and its disorders from the perspective of emotion theory. *American Psychologist, 55*, 1247–1263.

Barlow, D. H., Rapee, R. M. & Brown, T. A. (1992) Behavioral treatment of generalized anxiety disorder. *Behavior Therapy, 23*, 551–570.

Batelaan, N., Smit, F., van Balkom, T., *et al.* (2007) Societal costs of panic disorder and subthreshold panic disorder. *Journal of Affective Disorders, 104*, 127–136.

Baumeister, H. & Harter, M. (2007) Prevalence of mental disorders based on general population surveys. *Social Psychiatry and Epidemiology, 42*, 537–546.

Beasley, C. M., Koke, S. C., Nilsson, M. E., *et al.* (2000) Adverse events and treatment discontinuations in clinical trials of fluoxetine in major depressive disorder: an updated meta-analysis. *Clinical Therapeutics, 22*, 1319–1330.

Beck, A. T. & Emery, G., Greenberg, R. L. (1985) *Anxiety Disorders and Phobias: A Cognitive Perspective*. New York: Basic Books.

Becker, E., Goodwin, R., Holting, C., *et al.* (2003) Content of worry in the community: what do people with generalized anxiety disorder or other disorders worry about? *Journal of Nervous and Mental Disease, 191*, 688–691.

Bee, P., Bower, P., Lovell, K., *et al.* (2008) Psychotherapy mediated by remote communication technologies: a meta-analytic review. *BMC Psychiatry, 8*, 60.

Berg, A. L., Sandell, R. & Sandahl, C. (2009) Affect-focused body psychotherapy in patients with generalized anxiety disorder: evaluation of an integrative method, *Journal of Psychotherapy Integration, 19*, 67–85.

Berlin, J. A. (2001) Does blinding of readers affect the results of meta-analyses? *Lancet, 350*, 185–186.

Bielski, R. J. & Bose, A. (2005) A double-blind comparison of escitalopram and paroxetine in the long-term treatment of generalised anxiety disorder. *Annals of Clinical Psychiatry, 17*, 65–69.

Bishop, S. J., Duncan, J. & Lawrence, J. D. (2004) State anxiety modulation of the amygdale response to unattended threat-related stimuli. *Nature Neuroscience, 7,* 184–188.

Bitran, S., Barlow, D. H. & Spiegel, D. A. (2009) Generalized anxiety disorder. In *New Oxford Textbook of Psychiatry* (eds M. G. Gelder, M. G. Andreasen, J. J. Lopez-Ibor & J. R. Geddes), pp. 729–739. New York: Oxford University Press.

Bjorner, T. & Kjolsrod, L. (2002) How GPs understand patients' stories: a qualitative study of benzodiazepine and minor opiate prescribing in Norway. *European Journal of General Practice, 8,* 25–30.

Blair, D. T. & Ramones, V. A. (1996) The undertreatment of anxiety: overcoming the confusion and stigma. *Journal of Psychosocial Nursing and Mental Health Services, 34,* 9–18.

Blazer, D. G., Hughes, D., George, L. K., *et al.* (1991) Generalized anxiety disorder. In *Psychiatric Disorders in America: The Epidemiologic Catchment Area Study* (eds L. N. Robins & D. A. Regier). New York: The Free Press.

Blenkiron, P. (2001) Coping with depression: a pilot study to assess the efficacy of a self-help audio cassette. *British Journal of General Practice, 51,* 366–370.

Boardman, J., Henshaw, C. & Willmott, S. (2004) Needs for mental health treatment among general practice attenders. *British Journal of Psychiatry, 185,* 318–327.

Bond, A. J., Wingrove, J., Curran, H. V., *et al.* (2002) Treatment of generalised anxiety disorder with a short course of psychological therapy, combined with buspirone or placebo. *Journal of Affective Disorders, 72,* 267–271.[32]

Borkovec, T. D. & Costello, E. (1993) Efficacy of applied relaxation and cognitive-behavioral therapy in the treatment of generalized anxiety disorder. *Journal of Consulting and Clinical Psychology, 61,* 611–619.

Borkovec, T. D. & Roemer, L. (1995) Perceived function of worry among generalized anxiety disorder subjects: distraction from more emotionally distressing topics? *Journal of Behavior Therapy and Experimental Psychiatry, 26,* 25–30.

Borkovec, T. D., Newman, M. G., Pincus, A. L., *et al.* (2002) A component analysis of cognitive-behavioral therapy for generalized anxiety disorder and the role of interpersonal problems. *Journal of Consulting and Clinical Psychology, 70,* 288–298.

Bose, A., Korotzer, A., Gommoll, C., *et al.* (2008) Randomized placebo-controlled trial of escitalopram and venlafaxine XR in the treatment of generalized anxiety disorder. *Depression and Anxiety,* 25, 854–861.

Bourin, M. & Malinge, M. (1995) Controlled comparison of the effects and abrupt discontinuation of buspirone and lorazepam. *Progress in Neuro-Psychopharmacology and Biological Psychiatry, 19,* 567–575.

Bower, P. & Gilbody, S. (2005) Stepped care in psychological therapies: access, effectiveness and efficiency: narrative literature review. *The British Journal of Psychiatry, 186,* 11–17.

---

[32]This is the reference for study ID BOND2002B.

References

Bower, P., Rowland, N. & Hardy, R. (2003) The clinical effectiveness of counselling in primary care: a systematic review and meta-analysis. *Psychological Medicine, 33*, 203–215.

Bower, P., Gilbody, S., Richards, D., *et al.* (2006) Collaborative care for depression in primary care: making sense of a complex intervention: systematic review and meta-regression. *British Journal of Psychiatry, 189*, 484–493.

Bowman, D., Scogin, F., Floyd, M., *et al.* (1997) Efficacy of self-examination therapy in the treatment of generalized anxiety disorder. *Journal of Counselling Psychology, 44*, 267–273.

Brambilla, P., Cipriani, A., Hotopf, M., *et al.* (2005) Side-effect profile of fluoxetine in comparison with other SSRIs, tricyclic and new antidepressants: a meta-analysis of clinical trial data. *Pharmacopsychiatry, 38*, 69–77.

Brawman-Mintzer, O., Knapp, R. G. & Nietert, P. J. (2005) Adjunctive risperidone in generalized anxiety disorder: a double-blind, placebo-controlled study. *Journal of Clinical Psychiatry, 66*, 1321–1325.

Brawman-Mintzer, O., Knapp, R. G., Rynn, M., *et al.* (2006) Sertraline treatment for generalized anxiety disorder: a randomized, double-blind, placebo-controlled study. *Journal of Clinical Psychiatry, 67*, 874–881.

Brazier, J. E. & Roberts, J. (2004) The estimation of a preference based measure of health from the SF-12. *Medical Care, 42*, 851–859.

Brazier, J. E., Roberts, J. & Deverill, M. (2002) The estimation of a preference-based measure of health from the SF-36. *Journal of Health Economics, 21*, 271–292.

Breitholtz, E., Westling, B. E. & Öst, L. G. (1998) Cognitions in generalized anxiety disorder and panic disorder patients. *Journal of Anxiety Disorders, 12*, 567–577.

Briggs, A., Sculpher, M., Claxton, C. (2006) Making decision models probabilistic. In *Decision Modelling for Health Economic Evaluation* (eds A. Briggs, M. Sculpher & C. Claxton). New York: Oxford University Press.

British Medical Association & the Royal Pharmaceutical Society of Great Britain (2009) *British National Formulary (BNF) 57*. London: Pharmaceutical Press.

British Medical Association & the Royal Pharmaceutical Society of Great Britain (2010) *British National Formulary (BNF) 59*. London: Pharmaceutical Press.

Brooks, R., with the EuroQol Group (1996) EuroQol: the current state of play. *Health Policy, 37*, 53–72.

Brown, G. W. & Harris, T. O. (1993) Aetiology of anxiety and depressive disorders in an inner-city population: 1-Early adversity. *Psychological Medicine, 23*, 143–154.

Butler, G., Fennell, M., Robson, P., *et al.* (1991) Comparison of behavior therapy and cognitive behavior therapy in the treatment of generalized anxiety disorder. *Journal of Consulting and Clinical Psychology, 59*, 167–175.

Bystritsky, A., Wagner, A. W., Russo, J. E., *et al.* (2005) Assessment of beliefs about psychotropic medication and psychotherapy: development of a measure for patients with anxiety disorders. *General Hospital Psychiatry, 27*, 313–318.

Bystritsky, A., Kerwin, L., Niv, N., *et al.* (2010) Clinical and subthreshold panic disorder. *Depression and Anxiety, 27*, 381–389.

Caldwell, D. M., Ades, A. E. & Higgins, J. P. (2005) Simultaneous comparison of multiple treatments: combining direct and indirect evidence. *British Medical Journal, 331*, 897–900.

Carlbring, P., Westling, B. E., Ljungstrand, P., *et al.* (2001) Treatment of panic disorder via the internet: a randomised trial of a self-help program. *Behavior Therapy, 32,* 751–764.

Carlbring, P., Ekselius, L. & Andersson, G. (2003) Treatment of panic disorder via the internet: a randomized trial of CBT vs. applied relaxation. *Journal of Behavior Therapy and Experimental Psychiatry, 34,* 129–140.

Carlbring, P., Nilsson-Ihrfelt, E., Waara, J., *et al.* (2005) Treatment of panic disorder: live therapy vs. self-help via the internet. *Behaviour Research and Therapy, 43,* 1321–1333.

Carlbring, P., Bohman, S., Brunt, S., *et al.* (2006) Remote treatment of panic disorder: a randomized trial of internet-based cognitive behavior therapy supplemented with telephone calls. *American Journal of Psychiatry, 163,* 2119–2125.

Carter, R. M., Wittchen, H.-U., Pfister, H., *et al.* (2001) One-year prevalence of subthreshold and threshold DSM-IV generalized anxiety disorder in a nationally representative sample. *Depression and Anxiety, 13,* 78–88.

Chouinard, G. (2004) Issues in the clinical use of benzodiazepines: potency, withdrawal, and rebound. *Journal of Clinical Psychiatry, 65,* 7–12.

Christensen, H., Griffiths, K. & Jorm, A. (2004) Delivering interventions for depression by using the internet: randomised controlled trial. *British Medical Journal, 328,* 265.

Clark, D. M., Layard, R. & Smithies, R. (2008) *Improving Access to Psychological Therapy: Initial Evaluation of the Two Demonstration Sites.* CEP Discussion Papers, dp0897. London: Centre for Economic Performance, London School of Economics.

Clark, D. M., Layard, R., Smithies, R., *et al.* (2009) Improving access to psychological therapy: initial evaluation of two UK demonstration sites. *Behaviour Research and Therapy, 47,* 910–920.

Cloos, J. & Ferreira, V. (2009) Current use of benzodiazepines in anxiety disorders. *Current Opinion in Psychiatry, 22,* 90–95.

Cochrane Collaboration (2008) *Review Manager (RevMan) version 5.0.* Copenhagen: Nordic Cochrane Centre. [Computer programme]

Commander, M. J., Odell, S. M., Surtees, P. G., *et al.* (2004) Care pathways for south Asian and white people with depressive and anxiety disorders in the community. *Social Psychiatry and Psychiatric Epidemiology, 39,* 259–264.

Correll, C. U., Leucht, S. & Kane, J. M. (2004) Lower risk for tardive dyskinesia associated with second-generation antipsychotics: a systematic review of 1-year studies. *American Journal of Psychiatry, 161,* 414–425.

Cougle, J. R., Keough, M. E., Riccardi, C. J., *et al.* (2009) Anxiety disorders and suicidality in the National Comorbidity Survey – replication. *Journal of Psychiatric Research, 43,* 825–829.

Craske, M. G., Rapee, R. M., Jackel, L. *et al.* (1989) Qualitative dimensions of worry in DSM-III-R generalized anxiety disorder subjects and nonanxious controls. *Behaviour Research and Therapy, 27,* 397–402.

References

Crits-Christoph, P., Connolly Gibbons, M. B., Narducci, J., *et al.* (2005) Interpersonal problems and the outcome of interpersonally oriented psychodynamic treatment of GAD. *Psychotherapy: Theory, Research, Practice, Training, 2,* 211–224.

Culpepper, L. (2009) Generalized anxiety disorder and medical illness. *Journal of Clinical Psychiatry, 70* (Suppl 2), 20–24.

Curtis, L. (2009) *Unit Costs of Health and Social Care 2009.* Canterbury: University of Kent.

Darcis, T., Ferreri, M., Natens, J., *et al.* (1995) A multicentre double-blind placebo-controlled study investigating the anxiolytic efficacy of hydroxyzine in patients with generalized anxiety. *Human Psychopharmacology: Clinical and Experimental, 10,* 181–187.

Davidson, J. R. T., DuPont, R. L., Hedges, D., *et al.* (1999) Efficacy, safety, and tolerability of venlafaxine extended release and buspirone in outpatients with generalized anxiety disorder. *Journal of Clinical Psychiatry, 60,* 528–535.

Davidson, J. R. T., Bose, A., Korotzer, A., *et al.* (2004) Escitalopram in the treatment of generalized anxiety disorder: double-blind, placebo controlled, flexible-dose study. *Depression and Anxiety, 19,* 234–240.

Davidson, J. R. T., Wittchen, H.-U., Llorca, P. M., *et al.* (2008) Duloxetine treatment for relapse prevention in adults with generalized anxiety disorder: a double-blind placebo-controlled trial. *European Neuropsychopharmacology, 18,* 673–681

Davidson, J. R., Zhang, W., Connor, K. M., *et al.* (2010a) A psychopharmacological treatment algorithm for generalized anxiety disorder (GAD). *Journal of Psychopharmacology, 24,* 3–26.

Davidson, J. R. T., Feltner, D. E., Dugar, A. (2010b) Management of generalized anxiety disorder in primary care: identifying the challenges and unmet needs. *Primary Care Companion Journal of Clinical Psychiatry, 12,* 1–13.

Davis, M., Eshelman, E. R. & McKay, M. (1995) *The Relaxation and Stress Reduction Workbook.* 4th ed. Oakland, California: New Harbinger.

Davison, G. (2000) Stepped care: doing more with less? *Journal of Consulting and Clinical Psychology, 68,* 580–585.

Deacon, B. J. & Abramowitz, J. S. (2005) Patients' perceptions of pharmacological and cognitive-behavioural treatments for anxiety disorders. *Behavior Therapy, 36,* 139–145.

Decker, M. L., Turk, C. L., Hess, B., *et al.* (2008) Emotion regulation among individuals classified with and without generalized anxiety disorder. *Journal of Anxiety Disorders, 22,* 485–494.

Dedovic, K., Duchesne, A., Andrews, J., *et al.* (2009) The brain and the stress axis: the neural correlates of cortisol regulation in response to stress. *NeuroImage, 47,* 864–871.

Demyttenaere, K. & Jaspers, L. (2008) Bupropion and SSI-induced side effects. *Journal of Psychopharmacology, 22,* 792–804.

DH (1999) *National Service Framework for Mental Health: Modern Standards and Service Models.* Available from: http://www.dh.gov.uk/en/Publicationsand statistics/Publications/PublicationsPolicyAndGuidance/DH_4009598 [accessed June 2010]

DH (2010) *NHS Reference Costs 2008–09*. London: DH. Available from: http://www.dh.gov.uk/en/Publicationsandstatistics/Publications/PublicationsPolicy AndGuidance/DH_111591 [accessed May 2010]

Dhillon, S., Yang, L. P. H. & Curran, M.P. (2008) Bupropion: a review of its use in the management of major depressive disorder. *Drugs, 68*, 653–689.

Diefenbach, G. J., Stanley, M. A. & Beck, J. G. (2001a) Worry content reported by older adults with and without generalized anxiety disorder. *Aging and Mental Health, 5*, 269–274.

Diefenbach, G. J., Carthy-Larzelere, M. E., Williamson, D. A., *et al.* (2001b) Anxiety, depression, and the content of worries. *Depression and Anxiety, 14*, 247–250.

Dolan, P. (1997) Modelling valuations for EuroQol health states. *Medical Care, 35*, 1095–1108.

Dolan, P., Gudex, C., Kind, P., Williams, A. (1996) The time trade-off method: results from a general population study. *Health Economics, 5*, 141–154.

Dugas, M. J. & Robichaud, M. (2007) Description of generalized anxiety disorder. In *Cognitive-Behavioral Treatment for Generalized Anxiety Disorder: From Science to Practice* (eds M. J Dugas & M. Robichaud), pp. 1–21. New York: Routledge.

Dugas, M., Ladouceur, R., Leger, E., *et al.* (2003) Group cognitive-behavioral therapy for generalized anxiety disorder: treatment outcome and long-term follow-up. *Journal of Consulting and Clinical Psychology, 71*, 821–825.

Dugas, M. J., Savard, P., Gaudet, A., *et al.* (2007) Can the components of a cognitive model predict the severity of generalized anxiety disorder? *Behavior Therapy, 38*, 169–178.

Dugas, M. J., Brillon, P., Savard, P., *et al.* (2009) A randomized clinical trial of cognitive-behavioral therapy and applied relaxation for adults with generalized anxiety disorder. *Behavior Therapy, 10*, 1–13.

Duggan, S. E. & Fuller, M. A. (2004) Duloxetine: a dual reuptake inhibitor. *The Annals of Pharmacotherapy, 38*, 2078–2085.

DuPont, R. L., Rice, D. P., Miller, L. S., *et al.* (1998) Economic costs of anxiety disorders. *Anxiety, 2*, 167–172.

Durham, R. C., Murphy, T. Allan, T., *et al.* (1994) Cognitive therapy, analytic psychotherapy and anxiety management training for generalized anxiety disorder. *British Journal of Psychiatry, 165*, 315–323.

Durham, R. C., Fisher, P. L., Dow, M. G. T., *et al.* (2004) Cognitive behaviour therapy for good and poor prognosis generalized anxiety disorder. A clinical effectiveness study. *Clinical Psychology and Psychotherapy, 11*, 145–157.

Eccles, M., Freemantle, N. & Mason, J. (1998) North of England evidence based guideline development project: methods of developing guidelines for efficient drug use in primary care. *British Medical Journal, 316*, 1232–1235.

Edwards, J. G. & Anderson, I. (1999) Systematic review and guide to selection of selective serotonin reuptake inhibitors. *Drugs, 57*, 507–533.

Egan, G. (1990) *The Skilled Helper: A Systematic Approach to Effective Helping*. Pacific Grove, California: Brooks/Cole.

References

Egger, M., Juni, P., Bartlett, C., *et al.* (2003) How important are comprehensive literature searches and the assessment of trial quality in systematic reviews? Empirical study. *Health Technology Assessment, 7,* 1–76.

Engel, K., Bandelow, B., Gruber, O., *et al.* (2009) Neuroimaging in anxiety disorders. *Journal of Neural Transmission, 116,* 703–716.

ESEMeD/MHEDEA 2000 Investigators (2004) 12-month comorbidity patterns and associated factors in Europe: results from the European study of the epidemiology of mental disorders (ESEMeD) project. *Acta Psychiatrica Scandinavica, 109* (Suppl. 420), 28–37.

Ettigi, P., Meyerhoff, A. S., Chirban, J. T., *et al.* (1997) The quality of life and employment in panic disorder. *Journal of Nervous Mental Disorders, 185,* 368–372.

Fanselow, M. S. (2000) Contextual fear, gestalt memories and the hippocampus. *Behavioural Brain Research, 110,* 73–81.

Feltner, D. E., Crockatt, J. G., Dubovsky, S. J., *et al.* (2003) A randomized, double-blind, placebo-controlled, fixed-dose, multicentre study of pregabalin in patients with generalized anxiety disorder. *Journal of Clinical Psychopharmacology, 23,* 240–249.

Feltner, D., Wittchen, H-U., Kavoussi, R., *et al.* (2008) Long-term efficacy of pregabalin in generalized anxiety disorder. *International Clinical Psychopharmacology, 23,* 18–28.

Fenwick, E., Klaxton, K. & Schulpher, M. (2001) Representing uncertainty: the role of cost-effectiveness acceptability curves. *Health Economics, 10,* 779–787.

Fresquet, A., Sust, M., Lloret, A., *et al.* (2000) Efficacy and safety of lesopitron in outpatients with generalized anxiety disorder. *Annals of Pharmacotherapy, 34,* 147–153.

Furukawa, T. A., Barbui, C., Cipriani, A., *et al.* (2006). Imputing missing standard deviations in meta-analyses can provide accurate results. *Journal of Clinical Epidemiology, 59,* 7–10.

Garner, M., Mohler, H., Stein, D. J., *et al.* (2009) Research in anxiety disorders: from the bench to the bedside. *European Neuropsychopharmacology, 19,* 381–390.

Gelder, M., Harrison, P. & Cowen, P. (2006) *Shorter Oxford Textbook of Psychiatry.* London: Oxford University Press.

Gelenberg, A. J., Lydiard, B., Rudolph, R. L., *et al.* (2000) Efficacy of venlafaxine extended-release capsules in nondepressed outpatients with generalized anxiety disorder: a 6-month randomized controlled trial. *JAMA: the Journal of the American Medical Association, 283,* 3082–3088.

Gellatly, J., Bower, P., Hennessy, S., *et al.* (2007) What makes self-help interventions effective in the management of depressive symptoms? Meta-analysis and meta-regression. *Psychological Medicine, 37,* 1217–1228.

Gilbody, S., Bower, P., Fletcher, J., *et al.* (2006) Collaborative care for depression: a cumulative meta-analysis and review of longer-term outcomes. *Archives of Internal Medicine, 166,* 2314–2321.

Gili, M., Comas, A., Garcia-Garcia, M., *et al.* (2010) Comorbidity between common mental disorders and chronic somatic diseases in primary care patients. *General Hospital Psychiatry, 32,* 240–245.

Goodman, W. K., Bose, A. & Wang, Q. (2005) Treatment of generalized anxiety disorder with escitalopram: pooled results from double-blind, placebo-controlled trials. *Journal of Affective Disorders, 87,* 161–167.

Goodwin, R. D., Faravelli, C., Rosi, S., *et al.* (2005) The epidemiology of panic disorder and agoraphobia in Europe. *European Neuropsychopharmacology, 15,* 435–443.

GRADE Working Group (2004) Grading quality of evidence and strength of recommendations. *British Medical Journal, 328,* 1490–1497.

Grant, B. F., Hasin, D. S., Stinson, F. S., *et al.* (2004) The epidemiology of DSM-IV panic disorder and agoraphobia in the United States: results from the National Epidemiologic Survey on Alcohol and Related Conditions. *Journal of Clinical Psychiatry, 67,* 363–374.

Grant, B. F., Hasin, D. S., Stinson, F. S., *et al.* (2005) Prevalence, correlates, co-morbidity, and comparative disability of DSM-IV generalized anxiety disorder in the USA: results from the National Epidemiologic Survey on Alcohol and Related Conditions. *Psychological Medicine, 35,* 1747–1759.

Gray, J. A. (1982) *The Neuropsychology of Anxiety.* London: Oxford University Press.

Greenberg, P. E., Sisitsky, T., Kessler, R.C., *et al.* (1999) The economic burden of anxiety disorders in the 1990s. *Journal of Clinical Psychiatry, 60,* 427–435.

Gregorian, R. S., Golden, K. A., Bahce, A., *et al.* (2002) Antidepressant-induced sexual dysfunction. *The Annals of Pharmacotherapy, 36,* 1577–1589.

GSK (2002) A randomized, double-blind, placebo-controlled, flexible dosage trial to evaluate the efficacy and tolerability of paroxetine CR in patients with generalised anxiety disorder (GAD). Unpublished.

GSK (2005) Clinical evaluation of BRL29060A (paroxetine hydrochloride hydrate) in generalized anxiety disorder (GAD): a double-blind, placebo-controlled, comparative study. Unpublished.

Guest, J. F., Russ, J. & Lenox, S. A. (2005) Cost-effectiveness of venlafaxine XL compared with diazepam in the treatment of generalised anxiety disorder in the United Kingdom. *European Journal of Health Economics, 6,* 136–145.

Guizhen, L., Yunjun, Z., Linxiang, G., *et al.* (1998) Comparative study on acupuncture combined with behavioral desensitization for treatment of anxiety neuroses. *American Journal of Acupuncture, 2–3,* 117–120.

Gum, A. M., Arean, P. A., Hunkeler, E., *et al.* (2006) Depression treatment preferences in older primary care patients. *The Gerontological Society of America, 46,* 14–22.

Gunn, J., Diggens, J., Hegarty, K., *et al.* (2006) A systematic review of complex system interventions designed to increase recovery from depression in primary care. *BMC Health Services Research, 6,* 88.

Hackett, D., Haudiquet, V. & Salinas, E. (2003) A method for controlling for a high placebo response rate in a comparison of venlafaxine XR and diazepam in the short-term treatment of patients with generalised anxiety disorder. *European Psychiatry, 18,* 182–187.

Hakkart-van Roijen, L., van Straten, A., Al, M., *et al.* (2006) Cost-utility of brief psychological treatment for depression and anxiety. *The British Journal of Psychiatry, 188,* 323–329.

References

Hales R. E., Hilty, D. A. & Wise, M. G. (1997) A treatment algorithm for the management of anxiety in primary care practice. *Journal of Clinical Psychiatry*, *59* (Suppl. 3), 76–80.

Halligan, S. L., Murray, L., Martins, C., *et al.* (2007) Maternal depression and psychiatric outcomes in adolescent offspring: a 13-year longitudinal study. *Journal of Affective Disorders, 97*, 145–154.

Hansen, R. A., Gartlehner, G., Lohr, K. N., *et al.* (2005) Efficacy and safety of second-generation antidepressants in the treatment of major depressive disorder. *American International Medicine, 143,* 415–426.

Hanus, M., Lafon, J. & Mathieu, M. (2004) Double-blind, randomised, placebo-controlled study to evaluate the efficacy and safety of a fixed combination containing two plant extracts (Crataegus oxyacantha and Eschscholtzia californica) and magnesium in mild-to-moderate anxiety disorders. *Current Medical Research and Opinion, 20*, 63–71.

Hartford, J., Kornstein, S., Liebowitz, M., *et al.* (2007) Duloxetine as an SNRI treatment for generalized anxiety disorder: results from a placebo and active-controlled trial. *International Clinical Psychopharmacology*, *22*, 167–174.

Haslam, C., Brown, S., Atkinson, S., *et al.* (2004) Patients' experiences of medication for anxiety and depression: effects on working life. *Family Practice, 21,* 204–212.

Hazlett-Stevens, H., Craske, M. G., Roy-Byrne, P. P., *et al.* (2002) Predictors of willingness to consider medication and psychosocial treatment for panic disorder in primary care patients. *General Hospital Psychiatry, 24*, 316–321.

Healey, M., Pickens, R., Meish, M.D., *et al.* (1983) Effects of clorazepate, diazepam, lorazepam and placebo on human memory. *Journal of Clinical Psychiatry, 44*, 436–439.

Herrera-Arellano, A., Jimenez-Ferrer, E., Zamilpa, A., *et al.* (2007) Efficacy and tolerability of a standardized herbal product from Galphimia glauca on generalized anxiety disorder. A randomized, double-blind clinical trial controlled with lorazepam. *Planta Medica, 73*, 713–717.

Hettema, J. M., Neale, M. C. & Kendler, K. S. (2001) A review and meta-analysis of the genetic epidemiology of anxiety disorders. *American Journal of Psychiatry, 158*, 1568–1578.

Hettema, J. M., Prescott, C. A. & Kendler, K. S. (2004) Genetic and environmental sources of covariation between generalized anxiety disorder and neuroticism *American Journal of Psychiatry, 161*, 1581–1587.

Hettema, J. M., Prescott, C. A., Myers, J. M., *et al.* (2005) The structure of genetic and environmental risk factors for anxiety disorders in men and women. *Archives of General Psychiatry, 62,* 182–189.

Heuzenroeder, L., Donnelly, M., Haby, M. M., *et al.* (2004) Cost-effectiveness of psychological and pharmacological interventions for generalized anxiety disorder and panic disorder. *Australian and New Zealand Journal of Psychiatry, 38,* 602–612.

Hewett, K. (2001) A double-blind, placebo controlled study to evaluate the efficacy and tolerability of paroxetine in patients with generalised anxiety disorder (GAD). Unpublished.

Higgins, J. P. T. & Green, S. (eds) (2009) *Cochrane Handbook for Systematic Reviews of Interventions*. Version 5.0.2. The Cochrane Collaboration. Available at www.cochrane-handbook.org

Higgins, J. P. T. & Thompson, S. G. (2002) Quantifying heterogeneity in a meta-analysis. *Statistics in Medicine, 21,* 1539–1558.

Higgins, J. P. T. & Whitehead, A. (1996) Borrowing strength from external trials in a meta-analysis. *Statistics in Medicine, 15,* 2733–2749.

Houghton, V. (2008) A quantitative study of the effectiveness of mindfulness-based stress reduction treatment, using an internet-delivered self-help program, for women with generalized anxiety disorder. *Dissertation Abstracts International: Section B: The Sciences and Engineering, 69,* 3311.

Hoyer, J., Becker, E. S. & Margraf, J. (2002) Generalized anxiety disorder and clinical worry episodes in a representative sample of young women. *Psychological Medicine, 32,* 1227–1237.

Hoyer, J., Beesdo, K., Gloster, A. T., *et al.* (2009) Worry exposure versus applied relaxation in the treatment of generalized anxiety disorder. *Psychotherapy and Psychosomatics, 78,* 106–115.

Hunot, V., Churchill, R., Silva de Lima, M., *et al.* (2007) Psychological therapies for generalised anxiety disorder. *Cochrane Database of Systematic Reviews, 2007,* Issue 1. Art. No.: CD001848. DOI: 10.1002/14651858.CD001848.pub4

Hunt, C., Issakidis, C. & Andrews, G. (2002) DSM-IV Generalized anxiety disorder in the Australian National Survey of Mental Health and Well-Being. *Psychological Medicine, 32,* 649–659.

Iskedjian, M., Walker, J. H., Bereza, B. G., *et al.* (2008) Cost-effectiveness of escitalopram for generalized anxiety disorder in Canada. *Current Medical Research and Opinion, 24* 1539–1548.

Jadad, A. R., Moore, R. A., Carroll, D., *et al.* (1996) Assessing the quality of reports of randomised clinical trials: is blinding necessary? *Controlled Clinical Trials, 17,* 1–12.

Janbozorgi, M., Zahirodin, A., Norri, N., *et al.* (2009) Providing emotional stability through relaxation training. *Eastern Mediterranean Health Journal, 15,* 629–638.

Johne, A. & Roots, I. (2005) Clinical drug interactions with medicinal herbs. *Evidence-Based Integrative Medicine, 2,* 207–228.

Jørgensen, T. R., Stein, D. J., Despiegel, N., *et al.* (2006) Cost-effectiveness analysis of escitalopram compared with paroxetine in treatment of generalized anxiety disorder in the United Kingdom. *Annals of Pharmacotherapy, 40,* 1752–1758.

Jorm, A. F., Christensen, H., Griffiths, K. M., *et al.* (2004) Effectiveness of complimentary and self help treatments for anxiety disorders. *Medical Journal of Australia, 181,* 29–46.

Kadam, U. T., Croft, P., McLeod, J., *et al.* (2001) A qualitative study of patients' views on anxiety and depression. *British Journal of General Practice, 51,* 375–380.

Kahn, E. (1985) Heinz Kohut and Carl Rogers: a timely comparison. *American Psychologist, 40,* 893–904.

Kaltenthaler, E., Brazier, J., De Nigris, E., *et al.* (2006) *Computerised Cognitive Behaviour Therapy for Depression and Anxiety Update: a Systematic Review and Economic Evaluation.* Technical Report. Tunbridge Wells: Gray Publishing.

Kalueff, A. V. & Nutt, D. J. (2007) Role of GABA in anxiety and depression. *Depression and Anxiety, 24*, 495–517.

Kaplan, R. M. & Anderson, J. P. (1988) A general health policy model: update and applications. *Health Services Research, 23*, 203–235.

Kasper, S., Herman, B., Nivoli, G., *et al.* (2009) Efficacy of pregabalin and venlafaxine-XR in generalized anxiety disorder: results of a double-blind, placebo-controlled 8-week trial. *International Clinical Psychopharmacology, 24*, 87–96.

Kassinove, H., Miller, N. & Kalin, M. (1980) Effects of pre-treatment with rational emotive bibliotherapy and rational emotive audiotherapy on clients waiting at community mental health centre. *Psychological Reports, 46*, 851–857.

Kavoussi, R. (2006) Pregabalin: from molecule to medicine. *European Neuropsychopharmacology, 16*, S128–S133.

Keller, M. B. (2000) Citalopram therapy for depression: a review of 10 years of European experience and data from U.S. clinical trials. *Journal of Clinical Psychiatry, 61*, 896–908.

Kenardy, J. A., Dow, M. G. T., Johnston, D. W., *et al.* (2003)[33] A comparison of delivery methods of cognitive-behavioural therapy for panic disorder: an international multicentre trial. *Journal of Consulting and Clinical Psychology, 71*, 1068–1075.

Kendler, K. S. (1996) Major depression and generalised anxiety disorder. Same genes, (partly) different environments – revisited. *British Journal of Psychiatry, 30*, 68–75.

Kendler, K. S., Hettema, J. M., Butera, F., *et al.* (2003) Life event dimensions of loss, humiliation, entrapment and danger in the prediction of onsets of major depression and generalized anxiety. *Archives of General Psychiatry, 60*, 789–796.

Kennedy, B. L. & Schwab, J. J. (1997) Utilization of medical specialists by anxiety disorder patients. *Psychosomatics, 38*, 109–112.

Kessler, R. C. (2000) The epidemiology of pure and comorbid generalized anxiety disorder: a review and evaluation of recent research. *Acta Psychiatrica Scandinavica, 406* (Suppl.), S7–S13.

Kessler, R. C. & Wang, P. S. (2008) The descriptive epidemiology of commonly occurring mental disorders in the United States. *Annual Review of Public Health, 29*, 115–129.

Kessler, R. C., Brandenburg, N., Lane, M., *et al.* (2005a) Rethinking the duration requirement for generalized anxiety disorder: evidence from the National Comorbidity Survey Replication. *Psychological Medicine, 35*, 1073–1078.

Kessler, R. C., Chiu, W. T., Demler, O., *et al.* (2005b) Prevalence, severity, and comorbidity of 12-month DSM-IV disorders in the National Comorbidity Survey Replication. *Archives of General Psychiatry, 62*, 617–627.

Kessler, R. C., Berglund, P., Demler, O., *et al.* (2005c) Lifetime prevalence and age-of-onset distributions of DSM-IV disorders in the national comorbidity survey replication. *Archives of General Psychiatry, 62*, 593–602.

---

[33]This is the primary reference for KENARDY2003A. Secondary references can be found in Appendix 15e.

Kessler, R. C., Chiu, W. T., Jin, R., *et al.* (2006) The epidemiology of panic attacks, panic disorder, and agoraphobia in the National Comorbidity Survey Replication. *Archives of General Psychiatry, 63,* 415–24.

Kessler, R. C., Gruber, M., Hettema J. M., *et al.* (2008) Co-morbid major depression and generalized anxiety disorders in the National Comorbidity Survey follow-up. *Psychological Medicine, 38, 365–374.*

Khan, A., Brodhead, A. E., Kolts, R. L., *et al.* (2005) Severity of depressive symptoms and response to antidepressants and placebo in antidepressant trials. *Journal of Psychiatric Research, 39,* 145–150.

Kiropoulos, L. A., Klein, B., Austin, D. W., *et al.* (2008) Is internet-based CBT for panic disorder and agoraphobia as effective as face-to-face CBT? *Journal of Anxiety Disorders, 22,* 1273–1284.

Kitchiner, N., Edwards, D. & Wood, S. (2009) A randomized controlled trial comparing an adult education class using cognitive behavioural therapy ('stress control'), anxiety management group treatment and a waiting list for anxiety disorders. *Journal of Mental Health, 18,* 307 – 315.

Klein, B., Richards, J. C., Austin, D. W. (2006) Efficacy of internet therapy for panic disorder. *Journal of Behavioural Therapy, 37,* 213–238.

Klein, B., Austin, D., Pier, C., *et al.* (2009) Frequency of email therapist contact and internet-based treatment for panic disorder: does it make a difference? *Cognitive Behaviour Therapy, 38,* 100–113.

Kolts, R. L., *et al.* (2005) Severity of depressive symptoms and response to antidepressants and placebo in antidepressant trials. *Journal of Psychiatric Research, 39,* 145–150.

Koponen, H., Allgulander, C., Erickson, J., *et al.* (2007) Efficacy of duloxetine for the treatment of generalized anxiety disorder: implications for primary care physicians. *Primary Care Companion to the Journal of Clinical Psychiatry, 9,* 100–107.

Kroenke, K., Spitzer, R., Williams, J. B. W., *et al.* (2007) Anxiety disorders in primary care: prevalence, impairment, comorbidity and detection. *Annals of Internal Medicine, 146,* 317–25.

Lader, M. & Scotto, J. C. (1998) A multicentre double-blind comparison of hydroxyzine, buspirone and placebo in patients with generalized anxiety disorder. *Psychopharmacology, 139,* 402–406.

Ladouceur, R., Dugas, M. J., Freeston, M. H., *et al.* (2000) Efficacy of a cognitive-behavioral treatment for generalized anxiety disorder: evaluation in a controlled clinical trial. *Journal of Consulting and Clinical Psychology, 68,* 957–964.

Lang, A. J. (2005) Mental health treatment preferences of primary care patients. *Journal of Behavioral Medicine, 28,* 581–586.

Le Doux, J. E. (2000) Emotion circuits in the brain. *Annual Review of Neuroscience, 23,* 155–184.

Leichsenring, F., Salzer, S., Jaeger, U., *et al.* (2009) Short-term psychodynamic psychotherapy and cognitive-behavioral therapy in generalized anxiety disorder: a randomized, controlled trial. *American Journal of Psychiatry, 166,* 875–881.

References

Lenox-Smith, A. J. & Reynolds, A. (2003) A double-blind, randomised, placebo controlled study of venlafaxine XL in patients with generalised anxiety disorder in primary care. *British Journal of General Practice, 53*, 772–777.

Lenze, E. J., Mulsant, B. H., Shear, M. K., *et al.* (2005) Efficacy and tolerability of citalopram in the treatment of late-life anxiety disorders: results from an 8-week randomized, placebo-controlled trial. *American Journal of Psychiatry, 162*, 146–150.

Lenze, E. J., Rollman, B. L., Shear, M. K., *et al.* (2009) Escitalopram for older adults with generalized anxiety disorder: a randomized controlled trial. *JAMA: the Journal of the American Medical Association, 301*, 295–303.

Liddel, J., Williamson, M. & Irwig, L. (1996) *Method for Evaluating Research and Guideline Evidence.* Sydney: New South Wales Health Department.

Lieb, R., Becker, E. & Altamura, C. (2005) The epidemiology of generalized anxiety disorder in Europe. *European Neuropsychopharmacology, 15*, 445–452.

Linden, M., Zubraegel, D., Baer, T., *et al.* (2005) Efficacy of cognitive behaviour therapy in generalized anxiety disorders. *Psychotherapy and Psychosomatics, 74*, 36–42.

Llorca, P. M., Spadone, C., Sol, O., *et al.* (2002) Efficacy and safety of hydroxyzine in the treatment of generalized anxiety disorder: a 3-month double-blind study. *Journal of Clinical Psychiatry, 63*, 1020–1027.

Lohoff, F. W., Etemad, B., Mandos, L. A., *et al.* (2010) Ziprasidone treatment of refractory generalized anxiety disorder. *Journal of Clinical Psychopharmacology, 30*, 185–189.

Lovell, K. & Bee, P. (2008) Implementing the NICE OCD/BDD guidelines. *Psychology and Psychotherapy: Research and Practice, 81*, 365–376.

Lovell, K. & Richards, D. (2000) Multiple Access Points and Levels of Entry (MAPLE): ensuring choice, accessibility and equity for CBT services. *Behavioural and Cognitive Psychotherapy, 28*, 379–391.

Lovell, K., Bower, P., Richards, D., *et al.* (2008) Developing guided self-help for depression using the Medical Research Council complex interventions framework: a description of the modelling phase and results of an explanatory randomised controlled trial. *BMC Psychiatry, 8*, 1–19.

Lu, G. & Ades, A. E. (2004) Combination of direct and indirect evidence in mixed treatment comparisons. *Statistics in Medicine, 23*, 3105–3124.

Lucock, M., Padgett, K., Noble, R., *et al.* (2008) Controlled clinical trial of a self-help for anxiety intervention for patients waiting for psychological therapy. *Behavioural and Cognitive Psychotherapy, 36*, 541–551.

Lunn, D. J., Thomas, A., Best, N., *et al.* (2000) WinBUGS – a Bayesian modelling framework: concepts, structure, and extensibility. *Statistics and Computing, 10*, 325–337.

Lydiard, R. B., Ballenger, J. C. & Rickels, K. (1997) A double-blind evaluation of the safety and efficacy of abecarnil, alprazolam, and placebo in outpatients with generalized anxiety disorder. Abecarnil Work Group. *The Journal of Clinical Psychiatry, 58*, 11–18.

Machado, M., Iskedjian, M., Ruiz, I., *et al.* (2006) Remission, dropouts, and adverse drug reaction rates in major depressive disorder: a meta-analysis of head-to-head trials. *Current Medical Research and Opinion, 22*, 1825–1837.

Majercsik, E., Haller, J., Leveleki, C., *et al.* (2003) The effect of social factors on the anxiolytic efficacy of buspirone in male rats, male mice and men. *Progress in Neuro-pharmacology and Biological Psychiatry, 27,* 1187–1199.

Mann, C. & Staba, E. J. (1986) The chemistry, pharmacology, and commercial formulations of chamomile. *Journal of Herbs, Spices, Medicinal Plants, 1,* 235–278.

Mann, T. (1996) *Clinical Guidelines: Using Clinical Guidelines to Improve Patient Care Within the NHS.* London: NHS Executive.

Mantella, R. C., Butters, M. A., Amico, J. A., *et al.* (2008) Salivary cortisol is associated with diagnosis and severity of late-life generalized anxiety disorder. *Psychoneuroendocrinolgy, 33,* 773–781.

Marciniak, M., Lage, M. J., Landbloom, R. P., *et al.* (2004) Medical and productivity costs of anxiety disorders: case control study. *Depression and Anxiety, 19,* 112–120.

Marciniak, M. D., Lage, M. J., Dunayevich, E., *et al.* (2005) The cost of treating anxiety: the medical and demographic correlates that impact total medical costs. *Depression and Anxiety, 21,* 178–184.

Marks, I. M., Kenwright, M., McDonough, M., *et al.* (2004) Saving clinicians' time by delegating routine aspects of therapy to a computer: a randomised controlled trial in phobia/panic disorder. *Psychological Medicine, 34,* 9–18.

Marrs, R. (1995) A meta-analysis of bibliotherapy studies. *American Journal of Community Psychology, 23,* 843–870.

Maunder, L., Cameron, L., Moss, M., *et al.* (2009) Effectiveness of self-help materials for anxiety adapted for use in prison: a pilot study. *Journal of Mental Health, 18,* 262–271.

McLeod, D. R., Hoehn-Saric, R., Porges, S. W., *et al.* (1992) Effects of alprazolam and imipramine on parasympathetic cardiac control in patients with generalized anxiety disorder. *Psychopharmacology, 107,* 535–540.

McManus, S., Meltzer, H., Brugha, T., *et al.* (2009) *Adult Psychiatric Morbidity in England, 2007: Results of a Household Survey.* Leeds: The NHS Information Centre for Health and Social Care.

MHRA (2004) *Report of the CSM Expert Working Group on the Safety of Selective Serotonin Reuptake Inhibitor Antidepressants.* Available at: http://www.MHRA.gov.uk/home/groups/pl-p/documents/drugsafetymessage/con019472.pdf

Michalopoulos, C., Kiropoulos, L., Shih, S-T. F., *et al.* (2005) Exploratory economic analyses of two primary care mental health projects: implications for sustainability. *Medical Journal of Australia, 183,* S73-S76.

Miller, W. R. & Rollnick, S. (2002) *Motivational Interviewing: Preparing People for Change.* New York, Guilford.

Mohlman, J., Gorenstein, E. E., Kleber, M., *et al.* (2003) Standard and enhanced cognitive-behaviour therapy for late-life generalized anxiety disorder: two pilot investigations. *American Journal of Geriatric Psychiatry, 11,* 24–32.

Mojtabai, R., Olfson, M., Mechanic, D. (2002) Perceived need and help-seeking in adults with mood, anxiety, or substance use disorders. *Archives of General Psychiatry, 59,* 77–84.

Moller, H.-J., Volz, H.-P., Reimann, I.W., *et al.* (2001) Opipramol for the treatment of generalized anxiety disorder: a placebo-controlled trial including an alprazolam treated group. *Journal of Clinical Psychopharmacology, 21*, 59–65.

Montgomery, S. A., Tobias, K., Zornberg, G. L., *et al.* (2006) Efficacy and safety of pregabalin in the treatment of generalized anxiety disorder: a 6-week, multicenter, randomized, double-blind, placebo-controlled comparison of pregabalin and venlafaxine. *Journal of Clinical Psychiatry*, 67, 771–782.

Montgomery, S., Chatamra, K., Pauer, L., *et al.* (2008) Efficacy and safety of pregabalin in elderly people with generalised anxiety disorder. *The British Journal of Psychiatry: the Journal of Mental Science, 193*, 389–394.

Nadiga, D. N., Hensley, P. L., Uhlenhuth, E. H. (2003) Review of the long-term effectiveness of cognitive behavioral therapy compared to medications in panic disorder. *Depression and Anxiety, 17*, 58–64.

NCCMH (2010a) *Depression: the Treatment and Management of Depression in Adults.* Leicester & London: the British Psychological Society and the Royal College of Psychiatrists.

NCCMH (2010b) *Depression in Adults with a Chronic Physical Health Problem: Treatment and Management.* Leicester & London: the British Psychological Society and the Royal College of Psychiatrists.

NCCMH (2011) *Common Mental Health Disorders: Identification and Pathways to Care.* Leicester & London: the British Psychological Society and the Royal College of Psychiatrists. Forthcoming.

NHS, The Information Centre (2009) *Hospital Episode Statistics 2007–08.* London: The NHS Information Centre. Available at: http://www.hesonline.nhs.uk

NICE (2004a) *Anxiety: Management of Anxiety (Panic Disorder, with or without Agoraphobia, and Generalised Anxiety Disorder) in Adults in Primary, Secondary and Community Care.* Clinical Guideline 22. London: NICE.

NICE (2004b) *Depression: Management of Depression in Primary and Secondary Care.* Clinical Guideline 23. London: NICE.

NICE (2005a) *Post-traumatic Stress Disorder: The Management of PTSD in Adults and Children in Primary and Secondary Care.* Clinical Guideline 26. London: NICE.

NICE (2005b) *Obsessive-compulsive Disorder: Core Interventions in the Treatment of Obsessive-compulsive Disorder and Body Dysmorphic Disorder.* Clinical Guideline 31. London: NICE.

NICE (2006) *Computerised Cognitive Behaviour Therapy for Depression and Anxiety.* Technology Appraisal 97. London: NICE.

NICE (2007a) *Drug Misuse: Opioid Detoxification.* Clinical Guideline 52. London: NICE.

NICE (2007b) *Drug Misuse: Psychosocial Interventions.* Clinical Guideline 51. London: NICE.

NICE (2008a) *Guide to the Methods of Technology Appraisal.* London: National Institute for Health and Clinical Excellence.

NICE (2008b) *Social Value Judgements. Principles for the Development of NICE Guidance.* 2nd edition. London: NICE.

NICE (2009a) *The Guidelines Manual.* London: NICE.

NICE (2009b) *Depression: the Treatment and Management of Depression in Adults.* Clinical Guideline 90. London: NICE.

NICE (2009c) *Depression in Adults with a Chronic Physical Health Problem*: *Treatment and Management.* Clinical Guideline 91. London: NICE.

NICE (2010a) *Alcohol-Use Disorders: Diagnosis and Clinical Management of Alcohol-Related Physical Complications.* Clinical Guideline 100. London: NICE.

NICE (2010b) *Alcohol-Use Disorders: Preventing the Development of Hazardous and Harmful Drinking.* Public Health Guidance 24. London: NICE.

NICE (2011a) *Alcohol-Use Disorders: Diagnosis, Assessment and Management of Harmful Drinking and Alcohol Dependence.* Clinical Guideline 115. London: NICE.

NICE (2011b) *Common Mental Health Disorders: Identification and Pathways to Care.* London: NICE. Forthcoming.

Nicolini, H., Bakish, D., Duenas, H., *et al.* (2009) Improvement of psychic and somatic symptoms in adult patients with generalized anxiety disorder: examination from a duloxetine, venlafaxine extended-release and placebo-controlled trial. *Psychological Medicine, 39*, 267–276.

Nimatoudis, I., Zissis, N. P., Kogeorgos, J., *et al.* (2004) Remission rates with venlafaxine extended release in Greek outpatients with generalized anxiety disorder. A double-blind, randomized, placebo controlled study. *International Clinical Psychopharmacology, 19*, 331–336.

Nitschke, J. B., Sarinopoulos, I., Oathes, D. J., *et al.* (2009) Anticipatory activation in the amygdala and anterior cingulate in generalized anxiety disorder and prediction of treatment response. *American Journal of Psychiatry, 166*, 302–310.

Noyes, J., Clarkson, C., Crowe, R. R., *et al.* (1987) A family study of generalized anxiety disorder. *American Journal of Psychiatry, 144*, 1019–1024.

Olfson, M. & Gameroff, M. J. (2007) Generalized anxiety disorder, somatic pain and health care costs. *General Hospital Psychiatry, 29*, 310–6.

ONS (2009) *Mid-2008 Population Estimates: England and Wales; Estimated Resident Population by Single Year of Age and Sex.* London: Office for National Statistics. Available at: http://www.statistics.gov.uk/statbase/Product.asp?vlnk = 15106

Orsillo, S. M., Roemer, L. & Barlow, D. H. (2003) Integrating acceptance and mindfulness into existing cognitive-behavioral treatment for GAD: a case study. *Cognitive and Behavioral Practice, 10*, 222–230.

Öst, L. G. (1987) Applied relaxation: description of a coping technique and review of controlled studies. *Behaviour Research and Therapy, 25*, 397.

Öst, L. G. & Breitholtz, E. (2000) Applied relaxation versus cognitive therapy in the treatment of generalized anxiety disorder. *Behaviour Research and Therapy, 38*, 777–790.

Pande, A. C., Crockatt, J. G., Feltner, D. E., *et al.* (2003) Pregabalin in generalized anxiety disorder: a placebo-controlled trial. *American Journal of Psychiatry, 160*, 533–540.

Pandina, G. J., Canuso, C., Turkoz, *et al.* (2007) Adjunctive risperidone in the treatment of generalized anxiety disorder: a double-blind, prospective, placebo-controlled, randomized trial. *Psychopharmacology Bulletin, 40*, 41–57.

References

Pariante, C. M. & Lightman, S. L. (2008) The HPA axis in major depression: classical theories and new developments. *Trends in Neurosciences, 31*, 464–468.

Parker, G., Hadzi-Pavlovic, D., Greenwald, S., *et al.* (1995) Low parental care as a risk factor to lifetime depression in a community sample. *Journal of Affective Disorders, 33*, 173–180.

Pfizer (2005) *European Assessment Report: LYRICA*. London: European Medicines Agency.

Pfizer (2008) A 4-week, double-blind, randomized, multicenter, fixed dose, placebo-controlled, parallel group study of lorazepam and paroxetine in patients with generalized anxiety disorder: Assessment of a new instrument intended to capture rapid onset. Unpublished.

Phillips, M. L., Drevets, W. C., Rauch, S. L., *et al.* (2003) Neurobiology of emotion perception I: the neural basis of normal emotion perception. *Biological Psychiatry, 54*, 504–514.

Pies, R. (2009) Should psychiatrists use atypical antipsychotics to treat nonpsychotic anxiety. *Psychiatry, 6*, 29–37.

Pohl, R. B., Feltner, D. E., Fieve, R. R., *et al.* (2005) Efficacy of pregabalin in the treatment of generalized anxiety disorder. Double-blind, placebo-controlled comparison of BID versus TID dosing. *Journal of Clinical Psychopharmacology, 25*, 151–158.

Pollack, M., Worthington, J., Manfro, G., *et al.* (1997) Abecarnil for the treatment of generalized anxiety disorder: a placebo-controlled comparison of two dosage ranges of abecarnil and buspirone. *Journal of Clinical Psychiatry, 58*, 19–23.

Pollack, M. H., Zanelli, R., Goddard, A., *et al.* (2001) Paroxetine in the treatment of generalized anxiety disorder: results of a placebo-controlled, flexible-dosage trial. *Journal of Clinical Psychiatry, 62*, 350–357.

Pollack, M. H., Simon, N. M., Zalta, A. K., *et al.* (2006) Olanzapine augmentation of fluoxetine for refractory generalized anxiety disorder: a placebo-controlled study. *Biological Psychiatry, 59*, 211–215.

Porensky, E. K., Dew, M. A., Karp, J. F., *et al.* (2009) The burden of late-life generalized anxiety disorder: effects on disability, health-related quality of life, and healthcare utilization. *American Journal of Geriatric Psychiatry, 17*, 473–482.

Prins, M. A., Verhaak, P. F. M., Bensing, J. M., *et al.* (2008) Health beliefs and perceived need for mental health care of anxiety and depression: the patients' perspective explored. *Clinical Psychology Review, 28*, 1038–1058.

Prins, M. A., Verhaak, P. F. M., Meer, K. V. D., *et al.* (2009) Primary care patients with anxiety and depression: need for care from the patient's perspective. *Journal of Affective Disorders, 163*, 163–171.

Proudfoot, J., Ryden, C., Everitt, B., *et al.* (2004) Clinical efficacy of computerised cognitive–behavioural therapy for anxiety and depression in primary care: randomised controlled trial. *British Medical Journal, 185*, 46–54.

Ramasubbu, R. (2004) Cerebrovascular effects of selective serotonin reuptake inhibitors: a systematic review. *Journal of Clinical Psychiatry, 65*, 1642–1653.

Reardon, J. M. & Nathan, N. L. (2007) The specificity of cognitive vulnerabilities to emotional disorders: anxiety sensitivity, looming vulnerability and explanatory style. *Journal of Anxiety Disorders, 21*, 625–643.

Revicki, D. A. & Wood, M. (1998) Patient-assigned health state utilities for depression-related outcomes: differences by depression severity and antidepressant medications. *Journal of Affective Disorders, 48*, 25–36.

Revicki, D. A., Brandenburg, N., Matza, L., *et al.* (2008) Health-related quality of life and utilities in primary-care patients with generalized anxiety disorder. *Quality of Life Research, 17*, 1285–94.

Rezvan, S., Baghban, I., Bahrami, F., *et al.* (2008) A comparison of cognitive-behavior therapy with interpersonal and cognitive behavior therapy in the treatment of generalized anxiety disorder. *Counselling Psychology Quarterly, 21*, 309–321.

Richards, D., Richards, A., Barkham, M., *et al.* (2002) PHASE: a 'health technology' approach to psychological treatment in primary mental health care. *Primary Health Care Research and Development, 3*, 159–168.

Richards, D., Lovell, K. & McEvoy, P. (2003) Access and effectiveness in psychological therapies: self help as a routine health technology. *Health and Social Care in the Community, 11*, 175–182.

Richards, D. A., Weaver, A., Utley, M. *et al.* (2010) Developing evidence based and acceptable stepped care systems in mental health care: an operational research project. Final report. NIHR Service Delivery and Organisation programme. Available at: http://www.sdo.nihr.ac.uk/projdetails.php?ref = 08–1504-109

Richards, J., Klein, B. & Austin, D. (2006) Internet cognitive behavioural therapy for panic disorder: does the inclusion of stress management information improve end-state functioning? *Clinical Psychologist, 10*, 2–15.

Richardson, R., Richards, D. A. & Barkham, M. (2008) Self-help books for people with depression: the role of the therapeutic relationship. *Behavioural and Cognitive Psychotherapy, 38*, 67–81.

Rickels, K. & Rynn, M. A. (2001) What is generalized anxiety disorder? *Journal of Clinical Psychiatry, 62* (Suppl. 11), 4–12.

Rickels, K. & Schweizer, E. (1990) The clinical course and long-term management of generalized anxiety disorder. *Journal of Clinical Psychopharmacology, 10* (Suppl. 3), 101S-110S.

Rickels, K., Pollack, M. H., Sheehan, D. V., *et al.* (2000a) Efficacy of extended-release venlafaxine in nondepressed outpatients with generalized anxiety disorder. *American Journal of Psychiatry, 157*, 968–974.

Rickels, K., DeMartinis, N. & Aufdembrinke, B. (2000b) A double-blind, placebo-controlled trial of abecarnil and diazepam in the treatment of patients with generalized anxiety disorder. *Journal of Clinical Psychopharmacology, 20*, 12–18.

Rickels, K., Zaninelli, R., McCafferty, J., *et al.* (2003) Paroxetine treatment of generalized anxiety disorder: a double-blind, placebo-controlled study. *American Journal of Psychiatry, 160*, 749–756.

Rickels, K., Pollack, M. H., Feltner, D. E., *et al.* (2005) Pregabalin for treatment of generalized anxiety disorder. A 4-week, multi-center, double-blind, placebo-controlled trial of pregabalin and alprazolam. *Archives of General Psychiatry, 62,* 1022–1030.

Rijswijk, E. V., Hout, H. V., Lisdonk, E. V. D., *et al.* (2009) Barriers in recognising, diagnosing and managing depressive and anxiety disorders as experienced by family physicians: a focus group study. *BMC Family Practice, 10,* DOI: 10.1186/1471–2296-10–52.

Roemer, L., Borkovec, M., Posa, S., *et al.* (1995) A self-report diagnostic measure of generalised anxiety disorder. *Journal of Behavior Therapy and Experimental Psychiatry, 26,* 345–350.

Roemer, L., Molina, S., Litz, B. T., *et al.* (1996) Preliminary investigation of the role of previous exposure to potentially traumatizing events in generalized anxiety disorder. *Depression and Anxiety, 4,* 134–138.

Roemer, L., Molina, S. & Borkovec, T. D. (1997) An investigation of worry content among generally anxious individuals. *Journal of Nervous and Mental Disease, 185,* 314–319.

Roemer, L., Orsillo, S. M. & Salters-Pedneault, K. (2008) Efficacy of an acceptance-based behavior therapy for generalized anxiety disorder: evaluation in a randomized controlled trial. *Journal of Consulting and Clinical Psychology, 76,* 1083–1089.

Rogers, C. R. (1957) The necessary and sufficient conditions of therapeutic personality change. *Journal of Consulting Psychology, 21,* 95–103.

Rogers, C. R. (1986) Rogers, Kohut and Erikson. A personal perspective on some similarities and differences. *Person-Centered Review, 1,* 125–140.

Rollman, B. L., Belnap, B. H., Mazumdar, S., *et al.* (2005) A randomized trial to improve the quality of treatment for panic and generalized anxiety disorders in primary care. *Archives of General Psychiatry, 62,* 1332–1341.

Roth, A. & Fonagy, P. (1996) *What Works for Whom: A Critical Review of Psychotherapy Research.* New York: Guilford.

Rowe, S. K. & Rapaport, M. H. (2006) Classification and treatment of sub-threshold depression. *Current Opinion in Psychiatry, 19,* 9–13.

Royal College of Psychiatrists (2005) *Benzodiazepines: Risks, Benefits, or Dependence. A Re-evaluation.* Council report CR59. London: Royal College of Psychiatrists.

Roy-Byrne, P. P. & Wagner, A. (2004) Primary care perspectives on generalized anxiety disorder. *Journal of Clinical Psychiatry, 65* (Suppl. 13), S20–S26.

Roy-Byrne, P. P., Wagner, A.W. & Schraufnagel, T. J. (2005) Understanding and treating panic disorder in the primary care setting. *Journal of Clinical Psychiatry, 66* (Suppl. 4), 16–22.

Roy-Byrne, P. P., Davidson, K. W., Kessler, R. C., *et al.* (2008) Anxiety disorders and comorbid medical illness. *General Hospital Psychiatry, 30,* 208–225.

Roy-Byrne, P., Craske, M. G., Sullivan, G., *et al.* (2010) Delivery of evidence-based treatment for multiple anxiety disorders in primary care: a randomized controlled trial. *JAMA: the Journal of the American Medical Association, 19,* 1921–1928.

Ruan, J. I. Y. U. (2003) Clinical observation on treatment of 86 patients with anxiety neurosis by combination of traditional herbs with acupuncture. *Journal of Zhejiang College of TCM, 27,* 70–71.

Rubin, H. C., Rapaport, M. H., Levine, B., *et al.* (2000) Quality of well being in panic disorder: the assessment of psychiatric and general disability. *Journal of Affective Disorders, 57*, 217–221.

Ruscio, A. M. & Borkovec, T. D. (2004) Experience and appraisal of worry among high worriers with and without generalized anxiety disorder. *Behaviour Research and Therapy, 42*, 1469–1482.

Ruscio, A. M., Chiu, W. T., Roy-Byrne, P., *et al.* (2007) Broadening the definition of generalized anxiety disorder: effects on prevalence and associations with other disorders in the National Comorbidity Survey Replication. *Journal of Anxiety Disorders, 21*, 662–667.

Rynn, M., Russell, J., Erickson, J., *et al.* (2008) Efficacy and safety of duloxetine in the treatment of generalized anxiety disorder: a flexible-dose, progressive-titration, placebo-controlled trial. *Depression and Anxiety, 25*, 182–189.

Safren, S. A., Gershuny, B. S., Marzol, P., *et al.* (2002) History of childhood abuse in panic disorder, social phobia and generalized anxiety disorder. *Journal of Nervous and Mental Disease, 190*, 453–456.

Sareen, J., Jacobi, F., Cox, B. J., *et al.* (2006) Disability and poor quality of life associated with comorbid anxiety disorders and physical conditions. *Archives of Internal Medicine, 166*, 2109–2116.

Schneider, A., Mataix-Cols, D., Marks, I., *et al.* (2005) Internet-guided self-help with or without exposure therapy for phobic and panic disorders. *Psychotherapy and Psychosomatics, 74*, 154–164.

Schunemann, H. J., Best, D., Vist, G. *et al.* for the GRADE Working Group (2003) Letters, numbers, symbols and words: how to communicate grades of evidence and recommendations. *Canadian Medical Association Journal, 169*, 677–80.

Schwartz, T. L., Nihalani, N., Simionescu, M., *et al.* (2005) History repeats itself: pharmacodynamic trends in the treatment of anxiety disorders. *Current Pharmaceutical Design, 11*, 255–263.

Scogin, F., Hanson, A. & Welsh, D. (2003) Self-administered treatment in stepped-care models of depression treatment. *Journal of Clinical Psychology, 59*, 341–349.

SIGN (2001) *SIGN 50: A Guideline Developer's Handbook.* Edinburgh: Scottish Intercollegiate Guidelines Network.

Silove, D., Parker, G., Hadzi-Pavlovic, D., *et al.* (1991) Parental representations of patients with panic disorder and generalised anxiety disorder. *British Journal of Psychiatry, 159*, 835–841.

Simon, G., Ormel, J., von Korff, M., *et al.* (1995) Health care costs associated with depressive and anxiety disorders in primary care. *American Journal of Psychiatry, 152*, 352–357.

Sorby, N. G., Reavley, W. & Huber, J. W. (1991) Self help programme for anxiety in general practice: controlled trial of an anxiety management booklet. *British Journal of General Practice, 41*, 417–420.

Souêtre, E., Lozet, H., Cimarosti, I., *et al.* (1994) Cost of anxiety disorders: impact of comorbidity. *Journal of Psychosomatic Research, 38* (Suppl. 1), 151–60.

References

Spek, V. R. M., Cuijpers, P., Nyklicek, I., *et al.* (2007) Internet-based cognitive behaviour therapy for symptoms of depression and anxiety: a meta-analysis. *Psychological Medicine, 37*, 319–328.

Spiegelhalter, D. J., Thomas, A., Best, N. G., *et al.* (2001) *WinBUGS User Manual: Version 1.4*. Cambridge: MRC Biostatistics Unit.

Sramek, J., Tansman, M., Suri, A., *et al.* (1996) Efficacy of buspirone in generalized anxiety disorder with coexisting mild depressive symptoms. *Journal of Clinical Psychiatry, 57*, 287–291.

Stanley, M. A., Beck, J. G. & Glassco, J. D. (1996) Treatment of generalised anxiety in older adults: a preliminary comparison of cognitive-behavioral and supportive approaches. *Behavior Therapy, 27*, 565–581.

Stanley, M. A., Beck, J. G., Novy, D. M., *et al.* (2003) Cognitive-behavioral treatment of late-life generalised anxiety disorder. *Journal of Consulting and Clinical Psychology, 71*, 309–319.

Stanley, M. A., Wilson, N. L., Novy, D. M., *et al.* (2009) Cognitive behavior therapy for generalised anxiety disorder among older adults in primary care a randomized clinical trial. *JAMA: the Journal of the American Medical Association, 301*, 1460–1467.

Stein, M., Sherbourne, C., Craske, M., *et al.* (2004) Quality of care for primary care patients with anxiety disorders. *American Journal of Psychiatry, 161*, 2230–37.

Stocchi, F., Nordera, G., Jokinen, R.H., *et al.* (2003) Efficacy and tolerability of paroxetine for the long term treatment of generalized anxiety disorder. *Journal of Clinical Psychiatry, 64*, 250–258.

Stone, M., Laughren, T., Jones, M., *et al* (2009) Risk of suicidality in clinical trials of antidepressants in adults: analysis of proprietary data submitted to US Food and Drug Administration. *British Medical Journal, 339*, b2880.

Swenson, J. R., Doucette, S. & Fergusson, D. (2006) Adverse cardiovascular events in antidepressant trials involving high-risk patients: a systematic review of randomized trials. *Canadian Journal of Psychiatry, 51*, 923–929.

Tarrier, N. & Main, C. J. (1986) Applied relaxation training for generalised anxiety and panic attacks: the efficacy of a learnt coping strategy on subjective reports. *British Journal of Psychiatry, 149*, 330–336.

Tassone, D. M., Boyce, E., Guyer, J., *et al.* (2007) Pregabalin: a novel γ-aminobutyric acid analogue in the treatment of neuropathic pain, partial-onset seizures, and anxiety disorders. *Clinical Therapeutics, 29*, 26–48.

Taylor, D. (2008) Antidepressant drugs and cardiovascular pathology: a clinical overview of effectiveness and safety. *Acta Psychiatrica Scandinavica, 118*, 434–442.

Titov, N., Andrews, G., Robinson, E., *et al.* (2009) Clinician-assisted internet-based treatment is effective for generalized anxiety disorder: randomized controlled trial. *Australian and New Zealand Journal of Psychiatry, 43*, 905–912.

Truax, C. B. & Carkhuff, R. R. (1967) *Toward Effective Counseling and Psychotherapy: Training and Practice*. Chicago, Illinois: Aldine.

Tylee, A. & Walters, P. (2007) Underrecognition of anxiety and mood disorders in primary care: why does the problem exist and what can be done? *Journal of Clinical Psychiatry, 68*, 27–30.

Tyrer, P. & Baldwin, D. S. (2006) Generalised anxiety disorder. *Lancet, 368*, 2156–2166.

Tyrer, P., Seivewright, H. & Johnson, T. (2004) The Nottingham study of neurotic disorder: predictors of 12-year outcome of dysthymia, panic disorder and generalized anxiety disorder. *Psychological Medicine, 34*, 1385–1394.

Van Boeijen, C. A., van Oppen, P., van Balkom, A., *et al.* (2005) Treatment of anxiety disorders in primary care practice: a randomised controlled trial. *British Journal of General Practice, 55*, 763–769.

Van Straten, A., Tiemens, B., Hakkaart, L., *et al.* (2006) Stepped care vs. matched care for mood and anxiety disorders: a randomized trial in routine practice. *Acta Psychiatrica Scandinavica, 113*, 468–476.

Van Steenbergen-Weijenburg, K. M., van der Feltz-Cornelis, C. M., Horns, E. K., *et al.* (2010) Cost-effectiveness of collaborative care for the treatment of major depressive disorder in primary care. A systematic review. *BMC Health Services Research, 10*, 19.

Vera-Llonch, M., Dukes, E., Rejas, J., *et al.* (2010) Cost-effectiveness of pregabalin versus venlafaxine in the treatment of generalized anxiety disorder: findings from a Spanish perspective. *European Journal of Health Economics, 11*, 35–44.

Wade. A. & Rosenberg. C (2001) Citalopram in general practice: its efficacy and tolerability. *International Journal of Psychiatry in Clinical Practice, 7*, 123–128.

Wagner, A. W., Bystritsky, A., Russo, J. E., *et al.* (2005) Beliefs about psychotropic medication and psychotherapy among primary care patients with anxiety disorders. *Depression and Anxiety, 21*, 99–105.

Ware, J. E., Snow, K. K., Kolinski, M., *et al.* (1993) *SF-36 Health Survey Manual and Interpretation Guide.* Boston, MA: The Health Institute, New England Medical Centre.

Ware, J. E., Kolinski, M. & Keller, S. D. (1995) *How to Score the SF-12 Physical and Mental Health Summaries: a User's Manual.* Boston, MA: The Health Institute, New England Medical Centre.

Weinrieb, R. M., Auriacombe, M., Lynch, K. G., *et al.* (2003) A critical review of selective serotonin reuptake inhibitor-associated bleeding: balancing the risk of treating hepatitis C-infected patients. *Journal of Clinical Psychiatry, 64*, 1502–1510.

Weissman, M. M., Bland, R. C., Canino, G. J., *et al.* (1997) The cross-national epidemiology of panic disorder. *Archives of General Psychiatry, 54*, 305–9.

Wells, A. (1999) A metacognitive model and therapy for generalized anxiety disorder. *Clinical Psychology and Psychotherapy, 6*, 86–95.

Wells, A. (2005) The metacognitive model of GAD: assessment of meta-worry and relationship with DSM-1V Generalized Anxiety Disorder. *Cognitive Therapy and Research, 29*, 107–121.

Wells, A., Welford, M., King, P., *et al.* (2010) A pilot randomized trial of metacognitive therapy versus applied relaxation in the treatment of adults with generalised anxiety disorder. *Behavior Research and Therapy, 1*, 1–6.

Werneke, U., Northey, S., Bhugra, D., *et al.* (2006) Antidepressants and sexual dysfunction. *Acta Psychiatrica Scandinavica, 114*, 384–397.

References

Wernicke, J. F. (2004) Safety and side effect profile of fluoxetine. *Expert Opinion on Drug Safety, 3*, 495–504.
Wernicke, J., Lledo, A., Raskin, J. *et al.* (2007) An evaluation of the cardiovascular safety profile of duloxetine. *Drug Safety, 30*, 437–455.
Westra, H. A., Arkowitz, H. & Dozois, D. J. A. (2009) Adding a motivational interviewing pre-treatment to cognitive behaviour therapy for generalized anxiety disorder. A preliminary randomized controlled trial. *Journal of Anxiety Disorders, 23*, 1106–1117.
Wetherell, J. L., Gatz, M. & Craske, M. G. (2003) Treatment of generalised anxiety disorder in older adults. *Journal of Consulting and Clinical Psychology, 71*, 31–40.
Wetherell, J. L., Kim, D. S., Lindamer, L. A., *et al.* (2007) Anxiety disorders in a public mental health system: clinical characteristics and service use patterns. *Journal of Affective Disorders, 104*, 179–83.
White, J. (1995) Stresspac: a controlled trial of a self-help package for the anxiety disorders. *Behavioural and Cognitive Psychotherapy, 23*, 89–107.
White, J. (1998) 'Stress control' large group therapy for generalized anxiety disorder: two year follow up. *Behavioural and Cognitive Psychotherapy, 26*, 237–245.
White, J., Keenan, M. & Brooks, N. (1992) Stress control: a controlled comparative investigation of large group therapy for generalized anxiety disorder. *Behavioural Psychotherapy, 20*, 97–113.
WHO (1992) *The ICD-10 Classification of Mental and Behavioural Disorders: Clinical Descriptions and Diagnostic Guidelines.* Geneva, Switzerland: WHO
WHO (1993) *The ICD-10 Classification of Mental and Behavioural Disorders: Diagnostic Criteria for Research (ICD-10-DCR).* Geneva, Switzerland: WHO.
Wittchen, H.-U. (2002) Generalized anxiety disorder: prevalence, burden and cost to society. *Depression and Anxiety, 16*, 162–171.
Wittchen, H.-U. & Essau, C. A. (1993) Epidemiology of panic disorder: progress and unresolved issues. *Journal of Psychiatric Research, 27* (Suppl. 1), 47–68.
Wittchen, H.-U. & Jacobi, F. (2005) Size and burden of mental disorders in Europe: a critical review and appraisal of 27 studies. *European Neuropsycho-pharmacology, 15*, 357–376.
Wittchen, H.-U., Carter, R., Pfister, H., *et al.* (2000) Disabilities and quality of life in pure and comorbid generalized anxiety disorder and major depression in a national survey. *International Clinical Psychopharmacology, 15*, 319–328.
Wittchen, H.-U., Kessler, R. C., Beesdo, K., *et al.* (2002) Generalized anxiety and depression in primary care: prevalence, recognition, and management. *Journal of Clinical Psychiatry, 63* (Suppl. 8), 24–34.
Wittchen, H.-U., Zhao, S., Kessler, R. C., *et al.* (1994). DSM-III-R generalized anxiety disorder in the National Comorbidity Survey. *Archives of General Psychiatry, 51*, 355–36.
Woelk, H. & Schlafke, S. (2010) A multi-center, double-blind, randomised study of the lavender oil preparation silexan in comparison to lorazepam for generalized anxiety disorder. *Phytomedicine, 17*, 64–99.

Woelk, H., Arnoldt, K. H., Kieser, M., *et al.* (2007) Ginkgo biloba special extract EGb 761Reg. in generalized anxiety disorder and adjustment disorder with anxious mood: a randomized, double-blind, placebo-controlled trial. *Journal of Psychiatric Research, 41,* 472–480.

Yonkers, K. A., Warshaw, M. G., Massion, A. O., *et al.* (1996) Phenomenology and course of generalised anxiety disorder. *British Journal of Psychiatry, 168,* 308–313.

Yonkers, K. A., Dyck, I. R., Warshaw, M., *et al.* (2000) Factors predicting the clinical course of generalised anxiety disorder. *British Journal of Psychiatry, 176,* 544–549.

Yuan, Q., Li, J. N., Liu, B., *et al.* (2007) Effect of Jin-3-needling therapy on plasma corticosteroid, adrenocorticotrophic hormone and platelet 5-HT levels in patients with generalized anxiety disorder. *Chinese Journal of Integrative Medicine, 13,* 264–268.

Yuan, Y., Tsoi, K. & Hunt, R. H. (2006) Selective serotonin reuptake inhibitors and risk of upper GI bleeding: confusion or confounding? *The American Journal of Medicine, 119,* 719–727.

Zhang, Y., Young, D., Lee, S., *et al.* (2002) Chinese Taoist cognitive psychotherapy in the treatment of generalised anxiety disorder in contemporary China. *Transcultural Psychiatry, 39,* 115–129.

Zhang, H., Zeng, Z. & Deng, H. (2003) Acupuncture treatment for 157 cases of anxiety neurosis. *Journal of Traditional Chinese Medicine, 23,* 55–56.

Zhao, Y. H., Shan, Y. H., Ma, L. H., *et al.* (2005) Clinical efficacy of hypnotherapy in the treatment of generalized anxiety disorder. *Chinese Mental Health Journal, 19,* 8.

Zhiling, W., Yuhong, L., Hong, L., *et al.* (2006) Acupuncture treatment of generalized anxiety disorder. *Journal of Traditional Chinese Medicine, 26,* 170–171.

Zhou, Z-H., Yu, W-Y., Wu, Z-H., *et al.* (2003) Clinical observations on treatment of anxiety neurosis with combined acupuncture and medicine. *Shanghai Journal of Acupuncture and Moxibustion, 22,* 9.

Zhu, B., Zhao, Z., Ye, W., *et al.* (2009) The cost of comorbid depression and pain for individuals diagnosed with generalized anxiety disorder. *Journal of Nervous and Mental Disease, 197,* 136–139.

13   ABBREVIATIONS

5-HT	5-hydroxytryptamine
A&E	accident and emergency
ABP	affect-focused body psychotherapy
ACQ	Agoraphobic Cognitions Questionnaire
ADIS (-R)	Anxiety Disorders Interview Schedule (–revised)
AGREE	Appraisal of Guidelines for Research and Evaluation
AM(T)	anxiety management (training)
AMED	Allied and Complementary Medicine Database
AP	analytic psychotherapy
APA	American Psychiatric Association
AR	applied relaxation
ASPD	antisocial personality disorder
BAI	Beck Anxiety Inventory
BDZ/BZ	benzodiazepine
BID/b.i.d	twice daily
BNF	*British National Formulary*
BNI	British Nursing Index
BSI (-12)	Brief Symptom Inventory (12 items)
BT	behaviour therapy
BUS/bus	buspirone
CBT	cognitive behavioural therapy
CCA	cost-consequences analysis
CCBT	computerised cognitive behavioural therapy
CCMD (-2, -3, –R)	*Chinese Classification of Mental Disorders* (version 2, version 3, revised)
CCP	Centre for Clinical Practice (NICE)
CDSR	Cochrane Database of Systematic Reviews
CEA	cost-effectiveness analysis
CEAC	cost-effectiveness acceptability curve
CENTRAL	Cochrane Central Register of Controlled Trials
CGI (-I, -S)	Clinical Global Impressions (–Improvement; –Severity)
CGS	Clinical Global Severity
CI	confidence interval
CIDI	Composite International Diagnostic Interview
CINAHL	Cumulative Index to Nursing and Allied Health Literature
CNS	central nervous system

COM	combined treatment of Chinese medicine with acupuncture nurse
CORE-OM	Clinical Outcomes in Routine Evaluation (- Outcome Measure)
CR	controlled release
CRD	Centre for Reviews and Dissemination (University of York)
CrI	credible interval
CSM	Committee on Safety of Medicines
CSR	Clinician's Severity Rating
CT	cognitive therapy
CTCP	Chinese Taoist cognitive psychotherapy
CUA	cost-utility analysis
CVD	cardiovascular disease
d	day
DALYs	disability-adjusted life years
DARE	Cochrane Database of Abstracts of Reviews of Effects
DASS	Depression Anxiety Stress Scales
DB	double blind
DESS	Discontinuation Emergent Signs and Symptoms
DG	discussion group
DH	Department of Health
DSM (-III, -IV, -R, TR)	*Diagnostic and Statistical Manual of Mental Disorders* of the American Psychiatric Association (3rd edition; 4th edition; revision; text revision)
DUL/dul	duloxetine
EBM	evidence-based medicine
ECG	electrocardiogram
ECT	electroconvulsive therapy
EED	Economic Evaluation Database
EI	Efficacy Index
EMBASE	Excerpta Medica Database
EPQ	Eysenck Personality Questionnaire
EQ-5D	European Quality of Life – 5 Dimensions
ERSQ	Emotion Regulation Strategies Questionnaire
ESEMeD	European Study of the Epidemiology of Mental Disorders
FC CCBT	frequent contact computerised cognitive behavioural therapy
F-DIPS	Diagnostisches Interview Für Psychische Störungen–Forschungsversion
GABA	gamma-aminobutyric acid
GAD	generalised anxiety disorder
GAD-7	Generalized Anxiety Disorder Assessment – 7 items

Abbreviations

GAD-Q (-IV)	Generalized Anxiety Disorder Questionnaire (–IV)
GDG	Guideline Development Group
GHQ	General Health Questionnaire
GI	gastrointestinal/General Index
GP	general practitioner
GRADE	Grades of Recommendation Assessment, Development and Evaluation
GRP	Guideline Review Panel
GSI	Global Severity Index
GSK	GlaxoSmithKline
HADS (-A)	Hospital Anxiety and Depression Scale (–anxiety subscale)
HAM-A	Hamilton Anxiety Rating Scale
HCHS	Hospital and Community Health Services
HDRS	Hamilton Depression Rating Scale
HPA	hypothalamo-pituitary-adrenal axis
HR	hazard ratio
HRG	healthcare resource groups
HRQoL	health related quality of life
HTA	Health Technology Assessment
HUI	Health Utilities Index
IAPT	Improving Access to Psychological Therapies
IBSS	International Bibliography of the Social Sciences
IC	information control
IC CCBT	infrequent contact computerised cognitive behavioural therapy
ICD (-10, -DCR)	*International Classification of Diseases – the Classification of Mental and Behavioural Disorders* of the World Health Organization (10th revision; Diagnostic Criteria for Research)
ICER	incremental cost-effectiveness ratio
IPT	interpersonal therapy
ITT	intention to treat
J3N	Jin-3-Needling therapy
K	number of studies
LOCF	last observation carried forward
LTFU	long-term follow-up
LYs	life years
MADRS	Montgomery-Åsberg Depression Rating Scale
MAOI	monoamine oxidase inhibitor
MC error	Monte Carlo error
MCQ	Metacognitions Questionnaire

MCT	metacognitive therapy
MD	mean difference
MDD	major depressive disorder
MEDLINE	Medical Literature Analysis and Retrieval System Online
MHEDEA	Mental Health Disability: a European Assessment
MHRA	Medicines and Healthcare products Regulatory Agency
MI	motivational interviewing
MINI	Mini International Neuropsychiatric Interview
MMSE	Mini-Mental State Examination
N/n	number of participants
NA	not applicable
NCC	National Collaborating Centre
NCCMH	National Collaborating Centre for Mental Health
ND	non-directive
NDT	non-directive therapy
NHS	National Health Service
NICE	National Institute for Health and Clinical Excellence
NIHR	National Institute for Health Research
NIMH-CGI	National Institute of Mental Health – Clinical Global Impressions
NL	needling therapy
NMB	net monetary benefit
NOS	not otherwise specified
NSAID	non-steroidal anti-inflammatory drug
NSF	National Service Framework
OASIS	Overall Anxiety Severity and Impairment Scale
OCD	obsessive-compulsive disorder
ONS	Office for National Statistics
OR	odds ratio
Parox	paroxetine
PC	personal computer
PCT	Primary Care Trust
PD	panic disorder
PDSS	Panic Disorder Severity Scale
PGI (-I)	Patient Global Impression scale (–Improvement)
PGWB	Psychological Well-Being Index
PHQ-9	Patient Health Questionnaire – 9 items
PICO	patient, information, comparison, outcome
PL/pl	placebo
Pr	probability
PRIME-D	Primary Care Evaluation of Mental Disorders
PSS	personal social services

Abbreviations

PSSRU	Personal Social Services Research Unit
PSWQ	Penn State Worry Questionnaire
PsycINFO	Psychological Information Database
PTSD	post-traumatic stress disorder
QALY	quality-adjusted life year
Q-LES-Q (-SF)	Quality of Life Enjoyment and Satisfaction Questionnaire (-Short Form)
QoL	Quality of Life
QOLI	Quality of Life Inventory
QWB	Quality of Well Being Scale
RR	relative risk
SAS (-CR)	Self-rating Anxiety Scale (-revised)
SB	single blind
SC	stress control
SCD	self-control desensitisation
SCID	Structured Clinical Interview for DSM
SCL-90 (R)	Symptom Checklist – 90 items (revised)
SD	standard deviation
SDS	Sheehan Disability Scale
SE	standard error
SET	self-examination therapy
SF-12, -36, -6D (MCS, PCS)	12-/36-item short form health survey (6D = six multi dimensions) physical component summary scale and mental component summary scale
SG	standard gamble
SI	Severity Index
SIGH-A	Structured Interview Guide for the Hamilton Anxiety Rating Scale
SIGN	Scottish Intercollegiate Guidelines Network
SMD	standardised mean difference
SNRI	serotonin noradrenaline reuptake inhibitor
SP	supportive psychotherapy
SSRI	selective serotonin reuptake inhibitor
STAI (-S, -T)	State-Trait Anxiety Inventory (–State version, –Trait version)
TA	Technology Appraisal
TAU	treatment as usual
TCA	tricyclic antidepressants
TID/t.i.d	three times daily
TPQ	Treatment Perceptions Questionnaire
TTO	time trade-off